ATTITUDES

SITUATIONS

Problem
recognition

Information
search

Evaluation and
selection

Outlet selection and
decision implementation

Postpurchase processes

SITUATIONS

CONSUMER BEHAVIOR
Implications for
marketing strategy

Del I. Hawkins
University of Oregon

Kenneth A. Coney
Arizona State University

Roger J. Best
University of Arizona

1980

BUSINESS PUBLICATIONS, INC.   Dallas, Texas   75243
Irwin-Dorsey Limited   Georgetown, Ontario   L7G 4B3

© BUSINESS PUBLICATIONS, INC., 1980

ISBN 0-256-02290-9
Library of Congress Catalog Card No. 79–55225

Printed in the United States of America

1 2 3 4 5 6 7 8 9 0 MP 7 6 5 4 3 2 1 0

CONSUMER BEHAVIOR

Implications for
Marketing strategy

questions, the student can develop a feel for how the many concepts we discuss relate to each other in the context of a single product category.

We have attempted to write a useful and enjoyable text. The degree to which we have accomplished this goal was greatly increased by the assistance of numerous individuals and organizations. To all of them we express our gratitude. To our students, colleagues, friends, and families who suffered with us as we wrote, we express our love.

January 1980   **Del I. Hawkins**
                                                            Kenneth A. Coney
                                                            Roger J. Best

Preface

The purpose of this text is to provide the student with a usable, managerial understanding of consumer behavior. Most students in consumer behavior courses aspire to careers in marketing management. They hope to acquire knowledge and skills that will be useful to them in these careers. Unfortunately, some may be seeking the type of knowledge gained in introductory accounting classes, that is, a set of relatively invariant rules that can be applied across a variety of situations to achieve a fixed solution that is known to be correct. For these students, the uncertainty and lack of closure involved in dealing with living, breathing, changing, stubborn consumers can be very frustrating. However, if they can accept dealing with endless uncertainty, utilizing an understanding of consumer behavior in developing marketing strategy will become tremendously exciting.

The rules governing human behavior, although they do not operate like the rules developed for accounting systems, can be applied in a marketing context. Having students recognize this is a major challenge. It is our view that the utilization of a knowledge of consumer behavior in the development of marketing strategy is an art. This is not to suggest that scientific principles and procedures are not applicable. Rather, it means that the successful application of these principles to particular situations requires human judgment that we are not able to reduce to a fixed set of rules.

Let us consider the analogy with art in some detail. Suppose you want to become an expert artist. You would study known principles of the visual effects of blending various colors, of perspective, and so forth.

Then you would practice applying these principles until you developed the ability to produce acceptable paintings. If you had certain "natural" talents, the right teacher, and the right topic, you might even produce a "masterpiece." The same approach should be taken by one wishing to become a marketing manager. The various factors or principles that influence consumer behavior should be thoroughly studied. Then, one should practice applying these principles until acceptable marketing strategies result. However, while knowledge and practice can in general produce acceptable strategies, "great" marketing strategies, like "masterpieces," require special talents, effort, timing, and some degree of "luck" (what if Mona Lisa had not wanted her portrait painted?).

The art analogy is useful for another reason. All of us, professors and students alike, tend to ask: "How can I use this concept of, say, social class, to develop a successful marketing strategy?" This makes as much sense as an artist asking: "How can I use blue to create a great picture?" Obviously, blue alone will seldom be sufficient for a great work of art. Instead, the artist must understand when and how to use blue in conjunction with other elements in the picture to be successful. Likewise, the marketing manager must understand when and how to use a knowledge of social class in conjunction with a knowledge of other factors in designing a successful marketing strategy.

This book is based on the premise described above. That is, it is based on the belief that a knowledge of the factors that influence consumer behavior can, with practice, be used to develop sound marketing strategy. With this in mind, we have attempted to do three things. First, we present a reasonably comprehensive description of the various behavioral concepts and theories that have been found useful for understanding consumer behavior. This is generally done at the beginning of each chapter or at the beginning of major subsections in each chapter. We believe that a person must have a thorough understanding of a concept in order to successfully apply that concept across different situations.

Second, we present examples of how these concepts have been and can be utilized in the development of marketing strategy. We have tried to make clear that these examples are *not* "how you use this concept." Rather, they are presented as "how one organization facing a particular marketing situation used this concept." The difference, while subtle, is important.

Finally, at the end of each chapter, we present new marketing situations and ask the student to apply the concepts to these situations. We view this as an important part of the learning process. To provide continuity to the class and text, we describe in some detail in the first chapter a firm that must develop a marketing strategy for an addition to its product line. We do not refer back to this firm in the content part of the text; instead, several of the discussion and project situations presented at the end of each chapter relate to this firm. By discussing these

Contents

SECTION THREE
INTERNAL INFLUENCES

Individual development and learning. Individual characteristics. Attitudes. Lifestyle. Consumer decision process: *Problem recognition. Information search. Alternative evaluation and selection. Outlet selection and decision implementation. Postpurchase processes.* Future directions in consumer behavior: *Role accumulators. Adult life cycle. Family buying center. Imagery and linguistics. Cognitive response memory. Disposition.* Conclusion.

CONSUMER BEHAVIOR
Implications for
Marketing strategy

SECTION ONE
introduction and overview

What is consumer behavior? Why should we study it? Do marketing managers actually utilize knowledge about consumer behavior in developing marketing strategy? How can we organize our knowledge of consumer behavior in order to apply it more effectively? These and a number of other interesting questions are addressed in the first two chapters of the text. These two chapters seek to indicate the importance and usefulness of the material to be covered in the remainder of the text as well as providing an organizational overview of this material.

Chapter 3 is different from the first two chapters in that it sets some limits on our ability to generalize or rely completely on consumer behavior "principles." In this chapter, the important role of the situation is introduced. We can all recall shopping at a store toward which we held negative attitudes (did not like) because it was convenient and we were "in a hurry." Thus, our behavior was influenced more by the situation, i.e., our being in a hurry, than by the behavioral concept of attitude. An understanding of the role of the situation is necessary in order to properly appreciate the potential applications and limitations of the concepts presented in the remainder of the text.

1

Introduction

MARKETING STRATEGY AND CONSUMER BEHAVIOR

Before we embark on our presentation of consumer behavior and its implications for marketing strategy, let us first pause and examine the role consumer behavior plays in developing marketing strategy. A brief summary of the experience several different types of businesses have had in using consumer behavior in developing successful marketing programs will help you appreciate the importance and usefulness of consumer behavior in marking management.

Thomas S. Carroll, president and chief executive officer of the marketing-oriented Lever Brothers Company, makes the following statement concerning consumer behavior at Lever Brothers.:

> Understanding and properly interpreting consumer wants is a whole lot easier said than done. Every week our marketing researchers talk to more than 4,000 consumers to find out:
>
> What they think of our products and those of our competitors.
> What they think of possible improvements in our products.
> How they use our products.
> What attitudes they have about our products and our advertising.
> What they feel about their "roles" in the family and society.
> What their hopes and dreams are for themselves and their families.
>
> Today, as never before, we cannot take our business for granted. That's why understanding—and therefore, learning to anticipate—consumer behavior is our key to planning and managing in this ever-changing environment.[1]

---

[1] "Marketing-oriented Lever Uses Research to Capture Bigger Dentifrice Market Shares," *Marketing News* (February 10, 1978), p. 9.

Agree Creme Rinse and Agree Shampoo are both highly successful consumer products. The marketing research managers for Agree describe some of the development activities based on consumer behavior as follows:

> We fielded more than 50 individual research projects from late 1975 until national introduction of Agree Shampoo this past summer. There were focus groups, concept studies, concept product studies, product testing, advertising testing, extended use testing, a laboratory test market, and a test market. . . . We were called upon to establish market sizes and trends and generally review the attitudes of users and nonusers. . . . We conducted many focus groups among all types of women, but increasingly we came to zero in on the young, . . . we certainly didn't stop with focus groups, we conducted quantified concept tests among target users. . . . [One] test design used a blind-paired comparison among members of a mail panel. We placed products with 400 women and had them use each for two weeks. At the end of the use period, a telephone interview determined their preferences overall and their ratings on 15 to 20 performance attributes. And we asked open-end questions for supporting diagnostics.[2]

Hanes Corporation's L'eggs hosiery is one of the most outstanding consumer product successes in recent years. Babette Jackson, research director of Dancer, Fitzgerald and Sample, the advertising agency that helped develop the marketing mix for the product, describes their initial steps: "We talked to women to find out everything we could about hosiery. We did this through focus groups, in-home testing, national behavior study, and concept testing."[3]

The American Red Cross has recently changed its annual fund raising campaign from the passive "good neighbor" approach to the hard sell "Keep the Red Cross Ready" theme. The changes were the result of a series of research studies which indicated that previous campaigns had not effectively communicated the organization's message. Attitude research indicated widespread misconceptions about the services supplied by the Red Cross and a low level of personal identification with the organization's services.[4]

Toro Corporation currently commands more than half the total market for lightweight snow throwers. However, the firm's initial venture into the market was not a success. Toro's first lightweight snow thrower was called "Snow Pup," and "sales could be measured in the tens of thousands (a very small total) and even that would be an exaggeration." The company had Ogilvy & Mather develop a new strategy. After extensive research, "which included interviews with consumers at ski chalets,

---

[2] For a detailed description of the entire process, see "Key Role of Research in Agree's Success Is Told," *Marketing News* (January 12, 1979), pp. 14–15.

[3] "L'eggs Success Grew from Rumpled Bit of Cloth," *Marketing News* (December 29, 1978), p. 8.

[4] "Red Cross Drive Result of Research," *Advertising Age* (January 15, 1979), p. 36.

the agency's first recommendations were that Toro drop the name 'Snow Pup.' They said we needed a more masculine, macho name that implied power. The 'Pup' just didn't convey the image we wanted, as people couldn't believe it was anything but a high-priced toy. Subsequent name changes to 'Snowmaster' and later to simply 'Toro' brought success."[5]

In a recent speech, Tracy Weston, deputy director of the Federal Trade Commission's Bureau of Consumer Protection, cited an advertisement for Belair cigarettes which is "dominated by a full-page, color photograph of a happy couple frolicking in the surf." The text of the advertisement which claims that Belairs take you "all the way to fresh" are "trivial throw-aways" according to Weston. The real question is: What is the actual message or meaning conveyed by the advertisement? Perhaps it is that Belairs will make you "healthy" and "happy," a message that might be ruled deceptive if stated in words rather than pictures.

However, since pictures don't always have accepted meanings, it is "difficult to agree on the meaning or message communicated by a photograph—and thus to agree whether a theme or message in a picture is legally deceptive in FTC terms." FTC staffers are currently attempting to develop a method for assessing this aspect of an advertisement's meaning.[6]

The examples cited above reveal two main facts about the nature of our knowledge of consumer behavior. First, successful marketing decisions by commercial firms, nonprofit organizations, and regulatory agencies require extensive information on consumer behavior. The few examples cited above mentioned such diverse factors as demographics, perceptions, attitudes, preferences, roles, aspirations, and so forth. It should be obvious that from these examples that *firms are applying theories and information about consumer behavior on a daily basis*.

Each of the examples also involved the collection of information about the specific consumers involved in the marketing decision at hand. Thus, at its current state of development, *consumer behavior theory provides the manager with the proper questions to ask*. However, given the importance of the specific situation and product category in consumer behavior, it will often be necessary to conduct research to answer these questions.

Let us return now to our objective: to obtain a useable managerial understanding of consumer behavior. The key aspect of this objective is found in the phrase, *useable managerial understanding*. We want to

---

[5] J. Neher, "Toro Cutting a Wider Swath in Outdoor Appliance Market," *Advertising Age* (February 25, 1978), p. 21.

[6] S. Crock, "FTC Is Seeking Way to Decide if Pictures in Advertising Convey False Impressions," *The Wall Street Journal* (August 11, 1978), p. 4. See also "Bell Attacks Measuring Nonverbal Signals in Ads," *Advertising Age* (November 27, 1978), p. 94.

increase your understanding of consumer behavior in order to help you become a more effective marketing manager. Therefore, we have omitted some technical and theoretical considerations such as neurological aspects of perception or the structure of cognitive storage systems that might provide a small increase in understanding but probably would not prove useful to you as a marketing manager.

We believe that it is impossible to be an *effective* marketing manager without a useable understanding of consumer behavior. Therefore, we feel that the objective of this text is not only desirable but essential. However, we also agree with Mr. Carrol of Lever Brothers that "understanding and properly interpreting consumer wants is a whole lot easier said than done."[7] We have tried to make the task as easy as possible by stressing those areas of consumer behavior that appear to have direct applications in a number of areas.

Sufficient knowledge of consumer behavior currently exists to provide a useable guide to marketing practice. However, we must emphasize that the state of knowledge of consumer behavior is not sufficient for us to write a "cookbook" with "surefire recipes for success." We will illustrate how some firms were able to combine some ingredients for success under specific conditions. However, as conditions change, the quantities and even the ingredients required may change. Thus, we will attempt to present what is "known" about consumer behavior. It is up to you as a student and future marketing manager to develop the ability to apply this knowledge to specific situations. To assist you, we have supplied "situations" at the end of each chapter which you can use to develop your "application skills" and the ability to ask the appropriate questions concerning the potential impact of consumer behavior patterns on proposed marketing strategies.

Thus far we have stressed the applied, managerial approach we believe to be appropriate for this text. However, there is another reason for studying consumer behavior that is also important to all of us. Consider for a moment that most of us spend more time in consuming products than we do in either producing (work) or sleeping. Clearly, any attempt to understand ourselves, our society, or another society *must* include an understanding of consumer behavior. And this understanding goes beyond the mere flow of resources emphasized in economics, as the following quote makes clear:

> No behavior is simply economic. In every transaction *people deal in more than dollars and products.* A can of beans does not cost $.19; it costs $.19 plus or minus something. There is no word for the extra something that is negotiated in every sale. Sometimes what is negotiated is incremental amounts of status, or prestige or power or self-esteem. Sometimes . what is negotiated is as subtle as meanings or attitudes or values. And there

---

[7] "Marketing-Oriented Lever," p. 9.

is no single term that will satisfactorily refer to all these forms of *social currency*.[8]

Learning about the "social currency" described above is an exciting, rewarding task. Most successful marketing managers, as well as politicians, union leaders, and other individuals who must work with people, are intrigued and fascinated by such issues. However, we are going to limit ourselves to that subset of knowledge about consumer behavior that appears to offer a reasonable possibility of direct applicability across a variety of *managerial* situations. An increased awareness of the broader issues of consumer behavior is, fortunately, a natural by-product of this approach.

BASIC ASSUMPTIONS

Before we develop our approach to consumer behavior, we need to clarify some of our basic assumptions. Actually these are as much definitional problems as anything else.

When you hear the word *product,* what do you think of? Most likely you visualize a tangible item such as a book, a car, or a pencil. Some of you may have included such services as haircuts or visits to a psychiatrist. However, we are going to utilize an even broader definition. For our purposes a product will be defined as *anything available for exchange and perceived as having some value by the potential consumer.* Thus, education could be considered a product, as could membership in a social organization. We will use the term *product* frequently and it is important to remember that we are using this broad definition.

The second term that requires clarification is *behavior*. Most of us think of behavior in terms of visible, physical movements by individuals. Again, we are going to use a broader definition. In this text, behavior will refer to *any activity, physical or mental, performed by an individual.* While one could engage in extensive discussion on the appropriateness of separating "physical" and "mental" activities, we will avoid this by simply *defining* behavior to include such things as attitude change as well as purchasing a product.[9] Again, it is very important to remember that this broadened definition will be used throughout the text.

Measurement in consumer behavior[10]

In the remaining chapters, we will frequently be describing various *concepts* such as *social class, attitude,* and *motive*. Concepts are abstrac-

---

[8] W. T. Tucker, *The Social Context of Economic Behavior* (Holt, Rinehart and Winston, 1964), p. 4.

[9] See T. Shibutani, *Society and Personality* (Prentice-Hall, Inc., 1961).

[10] This section is based on D. S. Tull and D. I. Hawkins, *Marketing Research* (Macmillan Publishing Co., 1980).

tions based on observations of numerous particular occurrences. They aid in thinking by subsuming a number of events under one heading.[11] Thus, the concept *store* refers to the generalization of the characteristics that all stores have in common. The concept *store* is strongly anchored to a physical reality.

Most of the concepts in consumer behavior, however, do not have an observable physical property. That is, we cannot examine a physical example of *prestige, social mobility,* or *cognitive dissonance*. Therefore, we must be particularly careful to precisely define each concept that we utilize. To accomplish this, two definitional approaches are generally required to adequately define a concept: (1) *conceptual definition* and (2) *operational definition*.

Conceptual definitions   A conceptual definition *defines a concept in terms of related concepts*. It states the basic idea or essence of the concept. A good conceptual definition clearly delineates the major characteristics of the concept and distinguishes the concept from similar but different concepts. Consider *brand loyalty* as a concept. What is your definition? Based on your definition, is the person loyal to a brand who consistently buys that brand because it is the only brand available at the only store in the area? Is this person loyal in the same sense as the person who consistently selects the same brand from among the many carried at the store? A good conceptual definition of brand loyalty should distinguish that concept from other concepts such as "repeat purchasing behavior." The absence of such a conceptual definition has hindered research on brand loyalty.[12]

Operational definitions   An operational definition *describes the activities that must be completed in order to assign a value to the particular concept in a given instance*. Concepts are abstractions and are not observable. Operational definitions translate the concept into one or more observable events. Thus, a conceptual definition should precede and guide the development of the operational definition.

The need to transform a conceptual definition into an operational definition often leads to a major problem in the study of consumer behavior. The problem is the fact that the operational definition is sometimes a very inexact "translation" of the conceptual definition. Assume a manager is operating with a conceptual definition of brand loyalty as a *preferential response toward a brand in a product category over time based on underlying favorable attitudes toward the brand*.[13] A study

[11] C. Selltiz et al., *Research Methods in Social Relations* (Holt, Rinehart and Winston, 1959), p. 41.

[12] See J. Jacoby and D. Kyner, "Brand Loyalty vs. Repeat Purchasing Behavior," *Journal of Marketing Research* (February 1973), pp. 1–9.

[13] Based on G. S. Day, "A Two-Dimensional Concept of Brand Loyalty," *Journal of Advertising Research* (September 1969), pp. 29–35.

which classified individuals as brand loyal if at least 80 percent of their past year's purchases went to the same brand would therefore be a poor fit with the manager's definition.

A good operational definition would also have to measure attitudes toward the brand. This is an important point. Often a marketing study is conducted and the relationship (or lack of relationship) between two or more *concepts* is reported. However, it is always *the measurement* of the concepts that is studied, not the concepts themselves! Thus, a study that finds no relationship between, say, social class and type of movies preferred has in fact examined only one of several possible operational definitions of social class and the conclusions must be limited to the operational definition used.

The above discussion undoubtedly seems abstract for an applied text. However, application generally requires measurement. Therefore, it is important to be aware of the sometimes arbitrary links between the concept and the method by which it is measured. We will remind you of this distinction in those areas such as social class where it is particularly critical.

APPLYING YOUR KNOWLEDGE OF CONSUMER BEHAVIOR: THE MOPED

Throughout this text, we will present specific examples of how marketing managers have been able to utilize the concepts in developing marketing strategy. However, to develop a sound understanding of the material, you should attempt to apply it to an actual situation. To assist you with this task and to provide some continuity in the text, we are going to present you with the marketing problem facing a friend of ours. Then, at the end of each chapter, several of the discussion and project questions will refer to this problem. By responding to these questions, you can develop an ability to apply the material you have studied.

The person Jeff Stephenson received an MBA degree with an emphasis in marketing from the University of Oregon in 1972. Upon graduation, he took a position as a sales management trainee with Proctor and Gamble. After three years with Proctor and Gamble, he resigned and joined a company-owned distributor for Gallo Wine as a sales manager. In 1978, Jeff left Gallo to join his father's firm, Stephenson Marketing Company, as vice president. His primary motivation was his belief that the relatively small firm had an excellent chance to "hit it big" as an importer of Motron, a brand of moped.

The company Stephenson Marketing Company (SMC) of Rancho Palos Verdes, California, is primarily an importer of small engine-powered consumer products. SMC was established to assist manufacturers seeking distribution for their products through lawn, garden, and small farm equipment wholesalers in the United States. The company has access to sales representation throughout the United States with a dealer network of approximately 15,000 dealers.

The president of SMC is Stanley J. Stephenson who has spent 31 years in the manufacture and marketing of consumer hard goods. For over eight years Stephenson was vice president of marketing for McCulloch Corporation, one of the world's leading chain saw manufacturers. Prior to that position, he was president of AMF-Western Tool Division, Des Moines, Iowa, manufacturers of lawnmowers, riding mowers, snow throwers, and snowmobiles.

The product   The product that Jeff has staked his future on is known as a moped. *Moped* is a term used to describe a *mo*torized *ped*al bicycle. The vehicle is a two-wheeled cycle, which can be mounted, started, pedaled, controlled, and stopped like a bicycle (see Figure 1 – 2). It has a gearless automatic transmission and hand brakes. It typically weighs between 60 and 100 pounds. It was developed directly from the pedal bicycle, and its structure and controls are analogous to those of a bicycle. The pedals and automatic transmission are in contrast to the kick starter, manual clutch drive, and manually operated gear box found on the typical motorcycle.

A typical motorized bicycle is equipped with a small helper-motor of no more than 50 cc displacement which can move the cycle up to a maximum speed in the range of 17 to 30 miles per hour. Each state establishes a maximum allowable horsepower, between 1.0 and 2.0 BHP, and a maximum allowable speed, between 17 and 30 miles per hour. The vehicle is distinguished by its low acceleration, power, speed, and weight. Its engine limitations easily distinguish it from the higher powered motorcycle. The engine displacement of motorcycles generally varies from 70 cc to 1,200 cc (versus 50 cc for the motorized bicycle). The dry weight of motorcycles generally ranges from 300 to 700 pounds, depending upon their power (versus the 60- to 100-pound weight of the motorized bicycle). High-powered motorcycles can attain 70 mph (versus a maximum speed of 17 to 30 mph for the motorized bicycle).

The cost of motorized bicycles is in the $425 to $520 range, and its simple construction does not give rise to significant maintenance problems. Particularly attractive in these times of high fuel prices is the fact that the motorized bicycle will travel 120 to 170 miles per gallon of gasoline. Figure 1 – 1 provides a "typical" product description.

The industry[14]   Mopeds were initially developed by a French firm, Motobecane, shortly after World War II. The rapid development of the moped as a form of transportation throughout Europe and more recently the Far East was the result of the shortage and high cost of auto-

---

[14] For additional details see "Mopeds," *Consumer Reports* (June 1978), pp. 319–26; and "Boom in Mopeds Touches Off a Furor," *U.S. News and World Report* (October 17, 1977), p. 74.

FIGURE 1–1
Typical product specifications

Engine:	47–50 cc, single cylinder, two stroke, air cooled.
Weight:	70 to 100 pounds (dry)
Horsepower:	1.0–2.0 BHP
Speed:	17 to 30 miles per hour
Range:	120 to 170 miles per gal
Gas capacity:	0.33–1.3 gallons
Frame:	Bent tube or pressed steel
Transmission:	Automatic, centrifugal clutch
Drive:	Twin chain, one to pedal, one to engine
Brakes:	Hand-operated drum brake, front and rear
Lights:	Sealed-beam front light, combination stop/taillight, seven reflectors
Tires:	2.0–2.25 × 16″–17″
Ignition:	Magneto
Suspension:	Telescopic front fork, swing arm telescopic on rear
Other:	Tool kit, rear rack, fork lock, speedometer, horn
Price:	$420–$520

mobiles and fuel. Even motorcycles were expensive and out of reach for the average worker. The bicycle business boomed and many Europeans found this form of transportation suitable for nearly all their needs. The addition of a small helper-motor to the bicycle to help relieve tired muscles was a natural progression.

Today, it is estimated that there are approximately 30 to 40 million mopeds in use throughout the world. Over 2.7 million were sold in 1973. Approximately 6 million of the vehicles are in service in France alone—one per nine of population.

Worldwide, mopeds constitute a billion dollar industry. For years, foreign moped manufacturers had attempted to introduce their products into the United States without success. Prior to 1974, mopeds were in the same classification as motorcycles and were required to conform to the same regulations and standards. Due to their light weight and very small engine, the moped was not equipped to meet such standards. Collectively, several major European manufacturers petitioned the National Highway Traffic Safety Administration (NHTSA) of the Department of Transportation, to reclassify the moped as a "power assisted bicycle", separate from the motorcycle classification.

The NHTSA did not set up a separate classification but did establish a subcategory for mopeds that considerably relaxed certain requirements designed for the much bigger and heavier motorcycles. Although the federal regulations had been altered, each state had its own laws that needed to be changed. Again, the European manufacturers gathered together and financially backed the formation of the Motorized Bicycle Association (MBA) in Washington, D.C. The MBA has been working with the legislatures of each state to enact revised regulations allowing mopeds to operate under a separate category from motorcycles. Unfortunately, in the rush to change state laws, there has been a lack of consistency from state to state in areas of allowable horsepower, allowable top speed, and age limit for operation.

These changes, initiated in 1974, signaled the beginning of a new form of transportation in the United States. In 1974, only two models of moped were available in the United States and total sales were 2,500 units. There are now over 50 different brands of mopeds being marketed in the United States. Sales for 1977 were approximately 175,000 units with continued strong growth very possible. The major manufacturers of Europe: Puch (Austria), Sachs (Germany), Peugeot and Motobecane (France), Batavus (Holland), and Cimatti, Garelli, and Vespa (Italy) are the most widely distributed mopeds in the United States. Each of these has a long history in the manufacture of bicycles, motorcycles, or mopeds.

Only Puch (pronounced pook) has been successful at obtaining relatively broad distribution and significant penetration into those states with favorable moped laws. Most of the other mopeds enjoy satisfactory distribution along the East Coast and in southern California but are unevenly distributed in the balance of the country. Unlike the majority of other moped importer/distributors, Puch is being marketed in the United States by a division of the parent company, Steyr Daimler Puch of Germany. This organization has a long successful history in the marketing of mopeds and has the requisite knowledge and experience to be successful in the marketing of mopeds in the United States. Puch is clearly recognized as the leader in U.S. market penetration.

The moped is a hybrid breed from the marriage of a bicycle and a motorcycle. Price and design make it a "top end" sales extension for bicycle shops and a "low end" sales extension for motorcycle shops. Given this relationship, bicycle shops have become the primary sales outlet.

All current moped importer/distributors are concentrating on bicycle shops for initial distribution. Moped shops, specializing only in the sales of mopeds, are a minority and limited to the high density areas of the North, Southeast, and southern California. Motorcycle shops have shown little interest in mopeds due to their relatively low performance, the "trade-down factor" from higher priced motorcycles and the moped's considerably different consumer profile. The general distribution profile is shown in Table 1—1.

TABLE 1–1
Distribution profile

Bicycle shops	85.00%
Moped shops	8.00
Motorcycle shops	4.00
Mass merchandisers	2.00
Lawn and garden shops	0.50
Rental shops	0.25
Sporting goods	0.25
Resorts	0.05

Only a few brands utilize independent distributors or have attempted to develop a national distributor network. Where these distributors are established it is extremely rare to find one with any semblance of a sales force. Most simply serve as reception points for regional shipments and are not prepared to provide the dealer a full line of services typically found in the traditional wholesale function.

With many of the "bottom of the line" motorcycles selling in the $300 to $550 range, the moped with its lower performance may appear to be priced inordinately high. However the information shown in Table 1—2 indicates that moped sales are not extremely sensitive to price levels.

TABLE 1–2
Moped price range

Price Range	Percent of mopeds
$490–$550	5%
450– 489	70
430– 449	20
350– 429	3
300– 349	2

As an industry in its infancy stage, there is negligible competitive activity in the form of pricing, product differentiation, or advertising. The primary effort of manufacturers has been to establish a distribution network. With few exceptions, the little consumer-oriented advertising that is being done is of an informative or institutional nature.

FIGURE 1-2

Sprint
STANDARD EQUIPMENT:
Minarelli Z-10 2-cycle internally fan-cooled engine
Heavy-gauge steel fenders
Heavy-duty reinforced front-fork suspension
Rear shock absorbers on swing arm
Sealed-beam headlamp
Adjustable handlebars
Wraparound chain guard
Fully welded, heavy-duty tubular steel frame
Independent, easy-fill gas tank with metal cap
Reflectors, front and rear and on pedals
Deluxe electrical components

Classic
STANDARD EQUIPMENT:
Minarelli Z-10 2-cycle internally fan-cooled engine
Extra-strength, aluminum-cast rims
Top-quality, independently suspended speedometer
Spring-loaded carrier
Striking metallic paint finish
Over-sized, soft seat with independent spring
Tool Kit
Rack and frame covers for paint protection
Chrome mud guards on foot rests
Deluxe electrical components
Wraparound chain guard

Medalist
STANDARD EQUIPMENT:
Minarelli Z-10 2-cycle internally fan-cooled engine
Stainless-steel fenders
Top-quality, independently suspended speedometer
Spring-loaded carrier
Striking metallic paint finish
Over-sized, soft seat with independent springs
Tool Kit
Rack and frame covers for paint protection
Chrome mud guards on foot rests
Deluxe electrical components
Wraparound chain guard

FIGURE 1–3
Technical data for Motron

Engine
  Type: Air-cooled single cylinder
  2-cycle with internal fan
  Displacement: 49.6cc
  Bore-stroke: 38.8mm × 42mm
  Carburetor: Dell'Orio

Clutch
  Automatic centrifugal expansion
  clutch in oil bath

Power train
  Direct single chain drive
  Design efficient—minimum
  maintenance

Ignition—lighting
  Alternator flywheel magneto—6
  volt
  23 watt capacity. Sealed beam
  headlamp
  Combination tail-stop lamp
  SAE approved reflectors

Frame
  Heavy duty welded steel—tubular
  frame with extra strong tubular
  luggage rack

Gas tank
  Easy-fill independent tank
  Capacity: 1.0 gal. with reserve
  Consumption: 120—150 miles per
  gal.

Suspension
  Front: Cross-braced telescopic
  forkshock absorbers
  Rear: Independent swing-arm
  shock absorbers

Brakes
  Internal expansion drum brakes

Tires
  Pirelli 2¼ × 16"

Dry weight (approx.)
  Sprint—97 lbs.
  Medalist—100 lbs.
  Classic—104 lbs.

Wheel base
  43"

Overall length
  64"

Warranty
  Six months

Other standard equipment—all
models
  Mirror, horn, pedal reflectors,
  mudflap, low and wide footrest,
  screw-on metal gas cap, six-way
  adjustable seat, adjustable
  "safety weld" handlebars, steer-
  ing column lock, frame paint
  protector, wraparound chain
  guard, deluxe electrical switches,
  precision chain adjusters, long,
  quiet chrome muffler.

Medalist and Classic only
  Spring loaded rack, lighted
  speedometer, high lustre metallic paint finish, tool kit, super
  cushion seat, luggage rack paint
  protector, chrome footrest paint
  protector, stainless steel fenders
  (Medalist only).

Classic only
  Extra strong cast aluminum
  rims, all silver metallic paint
  finish.

* Data apply to all models except where noted

Product demand and awareness are still in an underdeveloped stage in most parts of the country. With the exception of trade journals (not public oriented) and two moped publications distributed through moped dealers, the industry is relying almost totally on the interest of the public media to inform the American public about the moped and the new laws affecting it.

The brand   SMC selected Motron from Italy as the best available brand and became the exclusive importer of this brand. The Motron comes in three models as shown in Figure 1−2. Additional technical data on the models is provided in Figure 1−3.

The marketing plan   SMC plans to use its existing network of distributors to establish a national distribution system for Motron. SMC will perform the marketing function for Motron in the United States. Thus, it will recommend product changes, design overall marketing strategy, conduct national advertising, and provide leadership and guidance for local distributors and retailers.

Jeff Stephenson has primary responsibility for the activities described above. In what ways, if at all, would a knowledge of consumer behavior assist Jeff in developing marketing strategy? He will be making recommendations on outlet locations, advertising themes, pricing strategies, model changes, and so forth. As you read each of the following chapters, try to visualize how Jeff could utilize the concepts covered in the chapter. The first discussion and project questions at the end of each chapter will help focus your thinking on specific aspects of developing a marketing strategy for mopeds based on an understanding of consumer behavior.

SUMMARY

Successful marketing decisions by commercial firms, nonprofit organizations and regulatory agencies require a sound understanding of consumer behavior. Numerous examples of actual business practices make it clear that successful firms can and do apply theories and information about consumer behavior on a daily basis.

A good basic knowledge of consumer behavior at its current state of development should provide you with, at the very least, the proper questions to ask concerning a proposed marketing activity. Frequently, however, it will be necessary to conduct research to answer these questions. It is our belief that, while much remains to be discovered, sufficient knowledge of consumer behavior currently exists to provide a usable guide to marketing practice.

Several basic assumptions and definitions are important to understand before embarking on the study of consumer behavior. The first of these is the definition and use of the word *product*. Product is defined in this text as anything available for exchange and perceived as having some value to the potential consumer. A second term that requires clarification is *behavior*. Behavior refers to any activity, physical or mental, performed by an individual.

Concepts in consumer behavior are frequently difficult to grasp immediately because they are not easily observed and are many times very abstract. Concepts are defined both conceptually (in terms of related concepts) and operationally (activities that must be completed to assign a value to the concept).

An example of an interesting consumer product, the Motron moped, has been presented to you in this chapter. You may find it helpful to consider the concepts presented in the rest of the text in light of how they might help to explain the purchase and use of a moped.

REVIEW QUESTIONS

1. What two conclusions can be drawn from the examples presented at the first of the chapter?
2. What is meant by the term *product* as used in this text?
3. What is meant by the term *behavior* as used in this text?
4. What is the relationship between a conceptual definition and an operational definition?

DISCUSSION QUESTIONS

1. a. Why would someone buy a moped?
    b. Why would someone else not buy one?
    c. How would *you* choose one brand over another? Would others use the same rules? What types of individuals would use different rules?
2. How would a text focusing on a "broad" understanding of consumer behavior differ from the applications-oriented approach of this text?
3. Is it possible for the FTC to evaluate the "total" or nonverbal meaning of an advertisement? If so, how should they proceed?

PROJECT QUESTIONS

1. Visit one or more stores that sell mopeds. Report on the sales techniques used (point-of-purchase displays, store design, salesperson comments, and so forth). What beliefs concerning consumer behavior appear to underlie these strategies. It is often worthwhile

for a male and a female student to visit the same store and talk to the same salesperson at different times. The variation in sales appeals is sometimes quite revealing.

2. Look through recent copies of a magazine such as *Advertising Age* or *Business Week* and report on three applications of consumer behavior knowledge (or questions) to marketing decisions.

2

Model and overview

As we stated in Chapter 1, the marketing manager with knowledge of why and how consumers act as they do will make better marketing mix decisions than one without that knowledge. This is because of an increased ability to accurately predict consumer responses to marketing mix variables. Just as every good salesperson must thoroughly know and understand their product, so must they know and understand their customer. Reflect for a moment on the situation facing Jeff Stephenson as described in the preceding chapter. It is readily apparent that the marketing mix decisions he will be making will be based on either a *knowledge* of consumer behavior or *intuitive guesses* about consumer responses. Most of us would prefer knowledge to guesswork.

Can a manager with a thorough understanding of consumer behavior still make a bad decision? Certainly! For one thing, we do not yet know all of what makes a consumer tick, though our knowledge is growing. But even with a sound storehouse of knowledge, decisions that marketing managers make sometimes turn out poorly because consumers are human and human beings change—unexpectedly and rapidly. In addition, consumers base their decisions not upon the marketing mix of one firm but on the relationship between each firm's marketing mix and the overall environment or situation in which the consumer is operating. This broader environment contains numerous factors such as competitors over which you, as a marketing manager, have no direct control. Does this mean we should not bother studying the consumer? Of course not! Every bit of information we gather about the consumer increases our chances of making better marketing decisions. And improved marketing decisions are, in effect, what it's all about.

In this chapter we are going to do two things. First, we are going to develop a "model" of consumer behavior. This model is not a predictive model. That is, it does not provide sufficient detail to allow a prediction of a particular purchase or brand choice even if we had adequate information on all the variables in the model. Instead, this model is a philosophical and organizational model. It reflects our philosophy or beliefs about the nature of consumer behavior. In addition, it provides a logical means of organizing the vast quantity of information on the variables that influence consumer behavior.

Our second objective will be developed simultaneously with the first. As we present our model, we will also present a fairly detailed overview of the material that is covered in the text. Since this is a detailed overview, it is natural to ask, "Why should I be concerned with all these concepts now if I'm going to cover them in more depth in just a few days or weeks?" The answer to this question is: "Because the factors that influence consumer behavior are all interrelated." Or, stated another way, "everything affects everything else." Thus, in the next chapter, we discuss the role situational influences have on purchase and consumption behavior. However, it is impossible to discuss situational influences without mentioning attitudes or the consumer decision process. This same type of problem arises in each chapter. Therefore, it is important that you develop an initial understanding of the major concepts so that their interrelationships will make sense to you.

MODEL OF CONSUMER BEHAVIOR

The marketing manager can most opportunistically view the consumer as a problem solver—*a decision-making unit (individual or family) that takes in information, processes that information in light of the existing situation, and takes the action that will hopefully achieve satisfaction and enhance lifestyle.* Problems arise for consumers in their attempts to develop, maintain, and/or change their lifestyle as shown in Figure 2–1. Past decisions, time-related events such as aging, and external events such as an illness or job change lead to lifestyle changes which pose additional consumption problems and result in new purchases, new attitudes, and so forth which in turn bring about further lifestyle changes. Marketing managers are seldom interested in a single individual's or a family's lifestyle. Rather, they are concerned with groups or market segments that exhibit similar lifestyles.

Consumer lifestyle

What do we mean by the term *consumer lifestyle* and why is it so vital to an understanding of how and why consumers act as they do?

FIGURE 2–1

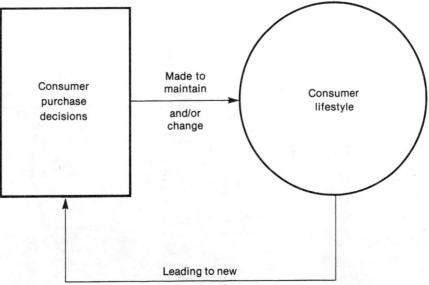

Lifestyle has been defined as "the way an individual chooses and uses possessions."[1] Others consider it to be composed of individuals' activities, interests, opinions, needs, and values which reflect who they are.[2] Quite simply your lifestyle is *how* you live. It is the products you buy, how you use them, and what you think about them. It is the manifestations of your self-image or self-concept—the total image you have of yourself as a result of the culture you live in and the individual situations and experiences that comprise your daily existence. It is the sum of your past decisions and future plans.

Both individuals and families exhibit distinct lifestyles. We often hear of "career-oriented individuals," "outdoor families," "devoted mothers," or "swinging singles." These expressions serve to summarize key aspects of individuals' or families' lifestyles. Lifestyle is both conscious and nonconscious. That is, we often make decisions with full awareness of their impact on our lifestyle. Perhaps more frequently we are unaware of the extent to which our decisions are influenced by our current or desired lifestyle.

It is important to understand that lifestyle serves a dual function—as a motivator of purchasing behavior and as the basic source of the information and rules we use to determine satisfaction and implement a particular behavior. Thus, lifestyle and consumer purchases are closely

---

[1] J. F. Engel, D. T. Kollat, and R. D. Blackwell, *Consumer Behavior* (Holt, Rinehart and Winston, 1973), p. 121.

[2] F. D. Reynolds and W. D. Wells, *Consumer Behavior* (McGraw-Hill Book Co., 1977), p. 35.

FIGURE 2–2

Factors that determine and influence consumer lifestyle

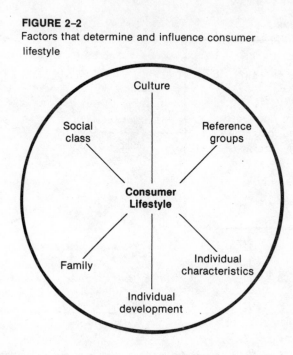

related. We buy and use products that we feel will maintain and/or positively change our desired lifestyle.

In the following chapters, we first discuss the many factors that influence our lifestyles. We focus particular attention on how marketing managers can apply what is known about each factor. Then, in Chapter 14, we return for a more complete discussion of lifestyle. Before discussing the factors that influence lifestyle, we are going to devote Chapter 3 to a discussion of situations. While we must, by necessity, discuss behavioral theories in general terms, it is important to keep in mind that consumption behaviors always occur in the context of a specific situation. A means of classifying situations is presented in Chapter 3 along with examples of how marketers can utilize situational influences.

We see six basic factors influencing consumer lifestyle: culture, social class, reference groups, family, individual development, and individual characteristics as illustrated in Figure 2−2. These six factors comprise a majority of the text and, of course, will be dealt with in detail. A brief overview of each at this point, however, will be helpful in forming your basic orientation toward consumer behavior as a marketing person as well as providing an overview of a major portion of this text.

EXTERNAL INFLUENCES

Section Two covers external influences affecting consumer behavior. Chapter 4 will focus on the subject of culture and cross-cultural influences. *Culture* is viewed in the traditional sense as representing "that complex whole which includes knowledge, belief, art, morals, law, custom, and any other capabilities and habits acquired by man as a member of society."[3] In other words, consumer behavior is the product of a particular culture. Our culture provides us with what we know to be "true." Our knowledge of "how things are" as consumers comes to us from the culture through our families, friends, and institutions. For instance, our particular culture has taught most of us that we should consume three meals per day with cereals, toast, eggs, bacon, or sausage being most appropriate for the morning meal. Other cultures prescribe differing numbers of meals as well as differing foods for each meal.

Probably one of the most important learned aspects of culture is a culture's *basic values*. These basic values provide us with guidelines as to what is right and wrong or good and bad in any given situation. Values vary across cultures and have significant impacts on consumer behavior. These impacts are evident not only in the product choices made but also in the advertising themes and symbols we respond to most positively or negatively. For instance, small children and puppies provide many people in our culture with positive and warm feelings which advertisers often utilize in attempting to obtain a positive association with a particular brand or product. Basic cultural values can also retard or accelerate new product innovation acceptance rates. Prepackaged and prepared foods were accepted slowly in the United States partially because of the strong cultural values attached to total food preparation at each meal as an expression of family love and concern on the part of the homemaker. The initial slow acceptance of credit cards is another example of the effect of strongly held values concerning thrift and security. Obviously, both of these values have changed considerably as we are now a society prone to utilize prepared foods and credit purchases.

We will also examine cultural variations in *nonverbal communications,* a subject of particular interest to those marketing managers dealing with major subcultures in the United States and other cultures in the world markets. Hall has done some fascinating work on how people across cultures vary in communicating trust, warmth, and respect.[4] Cross-cultural analysis will be dealt with in order to give the reader a methodology for investigating different cultures and a perspective on how marketing managers can deal with our own culture in making successful marketing decisions.

The changing American culture will be examined in Chapters 5 and 6. The intent here is to provide you with an overview of our own culture by describing how it affects consumers and how marketing managers can use knowledge of our culture in making marketing decisions. Our general discussion of basic cultural values in Chapter 4 will be extended to

---

[3] E. B. Taylor, *Primitive Culture* (Henry Holt, 1889), p. 1.

[4] E. T. Hall, *The Silent Language,* (Fawcett World Library, 1959).

an in-depth discussion of our own specific American cultural values in Chapter 5. The question of whether or not we face a rapidly changing set of values will be examined. The potential impact of these value shifts on consumer lifestyles and purchasing patterns is also discussed.

The second half of Chapter 5 contains detailed analysis of our changing values with respect to male and female *sex roles*. Culturally defined sex roles have gone through and, in fact, are still going through major changes that affect marketing management decisions. The working wife and mother is no longer an oddity. Many purchasing chores that traditionally have been carried out by women are now done by the male, either exclusively or on a shared basis. Traditional decision roles between husbands and wives have been substantially altered, not to mention types and kinds of products purchased and used by either sex.

In Chapter 6, the new *demographics* of America, particularly income, geographic, and age shifts, as they affect consumption patterns and marketing decisions are examined. The implications of these shifts for marketing managers are of critical importance and are discussed in some detail. In addition, major American *subcultures* will be analyzed, primarily using the characteristics of ethnic background, religious affiliation, and/or geographic identification. Subcultures are smaller, homogeneous segments of the dominant culture and are of interest to marketers when they require differential marketing activities because of unique values, attitudes, or behavior patterns. Differential marketing activities for specific market segments are expensive and therefore managers have to be sure that they identify as different only those subcultural groups that are distinct in a meaningful way with respect to consumption. For instance, blacks were initially viewed as being a separate subcultural unit of interest to marketers simply because of differences in race. Over time it has been ascertained that while there are many differences between blacks and whites, consumption patterns are often similar and apparent differences are frequently associated more with income than with race.

Social class influences on consumer lifestyle have been a much debated issue in consumer behavior. Chapter 7 will look at the issue in the broader perspective of *social stratification*. The major questions of interest are: (1) To what extent does our society structure and rank individuals? (2) On what characteristics is this structure built? and (3) In what ways does this structure influence consumer lifestyle and purchase decisions?

Generally, our society seems to be structured such that we are all ranked on a number of observable characteristics that represent underlying values that our culture holds to be worthwhile. For instance, one of the first things you inquire about when meeting a stranger is what he or she does for a living. That person's occupation (or lack of!) allows us to define them relative to ourselves and others so that we make an assessment of their position and how to act toward them. Sociologists have been able to group occupations and, together with other important variables, use them to identify categories of people that are composed of individuals holding similar jobs, values, attitudes, or, when viewed as a whole, somewhat similar lifestyles.

Marketers then can use social class as a consumer market identification tool. In fact, social class is one of the most commonly used variables for market segment identification. There is a large body of research that reports how social classes vary in store selection, media preference, desire for assistance from retail sales personnel, and so forth. Desired social class standing can be a major part of consumer lifestyle, not only reflecting what you are but serving as a goal for what you want to be.

Our cultural background and social class standing are primarily transmitted to us from two basic types of groups: reference groups and family. Certainly we also "learn" our culture and social class from institutions such as the educational and religious institutions and mass media, but the intimate groups we deal with on a daily basis are probably the most important influencers we face.

Reference groups and group theory in general will be the subject matter considered in Chapter 8. Most consumers belong to a large number of *groups*—two or more people who have a purpose for interacting over some extended period of time. These groups serve in effect as both a reference point for the individual and as a source of specific information. The group influences the individual in many ways and the individual uses the group to achieve his or her own goals. Marketing managers are particularly interested in the flow of information to and through groups. Here we examine the concept of opinion leaders within groups. We shall also study group conformity and how group norms often prescribe certain aspects of lifestyle, influencing clothing fashions and the adoption of specific brands of product. In addition we will analyze how new products, *innovations,* spread or diffuse through groups. Finally, *roles*—patterns of behavior expected of a position in a group rather than in an individual—are analyzed in light of their influence on purchasing patterns.

The *family* is a very special and influential form of reference group and is the subject of Chapter 9. Three specific areas of the family interest us as marketing managers—the composition of the family unit, family decision-making roles, and the family life cycle. Most consumers in the United States are members of families and many of the purchases they make are made as family decisions, even though only one person in the family may do the actual purchasing. In fact, the family is the primary purchasing unit for most consumer goods. Obviously it is important for the marketing manager to be fully aware of who is influencing the decision within a family so that a correct information campaign can be constructed and appropriately positioned and directed. We will examine the relative influence and roles of husbands, wives, and children at each stage in the decision process.

Another important variable for marketers is the *family life cycle.* Most consumers in our culture grow up, physically leave their original family and then begin a new family by marrying and having children. In other words, the institution we call a family has a fairly regular and predictable life cycle of its own. Marketers can look at each stage of this cycle and get accurate aggregate pictures of purchase needs and desires of individuals in that stage. When one combines other information, such as social class, with family life cycle, rather precise lifestyles emerge that are very useful to marketing managers in developing specific target market strategies. The chapter on families concludes Section Two of the text that focuses on external or group influences on lifestyle.

INTERNAL INFLUENCES

Section Three focuses on internal influences. Chapter 10, which covers *information processing,* describes the means by which consumers incorporate information from group influences, the situational context, and marketing efforts into their lifestyle and purchase decisions. Information processing is a process-oriented activity that links the various external influences and marketing practices to the consumer's decision process. It is the mechanism which makes our model function. We cover information processing at this point in the text because individual development and individual characteristics are determined in part by the information we receive and process from our culture, social class, reference groups, and family.

Information processing is particularly important in the consumer decision-making process, the final major section of the text. Information is the raw material for a decision. The consumer gathers information, processes it, discards some, stores some, combines new information with old, all to come up with solutions to problems in the form of decisions. Marketing managers are therefore vitally interested in where consumers get information, what makes them pay attention to it, what makes them believe some and disbelieve the rest. In short, the only way a marketing manager can influence consumer decisions is through the information he or she provides the consumer. In order to make it easier to understand the decision-making process described in the fourth major section of the text, Chapter 10 will deal with a discussion of the form, structure, and source of information and a general overview of human information processing.

The decision-making process requires inputs of information, and *perception* is the general study of how that information is selected, integrated, and organized. Chapter 10 will also explore in depth the nature of perception and what causes consumers to perceive or "see" stimuli or bits of information the way they do. We know that the perceptual process enables us to form stimuli into meaningful patterns. However, individual factors unique to all of us cause us to perceive selectively and frequently to give different meanings to the same stimuli. This problem of selective and unique perception is of major concern to marketers trying to communicate highly symbolic messages to a large group of diverse consumers.

Chapter 11 deals with a fairly new area of interest with respect to consumer behavior—*individual development*. Although we deal with children as consumers and influencers in the chapter on family, it is important to realize and understand how children learn to be consumers. Without a fundamental understanding of how learning occurs, it will be difficult for you as a marketing manager to affect and influence consumer learning. We will examine individual development in terms of consumer learning through age 18 while devoting special attention to such topics as children and advertising.

In terms of lifestyle and purchase decisions, we learn needs, tastes and preferences, price and quality relationships. As our purchase experience increases we learn the most effective sources of information, the best places to shop, the brand names to rely on and those to avoid. Thus, it is important for the marketer to understand how people learn and what must be done to affect their learning. For instance, if we learn to "like" through exposure (increased familiarity), it follows that the marketer can exert some direct influences upon taste preferences through the amount and timing of promotional efforts as well as the design and characteristics of products and services offered.

Chapter 12 analyzes those *individual characteristics* that energize, direct, and shape a particular pattern of purchase and consumption behavior. We will first look at *motives* —the forces that initiate and direct consumer behavior. Motives may be physiologically or psychologically based. However, most consumer behavior in developed economies is guided by psychological motives. We examine 12 basic motives as they relate to lifestyle and purchase decisions. While *motives* direct behaviors toward objectives, *personality* relates to the forms that behavior takes. Personality is generally considered to reflect a consistent pattern of responses to a variety of situations. Though Chapter 12 discusses motives and personality which are individual characteristics uniquely different to each of us, this chapter also discusses how this information can be used to improve the effectiveness of marketing efforts.

Chapter 12 also provides a brief discussion of the impact of individual *experiences* and *expectations* on consumption patterns. By experiences we mean the things that happen to us as a collective society (war, depression, technology advances) and as individuals (health, divorce). Expectations are also important in shaping consumer lifestyle and satisfaction. Expectations may serve as lifestyle goals (anticipated employment after graduation) or constraints (the need to save to send kids to college). One of the problems marketers have in accurately predicting consumer behavior is caused by the fact that consumers, in effect, live in the future.

Attitudes, the topic of Chapter 13, represent our basic orientation for or against some object such as a product or retail outlet. They are formed out of the interrelationship between personal experience and lifestyle and the factors discussed in the preceding ten chapters that help shape lifestyle. Attitudes are composed of cognitive (beliefs), affective (feelings), and behavioral (response tendencies) components. These three components tend to be consistent with one another. That is, if one believes that a brand has certain desirable attributes (cognitive component), one will probably like the brand (affective component) and, should the need arise, purchase that brand (behavioral component). Marketing strategies are, therefore, frequently based on influencing the cognitive component of the attitude with the expectation that success in this endeavor will eventually result in increased purchases of this brand or product.

The basic goal of marketing strategy with respect to attitudes can take one or a combination of three forms:

1. *To maintain present attitudes.* The goal here is to provide information to target market consumers that will help them maintain their current favorable attitude.
2. *To change attitudes.* This is the situation where the objective is to change a negative attitude into a positive one, further increase the strength of a positive attitude, or change a positive competing attitude (another brand for instance) into a less favorable or negative one.
3. *To create new attitudes.* This would be the situation of a new product on the market that is unfamiliar to consumers or trying to attract consumers who are unfamiliar with an existing product.

Chapter 13 provides a detailed discussion of the various techniques available to marketing managers for achieving these goals.

The final chapter in section three will draw together all we have discussed in Chapters 4 through 13 in a thorough discussion of consumer *lifestyles* and how they evolve and influence consumer behavior. Personality, motives, culture, social class, reference groups, family, and individual development, experiences, and expectations influence consumers in adopting a particular lifestyle that represents what they think they are and want to be. This is an ongoing process and there are continual, but generally moderate, changes in that lifestyle as our own personal situation changes.

In Chapter 14 we will also discuss *self-concept* as an internal representation of lifestyle. Self-concept is basically the attitudes one holds toward oneself. Lifestyle is the outward manifestation of the self-concept. After describing the self-concept and its relationship to lifestyle, *psychographics,* the most popular method of measuring lifestyle, will be described. Then, after focusing in some detail on consumer lifestyle and, in the previous chapters, on the factors that combine to influence lifestyle, we will turn our focus to the consumer decision process that is used to choose products and services that are a vital part of achieving and maintaining a particular lifestyle.

CONSUMER DECISION PROCESS

Section Four of the text focuses on the consumer decision process. We have already emphasized that consumers make purchase decisions that enhance their present or desired lifestyles. Marketing managers are, of course, interested in influencing consumers to purchase their particular product or brand and to do this they must have a thorough understanding of the decision-making process that consumers go through.

Chapters 15 through 19 deal with the decision-making process. Figure 2−3 illustrates the basic elements in the consumer decision process, and Figure 2−4 represents a comprehensive picture of our overall model that is conceptual rather than predictive as we stated at the start of this chapter. Again we would remind you that consumers have *specific problems* that require *specific solutions,* hence the *existing situation* must always be the framework within which the decision-making process is viewed.

FIGURE 2–3
Consumer decision-making
process

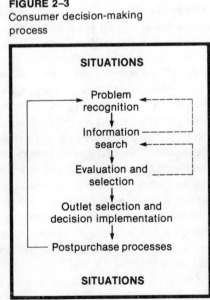

FIGURE 2–4

Overall model of consumer behavior

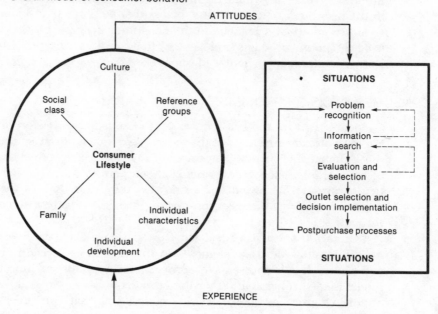

The consumer decision process begins with the recognition that a problem exists. A consumer problem is simply a difference between an existing state and a desired state. Once the consumer recognizes that a problem exists, the problem must be defined. This is a frequent source of frustration for consumers, as they know something is wrong but cannot put their finger on what bothers them. In such a case, it will then be difficult for consumers to come up with a relevant set of alternative solutions and there will be either a great deal of inefficient information search or a halt to the entire process as being too difficult to cope with.

We will be interested in determining the events and situations which cause problems for consumers. In a very real sense, this is the study of motivation or the impetus to action that is necessary for the decision-making process to begin. Obviously, marketers are interested in what motivates consumers and how they can influence that motivation. Managers can and do influence problem recognition, and this important aspect of marketing strategy will be closely examined. It is our basic contention that most consumption problems arise from a desire to maintain and enhance one's lifestyle. Figure 2–4 illustrates this relationship and represents our completed organizational model of consumer behavior.

Once the problem is recognized and defined, an information search is undertaken to come up with a suitable set of alternatives that could conceivably be solutions to the problem. This information search is the subject matter of Chapter 16. Additional information is usually gathered that will allow the consumer to evaluate the alternatives in order to decide which will best solve the problem. Depending on the particular situation and consumer, the information search may be extensive, very brief, or somewhere in between. For example, let us suppose that a newly married couple is in the market for a new car. Their problem is to find an automobile that will be extremely dependable, get good gas mileage, and yet be fun to drive and sporty in appearance. They have a limited income and this will be the only car they will have. Notice that in defining the problem we have also specified the information they will need in order to make a decision among the possible alternatives. Probably, because this car purchase represents a large part of their income and has to satisfy both of them, the information search will be relatively extensive and a joint husband/wife process. The purchase is an important one; they have to live with it for a long time and they do not want to make a mistake. They will also probably consider a reasonably large number of alternatives for the same reasons. This "evoked set" of products will probably not consist of all possible alternatives, however, as that would usually be too much to consider.[5] For instance, they might rule out foreign cars and consider only Chevette, Pinto, Concord, and Colt.

The other end of the information search continuum might be represented by someone who wants basically the same kind of car but is going to give it to a daughter at college. Since the buyer has a large income, the purchase does not represent a significant expense to the buyer. In this case, the time and effort spent in information search may be minimal and the evoked set of product alternatives may be smaller.

Conditions under which information search occurs will be examined in some detail as they will greatly affect marketing mix strategies. For instance, *perceived risk* is a phenomenon whereby consumers attach an estimate of the risk (chance and cost of purchasing a product that does not solve the problem) associated with a potential purchase. Information search is engaged in, in order to reduce the original risk assessment, and marketers can provide information to reduce the perceived risk, encourage purchase, and hopefully contribute to greater consumer satisfaction.

After information has been gathered that allows one to determine the relevant and feasible alternatives and to compare those alternatives, the decision can be made. Chapter 17 deals with how consumers select and evaluate relevant choice alternatives. Here we are concerned with which informational cues consumers use in choosing relevant alternatives and

---

[5] J. A. Howard and J. N. Sheth, *The Theory of Buyer Behavior* (John Wiley and Sons, Inc., 1969), p. 26.

how those cues are used to form product images. The actual *evaluative criteria* used will be examined and we will consider such questions as: Do consumers consider all product attributes to be equally important or are some more critical than others? How is this information evaluated and how is a brand choice made?

Chapter 18 focuses on the selection of the retail outlet and the actual purchase of the product. The attributes that influence store choice are examined and related to the needs of particular consumer groups. The actual acquisition of the product is analyzed with particular attention given to retailers' efforts to attract and satisfy consumers in the exchange process of the consumer purchase decision.

In Chapter 19 we examine four areas of particular concern to marketing managers that occur *after* purchase—use, satisfaction, disposition, and repurchase behavior. The uses of existing products are examined by marketing managers for clues to product improvements or themes for promotional campaigns. Satisfaction is influenced by both product performance *and* the purchasing process. We examine strategies that marketers can use to increase satisfaction in both areas. The disposition of products is an area of increasing concern for both public policymakers and marketing managers. In this chapter we review what is known of this process. Finally, we examine the repurchase motivation (or lack of it) for brands or products.

The bulk of this book is aimed at presenting "mainstream," useable knowledge of consumer behavior. The final chapter, Chapter 20, provides a managerial overview of all the major areas and then departs from this approach and presents a very brief glimpse at some new research areas such as the adult life cycle, cognitive response, imagery, role accumulators, and psycholinguistics which may be important in the future of consumer research.

SUMMARY

The purpose of the model presented in this chapter is to organize the major conceptual areas of consumer behavior and illustrate their relationships with one another. From a marketing standpoint this model outlines the major sources of influence that marketing managers should understand in developing marketing strategy to solve marketing problems and capitalize on marketing opportunities.

Within each major area outlined in our model of consumer behavior lie a large subset of related concepts. Because the number of these related concepts is quite large and their relative importance varies across consumers, products, and situations, a single comprehensive model of consumer behavior is not possible. Instead, for a given marketing situation a marketer must examine specific aspects of consumer behavior to develop a marketing strategy for that marketing situation.

At the hub of the consumer behavior model presented in this chapter is lifestyle. In the broadest sense possible, our culture by way of its values, norms, and traditions represents a major influence on the American style of life. Within any culture, social class distinctions create differing consumer lifestyles. However, specific groups within social classes also vary due to influences created by various reference groups and family influences. Each of these influences, culture, social class, reference groups, and family are external influences that contribute to a particular consumer lifestyle.

Those factors that influence consumer lifestyle but which are relatively unique to the individual consumer include individual development and individual characteristics. Individual development comprises learning and childhood socialization which contribute to a desired lifestyle and patterns of behavior. Individual characteristics represent those motivations and personality features that make each individual unique. Thus, the combination of these external and internal influences are manifested in consumer lifestyles and the products and services individuals consume to maintain and/or change that lifestyle.

Because of lifestyle, and indirectly all those factors that influence lifestyle, consumers establish certain attitudes toward consumption of products in various situations. The combination of a particular lifestyle, attitudes, and situational influences activates the consumer decision process. The consumer decision process involves problem recognition, information search, alternative evaluation, outlet selection, decision implementation, and postpurchase processes.

Our model of consumer behavior may appear static since it is difficult to graphically portray the dynamic nature of consumer behavior. However, consumers are continually evolving and changing as they process new information related to their lifestyle and the outcome of past purchase decisions. Thus, underlying the entire consumer behavior process shown in our model is the assumption that information processing is a never-ceasing activity.

REVIEW QUESTIONS

1. How should marketing managers view the consumer and how will this view of the consumer help them understand consumer purchasing behavior?
2. What is meant by a consumer's lifestyle?
3. What concepts make up and/or influence a consumer's lifestyle?
4. What do we mean by culture and how does it relate to the study of consumer behavior?

5. What is social stratification and why are marketing managers interested in the concept?
6. What are reference groups and what relationship do they have to consumer behavior?
7. Why is the family an important reference group of interest to marketing managers?
8. What is the role of information processing in consumer behavior?
9. What is meant by the phrase "consumer behavior is learned behavior"?
10. What are attitudes and why are they of interest to marketing managers?
11. Of what relevance is the study of the consumer decision-making process?
12. Why is correct problem recognition and definition so important to consumer decision making?
13. What do we mean by information search and what is its role in the decision-making process?
14. What are evaluative criteria?
15. What are the two components of consumer satisfaction?

DISCUSSION QUESTIONS

1. Of what use, if any, are models such as the one proposed in this chapter to practicing marketing managers?
2. Of what use would the model presented in this chapter be to Jeff as he develops marketing strategy for Motron?
3. What changes would you recommend in the model? Why?
4. Describe your "lifestyle." Does it differ significantly from your parents' lifestyle? What causes the difference?
5. Do you anticipate any major changes in your lifestyle in the next five years? If you do, what will be the cause of these changes?
6. Describe a recent, important purchase that you made. To what extent can your purchase be described by the consumer decision-making process described in this chapter? How would you explain the deviations?

PROJECT QUESTIONS

1. Interview a moped salesperson. Try to discover this individual's personal "model" of consumer behavior with respect to mopeds.
2. Repeat question 1 above for one of the following categories:
   a. Used cars.
   b. Men's suits

    c.   Women's shoes
    d.   Wine.
    e.   Bicycles
    f.   Houses
    g.   Paperback books

3.   Interview one person that recently made a major purchase and one person that recently made a minor purchase. In what ways were their decision processes similar? In what ways were they different?

3

Situational influences

The brand management of the L'Erin cosmetics decided to be the first complete line of cosmetics distributed through supermarkets. The rationale for this decision was a belief "that today's busy woman would respond to the convenience of having access to a line of cosmetics in a store she must visit anyway." However, the firm faced a vastly different environment in the supermarket from the traditional department store and specialty shop outlets with their trained personnel to "push" their products. In the supermarket, other tasks compete for the shopper's time and the "visually chaotic" environment has thousands of packages which compete for her attention. To compete in this environment, each of the 83 products in the line is displayed in distinctively colored burgundy boxes with "windows" which allow visual inspection of the product. These packages are contained in a "miniboutique"—a rotating display complete with mirrors.[1]

In effect, L'Erin recognized the problems posed for cosmetics by the supermarket shopping environment and sought to control some of the physical aspects of this environment. As we will see shortly, physical aspects are an important component of situational influences.

Frequently when a friend asks you how you would react or respond to

[1] B. Marona, "L'Erin Launch—A Food Store First," *Advertising Age* (February 26, 1979), p. S—27.

a certain event or occurrence, your answer is preceded by the statement "it depends." Depends on what? Generally, the action you will take depends on exactly what is the entire set of circumstances. In other words, your *action depends in part on the situation at hand*. For example, you would probably respond differently to a funny, but somewhat off-color joke told to you by a good friend while you were both at the local pub as opposed to being told the same joke by the same friend while visiting with your mother and grandmother. Note that the same stimulus input (the joke) is present and that the stimulus is being presented by the same source (your friend), but your overt response or reaction is different. This differential response is due to the fact that you were in two very different situations that called for different types of behavior on your part.

What is the moral of this for marketing managers? Simply that *one should view the consumer and the marketing activities designed to affect and influence that consumer in light of the situations that the consumer faces.* The relative effectiveness of an advertisement or personal sales presentation can vary tremendously as the situation changes. To the extent possible, we want to be able to predict how various situations and marketing mix strategies interact. In this chapter we define *situation* and then present a situation classification scheme that will be useful for you in judging when the situation is an active part of behavior and how it can affect the consumer. The final section of the chapter describes the managerial approach to situational analysis in making marketing decisions.

An initial word of caution is in order, however, before we delve into the situation. Like all aspects of consumption behavior, the effect of the situation will vary considerably. In some cases, the situation will have no influence whatsoever because the individual's characteristics or choices are so intense that they override everything else. For example, in a period of short supply for a particular product, say automobile tires, that you need very badly, the actual purchase situation may have very little effect on whether or not you will buy the tires. You would buy tires from a person you did not like in a store that you thought to be dirty and unattractive because you *needed* the tires immediately. On the other hand, there will be instances when the reverse is true and the situation is overwhelmingly dominant. As an example, when dining out on a special occasion such as the birthday of a good friend, the situation (physical environment, etc.) may well be the deciding factor on whether or not you purchase a bottle of wine to go with your meal. Do not look for hard and fast rules about the effect of situations. Rather, try to realize the potential effect and importance of the situation and develop a sensitivity to the clues that will indicate to you *when* a particular situation is likely to effect consumer's reactions to your product, *how strong* that reaction is likely to be, and in *what way* the situation influences purchase behavior.

SITUATION DEFINED

We will view a consumer situation "as comprising all those factors particular to a time and place of observation which do not follow from a knowledge of personal (intra-individual) and stimulus (choice alternative) attributes and which have a demonstrable and systematic effect on current behavior."[2] In other words, *a situation is a set of factors outside of and removed from the individual consumer as well as removed from the characteristics or attributes of the stimulus object (a product, a television advertisement, etc.) that the consumer is taking action on* (e.g., the *purchase* of a product or *watching* a television advertisement). We are also only interested in those situations that actually have a noticeable impact on consumer behavior. We can ignore situations when the characteristics of the buyer or the stimulus are so intense that they are influential across all relevant situations.[3] An example of this might be a consumer suffering from anxiety to the extent that the person perceives all possible purchases as being threatening or very risky.

Perhaps it would be helpful to diagram the relationship that the situation has with the consumer, the object of the consumer's interest, and the consumer behavior that results. Figure 3–1 shows the relationship

FIGURE 3–1
The situation in consumer behavior

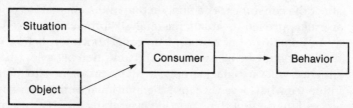

Source: Used with permission from R. Belk, "Situational Effects and Consumer Behavior," *Journal of Consumer Research* (December 1975), p. 158.

and, as we can see, there are basically three variables: the consumer, the object, and the situation that either directly or indirectly affect behavior. While marketers often study the effect the object has on the consumer's behavior, they may often ignore the motivating influence that the situation has on both how the object is perceived and used. Thus, marketers

[2] R. W. Belk, "Situational Variables and Consumer Behavior," *Journal of Consumer Research* (December 1975), p. 158.

[3] R. W. Belk, "An Exploratory Assessment of Situational Effects in Buyer Behavior," *Journal of Marketing Research* (May 1974), p. 156. See also P. H. Reingen, "Demand Bias in the Assessment of Situational Effects on Buyer Behavior," in *Advances in Consumer Research III,* ed. B. B. Anderson (Association for Consumer Research, 1976), pp. 130–33.

stand to gain a great deal by studying the roles their products play in different situations.

Traditionally, the marketer has controlled the object. If that object is a product, considerable effort is normally given to its design, color, function; and so forth. This is a very controllable variable for the marketing manager. In recent years, we have also become aware of the tremendous impact that individual consumer characteristics can have on whether or not that product will be purchased. Personality characteristics, demographic factors such as level of education and income, and lifestyle characteristics are all within each individual and affect overt behavior. This is a far less controllable variable for the marketing manager. However, through increased knowledge about individual characteristics and how those characteristics tend to affect people, marketers have been able to develop strategies that can influence product purchase because they account for and incorporate personal characteristics of the consumer into the product and its promotional appeals.

Only recently though have marketers become aware of the potentially powerful impact of the situation itself on behavior. With increased research in consumer behavior, it became apparent that something external to the person or persons and the object in question was frequently affecting the behavior of the consumer with respect to the product. This external influence is the situation. An example of this is presented below. The example is from a descriptive analysis of a young man's shift in beer preferences as his *social situation* changed.

In high school Bob had lived with his aunt and uncle. He participated very little in high-school activities and did not participate in high-school athletics. In short, his socialization prior to college was built primarily around his home and small group of friends he had known all his life. This limited interaction with others of his own age group tended to make Bob shy among strangers and somewhat insecure; however, he wanted desperately to be accepted by his friends in college. Bob pledged a social fraternity upon entering the University of Missouri.

At this point in his life Bob began drinking Michelob beer on draft. There are several reasons why Bob switched from being a constant Budweiser drinker to the use of draft Michelob.

First, the almost total acceptance of Budweiser did not prevail in Columbia, as it had in St. Louis. In his new environment Bob was confronted with people who preferred many other brands of beer and who had good reasons for their preference. Second, Bob was now in a social group that looked on a trip to the local beer garden as a normal everyday occurrence. Going down to get a beer in the afternoon or evening was an accepted social act. Third, Budweiser was looked upon as simply another of the "good" beers. Other brands such as Schlitz, Coors, Millers, and Falstaff were lumped in the same general class by most of his peers. Fourth, Michelob and several imported beers were generally regarded as the best

TABLE 3–1
Use context and desired product features: Nonalcoholic beverages

Use contexts (situations)	Context-specific ideal beverage clusters*	Desired Attributes
During the summer	Water-based drinks	Not relaxing Sour Thirst quenching
During the winter	Hot adult drinks	Served very hot Good for my health Energy giving
For breakfast	Juices	Primarily for children Good for my health Energy giving
For lunch	Hot adult drinks	Served very hot Best with food Not thirst quenching
When friends come for dinner	Hot adult drinks	Primarily for adults Sour Light
When you are thirsty	Water-based drinks	Not relaxing Sour Thirst quenching
When you wish to relax	Water-based drinks	Relaxing Sweet Not thirst quenching
When you need a pick-me-up	Milk-based drinks	Served very hot Good for my health Energy giving

* While the analysis yields unique context-specific beverages, only the beverage clusters are revealed here to protect the confidentiality of the results.
Source: T. P. Hustad, C. S. Mayer, and T. W. Whipple, "Consideration of Context Differences in Product Evaluation and Market Segmentation," *Journal of the Academy of Marketing Science* (Winter 1975), p. 42.

or highest quality. Drinking Budweiser did nothing to establish an individual's sophisticated taste within the group.

The change of circumstance forced Bob to re-evaluate his standards and tastes for beer. He soon began drinking Michelob on draft.[4]

The above example demonstrates both how important and yet how subtle the situation can be in influencing behavior. Note that the behavior that resulted depended on the *combined effects* of the situation, the customer, and the product, not just the situation by itself. Though this situation was primarily social in nature, there are many other kinds of situations that influence consumer behavior.

---

[4] J. L. Pullins, "Bob Palmer's Preference in Beer," in *Foundations for a Theory of Consumer Behavior*, ed. W. T. Tucker (Holt, Rinehart and Winston, 1967), p. 119.

Table 3–1 illustrates a number of situations (use contexts) utilized in a study of the nonalcoholic beverage market. The eight situations were derived from focus group interviews. As can be seen in the table, the ideal (best) type of beverage and the desired attributes differ markedly from one usage situation to another. Clearly, a marketing manager making product design or advertising copy decisions in this industry must consider the situational context in which the product is to be consumed. Figure 3–2 provides a further illustration of types of situations. In this

FIGURE 3–2
Situation descriptions relevant to fast-food restaurants

1. You are too tired to cook dinner either because you have been cleaning the house all day or you had a very busy day at the office or you had been shopping all day or the children have given you a hectic day.
2. Your neighbor came over to visit and you are having a pleasant chat, and you discover it is lunch time.
3. You are having a few friends over for a casual get-together.
4. You are planning a picnic with just your own family.
5. You have been watching the afternoon movie or you have been playing with the children, and they don't want you to stop the game, or you have been playing tennis or cards and you are having too good a time to cook dinner.
6. You want a change from the daily routine.
7. You are wondering what to serve yourself and the children since your husband is not going to be home for dinner.
8. You are planning a picnic with your friends.
9. You need food for some unexpected dinner guests.
10. The children are asking for something different for dinner.

Source: Based on R. W. Belk, "The Objective Situation as a Determinant of Consumer Behavior," in *Advances in Consumer Behavior II*, ed. M. J. Schlinger (Association for Consumer Research, 1975), p. 432.

case, the situations were developed for a study of fast-food and take-out restaurants. Again, preferences were found to vary by situation.[5] These two examples should highlight for you the necessity of situational considerations for marketing managers.

For instance, an advertisement showing a woman buying take-out

---

[5] R. W. Belk, "The Objective Situation as a Determinant of Consumer Behavior," in *Advances in Consumer Research II*, ed. M. J. Schlinger, (Association for Consumer Research, 1975), pp. 427–37. Similar results were found using slightly different situational definitions by K. E. Miller, "A Situational Multiattribute Attitude Model," in *Advances in Consumer Research II* ed. M. J. Schlinger (Association for Consumer Research, 1975), pp. 455–63.

food from a fast-food or convenience restaurant to serve good friends at a holiday picnic may be less believable and hence less effective than an advertisement showing the same woman making the same purchase in the situation where she has had a long, busy day and is very tired. It should be pointed out, that a fast-food restaurant may still run an advertisement showing purchase for friends at a holiday picnic with the specific goal in mind of educating consumers that it is an acceptable consumption situation for their product. The marketing goal here would be to increase the kinds of situations that consumers feel are appropriate in which to use the product and hence to increase consumption of the product.

While knowledge of the situation can help you make a better marketing mix decision in most cases, it is not a guarantee of success. The situation is not a major source of influence in all cases. Sometimes, as was noted earlier, the individual and/or object have such dominant characteristics that they wipe out the effects of the situation. Additionally, we are not always able to define the situation well. We do not always know when the situation will come to play and, if it does, how intense will be its influence. The entire process is complicated by the fact that these variables—the product, the consumer, and the situation—interact.[6] For example, "price-sensitive" individuals have been found to respond differently to purchase decision situations than other consumers.[7] The same study found price-related situational factors to vary in importance by product category.

Despite these difficulties, an objective consideration of the situation buyers will be in as they react to marketing stimuli can only improve your decision making.

SITUATION CLASSIFICATION

The purpose of classification systems is to combine items into a smaller number of groups, usually based on the similarity of the important characteristics that make up the items. For example, botanists classify plants into smaller groups based on certain characteristics of all plants and are therefore able to deal with plants more effectively by dealing with the similar groups instead of each separate plant. For this same reason, the marketing manager reduces large numbers of consumers into a smaller number of groups (market segments) based on

---

[6] See G. J. Szybillo, "A Situational Influence on the Relationship of a Consumer Attribute to New-Product Attractiveness," *Journal of Applied Psychology* (October 1975), pp. 652–55; W. O. Bearden and A. G. Woodside, "Interactions of Consumption Situations and Brand Attitudes," *Journal of Applied Psychology* (December 1976), pp. 764–69; J. F. Willenberg and R. E. Pitts, "Perceived Situational Effects on Price Sensitivity," *Journal of Business Research* (March 1977), pp. 27–38.

[7] Willenberg and Pitts, "Perceived Situational Effects," pp. 27–38.

similar characteristics. We, in turn, would like to classify situations in order to make it easier for you to use them in constructing more effective marketing strategies. There have been a number of recent attempts to classify situations relevant to consumer behavior.[8] It does not take a great deal of imagination to understand the tremendous difficulty of such a task. The main classification problem is twofold in nature—(1) how specific will the classes be and (2) whether to measure situations on an "objective" or "psychological" basis.[9]

The question of how specific to make a classification scheme is a difficult one to answer. The main concern here is the number of classes or sets of descriptive characteristics one should use in order to classify types of situations. A very large and specific set of classes will allow you to identify many situations very precisely but can become complex in terms of detail. Using a smaller set of classes is easier to handle but usually results in combining some unlike situations under the same class label. The problem is to find a happy medium—a classification scheme with enough classes to allow for accuracy and precision but few enough classes to be practically useful to the manager.

The second major question in classifying situations deals with how one should measure situations. The psychological approach uses the consumer's perceptions of what the situation is, that is, subjective assessments or interpretations by each individual consumer.[10] Objective measures are features of the situation as it exists before consumers' interpretations. We emphasize this latter perspective because it is more useful to the manager. This is not to say that the other view is incorrect or not useful. We feel, however, that objective descriptions of situations are realistic, practical, and to an extent include or encompass most

[8] See R. W. Belk, "Application and Analysis of the Behavioral Differential Inventory for Assessing Situational Effects in Buyer Behavior," in *Advances in Consumer Research I*, eds. S. Ward and P. Wright (Association for Consumer Research, 1974), pp. 370–80; Belk, "The Objective Situation, pp. 158–61; N. Frederickson, "Toward a Taxonomy of Situations," *American Psychologist* (February 1972), pp. 114–23; P. Kakkar and R. J. Lutz, "Toward a Taxonomy of Consumption Situations," in *Marketing in Turbulent Times*, ed. E. M. Mazze (American Marketing Association, 1975), pp. 206–10; R. J. Lutz and P. Kakkar, "Situational Influence in Interpersonal Persuasion," in *Advances in Consumer Research III*, ed. B. B. Anderson (Association for Consumer Research, 1976), pp. 370–78; and R. K. Srinivasan, A. D. Shocker, and G. S. Day, "An Exploratory Study of the Influences of Usage Situation on Perceptions of Product-Markets," in *Advances in Consumer Research, V*, ed. H. K. Hunt (Association for Consumer Research, 1978), pp. 32–38.

[9] The discussion of these two issues has been drawn from Belk, "Situational Variables," and Kakkar and Lutz, "Toward a Taxonomy."

[10] See R. J. Lutz and P. Kakkar, "The Psychological Situation as a Determinant of Consumer Behavior," in *Advances in Consumer Research II* ed. M. J. Schlinger, (Association for Consumer Research, 1975), pp. 439–53; A. Mehrabian and J. A. Russell, *An Approach to Environmental Psychology* (M.I.T. Press, 1974); J. A. Russell and A. Mehrabian, "Environmental Variables in Consumer Research," *Journal of Consumer Research* (June 1976), pp. 62–63; and K. E. Miller and J. L. Ginter, "An Investigation of Situational Variation in Brand Choice Behavior and Attitude," *Journal of Marketing Research* (February 1979), pp. 111–23.

subjective assessments. Marketing managers have to deal with large market segments (consumers that have a number of relevant similarities). They then can treat these large number of individuals as one unified whole and, if their initial segmentation definition has been done carefully, can make standardized decisions that are more efficient. By and large, we can make this same assumption for consumer situations, knowing full well that we will be wrong in some cases but more often than not we will be accurate enough for our purposes.

Belk has provided us with a useful classification scheme of five objectively measured situational variables.[11] They are as follows:

1. *Physical surroundings* are the most readily apparent features of a situation. These features include geographical and institutional location, decor, sounds, aromas, lighting, weather, and visible configurations of merchandise or other material surrounding the stimulus object.

2. *Social surroundings* provide additional depth to a description of a situation. Other persons present, their characteristics, their apparent roles, and interpersonal inter-actions occurring are potentially relevant examples.

3. *Temporal perspective* is a dimension of situations which may be specified in units ranging from time of day to seasons of the year. Time may also be measured relative to some past or future event for the situational participant. This allows conceptions such as time since last purchase, time since or until meals or payday, and time constraints imposed by prior or standing commitments.

4. *Task definition* features of a situation include an intent or requirement to select, shop for, or obtain information about a general or specific purchase. In addition, task may reflect different buyer and user roles anticipated by the individual. For instance, a person shopping for a small appliance as a wedding gift for a friend is in a different situation than he would be in shopping for a small appliance for personal use.

5. *Antecedent states* make up a final group of features which characterize a situation. These are momentary moods (such as acute anxiety, pleasantness, hostility, and excitation) or momentary conditions (such as cash on hand, fatigue, and illness) rather than chronic individual traits. These conditions are further stipulated to be immediately antecedent to the current situation in order to distinguish states which the individual brings to the situation from states of the individual which result from the situation. For instance, a person may select a certain motion picture because he feels de-

---

[11] Belk, "Situational Variables," p. 161. See also R. G. Barker, *Ecological Psychology: Concepts and Methods for Studying the Environment of Human Behavior* (Stanford University Press, 1968).

pressed (an antecedent state and a part of the choice situation), but the fact that the movie causes him to feel happier is a response to the consumption situation. This altered state may then become antecedent for behavior in the next choice situation encountered, such as passing a street vendor on the way out of the theater.

This classification scheme provides us with five basic types of situational characteristics that managers need to give consideration to in determining if a situation has an effect on the consumer's response to marketing mix strategies. Or in terms of our objective described in the first chapter, they provide the manager with a series of appropriate questions to ask concerning the consumption of the manager's product. We will examine these five groups and the kinds of effects they can have on consumer behavior in some detail.

Physical surroundings

Physical surroundings comprise a type of situational influence that is widely recognized. For example "there has been a growing recognition that store interiors can be designed to create specific feelings in shoppers that can have an important cuing or reinforcing effect on purchase."[12] A retail clothing store specializing in extremely stylish, modern clothing would want to reflect this to customers in the physical characteristics of the purchase situation. The fixtures, furnishings, and colors should all reflect an overall mood of style, flair, and newness. In addition, the store personnel should appear to carry this theme out also in terms of their own appearance and apparel. The effect that physical surroundings can have are derived from the following four sensory perceptions:

Visual perceptions
   Color, brightness, size, shapes
Aural perceptions
   Volume, pitch
Olfactory perceptions
   Scent, freshness
Tactile perceptions
   Softness, smoothness, temperature[13]

The retailer can manipulate the physical surroundings to create a set of perceptions which affect the overall perception a consumer has of the purchase situation. For example, the physical characteristics or atmo-

---

[12] Philip Kotler, "Atmospherics as a Marketing Tool," *Journal of Retailing* (Winter 1973−74), pp. 48−64.

[13] Ibid., p. 51.

sphere of many restaurants are one of the major competitive variables that significantly affect purchase and, more importantly, repeat purchase behavior. These physical aspects of the situation are of particular importance in the marketing of relatively undifferentiated products. Two retailing examples, furniture and the so-called bargain basement, will make this point clearer.

Progressive retailers are trying to create positive atmospheres consistent with the quality of their furniture. Colby, a large Chicago furniture retailer, opened a spacious suburban store nestled in a beautifully landscaped acre of land. Shoppers drive off the main highway and enter an ample parking lot. They proceed toward the main door passing handsome windows featuring tasteful living room ensembles. They enter the store and pass a leisurely collection of fine furniture. The store is finely scented of leather and maple furniture. Piped-in music provides a leisurely background and the buyer strolls from room to room immersed in a positive feeling toward furniture and Colby's. This store has designed an atmosphere to soothe the anxious buyer, give him a visually gratifying experience, and reinforce positive feelings toward the purchase of fine furniture.

. . . I was given a free hand to investigate how a department store could become more efficient in its sales effort. I very quickly became interested in bringing order out of the chaos that was a daily affair in the women's blouse subdepartment. On one counter, in particular, blouses were strewn about everywhere and the poor shopper was beside herself trying to locate her size. She wasted precious minutes because of the inefficiency of management. How easy it would be to arrange the merchandise neatly, and inaugurate a simple inventory replenishment scheme that would cut down the service times and make an orderly queue possible! After writing what I considered a masterful analysis of the problem I was invited to visit the store at opening time to see how the chaotic melange developed over time. Just before opening time, after the employees had got the entire stock neatly arranged and checked styles and sizes very carefully, they took the blouses out of their boxes, threw them on the counter and very methodically mixed them up. Things were so inefficiently arranged that half an hour after opening there was a crowd of women milling about the counter, and this crowd, like a magnet, lured other bargain hunters into the melee. I learned.[14]

We should be careful to mention at this point that in many instances physical situational characteristics are beyond the control of the marketer. For example, there are many forms of retailing such as mail order, door-to-door, and vending machines where control is minimal. Still, the marketer tries to account for the physical situation by carefully selecting appropriate outlets for vending machines and choosing which specific areas of the community are most acceptable to door-to-door selling.

As a marketing manager you should ask yourself if the physical sur-

---

[14] Ibid., pp. 56—57.

roundings could possibly effect the behavior you are interested in and, if so, in what ways. Note that there are many possible behaviors that a marketer could be interested in—actual purchase, shopping (looking), receiving information (such as watching TV advertisements), and so forth. Tauber, in an analysis of nonpurchase motivations for shopping, found physical activity and sensory stimulation to be two important motives.[15] Enclosed shopping malls offer clear advantages in providing a safe, comfortable area for leisurely strolls. The sights and sounds of a variety of stores and individuals also provide a high degree of sensory stimulation. Both these factors may play an important role in the overall success of shopping centers and other shopping areas.

If there are physical aspects of the situation that you can influence and/or control, then you should do so in a manner that would make the physical situation compatible with the lifestyle of your target market(s):

> Where goods or services are intended for specific social classes or life style groups, the vendors try to create an overall atmosphere suggestive of that market segment. That atmosphere provides cues as to the intended market segment and also enters as part of the consumption process since the consumer wants to enjoy the class qualities of that product. One can find clothing stores, restaurants, and jewelry stores differentially designed to cue buyers as to their intended market. Thus, stores appealing to upper-class patrons usually are laid out more spaciously and display less goods. Stores appealing to mod youth use moving lights, piped-in rock music, and bright colors.[16]

Often you can neither control nor influence the physical situation the consumer will encounter. Table 3—1 provides examples of physical situations over which the marketer has no control, that is, winter versus summer for beverage consumption. In these cases, it is appropriate to alter the various elements of the marketing mix to match the needs and expectations of the target market. Both Dr. Pepper and Lipton's tea have varied their advertising in terms of product usage between summer and winter based on physical changes in the environment and consumers' reactions to these changes.

Social surroundings

Social surroundings, the second set of situational factors or characteristics in our classification, *deal primarily with other persons present that could have an impact on the individual consumer's behavior*. Our actions are frequently influenced, if not altogether determined, by those around us. Our assessments of the relationship we have with others, based on experience with them and/or their role, status, and individual

---

[15] E. M. Tauber, "Why Do People Shop?" *Journal of Marketing* (October 1972), p. 47.

[16] Kotler, "Atmospherics," p. 53.

personalities can have a major impact on our behavior. Others, there-fore are part of our relevant situations.

Individuals tend to comply with group expectations, particularly when the behavior is visible.[17] Thus, shopping, a highly visible activity, and the use of many publicly consumed brands are subject to social influences. The behavior of others, even strangers, can affect an individual's perception.[18] For example, the presence and role of the other person (i.e., immediate family, close friend, young children, or church minister) has been shown to affect the perception of how similar various television programs are to each other.[19] We will present a more thorough analysis of group influence on behavior in Chapter 8, "Group Processes." For now it is enough to note that we can be affected by the others around us as we look for product information, receive that information, shop for the product and compare it with others, purchase the product, and dispose of it.

Tauber found social motives to be an important reason for visiting retail outlets.[20] Shopping can provide a social *experience outside the home* such as making new acquaintances, meeting existing friends, or just being near other people. It allows one to *communicate with others having similar interests.* For example, music lovers often gather at record stores while fishing devotees migrate to sporting goods stores. Sales personnel are often sought out because they share an interest with the shopper in a product-related activity. *Peer group attraction* is a related motive. Neighborhood or campus bars, record stores, coke stands, and so forth are often frequented more to meet one's friends than to make an explicit purchase. Finally, some people seek *status and authority* in shopping since the salesperson's job is to "wait on" the customer. This allows these individuals a measure of respect or prestige that may otherwise be lacking in their lives. Thus, consumers, on occasion, shop *for* social situations rather than, or in addition to, products.

Frequently, you will not be able as a marketing manager to have any control over the social characteristics of a situation. For example, when a television advertisement is sent into the home, the advertising manager cannot control who the viewer is with at the time of the reception or their relative status relationship. However, the manager can utilize the knowledge that some programs are generally viewed alone (weekday, daytime programs), some are viewed by the entire family (Walt Disney), and others by groups of friends (Superbowl). The message presented can

[17] H. C. Kelman, "Compliance, Identification, and Internalization: Three Processes of Attitude Change," *Journal of Conflict Resolution* (1958), pp. 51–60.

[18] S. E. Asch, "Studies of Independence and Conformity: A Minority of One against a Unanimous Majority," *Psychological Monographs* (1956), pp. 68–70.

[19] E. Dupnick, "The Effect of Context on Cognitive Structure," unpublished Ph.D. dissertation, University of Arizona, 1979.

[20] Tauber, "Why Do People Shop?" p. 48.

be structured to these viewing situations. For example, a message presented on a program frequently viewed by family groups might stress a family decision to purchase a given product, while an advertisement for the same product presented on daytime television might have a "surprise your family" theme.

There are a number of occasions where marketing managers can influence the social aspects of a situation to their advantage. For instance, the advertiser can encourage you to "ask a friend" or, better yet, "bring a friend along." Some firms, such as Tupperware have been ingenious in structuring social situations to encourage sales (this process is described in detail in Chapter 8).

Salespersons know that frequently they can use the shopper's companion as an effective sales aid by soliciting their opinion and advice. Alluding to the positive social implications of product purchase ("won't your friends think you look smart?") has long been a utilization of social situational effects by advertisers.

An interesting example of social surroundings and their effects on consumer behavior is provided by the study of *crowding* in retail stores. Harrell and Hutt have made an extremely interesting and perceptive study of this important situational phenomena which we will examine in some detail.[21]

According to environmental psychologists, crowding is a result of actual physical density and individuals' perceptions of how restricted they are in space. Crowding frequently results in confused and frustrated individuals. Crowding in shopping behavior seems to carry some of these same implications and can result in dissatisfied consumers. Figure 3–3 shows a model of supermarket shopping behavior under conditions of crowding. The model has three levels of interest: Level 1—the actual triggering of the crowding experience, both physically and psychologically; Level 2—the strategies that shoppers develop to handle the crowding experience; and Level 3—the outcomes or feelings that the shopper develops about the store as well as that particular shopping trip.

In combination with numbers of people, spatial limitations will produce some physical density factor. Perceptions of how restricted the physical space has become and how much interference is being experienced along with individual characteristics will produce the situation of crowding. It is important to point out here again that the situation interacts with the product (object) and the person to influence behavior. Therefore, such individual characteristics as geographic background may come into play. That is to say, someone from a small, rural town

---

[21] The following discussion of crowding behavior was drawn from Gilbert D. Harrell and Michael D. Hutt, "Crowding in Retail Stores," *MSU Business Topics* (Winter 1976), pp. 31–39. Used by permission of the publisher, Division of Research, Graduate School of Business Administration, Michigan State University.

FIGURE 3–3
Consumer behavior under conditions of crowding

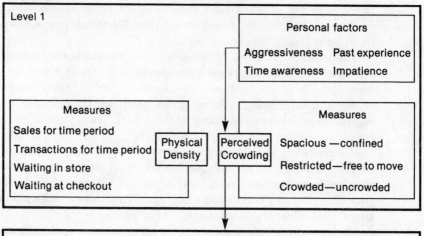

Source: Gilbert D. Harrell and Michael D. Hutt, "Crowding in Retail Stores," *MSU Business Topics* (Winter 1976), p. 35. Reprinted by permission of the publisher, Division of Research, Graduate School of Business Administration, Michigan State University.

may perceive a shopping experience as much more crowded than somebody from a large, metropolitan area.

As Figure 3–3 points out, shoppers can adopt a number of strategies to cope with the crowding. Social interaction with other shoppers and store personnel may be reduced. Certain purchases are delayed and, as shopping time is reduced, the probability of choosing more familiar national brands is increased. Much less time is likely to be spent in examining product label information and display advertising. Shoppers will also tend to conform to planned traffic flow patterns, much to the retailer's delight.

Level 3 of the model deals with the outcomes of crowding behavior that you as a marketing manager may have to contend with. If, in fact, consumers do become "confused and frustrated," they may develop negative attitudes toward future shopping at that store. On the other hand, a somewhat crowded shopping situation, particularly in a discount type operation could positively reflect an image of being "the place" for bargains as witnessed by the crowds of people there (similar to the myth about truck drivers and roadside restaurants!). As we can see, the social surroundings can produce a situational effect that, in combination with the individual consumer, can have important consequences for retailers.

Temporal perspectives

Temporal perspectives are situational characteristics that *deal with the effect of time on consumer behavior*. Howard and Sheth dealt with time pressure as an external variable that affected the decision-making process and have defined it as "the amount of time required (by the consumer) to perform these acts (purchase and consumption) in relation to the time he has allocated to himself for doing them."[22] In other words, the time element of the purchase situation, which is separate and distinct from the individual consumer and the product in question, can impose certain constraints on the purchase behavior.

We must be careful to note at this point, that we are not considering time as a product, at least in this context. Time, of course, is a purchaseable commodity and an increasingly important one. As has been pointed out:

> The affluent citizen of the next century will be oriented to buying time rather than product. He will take the myriad of sophisticated products at his disposal for granted. His chief concern will be to provide himself with free time in which he can conveniently use products that function to conserve time for leisure and pleasure. It is scarcity which creates value.

---

[22] J. Howard and J. Sheth, *The Theory of Buyer Behavior* (John Wiley & Sons, Inc., 1969), p. 77.

Hence, as scarcity of product disappears the scarcity of time ascends the value scale.[23]

Time as a situational factor can manifest itself in a number of different ways. It has been determined, for instance, that the length of time between your last meal and your grocery shopping trip will probably affect the amount of impulse purchasing you do.

> Intuitively it seems that behavior in the supermarket should reflect the differential attractiveness of food due to deprivation. For most people who shop on an empty stomach, supermarket aisles are lined with temptations. Imagination readily places potatoes and onions around roasts and transforms pancake mix into a steaming, buttered stack. An egg and milk run can turn out to cost considerable money and time. When one has recently eaten, on the other hand, roasts are examined with an efficient, dispassionate eye and pancake mix is just pancake mix. The trip may be less enjoyable, but escape with budget and schedule intact is more likely.[24]

It is interesting to note that in the study from which the above quote was taken, the effect of time on impulse purchase behavior was significantly affected by an individual characteristic—weight. Overweight people were not affected by the amount of time between eating and shopping, seemingly being unresponsive to internal "hunger" cues. Again, it is necessary to remember that usually a combination of the object, the situation, and the person brings about behavior.

The amount of time available for the purchase action has a substantial impact on the whole consumer decision process. Research indicates that the longer the period of time between purchases of a brand, the more likely it is that a consumer will engage in more information search and be less likely to engage in brand loyal behavior. As a generalization, we can say that the less time there is available (i.e., increased time pressure) the shorter will be the information search or even the utilization of available information.[25] Limited purchase time can also result in a smaller number of product alternatives relevant that a consumer would consider when making a purchase decision. Additionally, increased time pressures on working wives tend to increase the incidence of brand loyalty, particularly for nationally branded products. The obvious implication is that working wives feel safer with nationally branded or "known" products, particularly when they do not have the time to engage in extensive comparison shopping.[26]

[23] R. C. Ganetson and F. F. Mauser, "The Future Challenges Marketing," *Harvard Business Review*, (November–December 1963), p. 172.

[24] R. E. Nisbett and D. E. Kanouse, "Obesity, Food Deprivation and Supermarket Shopping Behavior," *Journal of Personality and Social Psychology* (August 1969), p. 290.

[25] P. Wright, "The Harassed Decision Maker: Time Pressures, Distractions, and the Use of Evidence," *Journal of Applied Psychology* (October 1974), p. 555–61.

[26] See J. Jacoby, G. J. Szybillo, and C. K. Berning, "Time and Consumer Behavior: and Interdisciplinary Overview," *Journal of Consumer Research* (March 1976), pp. 330–39.

A number of retail firms have taken advantage of the temporal perspective factor. Perhaps the most successful of these is the Seven Eleven chain which caters almost exclusively to individuals who either are in a hurry or who want to make a purchase after regular shopping hours.

Task definition

Task definition, the purpose or reason for engaging in the consumption behavior, can have substantial effects. Imagine the criteria you would use in purchasing an automobile for your personal or family use versus for business use. In Table 3−1 we saw that individuals preferred water-based beverages when the purpose was "to relax" and milk-based drinks when the purpose was a "pick-me-up." Sandell also found significant differences in beverage preferences between task definitions.[27]

To illustrate the potential influence of task definition as it interacts with a personal characteristic, we can examine the dogmatism-innovation relationship first explained by Jacoby.[28] *Dogmatism* is defined as the personality characteristic of closed mindedness and *innovation* the tendency to choose new and different items. It would seem logical that highly dogmatic individuals would not be highly innovative in product choice (i.e., they would not choose "new" or "different" brands over established ones), and indeed Jacoby found this inverse relationship between dogmatism and innovation to be true for college females. This finding was later replicated for college males.[29] Both studies posed a personal purchase situation. In order to see the effects of task definition, a study was conducted which presented a gift-giving situation to subjects. The original and second studies were replicated entirely except there were two task situations—gift giving versus personal use.[30] The normal inverse relationship (higher dogmatism-lower innovativeness) was found again for the self-purchase situation, but a direct relationship that was slightly positive (higher dogmatism-higher innovativeness) was found for persons in the gift purchase situation. Why this phenomenon occurs is not entirely clear. Perhaps when people purchase gifts for others they would like themselves to be perceived as progressive and innovative. The important point is, however, that the purchase intent or task definition did have an effect that reversed the normally predicted

[27] R. G. Sandell, "Effects of Attitudinal and Situational Factors on Reported Choice Behavior," *Journal of Marketing Research* (November 1968), pp. 405−8.

[28] J. Jacoby, "Personality and Innovation Proneness," *Journal of Marketing Research* (May 1971), pp. 244−47.

[29] K. A. Coney, "Dogmatism and Innovation: A Replication," *Journal of Marketing Research* (November 1972), pp. 453−55.

[30] K. A. Coney and R. R. Harmon, "Dogmatism and Innovation: A Situational Perspective," in *Advances in Consumer Research VI*, ed. W. L. Wilkie (Association for Consumer Research, 1979), pp. 118−21.

relationship between dogmatism and innovativeness. Gift-giving situations have also been found to influence perceived risk differently than personal use situations, further evidence that situational task characteristics must be considered by the marketing manager.[31]

Antecedent states

Antecedent states are the final type of situational characteristic. These are features of the individual person that are not lasting characteristics. Rather they can be more easily classified as momentary moods or conditions. For example, we all experience states of depression or high excitement from time to time that are not normally part of our individual makeup. Should we engage in shopping or purchase behavior during these periods, the outcome may be (radically) different than if we were in more "normal" states. So-called impulse purchases would seem to be very strongly influenced by temporary moods. How many times have we later regretted the money we spent on a whim as a result of feeling very good (or possibly very bad). We all know people for example, who at least profess the belief that buying something (many times anything) helps them feel better.

Momentary conditions differ somewhat from momentary moods. Whereas moods reflect states of mind, momentary conditions reflect actual states of being or conditions such as being tired, being ill, having a great deal of money, being broke, and so forth. Note again that for conditions, as for moods, to fit under the definition of antecedent states, they must be momentary and not constantly with the individual. Hence, an individual who is short on cash only momentarily will probably act differently than someone who is always short on cash (i.e., poor).

In Table 3—1, "when you are thirsty" represents an antecedent condition (a momentary condition) that influences beverage preferences. In Figure 3—2, situations 1, 5, and 6 represent antecedent conditions. Moods have been shown to influence individuals' attitudes toward consumer products.[32] Tauber's description of the influence of one response to moods, self-gratification, can have on the shopping process is worth repeating:

> Different emotional states or moods may be relevant for explaining why and when someone goes shopping. For example, a person may go to a store in search of social contact when he feels lonely. Likewise, he may go

[31] M. Vincent and W. G. Zikmund, "An Experimental Investigation of Situational Effects of Risk Perception," in *Advances in Consumer Behavior III,* in B. B. Anderson (Association for Consumer Research, 1976), pp. 125—29. For a somewhat different approach to task definition see G. Fennell, "Consumers' Perceptions of the Product-Use Situation," *Journal of Marketing* (April 1978), pp. 38—47.

[32] J. N. Axelrod, "Induced Moods and Attitudes toward Products," *Journal of Advertising Research* (June 1963), pp. 19—24.

to a store to buy "something nice" for himself when he is depressed. Several subjects in this study reported that often they alleviate depression by simply spending money on themselves. In this case, the shopping trip is motivated not by the expected utility of consuming, but by the utility of the buying process itself.[33]

MANAGERIAL USE OF SITUATION CLASSIFICATION

We have presented a basic classification system of situational characteristics and provided a number of examples of how managers could respond to specific situations in ways that are likely to increase the probability of purchase. Given that situations do have an impact, how do we as marketing managers respond to them; what actions do we take to influence the situation? Unfortunately, there is no magic formula which will allow you to recognize the potential influence of the situation other than simply being aware of situational characteristics and on the lookout for their impacts.

As we have indicated previously, situational variables not only have direct influences, they also interact with product and individual characteristics to influence behavior.[34] For example, research has found that fashion opinion leaders in contrast to nonleaders prefer new fashions that have limited distribution over similar fashions with more extensive distributions.[35] This suggests that messages designed to reach fashion opinion leaders should stress the exclusive nature of the new fashions while later messages could stress the availability of those fashions.

It should also be stressed that individuals do not encounter situations randomly. Instead, most people "create" many of the situations they face.[36] Thus, individuals who choose to engage in physically demanding sports such as jogging, tennis, or racquetball are indirectly choosing to expose themselves to the situation of "being tired" or "being thirsty." This allows marketers to consider advertising and segmentation strategies based on the situations that individuals selecting given lifestyles are likely to encounter. As we shall see in Chapter 14, "Consumer Lifestyles," marketers often describe their market segments in situational terms.

Product and market segment specific research may be required to isolate the appropriate situational factors. However, simply becoming sensitized to the potential impact of situational factors on the consumption process should make you a better marketing decision maker. The

---

[33] Tauber, "Why Do People Shop?" p. 47.

[34] Bearden and Woodside, "Interactions of Consumption Situations."

[35] Szybillo, "A Situational Influence."

[36] See K. S. Bowers, "Situationism in Psychology: An Analysis and a Critique," *Psychological Review* (September 1973), pp. 307–36.

examples presented throughout the chapter indicate some of the ways this sensitivity can be put to practice.

SUMMARY

Marketing managers should view the consumer and marketing activities designed to affect and influence that consumer in light of the situations that the consumer faces. A consumer situation is a set of factors outside of and removed from the individual consumer as well as removed from the characteristics or attributes of the product. Traditionally, marketers have always had a great deal of control over characteristics of the products. Additionally, we have recently learned much about individual consumer characteristics. However, situations that consumers face have largely been ignored.

Situations, for the purpose of helping to explain consumer behavior, have been classified into a scheme of five objectively measured variables. Physical surroundings comprise the first set of situational variables and are the most obvious and readily apparent features of the situation. Features of the physical surroundings include geographical and institutional location, decor, sounds, aromas, lighting, weather, and displays of merchandise or other material surrounding the product. Retailers are particularly concerned with the effect of situational features of physical surroundings.

Social surroundings deal primarily with other persons present that could have an impact on the individual consumer's behavior. The characteristics of the other persons present, their apparent roles, and interpersonal interactions are potentially important social situational influences. Crowding behavior in retail stores provides an excellent example of the effects of social surroundings on consumer behavior.

Temporal perspectives are situational characteristics that deal with the effect of time on consumer behavior. This dimension of situations may be specified in units ranging from time of day to seasons of the year. Time may also be measured relative to some past or future event for the situational participant. This allows conceptions such as time since last purchase, time since or until meals or payday, and time constraints imposed by prior or standing commitments. Convenience stores have evolved and been successful by taking advantage of the temporal perspective factor.

Task definition aspects of situational influence reflect the purpose or reason for engaging in the consumption behavior. The task may reflect different buyer and user roles anticipated by the individual. For example, a person shopping for dishes to be given as a wedding present is probably in a different situation than if the dishes were for personal use.

Antecedent states are the final type of situational characteristic.

These are features of the individual person that are not lasting or relatively enduring characteristics. They are momentary moods or conditions. Momentary moods are such things as temporary states of depression or high excitement which all people experience and that can affect behavior. Momentary conditions are such things as being tired, ill, having a great deal of money (or none at all), and so forth.

Situational influences may have very direct influences, but they also interact with product and individual characteristics to influence behavior. In some cases, the situation will have no influence whatsoever because the individual's characteristics or choices are so intense that they override everything else. But the situation is always potentially important and therefore should be of concern to marketing managers.

REVIEW QUESTIONS

1. What is meant by the term *situation?* Why is it important for a marketing manager to understand situational influences on purchasing behavior?
2. Why is it useful to develop a classification system for situations? What problems or issues are involved in developing such a system?
3. What are physical surroundings (as a situational variable)? Give an example of how they can influence the consumption process.
4. What are social surroundings (as a situational variable)? Give an example of how they can influence the consumption process.
5. What is temporal perspective (as a situational variable)? Give an example of how it can influence the consumption process.
6. What is task definition (as a situational variable)? Give an example of how it can influence the consumption process.
7. What are antecedent conditions (as a situational variable)? Give an example of how they can influence the consumption process.
8. What is meant by the statement, "Situational variables may interact with object or personal characteristics"?
9. Are individuals randomly exposed to situational influences? Why?

DISCUSSION QUESTIONS

1. Discuss the potential importance and applications of each situational variable to SMC for developing marketing strategy.
   a. At the national level.
   b. As a guide to their retail outlets.
2. What product categories seem most susceptible to situational influences? Why?
3. In those instances where marketers have little control over the pur-

chase situation, why is it importnt for them to understand how the situation relates to the consumption of their product?

PROJECT QUESTIONS

1. Discuss the purchase of a moped with someone who has recently purchased one. Determine the role, if any, played by situational factors.
2. Interview a moped salesperson. Determine the role, if any, this individual feels situational variables play in moped sales.
3. Conduct a study using a small (ten or so) sample of your friends in which you attempt to isolate the situational factors that influence the type or brand of (a) beer, (b) snack food, (c) restaurant, or (d) clothing store consumed. (Note: You can find details on how to do this by consulting the footnotes in the chapter.)

SECTION TWO
external influences

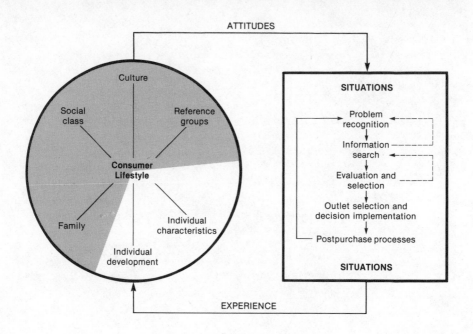

The shaded area of our model shown at left is the focal point for this section of the text. As we indicated in Chapter 2, any division of the factors that influence behavior into separate and distinct categories is somewhat arbitrary. For example, we have chosen to consider learning in the next section of the text on "internal influences." However, it is obvious that a substantial amount of human learning involves interaction with, or imitation of, other individuals. Thus, it could also be considered a group process. In Section Two we will examine groups as they operate to influence consumer behavior. Our emphasis will be on the functioning of the group itself and *not* the process by which the individual reacts to the group.

Our approach in this section is to start with large-scale, macrogroup influences and progress to smaller, more microgroup influences. As we progress, the nature of the influence exerted by the group will change from general guidelines to explicit expectations for certain behaviors. This pattern of influence is illustrated in Figure II—1.

We begin this section with an examination of *culture*. Chapter 4 describes the ways in which cultures differ. It is hoped that this description of cultural variations will increase our sensitivity to our own culture's influence on our behavior. Chapters 5 and 6 provide a fairly detailed description of the American society. The changing *values, demographic characteristics,* and *subcultural* makeup of the current society is described. Chapter 7 continues with an analysis of *social stratification* in America and its influence on consumer behavior. In Chapter 8, the focus moves to small group functioning. The critical role of *reference groups* in transmitting the influence of larger cultural and social class groups to the individual is described. In the last chapter of this section, the most critical reference group for most individuals, the *family,* is described. This description covers the existing family structure in the United States, the family life cycle, and decision roles within the family.

64

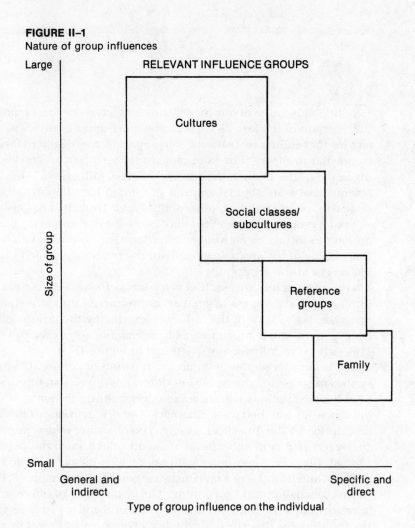

FIGURE II–1
Nature of group influences

4

The cultural environment: Cross-cultural variations in consumer behavior

General Mills tried to capture a share of the English breakfast cereal market with a package and promotional theme similar to several that had proven successful in the United States. In this case, the theme was a picture of a boy saying, "See kids, it's great." The campaign proved to be unsuccessful. One reason for its failure was the fact that British mothers and fathers, unlike American parents, were not accustomed to taking advice on food selection from children.[1] Thus, cultural variations can have a major impact on the success or failure of marketing programs.

As we saw in Chapter 3, consumer behavior always takes place within a specific situation or environment. A person's culture provides the most general situation in which consumption behavior occurs. All other situations, both concrete and abstract, take place within the boundaries of an individual's culture. In this chapter we are going to examine the general nature of culture and how culture functions to influence behavior. Four major types of cross-cultural variations in consumer behavior are described and the implications of culture for cross-cultural marketing strategies are discussed. A detailed examination of the American culture is presented in the next two chapters.

---

[1] E. A. McCreary, *The Americanization of Europe* (Doubleday and Co., 1964), p. 131.

THE CONCEPT OF CULTURE

What is this all-encompassing thing called culture? Before answering this question, we should remind ourselves that it is a *concept* not a physical object. As such, it is subject to all the problems of description and measurement associated with concepts and described in Chapter 1.

We will define *culture* as "that complex whole which includes knowledge, belief, art, law, morals, custom, and any other capabilities and habits acquired by man as a member of society."[2] Thus, culture, as the term is used by behavioral scientists, has a meaning different from the ordinary meaning of "high-brow" or "sophisticated" that is often attached to the term. As one author puts it: "National Culture is not found in museums or formed by graduate schools or universities. It is composed of common habits and patterns of living of people in daily activities, and of the common interest in entertainment, sports, news, and even advertising."[3] An understanding of culture is important to you as a marketing manager because "culture always provides approved specific goal objects for any generalized human want. A reasonably cosmopolitan culture provides a host of alternatives serving the same general end and, in an economically mature culture, most of the alternatives imply products."[4] Several aspects of this concept of culture require elaboration.

First, culture is a *comprehensive* concept. It includes almost everything that influences an individual's thought processes and behaviors. While culture does not determine the nature or frequency of biological drives, such as hunger or sex, it does influence if, when, and how these drives will be gratified. Second, culture is *acquired.* It does not include inherited responses and predispositions. However, since most human behavior is learned rather than innate, culture does affect a wide array of behaviors.

Third, while not explicit in the definition of culture, it should be emphasized that the complexity of modern societies is such that culture seldom provides detailed prescriptions for appropriate behavior. Instead, in most industrial societies, culture supplies *boundaries* within which most individuals think and act. In less complex and, therefore, usually more rigid societies, cultural pressures allow very limited ranges of behavior.[5]

Finally, the nature of cultural influences is such that we are *seldom*

---

[2] E. B. Taylor, *Primitive Culture* (Henry Holt, 1889), p. 1.

[3] L. Loevinger, "There Need Be No Apology, No Lament," *TV Guide Magazine* (April 6, 1968), pp. 8–9.

[4] W. T. Tucker, *The Social Context of Economic Behavior* (Holt, Rinehart and Winston, 1964), p. 37.

[5] An entertaining description of cultural prescriptions of behavior in a nonindustrialized society can be found in A. Haley, *Roots* (Doubleday and Co., 1976).

aware of them. One behaves, thinks, and feels in a manner consistent with other members of the same culture because it seems "natural" or "right" to do so. The influence of culture is similar to the air we breathe; it is everywhere and is generally taken for granted unless there is a fairly rapid change in its nature. As we will see later, it is often necessary to examine a different culture in order to appreciate the impact of our own.

THE FUNCTIONING OF CULTURE

The simpler the society, the more direct the role that culture plays in shaping thoughts and actions. At one extreme, virtually all actions may be prescribed by the culture. However, most industrialized societies are so complex that culture operates primarily by setting rather loose boundaries for individual behavior and by influencing the functioning of such institutions as the family structure, mass media, and so forth.

The boundaries that culture sets on behavior are called *norms*. Norms are simply rules that specify or prohibit certain behaviors in specific situations and are based on or derived from cultural values. *Cultural values* are (1) widely held beliefs that (2) affirm what is desirable and (3) have some impact on activities.[6] In a very simple society, cultural values may be limited to a few areas such as food production which relate directly to the short-run survival of the society. In more complex societies, cultural values tend to be more abstract and long run in nature. For example, some suggested values of the American culture include freedom of choice, egalitarianism, active use of time, and orientation toward the future. It is not necessary, at least in the short run, for a culture's values to be logically consistent. In fact, some tension or strain between conflicting cultural values is probably characteristic of most advanced societies due to rapid changes in such areas as technological development.

Violation of cultural norms results in *sanctions* or penalties ranging from mild social disapproval to, in extreme cases, banishment from the group. Conformity to norms is usually only given explicit and obvious rewards when a child is learning the culture (socialization) or an older person is learning a new culture (acculturation). In other situations, conformity is expected without reward. For example, in America we expect people to arrive on time for business and social appointments. We do not compliment them when they do arrive on time but we tend to become angry when they arrive late.

The preceding discussion may leave the impression that we, as individuals, are aware of cultural values and norms and that violating any

---

[6] F. M. Nicosia and R. N. Mayer, "Toward a Sociology of Consumption," *Journal of Consumer Research* (September 1976), p. 67.

given norm carries a precise and known sanction. This is not usually the case. We tend to "obey" cultural norms without thinking because to do otherwise would seem unnatural. For example, we are seldom aware of how close we stand to other individuals while conducting business. Yet, as we will see shortly, this distance is well defined and adhered to even though it varies from culture to culture. Nor do we consider consuming a vast array of plant and animal life that are considered delicacies in other parts of the world. In other words, we conform because it is the natural way to behave.

Cultures are not static. They typically evolve and change slowly over time. However, there can also be major changes during relatively short time periods. Cultural values are related to the physical and technological environment in an interactive manner. That is, they influence and are influenced by the existing and preceding physical and technological environments. Changes in these environments can produce corresponding changes in cultural values. For example, the introduction and widespread use of the automobile has strongly affected many cultural values in America.

Conflict between existing cultural values can lead to the emergence of new values. Likewise, the exposure to another culture's values can result in the incorporation or modification of these values into the original culture. Finally, dramatic events such as the advent of a great philosopher, a war, or a natural disaster can result in new or different cultural values. The next chapter will provide a detailed examination of the shifts that are taking place in some of the values and norms that characterize the American society and that affect consumer behavior.

CROSS-CULTURAL VARIATIONS IN CONSUMER BEHAVIOR

In our own culture there are commonly accepted thermal associations for various tastes (e.g., spicy foods are considered "hot") or the general opinion that reds, oranges, and yellows are "warm" colors whereas blues, greens, and violets are "cool." In Iran, all food and drink are categorized as either hot or cold in reference not to the temperature and spiciness but rather to the heavy or light feeling that results from eating or drinking.[7] This difference could have obvious importance for one exporting food to Iran. However, relatively few will become involved in this activity. Why then should we examine foreign cultures? The following quote provides the answer:

> Culture hides much more than it reveals, and strangely enough what it hides, it hides most effectively from its own participants. Years of study have convinced me that the real job is not to understand foreign culture but to understand our own. I am also convinced that all one ever gets from

___

[7] A. Mehrabian and J. A. Russell, *An Approach to Environmental Psychology* (M.I.T. Press, 1974), p. 10.

studying foreign culture is a token understanding (of that culture). The ultimate reason for such study is to learn more about how one's own system works.[8]

The above quote provides a statement of the philosophy and objectives of this section. We are going to examine aspects of foreign cultures, not to become experts in a given foreign culture, but to increase our appreciation of how culture operates. This appreciation will provide us with two advantages. First, we will better understand how culture influences consumer behavior in the United States. Second, our understanding of how culture functions will make us sensitive to the potential pitfalls that exist when one operates in a foreign culture or one of our own subcultures.[9]

In the following pages we will examine variations in cultural values and cultural variations in nonverbal communications. A number of examples of how these variations affect consumer behavior and thus marketing strategy will be presented. Since cultures are not static, these examples should be treated as illustrations of how cultures may differ rather than as concrete evidence of current cultural differences between two or more specific cultures.

Variations in cultural values

Cultural values are widely held beliefs that affirm what is desirable and have an impact on activities. These values affect behavior through norms which specify acceptable and unacceptable responses to specific situations. A useful approach to understanding cultural variations in behavior is to understand the values embraced by different cultures.[10]

If a marketing manager can determine the relevant cultural values for the market segment of interest and also knows the general type and strength of response those values will elicit, a much more effective marketing strategy can be developed. Therefore, we offer a simple but useful classification scheme consisting of three broad forms of behavioral responses—*control, direction,* and *feeling.*[11] The cultural values that impact the most on consumer behavior can be classified under one of these three general responses.

Basically, when we speak of *control* we are referring to the extent to which a person feels unrestricted or free to act in a variety of ways.

---

[8] E. T. Hall, *The Silent Language* (Fawcett World Library, 1959), p. 39.

[9] For a treatment of the role of culture in international business, see V. Terpstra, *The Cultural Environment of International Business* (South-Western Publishing Co., 1978).

[10] A discussion of this point is contained in T. O. Wallin, "The International Executive's Baggage: Cultural Values of the American Frontier," *MSU Business Topics* (Spring 1976), pp. 49–58.

[11] This general taxonomy is adopted from Mehrabian and Russell, *Environmental Psychology*, chap. 2.

Obviously, this is important for the marketing manager in determining the extent to which the consumer will be affected by the culture in making consumption decisions. For instance, if the culture values collective activity, consumers are likely to look toward others for guidance in purchase decisions. If that culture also values age more than youth and attributes wisdom and prestige to older members of the society, younger people will be more restricted in their activities and roles and look to older people for guidance.

Direction is our term for the set of responses people can make that determine, in effect, which way they will go in life. Knowing what these directional values are in any culture and how strongly they are held will allow us to better predict what kinds of actions consumers are likely to take. For example, a society that holds material goods and hard work in high esteem will tend to produce people who feel they should work long hours and that conspicious consumption is admirable.

The relative degree of pleasure or pleasantness evoked from a situation or activity is a *feeling* response. The acceptance and use of credit cards, for example, was very much determined by the commonly held cultural value of postponed versus immediate gratification. We would expect a society that encourages immediate gratification and sensual gratification to be much more receptive to pleasure-oriented products than one which does not.

Figure 4−1 provides a list of 18 values (six in each of the three response classes) which are important in most complex cultures. The list is not meant to be exhaustive but does include most of the major values that are relevant to consumer behavior in industrialized societies. You will note that most of the values are shown as dichotomies (e.g., materialistic versus nonmaterialistic); however, this is not meant to represent an either/or situation. Instead, there is a continuum between the two extremes. For example, two societies can each value tradition but one may value it more than the other and, therefore, lie closer to the tradition end of the scale. For several of the values, a natural dichotomy does not seem to exist. For a society to place a very low value on cleanliness does not necessarily imply that it places a high value on dirtiness. Each of the 18 values are described briefly in the following paragraphs.[12]

Control values

Individual − Collective　Does the culture emphasize and reward individual initiative and activity or are cooperation with and conformity to a group more highly valued? Are individual differences appreciated or condemned? Are rewards and status given to individuals or to groups?

---

[12] Additional details on cultural variations in these variables, particularly in relation to economic development, can be found in Terpstra, *Cultural Environment*.

FIGURE 4-1
Cultural values of relevance to consumer behavior

Control

1. *Individual—Collective* Are individual activity and initiative valued more highly than collective activity and conformity?
2. *Performance—Status* Is the culture's reward system based on performance or on inherited factors such as family or class?
3. *Tradition—Change* Are existing patterns of behavior considered to be inherently superior to new patterns of behavior?
4. *Masculine—Feminine* To what extent does social power automatically go to males?
5. *Competition—Cooperation* Does one obtain success by excelling over others or by cooperating with them?
6. *Youth—Age* Are wisdom and prestige assigned to the younger or older members of a culture?

Direction

1. *Active—Passive* Is a physically active approach to life valued more highly than a less active orientation?
2. *Material—Nonmaterial* How much importance is attached to the acquisition of material wealth?
3. *Hardwork—Leisure* Is a person who works harder than economically necessary admired more than one who does not?
4. *Risk taking—Security* Are those who risk their established positions to overcome obstacles or achieve high goals admired more than those who do not?
5. *Problem solving—Fatalistic* Are people encouraged to overcome all problems or do they take a "what will be, will be" attitude?
6. *Nature* Is nature regarded as something to be admired or overcome?

Feeling

1. *Adult—Child* Is family life organized to meet the needs of the children or the adults?
2. *Postponed gratification—Immediate gratification* Are people encouraged to "save for a rainy day" or to "live for today"?
3. *Sensual gratification—Abstinence* To what extent is it acceptable to enjoy sensual pleasures such as food, drink, and sex?
4. *Humor—Serious* Is life to be regarded as a strictly serious affair or is it to be treated lightly?
5. *Romantic orientation* Does the culture believe that "love conquers all"?
6. *Cleanliness* To what extent is cleanliness pursued beyond the minimum needed for health?

Answers to these questions reveal the individual or collective orientation of a culture and are of critical importance to the marketing manager. For example, techniques to motivate and compensate sales personnel should vary dramatically between individual- and collective-oriented societies. Likewise, such themes as "be yourself," "stand out," and "don't be one of the crowd" would not be as effective in a collective-oriented society such as China or parts of Africa as in an individually oriented one.

Performance – Status Are opportunities, rewards, and prestige based on an individual's performance or on the status associated with the person's family, position, or class? Do all people have an equal opportunity economically, socially, and politically at the start of life or are certain groups given special privileges? A status-oriented society is perhaps more likely to prefer "quality" or established brand names and high-priced items over functionally equivalent items with unknown brands or lower prices. The types of authority figures that would work in advertising would differ between cultures that varied on the performance – status orientation. In general, status-oriented societies are less socially mobile and have not developed a large "middle class."[13]

Tradition – Change Is tradition valued simply for the sake of tradition? Is change or "progress" an acceptable reason for altering established patterns? Societies that place a relatively high value on tradition tend to resist product changes. One study of the British housewife found that: "She regards the old styles as tried and trusted and, therefore, better than the new—the older the furniture, perhaps the better. Should it become necessary to replace it, she probably does so with the identical style and color."[14] This resistance to change has affected product development in Britain such that "in clothing, furniture, chinaware, housewares, and major and minor household appliances, British manufactures have been noticeably deficient (relative to Americans) in product design."[15]

Another study found that American women stated more of a preference for trying new grocery products and retail services than did French women.[16] Associated with this are more rapid changes in grocery products and retailing institutions in the United States than in France.

Masculine – Feminine Are rank, prestige, and important social roles assigned primarily to men? Can a female's life pattern be predicted at birth with a high degree of accuracy? Does the husband or wife or both make important family decisions? Basically, we live in a masculine-

---

[13] Wallin, "Cultural Values," p. 56.

[14] H. Boyd and I. Piercy, "Retailing in Great Britain," *Journal of Marketing* (January 1963), p. 31.

[15] H. Boyd and I. Piercy, "Marketing to the British Consumer," *Business Horizons* (Spring 1960), p. 79.

[16] R. T. Green and E. Langeard, "A Cross-National Comparison of Consumer Habits and Innovator Characteristics, *Journal of Marketing* (July 1975), p. 38.

oriented world. However, the degree of masculine orientation varies widely. At the extreme, women are viewed as little more than property.[17] In general, labor force participation by women as compared to men is lowest in Moslem countries, followed by Latin American countries. It is the highest in Caribbean, some African, and Soviet-type countries.[18] Even subtle aspects of business are affected by sex role perceptions. For example, most American executives feel compelled to have female secretaries. In Moslem countries this typically means hiring non-Moslem women. This presents a double affront to many of the Moslem executives.[19] In the next chapter, a detailed description of culturally defined sex roles and their implications for marketing practices in America is presented.

Competition – Cooperation   Is the path to success to be found by outdoing other individuals or groups or is success to be achieved by forming alliances with other individuals and groups? Does everyone "admire a winner"? Consider the following typical Australian's comment to an aggressive salesman: "Don't be greedy, mate, you've had yours for this time. Reckon I've got to save some for the next chap. Fair shares for all, you know."[20] Market share objectives, sales force compensation and motivation policies, and comparative advertising themes are among the decisions that would be affected by a culture's competition – cooperation orientation.

Youth – Age   Are prestige, rank, and important social roles assigned to younger or older members of society? Is the behavior, dress, and so forth of the younger or older members of a society imitated by the rest of the society? While the American society is clearly youth oriented, this conflicts sharply with the Confucian concept practiced in Korea which emphasizes age.[21] An advertising campaign for Reyno (Salem) failed in Germany because the young models in the ads were perceived as being *inexperienced* rather than someone to imitate.[22]

Direction values

Active – Passive   Are people expected to take a physically active approach to work and play? Are physical skills and feats valued more

---

[17] C. J. Omana, "Marketing in Sub-Sahara Africa," in *Marketing and Economic Development,* ed. P. D. Bennett (American Marketing Association, 1965), pp. 128 – 39.

[18] M. A. Ferber and H. M. Lowry, "Woman's Place: National Differences in the Occupational Mosaic," *Journal of Marketing* (July 1977), p. 24.

[19] J. A. Lee, "Cultural Analysis in Overseas Business," *Harvard Business Review* (March – April 1966), p. 108.

[20] J. Ewing, "Marketing in Australia," *Journal of Marketing* (April 1962), p. 56.

[21] Wallin, "Cultural Values," p. 53. See also S. O. Novotny, "American vs. European Management Philosophy," *Harvard Business Review* (March – April 1964), pp. 101 – 8.

[22] McCreary, *Americanization of Europe,* p. 131.

highly than less physical performances? Is emphasis placed on doing? A recent study identified American and French women who were socially active outside the home. The French women were characterized by agreement with the statement, "Fireside chats with friends are my favorite ways of spending an evening." In contrast, American women tended to agree with, "I like parties where there is lots of music and talk."[23] On a different dimension, Norwegian women spend two to four times more time participating in sports than do American women.[24] Vastly different products and advertising themes are required by these differing approaches to outside activities.

Material – Nonmaterial   Is the accumulation of material wealth a positive good in its own right? Does material wealth bring more status than family ties, knowledge, or other activities? A desire for material items can exist and grow despite official government attempts to reduce it, such as in the Soviet Union. As one observer of Russian society noted "it was apparent [in Russia] that while American bourgeois materialism might be officially censured, the American middle-class way of life embodied the aspirations of a growing number of Russians, especially in the cities. People wanted their own apartments, more stylish clothes, more swinging music, a television set and other appliances, and for those lucky enough, a private car."[25] Marketing in cultures that place less emphasis on the acquisition of material objects, such as the Middle East or Philippines, requires different strategies than those useful in more materialistic societies. A further description of cultural variation in the meaning of material items is presented in the section on nonverbal communication.

Hardwork – Leisure   Is work valued for itself independent of external rewards or is work merely a "means to an end"? Will individuals continue to work hard even when their minimum economic needs are satisfied or will they opt for more leisure time? In much of Latin America, work is viewed as a necessary evil at best. In the late 1940s and early 1950s American housewives were slow to accept instant coffee, TV dinners, and other frozen precooked products in part because they felt guilty about doing things the easy way.[26] It was necessary for marketers to downplay the convenience of these products and advertise the ben-

---

[23] S. P. Douglas and C. D. Urban, "Life-Style Analysis to Profile Women in International Markets," *Journal of Marketing* (July 1977), p. 49.

[24] D. K. Hawes, S. Gronmo, and J. Arndt, "Shopping Time and Leisure Time: Some Preliminary Cross-Cultural Comparisons of Time-Budget Expenditures," in *Advances in Consumer Research V*, ed. H. K. Hunt (Association for Consumer Research, 1978), pp. 151–59.

[25] H. Smith, *The Russians* (Quadrangle/The New York Times Book Co., 1976), p. 55.

[26] M. Haire, "Projective Techniques in Marketing Research," *Journal of Marketing* (April 1950), pp. 649–56.

efits that the other family members would derive from their use. In addition, the benefit to the housewife of increased free time had to emphasize that the free time would be used in worthwhile activities (e.g., more time with the children) and not just be idle "leisure" time. Obviously this value has changed in our culture over time. Product lines, advertising themes, and the nature of retail outlets will all vary based on a culture's orientation toward hard work and leisure. ·

Risk taking – Security Do the "heroes" of the culture meet and overcome obstacles? Is the person who risks established position or wealth on a new venture admired or considered foolhardy? The relationship between this value and entrepreneurship and economic development has been studied extensively.[27] The society that does not admire risk taking is unlikely to develop enough entrepreneurs to achieve great economic change and growth. New product introductions, new channels of distribution, and advertising themes would be particularly affected by this value. One would expect that the new product diffusion rate would be much slower in a society placing emphasis on security.

Problem solving – Fatalistic Do people react to obstacles and disasters as challenges to be overcome or do they take a "what will be, will be" attitude? Is there an optimistic, "we can do it," orientation? In the Dominican Republic, difficult or unmanageable problems are dismissed with the expression "no problem." This actually means: "There *is* a problem, but we don't know what to do about it—so don't worry!"[28] Advertising themes and the nature of products that are acceptable are affected by this value. For example, it would probably be more difficult to convince people in the Dominican Republic to save for unforeseen problems that may come up in the future than it would be to convince Americans.

Nature Is nature assigned a positive value or is it viewed as something to be overcome, conquered, or tamed? Americans have traditionally considered nature as something to be overcome or improved. In line with this, animals have either been destroyed as enemies or romanticized and made into heroes and pets.[29] In Thailand, animals are regarded as a lower form of creation and Thais are not attracted to advertising using animal themes. This rejection of animal themes included even the almost universally successful "Put a tiger in your tank" cam-

---

[27] The basic work in this area is D. C. McClelland, *The Achieving Society,* (Free Press, 1961). See also R. H. Tawney, *Religion and the Rise of Capitalism* (Harcourt, Brace & Co., 1926).

[28] J. Cerruti, "The Dominican Republic: Caribbean Comeback," *National Geographic* (October 1977), p. 545.

[29] For a discussion of this process, see B. Nietschmann, "The Bambi Factor," *Natural History* (August – September 1977), pp. 84 – 87.

paign by ESSO.[30] A culture's attitudes toward nature can influence advertising themes as well as product and package designs.

Feeling values

Adult – Child   To what extent do the primary family activities focus on the needs of the children as opposed to those of the adults? What role, if any, do children play in family decisions? What role do they play in decisions that primarily affect the child? One study found that 73 percent of a sample of Americans remembered influencing family decisions when they were around 16 years old. This can be compared with 48 percent of a sample of Italians.[31] The results of using child-centered promotional themes in a nonchild-centered society are generally unsuccessful as the General Mills English breakfast cereal example at the beginning of the chapter illustrated.[32]

Postponed gratification – Immediate gratification   Is one encouraged to "save for a rainy day" or should you "live for today"? Is it better to secure immediate benefits and pleasures or is it better to suffer in the short run for benefits in the future (or in the "hereafter" or for future generations)? One area in which this affects marketing is the maintenance and upkeep of products, including industrial products. One expert on international marketing concludes that the human qualities necessary for effective product maintenance such as discipline, responsibility, and thoroughness "go deeper than simple training and depend in large degree upon the culture of the society, the standards and attitudes to which people are raised and which their fellow men expect of them."[33] An example of the problem this can cause is seen in a recent examination of the Dominican Republic. Part of a power plant exploded killing and injuring several people. Because the equipment had received no maintenance, the investigator concluded: "The Tyranny of Maintenance is a pervasive nonproblem (i.e., an unsolvable problem), because the Dominican spirit cannot abide it. Why maintain when it is so much more romantic to build something new?"[34]

There are also strong implications for distribution strategies, efforts to encourage savings, and the use of credit. For example, one study found that some Americans, as compared to Germans, have an overrid-

---

[30] M. Carson, "Admen in Thailand, Singapore Find Unusual Problems, Novel Solutions," *Advertising Age* (November 27, 1967), p. 3. See also G. E. Miracle, "International Advertising Principles and Strategies," *MSU Business Topics* (Fall 1968), pp. 29–36.

[31] G. A. Almond and S. Verba, *Civic Culture: Political Attitudes and Democracy in Five Nations* (Princeton University Press, 1963), pp. 330–32.

[32] McCreary, *Americanization of Europe,* pp. 128–30.

[33] J. Fayerweather, *International Marketing* (Prentice-Hall, Inc., 1965), p. 59.

[34] Cerruti, "Caribbean Comeback," p. 546.

ing concern with buying the product which is available *now*.[35] In Germany and Holland, buying on credit is viewed as living beyond one's means. The largest mail-order company in Holland which specializes in credit sales uses unmarked packaging and unidentifiable trucks to make its deliveries![36]

Sensual gratification – Abstinence Is it acceptable to pamper oneself, to satisfy one's desires for food, drink, or sex beyond the minimum requirement? Is one who foregoes such gratification considered virtuous or strange? Smith describes the Russians as "lusty hedonists, devoted to such sensual pleasures as feasting, drinking, and bathing."[37] In contrast, Dichter explains the lesser usage of toothpaste, deodorant, and bath soap in France (than in America) as a reflection of their view (shared with many other Catholic and Latin countries) that excessive concern with the body and the unnecessary handling of it is immoral.[38] Both advertising themes and product lines should reflect a culture's position on this value dimension.

Humor – Serious Is life a serious and frequently sad affair or is it something to be taken lightly and laughed at when possible? Cultures differ in the extent to which humor is accepted and appreciated and in the nature of what qualifies as humor. Americans see little or no conflict between humor and serious communication. Latin Americans and Continental Europeans do see a conflict. In their view, if a person is serious, the talk is completely serious; when a person tells jokes or funny stories, the entire situation is to be taken lightly.[39] Personal selling techniques and promotional messages should be developed with an awareness of a culture's position on this value dimension.

Romantic orientation Is the "boy-meets-girl, overcomes obstacles, marries, and lives happily ever after" theme common in popular literature? Is there freedom of choice in the selection of mates? Is there a general feeling of support for the underdog and faith that the "good guys" will win? A Listerine ad in Thailand showing a boy and girl, obviously fond of each other, recommending Listerine failed. It was changed to two girls discussing Listerine and was judged successful.[40] Advertisements portraying courtship activities would be meaningless in much of

---

[35] R. Anderson and J. Engledow, "A Factor Analytic Comparison of U.S. and German Information Seekers," *Journal of Consumer Research* (March 1977), p. 196.

[36] G. Katona, B. Strumpel, and E. Zahn, "The Sociocultural Environment," in *International Marketing Strategy*, ed. H. B. Thorelli (Penguin Books, 1973), p. 145.

[37] Smith, *Russians*, p. 112.

[38] E. Dichter, "The World Customer," *Harvard Business Review* (July – August 1962), pp. 116 – 17.

[39] W. F. Whyte, "Must You Tell a 'Funny Story,'" *Columbia Journal of World Business* (July – August 1968), p. 86.

[40] R. S. Diamond, "Managers Away from Home," *Fortune* (August 15, 1969), p. 56.

India where marriages are still arranged by parents while the child is young.[41] Themes placing a product in an "underdog" position would also be unlikely to prove successful in cultures lacking a romantic orientation.

Cleanliness   Is cleanliness "next to Godliness" or is it a rather minor matter? Is one expected to be clean beyond any reasonable health requirements? In the United States a high value is placed on cleanliness. This does not conflict with our somewhat sensual orientation as described earlier. However, as was described in the section on sensual gratification, cultures which have a negative view of too much bodily concern do not place the same emphasis on cleanliness that the American society does. In fact, many Europeans consider the Americans to be paranoid on the subject of personal hygiene. A recent study found the following population percentages agreeing with the statement: "Everyone should use a deodorant."[42]

United States	89%
French Canada	81
English Canada	77
United Kingdom	71
Italy	69
France	59
Australia	53

In an impressive reflection of the impact of this value, the promotional theme "For people who can't brush after every meal" for Gleem toothpaste, did poorly in much of Europe where brushing after every meal would be considered strange.[43]

Clearly, the preceding discussion has not covered all of the values operating in the various cultures. However, it should suffice to provide a feel for the importance of cultural values and how cultures differ along value dimensions. We will now examine another dimension of cultural variation—nonverbal communications.

Cultural variations in nonverbal communications[44]

Differences in verbal communication systems are immediately obvious to anyone entering a foreign culture. An American traveling in Bri-

---

[41] D. W. Jacobson, "Life behind the Veil," *National Geographic* (August 1977), pp. 270—86.

[42] J. T. Plummer, "Consumer Focus in Cross-National Research," *Journal of Advertising* (November 1977), pp. 5—15.

[43] McCreary, *Americanization of Europe*, pp. 131—32.

[44] All of this section, except the subsections on colors and etiquette, is based on Hall, *The Silent Language;* and E. T. Hall, "The Silent Language in Overseas Business," *Harvard Business Review* (May–June 1960), pp. 87–96.

tain or Australia will be able to communicate, but differences in pronounciation, timing, and meaning will be readily apparent. These differences are easy to notice and accept because we realize that language is an arbitrary invention of man. Language is a part of culture and most individuals recognize that the meaning assigned to a particular group of letters or sounds is *not* inherent in the letters or sounds but is arbitrary. A word means what a group of people agree that it will mean. Thus even within cultures speaking the same language we can have ineffective communication (e.g., witness the problems older Americans have interpreting and understanding slang terms used by younger groups).

Attempts to translate marketing communications from one language to another can also result in ineffective communications. An American airline operating in Brazil advertised the plush "rendezvous lounges" on its jets only to discover that *rendezvous* in Portuguese means a room hired for lovemaking.[45] General Motors' "body by Fisher" was translated as "corpse by Fisher" in Flemish.[46] Colgate's Cue toothpaste had problems in France as *Cue* is a pornographic word in French.[47] In Germany, Pepsi's advertisement, "Come alive with Pepsi," was presented as "Come alive out of the grave with Pepsi." In China, an alert copy editor caught a similar mistranslation before it was presented that declared "Pepsi brings your ancestors back from the grave."[48]

The examples cited above are somewhat atypical. Generally, verbal language translations do not present major problems as long as we are careful. What many of us fail to recognize, however, is that each culture also has nonverbal communication systems or languages that, like verbal languages, are specific to each culture. Unlike verbal languages, most of us think of our nonverbal languages as being innate or natural rather than learned. Therefore, when we encounter a foreign culture we tend to assign our own culture's meanings to the nonverbal signs being utilized by the other culture. The problem is compounded by the fact that the "foreigner" is interpreting our nonverbal cues by the "dictionary" used in his or her own culture. The frequent result is misunderstanding, unsuccessful sales calls and advertising campaigns, and, on occasion, long-lasting bitterness. To the extent that we can recognize which nonverbal language variables are important to marketers and how they differ between cultures, the easier it will be to avoid making marketing mistakes when dealing with other cultures as well as our own.

---

[45] D. A. Ricks, J. S. Arpan, and M. Y. Fu, "Pitfalls in Advertising Overseas," *Journal of Advertising Research* (December 1974), p. 48.

[46] E. M. Mazze, "How to Push a Body Abroad without Making It a Corpse," *Business Abroad* (August 10, 1964), p. 15.

[47] H. Martyn, *International Business: Principles and Problems* (Collier-Macmillan, 1964), p. 78.

[48] K. Lynch, "Adplomacy Faux Pas Can Ruin Sales," *Advertising Age* (January 15, 1979), p. S−2.

In the following pages, we are going to examine seven variables which we consider to be nonverbal languages: time, space, friendship, agreements, things, colors, and etiquette. Since nonverbal languages, like verbal ones, evolve over time, the specific examples cited should be interpreted as illustrative of the nature of nonverbal communications, not as accurate descriptors of particular cultures at this point in time.

Time   The meaning of time varies between cultures in two major ways. First is what we call time perspective. This is a culture's overall orientation toward time. The second way in which the meaning of time varies is the interpretations assigned specific uses of time.

Time is also of specific interest to marketing managers with respect to consumption behavior. As Jacoby et al. noted:

> Time is both an antecedent to and a consequence of purchase. Consumers not only spend time and money to acquire products and services but also often use time as a substitute for money and vice versa. As early as 1748, in his Advice to a Young Tradesman, Benjamin Franklin wrote, "Remember that time is money." Once said products and services are acquired, consumers must necessarily also expend time in the consumption/utilization of them. Sometimes consumers attempt to minimize time expenditures, such as through the purchase of convenience goods. At other times, consumers seek to prolong time expenditures such as during an enjoyable shopping spree.[49]

Time perspective   Americans tend to view time as inescapable and fixed in nature. It is a road reaching into the future with distinct, separate sections (hours, days, weeks, etc.). Time is seen almost as a physical object: we can schedule it, waste it, lose it, and so forth. We have a strong orientation toward the future and consider the future to be anywhere from 5 to 25 years.

These views affect our lives as well as business practices in many ways. The scheduling of time for store hours, classes, construction projects, and so forth are based on our view of time. Individuals and business firms plan for the future. Current sacrifices are made in anticipation of future rewards.

Other cultures have different time perspectives. Latin Americans tend to view time as being less discrete and less subject to scheduling. This orientation leads to a different set of expectations concerning appointments and meetings. South Asians think of the future in terms of hundreds or even thousands of years. This can lead to a different outlook on investments as well as on the urgency of current activities. After all if one is thinking in terms of several hundred years, today's events are not as important.

Other cultures, generally nonindustrialized, operate with very short

---

[49] J. Jacoby, G. Szybillo and C. Berning, "Time and Consumer Behavior: An Interdisciplinary Overview," *Journal of Consumer Research* (March, 1976), p. 320.

time horizons. Both the Navajo and Sioux Indians had time perspectives limited almost totally to the present. Many Latin American countries are relatively present oriented. This leads to difficulties in encouraging individuals to save for the future and for firms to take a long-run orientation.

Time perspectives can influence the marketing of consumer products in a variety of ways. For example, an American firm introduced a filter-tip cigarette into an Asian culture. However, it soon became evident that the venture would fail. One of the main advertised advantages of filter cigarettes were that they would provide future benefits in the form of reduced risks of lung cancer. However, future benefits were virtually meaningless in this particular society which was strongly oriented to the present.[50]

Meanings in the use of time Specific uses of time have varying meanings in different cultures. In Ethiopia, the *time required for a decision* is proportional to the importance of the decision. Americans, by being well prepared with "ready answers" may adversely downplay the importance of the business being discussed. The *lead time* required for scheduling an event varies widely. One week is the minimum lead time for most social activities in America. However, a week represents the maximum lead time in many Arabic countries. The high value assigned to time by the Japanese has made them very receptive to many Western time-saving convenience goods.[51]

Promptness is considered very important in America. Furthermore, promptness is defined as being on time for appointments whether you are the person making the call or the person receiving the caller. The following quote indicates the variation in waiting time between cultures.

> Arriving a little before the hour (the American respect pattern), he waited. The hour came and passed; 5 minutes—10 minutes—15 minutes. At this point he suggested to the secretary that perhaps the minister did not know he was waiting in the outer office . . . 20 minutes—25 minutes—30 minutes—45 minutes (the insult period)!
>
> He jumped up and told the secretary that he had been "cooling his heels" in an outer office for 45 minutes and he was "damned sick and tired" of this type of treatment. . . .
>
> The principal source of misunderstanding lay in the fact that in the country in question the five-minute delay interval was not significant. Forty-five minutes, on the other hand, instead of being at the tail end of the waiting scale, was just barely at the beginning. To suggest to an American's secretary that perhaps her boss didn't know you were there after waiting 60 seconds would seem absurd, as would raising a storm about "cooling

---

[50] J. A. Lee, "Cultural Analysis in Overseas Operations," in *World Marketing,* eds. J. K. Ryons, Jr., and J. E. Baker (John Wiley and Sons, Inc., 1967), p. 59.

[51] J. N. Sheth and S. P. Sethi, "A Theory of Cross-Cultural Buyer Behavior," in *Consumer and Industrial Buying Behavior* eds. A. G. Woodside, J. N. Sheth, and P. D. Bennett (Elsevier North-Holland, Inc., 1977), p. 375.

your heels" for five minutes. Yet this is precisely the way the minister registered the protestations of the American in his outer office! He felt, as usual, that Americans were being totally unreasonable.[52]

Space   The use people make of space and the meanings they assign to that use of space constitute a second form of nonverbal communications.[53] In America, although there are some signs of change, "bigger is better." Thus, office space in corporations is generally allocated according to rank or prestige rather than need.[54] The president will have the largest office, followed by the executive vice president, and so on. The fact that a lower echelon executive's work may require a large space will seldom play a major role in office allocation.

American sales personnel and others learn to evaluate the prestige of those with whom they are dealing by the relative size of the individual's office among other things. However, in both Arabic and Latin American cultures a different perception of what is large exists. An office that seems large to a member of one of these cultures might easily appear small to an American. Unless Americans are attuned to culture differences, they may underestimate the standing of their contact.

Americans tend to separate supervisor offices from the work space of subordinates. The French tend to place supervisors in the midst of subordinates. In the United States, the chief executive offices are on the top floor, and production, maintenance, or "bargain basements" are located on the lowest floor. In Japanese department stores, the bargain basement is located on the top floor. Clearly, different cultures use physical space in different ways that are of direct relevance to marketing mix decisions.

A second major use of space is what we can term *personal space*. It is the nearest that others can come to you in various situations without your feeling uncomfortable. In the United States normal business conversations occur at distances of 5 to 8 feet and highly personal business from 18 inches to 3 feet. In parts of Northern Europe the distances are slightly longer, while in most of Latin America, they are substantially shorter. An American businessperson in Latin America will tend to back away from a Latin American counterpart in order to maintain his or her preferred personal distance. In turn, the host will tend to advance toward the American in order to maintain his or her personal space. The resulting "chase" would be comical if it were not for the results. Both parties are generally unaware of their actions or the reasons for them. Furthermore, each assigns a meaning to the other's actions *based on*

---

[52] Hall, *The Silent Language,* p. 18.

[53] For a detailed treatment see E. T. Hall, *The Hidden Dimension* (Doubleday and Co., 1966).

[54] For a lucid discussion of the use of office space in the Nixon White House see J. W. Dean, *Blind Ambition* (Simon and Schuster, 1976).

what the action means in his or her own culture. Thus, the North American considers the Latin American to be pushy and aggressive. The Latin American, in turn, considers the North American to be cold, aloof, and snobbish.

Friendship The rights and obligations imposed by friendship are another nonverbal cultural variable. Americans, more so than most other cultures, make friends quickly and easily and "drop" them easily also. In large part, this may be due to the fact that our society has always had a great deal of both social and geographic mobility. People who move every few years must be able to form friends in a short time period and depart from them with a minimum of pain. In many other parts of the world, friendships are formed slowly and carefully because they imply deep and lasting obligations. Friendship (and kinship) is expected to count more than good business practice, efficiency, or even legal requirements. While "favors" to friends which are counter to business rules or the law exist in the United States, they are not as common, socially accepted, and expected as in many other parts of the world.

Friendship often replaces the legal or contractual system for insuring that business and other obligations are honored. In countries without a well-established and easily enforceable commercial code, many people insist on doing business only with friends. The obligations imposed by friendship require the friend to protect one's interests. This often causes problems for representatives from American firms. The American is generally eager to move on to business, to "get things done." However, the host wants to establish a personal relationship prior to conducting business. And, establishing such a relationship is a slow process. A substantial amount of foreign business has been lost because of American impatience in this area.

Agreements Americans rely upon an extensive and, generally, highly efficient legal system for insuring that business obligations are honored and for resolving disagreements. Many other cultures have not evolved such a system and rely instead on friendship and kinship, local moral principles, or informal customs to guide business conduct.

When is an agreement concluded? Americans consider the signing of a contract to be the end of negotiations. However, to many Greeks such a signing is merely the signal to begin serious negotiations which will continue until the project is completed. At the other extreme, presenting a contract for a signature can be insulting to an Arab who considered the verbal agreement to be completely binding.

We also assume that in almost all instances prices are uniform for all buyers, related to the service rendered, and reasonably close to the going rate. We order many products such as taxi rides without inquiring in advance about the cost. In many Latin American and Arab countries the procedure is different. Virtually all prices are negotiated *prior* to the sale.

If a product such as a taxi ride is consumed without first establishing the price, the customer must pay whatever exorbitant fee is demanded by the seller.

The act of negotiating often has a positive value to both the buyer and the seller in many other cultures. It is the process itself that creates enjoyment not any monetary returns that may result from it. The following quote concerning a Peruvian woman illustrates this point: "When a visitor offered to buy the whole bushel early in the morning for a relatively high price, she refused. Although she had to earn a living, the satisfaction of spending a day in the market haggling with an assortment of buyers over the purchase of small fractions of her bushel was equally, if not more, important to her."[55]

Things

At my house he could talk freely and he impressed me with his knowledge and abilities; I was not invited back to his house. I only later found out where it was and realized how incongruous it was for him. *Having a house of European type was clearly a necessity for ToNori* (a native of New Britain), given the current fashion of house buying and given his own status aspirations.[56]

I asked Juan Navarro (a Mexican peasant) what were his major economic concerns. He answered very quickly, "food and clothes," he said. "How about housing?" I asked. "That is never a problem" he said, "for I can always make a house," . . . For Musio, Juan and the others, *a house is not a prestige symbol but simply a place to sleep, a place to keep dry in, a place for family privacy, and a place in which to store things.* . . . It seems difficult to overestimate the importance of clothing. A clean set of clothes is a pass into town, or a fiesta. Clothes are the mark of a man's self-respect, and the ability of a man to clothe his family is in many ways the measure of a man.[57]

The two quotes above demonstrate the vastly different meanings that housing has in two economically similar cultures. Such findings are common. Items conveying dependability and respectability to the English would often seem out of date and backward to Americans. Japanese homes would seem empty and barren to many Americans. In addition to assigning different meanings to the possession of various objects, cultures differ in the degree to which they value the acquisition of goods as an end itself. Such differences leads to problems in determining salary schedules, bonuses, gifts, product designs, and advertising themes.

---

[55] Fayerweather, *International Marketing,* p. 22.

[56] R. F. Salisbury, "ToNori Buys a House," in *Foundations for a Theory of Consumer Behavior,* ed. W. T. Tucker (Holt, Rinehart and Winston, 1967), p. 38.

[57] J. E. Epstein, "A Shirt for Juan Navarro," in *Foundations for a Theory of Consumer Behavior,* pp. 74—75.

Color If you were to see a baby wearing a pink outfit, you would most likely assume the child to be female. If the outfit were blue, you would probably assume the child to be male. These assumptions would be accurate most of the time in the United States but would not be accurate in many other parts of the world. White is unacceptable for packaging purposes in parts of the Far East where it is a symbol for mourning. A manufacturer of water-recreation products lost heavily in Malaysia because the company's predominant color, green, was associated with the jungle and illness in the culture.[58]

The examples cited above, indicate that colors acquire meanings over time. These meanings vary from culture to culture and must be taken into account when operating in various cultures. Packaging, advertising, company logos, and products should conform to the pertinent color language.

Etiquette Etiquette represents generally accepted ways of behaving in defined social situations. Assume that an American firm is preparing a commercial which shows children eating an evening meal with one child about to take a bite of food from a fork. The child will have the fork in the right hand and the left hand will be out of sight under the table. To an American audience this will seem natural for a well-mannered child. However, for many European cultures, a well-mannered child would have the fork in the left hand and the right hand on the table!

Behaviors that are considered rude or obnoxious in one culture may be quite acceptable in another. The American habit of picking up a sandwich or a hamburger with one's hands is considered rude or at least strange in much of Europe. On the other hand, many Europeans appear to eat entirely too rapidly by American standards.

A thorough examination of differing cultures reveals that many behaviors that we tend to consider natural are, in fact, socially prescribed. In America, three meals per day are considered normal if not necessary. However, an investigation of 12 countries found that "weekday patterns of *eating* behavior vary between an apparent single-evening meal per day pattern in Hoyerswerda (a town in the German Democratic Republic) to the four peak meal periods (6:00 A.M., 10:00 A.M., 3:00 P.M., and 8:00 P.M.) which characterize Kragujevac (a town in Yugoslavia)."[59] Thus, what we eat, how we eat, and how often we eat are, in part, culturally defined.

The importance of proper, culture specific etiquette for sales personnel and advertising messages is obvious. Although people are more apt to recognize that etiquette varies from culture to culture, there is still a strong emotional feeling that "our way is natural and right."

Conclusions on nonverbal communications Can you imagine yourself becoming upset or surprised because people in a different cul-

---

[58] "Key to Asia: Respect for Difference," *Printers Ink* (February 21, 1964), p. 48.

[59] A. Szalai, ed., *The Use of Time* (Paris: Mouton, 1972), p. 715.

ture spoke to you in their native language, say Spanish or French or German, instead of English? Of course not. We all recognize that verbal languages vary around the world. Yet we generally feel that our nonverbal languages are natural or innate. Therefore, we misinterpret what is being "said" to us because we think we are hearing English when in reality it is Japanese or Italian or Russian. As Hall says, "The error is in jumping to the conclusion that the foreigner feels the same way the American does even though his overt acts are identical."[60] It is this error that marketers must and can avoid.

CROSS-CULTURAL MARKETING STRATEGY

Our primary goal for examining foreign cultures was to gain a better understanding of how our own culture operates. The next two chapters focus specifically on the American culture. In the remainder of this chapter, we will further pursue our secondary goal of developing sufficient cultural sensitivity to avoid major pitfalls in international marketing.[61]

In the late 1960s, considerable debate focused on the extent to which cross-cultural marketing strategies, particularly advertising, could be standardized.[62] Standardized strategies can result in substantial cost savings. For example, a largely standardized program of advertising films saves Pepsi-Cola an estimated $8 million annually over a completely individualized approach.[63] However, a recent study of consumers in the United States, France, India, and Brazil found significant differences in the importance attached to 18 of 24 soft drink attributes.[64] The researchers concluded that standardized campaigns were risky.

The critical decision is whether or not utilizing a standardized marketing strategy, *in any given market,* will result in a greater return on investment than would an individualized campaign. Thus, the consumer response to the standardized campaign *and* to potential individualized campaigns must be considered in addition to the cost of each approach.

---

[60] Hall, *The Silent Language,* p. 161.

[61] See Sheth and Sethi, "Cross-Cultural Buyer Behavior;" and F. Hansen, "Managerial Implications of Cross-Cultural Studies of Buyer Behavior," in *Consumer and Industrial Buying Behavior,* eds. A. G. Woodside, J. N. Seth, and P. D. Bennett (Elsevier North-Holland, Inc., 1977), pp. 387–96, for a detailed treatment of this area.

[62] See for example E. Elinder, "How International Can European Advertising Be?" *Journal of Marketing* (April 1965), pp. 7–11; A. C. Fatt, "The Danger of 'Local' International Advertising," *Journal of Marketing* (January 1967), pp. 60–62; and R. D. Buzzell, "Can You Standardize Multinational Marketing?" *Harvard Business Review* (November–December 1968), pp. 102–13.

[63] N. Heller, "How Pepsi-Cola Does It in 110 Countries," in *New Ideas for Successful Marketing,* eds. J. S. Wright and J. L. Goldstucker (American Marketing Association, 1966), p. 700.

[64] R. T. Green, W. H. Cunningham, and I. C. M. Cunningham, "The Effectiveness of Standardized Global Advertising," *Journal of Advertising* (Summer 1975), pp. 25–29.

Figure 4–2 provides a listing of six key considerations that should be examined for each geographic area that a firm is considering. An analysis of these six variables provides the necessary background to decide whether or not to enter the area and to what extent, if any, an individualized marketing strategy is required. The suggested analysis may frequently not require a formalized research effort but rather be limited to an informal "armchair" analysis or discussion with a few knowledgeable sources. However, even at this level, it can help avoid major mistakes and oversights. Each consideration is examined in more detail below.

FIGURE 4–2
Key areas for developing a cross-cultural marketing strategy

1. Is the geographic area homogeneous or heterogeneous with respect to culture?
    Are there distinct cultures or subcultures in the geographic area under consideration? How narrow are the behavioral boundaries or norms imposed by the culture(s)? Is the culture(s) static or is it undergoing change?

2. What needs can this product fill in this culture?
    What needs, if any, does this product currently meet in this culture? Are there other needs it could satisfy? What other products are currently meeting these needs? How pressing or important are these needs to the people in the culture?

3. Can enough of the group(s) needing the product afford the product?
    How many people need the product and can afford it? How many need it and cannot afford it? Can a less expensive version be made? Can financing be obtained? Is a government subsidy possible?

4. What values or patterns of values are relevant to the purchase and use of the product?
    Is the decision maker the husband or wife? Adult or child? Will use of the product contradict any values such as hard work as a positive good? Will ownership of the product go against any values such as a nonmaterial orientation? Will the purchase of the product require any behaviors such as financing that might contradict a cultural value? What values support the purchase, ownership, or use of the product?

5. What is the distribution and legal structure concerning this product?
    Where do consumers expect to buy the product? Could a new channel reduce costs or reach more people? What legal requirements must the product meet? What legal requirements must the marketing mix meet?

6. In what way can we communicate about this product?
    What language(s) can we use? What forms of nonverbal communications will affect our salesmen, packages, and advertisements? What kinds of appeals will fit with the culture's value system?

Is the geographic area homogeneous or heterogeneous with respect to culture? Marketing efforts are generally directed at defined geographic areas, primarily political and economic entities. Legal requirements and existing distribution channels often encourage this approach. However, it is also often supported by the implicit assumption that geographical or political boundaries coincide with cultural boundaries. This assumption can be incorrect more often than not.

Canada provides a clear example. Many American firms treat the Canadian market as though it were a single cultural unit despite the fact that they must make adjustments for language differences. However, numerous studies have found French-Canadians to differ from English-Canadians in attitudes toward instant foods,[65] spending money,[66] and American cigarettes;[67] in spending patterns toward expensive liquors, clothing, personal care items, tobacco, soft drinks, candy, and instant coffee; in television and radio usage patterns; and in eating patterns.[68] A study of lifestyle differences concluded that compared to the English-Canadian female the French-Canadian female is:

a. More oriented toward the home, the family, the children and the kitchen.
b. More interested in baking and cooking and more negative toward convenience foods.
c. More concerned about personal and home cleanliness, and more fashion and personal appearance conscious.
d. More price conscious.
e. Much more concerned about a number of social, political, and consumer issues.
f. More religious, especially in feelings about the life hereafter.
g. More security conscious and less prone to take risks.
h. More positive toward television and less positive toward newspapers.
i. More negative toward the use of credit.[69]

The studies cited above should not be interpreted as a current portrayal of either English or French Canadians for Canadian culture is undergoing change.[70] Rather, they are illustrative of the heterogeneous

---

[65] G. W. Lane and G. L. Watson, "A Canadian Replication of Mason Haire's 'Shopping List' Study," *Journal of the Academy of Marketing Science* (Winter 1975), pp. 48–59.

[66] R. G. Wyckham, "Spending Attitudes of Consumers: Pilot Studies in French and English Canada," *Journal of the Academy of Marketing Science* (Winter 1975), pp. 109–18.

[67] W. J. Keegan, "Philip Morris International" (9-571-641.) (Intercollegiate Case Clearing House, 1968).

[68] These and other differences are described in W. J. Stanton, M. S. Sommers, and J. G. Barnes, eds. *Fundamentals of Marketing* 2d Candian ed. (McGraw-Hill Ryerson Ltd., 1975), pp. 108–9.

[69] D. J. Tigert, "Can a Separate Marketing Strategy for French Canada Be Justified: Profiling French Markets through Life Style Analysis," in *Canadian Marketing: Problems and Prospects,* eds. D. N. Thompson and D. S. R. Leighton (Toronto: Wiley, 1973), p. 128.

[70] B. Mallen, "The French-Canadian Customer: Changing? To What? So What?" *The Canadian Marketer* (Winter 1975), p. 33.

nature of Canadian culture. Approaching the Canadian market as a single cultural unit could be a mistake depending on the product and theme under consideration. This problem of *cultural pluralism* exists to an even greater extent in many other countries.

The discussion above has focused on the impact of one or more major subcultures in a given geographic area. A second aspect of cultural homogeneity is the range of behavior *not* prescribed by cultural norms. In some countries, particularly the United States, culture provides very loose boundaries on behavior and, therefore, provides less of a guideline for marketing practice. In other countries, the range of permissible behavior in any given situation is more restricted. In such cases, cultural norms must be closely adhered to.

What needs can this product or a version of it fill in this culture? While not exactly in accordance with the marketing concept, most firms examine a new market with an existing product or product technology in mind. The question they must answer is what needs their existing or modified product can fill in the culture involved.[71] For example, bicycles and motorcycles serve primarily recreational needs in the United States but provide basic transportation in many other countries. Sewing machines fulfill different needs in economically developed and economic undeveloped countries. Many people sew largely for pleasure in developed cultures such as ours and, therefore, must be approached differently than if sewing was a necessary aspect of a homemaker's job.

The marketer must not make the mistake of introducing filter cigarettes into a culture that does not fear lung cancer while using that benefit as the main sales pitch. To avoid mistakes of this type, one must be aware of the needs that exist in a culture, how they are currently being met, and how one's own product can better meet one or more needs.

Can enough of the group(s) needing the product afford the product? This requires an initial demographic analysis to determine the number of individuals or families that might need the product and the number that can probably afford it. In addition, the possibilities of establishing credit, obtaining a government subsidy, and making a less expensive version should be considered.

What values or patterns of values are relevant to the purchase and use of this product? The first section of this chapter focused on values and their role in consumer behavior. The value system should be investigated for influences on purchasing the product, owning the product, using the product, and disposing of the product. It is on this analysis that much of the marketing strategy will be based.

What is the distribution and legal structure concerning the product? The legal structure of a country can have an impact on each

---

[71] A discussion of this procedure is supplied by W. J. Keegan, "Multinational Product Planning: Strategic Alternatives," *Journal of Marketing* (January 1969), pp. 58—62.

aspect of a firm's marketing mix. For example, the Mexican government recently requested Anderson Clayton & Co. to "tone down" its commercials for *Capullo* mayonnaise because the advertisements were "too aggressive." The aggression involved direct comparisons with competing brands (comparative advertising) which is not acceptable in Mexico.[72] On the other hand, the Mexican government worked with Coca-Cola Company to develop a low-priced, nutritious soft drink aimed at improving the diets of Mexico's low-income children.[73]

The distribution channels and consumer expectations concerning where to secure products vary widely across cultures. In the Netherlands, supermarkets are virtually nonexistent, and drug stores do not sell prescription drugs (they are sold at an "apotheek" or apothecary which sells nothing else). Existing channels and consumer expectations generally must be considered as fixed at least in the short run.

In what way can we communicate about this product? This requires an investigation into (1) available media and who attends to each type, (2) the needs the product fills, (3) values associated with the product and its use, and (4) the verbal and nonverbal communications systems of the culture(s). All aspects of the firm's promotional mix (including packaging, nonfunctional product design features, personal selling techniques, and advertising) should be based on these four factors.

For example, BSR Ltd. of Japan, an importer of phonograph turntables and changers from Britain, was initially unsuccessful because of its packaging strategy. The Japanese consumer uses a product's package as an important indicator of product quality. Thus, the standard shipping carton used by BSR, while it protected the product adequately, did not convey a high quality image. To overcome this problem, BSR began packaging its phonograph equipment in two cartons: one for shipping and one for point-of-purchase display.[74]

Conclusions on cross-cultural marketing strategy It has been found that the assumptions made about culture by international advertising managers affect the approach taken in planning and placing foreign advertising.[75] This is undoubtedly true of other areas of the marketing mix.

To succeed in a foreign culture, the marketing managers must first evaluate each of the six key areas which may influence the success of marketing in a foreign culture and then decide on which of the following four marketing strategies is best suited for a particular situation.[76]

---

[72] S. Donner, "Capullo Labeled Too Aggressive," *Advertising Age* (August 14, 1978), p. 54.

[73] S. Donner, "Coke Launches Samson Nutritional Drink in Mexico," *Advertising Age* (August 14, 1978), p. 57.

[74] M. Tharp, "Getting Oriented," *The Wall Street Journal* (March 9, 1977), p. 1.

[75] J. H. Donnelly, Jr., "Attitudes toward Culture and Approach to International Advertising," *Journal of Marketing* (July 1970), p. 63. See also Wallin, "Cultural Values," pp. 49—58.

[76] M. Sommers and J. Kernan, "Why Products Flourish Here, Fizzle There," *Columbia Journal of World Business* (March—April 1967), pp. 89—97.

1. *Same product and the same promotion.* Promotional product claims and product usage are universal enough to be acceptable to consumers. Usually, this type of expansion strategy is most appropriate when expanding into a cultural market that is similar to the firm's original market. For example, Marlboro cigarettes have had good success with the same product and same promotion in a variety of cultures.

2. *Same product but different promotion.* Promotion must be changed to conform to the particular value orientations of the market to guarantee product acceptance. Products that are used differently must be promoted differently. The market reflects a culture whose way of life is similar but where implementation of lifestyles is along different lines. The Estee Lauder Cosmetic Company changed its store promotion strategy in Japan in order to appeal to the cultural needs of Japanese men in their purchase of men's cosmetics.

3. *Different product —same promotion.* This strategy is used in the multinational marketing of laundry detergents. Typically, the products differ among countries but the nature of promotional claims made in their behalf is similar. Laundering techniques may vary from culture to culture, but the "cleaningest" theme is universally subscribed to.

4. *Different product —different promotion.* This is the most risky kind of marketing strategy because it involves more than extending the firm's existing production and marketing capabilities and it often prompts firms to consider "buying their way into" such markets by acquiring existing firms in the market.

SUMMARY

The study of culture is an extremely important part of consumer behavior and of direct and immediate use to marketing managers. Culture is defined as that complex whole which includes knowledge, belief, art, law, morals, custom, and any other capabilities acquired by man as a member of society. Culture includes almost everything that influences an individual's thought processes and behaviors.

Culture operates primarily by setting boundaries for individual behavior and by influencing the functioning of such institutions as the family structure, mass media, and so forth. The boundaries or norms are derived from cultural values. Values are widely held beliefs that affirm what is desirable and that have some impact on activities. Cultures change when values change, the environment changes, or when dramatic events occur.

There are a great many cross-cultural variations in consumer behavior that are of particular interest to the marketer operating in more than one culture. Variations are particularly obvious when one looks at cultural values or nonverbal communications across cultures.

Cultural values are classified using three broad forms of behavioral response—control, direction, and feeling. *Control* refers to the extent to which a person feels unrestricted or free to act in a variety of ways. Some relevant values that reflect the control response are individual/collective, performance/status, tradition/change, masculine/feminine, competition/cooperation, and youth/age.

Direction refers to those values reflecting the set of responses people can make that determine which way in life they will go. Examples of directive values are active/passive, material/nonmaterial, hardwork/leisure, risk taking/security, problem solving/fatalistic, and nature.

The relative degree of pleasure evoked from a situation or activity is a *feeling* response. Feeling-related values include adult/child, postponed gratification/immediate gratification, sensual gratification/abstinence, humor/serious, romantic orientation, and cleanliness.

Differences in verbal communication systems are immediately obvious across cultures and must be taken into account by marketers wishing to do business in those cultures. Probably more important, however, and certainly more difficult to recognize are nonverbal communication differences. Major examples of nonverbal communication variables that affect marketers are time, space, friendship, agreement, things, colors, and etiquette.

A critical decision in cross-cultural marketing is whether or not utilizing a standardized marketing strategy in any given market will result in a greater return on investment than would an individualized campaign. The consumer response to the standardized campaign and to potential individualized campaigns must be considered in addition to the cost of each approach.

Six key questions for developing a cross-cultural marketing strategy are illustrated in the text. First, is the geographic area homogeneous or heterogeneous with respect to culture? Secondly, what needs can this product fill in this culture? Thirdly, can enough of the groups needing the product afford the product? Fourth, what values or patterns of values are relevant to the purchase and use of the product. Fifth, what is the distribution and legal structure concerning this product? And finally, in what way can we communicate about this product?

REVIEW QUESTIONS

1. What is meant by the term *culture?*
2. Is a country's culture more likely to be reflected in its art museums or its television commercials? Why?
3. Does culture provide a detailed prescription for behavior in most modern societies? Why or why not?
4. What does the statement "Culture sets boundaries on behaviors" mean?

5. Are we generally aware of how culture influences our behavior? Why or why not?
6. What is a *norm?* From what are norms derived?
7. What is a cultural value?
8. What is a sanction?
9. How do cultures and cultural values change?
10. Why should we study foreign cultures if we do not plan on engaging in international or export marketing?
11. Cultural values can be classified as affecting one of three behavioral responses—control, direction, or feeling. Describe each of these and differentiate it from the others.
12. How does a _____ orientation differ from a _____ orientation?

   a. individual—collective
   b. performance—status
   c. tradition—change
   d. active—passive
   e. material-nonmaterial
   f. hardwork—leisure
   h. masculine—feminine

   i. competition—cooperation
   j. youth—age
   k. problem solving—fatalistic
   l. adult—child
   m. postponed gratification— immediate gratification
   n. sensual gratification— abstinence.

13. What is meant by nonverbal communications? Why is this such a difficult area to adjust to?
14. What is meant by _____ as a form of nonverbal communications?

   a. time
   b. space
   c. friendship
   d. agreements

   e. things
   f. colors
   g. etiquette

15. Give an example of how each of the variables listed in question 14 above could influence marketing practice.
16. What are the advantages and disadvantages of standardized international advertising?
17. What are the six key considerations involved in deciding whether or not to enter a given international market?
18. What is meant by determining if a geographic area or political unit is "homogeneous or heterogeneous with respect to culture"? Why is this important.
19. What are the four basic marketing strategies that a manager can utilize in approaching an international market?

DISCUSSION QUESTIONS

1. The text provides a six step procedure for analyzing a foreign market. The United States is, in effect, a foreign market for the manufacturer of Motron. Using this six step procedure, analyze the U.S. market for Motron.

2. What cultural norms do you feel are relevant to the purchase and use of a moped?

3. What are the five most relevant cultural values as far as the success of mopeds is concerned? Describe how and why these values are particularly important.

4. What variations between the United States and the European societies such as France, other than cultural variations, may affect the relative level of usage of mopeds?

5. What, if any, nonverbal communication factors might be relevant in the marketing of Motron?

6. The text listed 18 cultural values of relevance to marketing practice. Describe and place into one of the three categories four additional cultural values that have some relevance to marketing practice.

7. Are the cultures of the world becoming more similar or more distinct?

8. Select two cultural values from each of the three categories; describe the boundaries (norms) relevant to that value in the American society and the sanctions for violating those norms.

9. If you have visited a foreign culture, describe any experiences you can recall involving variations in nonverbal communications.

PROJECT QUESTIONS

1. Interview two students from two different foreign cultures. Determine the extent to which mopeds are used in those cultures and the variations in the values of those cultures that relate to the use of mopeds.

2. Interview two students from two different foreign cultures. Report any differences they are aware of between their culture and the U.S. culture in nonverbal communications.

3. Interview two students from two different foreign cultures. Report their perceptions of the major differences in cultural values between their culture and the U.S. culture.

4. Imagine you are a consultant working with your state's tourism agency. You have been asked to advise the state on the best promotional themes to use to attract foreign tourists to the state. What would you recommend if West Germany and Japan were the two target markets selected by the state.

5

The American society: Changing values and sex roles

Chesebrough-Pond's Prince Matchabelli division recently introduced Chimere, a woman's fragrance, with a $4.5 million advertising and promotion budget. Michael Horowitz, group product manager, describes the development of Chimere as follows:

> *Windsong* came out in the 1950s, an era of romance; *Cachet* in the late '60s, when women were seeking their own identity, and *Aviance* in the early '70s, during the sexual revolution. Now, in the late '70s, you have women between the ages of 25 and 35 who have made it. Unlike the *Cachet* women, the *Chimere* woman doesn't have to prove she is there. She is a professional who wants to be treated as such.[1]

As the above quote makes clear, Prince Matchabelli has achieved success in part by monitoring shifting values and perceptions of the role of women in the American culture.

In this chapter we examine these two important aspects of the current American society—the value system and the social definition of appropriate sex role behavior. In the following chapter, we analyze the demographic characteristics of American society and some of the more important subcultures which make up our society. It is not our goal to paint a comprehensive portrait of America. Rather, we hope to highlight

---

[1] P. Sloan, "Chimere Aimed at Professional Women," *Advertising Age* (April 23, 1979), p. 40.

the fact that this society is neither unidimensional nor static. Instead, it is an evolving, multidimensional structure. By examining these major aspects of our society, hopefully we will develop an understanding of the critical importance that assumptions about the nature of society play in marketing decisions. In addition, we will see the absolute necessity for accurately anticipating shifts in society in order to develop or adapt marketing strategies to changing conditions.

To begin with, we will examine the current value system that seems to exist in our society. As we pointed out in the last chapter, cultural values are widely held beliefs that affirm what is desirable and that impact on our activities. We suggested a three type classification system—control, direction, and feeling—and described the kinds of values that make up the three types as well as the kinds of impacts those values could have. We will now deal with each value specifically as it relates to the American culture. We should note, however, that while the values we discuss are commonly held cultural values, there can be significant variations within the main culture. As we will see in the next chapter, subcultures often have values different from those held by the larger culture. As we indicated in the previous chapter, cultural values in America serve more as vague boundaries on permissible behavior than as explicit guides to specific behaviors.

CHANGING AMERICAN VALUES

"The United States is in the midst of one of the great transformations of Western civilization."[2] While this may appear to be an extreme statement, other authorities have expressed similar sentiments.[3] Such views are based on the belief that certain key "American" values are changing. However, predicting future values, while necessary, is a difficult task.

In the preceding chapter, we described the change of social values as an evolutionary process which could be accelerated by (1) technological changes, (2) conflicts between existing values, (3) exposure to another culture's values, and (4) dramatic events. Clearly, all four of these change agents have been operative in America over the past two decades. Technology, particularly in the development of effective birth control devices, and the fallibility of technology in the face of energy shortages, is a major factor. The Vietnam War emphasized conflicts between existing cultural values. Our mass media have provided extensive exposure to alternate life styles. Finally, the Vietnam War, Watergate, and shortages all qualify

---

[2] G. C. Lodge, "Business and the Changing Society," *Harvard Business Review* (March–April 1974), p. 59.

[3] See W. S. Harmon, "Toward a Transindustrial Society," *Management Review* (July 1976), p. 6.

as dramatic events that have shaken existing values. With these in mind, we will examine the values that were introduced in Figure 4−1 that appear to be changing. Figure 5−1 presents our estimate of the traditional values, the current value, and the emerging value for each of those values described in Figure 4−1. We must emphasize that this figure represents the opinions of the authors. You should feel free, if not compelled, to challenge any or all of it.

FIGURE 5–1
Traditional, current, and emerging American values

CONTROL

Individual	TV	CV	EV	Collective
Performance	TV CV	EV		Status*
Tradition		EV	CV TV	Change
Masculine	TV	CV EV		Feminine
Competition	TV CV		EV	Cooperation
Youth	CV TV		EV	Age

DIRECTION

Active	EV CV TV			Passive
Material	TV CV	EV		Nonmaterial
Hardwork	TV	CV	EV	Leisure
Risk taking	TV		CV EV	Security
Problem solving	TV CV	EV		Fatalistic
Admire nature		EV CV	TV	Overcome nature

FEELING

Adult	TV	EV CV		Child
Postponed gratification	TV		CV EV	Immediate gratification
Sensual gratification	EV	CV	TV	Abstinence
Humor	CV EV TV			Serious
Romantic orientation	TV	CV EV		Nonromantic orientation
Maximum cleanliness	TV CV EV			Minimum cleanliness

* The emerging value is not toward status in the traditional sense of the term but rather toward egalitarianism. See the text for discussion.
Note: TV = Traditional value; CV = Current value; EV = Emerging value.

Control values

Control refers to the extent to which a person feels unrestricted in his or her choice of actions. Americans have traditionally sought to maintain a high degree of individual control over their own lives. A number of specific values related to a high degree of individual control have been positively evaluated by Americans in the past. However, it appears that there has been a decline in this desire for individual control over the past few decades. Furthermore, it appears to us that this decline will continue in the future. Evidence of this decline can be seen by examining the specific value dimensions associated with control.

Individual – Collective   Although still more individualistic than most other cultures, the United States is increasingly accepting a more collective orientation. One reflection of this is the increased reliance on governmental intervention to solve what were previously viewed as individual problems. This is reflected in activities that range from social security programs to advertising regulation. As we assume more of a collective orientation, the regulation of marketing activities by both federal and state governments will increase.[4] Of course not everyone accepts these shifts and the growth of regulation is uneven. On the one hand we see decreased regulation of the airlines industry and increased freedom to advertise professional services. On the other hand, there are strong moves to strictly regulate advertising aimed at children. Such inconsistencies are common as cultural values evolve and change.

Performance – Status   Several authors have concluded that we are moving away from an emphasis on performance. However, rather than stress inherent status, the new stress is toward egalitarianism. That is, there is a shift from equality of opportunity toward an equality of results.[5] If this shift does occur, the management of marketing personnel as well as advertising themes would be profoundly altered. For example, a commission system of pay based on sales would not be acceptable to individuals (or unions) concerned with egalitarianism.

Tradition – Change   Change has long been viewed very positively by members of our society. The implicit assumption was that change was desirable, that an improvement always resulted because of the change. For many years, America's infatuation with change was evident in the yearly model and style change in everything from automobiles to cloth-

---

[4] See G. R. Laczniak, R. F. Lusch, and J. G. Udell, "Marketing in 1985: A View from the Ivory Tower," *Journal of Marketing* (October 1977), pp. 47 – 56; A. L. Seelye, "Societal Change and Business-Government Relationships," *MSU Business Topics* (Autumn 1975), pp. 5 – 11; and J. G. Udell, G. R. Laczniak, and R. F. Lusch, "The Business Environment of 1985," *Business Horizons* (June 1976), pp. 45 – 54. For a contradictory view, see P. N. Bloom and L. W. Stern, "Emergence of Anti-Industrialism," *Business Horizons* (October 1976), pp. 87 – 93.

[5] N. C. Hill and G. W. Dalton, "Business and the New Egalitarianism," *Business Horizons* (June 1977), pp. 5 – 11.

ing. Currently, we see some hesitation to accept all change as positive, and this has been reflected in a reduction of the number of and emphasis on new models and less encouragement by advertisers to buy something new simply for the change. Well-known authors have commented critically on the tremendous rate of change our society has experienced and its potentially negative results and people seem to be listening.[6] Evidence of this is reflected, in part, in the strong opposition to nuclear power plants that has surfaced in many parts of the country.

Masculine—Feminine   American society, like most others, has reflected a very masculine bias for a long time. That is to say, those things that were defined as masculine were preferred over those things that were defined as feminine. This has been more than obvious in such things as traditional man—woman roles in everything from jobs (a woman could not be a welder) to manners (gentlemen should open car doors for ladies). It takes only a cursory glance at the world around us to see that the current values relating to masculinity and femininity have changed a great deal and will probably continue to do so. These changes are resulting in matching changes in marketing practices. The following examples are typical: (1) the Mine Safety Appliances Company introduced a new hard hat designed specifically for the female construction worker; (2) the publishers of *Family Circle,* a magazine designed primarily for housewives, has introduced a new magazine titled *Women Who Work* to more effectively serve this market segment; and (3) an advertisement for Scott Paper Company's Baby Fresh, a premoistened paper towel, depicts a young father changing an infant.[7] The marketing implications of changes in this value are so vast that the second half of this chapter is devoted to this topic.

Competition—Cooperation   Americans have seemingly always been fierce competitors. This strong value may in part be responsible for the type of economic system we have and is in turn fostered by that system. However, in recent years there appears to have been a reduction in the competitive orientation of the society. This reduced level of competitiveness is reflected in marketing activities as well as by consumers. Many of the problems we face as individuals and as firms require cooperative efforts to solve. Many public and private schools emphasize "getting along" more than "getting ahead." As we move toward a steady-state population and economy, cooperation may well become even more important. Despite the decline in this value, we are and will most likely remain more competitive than most other societies. For example, the Head Division of AMF Corporation recently introduced the Prince tennis racquet, an oversized racquet that provides the user a distinct competi-

---

[6] For an example of the antichange literature, see Alvin Toffler's *Future Shock* (Random House, 1970).

[7] D. S. Yeager, "Women at Work," *The Wall Street Journal* (August 31, 1978), p. 1.

tive advantage. Wilson quickly followed with its own oversized racquet, the Wilson Extra. Such products would not enjoy the same degree of success in less competitive cultures.

Youth – Age Traditionally, age has been highly valued in almost all cultures. Older people were considered basically wiser than young people and were, therefore, looked to as models and leaders. This has never been true in our own culture, probably because it required characteristics such as physical strength, stamina, and youthful vigor and imagination to transform a wilderness into a new type of producing nation. This value on youth continued as we became an industrial nation and over the past three decades since World War II increased to such a point that products such as cars, clothing, cosmetics, and hairstyles seemed designed and sold only to the young! In our culture, to be young seems to mean to be beautiful, to be active, to be exciting—all highly valued things. Marketers have been responsive to this value and have reinforced it not only in terms of products for the increasingly affluent young market segments, but also as a basic selling theme for many products to all markets.

However, it appears that there may be a slight reversal of this currently held value on youth. Due to their increasing numbers and affluence in terms of disposable income, older citizens have developed political and economic clout and are beginning to use it. Retirement communities excluding younger people are being developed in large numbers. Cosmetics, medicines, and hair care products are being marketed specifically to older consumers. Middle-aged consumers will soon constitute the largest single market segment (see Chapter 6), and this segment will most likely develop and maintain lifestyles distinct from the "youth market." For example, a recent survey conducted for a major retail chain found that the "man in the middle" group (aged 29 – 40) had developed clothing preferences independent of and different from those of younger consumers.[8]

Directional values

The second major class of values Americans hold we have termed directional. These are the values that help to determine which way people will go in life. We see some shift in the direction that Americans are oriented and feel that a number of these values will shift even further in the future.

Active – Passive Traditionally, Americans have always been a very physically active people and this has increased over time. Currently, general physical fitness and interest in physical activities such as sport-

---

[8] "Men's Clothiers Zero in on Ages 29 through 40," United Press International (March 22, 1978).

ing events is at an all-time peak. This has opened up entirely new markets for "active leisure" products, everything from racquetball equipment to jogging shoes to $200 sweat suits to diet foods. This physical activity orientation has also negatively affected other kinds of products. Games such as Chess, for example, have never enjoyed the degree of acceptance in America that they have in many other cultures. However, intellectual pursuits and artistic endeavors do seem to be gaining more acceptance in our culture.

Material – Nonmaterial Americans have long been considered by other cultures to be excessively materialistic in orientation. Whether or not we actually have been "too" materialistic or just very fortunate economically is of little concern here. What is important, however, is to realize that material possessions and success are important values for Americans. Material possessions are indicators of who and what we are and, therefore, are an important part of our visible lifestyle. Imagine the different types of advertising appeals that would be used if we did not value material possessions as highly as we do. Also, a much reduced rate of new product innovation and introduction and a smaller number of available brands would result if we were significantly less materialistic. There are indications that at least some Americans are putting less emphasis on materialism. Kotler sees us in the transitional stage between an industrial and postindustrial society where there is a swing toward a less materialistic orientation.[9] Note, however, that a complete swing away from materialism is unlikely. Rather, a slight but significant shift may occur.

Hardwork – Leisure One of the most clearly evident shifts in current American values concerns the orientation toward work versus leisure. Traditionally, the belief in the benefits of hard work has been tremendously strong. Those who engaged in hard work were valued above those who "wasted time" in leisure activities. The so-called work ethic was meaningful because it did tend to produce an exceptional rate of upward social mobility.[10] Over time, there has been a shift in our orientation, such that leisure activities are seen as being more rewarding and more necessary than in earlier times. Hence new markets have opened up that are tremendously profitable, both to the participants and the sponsors, as witnessed by professional sports. This shift toward more leisure-time activities probably reflects the realities of our economic and social situation more than anything else. Technology has given us increased time. Most of our society can earn a reasonable income with a "normal" 40-hour workweek. Millions of Americans simply do not expect to climb any further on the ladder of social mobility and

---

[9] P. Kotler, "Generic Concept of Marketing," *Journal of Marketing* (April 1972), pp. 46–54.

[10] T. M. Kando, *Leisure and Popular Culture in Transition* (C. V. Mosby Co., 1975), p. 9.

hence divert that extra time toward the myriad of activities that signify recreation and leisure. One study found that the hours per week spent in total work-for-pay-related activities by employed men dropped from 51.3 hours per week in 1965 to 47.4 hours in 1975. Most of this "extra" time was devoted to leisure activities rather than sleep, family care, or personal care.[11]

Risk taking – Security   In a nation that developed in a manner such as ours, one would expect to see a generally higher propensity to take risks—gamble if you will—than in older more established cultures. This cultural "trait" of risk taking has traditionally been much admired in our society and has been widely adopted as a sound strategy for progressive marketers. Consumers were also more risk taking in their behavior and willing to try new products, wear new styles, and pick up, at least temporarily, new fads. This seems to have changed somewhat over time. There is an increasing emphasis on security. Perhaps this is because many of the risks we took for granted have become too large, with too critical of consequences. Resources are becoming too scarce, both physical and mental, to waste them on product ideas that have not been carefully thought out and given high probabilities of success. Recent "near-miss" accidents involving nuclear power plants will reinforce this concern.

Problem solving – Fatalistic   Our society has traditionally and currently taken a problem-solving orientation to life. In other words, people basically feel they can affect and to some extent control the world around them. Our tremendous technological success has largely been responsible for this strongly held value. For example, once landing on the moon was determined to be a national goal and given the proper resources, it was a relatively short time before we actually did land a man on the moon. This value has not changed a great deal, though there are groups within the society who take a far more passive orientation to life than does the majority. A failure to develop new energy resources could have a significant impact on this value. Marketing applications revolve around the way one can approach consumers—from advertising themes to new product introductions. For example, consumers generally do not accept problems as being "unsolvable" and they actively seek products to solve perceived problems. A more fatalistic approach would lead to more acceptance of problems as unsolvable and a reduced interest in new products.

Admire nature – Overcome nature   Traditionally, nature has been viewed as an obstacle. We as a people up until the past few decades have attempted to bend nature to our wants and desires. We have felt that we

---

[11] J. P. Robinson, *Changes in American's Use of Time: 1965–75* (Communication Research Center, Cleveland State University, 1977). Details of the 1975 data are presented in Table 5–2.

should reshape nature, both in form and cycle, to make for a more perfect world. Recently, however, this orientation has shifted dramatically and shows every sign of continuing to do so in the future. We now are more prone to admire nature, to coexist with it, and to learn from it. This shift affects us as marketers and consumers in many ways. For example, the nature and amount of packaging materials has changed to respond to this value shift. Biodegradable material is in higher demand and returnable package systems are frequently demanded when this cannot be done.[12] Natural foods and cosmetics have become a more highly demanded type of goods. Advertising themes can generally count on a favorable response when seeming to comply with the admiration of nature. In contrast, Du Pont recently spent $5 million in an advertising campaign designed to overcome negative attitudes toward synthetic chemical manufacturers.[13]

Feeling values

Our last general class of values has been designated as feeling values and deals with the relative degree of pleasure or pleasantness evoked from a situation or activity. It is difficult to make any generalization about overall changes in these values, as no clear trend is evident.

Adult – Child Children have always played an important role in our society and have been highly valued. However, historically the adult was the focus of our orientation and traditionally received more prestige and importance. In the 20th century this changed and the child became more and more to be the focus of the family unit. Increasingly, it seems that this value orientation is slowly shifting back toward the adult. Whether this shift will continue as children become less common due to a changing age distribution and falling birthrate remains to be seen.

Postponed gratification – Immediate gratification Traditionally members of our society have been encouraged to postpone gratification. A person was encouraged to pass up today's pleasures and save resources for a later reward. This value complemented our religious orientation which encouraged sacrifice (foregoing certain pleasures) for greater rewards after death. This value has undergone a profound change in the past 40 years. In part, this may be due to the fact that most of today's consumers have lived in a period of virtually uninterrupted prosperity. The potential for almost instant nuclear destruction may also encourage a "live for today" orientation.

Whatever the cause, most Americans are unwilling to delay important

---

[12] A number of states now require all beverages to be sold in returnable containers.

[13] "Du Pont Notes Importance of Chemicals to Consumers," *Advertising Age* (March 5, 1979), p. 63.

gratifications for any length of time. This is most clearly reflected in the enormous growth of credit purchases since the 1950s. Many of these credit purchases are for nonnecessities such as boats, second cars, vacation homes, hot tubs, and so forth.

Sensual gratification – Abstinence A fairly similar value to immediate versus postponed gratification is sensual gratification versus abstinence. Traditionally, the American culture prescribed that not only should one postpone gratification but also one should abstain from those activities that delight the senses—eating, drinking, sex, and other activities that provide sensual bodily pleasure. Our culture has for years considered these as relatively sinful, especially when done in excess (excess being defined as anything above bare minimum requirements). Over time, particularly the past 20 years, this value has been changing. People are now much more accepting of products that allow for and in fact encourage sensual gratification as well as the advertising themes that emphasize sensual gratification. However, this may be a cyclical phenomenon. Hedonism was widely accepted in this culture during the "roaring twenties" also.

Humor – Serious Generally, Americans have been humorous and appreciate humor in others. There seems to be relatively little change in this over time, though there may now be a slight shift back toward a more serious outlook, if only because some of the long-range problems mankind faces seem more serious. However, in our culture one can generally expect a favorable "emotional" response to humorous appeals. As a result, the use of humor in sales presentations and advertising is widespread.

Romantic – Nonromantic orientation America has always had a romantic orientation. We made heroes out of the cowboys and villians out of the Indians. Black hats lose and white hats prevail; underdogs can always be assured of popular support (to a point—then they become "losers"). This orientation may account for some of the success of the Avis "We're number 2 so we try harder" campaign. This theme matched both our competitive and romantic values. The "true love conquers all" theme is still quite popular as well.

Maximum – Minimum cleanliness Does the culture emphasize and, therefore, value a high degree of cleanliness or is it really a minor concern? In the American culture, cleanliness has been viewed as being extremely important and, though there may be a slight shift away from this great concern, the basic value remains intact. Clearly, the importance of this value has been responsible for the size of one of the biggest consumer product markets—soaps and detergents for clothes, cars, bodies, hair, floors, dishes, and so forth. This value also dictates to most people in the culture that they should use deodorants, brush their teeth, and change clothes frequently.

Conclusion on American values

We have tried to point out the nature and possible direction of change of some commonly held cultural values in America. We have not mentioned all the values that are relevant and we cannot say for certain that our views are correct. But they should give you a feel for how important values are and how they can affect consumer behavior and marketing strategy. When dealing with consumer behavior, you as a marketing manager should always ask yourself *which basic values exist that might affect, positively or negatively, the consumption of your product and brand.*

In the next section, we will provide a detailed analysis of the impact of the shift in one American value, the masculine–feminine value. As we indicated previously, our culture has always placed a higher value on the masculine dimension of this value. This has resulted in distinct social roles for males and females. However, it is clear that these roles are changing. The nature of this change is the subject of the remainder of this chapter.

SEX ROLES IN THE AMERICAN CULTURE

The past 20 years have witnessed a virtual revolution in the behaviors considered appropriate for females. The general nature of this shift has been for behaviors previously considered to be appropriate only or primarily for men to become more acceptable for women. The extent to which changes in sex roles will continue is a crucial issue to marketers as well as public policy planners. In this section, we are going to examine the changes that have taken place thus far and develop a foundation for understanding future changes in male and female sex roles.

The process of sex role differentiation

A *role* is a *prescribed pattern of behavior expected of a person in a given situation by virtue of the person's position in the situation* such as father in a family, a left end on a football team, or a passenger in a bus.[14] The key idea is that the behaviors are expected of a position *not* an individual. Thus certain behaviors are expected of all fathers, all left ends, and all bus passengers regardless of their individual characteristics or desires. While there are individual variations or *styles* in role performance, each role has a cluster of expected behaviors. (The concept of role is developed more fully in Chapter 8.)

Sex roles are *ascribed roles*. An ascribed role is *based on an attribute*

---

[14] T. Shibutani, *Society and Personality* (Prentice-Hall, Inc., 1961), p. 46.

over which the individual has little or no control. This can be contrasted with *achievement roles* which are based on performance criteria over which the individual has some degree of control. Individuals can, within limits, select their occupational roles (achievement roles) but they cannot influence their sexual category (ascribed role). The attributes used for ascribed role assignments such as sex category are generally evident from birth, so an individual's adoption to the appropriate sex role typically begins early in life. Therefore, the behavioral and psychological requirements of the role are acquired early and are probably very resistant to change.[15]

Male and female sex roles call for differing behavior in all societies. Furthermore, though there are major differences between cultures, the male role in any one culture is generally more similar to the male role in another culture than it is to the female role in either culture. Why are sex role differences so widespread? There are two opposing answers to this question.

Complete biological determinism holds that most observable differences between male and female behavior, temperament, and so forth are caused by biological and genetic factors. The other extreme, complete cultural determinism, is best represented by Margaret Mead's statement that "human nature is almost unbelievably malleable, responding accurately and contrastingly to contrasting cultural conditions."[16] Most current theories combine elements of each of these opposing approaches.

Our focus is on how societies maintain ascribed sex roles and how these roles are changing in our society rather than on the underlying causes of sex role differentiations. The process of child socialization is clearly the most important vehicle in establishing sex role differentiation. Boys are taught both directly and indirectly to be boys and girls to be girls. Formal and informal sanctions are applied to both children and adults who deviate from accepted sex role behavior. (If you are a male, try wearing red nail polish. Or if female, you could try smoking a pipe in public. This will provide you with intimate knowledge of informal social sanctions.)

There is little doubt that mass media play an important role in the socialization process. In addition, they provide continuing portrayals of "appropriate" sex role behaviors. In our culture advertising is an important part of the content of mass media. Based on this fact, a United Nations report concluded that advertising is "the most insidious form of mass-media perpetuation of the derogatory image of women as sex symbols and as an inferior class of human beings."[17] Holter lists "the

---

[15] H. Holter, *Sex Roles and Social Structure* (Oslo: Universitetsforlaget, 1970).

[16] M. Mead, *Sex and Temperament in Three Primitive Societies* (Morrow, 1935), p. 280.

[17] The New York Times News Service, "UN Report on Sexism 'Bluntly' Worded," United Nations, New York, 1974.

constant exposure to sex type role-models that, in modern society, are provided by various media of communication" as one of the two primary reinforcement mechanisms for existing patterns of sex differentiation.[18]

Empirical studies appear to support these allegations. A content analysis of the advertisements in seven popular magazines produced four prevalent stereotypes: (1) A woman's place is in the home, (2) Women do not make important decisions or do important things, (3) Women are dependent and need men's protection, and (4) Men regard women primarily as sexual objects; they are not interested in women as people.[19] This study was replicated 20 months later and a substantial improvement in both the percentage of women portrayed as working and in the types of jobs they were portrayed in was found. However, no significant changes were noted in the other aspects of women's roles as portrayed by ads.[20]

Advertisers are frequently criticized because of the female sex role portrayals described above. Some have replied that these portrayals merely reflect existing reality. However, critics contend that the endless portrayal of the existing sex role stereotypes by the mass media in general and advertisers in particular serves to reinforce and strengthen the existing stereotypes. This argument is shown in Figure 5–2.

Advertisers and the mass media have adjusted portrayals of racial and nationality groups based on this type of analysis. It seems evident that firms must also use care in how women are portrayed in advertising. A recent study found that a sizeable proportion of women were critical of the role portrayal of women in advertising.[21] Each advertising campaign should be tested to ensure that the role portrayals of women are not offensive to members of the target market.

Three sets of roles appear to be undergoing substantial changes—the workwife, housewife, and the workwife's husband. There are also increasing numbers of unmarried working women, but we lack sufficient data to describe this segment. The major changes taking place in the other three roles are described in the following sections.

---

[18] Holter, *Sex Roles,* p. 198.

[19] A. E. Courtney and W. Lockeretz, "A Woman's Place: An Analysis of the Roles Portrayed by Women in Magazine Advertisements," *Journal of Marketing Research* (February 1970), pp. 92–95.

[20] L. C. Wagner and B. Banos, "A Woman's Place: A Follow-up Analysis of the Roles Portrayed by Women in Magazine Advertisements," *Journal of Marketing Research* (May 1973), pp. 213–14. See also D. E. Sexton and P. Haberman, "Women in Magazine Advertisements," *Journal of Advertising Research* (August 1974), pp. 41–46; M. Venkatesan and J. Losco, "Women in Magazine Ads: 1959–1971, *Journal of Advertising Research* (October 1975), pp. 49–54; and A. Belkaoui and J. Belkaoui, "A Comparative Analysis of the Roles Portrayed by Women in Print Advertismenets: 1958, 1970, 1972," *Journal of Marketing Research* (May 1976), pp. 168–72.

[21] W. J. Lundstrom and D. Siglimpaglia, "Sex Role Portrayals in Advertising," *Journal of Marketing* (July 1977), pp. 72–79.

FIGURE 5–2

Mass media and existing sex role perceptions

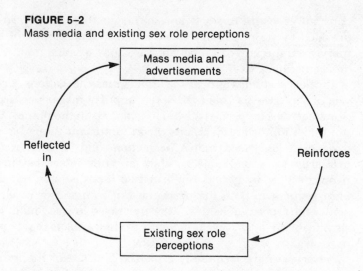

The workwife[22]

In 1950, the ratio of women to men in the work force was 41 percent. By 1974, that ratio had increased to 63 percent. Considering full-time workers only, the ratio of women to men was 29 percent in 1950 and 47 percent in 1974. Approximately 44 percent of all married women were employed in 1975 compared to only 25 percent in 1950. Clearly, more women are working outside the home than in previous years. It appears equally clear that more women will work outside the home in the future than do now.[23]

Marketing efforts have traditionally focused to a large extent on the housewife. With the housewife rapidly becoming a minority, marketers must learn about this new (in large numbers) phenomenon, the workwife. Table 5–1 illustrates some of the differences McCall found between housewives and workwives (the workwives in this study included part-time workers). As can be seen, the two groups differ in many respects relevant to marketing. However, there also appear to be areas, such as magazine readership, where only limited differences exist.[24]

Bartos, working with data from the J. Walter Thompson Company, has shown that the workwives are not a homogeneous group. The presence of children influences the consumption patterns of workwives. Of more significance is the fact that a woman's attitude toward her role as a

---

[22] The term *workwife* was introduced to the marketing literature by S. McCall, "Meet the 'Workwife'," *Journal of Marketing* (July 1977), pp. 55–65.

[23] W. Lazer and J. E. Smallwood, "The Changing Demographics of Women," *Journal of Marketing* (July 1977), pp. 14–22.

[24] S. P. Douglas, "Do Working Wives Read Different Magazines from Nonworking Wives?" *Journal of Advertising* (November 1, 1977), p. 434.

TABLE 5–1
Selected characteristics: Shopping by work status

Food shopping characteristics	Workwife	Housewife
Food shopping frequency:		
Once a day	4%	2%
Two or three times a week	43	52
Once a week	41	42
Two or three times a month	12	4
Time of day:		
Mornings	23	52
Afternoons	52	41
Evenings	25	7
Day of the week:		
Monday–Friday	60	80
Saturday–Sunday	39	19
Deciding where to shop:		
Always same store	17	21
Advertised price specials	13	17
Convenience	25	12
Low prices	16	16
Quality or assortment	28	33
Major shopper:		
Myself	83	94
Husband	15	4
Personal clothing shopping characteristics		
When you shop:		
Daytime	81%	97%
Evenings	19	3
Service you prefer:		
Self-service	50	39
Salesperson assists	32	41
No preferences	18	20
Store selection:		
Friend's advice	2	5
Newspaper ad	11	16
Impulse	15	15
Sale or special	34	34
Use sale store	29	22
Other	9	8
Average price of dress:		
$25 or less	38	30
$26–50	46	45
$51–100	14	21
More than $100	2	4
Leisure time characteristics		
Where free time spent:		
Yardwork	33%	49%
Reading	71	69
Watching TV	66	62
Shopping	39	46
Cooking	40	44
Helping husband with business	7	11
Sleeping or lounging	15	12
Talking with friends or relatives	34	45
Swimming, tennis, or golf	21	21
Bowling	5	1

TABLE 5–1 (continued)

Movies, plays, or musicals	28	23
Church work	32	29
Other	31	39
Eating out habits:		
Two or three times a week	24	18
Once a week	32	31
Two or three times a month	19	26
Only occasionally during the year	21	19
Rarely or never	4	6
Need advice or approval prior to purchasing the following:		
Paying bills	11	13
Car	73	89
Furniture	60	75
Household appliances	56	68
Food	1	1
Toys	1	2
Personal clothing	4	4
Children's clothing	4	4

Source: Developed with permission from S. McCall, "Meet the 'Workwife'," *Journal of Marketing* (American Marketing Association, July 1970), pp. 55–65.

workwife is related to her consumption patterns. Workwives can be divided into women who regard their occupation as "just a job" and those who regard it as a career. Bartos' data indicate, among other things, that career workwives are the predominate consumers of financial and travel services compared to housewives or just-a-job workwives. Career workwives constitute approximately 19 percent of all women over 16 in the labor force or keeping house, and 37 percent of the total female labor force. Significantly, this percentage is increasing over time.[25]

Other researchers have utilized similar attitudinal approaches. Reynolds, Crask, and Wells grouped female respondents to a 1975 survey into traditional and modern categories based on their selection of one of the two ways of life described below:

1. A traditional marriage with the husband assuming the responsibility for providing for the family and the wife running the house and taking care of the children.
2. A marriage where husband and wife share responsibilities more—both work, both share homemaking and child responsibilities.[26]

In this nationwide survey, 45 percent opted for the traditional arrangement (number 1) and 54 percent the "modern" alternative (number 2).

---

[25] R. Bartos, "The Moving Target: The Impact of Women's Employment on Consumer Behavior," *Journal of Marketing* (July 1977), pp. 31—37.

[26] Fred D. Reynolds, Melvin R. Crask, and William D. Wells, "The Modern Feminine Life Style," *Journal of Marketing* (July 1977), pp. 38—45.

These two groups differ in a number of demographic, attitudinal, and behavioral characteristics.

It is interesting to note that while 45 percent of the women interviewed selected the traditional way of life, only 26 percent of a separate sample of adult women agreed with the statement, "A woman's place is in the home." As Figure 5–3 shows, 60 percent agreed with this statement less than fifteen years ago. Thus, we see women increasingly rejecting the standard housewife stereotype.

FIGURE 5–3
Decline of the traditional feminine orientation

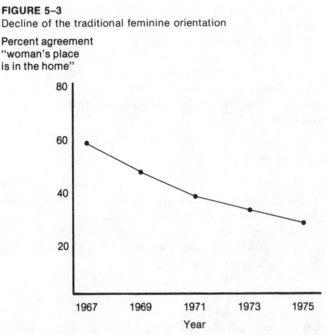

Percent agreement
"woman's place
is in the home"

Source: Fred D. Reynolds, Melvin R. Crask, and William D. Wells; "The Modern Feminine Life Style," *Journal of Marketing* (American Marketing Association, July 1977), p. 39. Used with permission.

The housewife

According to the J. Walter Thompson projections, 49 percent of all women 16 and over in the labor force or keeping house could be classified as housewives. Even so, housewives can be divided into two groups based on their future plans to "stay at home" or "go to work." In the Bartos study, over 40 percent of those classified as housewives planned to enter the labor market.[27] In a similar finding, 26 percent of the housewives in the Reynolds et al. study had a "modern" orientation.[28]

[27] Bartos, "The Moving Target," p. 33.
[28] Reynolds et al., "Modern Feminine," p. 41.

Those housewives who planned to enter the labor force at some future date differed from those without such plans in terms of travel, use of financial services, and automobile purchases.[29] Housewives are likely to have small children at home. Less than a third of married women with a child under three years of age works outside the home. In contrast, over half of those with a child between 6 and 17 work.[30]

Thus we find most women are housewives while their children are small. However, many plan to enter the work force and many have a modern or "liberated" view toward the role of women. As attitudes continue to change, the housewife will become a smaller segment of the total market. Furthermore, she will no longer be the traditional housewife of years past. It is likely that her time will be occupied with small children, community, political, or charitable organizations, advanced education, and other time-consuming activities. To the extent that this is true, differences between the workwife and the housewife will diminish. The trend will be for the housewife's behaviors to resemble those of the workwife.

The househusband?

Thus far we have examined the impact of changing sex roles on women. However, roles are based on the interaction of two or more positions. Therefore, changes in the traditional female sex role imply changes in the male sex role as well. While there has been limited attention focused on changes taking place in the male sex role, significant if slow changes are occurring.

Table 5−1 provides some evidence of this shift. For example, 15 percent of the workwives report that the husband is the major shopper for food items. In contrast, only 4 percent of the housewives report this. While there currently is little evidence of an equal sharing of the housework, as more women work full time, more men will become actively involved in housework and shopping.

It appears likely that shifts in the male role will occur more slowly and to a lesser degree than shifts in the woman's role. The "househusband" is not yet in sight. Nonetheless, the duties of the husband are and will continue to include more and more traditionally women's tasks.

Table 5−2 allows us to compare the time utilization patterns for employed men, workwives, housewives, and employed single females. In general the workwife works fewer hours for pay than the employed male but devotes substantially more time to family care and less time to "free time." Compared to the housewife, the workwife devotes considerably less time to family care and to "free time."

---

[29] Bartos, "The Moving Target."

[30] Lazer and Smallwood, "Changing Demographics," p. 17.

TABLE 5–2
1975 time use by urban husbands, housewives, workwives and single males and females*

| Activity | Employed men | | Employed women | | Housewives Married (N = 141) |
	Married (N = 245)	Single (N = 87)	Married (N = 117)	Single (N = 108)	
Sleep	53.4	54.1	55.1	54.3	56.8
Work for pay	47.4	40.0	30.1	38.8	1.1
Family care	9.7	9.0	24.9	16.6	44.3
Personal care	21.4	20.0	26.2	21.9	21.4
Free time	36.1	44.9	31.7	36.4	44.4
Organizations	3.7	4.8	2.2	4.4	4.8
Media	18.9	18.5	15.6	14.5	20.4
Social life	6.4	8.9	6.6	8.9	10.1
Recreation	1.3	4.1	0.8	0.5	0.7
Other leisure	5.8	8.6	6.5	8.1	8.4

* Average hours per week.
 Source: Derived from J. P. Robinson, *Changes in American's Use of Time: 1965–1975* (Communication Research Center, Cleveland State University, 1977), Table 4. Used with permission of the author.

Marketing Implications of the changing role of women

The implications for marketing practice of the ongoing shifts in our society's definition of the proper role of women are as numerous as they are profound. Eight important implications are briefly described below.

1. Sex-typed products Many products are losing their traditional sex typing.[31] In general, products that have been considered to be masculine are being considered appropriate for both sexes. Consider sporting goods. A few years ago, one could safely assume that a person purchasing a child's baseball glove was buying it for a boy. That is no longer the case. Along with this change in women's sex roles has come a greater interest and participation in sports traditionally stereotyped as masculine. This interest in sports is growing and marketers are responding to the needs of this new sports market. For example, Spalding is adjusting its products for the following reasons and in the following ways:

> By 1980 over one-third of all school sports participants will be women due to the women's rights movement and new legislation. Spalding, the oldest sporting goods producer in the United States, is redesigning golf clubs, baseball gloves, and other sporting equipment to more precisely fit the needs of sportswomen. No longer will women have to use scaled-down versions of men's sports equipment. Because of the increasing influence of women on the purchase of home pool tables, Spalding is producing

[31] See J. W. Gentry, M. Doering, and T. V. O'Brien, "Masculinity and Femininity Factors in Product Perception and Self Image," in *Advances in Consumer Research V*, ed. H. K. Hunt (Association for Consumer Research, 1978), pp. 151−59; and J. Dickens and B. Chappell, "Food for Freud? A Study of the Sexual Polarization of Food and Food Products," *Journal of the Market Research Society* (April 1977), pp. 76−92.

pool tables in several furniture styles such as Early American, Louis XV, Spanish and French Provincial in order to satisfy women's desires for pool tables that look more like furniture.[32]

The redefinition of women's products into men's is proceeding slowly. Women may wear slacks almost anywhere but men do not yet wear dresses. However, some products have shifted, such as hair spray.[33] Household products such as vacuum cleaners and dishwashers may be slowly losing their feminine identification. To the extent that these changes are occurring, marketers must alter their distribution, advertising, and product design policies to accommodate the shifts in the market.

The "Marlboro Story" illustrates the ability of marketers to influence perceptions of sex-typed products. Marlboro, which came equipped with both an ivory tip and a red "beauty tip," was originally perceived as a "woman's cigarette." However, a change in packaging, filters, and advertising rapidly reversed the brand's image to one of masculinity.[34]

2. *Increased importance of convenience* The workwife with a full-time job has a minimum of 40 hours a week less time to devote to household chores and other activities than does a nonworking wife.[35] Shifting chores to the children and husband still detracts from the total "free" time available to the family unit. Therefore, to workwife families, convenience is a critical variable, often more important than price.

The demand for convenience can be reflected in many ways. Labor-saving appliances, prepared foods, and minimum care homes and yards are one aspect of convenience.[36] Convenient locations, night and weekend hours, telephone shopping, and delivery services each add new importance to the retailing dimension. The demand for weekend and night services by workwife families will result in many people, including

---

[32] "The Woman's Influence on Sports," *Business Week* (August 17, 1974), p. 54.

[33] See G. P. Morris and E. W. Cundiff, "Acceptance by Males of Feminine Products," *Journal of Marketing Research* (August 1971), pp. 372 – 74; and J. R. Stuteville, "Sexually Polarized Products and Advertising Strategy," *Journal of Retailing* (Summer 1971), 3 – 13, for details on problems in changing sex-typed products.

[34] L. Brink and W. T. Kelly, *The Management of Promotion* (Prentice-Hall, Inc., 1963), pp. 161 – 65. See Stuteville, "Sexually Polarized Products," pp. 3 – 13, for other examples of shifting the sex role connotations of a product category or brand.

[35] For an excellent discussion of this issue, see J. Vanek, "Time Spent in Housework," *Scientific American* (November 1974), pp. 116 – 20.

[36] Empirical studies have thus far not documented differential levels of consumption of convenience food items, durables, or certain luxury items between workwife and housewife families when income is controlled. See S. P. Douglas, "Cross-National Comparisons and Consumer Stereotypes: A Case Study of Working and Non-working Wives in the United States and France," *Journal of Consumer Research* (June 1976), pp. 12 – 20; M. H. Strober, "Wives' Labor Force Behavior and Family Consumption Patterns," *American Economic Review* (February 1977), pp. 410 – 17; and M. H. Strober and C. B. Weinberg, "Working Wives and Major Family Expenditures," *Journal of Consumer Research* (December 1977), pp. 141 – 47.

other workwives, working during these times. This may cause a second round of pressures for traditional evening and weekend products such as movies, plays, and so forth to be offered at nontraditional times.

3. *Independence in purchase decisions* The workwife (and the modern women in general) exhibits a great deal more confidence and authority in making major purchase decisions than the traditional housewife. Marketing efforts directed at this segment of women should recognize this fact and not portray the woman in their advertising as dependent on the man. Sales personnel and credit policies should be oriented so that sales can be closed without the presence of the husband. For example, the management of Master Charge launched their "clout" advertising campaign with a 1979 budget of over $3 million to attract women consumers.[37] As the women in the Master Charge advertisements state: "I'm in charge."

4. *Increased male involvement in shopping and household duties* Males have different expectations and needs in terms of retail outlets. As they become increasingly involved in shopping for groceries, children's clothes, and so forth; store layout, advertising, product assortments, and sales force training will need to be adapted to the needs of the male shopper. In addition, household products and their advertising may require alteration. For example, a vacuum cleaner designed with the median height of women as a criteria may be too short for many men. It may be necessary to make such products adjustable so that males or females can use them comfortably.

5. *Increased importance of leisure* Increasingly time will become the scarce commodity in the workwife family rather than money. The firm attempting to market nonessential items to these households will find that it is competing with other firms, not for the families' money, but for their time. They simply do not have time to utilize more than a limited number of products.

6. *Increased affluence of workwife families* Workwife families are relatively more affluent than housewife families. This income gap will increase as women move into higher paying occupations. This affluence creates marketing opportunities among workwife families. However, it also creates opportunities among housewife families. Husbands in the lowest income categories are *least* likely to have working wives. Therefore, their family income is substantially below most workwife families. For this market segment, price should be a major consideration. In addition to low-income families, middle-income housewife families will have less disposable income than their peers whose wives work. For these families, price savings on "quality" goods should also be very important.

7. *Changing social class characteristics* Social class has tradi-

---

[37] J. Levine, "Interbank Touts Clout for Women," *Advertising Age* (April 16, 1979), p. 1.

tionally been based on characteristics of the husband, particularly his occupation. How do you classify a family whose husband is a truck driver and whose wife is a registered nurse? Will the family have the characteristics of a blue-collar family or a professional family? This issue is discussed in depth in Chapter 7. However, it is clear that the wife's occupational category must be considered in any analysis of a family's social class.

8. *Changing family role structures* As the role of the wife changes, the roles of the children and the husband also change. A workwife tends to be more independent than a housewife and plays more of a role in important decisions.[38] Husbands and children assume some of the tasks previously associated with the wife's role.

While all of the shifts described above represent opportunities for marketers, they must be handled with understanding and skill. Remember that almost half of the married women in this country *are* housewives. Advertising that directly or indirectly degrades this role could prove costly to the sponsor. One author examining attempts to totally eliminate gender as a basis for the division of labor in a kibbutz concluded that "this attempt to alter radically the sexual basis of the division of labor appears to have been a tragedy."[39] Mead stressed that "envy of the male role can come as much from an underevaluation of the role of wife and mother as from overevaluation of the public aspects of achievement that have been reserved for men."[40] It is important that marketers recognize both the changing role of women *and* the importance of the traditional role that women have fulfilled.

SUMMARY

The changing of social values is an evolutionary process which can be accelerated by (1) technological changes, (2) conflicts between existing values, (3) exposure to another culture's values, and (4) dramatic events. All of these change agents have been operative in our own culture over the past two decades. It is an important, though difficult, task for marketing managers to be aware of the extent and nature of value shifts as they relate to consumer behavior.

American society has changed dramatically in its value orientation and will continue to change as new values emerge. In terms of those values related to an individual's *control* in American society, Americans have moved from an extremely individualistic orientation to a

---

[38] See J. Scanzoni, "Changing Sex Role and Emerging Directions in Family Decision Making," *Journal of Consumer Research* (December 1977), pp. 185–88.

[39] R. G. D'Andrade, "Sex Differences and Cultural Institutions," in *The Development of Sex Differences,* ed. E. E. Maccoby (Stanford University Press, 1966), pp. 173–204, based on M. E. Spiro, *Kibbutz: Venture in Utopia* (Harvard University Press, 1956), pp. 221–30.

[40] M. Mead, *Male and Female* (Morrow, 1949), p. 771.

more balanced individualistic and collective orientation. Reward is still primarily based on performance but there is movement toward reward based on status. Americans have generally sought change in pursuit of a better lifestyle, but there is some evidence that less change will be preferred in the future. American society has an increasingly balanced male–female orientation and has moved from a highly competitive to a more cooperative orientation. Finally, American society has moved away from an identification with older members of society to one of an identification with youth, though this may change again in the near future.

American values related to the *direction* or preference for a particular way of life have also changed. Americans have always had and continue to have a preference for an active lifestyle. While still materialistic, American's emphasis on material wealth appears to have declined slightly. In terms of work versus leisure, American society values both, which creates a conflict between traditional values which were work oriented and emerging values which are leisure oriented. Americans are still primarily a problem-solving society that believes problems can be overcome and we can control the direction of our destiny. In terms of risk and security, American culture has moved dramatically from a tradition of risk taking to preference for greater security. And finally, American culture is moving away from the traditional value that regards nature as something that must be overcome in order to achieve a desired lifestyle.

American values related to *feelings* have changed also. Our view of family life is geared much more to meet the needs of children than traditional values that focused on the adults. Immediate gratification is now preferred over postponed gratification. Likewise, sensual gratification is now preferred over a traditional value which placed greater emphasis on abstinence. In American society a balanced preference for humor and seriousness prevails along with a balanced preference for a romantic and nonromantic orientation. Finally, maximum cleanliness has always been valued in American society and remains a preferred orientation in today's culture.

To operate successfully in American society, marketers must understand American values and how they influence attitudes and affect consumer behavior. Likewise, as new values emerge marketers must be prepared to understand how these new values affect consumption in order to develop marketing programs that serve the value-based needs of American society.

One aspect of American society that has undergone dramatic change in the past ten years is the role of women. Roles are prescribed patterns of behavior expected of a person in a situation. *Sex roles* are ascribed roles based on the sex of an individual rather than on characteristics which the individual can control. In contrast, an *achievement role* is acquired based on performance over which an individual does have some degree of control.

While male and female roles call for differing behavior in all societies, the male role is more similar to the male role in another culture than it is to the female role in either culture. Both biological and cultural influences have been used to explain these sex role similarities and dissimilarities.

In American society, sex roles are perpetuated, in part, by the role that mass media plays in both reflecting and reinforcing sex role stereotypes. Because sex roles are changing in American society, marketers must understand how they affect preferences for their products and the marketing programs they develop to market those products. The emergence of the workwife and her role in American society along with a change in the lifestyle and traditional feminine orientation have created new needs, product and store preferences, and attitudes that marketers must understand to serve target markets in contemporary American society. This has led directly to a reevaluation of sex-typed products, placed increased importance on convenience in terms of both consumption and purchase, necessitated changes in credit to allow for husband-independent purchases, increased male involvement in shopping and household duties, increased importance on leisure and leisure-time activities, increased the affluence of workwife families, altered social class characteristics, and changed the structure of family roles.

REVIEW QUESTIONS

1. What is a cultural value? Are cultural values shared by all members of a culture?
2. Do American cultural values provide explicit guides to specific behaviors? Explain.
3. What factors can accelerate the change of cultural values?
4. What is meant by a control value? a direction value? a feeling value?
5. Describe the current American culture in terms of the following values.

   a. Individual — Collective.
   b. Performance — Status.
   c. Tradition — Change.
   d. Masculine — Feminine
   e. Competition — Cooperation
   f. Youth — Age
   g. Active — Passive
   h. Material — Nonmaterial
   i. Hardwork — Leisure
   j. Risk taking — Security
   k. Problem solving — Fatalistic
   l. Admire nature — Overcome nature
   m. Adult — Child
   n. Postponed gratification — Immediate gratification
   o. Sensual gratification — Abstinence
   p. Humor — Serious
   q. Romantic — Nonromantic
   r. Cleanliness

6. What is a role? How does an ascribed role differ from an achievement role?
7. What is a sex role?
8. What role does mass media, including advertising, play in influencing sex roles?
9. What percentage of married women were employed in 1975? Has this percentage been increasing or decreasing?
10. What are some of the shopping and leisure-time differences between workwives and housewives? (See Table 5−1.)
11. How do career-oriented workwives differ from just-a-job workwives?
12. Are housewives a homogeneous group with respect to future work plans, spending patterns, and so forth? Explain your answer.
13. Is the househusband a widespread phenomenon?
14. What are the primary differences in time utilization between employed men, employed women, and housewives?
15. What are some of the major marketing implications of the changing role of women?

DISCUSSION QUESTIONS

1. Which values are most relevant to the purchase and use of a moped? Are they currently favorable or unfavorable for moped ownership? Are they shifting at all? If so, is the shift in a favorable or unfavorable direction?
2. In what way, if any, can the current shifts in sex roles be used to develop marketing strategy for Motron?
3. Describe additional values that you feel could (or should be added to Figure 5−1. Describe the marketing implications of each.
4. Pick the values that you feel the authors were most inaccurate in describing the *current* American values. Justify your answer.
5. Pick the three values that you feel the authors were most inaccurate in describing the *emerging* American values. Justify your answer.
6. Pick the three values you feel are undergoing the most rapid rate of change. How will these changes affect marketing practice?
7. Do you believe there are deep and fundamental shifts occurring in the role of women in our society or are the shifts described more like fads that will pass in a few more years? Justify your answer.
8. Do you believe the woman's role will continue to change? If so, in what ways?
9. What responsibilities do advertisers have to help change sex role stereotypes?
10. What are the primary marketing implications present in Table 5−1?

11. Do you think that housewives may become "defensive" or "sensitive" about not having employment outside of the home? If so, what implications will this have for marketing practice?
12. The househusband is rare. Why? Will there be an increase in the future?
13. What are the primary marketing implications present in Table 5−2?
14. Speculate on additional marketing implications associated with the changing roles of women.

PROJECT QUESTIONS

1. Interview a moped salesperson. Ascertain the interest shown in mopeds by males and females. Determine if males and females are concerned with different characteristics of mopeds or if they have different purchase motivations.
2. Interview ten male and ten female students. Ask each to describe a typical moped owner. If they do not specify, ask for the sex of the typical owner. Then probe to find out why they think the typical owner is of the sex they indicated.
3. Examine a magazine oriented to males such as *Playboy*, one oriented toward upper-income females such as *Cosmopolitan*, and one oriented toward lower-income females such as *True Romance*. Do the sex roles portrayed in the advertisements differ between these three magazine types? Speculate on the reasons for this.
4. Interview an appliance salesperson that has been selling appliances for at least ten years. See if this individual has noticed a change in the purchasing roles of women over time. Also interview the following salespersons:
   a. A furniture salesperson.
   b. An automobile salesperson.
   c. An insurance salesperson.
   d. A real estate salesperson.
5. Interview a career-oriented workwife and a housewife of a similar age. Report on differences in attitudes toward shopping, products, and so forth.

6

The American society: Demographics and subcultures

The American Association of Orthodontists began its first national advertising campaign in the fall of 1979. The campaign was aimed at young married people, especially women, and featured ads in *Good Housekeeping, Reader's Digest, Parents', Better Homes & Gardens,* and *People.* The rationale for aiming at young adults is explained by a spokesperson for the association as follows: "There's been a sharp drop in the birthrate, which has resulted in a significant reduction in the number of young patients coming into the orthodontist's office."[1] In other words, changing demographic characteristics of the American society have forced the orthodontists to identify and market to a new market segment.

In the preceding chapter we examined some basic American values and related changes in those values to marketing practices. Cultural values are not the only aspects of our society that are undergoing change. America's demographic characteristics are also changing. Changes in America's demographics have important implications for all aspects of the marketing mix. The first part of this chapter analyzes some of the more important demographic changes that are taking place and relates these changes to appropriate marketing practices.

---

[1] J. Neher, "Orthodontists Hope to Pull in Adults with First Drive," *Advertising Age* (July 2, 1979), p. 22.

We have been referring to "the American society" as though it were a homogeneous entity. In reality, our culture is composed of a large number of more or less distinct groups known as subcultures. Subcultures are of interest to marketing managers when they have unique consumption patterns for a particular product. In the second half of this chapter we will examine the major American subcultures and their impact on marketing decisions.

DEMOGRAPHICS

Demographics are *information on the size, distribution, structure, and change of populations*. Structure is defined broadly to encompass sex, age, ethnic, social, and economic categories.[2]

As we will see in the following sections and chapters, an appreciation of the nature of demographics and the factors that influence demographics are of major concern to marketing managers. In this chapter, we examine (1) changes in the size, distribution, and age of the American population, (2) changes in the economic conditions, (3) changes in the educational attainment of the population, and (4) changes in the occupational distribution of the population.[3] Each of these changing demographic variables has important implications for marketing strategy.

Population size, distribution, and age

The idea of zero population growth has received considerable publicity over the past decade. The importance of population growth and the potential impact of zero population growth in industry can best be seen by examining a specific industry. For example purposes, let us look at the coffee industry. The annual winter survey of coffee consumption by the Pan-American Coffee Bureau has shown a steady decline in per capita (over ten years of age) consumption of coffee from 3.12 cups per day in 1962 to 2.11 cups per day in 1976.[4] This is a drop of over 32 percent. Had the U.S. population remained stable over this 15-year period, the coffee industry would have faced a severe reduction in total demand. However, an increase in the population over ten years of age of approximately 25 percent greatly softened the impact of the decline in

---

[2] For a discussion on the boundaries of demographic analysis, see E. G. Stockwell, *The Methods and Materials of Demography* (Academic Press, 1976). The definition used here corresponds closely to the "operational" definition reported by A. M. Roscie, Jr., A. Le-Clare, Jr., and L. G. Schiffman, "Theory and Management Applications of Demographics in Buyer Behavior," in *Consumer and Industrial Buying Behavior,* eds. A. G. Woodside, J. N. Sheth, and P. D. Bennett (Elsevier North-Holland, Inc., 1977), p. 67.

[3] Similar information for Canada can be found in the most recent edition of *Canada Year Book* (Canada Year Book Section, Information Division, Statistics Canada).

[4] *Coffee Drinking in the United States: Winter 1976* (Pan-American Coffee Bureau, 1976), p. 1.

per capita demand. If the growth of the total population slows or stops, many industries will face stable or declining demand. This could lead to the failure of firms, increased diversification, a more highly competitive environment, and increased emphasis on export sales.

What is happening to the growth in the U.S. population? As Table 6 – 1 illustrates, the population is growing and is projected to continue to grow for at least the next 20 years.

Population growth is affected by fertility (the birthrate), mortality (the death rate), and net immigration. The prediction shown in Table 6 – 1 assumes a net annual immigration of 400,000. The mortality estimates used assume a slow and steady reduction in future mortality. The fertility rate shown in the table is the current "most likely" estimate.[5]

An examination of Table 6 – 1 shows the movement of the small number of babies born during the depression and the large number born during the "baby boom" following World War II through the age structure. As these groups change from one age category to another, the total demand for age specific products such as education, new homes, and so forth will shift rapidly. These shifts will create marketing opportunities for alert firms and crises for complacent ones.

The growth in the U.S. population has not been evenly distributed among the various regions of the country. The Western, Mountain, and South Atlantic states have grown more rapidly than the population as a whole since 1960. These regions and the West South Central region will probably continue to grow at a faster rate than the remainder of the country.

Just as regions of the country are growing at an uneven pace, so are the rural, suburban, and urban areas. The rural, or nonmetropolitan, areas grew as rapidly as the metropolitan areas in the first half of the 1970s. It appears that, in contrast to the last several decades, the nonmetropolitan areas will continue to grow at the same rate or slightly faster than the metropolitan areas. Urban or central city areas continue to lose population. However, most of this decline can be traced to the relatively large (population greater than 1 million) cities.[6] Table 6 – 2 provides estimates of the past, current, and future distribution of the population among these three areas.

As the geographic and urban characteristics of the population continue to change, firms will be required to alter sales territories, distribution systems, warehouse and plant locations, retail outlets, and so forth.

---

[5] This is known as a Series II projection, Series I and III projections are available and provide maximum and minimum likelihood population estimates. See U.S. Bureau of the Census, *Current Population Reports,* series P – 25, no. 704, "Projections of the Population of the United States: 1977 to 2050" (U.S. Government Printing Office, 1977).

[6] U.S. Bureau of the Census, *Current Population Reports,* series P – 23, no. 55, "Social and Economic Characteristics of Metropolitan and Nonmetropolitan Population: 1974 and 1970" (U.S. Government Printing Office, 1975), pp. 2 – 4.

TABLE 6-1

Estimates and projections of the population by age: 1950–2000

	Total, all ages (000)	Under 5	5–13	14–17	18–24	25–34	35–44	45–54	55–64	65 and over	Median age
Estimates											
1950	152,271	10.8	14.7	5.5	10.6	15.8	14.2	11.5	8.8	8.1	30.2
1955	165,931	11.1	16.8	5.6	9.0	14.6	13.8	11.4	8.8	8.8	30.2
1960	180,671	11.3	18.2	6.2	8.9	12.7	13.4	11.4	8.6	9.2	29.4
1965	194,303	10.2	18.4	7.3	10.4	11.6	12.6	11.2	8.8	9.5	28.1
1970	204,878	8.4	17.9	7.8	12.0	12.3	11.3	11.4	9.1	9.8	27.9
1975	213,540	7.4	15.7	7.9	12.9	14.5	10.7	11.1	9.3	10.5	28.8
Projections											
1980	222,159	7.2	13.6	7.1	13.3	16.3	11.6	10.2	9.5	11.2	30.2
1985	232,880	8.1	12.5	6.2	12.0	17.1	13.5	9.6	9.3	11.7	31.5
1990	243,513	8.0	13.4	5.2	10.3	16.9	15.0	10.4	8.5	12.2	32.8
1995	252,750	7.4	14.0	5.6	9.2	15.1	15.9	12.2	8.1	12.4	34.2
2000	260,378	6.9	13.5	6.2	9.5	13.2	15.9	13.8	8.9	12.2	35.5

Percent of population in various age categories

Source: U.S. Bureau of the Census, Current Population Reports, series P–25, no. 704, "Projections of the Population of the United States: 1977 to 2050" (U.S. Government Printing Office, 1977).

TABLE 6–2
Changes in the percent of the population in urban, suburban, and rural areas

Place of residence	1965	1970	1975	1980	1985
Metropolitan areas	67.8	68.6	68.3	68.0	67.5
Central cities	32.6	31.5	29.3	27.0	24.5
Outside central cities	35.3	37.1	39.0	41.0	43.0
Rural areas	32.2	31.4	31.7	32.0	32.5
Total	100	100	100	100	100

Source: F. Linden, "From Here to 1985," *Across the Board* (September 1977), p. 25. Used with permission of the publisher, The Conference Board, Inc.

Since many of these changes require a considerable amount of lead time, alert managers will react to approaching population shifts rather than to the results of past ones.

Income

The income level in the United States continues to rise. Table 6–3 illustrates several aspects of this growth. Two dimensions of this table are of particular importance. One is the continuing increase in per capita disposable income. It is for these funds that most consumer

TABLE 6–3
Income growth and distribution: 1965–1985*

	1965	1970	1975	1980	1985
Gross national product ($ billions)	$1,178.2	$1,368.3	$1,516.3	$1,880.0	$2,200.0
Disposable personal income ($ billions)	773.5	936.6	1,080.9	1,320.0	1,545.0
Per capita disposable income	3,981.0	4,571.0	5,062.0	5,925.0	6,600.0
Families by income class	100.0%	100.0%	100.0%	100.0%	100.0%
Under $5,000	15.6%	12.0%	12.0%	8.5%	6.8%
$5,000–10,000	24.2	20.5	21.1	16.2	14.7
$10,000–15,000	27.0	24.4	22.3	18.9	16.3
$15,000–25,000	25.0	30.5	30.3	32.4	32.1
$25,000 and over	8.2	12.6	14.1	24.0	30.2
Income by family income class .	100.0%	100.0%	100.0%	100.0%	100.0%
Under $5,000	3.7	2.6	2.6	1.3	1.0
$5,000–10,000	13.6	10.2	10.2	6.4	5.2
$10,000–15,000	25.2	20.0	18.0	12.3	9.6
$15,000–25,000	35.6	38.1	37.1	33.3	30.0
$25,000 and over	21.7	29.2	32.1	46.7	54.3

* Based on 1975 prices.
Source: F. Linden, "From Here to 1985," *Across the Board* (September 1977), p. 25. Used with permission of the publisher, The Conference Board, Inc.

goods marketers compete. A second factor of major importance is the changing shape of the income distribution. Family income is beginning to resemble an inverted pyramid rather than the standard pyramid of only a few years ago. *The increasing percentage of families with two income earners is a major factor contributing to this change.* As the table shows, it is predicted that by 1985 families with incomes over $15,000, 62 percent of all families, will have 84 percent of all personal income. This indicates that the marketplace will increasingly be dominated by relatively affluent individuals.

One impact of this change is reflected in the brand share distributions for the beer market. Low-price brands and, to a lesser extent, "popular" price brands have been losing market share to "prestige" or "high-priced" brands. To capitalize on this trend, a number of breweries are now introducing new prestige brands. For example, in March 1979, Schiltz placed its new super premium beer, Erlanger, into test market. The advertising theme stresses that "special moments deserve the best."[7]

Education

Like income, the level of education in the United States continues to rise. As Table 6–4 shows, more than half of the population over age 25 have completed high school and over one fourth have completed at least some college. As this trend continues, tastes in products, advertising,

TABLE 6–4
Educational attainment of individuals age 25 and over

	1965	1970	1975	1980	1985
Educational attainment	100.0%	100.0%	100.0%	100.0%	100.0%
Elementary or less	33.0	27.8	21.9	18.3	14.4
Some high school	18.0	17.0	15.6	16.3	15.4
High school graduate	30.7	34.0	36.2	37.9	38.9
Some college	8.8	10.3	12.4	12.5	13.7
College graduate	9.4	11.1	13.9	15.0	17.5

Source: F. Linden, "From Here to 1985," *Across the Board* (September 1977), p. 25. Used with permission of the publisher, The Conference Board, Inc.

and packaging will continue to shift. The ability of consumers to process information will improve with subsequent demands on the marketing communication systems of firms. As television viewing tends to decline as education increases, the impact of this media may be reduced somewhat.

---

[7] "Heralded by . . . ," *Advertising Age* (February 12, 1979), p. 90.

Occupation

Table 6 — 5 provides insights into the shifting occupational patterns in the United States. As can be seen, women are rapidly increasing their participation in the labor force. We examined the implications of this trend in detail in the preceding chapter. In addition, the United States is becoming a "white-collar" society with less than one third of the work force now considered to be blue collar. Chapter 7 explores the consumption process variations between occupational categories.

TABLE 6–5
Labor force participation and occupational categories: 1965–1985

	1965	1970	1975	1980	1985
Labor participation rates*					
Men	80.0%	79.1%	77.3%	77.2%	76.9%
Women	38.7	42.5	45.7	47.8	49.7
Total employment	100.0%	100.0%	100.0%	100.0%	100.0%
White-collar workers	44.8	48.3	49.8	50.7	51.5
Blue-collar workers	36.9	35.3	33.0	32.8	32.6
Service workers	12.6	12.4	13.7	13.9	14.1
Other	5.7	4.0	3.5	2.6	1.8

* Based on persons 16 and over.
   Source: F. Linden, "From Here to 1985," *Across the Board* (September 1977), p. 25. Used with permission of the publisher, The Conference Board, Inc.

Conclusions on demographics

Obviously the demographic characteristics of the United States are changing. The rate of population growth is slowing and the median age is increasing. The South and the West are growing more rapidly than the rest of the country. The mass movement to the urban areas appears to have stopped and the flight to the suburbs has slowed. The work force contains more women and more white collar employees than ever before. The educational and economic attainments of large segments of the population would have been considered impossible just a few years ago. Yet we also retain vast groups of poorly educated, low-income consumers. The challenges and problems presented to marketers by these demographic shifts are truly exciting.

SUBCULTURE

A subculture is a *segment of a culture which shares distinguishing patterns of behavior.*[8] There are two important features to this defini-

---
[8] T. S. Robertson, *Consumer Behavior* (Scott, Foresman and Co., 1970), p. 99.

tion. The first is the emphasis on *distinguishing patterns of behavior*. For a group to constitute a subculture, its members must share behaviors that differ from those of the larger or dominant culture. Thus, a group with a particular skin color, religious affiliation, or national background different from the larger culture will constitute a subculture *only* if, and to the extent, they have distinctly different behavior patterns.

A second important point is that members of subcultures *are also members of the broader culture*. This is particularly true of the United States and Canada. Therefore, subculture members generally have more behaviors that coincide with those of the larger culture than differ from it. In fact, our society is composed of a vast number of subcultures and each individual exists simultaneously in several subcultures. However, the commonalities of the broader culture are so great that we are often unaware of distinct subcultural influences.

Marketing managers are interested in subcultures only to the extent that they influence the consumption process for their products. If the behavior of a group differs with respect to *any* of the stages in the consumption process, the marketing manager must consider the possibility of altering the marketing mix variables in relation to this group. If the members of a particular subculture, no matter how distinct from the larger culture on other variables, do not differ in the acquisition, utilization, or disposition of the marketer's product, the subculture does *not* require recognition as a separate group or market segment.

The definition of subculture that we are using is not very precise in that almost any group has some unique behaviors. The marketing manager is generally interested only in subcultures containing substantial numbers of people, enough to comprise a potentially profitable market segment. Seven variables are often used to delineate such major subcultures: (1) race, (2) nationality, (3) religion, (4) age, (5) geographic location, (6) gender, and (7) social class. Social class will be considered in some detail in the next chapter. Some authorities consider gender (sex) to be a subculture variable. However, we have chosen to treat gender as a social role for reasons that were explained in the preceding chapter.

In the remainder of this section, brief descriptions of subcultures based on the remaining five variables are provided. A number of product categories will be utilized to illustrate variations in consumption patterns. To provide some consistency in explanation, coffee consumption as a product example will be discussed under each type of subculture. In addition, such factors as media usage, shopping behaviors, and information processing will be discussed where applicable. We must keep in mind that subcultures change over time. Therefore, some of the specific examples provided in the following discussion may not be appropriate for future decisions. Overall though, the existence and general nature of the subcultures will not change too dramatically in the short run.

Subcultures based on race

The major racial subcultures in the United States are the blacks, the orientals, and the American Indians. Since the black subculture is by far the largest of the three, we will examine some of the characteristics of this group. Before starting, it should be emphasized that the black subculture is not a homogeneous group any more than the white subculture is. The fact that a relatively high percentage of blacks are below or near the poverty level sometimes leads marketers to assume that all blacks share the behavior associated with low-income blacks. As we will see, such an assumption is dramatically false.[9]

Black demographics The demographics of black Americans differ significantly from white Americans. As Table 6—6 indicates, relative to

TABLE 6-6
Demographic differences between black and white Americans

Demographic variable	Black	White
Median Income	$7,800	$13,400
Median age: Males	21.9	28.5
Median age: Females	24.2	31.1
Families with income above:		
$10,000	38.0%	67.0%
$15,000	19.0	42.0
Families below the low-income level	31.4	8.9
Persons 18 to 24 who are enrolled in college	18.0	25.0
Persons 20 to 24 who are high school graduates	72.0	85.0
Geographic location:		
Central cities	58.0	26.0
Metropolitan rings	17.0	41.0
Nonmetropolitan areas	24.0	33.0
South	53.0	29.0
North	39.0	53.0
West	9.0	18.0
Female head of family	35.3	10.5
Average number of births to date (women 18–39)	2.4	1.9
Average number of total births expected (women 18–39)	2.9	2.5

Source: Derived from U.S. Bureau of the Census, *Current Population Reports*, series P–23, no. 54, "Social and Economic Status of the Black Population in the United States (U.S. Government Printing Office, 1974).

whites, blacks in general are poorer, younger, less educated, more fertile, and more concentrated inside central cities. The most salient of all

---

[9] Good discussions of the heterogeneous nature of the black subculture and the compounding effects of income are provided by T. W. Barry and M. G. Harvey, "Marketing to Heterogeneous Black Consumers," *California Management Review* (Winter 1974), pp. 50–57; D. E. Sexton, Jr., "Black Buyer Behavior," *Journal of Marketing* (October 1972), pp. 36–39; F. D. Sturdivant, "Subculture Theory: Poverty, Minorities, and Marketing," in *Consumer Behavior: Theoretical Sources*, eds. S. Ward and T. S. Robertson (Prentice Hall, Inc., 1973), p. 497.

these differences is the low-income level of many blacks. It is the state of poverty that accounts for many of the other differences. For example, of individuals between the ages of 18 to 24, 39 percent of whites and only 25 percent of blacks were enrolled in college in 1974. Likewise, 13 percent of whites in this group were *not* high school graduates while 29 percent of the blacks had not received a high school degree. Yet when income is held constant, these racial differences are greatly reduced.

The demographic differences shown in the table should alert us to the very real danger of assuming that consumption variations between blacks as a group and whites as a group are due directly to race. Such differences may be due to a different distribution of income, age, education, or other demographic factors instead of race. For example, a finding that blacks spend a higher percentage of their income on food than whites with a similar level of income might relate more directly to a difference in average family size than to race. This is not to suggest that there are not racially related differences in consumption patterns. Instead, it is a warning to examine such differences closely before assuming that the direct cause is race.

TABLE 6–7
Percentage of high income households owning selected appliances and automobiles: Fall 1973*

Appliance	Black	White
Refrigerator	84%	89%
Clothes dryer	47	76
Dishwasher	22	49
Home food freezer	36	44
Kitchen range	78	85
Clothes washing machine	74	86
Television sets		
One or more	99	99
Black and white only	26	20
Color only	19	28
Black and white and color	55	50
Air conditioning (available)	49	64
Room unit	30	35
Central system	19	29
Automobiles		
One or more	91	97
Two automobiles	35	34
Two or more automobiles	56	63
Latest model of automobile owned		
1973 or 1974	25	23
1970–1972	43	48
1968–1969	19	17
1967 or earlier	13	12

* Households are in highest income quartile and have incomes of approximately $15,000 or more.

Source: U.S. Bureau of the Census, *Current Population Reports*, series P–23, no. 54, "The Social and Economic Status of the Black Population in the United States" (U.S. Government Printing Office, 1974), p. 139.

Product usage There are numerous illustrations of variations between black and white product usage. For example, blacks consume only half the amount of coffee per person that whites consume. However, controlling for income level reduces or eliminates many of these differences. Table 6 – 7 shows the percentages of black and white households with an income in excess of $15,200 (1974 dollars) that own selected appliances. Black ownership was somewhat less than whites for most product categories. This may, in part, reflect past income patterns. Table 6 – 8 shows the number of purchases per 100 households and the

TABLE 6–8
Number of high income household purchases and average price paid for selected appliances and automobiles: Fall 1972 to Fall 1973*

Average purchase price	Household purchases per 100 households		Average price paid	
	Black	White	Black	White
Clothes washing machine	17	13	$ 239	$ 236
Clothes dryer	11	11	194	197
Dishwasher	1	8	201	246
Refrigerator	9	10	385	376
Home food freezer	6	6	350	248
Kitchen range	9	9	307	312
Room air conditioner	8	7	239	209
Television set				
Black and white	11	8	131	103
Color	15	14	417	434
Automobiles				
New	22	23	4,954	4,409
Used	18	20	2,354	1,858

* Households are in highest income quartile and have incomes of approximately $15,000 or more.
Source: U.S. Bureau of the Census, *Current Population Reports*, series P–23, no. 54, *"The Social and Economic Status of the Black Population in the United States"* (U.S. Government Printing Office, 1974), p. 139.

average price paid during the 12-month period preceding the survey. The purchasing rate of blacks is similar to whites. Likewise, the amounts paid are similar except that blacks paid substantially more for automobiles and home food freezers and less for dishwashers than did whites.

As we have seen, there are differential rates of product usage for certain product categories between blacks and whites even when income is held constant. After reviewing the available literature on black buying behavior, Sexton concluded that "blacks are more likely to be innovators in product classes that are socially visible, such as clothing; however, income does limit the extent of their innovativeness."[10]

A merchandising manager of Carson, Pirie, Scott, and Company

---

[10] Sexton, "Black Buyer Behavior," p. 38.

utilizes this information intuitively as evidenced by the statement: "The Negro shopper is my guide. If I see him buying yellow shirts, I start to buy greater quantities of the color which will filter down to white men a little later."[11]

Whether or not purchase motives differ between whites and blacks is an unresolved issue. It has been proposed that black purchasing reflects a desire to become part of mainstream America while whites purchase to obtain exclusiveness.[12] Others have proposed that "the basic dilemma of the Negro is whether to strive against odds for middle-class values as reflected in material goods or to give in and live more for the moment."[13] This could very easily also be the basic dilemma of anyone of lower income, however, and it appears that both of these proposals have some relevance for middle- and upper-income blacks.[14] At lower-income levels the impact of poverty appears to overwhelm other variables.

Media usage   Blacks use media differently and use different media than do whites. There are a number of black-oriented magazines such as *Ebony,* numerous black newspapers, and black-oriented radio stations. Blacks are the primary audience for these media. In addition, blacks utilize standard media as well.

Blacks listen to AM radio more than whites. Radio listening patterns among blacks are stable across most demographic variables, though those under 17 and over 50 listen somewhat less. A substantial amount of black radio listening is to black-oriented stations, although this declines sharply for those over 50 and somewhat as income and education increases.[15]

Black families and black women watch television more hours per week than do whites. Black males and white males watch about the same amount. Both black men and women watch less prime-time television than do whites. The situation is reversed for children between 7 and 17.[16] Blacks have also shown a preference for action-oriented shows and less of a preference for family-type shows or situation comedies compared to whites.[17]

Blacks not only utilize media differently but also react to the content of media in a distinctive manner. It appears safe to conclude that blacks

[11] *Men's Wear* (January 5, 1968), p. 3; quoted in Sexton, "Black Buyer Behavior."

[12] H. A. Bullock, "Consmer Motivation in Black and White," *Harvard Business Review* (May – June 1961), pp. 89 – 104; and (July – August 1961), pp. 110 – 24.

[13] R. A. Bauer, S. M. Cunningham, and L. H. Wortzel, "The Marketing Dilemma of Negroes," *Journal of Marketing* (July 1965), p. 3.

[14] See Sexton, "Black Buyer Behavior," p. 39.

[15] G. J. Glasser and G. D. Metzger, "Radio Usage by Blacks," *Journal of Advertising Research* (October 1975), pp. 39 – 45.

[16] "Black TV Viewing Study: Women Watch Most," *Advertising Age* (October 18, 1976), p. 20.

[17] J. W. Casey, "Variations in Negro-White Television Preference," *Journal of Broadcasting* (Summer 1966), pp. 199 – 211.

have a more positive attitudinal response to commercials utilizing black models than they do to commercials using white models.[18] Whites appear to respond in a similar manner to both types of commercials,[19] though there is limited evidence of white "backlash" against specific black or integrated advertisements.[20] There have been relatively few studies of sales response, as opposed to attitude or preference measures, of white and black responses to advertisements using white or black models. The studies that have been done show no difference in the short-run response of either blacks or whites to black, white, or integrated point-of-purchase advertisements in supermarkets.[21] Based on the existing research evidence, we can conclude that (1) all-black advertisements and, to a lesser extent, integrated advertisements will be favorably perceived by black consumers, (2) such ads will not automatically cause negative reactions in whites though specific ads should be tested prior to utilization, and (3) favorable response to the advertisement is *not* a certain indicator that a favorable sales response will follow.

An example of a marketing program directed at a black market segment   As stated at the beginning of this section, for most products there is no single black market. Black consumers, like white consumers, are heterogeneous. However, there are differences in the consumption patterns for at least some products between blacks and whites. These differences present opportunities and challenges for marketers. A useful warning on relying on racial differences that existed in the past is provided by Willard Savoy, who was in charge of creating an overall program

---

[18] See A. M. Barban, "The Dilemma of Integrated Advertising," *Journal of Business* (October 1969), pp. 477—96; A. M. Barban and E. W. Cundiff, "Negro and White Response to Advertising Stimuli," *Journal of Marketing Research* (November 1964), pp. 53—56; T. E. Barry and R. Hansen, "How Race Affects Children's TV Commercials," *Journal of Advertising Research* (October 1973), pp. 63—67; P. K. Choudbury and L. S. Schnid, "Black Models in Advertising to Blacks," *Journal of Advertising Research* (June 1974), pp. 19—22; and S. Tolley and J. T. Goett, "Reactions to Blacks in Newspaper Ads," *Journal of Advertising Research* (April 1972), pp. 11—17. For a contradictory view, see J. W. Gould, N. B. Sigbond, and C. E. Zoerner, Jr., "Black Consumer Reactions to 'Integrated' Advertising: An Exploratory Study," *Journal of Marketing* (July 1970), pp. 20—6.

[19] Barban, "Integrated Advertising"; Barban and Cundiff, "Negro and White Response"; R. F. Bush, R. G. Gwinner and P. J. Solomon, "White Consumer Sales Response to Black Models," *Journal of Marketing* (April 1974), pp. 25—29; L. Guest, "How Negro Models Affect Company Image," *Journal of Advertising Research* (April 1970), pp. 29—33; W. V. Muse, "Product-Related Response to Use of Black Models in Advertising," *Journal of Marketing Research* (February 1971), pp. 107—9; M. J. Schlinger and J. T. Plummer, "Advertising in Black and White," *Journal of Marketing Research* (May 1972), pp. 149—53; and J. E. Stafford, A. E. Birdwell, and C. E. Van Tassel, "Integrated Advertising—White Backlash?" *Journal of Advertising Research* (April 1970), pp. 15—20.

[20] C. E. Black, "White Backlash to Negro Ads: Fact or Fantasy?" *Journalism Quarterly* (Summer 1972), pp. 253—62; J. W. Cagley and R. N. Cardozo, "White Responses to Integrated Advertising," *Journal of Advertising Research* (April 1970), pp. 35—39; Muse, "Product-Related Response"; and Stafford et al., "Integrated Advertising."

[21] Bush et al., "White Consumer Sales"; and P. J. Solomon, R. F. Bush, and J. F. Hair, Jr., "White and Black Consumer Sales Response to Black Models," *Journal of Marketing Research* (November 1976), pp. 431—43.

for reaching the Negro market for Purex: "No company can build a program on the assumption that there'll be a social status quo between the races in the years to come."[22]

We can see many of the points made in the preceding pages by examining a successful case of treating part of the black market as a distinct market segment. Medical research demonstrated that there should be differences in the chemical composition of black cosmetic lines in part because of physiological differences between blacks and whites.[23] In addition, cosmetics designed for use on white complexions often produce an ashen or orange effect when used on darker skins. These findings, coupled with the increase in "black pride" and widespread acceptance of the idea that "black is beautiful," created a marketing opportunity that a number of firms sought to capitalize on.[24]

Avon sought to capture a share of the market through the following steps:

1. Focused on urban blacks.
2. Developed an entire product line based specifically on the cosmetic requirements of blacks.
3. Utilized a separate advertising agency to create advertisements designed to appeal to the black woman. These ads were based on the fact that Avon was not well known by black consumers.
4. Utilized special media to introduce the new line (spot radio in 43 markets, spot television in 55 markets, ads in 49 major black newspapers, and color pages in the Fall issues of *Ebony, Essence,* and *Jet*).[25]

Revlon followed a similar strategy but placed most of its advertising in black radio stations with print ads in *Essence.*[26]

Subcultures based on nationality

Nationality forms a basis for a subculture when members of that nationality group identify with it and base at least some of their behaviors on the norms of the national group. In the United States, Mexican-Americans, Puerto Ricans, Scandinavians, Italians, Polish, Irish, Japanese, and Chinese constitute important nationality subcultures. The subcul-

---

[22] J. Feehery, "Purex Launches Ads in *'Ebony'* in Test of 'Subtleties' of Negro Marketing," *Advertising Age* (February 1, 1965), p. 46.

[23] C. Marticarena, "Ethnic Market: Biggest Potential for Growth in Cosmetics Industry," *Chemical Marketing Reporter* (June 23, 1975), p. 37.

[24] For a discussion of the relationship between the rise of black pride and the decline of advertising for hair straightener and bleaching cremes and the rise of Afro hair models and Afro wigs, see J. S. Condie and J. W. Christiansen, "An Indirect Technique for the Measurement of Changes in Black Identity," *Phylon* (March, 1977), pp. 46−54.

[25] "Avon Aims New Line, Ad Effort at Fast-Growing Black Market" *Advertising Age* (July 28, 1975), p. 57.

[26] L. Baltera, "Ultra Sheen Losing Luster under Revlon Pressure," *Advertising Age* (July 11, 1977), pp. 3, 174.

tural influence tends to be strongest in cases where a significant number of the group members are geographically grouped together such as in Chinatown in San Francisco.

Food consumption appears to be the primary item affected by nationality subcultures. While no empirical evidence is available, it is likely that coffee consumption varies widely among nationality groups. Other products such as clothing, housing, or automobiles may also vary by nationality. In general, the preceding discussion on the functioning of racial subcultures is applicable to nationality groups and need not be repeated here. As with the case of race, it should be emphasized that nationality subcultures are heterogeneous. For example, one often sees references to the Hispanic market or the Spanish speaking market. This market consists of over 11 million people. However, 57 percent are of Mexican origin; 15 percent, Puerto Rican; and 6 percent, Cuban.[27] Each group has unique characteristics that may make a common marketing approach unsatisfactory. For example, only 2.6 percent of Puerto Rican Americans live outside metropolitan areas compared to over 23 percent of the Mexican Americans.[28] Thus, we must be careful in how we define nationality subcultures.

Subcultures based on religion

Most religions prescribe or prohibit certain behaviors including consumption behaviors. In addition, they have major influences on values and attitudes. There is evidence that the religious orientation of an individual's parents has a strong influence on the child's motivation to achieve. In fact, the prevailing religion of various cultures has been related to economic development and the rise of capitalism.[29]

Despite the immense power of religion and striking cross-cultural differences in religious practices, religious differences in the United States related to the consumption process are more apparent than real. With the exception of a few small sects such as the Amish, most religious-based differences focus on only a few products. A number of religions prohibit or restrict the use of alcoholic beverages. Orthodox Jews are required to consume kosher foods. The Mormons encourage the stockpiling of foods and prohibit the consumption of coffee. With the exception of such limited product areas, religious influences within the United States are indirect and are often more closely associated with social class or ethnic variations than with the religion itself.

---

[27] U.S. Bureau of the Census, *Current Population Reports,* series P—20, no. 310, "Persons of Spanish Origin in the United States: March 1976" (U.S. Government Printing Office, 1977).

[28] Ibid.

[29] See D. C. McClelland, *The Achieving Society* (Free Press, 1961); and R. H. Tawney, *Religion and the Rise of Capitalism* (Harcourt, Brace, & Co., 1926).

TABLE 6-9
Propensity to consume various products by age category*

Age	Beer, ale†		Car wax†	Ground coffee‡	Yogurt‡	Vege-tables‡	Frozen pizza‡	Metal polish‡	Insecti-cides‡	Hair-spray women†	Laxa-tives†	Diarrhea reme-dies†	Dry dog food‡
	Males†	Female†											
18–24	107	141	120	76	94	87	110	50	83	55	35	99	103
25–34	115	118	117	99	110	100	119	76	98	100	45	116	111
35–49	105	104	106	108	125	105	135	110	108	116	74	173	134
50–64	92	84	87	108	93	105	85	126	104	119	125	95	88
65⁺	67	49	60	95	62	94	39	114	96	100	271	65	47

* A value of 100 represents an average propensity to consume.
† Adults
‡ Homemakers
Source: Derived from "1977 Guide to Product Usage," *Progressive Grocer* (July 1977). Used with permission of the copyright holder Axiom Market Research Bureau, Inc., New York.

Subcultures based on age

Age specific behavior is widely recognized in the behavioral sciences and is frequently used as a segmentation variable by marketing practitioners. We will examine age-related behaviors in several chapters. In Chapter 11, "Individual Development," we will analyze the development processes of children as they relate to the consumption process. In Chapter 9, "The Family," the stages in the family life cycle are described. While age and stage in the family life cycle are not identical, they are closely associated. Since stage in the family life cycle provides a more useful approach to age-related behaviors, our primary treatment of age will occur in that context. For now, we will merely indicate the vast variation in product consumption by age category.

Table 6–9 provides insights into the relative propensity of various age categories to consume various products. Other variables interact with age to influence purchasing patterns. In Table 6–9, for example, it can be seen that younger females are substantially more important to total female beer consumption than young males are to total male beer consumption. Table 6–10 shows the percentage of individuals in various

TABLE 6–10
Incidence of consumption of major beverages on a "typical" winter day (in percent)

Age	Coffee	Coffee*	Milk and milk drinks	Fruit and vegetable juices	Soft drinks	Tea
10–14	6.0%	1.83	86.7%	54.1%	65.1%	12.6%
15–19	19.0	2.31	70.3	48.6	72.0	24.6
20–24	37.4	3.07	64.6	48.6	60.0	25.8
25–29	61.3	3.39	49.6	44.5	60.7	27.4
30–39	68.9	4.01	43.0	42.3	54.5	28.9
40–49	82.1	4.19	35.2	39.6	42.2	27.6
50–59	86.8	3.85	33.2	38.4	29.6	29.2
60–69	84.7	3.46	34.2	39.2	26.1	32.2
70 and over	88.2	2.77	34.7	44.8	19.4	28.3

* Average number of cups consumed by those that consumed coffee.
Source: Derived from *Coffee Drinking in the United States: Winter 1976* (Pan-American Coffee Bureau, 1976).

age categories that consumed various beverages on a specific winter day. It clearly demonstrates the strong relationship between age and coffee consumption. It also suggests the need for coffee manufacturers to attempt to generate brand sales (selective demand) among middle-aged consumers and product category (generic demand) sales among younger consumers.

Subcultures based on geographic factors

Geographic subcultures are often ignored and yet they are a major influence on American consumption patterns. There are two distinct types of geographic subcultures. One is based on the geographic region of the country, that is, Northwest, Southwest, and so forth. The second is the urban, suburban, rural distinction. Each of these two main variables tends to be associated with distinct lifestyles.

Different geographic regions of the country pose different problems that consumers must solve. The most obvious of these are the climatic conditions. Climatic conditions influence home construction, clothing requirements, and recreational opportunities to name but a few. In addition, different regions of the country have different age distributions and different social histories. These variables in combination with the climatic variables have produced differing values and lifestyles which newcomers to a region generally acquire after a period of time. These regional variations influence the use of particular media, the types of products used, and the product attributes considered important.

Table 6 – 11 illustrates regional variation in beverage consumption on a midwinter day. The large differences in consumption patterns cannot be explained solely by climatic differences, such as warm drinks being popular in colder climates. For example, the West has the lowest incidence of consumption of both coffee and soft drinks. Table 6 – 12 indicates that there are regional variations not only in *what* is consumed but in *how* it is prepared and *how* it is consumed.

TABLE 6–11
Incidence of consumption of major beverages (in percent)

Region	Coffee	Coffee*	Milk and milk drinks	Fruit and vegetable juices	Soft drinks	Tea
East	62.6%	2.98	43.8%	50.5%	47.2%	32.0%
Midwest ...	59.9	4.15	50.5	40.7	48.6	19.0
South	58.0	3.25	49.5	40.1	56.6	32.0
West	55.0	4.12	58.8	47.1	38.8	20.4

* Average number of cups consumed by those that consumed coffee.
Source: Derived from *Coffee Drinking in the United States: Winter 1976* (Pan-American Coffee Bureau, 1976).

Liquor products can be used to further illustrate the often subtle nature of regional influences. Large regional variations in the per capita consumption of distilled spirits are shown in Table 6 – 13. Even between areas with similar *levels* of consumption, the *content* of the consumption may vary. California and Massachusetts have similar per capita levels of consumption. Yet as Table 6 – 14 makes clear, the composition of that consumption differs dramatically. For example, on a per capita basis, people from Massachusetts consume three times as much blended whiskey as Californians, while Californians consume four times as much straight bourbon. The differences in consumption preferences can be even more subtle than suggested in Table 6 – 14. For instance, anisette is

TABLE 6–12

Regional variation in the preparation and consumption of coffee

	East	Midwest	South	West
How coffee is consumed at home—				
Black	15%	39%	30%	48%
Sweeteners only	6	10	14	14
Sweetners and creaming agents	53	27	38	24
Creaming agent only	26	24	18	14
How coffee is prepared—				
Electric percolator	33	58	48	53
Nonelectric percolator	38	12	13	12
Drip pot	8	4	8	1
Automatic electric drip maker	13	21	25	21
Filter cone	3	1	1	7
Steeping pot	4	3	4	3
Vacuum coffee maker	1	1	1	3
Container used for drinking coffee—				
Cup	49	59	58	37
Mug	44	34	35	55
Both	6	7	7	7

Source: *Derived from Coffee Drinking in the United States: Winter 1976* (Pan-American Coffee Bureau, 1976).

TABLE 6–13

Per capita liquor consumption by regional areas (wine gallons)

New England	2.59	East South Central	1.43
Middle Atlantic	1.99	West South Central	1.49
East North Central	1.86	Mountain	2.23
West North Central	1.67	Pacific	2.34
South Atlantic	2.26	United States	1.99

Source: *The Liquor Handbook 1977* (Gavin-Jobson Associates, 1977). Used with permission.

TABLE 6–14

Variation in per capita consumption of specific liquors (fifths per 100 population)

Beverage	Massachusetts	California
Rum	57.4	53.6
Brandy	39.3	71.9
Vodka	189.7	265.9
Gin	104.7	104.4
Canadian	183.3	83.0
Scotch	140.1	154.6
Bourbon	55.1	224.5
Blended whiskey	248.5	84.4
Tequila	5.5	49.3
Cordials	138.2	75.3
Total*	1,200.6	1,220.2

* Includes types not shown.
Source: *The Liquor Handbook 1977* (Gavin-Jobson Associates, 1977). Used with permission.

sold as a clear liqueur throughout the United States except for Louisiana where it must be colored red in order to achieve consumer acceptance.

Media usage and preference also varies widely by geographic region. Table 6–15 illustrates the range of variation in television ratings among the various regions of the country. For example, adventure programs received the lowest rating in the West Central region and the highest rating in the South.

TABLE 6–15

Household ratings of various television program types (evening 7:00 P.M.–11:00 P.M.) by region of the country: November 1977

Region	General drama	Suspense and mystery	Situation comedy	Adventure	Variety	Feature films
Northeast	14.6	16.2	20.4	14.1	16.6	18.5
East Central	19.6	20.9	21.1	19.2	16.1	21.3
West Central	18.3	17.9	19.7	16.8	17.4	18.7
South	18.2	18.9	20.0	21.6	17.3	21.3
Pacific	13.7	15.4	19.4	16.9	17.3	19.3
Total	16.8	17.9	20.1	17.8	17.0	19.8

Source: Used with permission of the A. C. Nielsen Company.

Clearly regional subcultures influence many aspects of the consumption process for numerous, though not all, products. Urban, suburban, and rural areas form a second aspect of geographic subcultures that influence the consumption process. Each group faces unique problems and has evolved unique lifestyles. In many ways suburban dwellers in Boston and Dallas share much in common as do rural dwellers in Massachusetts and Texas. Many of the apparent differences between urban-suburban-rural areas may be more directly related to income, education, and occupational differences.

Size of the metropolitan area and metropolitan—nonmetropolitan variations in the consumption of coffee appear to be negligible, although metropolitan areas under 500,000 population consume less coffee per capita than other areas. As Table 6–16 shows, there are other consumption differences among the urban, suburban, and rural areas some of which are probably caused by income differences. However, income variations cannot explain such facts as nonmetropolitan areas being relatively high in the ownership of home food freezers and clothes dryers and low in dishwashers.

Conclusions on subcultures

As we have seen in the preceding pages, geographic subcultures exert a substantial degree of influence on various aspects of the consumption

TABLE 6–16
Percent of urban, suburban, and rural households having available selected durables in Autumn 1974*

Durable	Urban	Suburban	Rural
Washing machine	60.0	77.0	77.9
Clothes dryer	39.6	61.6	55.0
Dishwasher...........................	23.5	38.5	21.2
Refrigerator	98.4	99.1	99.2
Home food freezer	20.3	33.9	47.0
Kitchen range	97.8	98.8	98.8
Any TV...............................	95.6	97.7	96.3
Color TV	56.1	69.4	57.0
Room air conditioning	33.1	32.2	30.1
Central air conditioner	17.3	23.4	14.5

* *Urban* is defined as the central city in a metropolitan area; *suburban* is the remainder of the metropolitan area, and *rural* is a nonmetropolitan area.
Source: H. Axel, ed., *A Guide to Consumer Markets 1976/1977* (The Conference Board, 1976), p. 192. Used with permission of The Conference Board.

process for many products. Product design, distribution, pricing, and promotion decisions should be made with these variations in mind *if they are relevant to the product category or brand under consideration*. As noted in the section on demographics, the growth rates of the various subcultures existing within the larger American culture are uneven. These uneven growth rates are creating new opportunities for forward-looking firms and problems for nearsighted ones.

FIGURE 6–1
Summary of subcultural influences on coffee consumption

1.	Race:	Blacks consume substantially less coffee than whites.
2.	Nationality:	No empirical evidence available. However, it is probable that there are strong nationality influences among rather small groups.
3.	Religion:	A few, relatively small denominations prohibit the consumption of coffee.
4.	Age:	There are major variations in the amount consumed and how it is consumed based on age. Middle-aged individuals (35 – 55) are the largest consumers.
5.	Geography:	Strong regional influences on almost all aspects of the consumption process. Apparently no influence from the rural – urban – suburban dimension.
6.	Gender:	Males consume slightly more coffee than females.
7.	Social class:	Lower socioeconomic status individuals consume slightly less coffee than other categories.

The preceding sections have demonstrated that the American society is not as homogeneous as we might assume. Subcultures influence the consumption process for many products. Yet, most Americans also share many behaviors and values. The marketing manager must consider each product individually in evaluating the relevance of subcultural influences. Figure 6–1 provides a brief summary of the subcultural influences on the consumption of coffee. Two variables, gender and social class, have been added to this figure. While they are treated elsewhere in this text, they are sometimes considered to be subcultures.

SUMMARY

American society is described in part by its demographic makeup which includes a population's size, distribution, and structure. A population's size, rate of growth, and distribution are the number of individuals in the population, the rate at which that number is increasing or decreasing, and how they are geographically distributed. The structure of a population refers to the population's demographics based on sex, age, income, education, and occupation. Because individuals of different sex, age, income, education, and occupation differ in their needs and preferences for products that fulfill their needs, population demographics have been and continue to be important variables in market segmentation and the management of marketing programs.

Population demographics, however, are not static. That is, population demographics continually change in American society. At present, the rate of population growth is slowing, average age is increasing, southern and western regions are growing, movement out of urban to suburban areas is slowing, and the work force contains more women and white-collar workers than ever before. These changes must be recognized by the marketers in order to best serve existing markets and new market segments that may evolve with the changing demographics of a population.

A subculture is formally defined as a segment of a culture which shares distinguishing patterns of behavior. Members of subcultures are also members of the broader culture which means that though they differ in some behaviors, most behaviors coincide with the predominant culture. This makes it difficult at times to recognize distinct subcultural influences.

American society is in fact a society of subcultures. That is, at one time or another either we or members of our family heritage moved to the United States from another culture. Thus, at one time Irish, Italian, Polish, Swedish, and German subcultures were very identifiable in major U.S. cities. Over time these subcultures have diffused and are less discernable in today's American society. Now, the black, Chinese,

Jewish, and Mexican-American subcultures are the dominant subcultures which influence the behavior of consumers who are members of these subcultures. Because unique needs and preferences often exist within subcultures, marketers of many products may find marketing opportunities in serving their specialized needs and preferences.

Though we often identify a subculture on the basis of race, nationality, or religion, other subcultures can exist on the basis of age, geographic location, gender, and social class. In any case the subculture is likely to have distinguishing patterns of behavior which may require a distinct marketing effort in terms of product form, pricing, promotion, and distribution in order to best serve the needs and behavior of a subculture. Marketing managers are interested in subcultures only to the extent that they influence the consumption process for their products. Blacks, for example, were originally considered to be a distinct and important consuming subculture. Recent evidence indicates fewer important product consumption differences between blacks and whites. What the research has clearly shown, however, is that a "poverty" subculture exists containing a wide mixture of ethnic types.

REVIEW QUESTIONS

1. What are demographics?
2. What trend(s) characterizes the size of the American population?
3. What trend(s) characterizes the geographic distribution of the American population?
4. What trend(s) characterizes the age distribution of the American population?
5. Why is "zero population growth" an important concept for marketers?
6. What trend(s) characterizes the level and distribution of income in the United States?
7. What trend(s) characterizes the level of education in the United States?
8. What trend(s) characterizes the occupational structure of the United States?
9. What is a subculture? When are subcultures important to marketing managers?
10. How do overall black demographics differ from white demographics? What happens to their differences when income level is controlled?
11. How does black product usage differ from white product usage? How does income affect these differences?
12. How does black media usage differ from white media usage?

13. What characterizes a good market segmentation strategy based on a racial subculture?

14. What are the major nationality subcultures in the United States?

15. What types of consumption are most strongly affected by nationality subcultures?

16. Are nationality subcultures homogeneous? Give an example to support your answer.

17. How important are religious subcultures in the United States? Why?

18. Provide five examples of differential rates of product consumption between age groups (see Table 6−9).

19. What are the two types of geographic subcultures?

20. Why do geographic subcultures exist?

21. Give ten examples of behavioral differences between geographic regions in the United States.

22. How does the ownership of appliances differ between urban, suburban, and rural households?

DISCUSSION QUESTIONS

1. Which demographic shifts, if any, do you feel will have a noticeable impact on the market for mopeds in the next ten years? Justify your answer.

2. Examine each of the subcultures described in this chapter. Do any of them constitute a unique market segment for mopeds? Justify your answer.

3. Do you think that America will reach zero population growth by the year 2000? If so, which industries will be most affected? In what ways?

4. What are five specific marketing implications of a continued population shift to the Western, Mountain, and South Atlantic states?

5. What industries will face particular problems in the year 2000 if Table 6−1 is accurate? Which will face particular opportunities?

6. Will the increasing median age of our population affect the general "tone" of our society? In what ways?

7. Will the large urban areas of the United States continue to decline?

8. Discuss the marketing implications of Table 6−3, assuming it is accurate for 1985.

9. Examine Table 6−4. Will the increases predicted have any noticeable impact on consumer behavior between 1980 and 1985?

10. Examine Table 6−5. Will the changes predicted have any noticeable impact on consumer behavior between 1980 and 1985?

11. How important are subcultures in the United States to marketing practices?

12. Will the black subculture become an increasingly or decreasingly distinct market segment over the next ten years?

13. Describe one or more unique consumption patterns associated with a nationality subculture with which you are familiar.

14. Describe one or more unique consumption patterns associated with a religious subculture with which you are familiar.

15. If you have lived in a different region of the country, describe some of the variations in consumption patterns between that region and the region you are currently in?

16. Why do the differences in Table 6–9 exist?

17. Why do the differences in Table 6–10 exist?

18. Why do the differences in Table 6–11 exist?

19. Why do the differences in Table 6–13 exist?

20. Why do the differences in Table 6–14 exist?

21. Why do the differences in Table 6–15 exist?

22. What are the marketing implications of the differences in:

    a. Table 6–9.   *d*. Table 6–13.

    b. Table 6–10.   *e*. Table 6–14.

    c. Table 6–11.   *f*. Table 6–15.

PROJECT QUESTIONS

1. Interview a moped salesperson and obtain a description of the "average" moped purchaser in demographic terms. Are the demographic shifts predicted in the text going to increase or decrease the size of this average purchaser segment?

2. Interview a moped salesperson and ascertain whether or not any particular subcultures are particularly important in his/her sales of mopeds.

3. Interview three members of one of the following subcultures. Ascertain the major ways, if any, that their consumption-related behaviors are unique *because of* their membership in that subcultural group.

    a. Racial.

    b. Nationality.

    c. Religion.

7

The nature of social stratification

In mid-1977, Perrier, bottled water from mineral springs in southern France, was successfully introduced into the United States. The product was positioned as a noncaloric, chic alternative to soft drinks and beverages. Using detailed demographic data as well as information on sales of imported beers and wine, Perrier was initially introduced into the most affluent market areas. Perrier was given a premium price "to enhance its appeal to well-heeled adults—or those trying to be like them. In other words, the approach was snob appeal."[1] This snob appeal was carried in advertisements in high-fashion women's magazines and in television commercials narrated by Orson Wells. Clearly, Perrier was successfully marketed by focusing on the upper and upper-middle social classes.

We are all familiar with the concept of *social class* if not with its formal definition. At the very least we are familiar with such terms as blue collar, white collar, middle class, upper class, and so forth and use them frequently to describe the world around us. But what exactly is a social class? A social class system is defined as the *hierarchical division of a society into relatively permanent and homogeneous groups with respect to attitudes, values, and lifestyles.* It is commonly stated that America really does not have social classes, or that if it does, it is so easy

---

[1] "Perrier: The Astonishing Success of an Appeal to Affluent Adults," *Business Week* (January 22, 1979), pp. 64–65.

to move from one class to another (mobility) that social class distinctions are relatively meaningless. There has also been a reluctance in our essentially equalitarian society to talk openly about class distinctions such as shopping differences between upper- and lower-class families. However, social classes do exist in America and marketers, such as the marketers of Perrier, do base marketing decisions on class-related behavior.

While discussing social classes, it is worthwhile to remember that social classes do exist because the individuals in a society feel the need to stratify themselves. Nobody arbitrarily decided that social classes should be established. Over time, *all* societies seem to naturally develop a social class system.

Since social classes differ in terms of at least some aspects of their lifestyles, marketing managers can often utilize social class variations in designing marketing strategies. However, the consumption process for many products is similar across social classes. We should recognize at the outset that the applicability of social class in the formulation of marketing strategies is product specific.

In this chapter, we are going to examine the characteristics of the social class concept, the measurement of social stratification, the nature of American social classes, and the impact of social stratification on the consumption process.

THE CONCEPT OF SOCIAL CLASS

For a social class system to exist in a society, the individual classes must meet five criteria: they must be (1) bounded, (2) ordered, (3) mutually exclusive, (4) exhaustive, and (5) influential.[2] *Bounded* means that there are clear breaks between each social class that separate one class from another. In other words, it is necessary that a rule be devised for each class that will include or exclude any particular individual. *Ordered* means that the classes can be arrayed or spread out in terms of some criteria, generally some measure of prestige or status, from highest to lowest. *Mutually exclusive* means that an individual can only belong to one social class (though movement from one class to another over time is possible). This requires that there be a generally accepted rule or rules in use to assign the same individual to the same social class.

Requiring social classes to be *exhaustive* means that every member of a social system must fit into some class. There must be no "undefined" individuals. Finally, the social classes must be *influential*. That is, there must be behavioral variations between the classes. This is closely related

---

[2] R. W. Hodge and P. M. Siegel, "The Measurement of Social Class," *International Encyclopedia of the Social Sciences* (Free Press, 1968), pp. 316—17. These authors used *awareness* as the final criteria but the term *influential* seems a better reflection of the point.

to the degree of class awareness or class consciousness by members of the society.

Based on these five criteria, it is clear that a strict and tightly defined social class system does *not* exist in the United States or most other industrialized nations. The first criteria, that the classes be distinctly bounded, obviously does not hold in the United States. The two classic studies of social class in America developed differing numbers of classes (and other researchers have reported yet other breakdowns).[3] If there were indeed firm boundaries, reasonably careful researchers would always identify the same number of classes. Likewise, various criteria of social class will place individuals into different categories. That is, a person may be considered upper-middle class if occupation is the criteria but upper-lower if education is the criteria. This casts some doubts on the ability to construct mutually exclusive social classes.

Social classes can be made exhaustive by simply constructing appropriate rules. However, these rules may distort the internal consistency of the various classes if substantial numbers of individuals clearly do not fit into one class. This is a common problem when families are assigned to social classes based on the husband's characteristics while ignoring those of the wife. As we saw in Chapter 5, working wives may contribute as much or more financial resources and prestige to the family as the husband.

Thus, "pure" social classes do not exist in the United States or most other industrialized societies. However, it is apparent that these same societies do have hierarchical groups of individuals and that individuals in these groups do exhibit some unique behavior patterns that are different from other groups. The following quote clearly represents the vague nature of social class in current American society:

> I would suppose social class means where you went to school and how far. Your intelligence. Where you live. The sort of house you live in. Your general background, as far as clubs you belong to, your friends. To some degree the type of profession you're in—in fact, definitely that. Where you send your children to school. The hobbies you have. Skiing, for example, is higher than the snowmobile. The clothes you wear . . . all of that. These are the externals. It can't be (just) money, because nobody ever knows that about you for sure.[4]

What exists is *not a set of social classes but a series of status continuums.* These status continuums reflect various dimensions or factors which the overall society values. In an achievement-oriented society

---

[3] See A. B. Hollingshead, *Elmstown's Youth* (Wiley, 1949); and W. L. Warner, M. Meeker, and K. Eels, *Social Class in America: A Manual of Procedure for the Measurement of Social Status* (Science Research Associates, 1949).

[4] R. P. Coleman and L. Rainwater, *Social Standing in America: New Dimensions of Class* (Basic Books, 1978).

such as the United States, achievement-related factors constitute the primary status dimensions or continuums. Thus, education, occupation, income, and, to a lesser extent, type of residence are important status dimensions in the United States. Race also serves as somewhat of a status dimension in our society although this is changing over time. The status characteristics of a person's parents is a second nonachievement-based status dimension that appears to exist in the United States. However, *heritage* is a more important dimension in a more traditional society such as England.

The various status dimensions are related to each other both functionally and statistically. In a functional sense, the *status of one's parents* or one's *race* influences one's *education* which is a type of investment that produces an *occupation* that generates *income* which sets limits on one's lifestyle.[5] Thus, there is a partially causal relationship between these various status dimensions. Does this mean that an individual with high status based on one dimension will have high status based on the other dimensions? This question is known as the question of *status crystallization* in the behavioral sciences. The more consistent an individual is on all status dimensions, the greater the degree of status crystallization for the individual. In general, status crystallization in the United States is relatively low.

A moment's reflection will make this apparent. Two individuals could have the same level of education (and thus the same status on this dimension) say a master's degree, one in business and one in library science. Yet the individual with the business degree might have twice the income of the other individual (and thus different levels of status on this dimension). One study found correlations of approximately 0.6 between education and occupation ratings, 0.33 between education and income ratings, and 0.4 between occupation and income ratings (where 1.0 indicates a perfect correlation and 0 indicates no correlation).[6]

The low degree of status crystallization in the United States is support for the contention that a social class system per se does not exist. This does not mean that the population cannot be subdivided into status groups which share similar lifestyles at least with respect to particular product categories or activities. Furthermore, there are many people with high levels of status crystallization. These individuals may exhibit many of the behaviors associated with a class system. Later in this chapter, we will describe some of the characteristics of these *class models*. Before we can describe the characteristics of a social class or a status group, we must devise a means to array the population into a status hierarchy (or status heirarchies).

---

[5] Based on Hodge and Siegel, "Measurement," p. 332.

[6] O. D. Duncan, D. L. Featherman, and B. Duncan, *Socioeconomic Background and Achievement* (Seminar Press, 1972), p. 38.

There are a number of types of social class structures available for use that vary by the number of categories included. The simplest type of structure is two categories, lower and upper. A more complex has nine categories as follows:

Lower – Lower ⎫
Middle – Lower ⎬ Lower class
Upper – Lower ⎭

Lower – Middle ⎫
Middle – Middle ⎬ Middle class
Upper – Middle ⎭

Lower – Upper ⎫
Middle – Upper ⎬ Upper class
Upper – Upper ⎭

We feel that marketing managers should avoid using any one specific type of social class structure all of the time. Rather, the particular structure that best suits the problem at hand should be utilized. It is wise to remember that there are advantages and disadvantages to both complex and simple structures.

THE MEASUREMENT OF SOCIAL STRATIFICATION

As described earlier, education, occupation, income, and, to a lesser extent, place of residence are the primary achievement-based status dimensions. Race and parent's status are ascribed (nonachievement) status dimensions. How do we measure these dimensions in the most useful manner? There are two basic approaches: (1) use a combination of several dimensions, a *multi-item index*; or (2) use a single dimension, a *single-item index*.

Multi-item indexes

The use of social class as an explanatory consumer behavior variable has been heavily influenced by two studies, each of which developed a multi-item index to measure social class.[7] The basic approach in each of these studies was to determine through a detailed, "clinical" analysis of a relatively small community the classes into which the community members appeared to fit. Then, more objective and measurable indicators or factors related to status were selected and weighted in a manner that would reproduce the original class assignments. One of these scales, the Hollingshead two-factor index, is well developed and widely used. The scales, weighting formulas, and class scores are shown in Table 7–1.

---

[7] A. B. Hollingshead and F. C. Redlich, *Social Class and Mental Illness* (John Wiley and Sons, Inc., 1958); and Warner et al., *Social Class in America*.

TABLE 7–1
The Hollingshead two-factor index of social class

A.   Occupation scale

Description	Score
Higher executives of large concerns, proprietors, and major professionals.	1
Business managers, proprietors of medium-sized businesses, and lesser professionals.	2
Administrative personnel, owners of small businesses, and minor professionals.	3
Clerical and sales workers, technicians, and owners of little businesses.	4
Skilled manual employees.	5
Machine operators and semiskilled employees.	6
Unskilled employees.	7

B.   Educational scale

Description	Score
Professional (M.A., M.S., M.E., M.D., Ph.D., LL.B., and the like).	1
Four-year college graduate (A.B., B.S., B.M.)	2
One to three years college (also business schools).	3
High school graduate.	4
Ten to eleven years of school (part high school).	5
Seven to nine years of school.	6
Under seven years of school.	7

C.   Weighting system

[Occupational score $\times$ 7] + [Educational score $\times$ 4] = Index score

D.   Classification system

Class	Range of scores
I	11–17
II	18–31
III	32–47
IV	48–63
V	64–77

It is important to note that this scale, like most multi-item indexes, was designed to measure or reflect an individual family's overall rank or social position within a community. Because of this, it is possible for a high score on one variable to offset a low score on another. Thus the following three individuals would all be classified in group III: (1) a successful owner of a medium-sized firm with an eight grade education, (2) a four-year college graduate working as a salesperson, and (3) a graduate of a junior college working in an administrative position in the civil service. All of these individuals may well have similar standing in the community. However, it seems likely that their consumption processes for at least some products will differ, pointing up the fact that overall status may mask or hide potentially useful associations between individual status dimensions and the consumption process for particular products.

An additional problem with multiple-item indexes has been a tendency on the part of some marketing researchers to arbitrarily substitute a convenient or more readily available factor for one of the factors called for in the original index. This process ignores the careful work required to develop a valid multiple-item index and may lead to incorrect conclusions.

Single-item indexes

Single-item indexes estimate social status based on a single dimension. Since an individual's overall status is influenced by several dimensions, single-item indexes are generally less accurate at predicting an individual's position in a community than are well-developed multi-item indexes. However, single-item indexes allow one to estimate the impact of specific status dimensions on the consumption process as well as making the classification process an easier one. The three most common single-item indexes are (1) income, (2) education, and (3) occupation.

Income   Income has traditionally been used as a measure of both purchasing power and status. Historically, the association between income and status has been high. However, this association is not as strong today as in the past. Correlations between income and education of 0.33 and income and occupational category of 0.4 have been reported[8] (where a 1.0 represents a perfect association and a 0 represents no association between the variables).

Using income directly poses a number of measurement problems. Basically the researcher must decide "which" income to measure. This involves such decisions as (1) individual or family income, (2) before or after taxes, and (3) salary or total income. Many individuals may not have accurate knowledge of their income as defined by the researcher (i.e., total family after-tax income). In addition, individuals are often reluctant to reveal their income, and if they do respond, they may not provide an accurate answer.

Income is clearly necessary to maintain a lifestyle. Likewise, there is a higher status attached to higher incomes than to lower incomes. Still, income does not explain lifestyles completely. A college professor or lawyer may have the same income as a truck driver or plumber. Nonetheless, it is likely that their consumption process for a variety of products will differ. As we will see shortly, income relative to other variables such as occupation may be quite useful, and a number of studies have found it useful when used alone.

Education   Education has traditionally been highly valued in our culture. It has served as the primary path for upward social mobility. Thus,

---

[8] Duncan et al., *Socioeconomic Background,* p. 38.

education is a direct measure of status and is used as a component of several of the multiple-item indexes. In addition, education may influence an individual's tastes, values, and information processing capacity, which have direct effects on marketing strategies.

Education is relatively simple to measure. It is generally broken into categories such as those shown in Table 7—2. Educational level is correlated with both occupation and income. In addition, it influences the lifestyle and therefore consumption patterns of individuals in a direct manner. Like income it is not a complete explanation. For example, physicians earning $30,000 per year probably have different lifestyles than physicians earning $150,000 per year, despite similar educational backgrounds.

Occupation   Occupation is the most widely used single-item index in marketing studies. In fact, occupation is probably the most widely used single cue that allows us to evaluate and define individuals that we meet. That this is true should be obvious when you stop to think of the most common bit of information we seek from a new acquaintance— "What do you do?" Almost invariably we need to know someone's occupation in order to make inferences about their probable lifestyle. Occupation is associated with both education and income, although the association is not as strong as it once was.[9] The type of work one does and the types of individuals one works with directly influence one's preferred lifestyle. Individuals can rank order occupations in terms of prestige, status, or desirability with little trouble. The rank position assigned a given occupation is very stable across both long time periods and cultures.[10] Interestingly enough, young children rate occupations almost identically to adults and older children.[11]

Like income and education, occupational scales have been widely used as an indicator of social status. However, in the case of occupational scales, there have been serious measurement problems. That is, how does one determine the relative status of the thousands of job titles that exist in an industrial society? A variety of approaches have been utilized, the most important of which are summarized in the following paragraphs.

The U.S. census uses the occupational group categories shown in Table 7—3.[12] The census or Edwards index was developed in the 1930s

---

[9] R. M. Hauser and D. L. Featherman, *The Process of Stratification* (Academic Press, 1977), xxiv.

[10] P. M. Blau and O. D. Duncan, *The American Occupational Structure* (Wiley, 1967), p. 119.

[11] R. G. Simmons and M. Rosenberg, "Functions of Children's Perceptions of the Stratification System," *American Sociological Review* (April 1971), pp. 235—49.

[12] A more detailed description of the occupations in each category can be found in U.S. Bureau of the Census, *1970 Census of Population: Classified Index of Industries and Occupations* (U.S. Government Printing Office, 1971).

TABLE 7-2

Distribution of parts of the day enjoyed most by educational level, sex, and employment status*

| | Men | | | Women | | | | | |
| | | | | Employed | | | Housewives | | |
Activity:	Less than high school (153)†	High school graduate (130)	Some college or more (167)	Less than high school (83)	High school graduate (119)	Some college or more (85)	Less than high school (96)	High school graduate (125)	Some college or more (74)
Work	24%	21%	30%	19%	18%	36%	2%	0%	0%
Housework	2	0	1	10	8	2	24	18	11
Child care	3	4	5	4	9	4	14	13	15
Shopping	4	4	5	10	8	4	8	10	8
Personal needs	17	18	18	12	16	4	10	12	8
Adult education	0	1	7	1	0	7	0	1	9
Organizations	2	2	2	1	1	0	1	2	5
Social life	6	14	16	16	17	24	18	22	24
Active leisure	9	9	12	9	9	6	8	16	23
Passive leisure	31	24	28	22	25	22	30	26	33
TV	17	13	10	12	9	3	16	10	4
Contextual:									
Financial	1	1	1	0	0	0	0	0	0
Activities of others	1	1	0	0	1	1	1	1	0
Interpersonal	12	13	17	10	11	12	3	12	13
Religious, moral	3	6	1	3	4	3	7	2	3
Property	4	5	4	1	1	2	6	1	1
General:									
Societal concerns	0	0	0	0	0	0	0	0	0
National	1	0	1	0	0	0	0	0	1
International	0	0	0	0	0	0	0	0	0
Miscellaneous	0	1	0	0	1	2	2	1	0
No part enjoyed most	9	13	4	12	9	4	8	3	4

* Percentages add to more than 100 because some respondents gave more than one reply.
† Number responding to an item is indicated in parentheses.
Source: Reprinted with permission from J. P. Robinson, *How Americans Use Time* (Praeger Publishers, 1977), p. 122.

TABLE 7–3
The census (Edwards) occupational index and scores from three status indexes

	Scales		
	---	---	---
Occupation group	*Duncan*	*Siegel (NORC)*	*Treiman*
Professional, technical, and kindred	75	60	57
Managers, officials, proprietors	57	50	64
Clerical and kindred	45	39	44
Sales and kindred	49	34	40
Craft and kindred.............................	31	39	41
Operatives	18	29	33
Service	17	25	31
Nonfarm labor................................	7	18	19
Farmers and farm managers	14	41	47
Farm laborers	9	19	27

Note: D. J. Treiman scores were calculated from an early appendix kindly supplied by the author.
Source: Reprinted with permission from R. M. Hauser and D. L. Featherman, *The Process of Stratification* (Academic Press, 1977), p. 17.

and was designed "intuitively" to provide a hierarchy in terms of education, income, and prestige. It is perhaps the most widely used scale.[13] Still, it suffers from several severe problems. The categories are not properly ordered with respect to prestige and the range in each category is too wide to be meaningful.[14] For example college presidents, surgeons, welfare workers, and music teachers are all in the same category as are newsboys, advertising agents, and insurance underwriters. Thus, the scale lacks sufficient specificity for effective use in most applied marketing studies. Unfortunately, as census occupational data is gathered in this form, marketers must frequently work with this index.

The North-Hatt or NORC (National Opinion Research Center) index was developed in 1947 and updated in 1963.[15] Using a rating scale approach, a large sample of individuals rated the "standing" of 90 occupations relative to each other. These ratings were converted into a prestige score for each occupation ranging from 96 (U.S. Supreme Court justice) to 33 (shoe shiner). The 1963 replication produced a correlation of 0.99 with the original study.

The primary shortcoming of the NORC index was the fact that only 90 occupations were rated. Siegel has developed scores for all of the 435 occupations listed in the U.S. census's *Classified Index of Industries and*

---

[13] C. M. Bonjean, R. J. Hill, and S. D. Lemore, *Sociological Measurement* (Chandler Publishing Co., 1967), p. 423.

[14] D. J. Treiman, "Problems of Concept and Measurement in the Comparative Study of Occupational Mobility," *Social Science Research* (1975), p. 188.

[15] C. C. North and P. K. Hatt, "Jobs and Occupations: A Popular Evaluation," *Opinion News* (September 1947), pp. 3 – 13.

Occupations.[16] The availability of these additional scores makes this a very useful index. The average NORC index values for the census categories are shown in Table 7 — 3.

Duncan developed a valuable scale based on the early NORC data, the Duncan Socioeconomic Index (SEI). Noting the relationship of education and income to status, Duncan developed an occupational scale based on the educational attainments and income of individuals in that occupation. The weight given each component was derived so that the score given each occupation was similar to the original NORC scores. Once the weights were derived, Duncan was able to assign scores to all of the 435 occupations covered in the census. Scores based on the 1970 census are available, making this the most up to date of the scales available.[17] Table 7 — 3 shows the average SEI scores for the census categories. Table 7 — 4 shows scores from an array of detailed occupations.

TABLE 7–4

Duncan SEI scores for various occupations

Occupation	SEI score	Occupation	SEI score
Dentist	96.0	Meter reader	44.0
Lawyer	92.3	Receptionist	44.0
Architect	85.2	Sales clerk	39.0
Geologist	80.0	Machinist	32.0
Bank officer	79.5	Brick mason	27.0
Airplane pilot	79.0	Plasterer	25.0
Optometrist	79.0	Bus driver	24.0
Accountant	76.8	Tailor	22.0
Office manager	75.1	Drill press operator	21.8
Sales manager	74.7	Bulldozer operator	19.7
Economist	74.4	Parking attendant	18.8
Buyer, retail	72.1	Gas station attendant	17.9
Advertising agent	66.1	Barber	17.0
Insurance agent	66.0	Stationary fireman	16.6
Computer programmer	65.0	Waiter	16.0
Stenographer	61.0	Janitor	12.7
Librarian	60.0	Dishwasher	11.0
Bank teller	52.0	Hucksters and peddlers	8.8
Telephone operator	45.0	Bootblack	8.0
Electrician	44.0		

This table illustrates the detail available using either the NORC or SEI approaches and the nature of the scores.

---

[16] P. M. Siegel "Prestige in the American Occupational Structure," unpublished Ph.D. dissertation, University of Chicago, 1971. Prestige scores for detailed occupations can be found in Hauser and Featherman, *The Process of Stratification,* pp. 320 — 29.

[17] See Hauser and Featherman, *Process of Stratification*. These authors also provide a detailed description of how to elicit appropriate information about a respondent's occupation.

A third useful scale is Treiman's Standard International Occupational Prestige Scale. Since it is based on data from a number of countries, it is particularly appropriate for cross-cultural studies.[18] Treiman scale values for the census categories are shown in Table 7−3.

The NORC, Duncan, and Treiman scales all provide similar, though not identical, results. There is also a useful prestige scale developed specifically for Canadian occupations.[19]

Which scale should be used?

The selection of a measure of social status or prestige is not as complex a problem as it might appear. What must be realized is that, as we stressed earlier in this chapter, there is no one, unidimensional prestige or class continuum. Thus, the problem is not one of selecting the best measure, rather it is to select the most appropriate prestige or status dimension for the problem at hand. When an individual's total personal prestige is the dimension of concern, perhaps in a study of opinion leadership, a multi-item index such as the Warner or Hollingshead index would be most appropriate. Studies of taste and intellectually oriented activities such as magazine readership or television viewing should consider education as the most relevant dimension. Occupation might be most relevant for studies focusing on leisure-time pursuits.

The task of the marketing manager is to think the problem through and select the measure of social stratification that is conceptually most relevant to the problem. Given this perspective, it is not surprising that studies attempting to determine the "best" measure of social class have found a variety of "answers."

A study of the use of bank credit cards for convenience versus installment purposes compared income versus the Hollingshead two-factor index of social class. Both measures were found to differentiate credit card usage, although the correlation, that is, the association, between the two measures was fairly low ($r = 0.53$).[20] Lower income and lower social class individuals were more likely to utilize credit cards for installment purposes (not pay off the entire bill at the end of each month) than were higher income or higher social class individuals. Within income categories, lower social class individuals were generally more likely to use credit cards for installment purposes.

---

[18] For a complete description of this scale and its construction, see D. J. Treiman, *Occupational Prestige in Comparative Perspective* (Academic Press, 1977). A summary description and representative occupation scores are provided in D. J. Treiman, "Problems and Concept and Measurement in the Comparative Study of Occupational Mobility," *Social Science Research* (September 1975), pp. 183−230.

[19] B. R. Blishen, "The Construction and Use of an Occupational Class Scale," *Canadian Journal of Economic and Political Science* (1958), pp. 519−31.

[20] J. W. Slocum, Jr., and H. L. Mathews, "Social Class and Income as Indicators of Consumer Credit Behavior," *Journal of Marketing* (April 1970), pp. 69−74.

Another study compared the ability of income classes and Carmen's multi-item index[21] (a weighted combination of education, property value, and occupation) to predict *ownership* of a wide variety of food and personal care items (the correlations between the two measures was 0.52).[22] For most, but not all items, income was a better predictor of ownership. A second study using the same basic methodology, focused on the purchase of durable goods or services within the past year, found similar results.[23] Neither of these studies considered specific brands purchased or frequency of use. A study comparing Warner's multi-item index and income found that income was generally a better predictor of use-nonuse of a product category but that social class (as measured by Warner's four-item index) was generally more highly correlated with frequency of use.[24]

For many of the product categories examined in the studies described above there is no obvious reason to expect one status dimension to be uniquely related to the consumption of the product category. However, a recent study of social class and fine arts consumption allows us to see the value of selecting the most relevant status dimension.[25] In this study, education, income, and occupation were compared. Logically, one would expect education to be most highly associated with the consumption of fine arts and this was the finding of this study. A comparison of relationships between income and education with art consumption is shown in Table 7−5. As can be seen, education is the better predictor except for the popular arts: the cinema and popular music.

Relative occupational class income Thus far we have been discussing the relative merits of one status dimension over another. However, in some cases it may be more productive to consider using one status dimension *in conjunction with another*. This is what the concept of relative occupational class income (ROCI) involves. ROCI is the "relationship of a family's total income to the median income of other families in the same occupational class."[26] Thus, occupational class is viewed as setting the basic lifestyle, while *relative* income provides (1) excess funds (2) neither excess nor deficient funds, or (3) deficient funds for the desired

---

[21] J. M. Carmen, *The Application of Social Class in Market Segmentation* (IBER Special Publications, University of California, 1965).

[22] J. M. Myers, R. R. Stanton, and A. T. Haug, "Correlates of Buying Behavior: Social Class vs. Income," *Journal of Marketing* (October 1971), pp. 8−15.

[23] J. H. Myers and J. F. Mount, "More on Social Class vs. Income as Correlates of Buying Behavior," *Journal of Marketing* (April 1973), pp. 71−73.

[24] R. D. Hisrich and M. P. Peters, "Selecting the Superior Segmentation Correlate," *Journal of Marketing* (July 1974), pp. 60−63.

[25] P. Dimaggio and M. Useem, "Social Class and Arts Consumption," *Theory and Society* (March 1978), pp. 141−61.

[26] W. H. Peters, "Relative Occupational Class Income: A Significant Variable in the Marketing of Automobiles," *Journal of Marketing* (April 1970), p. 74.

TABLE 7-5
Consumption of seven cultural forms, 1975

	Percentage consuming during previous 12 months						
	Art museum	Theater	Classical music	Science museum	Book reading	Cinema	Popular music
Education							
<High school graduate (A)	20%	18%	23%	17%	26%	56%	25%
<College graduate	44	44	50	34	46	75	41
College graduate (B)	78	73	77	59	60	85	40
Education gap (B–A)	58	55	47	42	34	29	15
Income							
<$5,000 (C)	20	17	9	12	29	46	21
$5,000–10,000	37	32	11	32	43	68	34
$10,000–15,000	39	41	15	32	43	76	32
>$15,000 (D)	59	57	27	45	49	82	45
Income gap (D–C)	39	40	18	33	20	36	24

Source: National Research Center of the Arts, *Americans and the Arts* (New York, 1976), pp. 77, 77, 79, 81–82, 84, 86, 118. Reprinted with permission from P. Dimaggio and M. Useem, "Social Class and Arts Consumption:" *Theory and Society* (March 1978). p. 145.

lifestyle. The three categories are referred to as overprivileged, average, and underprivileged respectively.

Table 7−6 shows the results of one study using this concept. The study used ten occupational categories. The authors concluded that with respect to automobiles "the buying behavior of relatively well-off, blue-collar workers is more like that of affluent, white-collar and professional workers than that of less well-off, blue-collar workers."[27] Similar results were obtained in a study of automobile ownership which used relative income within Warner's social class structure.[28] A third study found ROCI to be associated with the purchase of high-priced versus lower-priced coffee.[29] Other combinations of status dimensions such as *relative income class education* may prove very useful for other product categories.

TABLE 7–6

Variance (in percent) of actual ownership share from expected share of each automobile class by each income status group

Income status	Automobile class						
	No car	Used car	Com-pact	Inter-mediate	Foreign economy	Medium-sized car	Large car
Underprivileged	78%	−17%	−25%	−25%	−40%	−53%	−75%
Average	−21	5	16	27	50	0	−37
Overprivileged	−53	11	13	9	−11	42	76

Source: W. H. Peters, "Relative Occupational Class Income: A Significant Variable in the Marketing of Automobiles," *Journal of Marketing* (April 1970), p. 76. Reprinted with permission of the publisher, the American Marketing Association.

SOCIAL STRUCTURE OF THE UNITED STATES

As we have been emphasizing, there is not one specific social structure in the United States. Instead, there are several depending on the status dimension being utilized. In Chapter 6, the percentages of Americans falling in various income, education, and occupational categories were presented. As these tables indicated, the overall social structure of the United States is shifting in an upward direction in terms of income, education, and occupation.

Despite the general lack of well-defined classes, there are large numbers of individuals with a high degree of status crystallization. As has

[27] Ibid., p. 77.

[28] R. P. Colemàn, "The Significance of Social Stratification in Selling," in *Marketing: A Maturing Discipline*, ed. M. L. Bell (American Marketing Association, 1960), pp. 171−84.

[29] R. E. Klippel and J. F. Monoky, "A Potential Segmentation Variable for Marketers: Relative Occupational Class Income," *Journal of the Academy of Marketing Science* (Spring 1974), pp. 351−56.

been discussed before, classes do exist in our society and individuals within those classes can serve as models or stereotypes. It is useful to the marketing manager to know the characteristics of these relatively pure class types, even though the descriptions represent a simplified abstraction from reality, in order to develop marketing strategies for specific segments. We will describe four classes: poverty, working, white collar and managerial-professional.

Poverty class

The poor represent the nearest thing to a pure class or caste in America. Most of those with poverty level incomes have limited educations, no jobs or at best menial ones, and come from families with similar characteristics. Marriage is generally limited to members of the same class and only a small percentage escape from this class. A high percentage of those in this category are from a racial minority, particularly the blacks.

Heilbroner describes the poverty class as compared to the middle class in our society as follows:

> A great divide separates the poor from the economic middle class, but the poor nonetheless affect middle-class prosperity in two ways. First, many of the amenities of middle-class existence are made possible because the bottom group includes large numbers of working poor. Here are the nation's bellhops, porters, washroom attendants, shoeshine boys, hotel maids, parking lot attendants, restaurant kitchen help. It would be too much to say that the middle class lives off the low-cost services of the working poor. It is not too much to say that it enjoys them.
>
> Second, the poor are the class that the economic middle class pays for. The poor are major beneficiaries of the taxes paid by the nation—almost a third of their income comes from public assistance. The middle class is not, to be sure, the only class that supports the nonworking poor. It shares that burden with the rich and the working class. It shares as well the mixed attitudes of pity, contempt, hatred, and fear with which upper and working-class America regards the bottom group.[30]

It is difficult for others in society to understand members of the poverty class. What is difficult to grasp is the overwhelming impact of having been raised from birth in an environment of hopelessness. Children in poverty level households are frequently raised by only one parent and with a complete absence of successful middle-class or mainstream role models. Many of these children adopt attitudes of despair and hopelessness that tend to keep them in the "cycle of poverty."

---

[30] R. L. Heilbroner, "Middle-Class Myths, Middle-Class Realities," *The Atlantic Monthly* (October 1976), pp. 37–38.

Perhaps the trait that most clearly distinguishes this group from other members of society is its lack of a feeling of control. Members of the poverty class generally view the environment as the controlling force and themselves as pawns acted on by the environment. This view is not inconsistent with their life experiences. However, it is in marked contrast to the perceptions and experiences of most of the larger culture.

One result of this feeling of powerlessness is a short time perspective. If one cannot influence or control the future, one should "live for today." This results in a failure to invest in personal development (e.g., education) which further strengthens the poverty cycle. It also creates a great difficulty in taking advantages of opportunities that may present themselves.

This concern for the present also produces consumption behaviors that deviate from those of the larger society. The consumption of escape products such as liquor and drugs is unusually high. Credit purchases, often at exorbitant interest rates, are common primarily because of economic necessity. The entire consumption process is frequently oriented toward immediate gratification with a lack of comparative shopping or other attempts to maximize the value received.[31]

As we saw in Chapter 6, the distribution of family incomes in the United States is predicted to continue its upward trend. One of the major reasons for this is the continuing increase in the number of working wives. However, in the poverty group it is rare for both spouses to be employed due to broken homes and inadequate job training. Thus, the income gap between poverty families and nonpoverty families will most likely increase in the future. The impact of this income gap is even more pronounced than one might expect because of the larger than average family sizes that characterize the poor.

The poor represent a problem for public policymakers as they attempt to eliminate or at least minimize poverty. Likewise, serving the poor has been viewed as a problem for the marketing system as a whole and for individual firms. The evidence suggests that marketers have not dealt with this problem very successfully.[32] As the income, and thus expenditures, of the nonpoverty groups grow, it will be increasingly easy to ignore the low-income segment of the market. To ignore this segment completely is to forego a large and potentially profitable market segment. Marketers should at least examine the possibility of developing marketing strategies for this market segment. The motive for such decisions can be profit instead of (or in addition to) social responsibility.

---

[31] An overview of this area can be found in F. D. Sturdivant, "Subculture Theory: Poverty, Minorities, and Marketing," in *Consumer Behavior Theoretical Sources* eds. S. Ward and T. S. Robertson (Prentice Hall, Inc., 1973), pp. 469−520.

[32] One of the best-known critiques in this area is D. Caplovitz, *The Poor Pay More* (Free Press, 1967).

Working class

The working class is known by a variety of titles such as blue-collar group, upper-lower class, or "hard hats." The characteristic feature of this group is that the husband's occupation involves some degree of manual labor either skilled or unskilled. Historically, a high percentage of blue-collar workers did not complete high school, and both income and job security were low. Today the percentage completing high school is higher, as is the median income. In fact, for some unionized occupations and certain highly skilled occupations, income is as high as many professional occupations. Job security remains low as strikes and layoffs may disrupt a family's normal income flow. Working wives are still relatively uncommon in this category.

Drawing on Heilbroner's perspective again, we see the working class as contrasted with the middle class as:

> The working class affects the economic middle class in a way that is different from what the poor does. The middle class feels that it is bled by the poor, but that it is challenged by the working man. When a middle-class engineer making $20,000 reads about a building trades worker who pulls down $8 an hour, he feels pressured. He complains that "unions are pushing the country into bankruptcy." Well, maybe unions are pushing some parts of the country, especially the cities, into bankruptcy, but the hard facts of income distribution nonetheless draw a clear line between working-class incomes and middle or upper-class ones. Average annual earnings for male craft workers, the aristocracy of the working class, were just over $8,000 in 1969—perhaps they are up to $10,000 today. Most working-class families who make it up to the $15,000 level do so because they have two earners in the family. But realities are often less important than perceptions. And there is no doubt that the middle class feels the union man breathing down its neck.[33]

The family group, including the extended family, is very important to the blue-collar family. Most social activities evolve around the family. Work is not as important to this group as it is to white-collar and managerial groups. Often, one's occupation is viewed as a necessary evil which must be tolerated in order to be able to purchase aspects of "the good life." There is some orientation toward preparing the children to move up by pursuing education, but the overall focus is on getting by and living comfortably now.[34]

White-collar class

The white-collar category is composed of individuals whose occupations involve neither manual labor nor extensive decision making. Bank

---

[33] Heilbroner, "Middle-Class Myths," p. 38.

[34] An excellent overview of the value system of this group and changes in these values over time can be found in R. F. Coup, S. Greene, and B. B. Gardner, *A Study of Working Class Women in a Changing World* (Social Research, Inc., May 1973).

tellers, store clerks, and dental technicians are representative occupations. Most members of this group have completed high school and many have advanced training including a college degree. For the majority their job offers limited hope for advancement, and many are concerned that less-trained manual laborers earn more than they do. These people tend to perceive themselves as being middle-class, even though their incomes may be no higher than many in the working class.

This group has a high percentage of working wives necessitated in part by their desire to maintain the lifestyle they feel they deserve. This group is somewhat future oriented and stresses the importance of education for their children. There is also a tendency to emphasize "respectability." Home is important to this group both as a concept and as a physical reality. They tend to strive for neat, well-furnished homes in respectable neighborhoods. Like the blue-collar classes, they desire products of an affluent society, but are more apt to place some concern and plans for the future as opposed to current consumption.

Managerial-professional class

These are the owners and managers of business firms, teachers, lawyers, doctors, and so forth. They are generally highly educated and, with some exceptions, have relatively high incomes. Careers (not jobs) are very important to these individuals for both financial rewards and personal satisfaction. These individuals tend to be "competitive, mobile, industrious, and very concerned about the education and career plans of their children."[35]

Conclusions on social structure in the United States

The descriptions provided above are very brief. In part, this reflects our belief that it is relatively unproductive to attempt to provide very specific descriptions for social classes. The complexity and variety of behaviors and values involved precludes doing a thorough job. Rather, marketing managers must investigate the various status dimensions to determine which, if any, affect the consumption process for their products. In the next section we will provide brief descriptions of some of the products and situations in which social status has affected consumption behavior.

SOCIAL STRATIFICATION AND THE CONSUMPTION PROCESS

Four sets of behaviors relative to the consumption process vary significantly with social status: (1) media usage, (2) information search, (3) store choice, and (4) product consumption.

---

[35] Sturdivant, "Subculture Theory," p. 480.

Media usage

Education is generally the best predictor of media usage. Better-educated individuals have different media patterns than do less well educated individuals, and these differences cannot be attributed to differences in the amount of free time available to the two groups. Better-educated individuals spent more time reading magazines and books, listening to the radio, and going to the movies; and less time watching television than the less well educated.[36] Table 7−7 illustrates the relationship between education and television viewing.

TABLE 7–7
Education and income effects on television viewing

	Minutes per day above or below average	
	Female	Male
Total sample average	80	107
Education		
Grade school	+32	+5
Some high school	+17	+14
High school graduate	−4	+8
Some college	−17	−20
College graduate	−25	−24
Income		
Under $5,000	+12	+26
$5,000–5,999	+7	−2
$6,000–7,499	−4	−13
$7,500–9,999	−2	−4
$10,000–14,999	−4	−3
$15,000 and over	−9	−1

Source: Reprinted with permission from J. P. Robinson, *How Americans Use Time* (Praeger Publishers, 1977). p. 104.

In addition to the time spent on various mass media, education level also influences the content of the media attended to. The better educated read more news and analysis magazines, nonfiction books, and editorial material in the newspaper. The less educated read more fiction books, general women's magazines, and general news stories in the newspaper. Better educated listen to more classical and background radio music, while less educated listen more to the "top 40" stations. The decline in television viewing as education increases is caused almost entirely by a reduction in viewing of fictionalized entertainment pro-

---

[36] The results in this and the following paragraph are from J. P. Robinson, *How Americans Use Time: A Social Psychological Analysis of Everyday Behavior* (Praeger Publishers, 1977), pp. 103−6.

grams. News and sports viewership varies little between educational levels.[37]

Information search

As described earlier, the lowest social groups appear to engage in less information search than the other groups. Those at the bottom rung have limited access to information sources and limited training in processing purchase-related information. Table 7–8 illustrates variations in

TABLE 7–8
Prepurchase sources of information (domestic appliances) by social class

Source	Lower class (n = 236)	Middle class (n = 278)
Brochures and leaflets	17.1%	26.6%
Newspaper and magazine ads	6.7	12.2
Friends, neighbors	2.6	13.7
Test reports	—	12.2
In-store sources	42.3	15.8
No source specified	34.6	30.2
No answer	0.8	10.1

Source: G. R. Foxall, "Social Factors in Consumer Choice: Replication and Extension," *Journal of Consumer Research* (June 1975), p. 62. Reprinted with permission of the publisher.

types of information sources used by the lower and middle class (defined by Warner's ISC) in a recent United Kingdom study. These findings are consistent with earlier research in the United States. For example, in a Cleveland study, 39 percent of the lower-income housewives (Warner's ISC) reported using newspaper ads for information on fashion trends compared to 68 percent of the upper-middle-income housewives.[38] While there is a lack of direct evidence, it seems likely that education is a major factor in search behavior.[39] At high-income levels search may decline because the relative value gained by search may not be perceived as being worth the time cost.

A Canadian study demonstrates the variation in the perception of the shopping task between working-class and middle-class housewives (defined primarily by place of residence). The study involved making simu-

---

[37] Ibid.; for additional details, see S. J. Levy, "Social Class and Consumer Behavior," in *On Knowing the Consumer,* ed. J. W. Newman (John Wiley and Sons, Inc., 1966).

[38] S. V. Rich and S. C. Jain, "Social Class and Life Cycle as Predictors of Shopping Behavior," *Journal of Marketing Research* (February 1968), pp. 41–49.

[39] See J. W. Newman and R. Staelin, "Prepurchase Information Seeking for New Cars and Major Appliances," *Journal of Marketing Research* (August 1972), pp. 249–57.

lated purchases from a homogeneous product set. The authors conclude:

> The reaction set of the working class housewife was subjective; she reacted as if the difficulties and uncertainties encountered were centered in her own inadequacies rather than the objective nature of the problem. This led, for example, to high reliance on a general belief in a price/quality association in handling price level choice. The middle class housewife reaction set was objective, treating the difficulties and uncertainties as centered in the nature of the problem presented her.[40]

Store choice

The types of stores shopped varies by social status. In the study of shopping behavior in Cleveland, it was found that 68 percent of the lower-lower class housewives did a high proportion of their shopping downtown compared to 33 percent of the upper-middle class housewives.[41] The discount store originally appealed primarily to the middle class who had both the confidence (often lacking in the lower classes) and the motivation (often lacking in the upper classes) to shop in such outlets. However, this varies by product type. For example, as social class increases, purchases of clothing at discount stores tend to decrease.[42] These findings may be generalized to include products with a high perceived level of social risk (clothing, jewelry, draperies, and so forth). A recent study found that higher social classes (based on Hollingshead's two-factor index) "exhibited generally *less* favorable patronage attitudes toward discount stores than those in the lower social classes for purchases of products with higher social risk."[43] No differences were found between the classes for other products.[44]

Social class differences seem to exist not only in store choice but also in whether or not shopping is done in a store at all.[45] Table 7−9 gives the results of a study comparing persons shopping at home versus in a store. In-home shopping was defined as mail or telephone orders from the home or from a catalog store. Levels of income, type of occupation, and amount of education seem to differentiate well between the tendency to shop from the home or in a store.

---

[40] J. N. Fry and F. H. Siller, "A Comparison of Housewife Decision Making in Two Social Classes," *Journal of Marketing Research* (August 1970), pp. 333−37.

[41] Rich and Jain, "Social Class," p. 441.

[42] R. Dardis and M. Sandler, "Shopping Behavior of Discount Store Customers in a Small City," *Journal of Retailing* (Summer 1971), pp. 60−72.

[43] V. K. Prasad, "Socioeconomic Product Risk and Patronage Preference of Retail Shoppers," *Journal of Marketing* (July 1975), p. 45.

[44] Additional details on store choice and social strata are in Levy, "Social Class."

[45] P. L. Gillett, "A Profile of Urban In-Home Shoppers," *Journal of Marketing* (July 1970), pp. 40−45.

TABLE 7–9
Shopper profile

Socioeconomic and demographic variables	Shopping Behavior	
	Shopped at home	Did not shop at home
Family income:		
$0–$3,999	12.5%	15.9%
$4,000–6,999	23.6	36.5
$7,000–9,999	28.5	27.0
$10,000–14,999	22.9	15.9
$15,000 and over	12.5	4.7
	100.0%	100.0%
Occupation of household head:		
Professional, technical	15.2%	6.4%
Managers, proprietors, officials	20.0	13.0
Clerical and sales	12.4	6.4
Foremen, craftsmen, operatives	22.8	32.2
Private household, service laborers	13.1	21.0
Retired	12.4	13.0
Unemployed, others	4.1	8.0
	100.0%	100.0%
Shopper education:		
To 6 years	2.8%	9.5%
7–11 years	32.6	39.7
12 years	43.8	39.7
Over 12 years	20.8	11.1
	100.0%	100.0%

Source: P. L. Gillett, "A Profile of Urban In-Home Shoppers," *Journal of Marketing* (July 1970), pp. 40–45. Reprinted with permission of the publisher, the American Marketing Association.

Product utilization

Product utilization varies widely among social strata. Income clearly restricts the purchase of some products such as expensive sports cars and boats. We have already seen the relationship between education and the consumption of fine art. Occupation appears to be related closely to leisure pursuits.[46] Relatively high status occupational groups generally prefer more active leisure pursuits, though there are many exceptions.

---

[46] D. W. Bishop and M. Ikeda, "Status and Role Factors in the Leisure Behavior of Different Occupations," *Sociology and Social Research* (January 1970), pp. 190–208; and A. C. Clarke, "Leisure and Occupational Prestige," *American Sociological Review* (June 1956), pp. 305–6.

FIGURE 7–1

SOCIOECONOMIC/LIFE CYCLE GRID

Population _____ Characteristic _____

		Socioeconomic class				Life cycle totals
		Lower	Lower-middle	Upper-middle	Upper	
Life cycle category — Younger households	No children	1.5	5.7	6.8	2.9	16.9
	Younger children	0.9	6.2	8.1	4.3	19.5
	Older children	1.4	8.7	10.8	4.8	25.7
Older households		12.5	13.5	8.8	3.1	37.9
SES class totals		16.3	34.1	34.5	15.1	100.0

COMPOSITE TOTALS

SES	Life cycle		Total
Middle-class*	Family households+	Younger households	Middle-class family households
68.6	45.2	62.1	33.8

*Lower-middle and upper-middle classes   +Young households-younger and older children

Source: R. B. Ellis, "Composite Population Descriptors: The Socio-Economic/Life Cycle Grid," in *Advances in Consumer Research II,* ed. M. J. Schlinger (Association for Consumer Research, 1975), p. 490. Reprinted with permission.

SOCIAL STRATIFICATION AND MARKETING MANAGEMENT

The problem the marketing manager faces is not whether or not social stratification is relevant to a range of products and activities. Instead, the manager must determine *if* and *how* social status affects the consumption process for his/her products. Often, this may involve combining the social status variable with a second variable such as family life cycle. This approach has been used successfully by the American Telephone & Telegraph Company (AT&T).[47]

AT&T's approach, which has been used successfully by a number of consulting firms, is to develop a socioeconomic life cycle grid (SES/LC grid). The SES/LC grid used by AT&T and the percentage of the population falling in each cell is shown in Figure 7–1.[48] The two axes can be broken into as many categories as necessary in relation to the problem at hand. Thus, for some studies the "no children" category would be divided into married and single categories. This matrix approach has been used successfully to segment markets and guide marketing strategy for telephone services, motion pictures, bread, shoe retailers, travel trailers, and a number of other products.

SUMMARY

A social class system is defined as the hierarchical division of a society into relatively permanent and homogeneous groups with respect to attitudes, values, and lifestyles. Social classes clearly do exist in America and marketers do base many decisions on class-related behavior. However, it must be stressed that the applicability of social class to marketing strategy is product specific.

For a social class system to exist in a society, the individual classes must meet five criteria: (1) bounded, (2) ordered, (3) mutually exclusive, (4) exhaustive, and (5) influential. Using these criteria, it is obvious that a strict and tightly defined social class system does not exist in the United States. What does seem to exist is a series of status continuums that reflect various dimensions or factors which the overall society values. Education, occupation, income, and, to a lesser extent, type of residence are important status dimensions in this country. Status crystallization refers to the consistency of individuals on all relevant status dimensions (e.g., high income, high educational level, etc.). In general, status crystallization in the United States is relatively low.

There are two basic approaches to the measurement of social

---

[47] R. B. Ellis, "Composite Population Descriptors: The Socio-Economical Life Cycle Grid," in *Advances in Consumer Research, II,* ed. M. J. Schlinger (Association for Consumer Research, 1975), pp. 481–93.

[48] For details on how individual households are classified, see ibid.

classes: (1) use of a combination of several dimensions, a multi-item index; or (2) use of a single dimension, a single-item index. Multi-item indexes are designed to measure an individual's overall rank or social position within the community. Problems occur in doing this because of differences (inconsistencies) between status items.

Single-item indexes estimate status based on a single status dimension, which is easier to do than in multi-item measures. Income, education, and occupation are the most frequently used measures of social status. Since there is no one, unidimensional prestige or class continuum, it is impossible to state which is the best measure. Rather the choice of the measure to be used should depend on its appropriateness or relevancy to the problem at hand. Increasingly, the use of one status dimension in conjunction with another seems appropriate. Relative occupational class income (ROCI) is a good example of such an approach.

For purposes of most marketing decisions for mass consumer goods, we can look at four "classes": poverty, working, white collar, and managerial-professional. The poverty class contains people who came from families with similar backgrounds, with low incomes, limited educations, and no jobs (or at best menial ones). Unique marketing opportunities as well as responsibilities are open to marketers aiming at this group of people.

The working class represents a larger market opportunity in many respects. The characteristic feature of this group is that the husband's occupation involves some degree of manual labor, either skilled or unskilled. The middle-class or white-collar category is composed of individuals whose occupations involve neither manual labor nor extensive decision making. These individuals tend to perceive themselves as being middle class, even though their income may be no higher than many in the working class. The managerial-professional category is generally highly educated and has relatively high incomes. Careers (not jobs) are very important to these individuals.

Marketing managers must investigate the various status dimensions to determine which, if any, affect the consumption process for their products. For example, educational level seems to directly affect time spent on various mass media and media attended to. Such things as store choice are also heavily affected by social class membership.

REVIEW QUESTIONS

1. What is a social class system?
2. Describe the five criteria necessary for a social class system to exist.
3. Does a tightly defined social class system exist in the United States? Explain your answer.

4. What is meant by the statement, "What exists is not a set of social classes but a series of status continuums?"
5. What underlying cultural value determines most of the status dimensions in the United States?
6. What status dimensions are common in the United States?
7. What is meant by status crystallization? Is the degree of status crystallization relatively high or low in the United States? Explain your answer.
8. What are the two basic approaches used by marketers to measure social class?
9. What are the advantages of multi-item indexes? The disadvantages?
10. Describe the Hollingshead two-factor index.
11. What are the primary advantages of single-item indexes?
12. What are the problems associated with using income as an index of status?
13. Why is education sometimes used as an index of status?
14. Describe three scales for measuring occupational status.
15. What are the advantages of using occupation as an indication of status?
16. How should a marketing manager select the most appropriate measure of status?
17. What is meant by relative occupational class income? Why is the general idea behind this concept particularly appealing?
18. Briefly describe the primary characteristics of each of the classes listed below (assume a high level of status crystallization).
    a. Poverty class.
    b. Working class.
    c. White-collar class.
    d. Managerial-professional class.
19. How does social stratification affect:
    a. Media usage.
    b. Information search.
    c. Store choice.
    d. Product usage.

DISCUSSION QUESTIONS

1. Which status variable, if any, is most related to moped ownership?
2. How could a knowledge of social stratification be used in the development of a marketing strategy for Motron?
3. Do you think the United States is becoming more or less stratified over time?
4. Which status continuum do you think conveys the most status?
5. Did your parents have a high or low level of status crystallization? Explain.

6. Based on the Hollingshead two-factor index, what social class would your father be in? your mother?
7. Name four products for which each of the three following single-factor indexes would be most appropriate. Justify your answer.
   a. Income.
   b. Education.
   c. Occupation.
8. What are some of the marketing implications of Table 7−2?
9. Name four products in addition to automobiles for which the relative occupational class income concept would be particularly useful.
10. How should marketers approach the poverty class?
11. Is it ethical for marketers to use the mass media to promote products that most members of the poverty class and working class cannot afford?
12. Would your answer to question 11 change if the products were limited to childrens' toys?
13. What are the marketing implications of Table 7−7?
14. What are the marketing implications of Table 7−8?
15. What are the marketing implications of Table 7−9?
16. Explain Figure 7−1.

PROJECT QUESTIONS

1. Interview a moped salesperson and determine the social class or status characteristics of moped purchasers.
2. Using *Standard Rate and Data* pick three magazines that are oriented toward different social classes. Comment on the difference in content and advertising.
3. Interview two salespersons from one of the following product categories. Ascertain their perceptions of the social classes or status of their customers. Determine if their sales approach differs with differing classes.
   a. Automobile.
   b. Kitchen appliance.
   c. Men's shoes.
   d. Furniture.
   e. Women's dresses.

8

Group processes

Glenmore Distilleries markets Amaretto di Saronne, the second best selling imported liqueur in the United States. The firm is now introducing a creamy mint-flavored English liqueur. In-store displays in Chicago, where the product is being introduced, ask purchasers to share their first bottle with five friends and to submit their names and addresses to the company. The purchasers will receive a free bottle for their efforts. This approach in marketing represents, in part, an attempt to accelerate normal within-group communications about a new product.[1]

In deciding what to wear to the last party you attended, you probably based your decision in part on the anticipated responses of the other individuals at the party. Likewise, your behavior at an anniversary celebration for your grandparents would probably differ from your behavior at a graduation party for a close friend. Your general personal grooming and dress would probably differ between an 8:30 A.M. interview and a large lecture class at the same time. All of the behaviors described above are subject to group influences.

The term *group* considered in its broadest sense refers to *two or more individuals who share a set of norms, values, or beliefs and have certain implicitly or explicitly defined relationships to one another such that*

---

[1] N. F. Millman, "Glenmore Moves to Follow Up Amaretto Success," *Advertising Age* (June 25, 1979), p. 4.

their behavior is interdependent.[2] Almost all consumer behavior takes place within a group setting. Therefore, an understanding of how groups function is essential to an understanding of consumer behavior.

The general definition of a group presented above encompasses a number of distinct types of phenomena. Cultures, as described in Chapter 4, are the most general type of group. Subcultures (Chapter 6) and social strata (Chapter 7) are also groups. However, they differ in important ways from families (Chapter 9), which are also groups.

In this chapter, we examine the manner in which groups function. Our first concern is with the various ways in which groups can be classified. Next, we analyze three important aspects of group dynamics—roles, conformity, and communications. Finally, the function of group processes in the spread of new products is described.

TYPES OF GROUPS

The terms *group* and *reference group* need to be distinguished. A group was defined earlier as two or more individuals who share a set of norms, values, or beliefs and have certain implicitly or explicitly defined relationships to one another such that their behavior is interdependent. A reference group is *that group whose presumed perspectives or values are being used by an individual as the basis for his or her current behavior.*[3] Thus, a reference group is simply a group that an individual is using as a guide for behavior in a specific situation. Most of us belong to a number of different groups. When we are actively involved with a particular group, it is probably functioning as a reference group. As the situation changes, we may base our behavior on an entirely different group which would then be our reference group. In essence, while we may belong to many groups simultaneously, we generally use only one group as a point of reference in any given situation.

Groups and/or reference groups may be classified on a number of variables. Marketers have found three classification criteria to be particularly useful—membership, type of contacts, and attraction.

The *membership* criteria is dichotomous: either one is a member of a group or one is not a member of a group. Of course, some members are more secure in their membership than are others. That is, some members feel they really "belong" to a group while others lack this confidence. However, membership is generally treated as an either/or criterion for classification purposes.

Type of contact refers to the degree of interpersonal interaction

---

[2] L. E. Ostlund, "Role Theory and Group Dynamics," in *Consumer Behavior: Theoretical Sources,* ed. S. Ward and T. S. Robertson (Prentice-Hall, Inc., 1973), p. 232.

[3] Adopted from T. Shibutani, *Society and Personality* (Prentice-Hall, Inc., 1961), pp. 257–60.

among the group members. This is necessarily related to group size. As group size increases, interpersonal contact tends to decrease. For example, you probably have less interpersonal contact with other members of the American Marketing Association than you do with your family or close friends. Type of contact is also generally treated as having two categories. Those groups characterized by "frequent" interpersonal contact are called *primary groups*. Those groups characterized by "infrequent" interpersonal contact are referred to as *secondary groups*.

Attraction refers to the degree of desirability group membership has for the individual. This can range from negative to positive. Groups with negative desirability can influence behavior just as do those with positive desirability. For example, at some point in time motorcycles became associated with "disreputable" groups in the United States such as the Hell's Angels. Sales of motorcycles were limited because many people did not want to utilize a product associated with such groups. Thus, motorcycle gangs served as negative reference groups for these individuals. It took extensive advertising by such firms as Honda ("You meet the nicest people on a Honda") to change this image and increase the market acceptance of motorcycles.

Attraction is often a more important determinant of group influence than membership. For example, *aspiration reference groups,* nonmembership groups with a positive attraction, have been found to exert a strong influence on product aspirations.[4] That is, individuals may purchase those products thought to be used by the desired group in order to achieve actual or symbolic membership in the group.

Having briefly looked at some of the types of groups that exist, let's examine in more detail some of the ways in which these groups influence consumer behavior.

ROLES

Roles are defined and enacted within groups. In Chapter 5, we defined a role as *a prescribed pattern of behavior expected of a person in a given situation by virtue of the person's position in the situation.*[5] Thus, while an individual must perform the behavior, the expected behaviors are based on the position and *not* the individual involved. For example, in your role as a student, certain behaviors are expected of you such as attending class, studying, and so forth. The same general behaviors are expected of all other students. Roles are based on positions, not individuals.

While all students in a given class are expected to exhibit certain

---

[4] A. B. Cocanougher and G. D. Bruce, "Socially Distant Reference Groups and Consumer Aspirations," *Journal of Marketing Research* (August 1971), pp. 379–81.

[5] Shibutani, *Society and Personality*, p. 46.

behaviors it is obvious that the manner in which these expectations are fulfilled varies dramatically from individual to individual. Some students arrive at class early, take many notes, and ask numerous questions. Others come to class consistently but never ask questions. Still others come to class only occasionally. *Role style* refers to these individual variations in the performance of a given role. *Role parameters* represent the range of behaviors acceptable within a given role. The role of college student has wide parameters while the role of private in the Marines carries very narrow parameters.

Sanctions are punishments imposed upon individuals for violating role parameters. Thus, a student that fails to attend class or disrupts the conduct of the class is generally subject to sanctions ranging from mild reprimands to dismissal from school. The most severe sanction for most role violations is disqualification from that role. Therefore, an individual's *role commitment* or desire to continue in the role position is an important determinant of the effectiveness of the sanctions and the likelihood that the individual will remain within the role parameters.

All of us fulfill numerous roles and occasionally two roles demand different behaviors. For example, the student role may require one to study on a weekend while the dating role may require one to spend time in social activities. This is known as *role conflict*. Most career-oriented individuals experience strong conflicts between their role as family member (husband, wife, father, or mother) and their career role. As we saw earlier, these conflicts are particularly strong for working wives.

A *role stereotype* is a shared visualization of the ideal performer of a given role. For example, most of us would share a common view of the physical and behavioral characteristics of a doctor, a lawyer, or a grade-school teacher. Close your eyes and imagine any of these occupational types. The chances are that your mental image is similar to the image held by your classmates. In fact, large numbers of people share such common images. As we will see shortly, this fact is quite useful to marketing managers.

Applications of role theory in marketing practice

The most important application of role theory in marketing practice is found in the concept of a *role-related product cluster.*[6] A role-related product cluster is *a set of products generally considered necessary to properly fulfill a given role*. The products may be *functionally* necessary to fulfill the role or they may be *symbolically* important. For example, the boots associated with the cowboy role were originally functional. The

---

[6] This concept is developed in depth in J. B. Kernan, W. P. Dommermuth, and M. S. Sommers, *Promotion: An Introductory Analysis* (McGraw-Hill Book Co., 1970).

pointed toe allowed the foot to enter the stirrup quickly and easily while the high heel prevented the foot from sliding through the stirrup. The high sides of the boot protected the rider's ankles from thorns. Today, the cowboy role still calls for boots, although few cowboys spend much time in the saddle. The boot is now symbolically tied to the cowboy role.

Role-related product clusters are important because they define both appropriate and inappropriate products for a given role. Since most products are designed to enhance role performance, marketing managers must be sure that their products fit with existing and/or evolving roles. For example, instant coffee faced the problem of a poor fit with existing role perceptions when it was initially introduced and promoted for its convenience. Taste tests had shown that many consumers could not distinguish instant coffee from drip grind. However, sales were substantially below expectations.

In an attempt to isolate the reason for the resistance to the new product, Mason Haire supplied two similar groups of housewives with shopping lists that were identical except for one item—coffee. Each list contained: one and one-half pounds of hamburger, two loaves of Wonderbread, one can of Rumford baking powder, two cans of Del Monte peaches, and five pounds of potatoes. In addition, one list contained one-pound can of Maxwell House coffee (drip grind), while the other contained Nescafe instant coffee. The housewives were asked to describe the type of person that would go shopping with such a list. Some of the descriptions are shown below:

Descriptions of a woman who bought, among other things, Maxwell House coffee

I'd say she was a practical, frugal woman. She bought too many potatoes. She must like to cook and bake as she included baking powder. She must not care much about her figure as she does not discriminate about the food she buys.

I have been able to observe several hundred women shoppers who have made very similar purchases to that listed above, and the only cue that I can detect that may have some bearing on her personality is the Del Monte peaches. This item, when purchased singly, indicates that she may be anxious to please either herself or members of her family with a "treat." She is probably a thrifty sensible housewife.

Descriptions of a woman who bought, among other things, Nescafe Instant coffee

This woman appears to be either single or living alone. I would guess that she has an office job. Apparently she likes to sleep late in the morning, basing my assumption on what she bought, such as instant coffee which can be made in a hurry. She probably also has can (sic) peaches for breakfast, cans being easy to open. Assuming that she is just average, as opposed to those dazzling natural beauties who do not need much time to make up, she must appear rather sloppy, taking little time to make up in the morning. She is also used to eating supper out, perhaps alone rather than with an escort. An old maid probably.

She seems to be lazy, because of her purchases of canned peaches and instant coffee. She doesn't seem to think because she bought two loaves of bread, and then baking powder, unless she's thinking of making a cake. She probably just got married.

I think the woman is the type who never thinks ahead very far—the type who always sends Junior to the store to buy one item at a time. Also she is fundamentally lazy. All the items with the possible exception of the Rumford's are easily prepared items. The girl may be an office girl who is just living from one day to the next in a sort of haphazard sort of life.[7]

Clearly, instant coffee was not viewed as part of the approprite product cluster for a good housewife. As a result, advertising for instant coffee shifted from an emphasis on convenience to an emphasis on taste and the appropriateness of the product for the housewife role. The success of these efforts can be seen by the large market share enjoyed by instant coffee today. Perhaps even more impressive is the fact that now when Haire's original study is repeated, the instant coffee shopper is generally described in favorable terms, while the drip grind shopper is described somewhat negatively as "old-fashioned" and "out-of-date."[8]

Since marketers were able to shift instant coffee from an inappropriate to an appropriate member of the product cluster associated with the housewife role, an examination of the procedures used will shed some light on this process. Notice in the stories above that the instant coffee shopper is seen as being lazy, a poor planner, and not devoted to her family. Now think about advertisements for instant coffee. Perhaps you recall an ad that shows a woman using instant coffee and her husband saying something like "Honey, this coffee tastes great." This is an example of a *reward* being promised if the individual will utilize this product to fulfill her role.

Or perhaps you recall an ad in which a lady obviously entertaining a small group of women overhears them talking about her after she leaves the room: "Maggie is a hard worker and a great chairperson for our committee, but her coffee tastes terrible. She should use Instant X." While we may smile about such an ad, notice how it addresses some of the key concerns from the projective stories presented earlier. Maggie is a hard worker (not lazy) and a great chairperson (good planner), and instant coffee is appropriate for her. In addition, the ad implies that not

---

[7] M. Haire, "Projective Techniques in Marketing Research," *Journal of Marketing* (April 1960), pp. 649–56.

[8] See F. E. Webster, Jr., and F. Von Pechman, "A Replication of the 'Shopping List' Study," *Journal of Marketing* (April 1970), pp. 61–63; D. H. Robertson and R. W. Joselyn, "Projective Techniques in Research," *Journal of Advertising Research* (October 1974), pp. 27–31; and G. S. Lane and G. L. Watson, "A Canadian Replication of Mason Haire's 'Shopping List' Study," *Journal of the Academy of Marketing Science* (Winter 1975), pp. 48–59.

using instant coffee can lead to *sanctions,* that is, people will talk about you behind your back.

A final type of ad that you may recall involves a particular type of person advising someone to utilize a particular brand of instant coffee. In one such sequence, a newly married woman (therefore not knowledgeable about her new role) seeks advice from a middle-aged, solid woman (a role stereotype for a good housewife) who, of course, recommends instant coffee.

The above examples of promises of rewards and sanctions, showing appropriate individuals using the product, and having role stereotypes use or recommend the product, are common and frequently necessary strategies. The fact that instant coffee might have had several functional advantages over regular coffee was not sufficient to ensure its success without the use of these techniques.

Roles are not static. New roles evolve as do the appropriate behaviors for existing roles. In Chapter 5, we examined in detail the changing role of women in our society. As roles evolve and change, challenges and opportunities are created for marketers. For example, the shifting role of women now includes active sports. In response, four apparel companies introduced sports bras in 1979. In fact, the market is already segmenting into special products for various types of sports, such as casual running versus marathon running.[9] These products are more than name and advertising changes. They are functionally different products based on the differing physiological requirements of active sports.

As roles evolve and change, new types of role conflicts will come into existence. These role conflicts will offer opportunities for marketers. For example, many airlines have altered their pricing policies and promote "take your spouse along on your business trip" in an attempt to capitalize on conflicts between career and family roles. Students are frequently advised of the existence of speed reading courses which promise both to improve classroom performance and reduce conflict between the student role and other roles by reducing the time required for studying.

The importance of roles to marketing managers should be obvious by now. We will return to the concept of roles when we examine within group communications and the diffusion process.

CONFORMITY

Conformity is a behavioral concept which frequently gives rise to negative feelings on the part of the reader. Traditionally in our society, it has been felt that to conform meant to follow the crowd, not acting

---

[9] P. Sloan, "Bra Makes Sprint to Fill Sports Market," *Advertising Age* (December 25, 1978), p. 4.

and thinking as an individual. It is important that we achieve a more realistic view of conformity for it is the mechanism that makes groups influential. Conformity refers to the *seemingly natural human tendency to want to be like relevant and significant others and which brings about some degree of adherence to group norms.*

We all conform in a variety of ways to numerous groups and by conforming we make our lives more pleasant. For example, the very fact that we are all wearing clothes when attending class is conforming to a basic societal norm. The fact that most of us would not wear shorts, sandals, and no shirt to church on Sunday is also conforming to norms. Note that we, as individuals, do not generally consider these behaviors to constitute conformity. It is also important to point out that there are many situations where individuals choose not to conform to expected behaviors or norms. We are not forced to conform. Normally, we conform without even being aware of doing so but we also frequently face conscious decisions on whether or not to go along with the group. Conformity, therefore, is a complex phenomenon that is a part of our daily lives and which helps explain how groups influence behavior. Let us now turn to a specific discussion of how conformity operates and its relationship to marketing practice.

Roles are behaviors expected of a position in a social situation. *Norms* are more *general expectations about behaviors that are deemed appropriate for all persons in a social context, regardless of the position they hold.*[10] Norms arise quickly, often without verbal communication or direct thought, anytime a group exists. The norms tend to cover all aspects of behavior relevant to the group's functioning and violation of the norms results in sanctions. For example, in most classrooms in which the teacher does not use a seating chart, students select and maintain one seat throughout the term. As an experiment, try sitting in someone else's seat in such a class. Chances are you will receive some form of a social sanction such as a dirty look.

Asch phenomenon   The tremendous power of group norms has been demonstrated in a series of studies now generally referred to as the Asch experiments or the Asch phenomenon. The basic Asch study is conducted as follows:

> Eight subjects are brought into a room and asked to determine which of a set of three unequal lines are closest to the length of a fourth line shown some distance from the other three. The subjects are to announce their judgments publicly. Seven of the subjects are working for the experimenter and they announce incorrect matches. The order of announcement is arranged such that the naive subject responds last. In a control situation 37 naive subjects performed the task 18 times each without any information about other's choices. Two of the 37 subjects made a total of

---

[10] L. S. Wrightsman, *Social Psychology* (Brooks/Cole Publishing Co., 1977), p. 17.

3 mistakes. However, when another group of 50 naive subjects responded *after* hearing the unanimous but *incorrect* judgment of the other group members, 37 made a total of 194 errors, all of which were in agreement with the mistake made by the group.[11]

This basic study has been repeated in a variety of formats, including the selection of the best suit from among three identical suits, and has generally achieved the same results.[12] Interviews with respondents after the experiments indicate that many actually change their beliefs concerning which answers were correct. Thus, more than verbal conformity is occurring. In addition, many of those respondents that express correct judgments indicate doubts of their accuracy afterward. It is important to note that the conformity being obtained is among strangers with respect to a discrete, physical task that has an objective, correct answer. Imagine how much stronger the pressures to conform are among friends or when the task is less well defined such as preferring one brand or style over another.

The Asch phenomenon has been applied by marketers in a personal selling situation. Notice the similarities between the basic Asch experiment described above and the sales technique described below.

(A group of potential customers—owners and salesmen of small firms—are brought together in a central location for a sales presentation). As each design is presented, the salesman scans the expresssions of the people in the group, looking for the one who shows approval (e.g., head nodding) of the design. He then asks that person for an opinion, since the opinion is certain to be favorable. The person is asked to elaborate. As he does so, the salesman scans the faces of the other people, looking for more support. He then asks for an opinion of the next person now showing most approval. He continues until he reaches the person who initially showed most disapproval (who initially might have reacted negatively). In this way, by using the first persons as a model, and by social group pressure on the last person, the salesman gets all or most of the people in the group to make a positive public statement about the design.

If the group includes a highly authoritarian owner accompanied by submissive subordinates, there will be a tendency for the subordinates to look to the boss before expressing an opinion. This is solved by seating the boss so that the subordinates cannot see his expression. The ensuing social pressure works on the boss even though it comes from subordinates, because often such a boss has a great need for social approval.[13]

---

[11] Adopted from S. E. Asch, "Effects of Group Pressure upon the Modification and Distortion of Judgments," in *Readings in Social Psychology,* eds. E. E. MacCoby et al. (Holt, Rinehart and Winston, 1958), pp. 174—83.

[12] M. Venkatesan, "Experimental Study of Consumer Behavior Conformity and Independences," *Journal of Marketing Research* (November 1966), pp. 384—87. See also J. T. Sims, "Comparison of Consumer Behavior Conformity and Independence between Blacks and Whites: An Exploratory Study," in *Proceedings of the 2d Annual Conference,* ed. D. M. Gardner (Association for Consumer Research, 1971), pp. 76—81.

[13] P. Zimbardo and E. Ebbesen, *Influencing Attitudes and Changing Behavior* (Addison-Wesley Publishing Co., 1970), pp. 114—22.

The selling approach described above is an extreme example of the use of Asch phenomenon in selling. However, Tupperware and other party sales situations employ many of the same techniques.

The groups in the Asch situation and the sales example cited above are membership groups with limited attraction to the individual members, having characteristics closer to a secondary group than to a primary group. If high levels of conformity exist in these groups, one would expect equally high levels to exist within more desirable, primary groups. Research indicates that this is indeed the case. Housewives have been found to conform with friends with respect to brands of bread preferred.[14] A study of children's preferences for cookies also found peer groups to influence brand choices.[15]

Determinants of conformity

Groups do not always appear to influence consumer decisions with respect to product and/or brand usage.[16] Figure 8–1 indicates that reference groups can influence product usage, brand choice, both, or neither. A close examination of this figure suggests that reference group influence is strong when the use of the product or brand is public and conspicuous but weak when the use is private and inconspicuous. Other research has supported this generalization.[17] Therefore, we can conclude that *the degree of reference group influence on product or brand usage is, in part, a function of the visibility of the usage situation*.

The visibility of the usage situation is not the only factor that explains reference group influence. Three other factors must also be considered. One is the degree of commitment the individual has to the group. In general, we can say that *the more commitment an individual feels to a group, the more the individual will conform to the group norms.*[18]

The second factor that influences the impact of a reference group on an individual's behavior is the relevance of the behavior for the group. *The*

---

[14] J. E. Stafford, "Effects of Group Influence on Consumer Brand Preferences," *Journal of Marketing Research* (February 1966), pp. 68–75.

[15] D. I. Hawkins and K. A. Coney, "Peer Group Influences on Children's Product Preferences," *Journal of the Academy of Marketing Science* (Spring 1974), pp. 322–31. See also R. E. Witt, "Informal Social Group Influence on Consumer Brand Choice," *Journal of Marketing Research* (November 1969), pp. 473–76; and R. E. Witt and G. D. Bruce, "Purchase Decisions and Group Influence," *Journal of Marketing Research* (November 1970), pp. 533–35.

[16] F. S. Bourne, "Group Influences in Marketing and Public Relations," in *Some Applications of Behavioral Research*, eds. R. Likert and S. P. Hayes, Jr. (UNESCO, 1961); and V. P. Lessig and C. W. Park, "Promotional Perspectives of Reference Group Influence: Advertising Implications," *Journal of Advertising* (Spring 1978), pp. 41–74.

[17] Witt and Bruce, "Purchase Decisions."

[18] See D. Cartwright and A. Zonder, *Group Dynamics* (Harper and Row, 1968), pp. 139–51; and Hawkins and Coney, "Peer Group Influences." A somewhat similar approach focusing on the co-orientation between the individual and the group is supported by B. P. Moschis, "Social Comparison and Informal Group Influence," *Journal of Marketing Research* (August 1976), pp. 237–44.

FIGURE 8–1

Reference group influence on brand and product choice

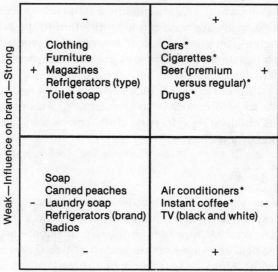

Weak—Influence on product—Strong

	−	+
+	Clothing Furniture Magazines Refrigerators (type) Toilet soap	Cars* Cigarettes* Beer (premium versus regular)* Drugs*	+
−	Soap Canned peaches Laundry soap Refrigerators (brand) Radios	Air conditioners* Instant coffee* TV (black and white)	−
	−	+

Weak—Influence on brand—Strong

* The classification of all products marked with an asterisk is based on actual experimental evidence. Other products in this table are classified speculatively on the basis of generalizations derived from the sum of research in this area and confirmed by the judgment of seminar participants.

Source: F. S. Bourne, "Group Influences in Marketing and Public Relations," in *Some Applications of Behavioral Research*, eds. R. Likert and S. P. Hayes, Jr. (UNESCO, 1961).

more salient a particular activity is to the functioning of a group, the stronger the pressure to conform to the group norms concerning that activity. Examine Figure 8 – 1 again. It is suggested that both the type and brand of automobile are subject to reference group influence. However, for many reference groups, the purchase and use of a car is irrelevant. These groups would exert little or no influence on the brand or type of car owned. Canned peaches, a product Figure 8– 1 suggests is immune to reference group influence, may be quite susceptible to influence by family reference groups.

The salience of a product to a group is difficult to determine. This difficulty is due to the fact that both functional and symbolic aspects of the products are important to groups. Thus, cars have little or nothing to do with the functioning of those work groups composed of professors. However, you will have a difficult time finding a Cadillac parked in a faculty parking lot. You may find numerous cars in the same price range, but Cadillacs are generally considered inappropriate for professors, even if they can afford to purchase one.

The third factor that appears to affect the degree of reference group influence is *the individual's own perceived confidence in the purchase situation*. One study found color television, automobiles, home air conditioners, insurance, refrigerators, physician selection, magazines or books, clothing, and furniture to be particularly susceptible to reference group influence.[19] Several of these products such as insurance and physicians are neither visible nor important to group functioning. However, they are important products to the individual and they are products about which most individuals have limited information.

Types of conformity

Thus far, we have discussed conformity to group norms as though it were an unidimensional concept. However, at least four types of conformity are of interest. It is important to distinguish the type of conformity desired since the marketing strategy required depends on the type of conformity sought.[20]

Informational conformity occurs when an individual uses the behaviors and opinions of reference group members as potentially useful bits of information. Thus, a person may notice several members of a given group utilizing a particular brand of coffee. The individual may then decide to try that brand simply because there is some evidence (its use by friends) that it may be a good brand.[21] In this case, the apparent conformity is simply the result of information shared by the group members.

Compliance conformity occurs when an individual fulfills group expectations to gain a direct reward or to avoid a sanction.[22] An individual may purchase a given brand of coffee to win approval from a spouse or a neighborhood group. Or one might refrain from maintaining too nice of a yard to avoid wisecracks or even ostracism by one's neighbors.[23]

Identification and *internalization conformity* differ from the previously described types in that they focus on internal, i.e., attitudinal and value, rather than just external or behavioral conformity. Identification involves conformity to group norms to sustain a relationship with the group that supports the individual's self-concept or identity. The individual perceives himself as similar to the group and conforms to the

---

[19] Lessig and Park, "Promotional Perspectives."

[20] Three of these—compliance, identification, and internalization—were initially described by H. C. Kelman, "Process of Opinion Change," *Public Opinion Quarterly* (Spring 1961), pp. 57–78. See also C. W. Park and V. P. Lessig, "Students and Housewives: Differences in Susceptibility to Reference Group Influence," *Journal of Consumer Research* (September 1977), pp. 102–10; and Lessig and Park, "Promotional Perspectives."

[21] For research evidence on this point, see R. E. Burnkrant and A. Cousineau, "Informational and Normative Social Influence in Buyer Behavior," *Journal of Consumer Research* (December 1975), pp. 206–15.

[22] See G. Homans, *Social Behavior: Its Elementary Forms* (Harcourt, Brace, Jovanovich, Inc., 1961).

[23] See H. J. Gans, "The Levittowners: Ways of Life and Politics in a New Suburban Community," in *Studies in American Society*, ed. F. L. Sweetser (Crowell, 1970), pp. 185–220.

FIGURE 8–2
Text from a Dewar's print advertisement

DEWAR'S® PROFILES

(pronounced Do-ers "White Label")

ARLENE PORTNEY

HOME: Meadowbrook, Pennsylvania

AGE: 27

PROFESSION: Concert pianist

HOBBIES: Mountain climbing, model-railroading, squash.

MOST MEMORABLE BOOK: "Ada" by Vladimir Nabokov

LATEST ACCOMPLISHMENT: First American woman ever to have won first prize in a major international piano competition: The Prix Beracasa, Paris, France.

QUOTE: "I've always felt that art is to be cherished. It convinces us of the dignity of life, and that for which civilizations have been remembered."

PROFILE: Sensitive, gifted and thoroughly dynamic. A true romantic, she's committed to making music more accessible to every one.

SCOTCH: Dewar's "White Label®"

Source: Used with permission from Schenley Industries, Inc.

group's norms to validate or justify this self-concept.[24] While compliance involved a behavioral conformity to group norms without the necessity for attitudinal or value conformity, identification suggests conformity at the attitudinal and value level as well.

Internalization occurs when the individual completely accepts the norms and values of the group as his or her own. Conformity occurs in this situation because the group norms are the same as the individual's

---

[24] This is similar to the co-orientation concept, see Moschis, "Social Comparison."

and the required behaviors appear intrinsically rewarding and appropriate.

Marketers frequently attempt to utilize conformity pressures in both personal selling situations and in advertising. We have already examined a situation in which conformity to group norms was used in a selling situation. In that case, both informational and compliance influences were operating. In Figure 8—2 we see a use of reference group theory in advertising. Basically, the advertisement is saying that "this is the kind of person that uses Dewar's Scotch. If you are this type of person, you should use it also." Thus, the advertisement appears to be seeking conformity to the message by relying on identification. Numerous other advertisements attempt to gain conformity through compliance by implying that using (or not using) a given brand or product will result in rewards (punishments) from relevant reference groups.

COMMUNICATION WITHIN GROUPS

Information is the primary tool used by marketers to influence consumer behavior. In Chapter 10, we present a model of how an *individual* processes information. While information is ultimately processed by an individual, in a substantial number of cases one or more groups filter, interpret, or provide the information for the individual group members. The individual that performs this task or role is known as an *opinion leader* and the process of one individual receiving information from the mass media and passing that information on to others is known as the *two-step flow of communications.* Figure 8—3 illustrates both the direct flow and the two-step flow of mass communications.

Imagine for a moment that you are going to make a purchase in a product category with which you are not very familiar. Further imagine that the purchase is important to you—perhaps a new stereo system, skis, a sports car, or jogging shoes. How would you go about deciding what type and brand to buy? Chances are you would consult a friend that you believe to be knowledgeable about the product category. This friend would be an opinion leader for you. (The situations in which an individual is likely to seek out information from an opinion leader are described in detail in Chapter 16.)

What characterizes opinion leadership? The most salient characteristic of an opinion leader is greater *interest in* and *knowledge of* the product category than the nonopinion leaders in the group. Thus, an individual tends to be an opinion leader only for specific product or activity clusters.[25] Opinion leaders are exposed to more mass media and

---
[25] E. Katz and P. F. Lazarsfeld, *Personal Influence* (Free Press, 1955); E. Katz, "The Two-Step Flow of Communications: An Up-to-Date Report on a Hypothesis," *Public Opinion Quarterly* (Spring 1957), pp. 61—78; A. J. Silk, "Overlap among Self-Designated Opinion Leaders: A Study of Selected Dental Products and Services," *Journal of Marketing Research* (August 1966), pp. 255—60; T. S. Robertson and J. H. Myers, "Personality Correlates of Opinion Leadership and Innovative Buying Behavior," *Journal of Marketing Research* (May 1969), pp. 164—68; D. B.

FIGURE 8–3

Mass communication information flows

Direct flow

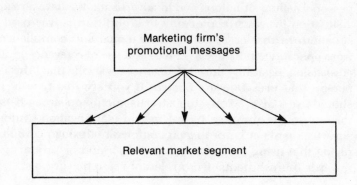

Two-Step flow

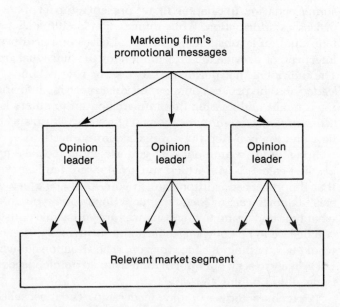

Montgomery and A. J. Silk, "Patterns of Overlap in Opinion Leadership and Interest for Selected Categories of Purchasing Activity," in *Marketing Involvement in Society and the Economy,* ed. P. R. McDonald (American Marketing Association, 1969), pp. 377 – 86; C. W. King and J. O. Summers, "Overlap of Opinion Leadership across Consumer Product Categories," *Journal of Marketing Research* (February 1970), pp. 43 – 50; J. O. Summers, "The Identity of Women's Clothing Fashion Opinion Leaders," *Journal of Marketing Research* (May 1970), pp. 178 – 85; and D. B. Montogomery and A. J. Silk, "Clusters of Consumer Interests and Opinion Leaders' Spheres of Influence," *Journal of Marketing Research* (August 1971), pp. 317 – 21.

particularly to mass media oriented toward their area of leadership than are nonopinion leaders.[26]

Opinion leadership functions primarily through interpersonal communications, and interpersonal communications occur most frequently among individuals with similar demographic characteristics. Thus, it is not surprising that opinion leaders are found within all demographic segments of the population and seldom differ significantly on demographic variables from the nonopinion leaders they influence.[27] For certain product categories, such as fashions, movies, or foods, some demographic groups are more informed and thus more likely to serve as opinion leaders.[28]

Opinion leaders tend to be more gregarious and outgoing than nonopinion leaders.[29] Other personality factors do not appear to differ between the two groups.[30] There is some evidence to suggest that psychographic or lifestyle (see Chapter 14) differences between opinion leaders and nonopinion leaders for particular product categories may be significant.[31]

Applications of opinion leadership

The importance of opinion leadership varies radically from product to product and from target market to target market. Therefore the initial step in utilizing opinion leaders is to determine, either through research or logic, the role of opinion leadership in the situation at hand.

Utilizing existing knowledge of opinion leadership and the two-step (or multistep) flow of communication is complicated by the fact that opinion leaders are difficult to identify. They tend to be similar, both demographically and in personality, to those they influence. The fact that opinion leaders are heavily involved with the mass media, particu-

---

[26] Summers, "Identity of Women's"; F. D. Reynolds and W. R. Darden, "Mutually Adaptive Effects of Interpersonal Communication," *Journal of Marketing Research* (November 1971), pp. 449–54; and L. H. Corey, "People Who Claim to be Opinion Leaders: Identifying Their Characteristics by Self-Report," *Journal of Marketing* (October 1971), pp. 48–53; and G. M. Armstrong and L. P. Feldman, "Exposure and Sources of Opinion Leaders," *Journal of Advertising Research* (August 1976), pp. 21–27. Contradictory findings are reported in J. H. Myers and T. S. Robertson, "Dimensions of Opinion Leadership," *Journal of Marketing Research* (February 1972), pp. 41–46.

[27] Robertson and Myers, "Personality Correlates"; Corey, "People Who Claim."

[28] Robertson and Myers, "Personality Correlates"; and Katz and Lazarsfeld, *Personal Influence*.

[29] Robertson and Myers, "Personality Correlates"; Reynolds and Darden, "Mutually Adaptive Effects"; Summers, "Identity of Women's"; J. N. Sheth, "Word-of-Mouth in Low Risk Innovations," *Journal of Advertising Research* (June 1971), pp. 15–18; and L. G. Schiffman and V. Gaccione, "Opinion Leaders in Institutional Markets," *Journal of Marketing* (April 1974), pp. 49–53.

[30] Robertson and Myers, "Personality Correlates."

[31] D. J. Tigert and S. J. Arnold, *Profiling Self-Designated Opinion Leaders and Self-Designated Innovators through Life Style Research* (University of Toronto, 1971).

larly media that focus on their area of leadership, provides a partial solution to the identification problem. For example, Osaga (a marketer of running shoes) could assume that many subscribers to *Runners World* serve as opinion leaders for jogging and running shoes. Likewise, the fact that opinion leaders are gregarious and tend to belong to clubs and associations suggests that Osaga could also consider members and officials of local running clubs to be opinion leaders.

For some product categories there are professional opinion leaders. For products related to livestock, the county extension agent is generally very influential. Barbers and hairstylists serve as opinion leaders for hair care products. Pharmacists are important opinion leaders for a wide range of health care products.

Thus, for many products it is possible to identify individuals who have a high probability of being an opinion leader. Once these individuals are identified, what should the marketer do?

Since opinion leaders receive, interpret, and retransmit marketing messages on to others, marketing research should focus on opinion leaders rather than "representative" samples in those product categories and groups in which the opinion leaders play a critical role. Thus, product usage tests, pretests of advertising copy, media preference studies, and so forth *should be conducted on samples of individuals likely to be opinion leaders.* It is essential that these individuals be exposed to, and respond favorably to, the firm's marketing mix elements. Of course, for those product categories or groups in which opinion leadership is not important such a strategy would be unwise.

Sampling—sending a sample of a product to a group of potential consumers—has been found to be an effective means of generating interpersonal communications concerning the product. In one study, 33 percent of a randomly selected group of women who received a free sample of a new brand of instant coffee discussed it with someone outside their immediate family within a week.[32] Instead of using a random sample, a marketer should attempt to send the product to a group of individuals likely to be opinion leaders. This should produce even more effective results than those described above.

Rather than identifying current opinion leaders, it is sometimes possible to create them. Remember that opinion leaders are characterized by gregariousness, interest in the product category, and knowledge about the product. It is sometimes possible for a firm to identify gregarious individuals and then to create interest and knowledge about a particular product among those individuals. Figure 8–4 illustrates the way one record company went about this. Versions of this technique have also been used in the electronics and metalworking industries.[33] An ap-

[32] J. H. Holmes and J. D. Lett, Jr., "Product Sampling and Word of Mouth," *Journal of Advertising Research* (October 1977), pp. 35–40.

[33] J. R. Mancuso, "Why Not Create Opinion Leaders for New Product Introductions?" *Journal of Marketing* (July 1969), pp. 20–25.

FIGURE 8–4
Creation of high school opinion leaders for rock records

Procedure

1. Social leaders (presumably gregarious) such as class presidents, secretaries, sports captains, and cheerleaders were selected from geographically diverse high schools in test cities. Research indicated that few of those selected were currently opinion leaders for records.

2. These individuals were asked to join a panel composed of "leaders" who "should be better able to identify potential rock-and-roll hits." In return for participation, the student would receive free records.

3. Information about the record and singing star were provided for each record the student was to evaluate. In addition, the students were encouraged to investigate other sources of information such as *Billboard* magazine and record stores.

4. The students were also encouraged to discuss each record with their friends before voting.

Results

Several test records reached the top ten in the cities with the student panels. None of these records reached the top ten in other cities. Thus, the firm was apparently successful in creating opinion leaders who, in turn, influenced sales.

Source: Adopted from J. R. Mancuso, "Why Not Create Opinion Leaders for New Product Introductions," *Journal of Marketing* (July 1969), p. 21.

proach similar to this would seem to have a particularly high potential for retailers.

DIFFUSION OF INNOVATIONS

The manner by which a new product is accepted or spreads through a market is basically a group phenomenon. As with all consumer behaviors, other factors such as the product, the situation, and the individual also play a part. In this section, we will examine this process in some detail.[34]

---

[34] Due to the vast amount of research in this area only representative studies will be cited. Detailed reviews are available in E. M. Rogers and F. F. Shoemaker, *Communication of Innovations: A Cross-Cultural Approach* (Free Press, 1971); T. S. Robertson, *Innovative Behavior and Communication* (Holt, Rinehart & Winston, 1971); and G. Zaltman and R. Stiff, "Theories of Innovation," in *Consumer Behavior: Theoretical Sources,* eds. S. Ward and T. S. Robertson (Prentice-Hall, Inc., 1973), pp. 416−68. A discussion of the development, problems, and potential of diffusion research can be found in E. M. Rogers, "New Product Adoption and Diffusion," *Journal of Consumer Research* (March 1976), pp. 290−301.

Nature of innovations

An innovation is *any idea, practice, or material artifact perceived to be new by the relevant individual or group*.[35] It is important to note that whether or not a given product is an innovation is determined by the perceptions of the potential market, *not* by an objective measure of technological change. Thus, the social concept of a "negative income tax" may, in fact, differ only marginally from current welfare programs. However, as long as the market (the voting public) perceives it as being radically different, it will be difficult to implement.

Under this definition, a product does not have to be new in terms of the length of time it has been in existence to be an innovation. Yogurt, as well as many other health foods, has been used for hundreds of years. Recent marketing efforts have introduced these products to market segments that were not familiar with them. To these market segments, the products were innovations and were responded to as such. Computer-designed, "passive" solar-heated homes represent a major innovation to many perspective consumers. Yet the same principles were used in the design of the Pueblo dwellings centuries ago.[36]

Categories of innovations

Try to recall innovations that you have encountered in the past two or three years. As you reflect on these, it may occur to you that there are degrees of innovation. For example, an electric razor was more of an innovation than a double-blade safety razor. We can picture any given product as falling somewhere on a continuum ranging from no change to radical change depending on the target markets' response to the item. This is portrayed in Figure 8—5.

FIGURE 8-5
Degrees of innovation

No change	Continuous innovation	Dynamically continuous innovation	Discontinuous innovation	Radical change

Change in Figure 8—5 refers to *changes required in the consumer's behavior if the innovation is adopted or utilized, not to technical or functional changes in the product*. Also indicated in this figure are three categories into which it is useful to classify a given innovation as viewed by a specific market segment. Each of these categories is described below.[37] It should be noted that no boundaries are shown between the

---

[35] Zaltman and Stiff, "Theories of Innovation."

[36] "Passive Solar: Yesterday Is Tomorrow," *Sunset* (February 1979), p. 77.

[37] Based on T. S. Robertson, "The Process of Innovation and the Diffusion of Innovation," *Journal of Marketing* (January 1967), pp. 14—19.

categories. This is because there are no clear-cut or distinct breaks between each category.

> *Continuous innovation.* Adoption requires relatively minor changes in behavior. Examples would include a new flavored toothpaste, an improved cigarette filter, a new motor oil, or freeze-dried coffee.
>
> *Dynamically continuous innovation.* Adoption requires a major change in an area of behavior that is relatively unimportant to the individual. Examples would include electric razor, touch-tone telephones, Weed Eater lawn trimmer, or variable-rate home mortgages.
>
> *Discontinuous innovation.* Adoption requires major changes in behavior in an area of importance to the individual or group. Examples would include snuff (moist tobacco), no-fault insurance, bicycle (as a primary means of transportation), and solar heating.

A moment's reflection will reveal that most of the thousands of new products or alterations introduced each year tend toward the no change end of the continuum. Much of the theoretical and empirical research has been based on discontinuous innovations. The material we present below is most valid for discontinuous innovations and least applicable for continuous innovations.

Diffusion process

The *diffusion process* is *the process by which innovations spread to the members of a social system.*[38] From a marketing context, the term *spread* refers to purchase behavior in which the members of the social system purchase the product with some degree of continuing regularity, i.e., they adopt the product. The *social system* for a marketer would refer to the target market. The social system (group) could range from virtually the entire American society (for a new soft drink perhaps) to the students at a particular junior high (for an automated fast-food and snack outlet).

No matter what innovation is being studied or which social group is involved, the diffusion process appears to follow a similar pattern over time: a period of relatively slow growth followed by a period of rapid growth followed by a final period of slower growth. This pattern is shown in Figure 8—6. However, there may be some exceptions to this pattern. In particular, it appears that for continuous innovations such as new ready-to-eat cereals, the initial slow growth stage may be skipped.[39]

An overview of innovation studies reveals that the time involved from introduction until the given market segment is saturated (i.e., sales growth has slowed or stopped) varies from a few days or weeks to years.

---

[38] Rogers and Shoemaker, *Communication of Innovations,* p. 12.

[39] Robertson, "Process of Innovation," pp. 33—34.

194

FIGURE 8–6
Diffusion rate of an innovation over time

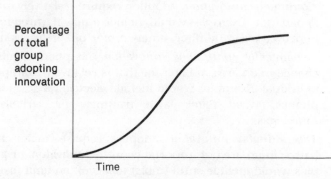

This leads to two interesting questions: (1) *What determines how rapidly a particular innovation will spread through a given market segment?* and (2) *In what ways do those who purchase innovations relatively early differ from those who purchase them later?*

Factors affecting the time required for an innovation to spread through a group   The rate at which an innovation is diffused is a function of five factors: (1) nature of the group involved, (2) type of innovation decision required, (3) communication channels used, (4) extent of marketing effort, and (5) perceived attributes of the innovation.[40]

The definition of the *relevant group* is a critical issue in this area. For example, a group defined as young, single white-collar males might be expected to adopt a new clothing style more rapidly than a group defined as all males over 21 or all males over 55. Therefore, most studies of the diffusion of innovation define the relevant group as all potential adopters (consumers) within a defined geographic area such as a city, state, or farming area. Even with this approach, the rate of adoption of a product aimed at a relatively young, change-oriented group will generally spread faster than a product designed for an older, more traditionally oriented group.

The *type of innovation decision* is basically an individual versus collective dimension. The fewer the individuals involved in the decision, the more rapidly the innovation will spread. The rate of diffusion is also increased as *the use of mass media increases.* Although there is clearly a limit to this effect, a move from solely interpersonal communications to some mass media can greatly accelerate the process. Closely related to this is the *extent of marketing effort* involved. That is, the rate of diffusion is not completely beyond the control of the firm. A good example of this is provided by Johnson Wax's decision to spend $30 million in

---

[40] Rogers and Shoemaker, *Communication of Innovations,* p. 158.

advertising, sampling, couponing, trade deals, and public relations to introduce Agree Shampoo.[41]

Although the factors described above all influence the rate of diffusion, the *perceived attributes of the innovation* appear to be the most important determinants.[42] The most important of these attributes are described below:[43]

1. *Fulfillment of felt need.* The more manifest or obvious the need that the innovation satisfies, the faster the diffusion. One of the difficulties in persuading large segments of the American society to quit smoking because of the health hazard (a new idea not many years ago) has been the fact that reduced risk of lung cancer is not a strongly felt need in most healthy individuals.

2. *Compatibility.* The more the purchase and use of the innovation is consistent with the individual's and group's values, the more rapid the diffusion. Television was quite compatible with the existing values of large segments of the American society, while dishwashers were not (they conflicted with the perceived role of the housewife personally caring for her family).

3. *Relative advantage.* The better the innovation is perceived to meet the relevant need compared to existing methods, the more rapid the diffusion. For example, Weed Eater appears to offer substantial advantages over hand-trimming lawns. Included in relative advantage is *price*. Thus, while Weed Eater enjoys tremendous advantages over hand trimming in terms of effort involved, this aspect of relative advantage is somewhat offset by the higher cost.

4. *Complexity.* The more difficult the innovation is to understand and use, the slower the diffusion. This has particular importance with respect to farm products.[44] It may also be important for such consumer products as pesticides, diets, and games.

5. *Observability.* The more easily observed the positive effects of adopting an innovation are, the more rapid the diffusion. Television, clothing fashions, and automobile changes are all highly visible in their use. New types of magazines, while less visible in use, are often the topic of conversation. On the other hand, dishwashers, deodorants, and vitamins are less obvious and generally less likely to be a topic of conversation.

6. *Trialability.* The easier it is to have a low-cost or low-risk trial of the innovation, the more rapid the diffusion. The diffusion of such

---

[41] "Key Role of Research in Agree's Success Is Told," *Marketing News* (January 12, 1979), p. 15.

[42] Rogers and Shoemaker, *Communication of Innovations,* p. 157.

[43] Ibid., pp. 137−57; and E. M. Rogers and J. D. Stanfield, "Adoption and Diffusion of New Products: Emerging Generalizations and Hypotheses," paper presented at the Conference on the Application of Sciences to Marketing Management (Purdue University, 1966).

[44] Rogers and Shoemaker, *Communication of Innovations,* p. 154.

products as dishwashers, prefabricated homes, and contact lens have probably been hampered by the difficulty of trying out the product. This is much less of a problem with low-cost items such as toothpaste or items which can be rented, borrowed, or tried at a retail outlet such as color televisions.

How can we utilize this information? First, by combining research and judgment, we can estimate how a given market segment will perceive a proposed innovation on each of these six attributes. Based on this we can estimate both the probability of success and the rate of diffusion.

However, limiting ourselves to prediction would be to forego a useful strategy tool. For example, suppose a proposed innovation scores high (favorably) on all attributes except compatibility. What marketing strategy does this suggest? Obviously, the firm's communications, particularly advertising, will have to attempt to minimize this problem. For example, "light" (diet) beers were successfully introduced by relating them to active, masculine individuals and avoiding direct references to diet which many "real beer drinkers" may feel to be for women and sissies.[45]

Suppose the example were changed to a proposed innovation which scored high on all attributes except observability. What marketing strategy would be suggested?

Characteristics of individuals that adopt an innovation at varying points in time The curve shown in Figure 8–6 was a cumulative curve that illustrated the increase in the percentage of adopters over time. If we change that curve from a cumulative curve to one that shows the percentage of a market that adopts the innovation at *any given point* in time, we will find the familiar bell-shaped curve shown in Figure 8–7.

FIGURE 8–7
Adoptions of an innovation over time

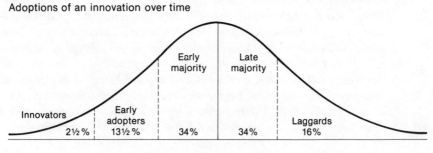

Time of adoption of innovations

Figure 8–7 reemphasizes the fact that a few individuals adopt an innovation very quickly, another limited group is very reluctant to adopt

---

[45] "How Miller Won a Market Slot for Lite Beer," *Business Week* (October 13, 1975), p. 116.

the innovation, and the majority of the group adopts at some time in between the two more extreme groups.

Researchers have found it useful to divide the adopters of any given innovation into five groups based on the relative time at which they adopt. These groups, called *adopter categories,* are shown in Figure 8−7 and are defined below:

Innovator: The first 2.5 percent of the individuals to adopt an innovation.
Early adopter: The next 13.5 percent to adopt.
Early majority: The next 34 percent to adopt.
Late majority: The next 34 percent to adopt.
Laggards: The final 16 percent that adopt.

The question of interest is, how do these five groups differ?

The first answer to this question is: *It depends on the product category being considered.* Thus, while we will propose some broad generalizations, they may not hold true for a particular product category. Indeed, they should generally be treated as hypotheses or ideas to test for the product category you are involved with rather than as established facts.

With the above qualification in mind, let us examine each category as an ideal type—a generalization that may not hold true in particular cases. These generalizations are based heavily on studies of farm innovations.[46]

Innovators are venturesome risk-takers. They are capable of absorbing the financial and social costs of adopting an unsuccessful product. They are cosmopolitan in outlook and use other innovators as a reference group rather than local peers. They tend to be younger, better educated, and more socially mobile than their peers. They make extensive use of commercial media, sales personnel, and professional sources in learning of new products.

Early adopters tend to be opinion leaders in local reference groups. They tend to be successful, well educated, and somewhat younger than their peers. They are willing to take a calculated risk on an innovation but are also concerned with failure. They also utilize commercial and professional information sources.

Early majority tend to be cautious with respect to innovations. They adopt prior to most of their social group but also after the innovation has proven successful with others. They are socially active but seldom are leaders. They tend to be somewhat older, less well educated, and less socially mobile than the early adopters. They rely heavily on interpersonal sources of information.

Late majority are skeptical about innovations. They often adopt more

---

[46] The following is based on Rogers and Shoemaker, *Communication of Innovations,* pp. 183−85, as well as subsequent research in the area.

in response to social pressures or a decreased availability of the previous product than because of a positive evaluation of the innovation. They tend to be older and have less social status and mobility than those who adopt earlier.

Laggards are locally oriented and engage in limited social interaction. They tend to be relatively dogmatic and oriented toward the past. Innovations are adopted only with reluctance.

Figure 8–8 illustrates some of the generalizations just described. Again, it must be emphasized that the ideal types presented above and the generalizations shown in Figure 8– 8 are abstractions that may not

FIGURE 8–8

Generalized relationships of selected variables with adopter categories

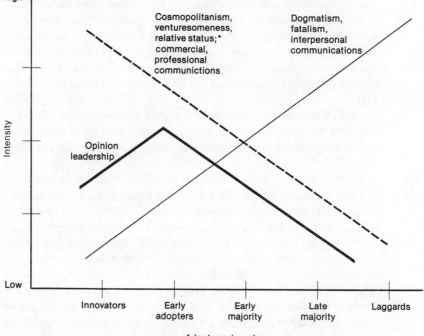

* Measured in a variety of ways, such as income, occupation, education, lifestyles, and so forth.

hold true for a particular product category. For example, a study of the push-button phone found that cosmopolitanism—an orientation outside the local area—had a negative correlation with adoption.[47] This is exactly the opposite of the prediction one would make based on the ideal types described earlier.

[47] T. S. Robertson and J. N. Kennedy, "Prediction of Consumer Innovators: Application of Multiple Discriminant Analysis," *Journal of Marketing Research* (February 1968), pp. 64 – 69.

What can we conclude from this and how can we utilize it? The only firm conclusion is that while adopter categories exist, are different from each other on a number of dimensions, and are relatively stable over time; the adopter categories are product or activity specific. That is, the adopter categories that exist for kitchen appliances are distinct from those that exist for skiing equipment.

This does not mean that adopter categories cannot be used by marketing managers. Rather, it means that the marketing manager must first isolate or define the characteristics of the adopter categories for the product of interest. Since the manager will be dealing with a new product (or an extension of an existing product into a new market segment), it will generally be necessary to determine the characteristics of the adopter categories for a similar product in a similar market segment.

Once adopter categories have been defined, the marketing mix can be designed with the characteristics of each group in mind. For example, assume the ideal types described earlier were accurate for a farm innovation your firm was planning to introduce. How would your marketing mix change as the majority of the market shifted from innovators to early adopters to early majority, and so forth?

Conclusions on the diffusion of innovations There have been over 2,000 published studies of the diffusion process. From this volume of research, a number of useful generalizations have emerged as described in the preceding sections. Despite our knowledge in this area, most new consumer products are commercial failures.[48] The primary reason for this high failure rate is not a lack of knowledge, but a failure to apply what is known.[49] Executives too often utilize *their* own evaluation of the attributes of the innovation rather than those of the relevant market segments. Or, the initial introduction is aimed at the average consumer; however, the average consumer often is *not* the innovator or early adopter who must try the product first.

SUMMARY

A group in its broadest sense includes two or more individuals who share a set of norms, values, or beliefs and have certain implicit or explicit relationships such that their behavior is interdependent. Groups may be classified on the basis of membership, nature of contact, and attraction.

Some groups require membership; others such as aspiration groups do not. The *nature of contact* is based on the degree of interpersonal group interaction. Groups that have frequent personal contact are called *primary groups*, while those with infrequent or minimal

---

[48] C. M. Crawford, "Marketing Research and the New Product Failure Rate," *Journal of Marketing* (April 1977), pp. 51–61.

[49] Ibid., see especially Exhibit 1.

interpersonal contact are called *secondary groups*. *Attraction* refers to the degree of positive or negative desirability the group has to the individual.

A role is defined as a prescribed pattern of behavior expected of a person in a given situation by virtue of the person's position in that situation. Thus, roles are based on positions and situations and not individuals. There are many characteristics that affect role behavior such as role style and parameters, one's commitment to a certain role, and role conflict. The most important use of role theory in marketing revolves around the fact that there is usually a set of products generally considered necessary to properly fulfill a given role.

Norms are general expectations about behaviors that are deemed appropriate for all persons in a social context, regardless of the position they hold. Norms arise quickly and naturally in any group situation. The degree of conformity to group norms is a function of the visibility of the usage situation, the level of commitment the individual feels to the group, the relevance of the behavior to the functioning of the group, and the individual's confidence in his or her own judgment in the area. Since product acquisition and utilization vary along each of these four dimensions, the pressure to conform in the purchase of products or brands also varies in terms of reference group influence.

Conformity can vary across situations, and as a result an individual may experience different types of conformity. *Informational conformity* represents the lowest level of conformity as individuals simply acquire information shared by group members. *Compliance conformity* is stronger because an individual conforms to group expectations to gain approval or avoid disapproval. *Identification conformity* is still stronger since an individual utilizes the group norms and identifies with them as a part of their own self-concept and identity. Finally, the highest level of individual conformity is *internalization*. This occurs when an individual completely accepts (internalizes) the norms and values of the group.

Communication within groups is a major influence affecting word-of-mouth communication about certain products. Because good word-of-mouth brand communication is a valuable marketing asset, marketers attempt to identify and/or create opinion leaders that affect the within-group information acquisition of members. When opinion leaders can be reached, a two-step flow of information is utilized by the firm, which directs marketing communications to opinion leaders and opinion leaders then communicate this information to group members. When done successfully this method of communication is very effective in promoting brand specific word-of-mouth communication.

Groups, because of their interpersonal interaction and influence, greatly affect the diffusion of innovations. Innovations vary in terms of degree of innovation and the rate at which they are diffused. The first purchasers of an innovative product or service are termed innovators; those that follow in adoption over time are subsequently identified as early adopters, early majority, late majority, and laggards. Each of these groups differs in the time of adoption of an innovation and in terms of personality, age, education, and reference group membership. These characteristics make it feasible for marketers to identify and appeal to different classes of adopters at different stages of the innovation's diffusion.

The time it takes for an innovation to spread from innovators to laggards is affected by several factors: (1) nature of the group involved, (2) type of innovation decision required, (3) communication channels used, (4) extent of marketing effort, and (5) perceived attributes of the innovation. The perceived attributes of an innovation include: (1) fulfillment of felt need, (2) compatibility of the innovation with existing behavior, (3) relative advantage, (4) complexity of the innovation, (5) ease in observing usage of the innovation, and (6) ease in trying the innovation at a relatively low cost.

REVIEW QUESTIONS

1. What is a negative reference group? In what way can negative reference groups influence consumer behavior?
2. What criteria are used by marketers to classify groups?
3. What is an aspiration reference group? How can an aspiration reference group influence behavior?
4. How does a group differ from a reference group?
5. What is a *role?*
6. How does role style relate to role parameters?
7. How does a role sanction relate to a role parameter?
8. How does role commitment relate to role sanctions?
9. What is role conflict? How can marketers utilize role conflict in product development and promotion?
10. What is a role stereotype? How do marketers utilize role stereotypes?
11. What is a role-related product cluster? Why is it important to marketing managers?
12. How does a group norm differ from a role?
13. What is the Asch phenomenon?
14. What factors determine the degree of influence a reference group will have for a given consumer decision?
15. What types of conformity exist? Why is it important for a marketing manager to be aware of these separate types of conformity?
16. What is an opinion leader? How does an opinion leader relate to the two-step flow of communications?
17. What characterizes an opinion leader?

18. How can marketing managers identify opinion leaders?
19. How can marketers utilize opinion leaders?
20. How could one "create" opinion leaders?
21. What is an innovation? Who determines whether a given product is an innovation?
22. What are the various categories of innovations? How do they differ?
23. What is the diffusion process? What pattern does the diffusion process appear to follow over time?
24. What factors affect the diffusion rate for an innovation?
25. Describe the perceived attributes of the innovation that influence its rate of diffusion. How can these factors be utilized in developing marketing strategy?
26. What are adopter categories? Describe the "ideal type" adopter categories.
27. How can a marketer utilize a knowledge of adopter categories?

DISCUSSION QUESTIONS

1. Refer to the discussion of mopeds in Chapter 1 in answering the following questions.

   a. Is the moped an innovation? Justify your answer.

   b. Assume the moped becomes widely used on your campus. Speculate on the characteristics of the adopter categories.

   c. Using the student body on your campus as a market segment, evaluate the perceived attributes of the moped.

   d. Who, on your campus, would serve as opinion leaders for the moped?

   e. How important are reference groups to the purchase of mopeds? Would the influence also affect the brand or model? Justify your answer.

   f. What reference groups would be relevant to the decision to purchase a moped (based on students on your campus)?

   g. What are the norms concerning transportation of the social groups of which you are a member?

   h. Could Jeff (or the local dealers) use an Asch-type situation to sell mopeds?

   i. How could Jeff associate moped with the student role on your campus?

   j. Describe how you would "create" moped opinion leaders on your campus.

2. The figure below approximates the diffusion rate for television sets and automatic washers in the Milwaukee area. On an after-the-fact basis, analyze the attributes of each product to see if such an analysis would predict their relative rates of diffusion.

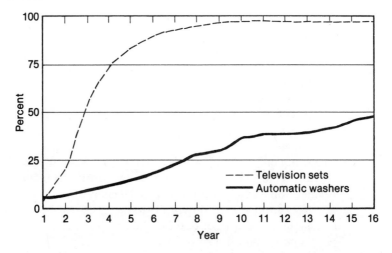

3. Assume that you are a consultant to firms with new products. You
   have members of the appropriate market segments rate the innovation on the six attributes described in the chapter. Based on these
   ratings you develop marketing strategies. Assume that a rating of 10
   is extremely favorable (strong relative advantage or a lack of complexity), and 0 is extremely unfavorable. Develop appropriate strategies for each of the nine products rated below.

	Product								
Attribute	A	B	C	D	E	F	G	H	I
Fulfillment of felt need	3	9	8	8	5	4	8	9	9
Compatibility	8	2	8	9	2	8	9	8	8
Relative advantage	8	8	9	4	6	9	8	8	9
Complexity	9	9	9	9	3	3	8	2	9
Observability	8	9	1	9	4	8	3	8	8
Trial ability	9	8	9	9	2	9	2	9	2

4. Speculate on the characteristics of the adopter categories for each of
   the following products:
   a. Video recorders for televisions.
   b. Soy protein meat substitutes.
   c. Microwave ovens.
   d. Solar-heated houses.
   e. Soft contact lens.
   f. Hearing aid that is inserted under the skin behind the ear.
   g. Home computers that calculate taxes, keep check books bal-
      anced, keep budgets, etc. (cost, $500).

5. Speculate on the characteristics of opinion leaders for college students for the following product categories:
   a. Cross-country skis.
   b. Physicians.
   c. Laundry detergent.
   d. Baby food.
   e. Health insurance.
   f. Overseas vacations.
   g. Clothing styles.
6. Assuming college students as the market segment, describe the most relevant reference group(s) and indicate the probable degree of influence for each of the following decisions:
   a. Decision to learn downhill skiing.
   b. Type and brand of downhill ski to purchase.
   c. Type of clothing to wear to class.
   d. Decision to bicycle to school daily.
   e. Brand of beer or soft drink to consume.
   f. Area in which to major.
   g. Brand of aspirin to use.

PROJECT QUESTIONS

1. Identify and interview several moped innovators on your campus. To what extent do they match the "ideal type" innovator?
2. Repeat question 1 for early adopters *if* early adopters exist on your campus.
3. Find three advertisements that utilize reference groups in an attempt to gain patronage.
   a. Describe the advertisement.
   b. Describe the type of reference group being utilized.
   c. Describe the type of conformity being sought.
4. Find three advertisements that utilize role stereotypes and describe the type of role being portrayed.
5. Find and describe an advertisement, product, or other use of the marketing mix based on role conflict.
6. Find and interview two opinion leaders for one of the product categories listed in discussion question 5. To what extent do they match the description provided in the chapter?

9

The family

After a research project to determine which family members are involved in the purchase of crayons, Crayola shifted their $1 million advertising budget from childrens' television to womens' magazines. The research revealed that mothers rather than children were most likely to recognize the problem, evaluate the alternatives, and make the purchase.[1] Thus, for this product category, a family member other than the one that uses the product is the primary decision maker.

The family is the basic consumption unit for consumer goods in the American society. Such major items as food, housing, automobiles, and appliances are, in effect, consumed more by family units than by individuals. Furthermore, the consumption patterns of individual family members are seldom independent from those of other family members. For example, the decision to grant a child's request for a bicycle may require using discretionary funds that could have been used to purchase an evening out for the parents, new clothing for a brother or sister, or otherwise used by another family member.

Families are important not only for their direct role in the consumption process but also for the critical role they perform in child socialization. The family is the primary mechanism whereby cultural and social class values and behavior patterns are "passed on" to the next genera-

---

[1] "Research, High TV Costs Push Crayola into Print," *Advertising Age* (September 18, 1978), p. 3.

tion. Purchasing and consumption patterns are among those attitudes and skills strongly influenced by the family unit. We examine this learning process in some detail in Chapter 11.

In this chapter, we first examine the nature and importance of families in contemporary American society. Following this, we analyze the concept of the family life cycle. The final major section of the chapter examines the nature of the family decision process.

THE NATURE OF AMERICAN FAMILIES

The term *family* is used to designate a variety of distinct social groups. This can cause confusion unless each type of family unit is clearly distinguished. The *nuclear family* consists of two adults of opposite sex, living in a socially approved sex relationship, and their own or adopted children.[2] The nuclear family is virtually universal in every culture. That is, it appears to exist in and play an important role in all, or virtually all, societies.

The nuclear family as described above represents the prescriptive (culturally desirable) and descriptive (most common) version of the nuclear family. However, there are several variations of the nuclear family. The most common variation in the United States is the single-parent family caused by the death of one spouse or, more commonly, divorce. In both cases, the children and the mother are likely to remain together as a nuclear family. In general, the single-parent family is a temporary occurrence. Although the divorce rate continues to increase, approximately 80 percent of those who obtain a divorce will eventually remarry.[3]

Most members of the American society function in two distinct nuclear families during their lifetime. The first nuclear family, the one a person is born or adopted into, is the *family of orientation*. The term *orientation* is particularly apt as this social group supplies the individual with many permanent values and "orientations" toward life. The second nuclear family that most individuals belong to is the *family of procreation*. It is the family unit that, in our society, is formed by marriage. While one always belongs to the family of orientation and is influenced by it, the establishment of the family of procreation signals a definite shift in lifestyle and the addition of a new purchasing unit to the census.

The extended family is the nuclear family plus additional relations. The most common form of the extended family involves the inclusion of one or both sets of grandparents. In addition, aunts, uncles, cousins, in-laws, and so forth may be included. The extent and importance of the

---

[2] G. R. Leslie, *The Family in Social Context* (Oxford University Press, 1976), p. 15. The following discussion is based primarily on this source, pp. 15–26.

[3] U.S. Bureau of the Census, *Current Population Reports*, "Marriage, Divorce and Remarriage by Year of Birth: June 1971", series P–20, no. 239 (1972).

extended family varies from culture to culture. In the United States, extended families are narrowly defined and, with exceptions, are of relatively limited importance to the individual. Extended families are much more important in most other cultures and within certain ethnic subcultures in the United States.[4]

The nuclear family is particularly important in the United States as the nuclear family is the basic *residential family unit*. That is, most Americans live with the other members of their nuclear family and no one else lives with this group. This correspondence of the nuclear family and the residential family does not exist in many other cultures. The term *primary family* is used to describe a nuclear family which is also the residential family.[5]

Residential units that are not families are also of interest to marketing managers. A *household* is an individual or group of people who share a common dwelling. Most nuclear families constitute households. Single parents living alone, same-sex couples, unmarried couples "living together," and larger groups living under the same roof are also households. Households are important to the marketing manager because they constitute consumption units, and many published statistics are reported in terms of households.

Table 9–1 shows the current distribution of family types in the United States as well as changes in that distribution since 1950. The total number of households has increased by 70 percent to almost 75 million since 1950. During this same period, primary families increased by only 45 percent. As a percent of total households, primary family units declined from almost 90 percent in 1950 to slightly over 75 percent in 1977.

In contrast to the decline in the percentage of primary family units, the percentage of total households composed of primary individuals more than doubled from 10.8 to 23.8 percent. Most of this growth was caused by an increase in the number of young individuals living alone. In examining changes in the nature of families since 1950, we can see that the husband-wife family has declined from 87.6 percent of all families in 1950 to 83.8 percent in 1977.

What are the marketing implications of these shifts? The rapid growth of new household formation implies a strong demand for housing and household furnishings. The fact that much of this growth is coming from single-person households suggests, for example, that apartment, appliance, and food containers be produced in sizes appropriate for the single individual. The growth in single-parent families implies a need for convenience items, day-care centers, and appliances

---

[4] A description of the degree and importance which extended families can assume is provided by R. F. Salisbury, "ToNiri Buys a House," in *Foundations for a Theory of Consumer Behavior*, ed. W. T. Tucker (Holt, Rinehart and Winston, 1967), pp. 34–45.

[5] In some cases the primary family also includes married children and/or grandparents that live with the nuclear family.

TABLE 9–1

Household and family units by type: 1950–1977 (000)

	1977		1970		1960		1950	
	Number	Percent	Number	Percent	Number	Percent	Number	Percent
Households	74,142	100.0	63,401	100.0	52,799	100.0	43,554	100.0
Primary families	56,472	76.2	51,456	81.2	44,905	85.0	38,838	89.2
Husband–wife	47,471	64.0	44,728	70.5	39,254	74.3	34,075	78.2
Male head only	1,461	2.0	1,228	1.9	1,228	2.3	1,169	2.7
Female head only	7,540	10.2	5,500	8.7	4,422	8.4	3,594	8.3
Primary individuals*	17,669	23.8	11,945	18.8	7,895	15.0	4,716	10.8
Male	6,971	9.4	4,063	6.4	2,716	5.1	1,668	3.8
Female	10,698	14.4	7,882	12.4	5,179	9.8	3,048	7.0
Living alone	15,532	20.9	10,851	17.1	6,896	13.1	3,954	9.1
Families	56,710	100.0	51,586	100.0	45,111	100.0	39,303	100.0
Husband–Wife	47,497	83.8	44,755	86.8	39,329	87.2	34,440	87.6
Male head only	1,500	2.6	1,239	2.4	1,275	2.8	1,184	3.0
Female head only	7,713	13.6	5,591	10.8	4,507	10.0	3,679	9.4

* A household unit occupied by unrelated individuals.

Source: Derived from Bureau of the Census, *Current Population Reports*, "Population Characteristics: Households and Families by Type: March 1977," series P-20, no. 313 (September 1977), p. 6.

which relatively young children can operate. The timing and content of advertising aimed at single and single-parent families may need to differ from those aimed at standard nuclear families. As is the case with most variables affecting consumer behavior, the marketing manager must examine the shifts in the American family structure for specific product category implications.

THE FAMILY LIFE CYCLE

The family life cycle (FLC) is the classification of the family into stages over a period of time. The basic assumption is that families, like individuals, move through a series of relatively distinct and well-defined stages with the passage of time. Sociologists did not create the FLC, they merely observed the fact that families change over time at relatively predictable intervals based on largely demographic (and thus readily measurable) variables. These changes affect product needs and wants and present marketers with opportunities to help solve consumer problems. Much like the concepts of social class and subcultures, stages in the FLC provide marketers with relatively homogeneous segments that share similar values and lifestyles with respect to family-related problems and purchases.

FLC then represents a tool that marketing managers can use to better understand their potential market segments. Like all tools, FLC is not universally applicable and managers must be sure to first establish whether the purchase and use of their product is in any significant way affected by stages in the FLC before trying to "force" the product to fit the tool.[6]

The demographic variables most frequently used to define family life cycle reflect the number, age, and income-producing capacity of the family members. The following list reflects the most commonly used variables.

1. Marital status—single, married, or widowed.
2. Number of children at home.
3. Age of children at home.
4. Working status of head of household—working versus retired.

Note that, unlike social classes, it will be difficult for FLC to be collectively exhaustive. In other words, not all people in our society can be placed in some stage of the FLC. Single people, divorced, and so forth are often excluded. However, this does not make the classification system any less useful. *Most* people in the United States get married, *most*

---

[6] For a discussion of the value of the FLC concept, see J. B. Lansing and L. Kish, "Family Life Cycle as an Independent Variable," *American Sociological Review* (October 1957), pp. 512–19; and E. P. Cox, III, "Family Purchase Decision Making and the Process of Adjustment," *Journal of Marketing Research* (May 1975), pp. 189–95.

people have children, *most* children leave home sometime between the ages of 18 and 22, and *most* people retire at some point (generally around the age of 65). Thus, the FLC is a useful concept for analyzing and predicting the consumption patterns of many consumers.

Each stage in the family life cycle poses a series of problems which family decision makers must solve. The solution to these problems is intimately bound to the selection and maintenance of a lifestyle and thus to product consumption. For example, all young married couples with no children face a need for relaxation or recreation. Resolutions to this common problem will differ. Some will opt for an outdoors-oriented lifestyle and will consume camping equipment and related products. Others will choose a "sophisticated" urban lifestyle and will consume tickets to the theater and opera, restaurant meals, and so forth. The solutions differ but they are addressed to the same general problem. As these families move into the next stage in the FLC, generally the "young married, youngest child under six" stage, the problems they face will change. The amount of time and resources available for recreation will diminish. New problems relating to "raising" a family will become more urgent.

Most of the remainder of this section is devoted to a description of the various stages in the FLC and the consumption problems posed by each stage. First, we want to relate the FLC to the individual life cycle. Table 9−2 presents a combination of the individual and family life cycles showing the approximate age range, the major lifestyle problems and tasks, the income-to-expense ratio, and the approximate numbers of individuals or families by each stage. The individual is stressed throughout the family of orientation period. The individual is also the primary unit in the intermediate period when he or she often lives alone or with other unrelated individuals after leaving the family of orientation. Once a new family unit is formed, the emphasis shifts from the individual to the family as the unit of analysis.

Obviously, the individual and family life cycles are interrelated. For example, the infant and preschool stages coexist with the young married, youngest child under six stage. For analytical purposes, it is useful to focus on individual processes in analyzing child development and socialization. Chapter 11 deals with individual life cycles through teenage and discusses how these consumers are socialized. FLC only includes the stages beginning with the young single and hence deals with the family of procreation, not the family of orientation.

The following sections describe each stage of the FLC. A series of tables are presented in support of some of the generalizations. An examination of these tables reveals the fact that they use differing parameters for the various stages of the FLC. This reflects one of the primary practical problems involved in utilizing the FLC—there is no widely accepted and used set of operational definitions for each stage of the cycle.

TABLE 9–2
Characteristics of the individual and family life cycles

		Family type: Orientation		
Category	General range age	Major lifestyle problems and tasks	Income/ Expense ratio	Size (000)*
Infant	0–2	No expected tasks. Completely cared for by other family members. A major focus of attention and concern by others.	—	9,030†
Preschool	3–5	Has developed a definite personality. Can interact and communicate well with others. Still largely cared for but expected to conform to basic family behavior patterns.	—	9,877†
Preteenage	6–12	Through interaction with peers and experience with extra-family institutions (school, church, etc.) a definite lifestyle approach begins to emerge. Task responsibilities, both in and out of the family, begin to be assigned.	Moderate	25,316†
Teenager	13–18	Development of an independent lifestyle. Many identification problems. Relationship with family begins to be strained as need for independence increases.	Moderate	25,220†
Young single	19–44	Attainment of independent lifestyle. Mate search and selection. Occupation choice and preparation.	High	8,350†
Older single	45–64	Adjustment to divorce and/or renewed mate search, career advancement.	Very high	5,034†

TABLE 9–2 (continued)

		Family type: Procreation		
Category	General range age	Major lifestyle problems and tasks	Income/ Expense ratio	Size (000)*
Younger married, no children	20–44	Development of a joint lifestyle. Career decisions and development.	High	5,134‡
Younger married, youngest child under 6	20–38	Adjustment to parenthood. Decline in discretionary income, decline in freedom. Career development, raising a family.	Low	11,014‡
Married, youngest child 6–18	30–55	Career advancement and moves. Acceptance of a stable lifestyle.	Moderate	13,913‡
Older married, no children home	45–65	Adjustment to removal of children. Realization of a finite lifespan. Career stabilization/decline.	High	10,518‡
Married, retired	60–85	Adjustment to retirement. Health problems. Adjustment to reduced income.	Low	6,248‡
Solitary survivor, retired	60–85	Adjustment to loss of mate. Health problems.	Low	6,851†

* Size estimates are only rough approximations and, for the family of procreation groups, do not correspond precisely with the general age range shown in the table. Note also that the units are sometimes shown as individuals and sometimes as families. Size is as of 1976.

† Individuals.

‡ Families.

Source: The size estimates are derived from U.S. Bureau of the Census, *Current Population Reports,* "Estimates of the Population of the United States by Age, Sex, and Race: July 1, 1974 to 1976," series P–25, no. 643 (1977); and "Household and Family Characteristics: March 1976," series P–20, no. 311.

Young single

The young single group is composed of unmarried individuals between 19 and 44 years of age with the vast majority under 26. This group exists between the family of orientation and the family of procreation. Obviously, some individuals marry without spending any time "on their own." However, most Americans spend at least some time in this stage. As the value placed on early marriage, particularly for women, continues to decline, the average length of time spent in this stage of the FLC will increase.[7] The impact of this trend will be partially offset by the declining percentage of the population contained within this general age group (see Table 6−1).

As Table 9−2 indicates, the ratio of income to expenses is relatively high in this stage. Most members of this group live in rented housing and frequently share these expenses with other individuals. Good health, limited use of savings and insurance, and limited expenditures on others produces the relatively high level of discretionary income despite relatively low levels of absolute income.

Individuals in this group are generally attempting to evolve and develop their own lifestyle. They want to establish a lifestyle independent of the lifestyle associated with their family of orientation. This represents an extension of a process begun during the teenage stage in the family of orientation. There is considerable experimentation with various lifestyles and consumption patterns during this stage. Many individuals view their style of life during this stage as temporary and take a short-run time perspective toward their consumption decisions. Most anticipate marriage and substantial lifestyle changes before reaching 30.

In addition to developing an independent lifestyle, two major activities occur during this stage: (1) mate search and selection, and (2) occupational selection and preparation. The mate search and selection process becomes intertwined with the general recreational patterns of this group and occupies a substantial amount of time and effort. Occupational choice and preparation serves to determine the income patterns, educational attainment, reference groups, and ultimate social class of the individual. Despite the importance of the occupational decision, most individuals approach it rather casually.

Table 9−3 provides some evidence of the state of mind of individuals during this stage. The picture presented in this table is less rosy than the stereotype of the "swinging singles." A substantial percentage feel life is hard, and only half express a high degree of satisfaction with life as a whole. However, feeling tied down, rushed, or worried about bills is limited at this stage. In general, men are substantially more pleased with this time of their lives than are women. Advertising appeals that recognize the psychological stresses that occur during this period may be particularly effective.

Table 9−4 illustrates the propensity to eat out in the evening by the stages in the FLC. This table can be used as a reasonably accurate indicator of the general usage of evening activities outside the home. As the

---

[7] For a discussion of this phenomenon see P. C. Glick, *Current Population Reports,* "Some Recent Changes in American Families," series P−23, no. 52 (1975).

TABLE 9–3
Psychological stress and satisfaction at stages of the family life cycle

	Percent who									
	Feel life is hard		Feel tied down		Always feel rushed		Worry some about bills		Are satisfied with life as a whole	
Stage in the life cycle	Male	Female	Male	Female	Male	Female	Male	Female	Male	Female
Never married, between ages of 18 and 29	27	35	15	19	13	16	22	33	46	57
Married, 18 to 29, no children	34	18	14	4	24	13	38	20	72	89
Married, youngest child less than 6	34	28	25	25	23	28	47	46	64	65
Married, youngest child 6 to 17	30	24	14	11	29	28	44	38	65	67
Married, youngest child over 17	25	15	7	12	21	17	24	24	66	69
Widowed	28	23	6	12	8	12	27	29	50	56
Married, over 29, no children	20	18	11	12	18	25	22	24	75	69
Never married, over 29	23	19	10	13	5	26	28	39	41	53
Divorced or separated	25	42	15	20	12	34	35	63	42	33

Source: Derived from A. Campbell, P. E. Converse, and W. L. Rodgers, *The Quality of American Life* (Russell Sage Foundation, 1976). © 1976 by Russell Sage Foundation, New York.

TABLE 9–4

Eating out in the evenings by stage in the family life cycle

Stage in the family life cycle	Index of eating out			
	Frequently	Sometimes	Seldom	Never
Single	133	111	93	86
Married	95	103	110	92
Widowed/divorced/separated	83	74	63	153
Parents	75	100	128	86
No child in home	120	99	78	111
Child less than 2	62	101	126	93
Child 2–5	69	96	124	95
Child 6–11	77	99	121	93
Child 12–17	82	97	116	96

* The index is derived by dividing the percentage of individuals in a given group that engage in the specific pattern of behavior by the percentage of the total population contained in that group. The higher the index number the more that group engages in that behavior relative to the general population.

Source: Derived from *Spring 1976 Target Group Index*. Used with the permission of the copyright holder, Axiom Market Research Bureau, Inc.

table indicates, young singles are particularly heavy consumers of this type of product. This high level of consumption of evening activities is related to the high income/expense ratio, the mate search, and the desire for companionship that is not available in an empty apartment. Among other things, the use of nonhome evening entertainment suggests that evening television could be an inefficient way to reach this market.

Table 9–5 shows the propensity to purchase various products by stage in the FLC. Singles are particularly good markets for recreational equipment (camping and backpacking), entertainment (combination stereo equipment), and specialized items with sexual connotations (waterbeds). The importance of the situation in market segmentation can also be seen in this table. Singles have the highest propensity to purchase combination stereo equipment when the purchase is for their personal use. However, when the purchase is a *gift* for another, parents with teenage children are the most likely purchasers. In general, singles are limited gift givers. Singles are also a limited market for household items and children's products.

Singles not only purchase different items but they have unique purchasing styles. Table 9–6 shows some of the purchasing strategies used at various stages in the FLC. Singles appear to be particularly susceptible to peer group influences, to experimentation, to impulse purchases, and to style-oriented purchasing.

Older singles

The older single group is composed primarily of two types of members: (1) the never marrieds, and (2) the divorced. Most divorced individ-

TABLE 9–5
Index of purchases by stage in the family life cycle (purchased in past year for self)*

Stage in the life cycle	Combination stereo equipment (for self)	Combination stereo equipment (for other)	Encyclopedia	Massager	Camping backpacking	Microwave oven	Piano	Children's furniture	Water beds
Single	161	62	46	53	148	92	46	39	235
Married	97	124	119	108	103	115	119	129	76
Widowed/divorced/separated	43	35	74	116	34	42	73	36	54
Parents	104	158	173	88	122	117	173	188	65
No child in household	83	49	36	121	80	91	46	32	114
Child less than 2	93	93	160	53	101	77	119	502	94
Child 2–5	122	97	274	85	136	56	122	224	129
Child 6–11	113	141	177	96	138	143	186	122	87
Child 12–17	110	182	90	68	107	115	126	64	69

* The index is derived by dividing the percentage of total purchases that a given group contains by the percentage of the total population contained in that group. The higher the index number the more that group purchases the product relative to the general population. An index of 100 represents a purchase rate similar to the general population.
Source: Derived from the Spring 1976 Target Group Index. Used with the permission of the copyright holder, Axiom Market Research Bureau, Inc.

TABLE 9-6
Index of buying styles by stage in family life cycle*

				Stage in the life cycle					
Buying style	Single	Married	Widowed/divorced/separated	Parents	No child in household	Child less than 2	Child 2–5	Child 6–11	Child 12–17
Brand loyal: I always look for the name of the manufacturer on the package	82	105	99	100	105	93	93	97	96
Cautious: I do not buy unknown brands merely to save money	83	103	106	97	108	83	86	91	95
Conformists: I prefer to buy things that my friends or neighbors would approve of	128	92	102	82	112	99	73	80	95
Ecologists: All products that pollute the environment should be banned	97	99	111	92	110	88	91	90	89
Economy minded: I shop around a lot to take advantage of specials or bargains	81	105	97	106	97	107	102	101	107
Experimenters: I like to change brands often for the sake of variety and novelty	115	98	94	100	98	107	100	96	101
Impulsive: When in the store, I often buy an item on the spur of the moment	109	98	100	102	97	109	104	105	97
Persuadable: In general, advertising presents a true picture of the products of well-known companies	91	102	103	98	105	103	95	91	97
Planners: I generally plan far ahead to buy expensive items such as automobiles	94	105	84	101	101	98	98	97	98
Style conscious: I try to keep abreast of changes in styles and fashions	113	96	104	97	101	106	96	98	100

* The index is derived by dividing the percentage of total users of a style that a given group contains by the percentage of the total population.
Source: Derived from the *Spring 1976 Target Group Index*. Used with the permission of the copyright holder, Axiom Market Research Bureau, Inc.

uals eventually remarry and tend to view their membership in this category as a temporary phenomenon. The never marrieds are more likely to view their position as permanent. For a substantial number, the search for a mate continues but with less energy and sense of urgency than during the earlier years. For the never marrieds, careers are generally developing and consuming time and energies. For the divorced, finances are often a renewed problem with many women entering the work force in low paying jobs and many men making child support and/or alimony payments.

Table 9—3 allows us to compare these two groups of older (over 30) singles with each other and with other stages in the FLC on several psychological dimensions. In general, never marrieds are more content than divorced individuals. Within each group, men are generally more content than women. Divorced or separated women are particularly concerned about bills, and only a third express a high degree of satisfaction with their life as a whole. Compared to younger singles, the older never marrieds are somewhat more worried about bills but otherwise tend to be more pleased with their lives.

Unfortunately, there is a lack of data concerning the purchasing patterns of this group. In fact, this group represents one of the least studied market segments. Yet Table 9—3 suggests that they differ from other stages in the life cycle along several psychological dimensions. In addition, as Table 9—2 illustrates, older singles represent a large group with a relatively high level of disposable income. Finally, it appears that this group will increase in importance as the age distribution of the population shifts over the next 10 to 20 years. Therefore, it appears marketers should focus additional attention on this market segment. The never-married segment in particular may represent a major market for high-quality items of all types.

Younger married, no children

Young people may enter marriage directly upon leaving the family of orientation or after a period of independence as a young single. In either case, the primary task facing the young couple is to develop a joint lifestyle that is acceptable to both partners. This frequently involves experimentation, conflict, and compromise. Since many young couples live a substantial distance from their parents, other young couples may serve as primary role models (someone whose behavior is observed and often copied). Many couples take a relatively short-run time perspective concerning the lifestyles they develop during this stage in the FLC. These couples anticipate major changes after they "have kids and settle down."

While they are developing a joint lifestyle, one and often both spouses are also developing a career. While most wives work during this stage, some view this as a temporary position until children are born. Increasingly, however, both spouses view their careers as lifetime commitments. This produces conflicts and marital strain when the requirements of one spouse's job conflicts with the requirements of the other's. The solutions to these conflicts may alter the nature of the family's decision making for a wide range of activities and products.[8]

Table 9–3 shows that males and females react very differently to this stage of the life cycle. Males appear to have substantially more difficulty adjusting to marriage than do females. Advertisers aiming at this group could utilize these concerns of the husband to create more effective copy. Despite the specific concerns of the husbands, both males and females express as much or more satisfaction with life as a whole during this stage than any other stage in the FLC.

Tables 9–4, 9–5, and 9–6 are difficult to use with respect to this group since the category "no children in the house" includes both young and older couples. There is evidence in Table 9–4 that young marrieds represent a prime market segment for evening entertainment outside the house. Table 9–5 indicates that they may be heavy consumers of such semiluxury home products as waterbeds. In fact, other sources indicate that newlyweds constitute a major market segment for most home appliances, sewing machines, kitchenware, and so forth. The importance of this market can be seen in the estimate that 58 percent of all sterling flatware is purchased by or for couples within three months of marriage.[9]

Table 9–6 implies that peer group influence is strong at this stage, as is a concern for ecology. The general picture that emerges is of a couple with a relatively high level of disposable income (both spouses working and limited fixed expenses) which enables them to pursue an active, externally oriented lifestyle.

Married, youngest child under six

The arrival of the first child generally results in a major adjustment in the lifestyle of the couple. The medical expenses associated with the child's birth and the acquisition of clothing, baby furniture, and so forth reduces or eliminates the couple's liquid assets and may produce short-term debt. The expenses of clothing, feeding, and caring for the child continue after the initial expenses have been covered. This increase in expense is generally accompanied by a sharp decline in income as the wife frequently withdraws from the labor force. In fact, only a third of those women with a child under three are employed.[10]

---

[8] For a discussion of this issue, see J. Scanzoni, "Changing Sex Roles and Emerging Directions in Family Decision Making," *Journal of Consumer Research* (December 1977), pp. 185–88.

[9] B. J. Wattenberg, "The Forming-Families: The Spark in the Tinder, 1975–1985," in *Marketing in Turbulent Times*, ed. E. M. Mazze (American Marketing Association, 1975), p. 54.

[10] W. Lazer, and J. E. Smallwood, "The Changing Demographics of Women," *Journal of Marketing* (July 1977), p. 17.

Table 9–3 reflects some of the psychological stress that occurs during this stage of the FLC. This period is especially difficult for women, with a substantial minority reporting that they feel "tied down" and "rushed." About half of both males and females report worrying about bills, and there is a sharp decline in the percentage reporting satisfaction with life as a whole.

The reduced level of disposable income and the cost and effort involved in using babysitters results in a dramatic reduction in evening activities outside the home. This is clearly reflected in Table 9–4. Table 9–7 also supports this contention. Here we see that families with chil-

TABLE 9–7
The impact of children on television viewing*

Program	All age groups	Age of children			
		0–2	2–5	6–11	12–17
"Baretta"	120	131	128	114	110
"Happy Days"	125	154	132	122	117
"Welcome Back, Kotter"	127	160	148	121	110
"Starsky & Hutch"	122	138	139	126	107
"Rhoda"	97	119	107	92	83
"CBS Thursday Night Movie"	112	120	120	111	107
"Rockford Files"	98	111	102	99	91
"General Hospital"	106	172	140	100	88
"Days of Our Lives"	119	171	151	121	95
"Love of Life"	114	185	143	115	98

* The index is derived by dividing the percentage of total viewers that a given group contains by the percentage of the total population contained in that group. The higher the index number the more that group views the show relative to the general population. An index of 100 represents a viewing rate similar to the general population.
Source: Derived from the *Spring 1976 Target Group Index.* Used with permission of the copyright holder. Axiom Market Research Bureau, Inc.

dren are above-average viewers of evening television programs. Furthermore, the younger the child, the greater the tendency to watch most programs.

Table 9–5 illustrates some of the purchase patterns of this group. The purchasing of such necessities as children's furniture is clearly evident as is the purchase of child-centered luxuries such as encyclopedias and pianos. In addition, family recreation items such as camping equipment become popular as the child grows older.

A mixed pattern of purchasing styles is reflected in Table 9–6; the financial status of the household is reflected in the economy-minded orientation. However, the need for new products and a lack of familiarity with many of these products is reflected in the experimentation, impulsive orientations. The style consciousness of this group probably reflects their youth as much as anything.

Married, youngest child six to 18

During this stage of the FLC the family unit is characterized by activity. One or both parent's careers are advancing. The children are becoming more mobile and independent. They are involved in school, school activities, and other youth-oriented activities. The members of the family are learning to adjust to each other as they grow and change over time. Parents tend to be concerned with "getting along with" and "raising" the kids. A number of families, particularly lower-income families, have a female head of household by now because of divorce.

Table 9−3 shows an increase in satisfaction with life during this stage. Indeed, the only measure of stress to increase is the feeling of being rushed. This is associated with the need to support the children in their various activities as well as attend to careers. This feeling of being rushed is heightened by the fact that many women return to work during this period. Reflecting this feeling of being rushed is a positive orientation toward convenience goods.[11]

Table 9−4 indicates a substantial increase in evening activity over the stage in which younger children are present. This trend is probably stronger than suggested by Table 9−4 since it shows the presence of any children in the age category, not just the youngest child (the same is true for Table 9−5, 9−6, and 9−7). Table 9−7 reflects this increase in evening activities by showing a decline in evening television viewing.

There is an increase in luxury purchases both for the parents and as gifts for the children. Table 9−5 shows increased purchases of combination stereo equipment (for self and for gifts), microwave ovens, pianos, and backpacking equipment. Purchasing strategies become very diverse during this stage. Economy is still important while conformity and ecology are relatively unimportant (Table 9−6).

Married, no children at home

This group is composed of older families whose children have left home and families who have never had children. The former group of families must adjust to the fact that their children are grown, which is sometimes difficult, particularly for the mother. As Table 9−3 shows, both groups are content with life as a whole and with specific aspects of their life. The improved financial status that typically occurs during this stage is reflected in the sharp decrease in the number who report worrying about bills.

Tables 9−4 through 9−6 do not allow us to separate this group from retired couples or younger couples with no children. However, a number of characteristics of this group are apparent. They tend to be in good

---

[11] W. T. Anderson, Jr., "Identifying the Convenience-Oriented Consumer," *Journal of Marketing Research* (May 1971), pp. 181−82.

health and to have relatively high levels of discretionary income. They constitute a primary market for vacation services and for quality home furnishings. They can afford nicer automobiles and more expensive restaurants and clothes. Advertisements aimed at these "empty nesters" by the Old West Regional Commission (a tourism group) for example, appeal to this group's ability to travel independent of child-school responsibilities and touts the advantages of being together and rediscovering each other. Luxury products that there was either not income for or time for previously are realistic purchases for this group. As the population distribution continues to shift (see Chapter 6), this group will become the most important single market segment for a wide range of quality products.

Married, retired, and solitary survivor, retired

We will consider these two groups together. However, widows (most solitary survivors are female) frequently suffer more from loneliness, reduced income, and general dissatisfaction with life than retired couples. Generally, income drops rather sharply with retirement while expenses decline only slightly. Thus, discretionary income is often reduced substantially. It has been suggested that the spending power of the elderly will improve over the next two decades.[12] The extent to which this will occur depends largely on the inflation rate and the ability of the elderly to develop effective political power.[13]

The elderly tend to spend proportionally more of their income on housing, food, medical care, and gifts than the nonelderly.[14] They are frequently among the last to adopt new products and ideas.[15] Thus, new products and services aimed at the elderly market should be closely tied to existing products if possible. If not, free samples or easy trial should be made available.

Reflecting the limited discretionary income is a heightened degree of price sensitivity among this group.[16] Restricted physical mobility may reduce shopping behavior and the distance traveled to shop. For those with limited ability to shop, convenient locations, mail and telephone shopping, and home delivery may be important. The development of

---

[12] J. Schuly, *The Search for Retirement Income Adequacy* (Brandeis Univeriity Press, 1975).

[13] For a discussion of this issue, see B. D. Geld, "Gray Power: Next Challenge to Business," *Business Horizons* (April 1977), pp. 38–45.

[14] "Expenditure Patterns of Welfare, Aged and Disabled Households," *Social Security Bulletin* (August 1974), p. 41.

[15] T. S. Robertson, *Innovative Behavior and Communication* (Holt, Rinehart and Winston, 1971), pp. 100, 131.

[16] See J. Howell and D. Loeb, "Income, Age and Food Consumption," *Gerontologist* (February 1975), pp. 7–16; and J. McCann, "Market Segment Response to the Marketing Decision Variables," *Journal of Marketing Research* (November 1974), pp. 399–412.

retirement centers which concentrate numerous elderly individuals may make such services as home delivery economically viable.

The elderly tend to use different sources of information and to process this information differently than younger consumers.[17] The elderly tend to reduce their contacts with social groups as they age but maintain close contacts with the extended family and nearby friends. They tend to utilize the mass media more for information than do younger individuals and they make more use of newspapers. With increasing age, individuals appear less able to process information that is presented rapidly.

Conclusions on the family life cycle

In summary, it can be seen that the FLC is a very useful tool for the marketing manager of many products to use to identify market segments and explain their behavior. Other, similar concepts, such as social class, can frequently be combined with FLC to provide an even more meaningful picture of consumer markets.

For example, in a study for a savings and loan association, one of the authors used the FLC/social class (SC) matrix shown in Table 9−8 to

TABLE 9–8
Market segment identification matrix

Stage in family life cycle	Social class by occupation		
	Working class	White collar	Management/ professional
Young single			
Younger married, no children			
Younger married with children			
Older married, no children at home			
Married, retired			
Solitary survivor, retired			

identify relevant market segments. The association was in a geographical area that traditionally had attracted a large number of retired or semiretired people who were good savings customers. They seemed to repre-

---

[17] An overview of this area is provided by L. W. Phillips and B. Sternthal, "Age Differences in Information Processing: A Perspective on the Aged Consumer," *Journal of Marketing Research* (November 1977), pp. 444−45. The following generalizations are derived from this review.

sent the largest market segment, and hence a majority of the association's marketing effort was directed at them. It was felt that this might not be an extremely profitable segment because they tended to initially deposit money and then over time reduce that amount in order to meet living expenses.

In order to try and define other relevant market segments, the FLC was felt to be a logical starting place because of a natural relationship between saving and a family's financial needs. The need to save for emergencies, children's schooling, retirement, and so forth appears to be a major family concern. Not all families at the same stage of the FLC can afford to save nor do they feel about saving in the same way. Hence, it was felt that another variable, occupation as a measure of social class, would provide a finer definition. Occupation should reflect income differences reasonably well and also orientations to future savings versus present expenditures. Based on the FLC and the occupational categories of working, white collar, and managerial/professional, one could hypothesize that younger married with children in the white-collar and, particularly, the managerial/professional class would be an excellent target market. These people have higher incomes and family responsibilities that increase their potential as good savings customers. They are oriented to future planning, anticipate sending their children to college, see the need for retirement savings, plan early in their career and so forth.

In the study conducted to determine size and potential of market segments, the hypothesized FLC/SC group proved to be the ideal target market. They had a high motivation to save and the income necessary, and were likely to leave the money in for a long time as opposed to withdrawing it on a regular basis. The association changed its marketing activities (types of accounts, advertising appeals, branch locations) to take advantage of this previously neglected market.

FAMILY DECISION MAKING

It should be obvious that decisions made by and/or for a group such as a family may differ in important respects from completely individual decisions. Since marketers frequently wish to influence the decisions made by families, it is essential to understand *how* consumption decisions are made within the family unit.[18] For example, recall the purchasing process for crayons described at the beginning of this chapter in which the child used the product but the mother recognized the problem, evaluated the alternatives, and made the purchase.[19]

---

[18] An overview of this area and the research issues involved is presented by H. L. Davis "Decision Making within the Household," *Journal of Consumer Research* (March 1976), pp. 241–60. See also R. Ferber, "Family Decision Making and Economic Behavior: A Review," in *Family Economic Behavior*, ed. E. B. Sheldon (J. B. Lippincott Co., 1973), pp. 29–61.

[19] "Research, High TV Costs."

Suppose you are the marketing manager for a firm that has developed a new breakfast cereal with nutritional content particularly appropriate for children. Do you try to persuade the child, the mother, or the father to purchase the item? Who in the family would recognize the problem? Seek out information? Evaluate the information? Make the purchase? Consume the product? Evaluate the product? Would the same individual perform each of these activities or would different members of the family be involved at each stage? How would disagreements be resolved? Are the answers to the above questions general or do they vary by culture, subculture, social class, stage in the family life cycle, and so forth?

Obviously, we are entering a complex area. Furthermore, marketing researchers only recently began considering these questions. There are still a large number of unresolved issues. As we will see by the end of this section, however, enough is known to provide a research framework for any specific product category.

Prior to beginning our discussion, two cautions are appropriate. First, virtually all studies to date have focused not on family decision making but on husband-wife decision making. The influence of children has been largely ignored. Yet there is evidence that children often exert a substantial influence on the consumption process.[20] Second, most studies have focused on direct influence and ignored indirect influence. Thus, a husband might report purchasing an automobile without discussing it with any member of his family. Yet he might purchase a blue station wagon to meet his perceptions of the demands of the family rather than the red sports car that he would personally prefer. Most research studies would classify the above decision as strictly husband dominated. Clearly, however, other family members influenced the decision.

Family member involvement by stage in the consumption process

At any stage of the consumption process one or more members of the family may be involved. Involvement is not an either/or proposition but rather one of degree. For example, one spouse may examine a large number of automobiles and eventually narrow the alternatives down to three. At this point, the other spouse becomes involved and helps make the final choice. Both spouses were involved in the alternative evaluation stage but one was more involved than the other.

One of the more consistent findings of research in this area is that which family members are involved varies by the stage of the consumption process. Table 9 – 9 illustrates this point for two products the use of

---

[20] J. L. Turk and N. W. Bell, "Measuring Power in Families," *Journal of Marriage and the Family* (May 1972), pp. 215– 22; and E. H. Bonfield, "Perceptions of Marital Roles in Decision Processes: Replication and Extensions," in *Advances in Consumer Research V,* ed. H. K. Hunt (Association for Consumer Research, 1978), pp. 300 – 7.

TABLE 9–9
Family role structures across decision stages within service decisions

Decision stages	Role structures (percent)*						
	(1)	(2)	(3)	(4)	(5)	(6)	(7)
Fast food restaurant							
Initiate purchase	1%	—	6%	11%	11%	16%	55%
Provide information	—	3%	4	10	8	14	61
Final decision	1	1	10	4	5	8	71
Family trip							
Initiate purchase	4	2	34	2	4	6	48
Provide information	4	4	35	—	6	4	47
Final decision	4	1	37	1	1	2	54

* Role structures: (1) Husband, (2) wife, (3) husband and wife, (4) child/children, (5) husband and child, (6) wife and child, (7) husband, wife and child. Sample size = 190.
Source: G. J. Szybillo and A. Sosanie, "Family Decision Making: Huband, Wife and Children" in *Advances in Consumer Research IV*, ed. W. D. Perreault, Jr. (Association for Consumer Research, 1977), p. 47. Used with permission.

which affects the entire family. For these products, there is an increase in multimember involvement as one moves from initiating the purchase to making the final decision. A study focusing on husband-wife decision making found a similar pattern for a number of other products.[21]

Family decision making not only allows different family members to become involved at different stages of the process, it also makes it possible for different members to make specific subdecisions of the overall decision. When an individual makes a decision, he or she evaluates all the relevant attributes of each alternative and combines these evaluations into a single decision. In a family decision, different members often focus on specific attributes. For example, a child may evaluate the taste of a cereal while a parent evaluates its cost and nutritional value. Table 9–10 illustrates this process for automobiles and home furniture.[22] Table 9–10 not only indicates that family members make specific sub-

---

[21] H. L. Davis and B. P. Regaux, "Perception of Marital Roles in Decision Process," *Journal of Consumer Research* (June 1974), pp. 51–61. See also R. L. Wilkes, "Husband-Wife Influence in Purchase Decisions—A Confirmation and Extension," *Journal of Marketing Research* (May 1975), pp. 224–27.

[22] For additional evidence, see D. J. Hempel, "Family Buying Decisions: A Cross-Cultural Perspective," *Journal of Marketing Research* (August 1974), pp. 295–302; A. G. Woodside, "Effects of Prior Decision-Making, Demographics and Psychographics on Marital Roles for Purchasing Durables," in *Advances in Consumer Research II*, ed. M. J. Schlinger (Association for Consumer Research, 1975), pp. 81–91; G. M. Munsinger, J. E. Weber, and R. W. Hansen, "Joint Home Purchasing Decisions by Husbands and Wives," *Journal of Consumer Research* (March 1975), pp. 60–66; A. C. Burns, "Spousal Involvement and Empathy in Jointly-Resolved and Authoritatively-Resolved Purchase Subdecisions," in *Advances in Consumer Research III*, ed. B. B. Anderson (Association for Consumer Research, 1976), pp. 199–207; G. J. Szybillo and A. Sosanie, "Family Decision Making: Husband, Wife and Children," in *Advances in Consumer Research IV*, ed. W. D. Perreault, Jr. (Association for Consumer Research, 1977), pp. 46–49; and A. C. Burns and D. H. Granbois, "Factors Moderating the Resolution of Preference Conflict in Family Automobile Purchasing," *Journal of Marketing Research* (February 1977), pp. 77–86.

TABLE 9–10

Family member variation in attribute evaluation in automobile and furniture
purchase decisions

	Patterns of influence (percent)		
	Husband has more influence than wife	Husband and wife have equal influence	Wife has more influence than husband
Automobile purchase			
When to buy the automobile?	68%	29%	3%
Where to buy the automobile?	62	35	3
How much to spend for the automobile?	62	37	1
What make of automobile to buy?	60	32	8
What model of automobile to buy?	41	50	9
What color of automobile to buy?	25	50	25
Furniture purchase			
How much to spend for furniture?	22	47	31
When to buy furniture?	16	45	39
Where to buy furniture?	7	53	40
What furniture to buy?	3	33	64
What style of furniture to buy?	2	26	72
What color and fabric to buy?	2	16	82

Source: H. L. Davis, "Dimensions of Marital Roles in Consumer Decision Making," *Journal of Marketing Research* (American Marketing Association, May 1970), p. 169.

decisions or evaluations within the overall decision, it also indicates that there is considerable variation across products and across families. This emphasizes the point that *the marketing manager must analyze the family decision process separately for each product category within each target market.*

What factors influence involvement by a family member in a purchase decision? *Involvement* with the product is probably the most important single determinant. This is clearly indicated in Table 9–11 which shows children's requests for products and the mother's granting of these requests to be closely related to the child's involvement (interest and use) with the product. Similar results were found in an analysis of husband-wife evaluations of specific attributes across a variety of decisions.[23] The degree to which the purchase of one product will influence the family's ability to purchase other products, that is, the purchase of an expensive item, also increases the involvement of other family members.[24]

---

[23] Burns, "Spousal Involvement." See also S. Mehrotra and S. Torges, "Determinants of Children's Influence on Mother's Buying Behavior," in *Advances in Consumer Research IV*, ed. W. D. Perreault, Jr. (Association for Consumer Research, 1977), pp. 56–60.

[24] R. Ferber, "Applications of Behavioral Theories to the Study of Family Marketing Behavior," in *Behavioral Models for Market Analysis*, eds. F. N. Nicosia and Y. Wind (Dryden Press, 1977), p. 89.

TABLE 9–11

Frequency of children's attempts to influence purchases and percentages of mothers "usually" yielding

Products	Frequency of requests*				Percentage of yielding			
	5–7 years	8–10 years	11–12 years	Total†	5–7 years	8–10 years	11–12 years	Total†
Relevant foods:								
Breakfast cereal	1.26	1.59	1.97	1.59	88.0	91.0	83.0	87.0
Snack foods	1.71	2.00	1.71	1.80	52.0	62.0	77.0	63.0
Candy	1.60	2.09	2.17	1.93	40.0	28.0	57.0	42.0
Soft drinks	2.00	2.03	2.00	2.01	38.0	47.0	54.0	46.0
Jello-o	2.54	2.94	2.97	2.80	40.0	41.0	26.0	36.0
Overall mean	1.82	2.13	2.16	2.03				
Overall percentage					51.6	53.8	59.4	54.8
Less relevant foods:								
Bread	3.12	2.91	3.43	3.16	14.0	28.0	17.0	19.0
Coffee	3.93	3.91	3.97	3.94	2.0	0.0	0.0	1.0
Pet food	3.29	3.59	3.24	3.36	7.0	3.0	11.0	7.0
Overall mean	3.45	3.47	3.49	3.49				
Overall percentage					7.6	10.3	9.3	9.0
Durables, for child's use:								
Games, toys	1.24	1.63	2.17	1.65	57.0	59.0	46.0	54.0
Clothing	2.76	2.47	2.29	2.52	21.0	34.0	57.0	37.0
Bicycle	2.48	2.59	2.77	2.61	7.0	9.0	9.0	8.0
Hot wheels	2.43	2.41	3.20	2.67	29.0	19.0	17.0	22.0
Record album	3.36	2.63	2.23	2.78	12.0	16.0	46.0	24.0
Camera	3.91	3.75	3.71	3.80	2.0	3.0	0.0	2.0
Overall mean	2.70	2.58	2.73	2.67				
Overall percentage					25.6	28.0	35.0	29.4
Notions, toiletries:								
Toothpaste	2.29	2.31	2.60	2.39	36.0	44.0	40.0	39.0
Bath soap	3.10	2.97	3.46	3.17	9.0	9.0	9.0	9.0
Shampoo	3.48	3.31	3.03	3.28	17.0	6.0	23.0	16.0
Aspirin	3.64	3.78	3.97	3.79	5.0	6.0	0.0	4.0
Overall mean	3.13	3.09	3.26	3.16				
Overall percentage					16.8	16.3	18.0	17.0
Other products:								
Automobile	3.55	3.66	3.51	3.57	2.0	0.0	0.0	1.0
Gasoline brand	3.64	3.63	3.83	3.70	2.0	0.0	3.0	2.0
Laundry soap	3.69	3.75	3.71	3.72	2.0	0.0	3.0	2.0
Household cleaner	3.71	3.84	3.74	3.76	2.0	3.0	0.0	2.0
Overall mean	3.65	3.72	3.70	3.69				
Overall percentage					2.0	0.75	1.50	1.75

* On a scale from 1 (often) to 4 (never).

† For 5–7 years, $n = 43$; 8–10 years, $n = 32$; 11–12 years, $n = 34$; total $n = 109$.

Source: S. Ward and D. B. Wackman, "Children's Purchase Influence Attempts and Parental Yielding," *Journal of Marketing Research* (American Marketing Association, August 1972), p. 317.

Role specialization within the family influences which family members are most likely to be directly involved in a purchase decision. Role specialization takes time to develop. Thus we find joint decision making more common in younger and relatively new families.[25] The develop-

---

[25] Ibid.

TABLE 9–12
Identity of family financial officer by year of marriage

Family financial officer	Year of marriage	
	First	Second
Husband	26%	27%
Wife	25	36
Both	49	37

Source: R. Ferber and L. C. Lee, "Husband-Wife Influence in Family Purchasing Behavior," *Journal of Consumer Research* (June 1974), p. 45.

ment of role specialization over time is illustrated in Table 9—12. As can be seen, joint decision making with respect to financial affairs dropped dramatically between the first and second year of marriage. Role specialization does *not* mean that the desires of other family members are ignored. In fact, it probably reflects the fact that one member of the family has developed the ability to effectively recognize and solve certain problems for other family members without their direct input or participation.

The nature of role specialization and the product categories which individual family members become involved with are related to the demographic characteristics of the family and the intrapersonal characteristics of the individual family members. For example, a child's age is directly related to the mother's tendency to grant the child's request for any given product as can be seen in Table 9—11.[26] Middle-class families tend to engage in more joint decision making than upper- or lower-class families.[27] Wives with a modern or liberated view of the female role tend to be more active in the decision-making process, particularly the financial aspects of this process, than more traditional wives. This difference is most pronounced in younger families with relatively high incomes.[28]

Conflict resolution within the decision process

Conflicts between family members may arise at any stage of the decision process. Perhaps the most frequent areas of conflict are (1) whether or not a problem is of sufficient magnitude to require a solution and (2) the evaluative criteria to be used in reaching a decision. Despite the opportunities for conflict, agreement appears to be more common than disagreement.[29]

---

[26] See S. Ward, D. B. Wackman, and E. Wartella, *How Children Learn to Buy* (Sage Publications, 1977), p. 133.

[27] Ferber, "Applications of Behavioral Theories."

[28] R. T. Green and I. C. M. Cunningham, "Feminine Role Perception and Family Purchasing Decisions," *Journal of Marketing Research* (August 1975), pp. 325—32.

[29] See Burns and Granbois, "Family Automobile Purchasing," p. 85.

When conflict does arise, there are three basic ways of resolving it — consensus, compromise, and authority.[30] Consensus involves reaching mutual agreement such that all involved are completely satisfied. This may involve the acquisition of additional information, reevaluation of existing information, or consideration of new alternatives. Once conflict is aroused, consensus is difficult to achieve. Unless the purchase is of considerable importance to two or more family members, compromise or resort to authority is the most likely solution.

Compromise is a frequently used means of conflict solution. In a compromise, each party settles for something less than they desired. Compromises may take many forms. A few examples are (1) purchase a brand or product that satisfies all those involved but does not meet anyone's desires completely, (2) yield this time with the understanding that the next purchase relating to this need will be made by the yielding party, (3) yield on this decision for increased power in an unrelated decision, or (4) yield in anticipation of emotional rewards (sympathy, love, etc.). These are but a few of the forms and they are frequently implicit rather than explicit. The participants may not even be aware of the exact nature of the compromises that they have reached or the manner in which the negotiations took place.

The third solution to conflict is to rely on authority. This position is often taken between parents and younger children.[31]

Child: Can I have one of these?

Parent: No!

Child: Why not?

Parent: Because I said so.

Such solutions also occur between spouses. One spouse may be the general authority with respect to *all* decisions. This is a rare occasion however. Instead, role specialization occurs and all family members recognize one member as *the* authority in a specific area. The authority has the final say in any disagreement concerning his/her areas of specialization.

Conclusions on family decision making

While much remains to be learned about family decision making, we can offer five general conclusions.

1. Different family members may be involved at different stages of the consumption process.

---

[30] A substantially more detailed breakdown is provided by Davis, "Dimensions of Marital Roles," pp. 254–56.

[31] See Ward, Wackman, and Wartella, *How Children*.

2. Different family members may evaluate specific attributes of a product or brand.

3. The direct involvement of family members in each stage of the decision process represents only a small part of the picture. The "taking into account" of the desires of other family members is more important (though seldom studied).

4. Who participates at each stage of the consumption process and the method by which conflicts are resolved are primarily a function of the product category and secondarily a function of the characteristics of the individual family members and the characteristics of the family. The product category is important because it is closely related to who uses the product.

5. Overt conflicts in decision making are less common than agreement. Conflicts are resolved through consensus or, more frequently, compromise or resort to authority.

These conclusions are too broad to provide specific guidelines to the marketing manager. However, they do provide managers the framework necessary to guide research for their specific products. This framework is presented in Table 9−13. Since there is substantial variation across product categories, a separate analysis is required for each product category. Once the cells in the matrix have been completed, the marketing manager is in a position to make informed decisions on product design, media selection, advertising copy, and so forth.

TABLE 9–13
Framework for managerial research into the family consumption process for a specific product category

Product: X

A Stage in the consumption process	B Members involved	C Variables affecting B	D Method of conflict resolution	E Variables affecting D
Problem recognition				
Information acquisition				
Alternative evaluation				
Purchase				
Utilization				
Disposition				
Evaluation				

TABLE 9-14
Hypothetical family consumption process: School shoes for preteens (age 10–12)

A Stage in the consumption process	B Members involved*	C Variables affecting B	D Method of conflict resolution	E Variables affecting D
Problem recognition	Child (40%) Mother (40) Father (20)	Social class Sex of child Employment status of wife	Parent authority (80%) Consensus (10) Compromise (10)	Social class
Information acquisition	Mother-child (50) Father-child (15) Parent (20) Child (15)	Employment status of wife Sex of child Social class	Parent authority (80) Consensus (10) Compromise (10)	Social class
Alternative evaluation Price Style Fit	Mother (80) Child (70) Parent-child (60)	Social class Social class Social class	Parent authority (95) Child authority (60) Consensus (60)	Social class Social class Social class
Purchase	Mother (65) Father (20) Child (15)	Employment status of wife Sex of child Social class	Not applicable	Not applicable
Utilization	Child (100)	Not applicable	Not applicable	Not applicable
Disposition	Mother (80) Father (15) Child (5)	None	Parent authority (90)	Not applicable
Evaluation* Overall Durability	Child (90) Mother (80)	None Social class	Child authority (60) Parent authority (90)	Social class None

* Only the predominate member(s) are shown to conserve space.

Table 9—14 presents the hypothetical results of an analysis of the decision process for school shoes for preteenagers. A number of marketing implications are readily apparent from this analysis. First, parents are more involved in problem recognition than are children. Furthermore, social class, the employment status of the wife, and the sex of the child influence this. In almost all cases of disagreement, the conflict is resolved by resort to the parent's authority. This suggests that it is critical that the firm encourage problem recognition among parents. In addition, it suggests the possibility of a segmented approach to advertising based on the three variables in column C. A thorough analysis of the table and the data supporting it would allow the development of a complete marketing strategy.

Collecting the data for a table such as this is neither unduly difficult nor expensive for most consumer goods manufacturers. However, it should be emphasized that there can be measurement problems involved.[32]

SUMMARY

The family is the basic purchasing and consuming unit in the American society and is therefore of great importance to marketing managers of most products. Families are also the primary mechanism whereby cultural and social class values and behavior patterns are "passed on" to the next generation, thus performing the child socialization function.

The nuclear family consists of two adults of opposite sex, living in a socially approved sex relationship, with their own or adopted children. There are really two forms of the nuclear family that are of interest to marketers. The first is the family of orientation or the family that a person is born or adopted into. The second nuclear family that most individuals belong to is the family of procreation or the family unit that is formed by marriage. The family is also classified as to whether or not one is dealing with the extended family—nuclear plus additional relations—or the residential family—the family living in a single household.

The family life cycle is the classification of the family into stages through which it passes over time. Families, as institutions, change over time at relatively predictable intervals based on largely demographic (and thus readily measurable) variables. The family life cycle is therefore a very valuable marketing tool because its stages provide marketers with segments that face similar consumption problems.

---

[32] These are reviewed in M. M. Dunsing and J. L. Hafstrom, "Methodological Considerations in Family Decision-Making Studies," in *Advances in Consumer Research II*, ed. M. J. Schlinger (Association for Consumer Research, 1975), pp. 103—11.

The demographic variables most frequently used to define family life cycle reflect the number, age, and income-producing capacity of the family members. Using these variables, specific stages can be determined and described. One common form of the life cycle involves the following stages: young singles; older singles; younger married, no children; married, youngest child under 6; married, youngest child 6 to 18; married, no children at home; married, retired; and solitary survivor, retired.

Family decision making involves consideration of some very important and very complex questions. Who buys, who decides, and who uses are only a few of the questions that marketers must ask in dealing with products purchased and used by and for families.

Among the important findings to emerge from the research in family decision making is that marketing managers must analyze the family decision process separately for each product category within each target market. Family member involvement in the decision process varies by involvement with the specific product as well as by stage in the consumption process. Role specialization within the family also influences which family members are most likely to be directly involved in a purchase decision.

Conflict between family members with respect to purchase and consumption decisions may arise at any stage of the decision process. There appear to be three common ways that families resolve such conflicts—consensus, compromise, and authority.

REVIEW QUESTIONS

1. The family is described as "the basic consumption unit for consumer goods." Why?
2. What is a nuclear family? Can a single-parent family be a nuclear family?
3. How does a family of orientation differ from a family of procreation?
4. What is an extended family?
5. What is a residential family? How is a residential family related to a primary family? a nuclear family?
6. What is a household? Why are households important to marketing managers?
7. How has the distribution of family types in the United States changed over the past ten years? What are the implications of these shifts?
8. What is meant by the family life cycle? Does everyone progress through this cycle?

9. What is meant by the statement: Each stage in the family life cycle poses a series of problems which family decision makers must solve?

10. Describe the general characteristics of each of the following stages in the family life cycle:

 a. Young single.

 b. Older single.

 c. Younger married, no children.

 d. Younger married, youngest child under 6.

 e. Married, youngest child 6 to 18.

 f. Older married, no children at home.

 g. Married, retired.

 h. Solitary survivor, retired.

11. Why is the income/expense ratio relatively high for the (*a*) young single; (*b*) older single; (*c*) younger married, no children; and (*d*) older married, no children home stages?

12. Why is the income/expense ratio low for the younger married, youngest child under six stage?

13. Members of which stages of the FLC appear to be subject to the most stress and least satisfaction?

14. Members of which stages of the FLC eat out most frequently?

15. Members of which stage of the FLC consume the most of the following products on a per capita basis?

 a. Combination stereo equipment.

 b. Encyclopedias.

 c. Massagers.

 d. Pianos.

 e. Water beds.

16. Members of which stage in the FLC are most concerned with conforming to friends' and neighbors' expectations?

17. What is meant by family decision making? How can different members of the family be involved with different stages of the decision process?

18. The text states that "the marketing manager must analyze the family decision process separately for each product category within each target market." Why is this true?

19. What factors influence involvement by a family member in a purchase decision?

20. What factors are most closely related to a parent's yielding to a child's request for a particular product?

21. What is meant by role specialization with respect to family purchase decisions?

22. Describe the three basic ways of resolving conflict within the family decision process.

DISCUSSION QUESTIONS

1. Rank the stages of the family life cycle (from young single on) in terms of their probable acceptance of the moped. Justify your answer.

2. Pick two stages in the FLC. Describe how your marketing strategy for Motron would differ depending on which group was your primary target market.

3. Assume you are going to focus on high school students as a market segment for mopeds. Reconstruct Table 9−14 for this target market. Justify your assumptions. Describe the marketing strategy you would develop based on your table.

4. Do you think the trends shown in Table 9−1 will continue? Justify your response.

5. What are the primary marketing implications of a continuation of the trends shown in Table 9−1?

6. Based on Table 9−2 and the text material related to it, describe how the marketing strategies for the following products would vary with each stage in the FLC (starting with young single).
   a. Toothpaste.
   b. Camera.
   c. Car.
   d. Restaurant.
   e. Washing machine.

7. Why is the income to expense ratio an important concept?

8. Describe three potential applications of the material in Table 9−3. Be specific.

9. How could the material in Table 9−4 be used by the management of a chain of medium-priced steak houses?

10. Pick one of the product categories in Table 9−5. Describe how the material in the table could be used by a product manager for a brand in that product category. Be specific.

11. Select three of the "buying styles" shown in Table 9−6. Explain why the highest and the lowest indexes are associated with the group they are associated with.

12. Discuss the marketing implications of the material in Table 9−6.

13. Government publications frequently describe the stages in the family life cycle in terms of the age of the oldest child. The textbook uses the age of the youngest child. Which is most relevant for marketing purposes? Why?

14. To what extent do the percentages shown in Table 9−10 reflect the current situation? Why?

15. Assume that the percentages in Table 9−10 are an accurate reflection of a particular target market. What are the marketing strategy implications for the two product categories?

16. What are the general marketing implications of Table 9—11?
17. Develop a marketing strategy based on Table 9—14.

PROJECT QUESTIONS

1. Interview a high school student that owns a moped. Determine and describe the family decision process involved.
2. Interview two moped salespersons from different outlets. Try to ascertain which stages in the family life cycle constitute the primary markets and why this is so.
3. Interview one individual from each stage in the family life cycle. Determine and report the extent to which these individuals conform to the descriptions provided in the text.
4. Interview a family with at least one child at home. Interview both the parents and the child but interview the child separately. Try to determine the influence of each family member for the following products for the child's use:
   a. Toothpaste.
   b. Breakfast food.
   c. Shoes.
   d. Television programs.
   e. Bath soap.
   In addition, ascertain the method(s) of conflict resolution used.
5. Interview a couple that have been married between three and six years. Ascertain and report the degree and nature of role specialization that has developed with respect to the consumption process.

SECTION THREE
internal influences

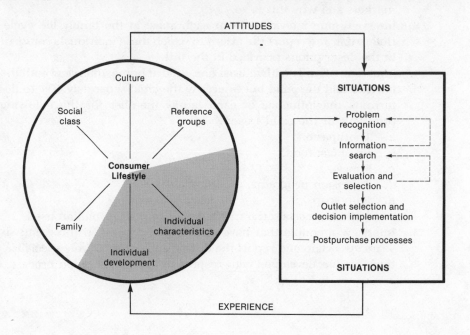

The shaded area of our model shown at left is the focal point for this section of the text. That is, our attention now shifts from group influences to the processes by which *individuals* react to and initiate group influences, environmental changes, and marketing efforts.

The perception and processing of information necessary for consumer decision making to enhance or maintain lifestyle is the subject of Chapter 10. Then the learning process necessary for consumer behavior to function is discussed in Chapter 11. This process of individual development is looked at generally for all consumers, and specifically in terms of how children learn to be consumers. Next we examine motivation in the individual and those overall characteristics that we term personality. Both of these aspects of the individual discussed in Chapter 12 are vital determinants of consumer lifestyle. Attitudes are the focus of Chapter 13 and we look at them as representing our basic orientations about products and marketing activities. Attitudes are brought out at this stage in the text because they are the actual manifestations of our learning about products and are the basic concept that marketers can measure and use to predict purchase tendencies. Finally, in Chapter 14 we tie together the first two sections of this text in an overall discussion of consumer lifestyle.

10

Information processing

Pizza Inn's 1979 advertising campaign involves almost $9 million and a break with past creative themes. For the past several years, most pizza chain advertising and a substantial amount of other fast-food chain advertising has featured jingles and interior views showing smiling employees and customers. Ray Kelley, marketing vice president for Pizza Inn, explains the firm's decision to use a mystical, humorous campaign as follows: "There's a lot of air noise" and Pizza Inn has "less bucks to spend than a Pizza Hut or McDonald's." Therefore, "it's time to be unique."[1]

Pizza Inn is basing its $9 million advertising decision on certain assumptions about how people react to television commercials, that is, about how consumers process information. Information processing then is the activity that links the consumer and the marketer. In addition, information processing is the activity that permits group influences, such as those described in the preceding six chapters, to influence individual behavior, development, and characteristics. Thus, *information processing is the critical activity that links the individual consumer to both group and marketer influences.*

In this chapter, we are going to discuss three major aspects of consumer information processing: (1) the nature of information, (2) the

---

[1] H. R. Bernstein, "Taco Pizza Joins Pizza Inn Line," *Advertising Age* ((April 23, 1979), p. 3.

nature of information processing activities, and (3) the factors that influence the amount of information processed.

NATURE OF INFORMATION

Information defined

Information is such a common word that everyone assumes they know exactly what it means. Try to come up with an exact definition of the term, one that is similar to your neighbors'; and you will immediately see the problem we face. In a major assessment of this area, Wilkie concluded:

> It is natural to expect that research on consumer information processing would utilize a reasonably precise definition of "information" both to delimit its scope of inquiry and to guide operationalizations. In fact, we find no such definition at present. The difficulty does not rest with consumer research alone, but extends to the underlying disciplines of cognitive psychology, economics, and communications.[2]

Since we are concerned with information within the context of consumer decisions, we will use the following definition:

> Information consists of all facts, estimates, predictions, and generalized relationships which affect a decision maker's perceptions of the nature and extent of the uncertainties associated with a given consumer problem or opportunity.[3]

In other words, information is stimuli that have been acquired and given meaning, and are available in a problem-solving context by a consumer.

What do we mean by facts, estimates, predictions, and generalized relationships and what do they have to do with information? Information is defined as that material used to arrive at a decision and therefore is actually knowledge or intelligence in a dynamic context. Webster defines information as "the communication or reception of knowledge or intelligence" which directly implies that information is an active concept.[4] Facts, estimates, predictions, and generalized relationships then are various types or levels of information as follows:

1. *Facts.* The simplest (theoretically at least) kind of information, facts are defined as an event or condition that is directly observed. As will be discussed later, even the same, simple fact can be given different meanings by two individuals through perceptual distortion.

---

[2] W. L. Wilkie, *How Consumers Use Product Information: An Assessment of Research in Relation to Public Policy Needs*. Report prepared for the National Science Foundation, Washington, D.C..

[3] This definition and much of the discussion explaining it was derived from R. D. Buzzell, D. F. Cox, and R. U. Brown, *Marketing Research and Information Systems: Text and Cases* (McGraw-Hill Book Co., 1969), pp. 11–13.

[4] *Webster's New Collegiate Dictionary* (G. & C. Merriam Co., 1973), p. 592.

2. *Estimates.* Estimates are different from facts in that they are based on inference (either logical or statistical) rather than on direct observation. We would prefer to have facts, but frequently must use estimates due to time and cost savings.

3. *Predictions.* Facts and estimates deal with the past and the present, while predictions deal with the future, an obvious necessity for many consumer problems and opportunities.

4. *Generalized relationships.* In order to obtain estimates and predictions, particularly for complex problems, specific facts concerning specific situations must be related to each other (cause and effect) and generalized to other, similar situations and facts.[5]

FIGURE 10–1
Components of information for a specific consumer decision

Decision:	Should I purchase a 100-aspirin bottle of Bayer aspirin or should I purchase a 200-bottle of Safeway aspirin.
1. Facts:	The Bayer aspirin costs $1.39 per bottle while the Safeway aspirin costs $.68 per bottle. According to the labels, each aspirin contains five grains.
2. Estimates:	The Bayer aspirin costs about four times as much as the Safeway aspirin on a per aspirin basis. (Note: This could be computed and become a fact. However, because of time pressures while shopping an estimate is used.)
3. Predictions:	My roommate and I will probably use about 20 aspirins a month unless one of us gets a cold. If that happens we may use 30 aspirins, but I don't think either of us will get a cold.
4. Generalized relationships:	I believe that you usually get what you pay for, particularly with health care items. Therefore, since Bayer aspirins cost more, they are probably better.

Figure 10–1 illustrates each of these four components for a particular consumer deciding between two brands of aspirin. It is important for the marketing manager to understand the differences between these types of information since the appropriate marketing strategy may de-

---

[5] Buzzell et al., *Marketing Research,* pp. 12–13.

pend on the type of information required. For example, assume that the consumer described in Figure 10−1 is typical of a market segment that Safeway (a national grocery chain) wishes to attract. What should Safeway do? It has effectively communicated both its price and product characteristics. To succeed in this market segment, Safeway must either alter the generalized relationship held by this market segment or produce a second, high-priced brand to capitalize on this relationship.

Now that we have an idea of the nature of information and its importance to the marketing manager, let us examine the ways consumers process information.

INFORMATION PROCESSING ACTIVITIES

Information processing is a series of activities by which stimuli are transformed into information and stored. As we discussed earlier, information itself provides two very important functions as a link between the individual and the various groups that influence the individual's development and lifestyle as well as a link between the marketer and the individual. However, it is the processing activities that gives overall meaning to this information.

Figure 10−2 illustrates a useful information processing model. This model views information processing as having three major components.

FIGURE 10–2
Information processing for consumer decision making

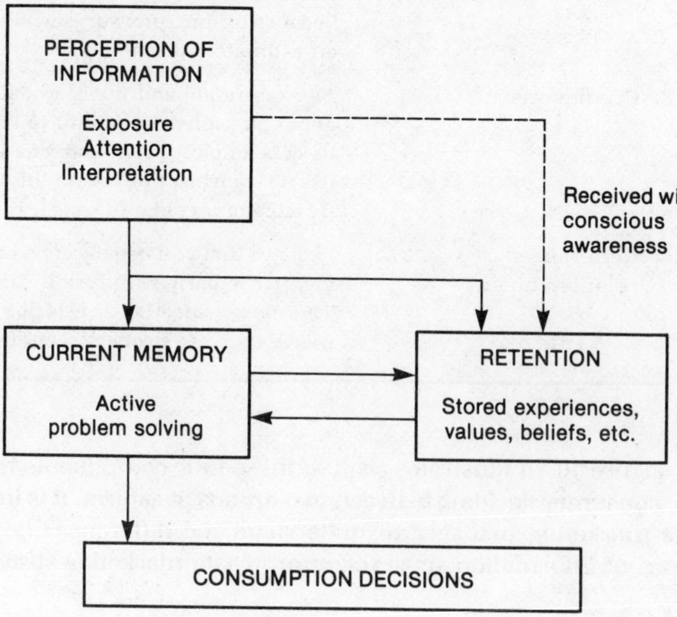

Perception is the process of selecting, integrating, and organizing stimuli from the environment into a meaningful pattern. *Current memory* is new information and previously acquired information that the consumer is utilizing to reach a decision. *Retention* is information that has been acquired and is not currently being utilized although it could be transferred to current memory if needed. We will examine each of these components in some detail and see how they are used in marketing.

Perception of information

The perception process involves those activities by which an individual acquires and assigns meaning to stimuli. A useful model of this process is illustrated in Figure 10–3. This model indicates that, of the

FIGURE 10–3
The perception process

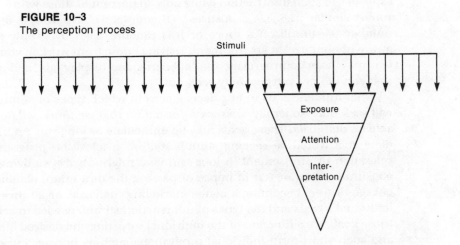

massive amount of information presented in our environment, an individual can be exposed to only a limited amount. Of the information to which the individual is exposed, only a relatively small percentage is attended to and passed on to the central processing part of the brain for interpretation. It is the final interpretation of a stimulus, such as a package design, that ultimately influences behavior, but interpretation is preceded and therefore dependent on exposure and attention. It is, therefore, necessary for marketing managers to be aware of each stage in the perception process in order to try and increase the probability that consumers will be exposed to, pay attention to, and assign the desired meaning to the messages aimed at them.

Exposure   Exposure occurs *when a stimuli comes within range of our sensory receptor nerves.* The primary sensory receptors of concern to marketing managers are those involved with vision, hearing, taste, smell, and touch. For an individual to be exposed to a stimuli requires only that the stimulus be placed within the person's relevant environment. The individual need not receive the stimuli for exposure to have occurred.

As the model in Figure 10−3 shows, an individual is generally exposed to no more than a small fraction of the available stimuli. One normally watches only one television station at a time; reads one magazine, newspaper, or book at a time and so forth. What determines which specific stimuli an individual will be exposed to? Is it a random process or purposeful? Why are you reading this text at this point in time? Clearly you are doing so for a reason. Most of the stimuli to which an individual is exposed are "self-selected." That is, we deliberately seek out exposure to certain stimuli and avoid others. For example, exposure to articles on smoking and cancer is selective, as 67 percent of nonsmokers report exposure to such information while only 40 percent of those who smoke report similar message exposures.[6] Of course, we also sample a large number of stimuli on a more or less random basis by simply being aware of our current environment. Driving home from work in your car you may hear commercials, see billboards and display ads, and so on that you did not purposefully seek out.

What influences us in our decisions as to which types of stimuli we will seek out? Generally, *we seek information that we think will help us achieve our goals*. These goals may be immediate or long run. An immediate goal would be seeking stimuli such as a television program for relaxation or amusement. A long-run goal might involve studying this consumer behavior text in hopes of passing the next exam, obtaining a college degree, becoming a better marketing manager, or all three. An individual's goals and the types of information stimuli needed to achieve those goals are a function of the individual's existing and desired lifestyle and such short-term individual motivations such as hunger, curiosity, need for approval, and so forth.

Exposure, from the marketing manager's viewpoint, involves having the message at the proper place at the correct time, so that the desired consumer segment has a chance to pay attention to it. This arises most often in media decisions, although store location and layout decisions are also affected by the exposure patterns of potential customers.[7]

The fact that the exposure process is selective rather than random is the underlying basis for effective media strategies. If the process were random, a shotgun approach of trying to place messages randomly in the environment would make sense. Since exposure is not random, the proper approach is to determine which media consumers in the target

---

[6] C. Connell and J. C. MacDonald, "The Impact of Health News on Attitudes and Behavior," *Journalism Quarterly* (Summer 1956), pp. 315−23.

[7] For a detailed discussion of media selection strategies, see J. Z. Sissors and E. R. Petray, *Advertising Media Planning* (Crain Books, 1976).

market are most frequently exposed to and then to place the advertising messages in those media.

For some products and target markets, the consumers are interested in the product category itself and will go to considerable trouble to secure product relevant information. This occurs most frequently for heavy users of hobby and luxury items such as skis and mountaineering equipment or for fashion items.

For other products and target markets, the consumers have limited interest in the product category. Products such as salt or detergents are examples. In a situation such as this, the marketer must find media that the target market is interested in and place the advertising message in those media. As we learned earlier, potential target markets as defined by age, ethnic group, social class, or stage in the family life cycle have differing media preferences.

Attention   Attention occurs *when the stimulus activates one or more sensory receptor nerves and the resulting sensations go into the brain for processing.* We are constantly exposed to thousands of times more stimuli than we can process.[8] Therefore, we have to be selective, both consciously and unconsciously, in terms of which stimuli we actually process. For example, consumers are exposed to about 1,600 advertisements each day, yet consciously attend to about 5 percent of these stimuli.[9]

At this moment you are focusing on these words. If you shift your concentration to your feet you will most likely become aware of the pressure being exerted by your shoes. A second shift in concentration to sounds will probably produce awareness of a number of background noises. These stimuli are available all the time but are not processed until a deliberate effort is made to do so. However, no matter how hard you are concentrating on this text, a loud scream or a sudden hand on your shoulder would probably get your attention. Attention, therefore, is determined by two factors—stimulus and individual.

Stimulus factors   Stimulus factors are *physical characteristics of the stimulus itself.* The stimulus can have the ability to make us pay attention due to the effects it (the stimulus) has on our nervous systems. Let us look at a few examples more closely.

Contrast refers to the tendency we have to attend more closely to those stimuli that contrast with their background than we do to those that blend with it. This principle appears to underlie Pizza Inn's new advertising campaign described at the beginning of this chapter. The *size* of the stimulus influences the probability of paying attention. Basically,

---

[8] W. J. McKeachie and C. L. Doyle, *Psychology* (Addison-Wesley Publishing Co., 1966), p. 171.

[9] R. A. Bauer and S. A. Greyser, *Advertising in America: The Consumer View* (Harvard University, 1968).

but only up to a point, we can say that larger stimuli are more likely to be noticed than smaller ones. Thus, a full-page advertisement is more likely to be noticed than a half-page advertisement. The *intensity* (e.g., loudness, brightness) of a stimulus operates in much the same manner as size.

Color and *movement* both serve to attract attention with brightly colored and moving items being more noticeable. A brightly colored package is more apt to receive attention than a dull package. *Position* refers to the placement of an object in a person's visual field. Objects placed near the center of the visual field are more likely to be noticed than those near the edge of the field. This is a primary reason why consumer goods manufacturers compete fiercely for eye level space in grocery stores. In one study the simple addition of a mobile over the dairy case improved the sales of cheese 30 percent as long as the mobile was at the right height; if it was too high or too low no improvement in cheese sales resulted.[10] *Isolation* is separating a stimulus object from other objects. The use of "white space" (placing a brief message in the center of an otherwise blank or white advertisement) is based on this principle.

Individual factors Individual factors are *characteristics of the individual. Interest* or *need* seems to be the primary individual characteristic that influences attention. Interest is, as was stated earlier, a reflection of overall lifestyle as well as a result of long-term goals and plans (e.g., development of a "perfect" golf swing) and short-term needs (e.g., hunger). If consumers have a high interest or need for information, it will be much easier to attract their attention.

How can a marketing manager utilize this information? As with most aspects of the marketing process, it depends on the target market. If the target market is actively interested in the product category and in the firm or brand, then attention will not constitute much of a problem. Once consumers are exposed to the message, they will most likely attend to it. Unfortunately, most of the time consumers are not actively interested in a particular product. Interest in a product tends to arise only when the need for the product arises. Since it is difficult to reach consumers at exactly this point in time, marketers have the difficult task of trying to communicate with them at times when their interest in the product category is low or nonexistent.

If interest in or need for the information is lacking, stimulus factors become more important for their ability to attract attention. Both individual and stimulus factors are inherent in every attention-attraction occasion. Their relative influence with respect to attention varies though. If interest is high, stimulus factors are less important. If interest or need is low, *as is the case with many consumer good items,* stimulus factors play a much larger role in attention attraction.

---

[10] "How to Turn P-O-P into Sales Dollars," *Progressive Grocer* (June 1977), pp. 83–100.

Assume you are responsible for developing a campaign designed to increase the market (number of users) for your firm's toilet bowl freshener. Research indicates that the group you wish to reach has very little interest in the product. What do you do? Two strategies seem reasonable. One is *to utilize stimulus* characteristics such as full-page ads, bright colors, animated cartoons, or magical characters to attract attention to the advertisement. The second is *to tie the* message *to a topic the target market is interested in.* Celebrities are often used in advertisements in part for this reason,[11] as is humor.[12] Sex, in the form of attractive models is also frequently utilized.[13]

Using either stimulus characteristics or consumer interests unrelated to the product category to attract attention presents two dangers. The first is that the strategy will be so successful in attracting attention to the stimulus object that it will reduce the attention devoted to the sales message. Thus, the reader may observe an attractive member of the opposite sex in an advertisement and *not* attend to the sales message or copy. A second danger is that the interpretation of the message will be influenced in a negative manner by the use of the stimulus objects. For example, using the sound of a siren to attract attention to a television commercial may result in the product being considered dangerous. Thus, the marketer must use care in creating advertisements, packages, and other messages which rely on factors other than the target market's interest in the product itself.   •

Interpretation   Interpretation is *the assignment of meaning to sensations.* Like attention, it is a function of both stimulus and individual factors. The stimulus sets the basic structure to which an individual responds. However, the interpretation is almost entirely a function of the individual. Whether or not an object is considered sexually attractive, beautiful, dangerous, or edible depends primarily on the individual not the object. Furthermore, it is the individual's interpretation that will influence behavior, not "objective" reality. For example, a firm may

---

[11] The use of celebrities is discussed in J. M. Kamen, A. C. Azhari, and J. R. Kragh, "What a Spokesman Does for a Sponsor," *Journal of Advertising Research* (April 1975), pp. 17–24.

[12] An overview of the use and problems of using humor in advertising is provided in B. Sternthal and C. S. Craig, "Humor in Advertising," *Journal of Marketing* (October 1973), pp. 12–18.

[13] For studies on the effectiveness of "sexiness" in ads, see S. Baker, *Visual Persuasion* (McGraw-Hill Book Co., 1961), p. 4.; M. Steadman, "How Sexy Illustrations Affect Brand Recall," *Journal of Advertising Research* (March 1969), pp. 15–19; B. J. Morrison and R. C. Sherman, "Who Responds to Sex in Advertising," *Journal of Advertising Research* (April 1972), pp. 15–19; G. L. Wise, A. L. King, and J. P. Merenski, "Reactions to Sexy Ads Vary with Age," *Journal of Advertising Research* (August 1974), pp. 11–16; and R. A. Peterson and R. A. Kerin, "The Female Role in Advertisements: Some Experimental Evidence," *Journal of Marketing* (October 1977), pp. 59–63. The related topic of model attractiveness is evaluated in M. J. Baker and G. A. Churchill, Jr., "The Impact of Physically Attractive Models on Advertising Evaluations," *Journal of Marketing Research* (November 1977), pp. 538–55.

introduce a new brand at a lower price than existing brands because the firm has a more efficient production or marketing process. If consumers interpret this lower price to mean lower quality, the new brand will not be successful regardless of the objective reality. Research has frequently shown that many consumers cannot differentiate between various brands of aspirin, beer, liquors, cigarettes, and carbonated beverages in "blind" taste or usage tests. Yet large price differentials exist within these product categories, indicating the critical importance of interpreted reality over objective reality. For marketers of products for which consumers do not have good sensory discrimination abilities (see Chapter 17), such as those mentioned above, interpreted reality is synonymous with brand image.

Interpretation appears to involve a process whereby new stimuli are placed into existing categories of meaning. Consider the following example:

> A savage who has never seen a white man or any of the paraphernalia of the white man's civilization sees an Army airplane descend from the skies and make a three point landing and sees Second Lieutenant Arbuthnot come out of the plane. Obviously, our savage will see the airplane and Arbuthnot as organized objects but will they, because he has never seen their like before, be completely meaningless to him? Again, the meaning he experiences may be wrong, but there will be meaning. He may experience the meaning of a "bird" as part of his purely visual precept of the airplane; he may ascribe the meaning of "God" or its equivalent to Arbuthnot, 2nd Lieutenant AUS. He will not have to wait until he has had further and extended experiences with these strange objects before his cognitive field is organized into a meaningful one."[14]

The "savage" in the example above was exposed to and paid attention to the information stimuli he was presented with. Because perception is the process of giving us an organized and meaningful world, he was literally forced to assign some meaning to these new and strange stimuli. He did so by *categorizing* them as being similar to things that already had meaning, birds and godlike figures. We, as consumers, do exactly the same thing when presented with new and different products, communication sources, and so forth. For example, when the microwave oven was first introduced to consumers, most undoubtedly grouped it in the general category of ranges, ovens, and cookers in order to be able to evaluate it. With further experience and information, of course, the category for microwaves will become more clearly and sharply defined.

---

[14] D. Krech and R. S. Crutchfield, "Perceiving the World." Reprinted in *Behavioral Sciences Foundations of Consumer Behavior,* ed. J. B. Cohen (Free Press, 1972), pp. 148–49.

The initial assignment of meaning through categorization has been described as a four-stage decision sequence:

1. *Primitive categorization.* Before any more elaborate inferential activity can occur there must be a first, "silent" process that results in the perceptual isolation of an object or an event with certain characteristic qualities. The event may have no more "meaning" than that it is an "object," a "sound," or a "movement." For example, from the physical characteristics the consumer infers it is a product as opposed to a service or communication.

2. *Cue search.* This is the second-stage process of more precise category placement based on scanning the environment for cues or identification "clues." For example, the product is categorized as a detergent.

3. *Confirmation check.* When a tentative categorization has occurred, cue search changes. The "openness" to stimulation decreases sharply in the sense that now, a tentative placement or identity having occurred, the search is narrowed for additional confirmatory clues to check this placement. For example, the product is categorized as a brand of detergent.

4. *Confirmation completion.* The final stage in the process occurs as the object or stimuli is successfully, at least to the individual, categorized. Further cue search is eliminated and incongruent or "confusing" information is ignored or rationalized away. For example, a brand of detergent is classified as a "good" brand of detergent.[15]

As noted before, exactly how these basic steps in categorization for meaning take place vary widely between consumers based on age, experience, and other factors such as educational level. It may be that genetic factors also determine the ability to categorize. We do know that some individuals have a larger number of more discrete categories than others and hence are able to more specifically identify a wider number of diverse objects. The time it takes to categorize for meaning will also vary. The sequence may be completed almost simultaneously and instantly for many stimulus objects or require a relatively longer period of time for unfamiliar, more difficult ones.

Marketing managers can aid consumers in the task of correctly categorizing information stimuli by providing them with appropriate cues. In fact, *product positioning* is in reality a marketing strategy the goal of which is "correct" consumer categorization. For example, Anheuser-Busch has developed unique product positions for its Michelob, Budweiser, and Busch beers. Each beer is differentiated phys-

---

[15] J. S. Bruner, "On Perceptual Readiness," *Psychological Review* (1957), pp. 130–31.

ically on the basis of price and taste. However, to emphasize categorization of these product positions, differential advertising copy is used to stress a different consumer lifestyle. Busch ad copy stresses quality and price while using baseball as a theme; Budweiser ad copy stresses fun, fellowship, and quality while using football and hockey themes; Michelob ad copy emphasizes superior quality and uses country club sports.

By product positioning in a marketing strategy sense, we mean the perceptual location of the brand in the consumer's mind in relation to competing brands of the same product. For example, Anheuser-Busch attempted to position Chelsea as an adult soft drink. The product characteristics, name, packaging, and advertising are all oriented toward the adult market. Whether or not the product will actually be perceived in this manner is not yet clear.

The stimuli that marketing managers utilize to influence categorization and thus interpretation can be quite subtle. Sunkist Growers has a pectin (a carbohydrate obtained from orange and lemon peels) based candy that is available in orange, lemon, lime, raspberry, and cherry flavors. It contains no preservatives and less sugar than most fruit jelly candies. Until recently the candy was available in restaurants, hospitals, and, to a limited extent, supermarket candy sections. Now, Sunkist Growers is actively promoting the candy, called Sunkist Fruit Gems, as a "healthful, natural" snack. They hope to attract adults as well as children. As part of the overall marketing strategy, Sunkist is attempting to distribute the candy *through the produce departments of supermarkets*.[16] Notice how the distribution plan supports the desired product position or image. A consumer receiving a message that this is a healthful, natural product may, through cue search and confirmation check, agree with this when the product is found with other healthful, natural products such as apples and oranges. Figure 10−4 illustrates how U.S.I. Chemicals was able to create a distinct product position for a commodity item—ethyl alcohol.

Marketing managers frequently fail to achieve the type of product image or position they desire because they fail to anticipate or test for consumer reactions. Recall from Chapter 1 that Toro's initial lightweight snowthrower was not successful. Why? It was named the Snowpup, and consumers interpreted this to mean that it was a toy (incorrect categorization) or lacked sufficient power. Sales success came only after a more macho, power-based name was utilized—first Snowmaster and later Toro.[17]

A number of principles or generalizations about interpretation are available to assist the manager. First, the meaning assigned to stimuli is

[16] J. Pendleton, "Sunkist Launching Candy via Store Produce Sections," *Advertising Age* (December 4, 1978), p. 17.

[17] J. Neher, "Toro Cutting a Wide Swath in Outdoor Appliance Marketing," *Advertising Age* (February 25, 1978), p. 21.

FIGURE 10–4
U.S.I. Chemicals development of punctilious alcohol

The problem: How do you create a brand position for a commodity chemical that is essentially the same as your competitors? The message U.S.I. wanted to convey was: We have a high-quality product and this high quality is due to our own demanding standards. The problem was to convey this message to the wide range of commercial and industrial buyers of ethyl alcohol.

The solution: Use the registered trademark "Punctilious Ethyl Alcohol" and advertise the quality message heavily. *Punctilious* is a seldom used word that means "precise; exact according to detail."

Rationale:

1. The word *punctilious* matched the high quality and attention to detail we had articulated previously. It was also in keeping with the character of the company.

2. It was an unusual word, not normally used in the vernacular, and would wake the reader up. Why not make him or her stretch his/her mind a bit to learn what this word really meant? That is one way of being intrusive, which is what you want your advertising to be.

3. It was a simple, one-word slogan. And it was unusual enough to be memorable.

4. *Punctilious* probably would have long-term usage for us and, like our product, would probably not have to be changed every few years.

5. By using an offbeat word to describe our quality product, we would probably preempt anyone else in the ethyl alcohol category from dramatizing quality. Thus the word offered a competitive advantage.

6. The word lacked any negative connotations and could not confuse the reader. In fact, it even promised something new or different, because every other chemical product was identified with a number or a name derived from chemical terminology.

7. The unusual word would be measurable. Because it was controversial, it would create feedback from the field. And it was definitely something that research studies could track and report on.

The results: In the words of a U.S.I. executive: "It is a smashing success."

Source: Derived from G. D. Miknich and W. F. Foley, "Punctilious Alcohol Sells for U.S.I.," *Advertising Age* (June 25, 1979), pp. S.28–S.30.

learned. We saw in Chapter 4 that the meaning attached to such natural things as time, space, friendship, and colors is learned. In Malaysia, green is closely associated with the jungle, sickness, disease, and death. A peanut butter manufacturer that attempted to market its product in Malaysia in green containers was unsuccessful.[18] However, the color green does not have these negative connotations in other cultures (e.g., the Jolly Green Giant in the United States).

Even within the same culture, different subcultures assign different meanings to similar stimuli. For example, dinner refers to the noon meal for some social classes in some geographic regions of the United States, and to the evening meal for other social classes and geographic regions. Marketers must be certain that the audience has learned the same meanings that they wish to portray.

Individuals tend to interpret stimuli consistently with their *expectations*. This has been demonstrated in a wide variety of contexts. Managers have frequently evaluated a given level of performance by a male higher than a similar level of performance by a female because they expected the male to perform better.[19] Consumers will frequently evaluate the performance of a well-known brand or a more expensive brand higher than an identical product with an unknown brand name or a lower price.[20] Consumers also frequently attribute advertisements for new or unknown brands to well-known brands.[21] These are important factors for the marketing manager to consider, particularly in the areas of personnel evaluation, interpretation of marketing research, and the design of marketing communications.

Proximity refers to a tendency to perceive objects or events that are close to one another as being related. While sales of cheese were increased when a display mobile was placed at the right height over a store's dairy case, when the mobile was placed over the aisle adjacent to the dairy case, cheese sales did not improve.[22] In this case the proximity of the display mobile and dairy case were such that they were not related. The principle of proximity is constantly evoked when beer is shown in social settings, cigarettes in outdoor or fun-loving situations,

---

[18] D. Sator, "Differences in Tastes, Cultures, and Language Translations Make International Marketing Tricky," *Marketing News* (March 28, 1975), p. 5.

[19] E. A. Shaw, "Differential Impact of Negative Stereotypes in Employee Selection," *Personnel Psychology* (1972), pp. 333–38; B. Rosen and T. H. Jerdee, "Influence of Sex Role Stereotypes on Personnel Decisions," *Journal of Applied Psychology* (1974), pp. 9–14; and B. Rosen and T. H. Jerdee, "Effects of Applicant's Sex and Difficulty of Job on Evaluations of Candidates for Managerial Positions," *Journal of Applied Psychology* (1974), pp. 511–12.

[20] A summary of research findings in this area is contained in J. H. Myers and W. H. Reynolds, *Consumer Behavior and Marketing Management* (Houghton Mifflin Co., 1967), pp. 15–20. The problems this can cause management are illustrated in "Twink: Perception of Taste" in R. D. Blackwell, J. F. Engle, and D. T. Kollat, *Cases in Consumer Behavior* (Holt, Rinehart and Winston, 1969), pp. 38–43.

[21] See F. E. Webster, Jr., *Marketing Communications* (Ronald Press, 1971), pp. 71–72.

[22] "How to Turn," pp. 83–100.

and expensive cars in luxurious settings such that the advertised products and the settings are perceived as being related.

Closure occurs out of our need for completeness. When presented with incomplete stimuli, we have a need to fill in the missing elements in order to complete the meaning of the stimuli. Salem cigarettes has used the principle of closure to increase ad attention and comprehension by omitting the second half of earlier advertisements which began with "You can take Salem out of the country, but. . . ." On hearing the first half of the commercial, listeners tended to complete the ad because of a need for closure.

Individuals' *personal characteristics* also affect their interpretation of stimuli. For example, some individuals are more trusting than others and may be easily misled by unscrupulous sales personnel or misleading advertising.[23] *Temporary characteristics* such as hunger or loneliness influence interpretation of a given stimulus[24] as do moods.[25]

The final generalization that we can reach concerning interpretation is the fact that interpretation is *holistic* or Gestalt in nature. That is, stimuli are evaluated in the context of a structure rather than in isolation. A price of $2.50 for a gallon of gasoline seems expensive to most Americans. This is because we are accustomed to much lower prices. A European would interpret a price of $2.50 per gallon in a substantially different manner. Likewise, the *source* of the message affects the interpretations of the message as does the *media* in which the message appears. Previous experiences with the same firm, current and previous experiences with competing firms, and relevant external factors such as the state of the economy all influence the interpretation of a message.[26]

Determining the exact meaning a consumer will or has assigned to a particular advertisement, package, and so forth is difficult. As we saw in Chapter 1, the Bureau of Consumer Protection, a division of the Federal Trade Commission (FTC), is beginning to consider the "total" advertisement rather than just the verbal portions in assessing whether or not the ad is misleading. As an example, the bureau's deputy director cited an ad for Belair cigarettes which is "dominated by a full-page color photograph of a happy couple frolicking in the surf." The words used in the ad

---

[23] See M. W. DeLozier, *The Marketing Communications Process* (McGraw-Hill Book Co., 1976), pp. 47–48.

[24] Ibid., pp. 45–46.

[25] R. Barton, *Media in Advertising* (McGraw-Hill Book Co., 1964), p. 47. See also C. Leuba and C. Lucas "The Effects of Attitudes on Descriptions of Pictures," *Journal of Experimental Psychology* (1945), pp. 517–24; and I. A. Horowitz and R. S. Kaye," Perception and Advertising," *Journal of Advertising* (June 1975), pp. 15–21.

[26] A detailed discussion of the nature of Gestalt principles and their relationship to advertising can be found in D. A. Aaker and J. G. Myers, *Advertising Management* (Prentice-Hall, Inc., 1975), pp. 287–99.

were not misleading. However, if the message (interpretation) of the entire ad is that smoking Belairs will make you "healthy" and "happy," it might be considered deceptive.[27]

In fact, the FTC has already begun taking action based on the total impression conveyed by an advertisement or package. For example, General Mills was fined $90,000 for an advertisement which allegedly implied that a toy horse could stand upright by itself when in fact it required support. In addition, they were fined $10,000 for certain model kits which the FTC claimed were packaged in oversize containers or with pictures or written material that created a false idea of the toy's size.[28] As the FTC proceeds with this approach, manufacturers and retailers will have to utilize increasing skill to design total advertisements and packages that convey a favorable and accurate message.

Subliminal perception   The steps described above may also occur at the subliminal (below awareness) level. Awareness refers to the ability of the individual to report the presence and/or nature of the stimulus influencing him/her. A stimulus may be subliminal if (1) it is presented in a manner such that the individual cannot recognize it even if trying (most studies present the stimulus for very brief time periods) and (2) the individual devotes insufficient attention to the stimulus to recall its presence. Most studies have focused on the first approach, while the second is probably more common in actual consumer decision making. This focus seems to occur because people are both fascinated and repelled by the possibility of influencing others without their awareness.

Initial interest in the topic of subliminal perception seems to be due to a much discussed, but never published, demonstration by a commercial firm of the potential effects of subliminal advertising. The firm presented two subliminal messages, "Eat Popcorn" and "Drink Coca-Cola," during the regular presentation of a movie. Unconfirmed reports indicate that due to these messages, popcorn sales increased more than 50 percent and Coke sales by 18 percent.[29] Even though these results and the subliminal methods used to obtain them were never verified, there is evidence which indicates that subliminal messages can have limited influences on behavior.[30] One of these studies found that, while subliminal advertisements could affect basic drives such as hunger level, they could

---

[27] S. Crock, "FTC Is Seeking Way to Decide if Pictures in Advertising Convey False Impressions," *The Wall Street Journal* (August 11, 1978), p. 4.

[28] "Biggest FTC Ad Fine Hits General Mills," *Advertising Age* (May 28, 1979), p. 2.

[29] N. Cousins, "Smudging the Subconscious; Subliminal Projection," *Saturday Review* (1957), p. 20.

[30] N. F. Dixon, *Subliminal Perception: The Nature of a Controversy* (McGraw Hill Book Co., 1971); and D. I. Hawkins, "The Effects of Subliminal Stimulation on Drive Level and Brand Preference," *Journal of Marketing Research* (August 1970), pp. 322–26. For a related discussion, see H. E. Krugman, "Memory without Recall, Exposure without Perception," *Journal of Advertising Research* (August 1977), pp. 7–12.

not influence brand preferences.[31] This is not surprising considering the following characteristics of subliminal messages:

1. Stimulus message duration must by necessity be short and simple (Drink Coke, Eat Popcorn).
2. Individual perceptual thresholds vary such that something that you are consciously aware of, another person may not be.
3. Perception is highly selective, consciously as well as subconsciously.
4. Human beings due to individual background factors, needs, and so forth frequently distort stimuli.

We are all aware that information stimuli presented by marketers with the intent of persuading consumers are somewhat less than totally effective in achieving that goal. Exposure is not guaranteed, attention is hard to bring about, particularly for low-interest products, and correct interpretation is extremely difficult to bring about except for the simplest product information and claims. It is then extremely difficult to imagine any marketer being successful in using subliminal techniques. This would simply make the task harder. In fact, a study has shown that subliminal advertising is ineffective in generating sales.[32]

Although purely subliminal messages appear to be extremely inefficient at best, accelerated or compressed messages may produce some benefits. In one experiment, 30-second commercials were reduced to 24 seconds via a device that does not produce sound distortions. The compressed commercials were found to be more interesting and to generate at least the same level of product recall as standard commercials. Thus, there appears to be some potential to accelerate all or selected parts of advertisements presented via broadcast media.[33]

Information storage and retrieval

Having assigned meaning to a stimulus, the consumer will place it either in retention (e.g., long-term memory) for future reference or in current memory for immediate use in a decision.

The current memory concept of active problem solving and its relationship to retention has been appropriately described as being analogous to a desk:

> When working on a problem, an individual may assemble materials related to the topic from various files and books and place them on the desk top.

[31] Hawkins, "Effects of Subliminal Stimulation."

[32] M. L. DeFleur and R. M. Petranoff, "A Televised Test of Subliminal Persuasion," *Public Opinion Quarterly* (Summer 1959), pp. 169–70.

[33] J. Machlan and P. LaBarbera, "Time-Compressed TV Commercials," *Journal of Advertising Research* (August 1978), pp. 11–15. See also P. LaBarbera and J. Machlan, "Time-Compressed Speech in Radio Advertising," *Journal of Marketing* (January 1979), pp. 30–36.

When he is finished, he may stuff the materials placed on the desk into a drawer and keep them as a unit. Or he may return the items to their original locations, perhaps storing the problem solution.[34]

In other words, when consumers are engaged in decision making to solve a problem, they are actively involved in the use of newly perceived information in conjunction with previously perceived information that has been stored. Thus, new and stored information are brought together through cognitive mental processes in order to arrive at problem solutions. This active problem solving can and does occur at various stages of the decision-making process. For instance, problem recognition calls for active information processing as does alternative evaluation, but with different kinds and amounts of information stimuli.

Current memory   Current memory has been described in terms of two basic kinds of information processing activities—*maintenance rehearsal* and *elaborative activities*.[35] Maintenance rehearsal is the continual repetition of a piece of information in order to hold it in current memory for use in problem solving. Elaborative activities are the use of the stored experiences, values, attitudes, beliefs, and so forth to interpret and evaluate information in current memory, as well as add relevant previously stored information.

What we commonly term as forgetting may also be an information processing activity closely associated with current memory. The success of maintenance rehearsal will, to a large extent, determine what new information we retain during the problem-solving activity. In addition, new and/or reinterpreted information that seems incorrect or not of further use to the individual may be thrown out at this point and not taken into retention.

Retention   Retention is the term we use for what has also been called *secondary* memory or *long-term* memory. Basically, it is information from previous information processing. Current opinion holds that retention, unlike current memory, has unlimited capacity for information storage.[36] It also appears that much more information is retained than we have the ability to recall, an interesting form of forgetting.[37]

Retrieval is the process of obtaining information from retention for use in elaborative operations in current memory. In other words, "retrieval is the process by which information stored in long-term memory is activated to recognize new input or solve a problem."[38] The success of

---

[34] M. I. Posner, *Cognition: An Introduction* (Scott, Foresman and Co., 1977), p. 16.

[35] A. A. Mitchell, "An Information Processing View of Consumer Behavior," in *Research Frontiers in Marketing: Dialogues and Directions*, ed. S. C. Jain (American Marketing Association, 1978), pp. 188—97.

[36] Ibid., p. 189.

[37] Posner, *Cognition*, pp. 38—39.

[38] Ibid., p. 40.

information retrieval may depend on which of the two types of retention one is dealing with—episodic or semantic.[39]

By *episodic memory*, we mean memory of those events or episodes an individual paid attention to over time. When an individual is asked to recall a particular advertisement presented the previous night during "Three's Company," the sequence probably involves starting with last night's show at the beginning and searching forward until that ad is reached. Failure to recall the ad could mean that it never made it into retention or that there are other factors blocking retrieval.

The other form of retention is *semantic memory*, which is the stored representations of our generalized knowledge about the world we live in. It is this form of longer-term memory that is concerned with the association and combinations of various "chunks" of information. Mitchell provides an example of semantic memory by showing how one might associate various concepts to 7up in order to come up with a complete network of meaning for that brand (see Figure 10–5). We will deal more directly with how these associative structures are formed (learned) in Chapter 11.

FIGURE 10–5
7up associative memory network

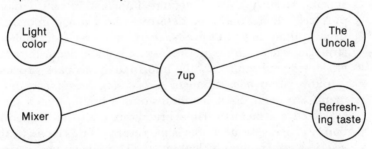

Source: A. A. Mitchell, "An Information Processing View of Consumer Behavior," in *Research Frontiers in Marketing: Dialogues and Directions*, ed. S. C. Jain (American Marketing Association, 1978), p. 189.

Conclusions on information processing activities

It would be wise at this point to again stress that in actuality consumer information processing is not as neatly segmented, labeled, and ordered as Figure 10–2 might indicate. The entire process for any given situation might be almost instantaneous or it may take some time. The main factors affecting the time for processing would seem to be the complexity and familiarity with the information stimuli and the problem/decision at hand. Also, information processing can and does happen at one time for the entire decision process or at various stages.

[39] Mitchell, "Information Processing," p. 189.

For example, problem recognition may require a fairly lengthy and complex information processing activity that is unrelated to that required for alternative evaluation.

AMOUNTS OF INFORMATION PROCESSED

Consumers process information in order to make decisions. Traditionally, we have assumed that the more information one has available, the better the resultant decision. The amount of information available is known as the *information load*. There is currently a great deal of controversy over an exact definition of what constitutes information load, but it is generally considered in a marketing sense to consist of the number of brands and the number of attributes per brand.[40]

Information acquisition strategies

Information load may be most clearly illustrated by examining the strategies that consumers use to acquire information for a purchase decision. As we have stated, information load consists of the number of brands and the number of attributes per brand. It follows then that the specific strategy used to acquire information with which to make a purchase choice may well determine how much information (load) is used in that choice. Basically, there are three information acquisition strategies—acquisition by processing brands, acquisition by processing attributes, and acquisition by information feedback processing.

Information acquisition *by processing brands* occurs when judgments are made on all attributes of one brand, then a second brand is evaluated, and so forth. Thus, brands are evaluated sequentially. Acquisition *by processing attributes* is the reverse of this whereby the consumer acquires information by looking at all brands on one attribute, then the next attribute, and so forth. In this case, attributes are evaluated sequentially. Finally, acquisition *by information feedback processing* is a combination strategy whereby consumers alternate short sequences of brand and attribute processing. In other words, a consumer may begin to evaluate brands, then based on an evaluation of a certain attribute on one brand (feedback) move to evaluate (information acquisition) the other attributes of that brand. Table 10−1 provides you with a graphic

---

[40] J. Jacoby, D. E. Speller, and C. A. Kohn, "Brand Choice Behavior as a Function of Information Load," *Journal of Marketing Research* (1974), pp. 63−69; J. Jacoby, D. E. Speller, and C. A. Kohn, "Brand Choice Behavior as a Function of Information Load: Replication and Extension," *Journal of Consumer Research* (1974), pp. 33−42; J. E. Russo, "More Information Is Better: A Reevaluation of Jacoby, Speller, and Kohn," *Journal of Consumer Research* (1974), pp. 68−72; W. Wilkie, "Analysis of Effects of Information Load," *Journal of Marketing Research* (1974), pp. 462−66; J. Jacoby, "Information Load and Decision Quality: Some Contested Issues," *Journal of Marketing Research* (1977), pp. 569−73; and R. Best and D. Williams, "Structural Properties of Consumer Information and Perceptions of Information," in *Advances in Consumer Resarch VII*, ed. J. Olson (Association for Consumer Research, 1980).

TABLE 10–1

Information acquisition strategies for an apartment

	Apartment brands		
Apartment attributes	A	B	C
Location	Good	Excellent	Fair
Price per month	350	400	290
Pets allowed	No	No	Yes
Appearance	Fair	Good	Fair

Strategies

I. *Acquisition by processing brands.*
   Evaluate apartment A on attributes 1 through 4, then apartment B on the same attributes, and so on for apartment C.

II. *Acquisition by processing attributes.*
    Evaluate the location of each apartment, then evaluate price of each, and continue to acquire other attribute specific information for each apartment until one apartment is preferred.

III. *Acquisition by information feedback processing.*
     Evaluate apartments A and B on location, become interested in apartment B because of its location, and then evaluate B on all other attributes. Either select apartment B or continue evaluating apartments A and C.

example of the three strategies for three hypothetical apartments and four attributes.

One study of 60 consumers of breakfast cereal found that 30 percent used acquisition by processing brands; 37 percent used acquisition by processing attributes; 13 percent used acquisition by feedback processing; and 20 percent acquired information and made a brand choice using a choice by brand name strategy (i.e., simply choose based on brand name rather than by judging attributes).[41] Table 10–2 illustrates the differences for each of these patterns of information acquisition in terms of the amount of the information examined prior to choice (i.e., information load), amount of time used, number of brands examined, number of evaluative criteria examined, and perceived difference in quality of alternative brands. This table illustrates that consumers who used the acquisition by feedback processing strategy examined more information both in terms of evaluative criteria and number of brands than consumers using one of the other two strategies. Also important is the fact that these consumers perceived a greater difference in quality among alternatives than did the others.

---

[41] J. Bettman and J. Jacoby, "Patterns of Processing Consumer Information," in *Advances in Consumer Research III*, ed. B. B. Anderson (Association for Consumer Research, 1976), pp. 315–20.

TABLE 10-2
Information acquisition characteristics associated with three information processing strategies

Information acquisition strategy	Amount of information examined	Amount of time used (seconds)	Number of brands examined	Number of criteria examined	Perceived difference in quality*
Choice by processing brands	12.40	202	2.89	6.06	3.50
Choice by processing attributes	13.10	178	4.86	3.64	3.41
Choice by feedback processing	22.40	314	5.71	6.29	2.57

* Perceived difference in quality ranged from 1 (very large difference) to 5 (hardly any difference).
Source: J. Bettman and J. Jacoby, "Patterns of Processing Consumer Information." in *Advances in Consumer Research III*, ed. B. B. Anderson (Association for Consumer Research, 1975), pp. 315–20.

A second study of information evaluation strategies with respect to breakfast cereals obtained similar results. However, this study also showed that consumers evaluate only a small portion of the available information prior to making a brand choice. Of the 560 pieces of information available, half of the consumers acquired less than 2 percent of this information prior to making a brand choice.[42]

While utilizing less than 2 percent of the available information may seem ineffective, you will recall that there are definite limits to our ability as humans to process large quantities of information. To illustrate the amount of information processing that would be required to utilize all available data, consider the decisions necessary to develop a single day's menu. A study of this topic evaluated 57 branded food items that could be included in a nutritiously balanced breakfast, lunch, and dinner for a single consumer. Using a computer program to process the information, it took an IBM Model 370 computer seven and one-half minutes of computer time to select a single day's menu which would meet minimum daily requirements for nutrition at the lowest cost to the consumer.[43] Clearly, most consumers use satisfying strategies in order to make such information processing tasks manageable. The primary approach to shortening this information acquisition and processing task is the use of decision rules which will be discussed in Chapter 17.

Information overload

Although there is substantial variation between individuals, all consumers have limited capacities to process information. Despite the fact

---

[42] J. Jacoby, R. Chesnut, K. Weigel, and W. Fisher, "PrePurchasing Information Acquisition: Description of a Process Methodology, Research Paradigm, and Pilot Investigation," in *Advances in Consumer Research III*, ed. B. B. Anderson (Association for Consumer Research, 1976), pp. 306–14.

[43] Z. Lambert, "Nutrition Information: A Look at Some Processing and Decision Making Difficulties," *Advances for Consumer Research IV*, ed. W. D. Perreault, Jr. (Association for Consumer Research, 1977), pp. 126–32.

that these capacities can be expanded by training, both marketing managers and regulatory agencies recognize the potential dangers of *information overload*. Information overload occurs when consumers are confronted with so much information that they cannot or will not process it. Instead they become frustrated and either postpone or give up on the decision, make a random choice, or utilize a suboptimal portion of the total information available. You have probably experienced information overload yourself. If not, go to the supermarket and try to select the brand of breakfast cereal that provides the most nutrition per dollar.

There are no general rules or guidelines concerning how much information consumers can or will utilize. Marketers, the federal government, and various consumer groups want product labels, packages, and advertisements to provide *sufficient* information to allow for an informed decision. One approach would be to provide all potentially relevant information. This approach is frequently recommended by regulatory agencies and is required for some product categories such as drugs. Problems with this approach can arise, however. For example, a relatively simple, one-page advertisement for ModiCon oral contraceptive required a second full page of small type telling of dosage, precautions, warnings and so forth in order to comply with federal full disclosure regulations.[44]

The assumption behind this approach is that each consumer will utilize those specific information items required for their particular decision. Unfortunately, consumers frequently will not react in this manner. Instead, they may experience information overload as described above and make a less than optimal decision.

How should the marketing manager or regulator approach this issue? The consumer research cited earlier indicates that information overload may be a problem in some situations (something which was not recognized a few years ago) but, as yet, does not specify exactly when it will be a problem. As we have stressed a number of times, it merely provides us with an appropriate question which must be answered in light of the product category and target market involved.

INFORMATION PROCESSING AND DECISION MAKING

We have chosen to stop our coverage of information processing prior to the actual decision-making process. We consider information processing to consist of those activities that transform stimuli into information that can be used for decision making. However, we are going to treat the actual decision-making process as a separate, though closely related activity. Decision making basically involves applying rules to information

---

[44] W. G. Castagnoli, "Deregulation of Ads Is Still in Line for Rough Times," *Advertising Age* (April 2, 1979), p. S.4.

to choose among alternatives. The consumer makes an almost infinite series of decisions daily. We will discuss the major types of consumer decisions in later chapters; that is, problem recognition decisions (Chapter 15), information search decisions (Chapter 16), alternative selection decisions (Chapter 17), purchase and outlet decisions (Chapter 18), and usage decisions (Chapter 19).

SUMMARY

Marketing managers influence consumer decision making primarily by presenting the consumer with information. Hence it is necessary to understand what kind of information consumers want and need and how that information is acquired and processed.

Information consists of facts, estimates, predictions, and generalized relationships that are used by consumers to recognize and solve problems. Different marketing strategies may be appropriate depending on which of the four aspects or types of information are being utilized by consumers.

Information processing consists of three major activities—perception of information, current memory, and retention. Perception involves those activities by which an individual acquires and assigns meaning to stimuli. Initially, perception begins with exposure to various stimuli. Exposure occurs when a stimuli comes within range of one of our five primary sensory receptors—vision, hearing, taste, smell, or touch. We are exposed to only a small fraction of the available stimuli and this is usually the result of "self-selection." That is to say, our exposure is usually the result of purposeful, goal-directed behavior. Marketing managers must be cognizant of the fact that if they cannot obtain consumer exposure they will not be able to influence that consumer, thus the intense interest in target markets' media preferences.

Attention, the second step in the perception of information, occurs when the stimulus activates one or more of the sensory receptors and the resulting sensations go into the brain for processing. Because of the amount of stimuli we are exposed to, we selectively attend to those stimuli that physically attract us (stimulus factors) or personally interest us (individual factors). Stimulus factors are physical characteristics of the stimulus itself such as contrast, size, intensity, color, movement, and so forth. Individual factors are characteristics of the individual such as interests and needs. Both factors are complimentary determinants of attention with their relative influence depending on the particular person and situation.

Interpretation, the final stage of perception, is the assignment of meaning to stimuli that have been attended to. Interpretation is primarily a function of the individual. In other words, we assign meaning to stimuli based on our individual experiences. Interpretation appears to involve a process whereby new stimuli are placed into existing categories of meaning with the number and width of categories being dependent upon a number of individual factors. Product positioning provides us with an excellent example of a marketing strategy that has the goal of correct consumer categorization. The meanings assigned to stimuli can be said to reflect the following generalizations: they are learned, they are consistent with expectations, they are influenced by proximity and the need for closure, they can be affected by temporary characteristics such as hunger, and they are holistic or Gestalt in nature.

Subliminal perception is a concept that describes how meaning is attached to stimuli presented at a "below-awareness" level. A great deal of concern has been raised about the possibility that stimuli can influence individuals without their being aware of the stimuli. The evidence seems to indicate that subliminal stimuli have at most a mild and generalized effect.

After perception has occurred, the meaningful information is stored. Most commonly, information goes directly into current memory for problem solving where two basic activities occur—maintenance rehearsal and elaborative activities. Maintenance rehearsal is the continual repetition of a piece of information in order to hold it in current memory. Elaborative activities are the actual use of the stored experiences, values, attitudes, and so forth to interpret and evaluate information in current memory, as well as add relevant previously stored information.

Retention is information from previous information processing that has been stored for future use. Information in retention reflects previous experiences, values, attitudes, and so forth. It undergoes continual restructuring because the environment is changing as well as the problem-solving tasks that consumers face. Information is retrieved from retention for problem solving and the success of the retrieval seems dependent on whether one is dealing with episodic or semantic memory. Episodic memory refers to memory of events over time. Semantic memory is the stored representations of our generalized knowledge about the world we live in.

As information is used to make decisions, we are interested in the amount or load of information that consumers use. Information load is normally defined as the number of brands and the number of attributes per brand. Both marketing managers and public policy officials are concerned with possible consumer information overload. Information acquisition strategies may well determine how much information is used. Three basic acquisition strategies exist—acquisition by processing brands, acquisition by processing attributes, and acquisition by information feedback processing.

REVIEW QUESTIONS

1. What is information? What does it consist of?
2. Why is information important to the consumer?
3. Why is information important to the marketing manager?
4. What is information processing? How does information processing differ from perception?
5. How is current memory related to retention?
6. What is meant by exposure? What determines what stimuli an individual will be exposed to? How do marketers utilize this?
7. What is meant by attention? What determines what stimuli an individual will attend to? How do marketers utilize this?
8. What stimulus factors can be used to attract attention? What problems can arise when stimulus factors are used to attract attention?
9. What is meant by interpretation? What determines how an individual will interpret a given stimulus?
10. What is meant by interpreted reality? Why is this important?
11. What is meant by categorization? What steps are involved?
12. What is meant by product positioning? How does this relate to categorization?
13. What principles or generalizations about interpretation are available to assist the manager?
14. What is meant by the term Gestalt as it relates to interpretation? Why is it important?
15. What is meant by subliminal perception? Is it a real phenomena? Is it effective?
16. What is an accelerated or compressed message?
17. What is episodic memory? How does it differ from semantic memory?
18. What is information overload? How should marketers deal with information overload?

DISCUSSION QUESTIONS

1. What information do you think the average male student and, secondly, the average female student on your campus has in retention about (a) mopeds and (b) Motron mopeds? List the information by the four information components.
2. What product position do you think (a) mopeds and (b) Motron mopeds occupies among students on your campus? Do you think these product positions differ significantly among different target markets such as high school students, young blue-collar workers, or ethnic groups?
3. How could Jeff use the material in this chapter on perception to guide the development of a national advertising campaign? to assist

local retailers in developing their promotional activities? Would the usefulness of this material be limited to advertising decisions? Explain your answer.

4. In 1978, Anheuser-Busch test marketed a new soft drink for adults called Chelsea.[45] The product was advertised as a "not-so-soft drink" that Anheuser-Busch hoped would become socially acceptable for adults. The advertisements featured no one under 25 years of age, and the product contained one half of 1 percent alcohol (not enough to classify the product as an alcoholic beverage).

   The reaction in the test market was not what the firm expected or hoped for. The Virginia Nurses Association decided to boycott Chelsea claiming that it "is packaged like a beer and looks, pours, and foams like beer, and that children are pretending the soft drink is a beer." The Nurses Association claimed that the product was an attempt to encourage children to become beer drinkers later on. Secretary of Health, Education and Welfare, Joseph Califano, urged the firm to "rethink their marketing strategy." Others made similar protests. Eventually Anheuser-Busch reformulated the product and altered the marketing mix substantially.

   Assuming Anheuser-Busch was in fact attempting to position Chelsea as an adult soft drink (which it appears was their objective), why do you think it failed?

5. A television advertisement for General Mill's Total cereal makes the following claim: "It would take 16 ounces of the leading natural cereal to equal the vitamins in one ounce of fortified Total." The Center for Science in the Public Interest filed a petition against General Mills claiming that the advertisement is deceptive. It is the center's position that the claim overstated Total's nutritional benefits because the cereal is not 16 times higher in other factors important to nutrition.[46]

   a. Is the claim misleading? Justify your answer.

   b. How should the FTC proceed in cases such as this?

   c. What are the implications of cases such as this for marketing management?

6. In recent years, manufacturers of meat products have introduced a product labeled as "turkey-ham." The product looks like ham and tastes like ham but it contains *no ham;* it is all turkey. A nationwide survey of consumers showed that most believed that the meat product contained both turkey and ham.[47] The USDA approved this label

---

[45] This problem is based on "Nurses Foaming over Chelsea," *Advertising Age* (October 23, 1978), p. 8.

[46] "FTC Urged to Review Total Spots," *Advertising Age* (October 23, 1978), p. 114.

[47] P. Kuehl and R. Dyer, "An Experimental Examination of Deception in Labelling: Consumer Research and Public Policymaking," in *Advances in Consumer Research,* ed. H. K. Hunt (Association for Consumer Research, 1978), pp. 206–12.

based on a dictionary definition for the technical term *ham* —the thigh cut of meat from the hind leg of any animal. Using Figure 10 −2, discuss how consumers processed information concerning this product and used this information in purchasing this product. From a public policy standpoint, should the FTC and/or USDA take some corrective action since consumers are being deceived?

PROJECT QUESTIONS

1. Fulfill the requirements of the first discussion question by interviewing five male and five female students.
2. Find examples of marketing promotions that specifically use stimulus factors to create attention. Look for examples of each of the various factors discussed earlier in the chapter, and try to find their use in a wide variety of promotions (e.g., point-of-purchase, billboards, print advertisements, and so forth). For each example, evaluate the effectiveness of the stimulus factors used.
3. Repeat question 2 above, but this time look for promotions using individual factors.
4. Read *Symbolic Seduction* by Wilson Bryan Key. Is the author really describing subliminal perception? Do you feel he makes a valid point that marketers should be aware of?
5. Develop a series of statements that describe different ways in which information is acquired when purchasing an automobile. Develop a second set of statements for acquisition of information when purchasing a shampoo. Then have other students not enrolled in your class read your description of how information can be acquired and have them indicate which one best describes their style of acquiring information in purchasing a car and shampoo. Then as a class discuss your results in terms of differences in acquisition strategies among individuals and between types of products.

---

[48] *Business Week,* April 21, 1973, p. 85.

11

Individual development: Learning and consumer socialization

Honda, the Japanese automobile and motorcycle manufacturer, recently entered the U.S. lawn mower market. A unique feature of the Honda lawn mower is that the cutting blade automatically stops rotating within seconds after the operator releases the handle. This greatly increases the safety of the unit. Before Honda can become successful in the marketplace, consumers must *learn* of the product's existence and features. To assist with this learning process, Honda will spend about $1 million in spot television ads and magazines.[1]

As the above example indicates, learning is essential to the consumption process. In fact, consumer behavior is largely learned behavior. That is, we acquire most of our attitudes, values, tastes, preferences, symbolic meanings, and so forth through learning. Our culture and social class, through such institutions as schools and religious organizations, as well as our family and friends, provide learning experiences that greatly influence the type of lifestyle we seek and the products we consume.

The purpose of this chapter is to show how individuals develop and learn to become consumers. As indicated in Chapter 4, culture provides a basic framework of knowledge, values, and attitudes which all individuals in that culture must learn in order to function effectively.

---

[1] J. Neher, "Market Buzzing over Mower Moves," *Advertising Age* (March 5, 1979), p. 10.

Included in this framework is information about acceptable lifestyles and purchasing processes. This information must be processed (see Chapter 10) and learned if the consumer is to cope successfully with the environment. Thus, individual development, while it includes critically important physiological changes, is also very much a learning process.

We are going to examine two aspects of the learning process. The first is the general nature of learning. The focus of this discussion will be toward answering questions such as "How can Honda be sure that consumers will *learn* about the safety features of its new lawn mower?" We will focus here on theories of how adults learn specific facts or behaviors. The second aspect that we will cover is consumer socialization. That is, we want to examine what is known about how children learn to consume.

THE NATURE OF LEARNING

Think for a moment of the many things it has been necessary for you to learn in order to make consumption decisions. For example, one consumer might have learned the following:

When buying durable goods such as a microwave oven, a national brand is a *safer* buy than a retailer's private brand.

A sale price of $4.69 is far *too much* to pay for a six pack of beer brewed in America.

The *best* values for television sets are found in discount appliance stores rather than in full-service department stores.

All brands of aspirin are really the *same,* regardles of advertised claims.

When buying a new suit to wear to work, *disregard* bright colors and the latest style and consider only styles similar to those the other people you work with wear.

To not order snails as an appetizer at a restaurant because they taste *bad.*

To read the food advertising in the newspaper very closely on Wednesday because that is *when* all the good buys are advertised.

Of course, this consumer would have learned thousands of other things such as store locations and hours and such general skills as how to read, drive, and so forth.

All of the above are specific examples of learned needs, preferences, behaviors, and so on that influence important parts of consumer decisions. For instance, the consumer described above probably would shop only for nationally branded microwave ovens. Perhaps because he or she had learned that for new and complex products, national brands meant that the chance of product failure was lower and if the product did fail, the risk was still reduced because the company would stand behind the product.

It should be apparent from this example that what is learned does not necessarily correspond with "truth." It may well be that private brands are no less risky than national brands in terms of either failure or warranty. But to the extent that consumers have learned a preference for brand names in such purchase circumstances, they will act as if their information is the truth. One could have as easily learned that private brands are no less risky and considerably cheaper than national brands and therefore make an entirely different purchase decision.

It is important to understand the origins of what is learned. In our microwave example, the consumer could have learned about the low risk involved in purchasing national brands from family or friends, from direct experience with the product, from information deliberately gathered from the mass media, or from years of low-level involvement with television commercials promoting national brands. Also this learned preference for national brands could be changed. The consumer could have a favorable experience with a private brand (perhaps acquired as a gift), an unfavorable experience with a national brand, or perhaps acquire additional information from family, friends, or other sources.

As the above discussion indicates, marketing managers need to be aware of what consumers have learned about their firm, product category, and brand. Without such a knowledge, and a knowledge of how learning occurs, it will be difficult to influence what consumers know about a given brand or firm. For example, many consumers have learned the rule: "Red wine with heavy meats, white wine with fish and poultry." With the increasing popularity of wine, particularly white wine, at meals and as a cocktail, wine producers have attempted to alter this learned rule by advertising that "the appropriate wine for any meal is the wine you prefer." The reason for such a communications campaign may be that it is easier to get people to learn a new rule for wine and food selections than it is to get people who like only white, light wines to learn to also like red, heavy wines.

Learning defined

Having developed a feel for the nature and importance of learning, let us consider a formal definition: *Learning is the process that results in changes in behavior, immediate or expected, which come about from experience and practice or the conceptualization of that experience and practice in response to stimuli and/or situations.*

Several aspects of this definition require elaboration. First, learning is a *process*. That is, it is an ongoing activity that is dynamic, adaptive, and subject to change. While learned behaviors are the outcome of the process, these behaviors may be temporary due to additional learning.

Secondly, we can see that it is *experience* and *practice* that actually bring about changes in behavior. For example, in order to learn how to play racquetball you may participate in it to gain experience (be exposed to the different skills required, the rules, and so forth). However, the experience does not have to be an actual, physical one. It could be a conceptualization of a potential experience. In other words, you could learn to play racquetball by reading about how to play without actually doing it. Certainly, most of us would feel that you would not learn as well as through actual experience, but you could still learn. Of course, combining reading and direct experience might accelerate the total process.

Nonexperiential learning (conceptual learning) is particularly important in consumer behavior. For example, assume that you are considering purchasing a bottle of liqueur to serve as afterdinner drinks. A bottle of a Greek liqueur attracts your attention. The sales clerk tells you that it has a strong, licorice flavor. Not liking licorice, you decide that you do not like Ozou. Thus, you have learned that you do not like Ozou without having a direct, taste experience with the product. This is an extremely common form of learning.

Finally, we should note that learning can result in *immediate* changes in behavior or *anticipated* ones. In other words, we do not have to see the immediate results of the learning process to assume that learning has occurred. We can store our learning until it is needed and frequently do this in terms of making purchase decisions. For example, we can learn product attribute characteristics even though we do not expect to make the purchase decision for several months or even years. Marketers know that in many circumstances the learning involved in a complex product choice is the result of a lengthy process and cannot be brought about in a short period of time. Television advertising often appears to influence our perception of desirable brands and product attributes through a slow, incremental process of low-involvement learning.[2]

The strength of learning

What is required to bring about a strong and long-lasting learned response? How can the promotion manager of Levis teach you the advantages of this brand? How can this be done so that you will not quickly forget them? These questions all relate to the strength of learning. The strength of learning is heavily influenced by three factors: importance, reinforcement, and repetition or practice. Generally, learning will come about more rapidly and last longer *the more important the material* to be learned, *the more reinforcement received* during the process, and *the greater the number of stimulus repetitions* (or practice) that occurs.

---

[2] H. E. Krugman, "The Impact of Television Advertising: Learning without Involvement," in *Perspectives in Consumer Behavior*, eds. H. H. Kassarjian and T. S. Robertson (Scott, Foresman and Co., 1973), pp. 98–104.

Importance Importance refers to the value that the consumer places on the information to be learned. The more important it is for you to learn a particular behavior or information, the more effective and efficient you become in the learning process. The information stimuli become easier for you to pay attention to and to attach meaning to when you see it as important and relevant to your needs. You will probably also put more effort into the process because the consequences are of value to you. Your practice will probably be more consistent and occur at more frequent intervals, both factors that increase the speed of learning and the quality of that learning.

Typically, we can use involvement and motivation interchangeably when dealing with learning. That is to say that the motivation to learn will be high when involvement is high and vice versa. However, there is a body of literature and research being developed that points out that meaningful learning can and does occur when involvement, and hence motivation to learn, is low. This is called *low-involvement learning.*[3] The basic point of low-involvement learning is that when a consumer is receiving unimportant information, such as in television advertising for many convenience products, a unique type of learning occurs. In such situations, parts of the message are processed and stored without an active evaluation of its meaningfulness or accuracy. Over time such partial messages exert a strong influence on the images we hold of particular brands, the product attributes we consider important, and so forth.

Reinforcement Many learning theorists believe that learning is brought about only through reinforcement (reward or punishment). While there are theories of learning that do not emphasize reinforcement as the central explanatory concept, it is apparent that reinforcement has a significant impact on the motivation to learn as well as the speed with which learning occurs and the duration of its effect.

We have made the statement many times throughout the text that consumer behavior is purposeful, goal-directed behavior. Marketers attempt to teach us that their products have attributes that will satisfy one or more of our goals. Eventually, if their promotional campaigns are successful and the goal or need the product can satisfy is sufficiently important, we will try the product. To the extent that it satisfies our goal(s), we will be reinforced and the probability of our purchasing that brand again increases. To the extent that the product does not fulfill our goal(s), we will not be reinforced and the probability of our purchasing that brand again will decrease.

From the above discussion, we can see that there are two very important reasons for marketers to determine precisely what reinforces specific consumer purchases. First, to obtain repeat purchases the product must satisfy the goals sought by the consumer. Second, to in-

---

[3] Ibid.

duce the consumer to make the first purchase, the promotional messages must promise reinforcement, that is, satisfaction, of the consumer's goals.

We will formally define reinforcement as—*anything which increases the likelihood that the desired response will be repeated in the future.*[4] This means, of course, that there are negative (punishment) as well as positive (rewards) reinforcements. The use of *fear appeals* in advertising provides an excellent example of the use of negative reinforcement. We will talk in some depth about fear appeals and their use in marketing persuasion attempts in Chapter 13, but for now we can simply define a fear appeal as an attempt to point out negatively valued consequences of performing (or not performing) some act. For instance, perhaps you can recall various advertisements for life insurance that portray a family left without financial resources causing the loss of the home or the children not being able to go to college because Dad did not have life insurance! Such advertisements are using the potential of negative reinforcement and conceptual learning in an attempt to stimulate a particular insurance purchase.

Repetition   Repetition (or practice) increases the strength and speed of learning. Quite simply, the more times we are exposed to information or practice a behavior the more likely we are to learn it. The effects of repetition are, of course, directly related to the importance of the stimuli and the reinforcement given. In other words, less repetition of an advertising message is necessary for you to learn that message if the subject matter is very important to you and/or if there is a great deal of relevant reinforcement. Since many advertisements do not contain information of current importance to consumers, repetition plays a critical role in the promotion process.

Both the number of times a message is repeated and the timing of those repetitions affect the extent and duration of learning. Figure 11−1 illustrates the relationship between repetition timing and product recall for a food product. One group of housewives, represented by the curved line in the figure, were exposed to the product advertisement once a week for 13 consecutive weeks. For this group, product recall (learning) increased rapidly and reached its highest level during the 13th week, forgetting occurred rapidly, and recall was virtually zero by the end of the year.

The second group of housewives were exposed to the same 13 direct mail advertisements. However, they received one ad every four weeks. The recall pattern for this group is shown by the zigzag line in the figure. Here learning increased throughout the year but with substantial forget-

---

[4] H. C. Ellis, *Fundamentals of Human Learning and Cognition* (William C. Brown Co. Publishers, 1972), p. 15.

FIGURE 11–1

Repetition timing and advertising recall

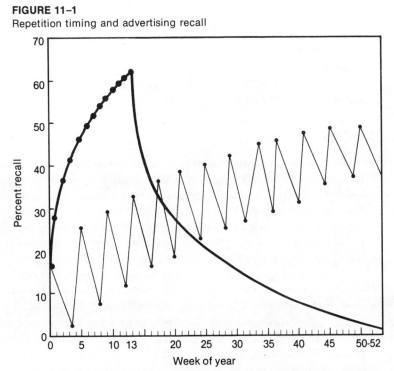

Source: Reprinted from H. J. Zielske, "The Remembering and Forgetting of Advertising," *Journal of Marketing* (January 1959), p. 240, with permission from the American Marketing Association.

ting between message exposures.[5] Of course, the best exposure strategy depends entirely on the objectives of the organization. Obviously, if it is important to produce widespread knowledge of the product rapidly, frequent (close-together) repetitions should be used. Thus, political candidates frequently hold back a significant proportion of their media budgets until shortly before the election and then use a "media blitz" to ensure widespread knowledge of their desirable attributes. More long-range programs, such as store image development, should consider more widely spaced repetitions.

Consumers frequently complain about repetition in advertising, and some even declare that because of excess repetition "they would never buy that product!" However, look at it from the advertiser's point of view. First, advertisers are never sure when all of the relevant markets are exposed to the ad, so to the extent that it is economically feasible, they blanket, via repetition, the market. Secondly, for many products,

---

[5] H. J. Zielski, "The Remembering and Forgetting of Advertising," *Journal of Marketing* (January 1959), pp. 239–43.

particularly convenience items, advertisers are primarily interested in consumers learning the brand name, that is, learning familiarity, and familiarity is directly related to number of exposures. There is, however, a fine line for the marketer to balance in terms of repetition. Too much repetition can, at some point, cause people to actively shut out the message, evaluate it negatively, or pay no attention to the message because it is too familiar (habituation).

THEORIES OF LEARNING

In this part of our discussion concerning learning we are going to examine how learning occurs. Our purpose is not to engage in an extremely theoretical explanation nor to compare and contrast various theories with the goal of deciding which best explains learning. Rather, we want to present you with a general picture of accepted theory as to how learning occurs that can be useful across the wide variety of learning-related situations confronting consumers.

Consumers face a great many tasks or situations that require learning to take place, and the nature of the learning mechanisms employed will vary as the situations faced vary. We will look at two basic approaches to learning, *conditioning* and *cognition,* in order to give you a broad view of how learning occurs. They both are correct descriptions of learning but are applicable *in different situations*.

Conditioning

Conditioning represents the simplest form of learning. In a broad sense, conditioning refers to learning based upon association of stimulus (information) and response (behavior). We realize that the word *conditioning* has a negative connotation to some and brings forth images of robotlike humans who have literally been conditioned by some outside force. Nothing could be further from the actual meaning of the term as it relates to real world consumer learning situations. Generally, conditioned learning simply means that through continuous exposure to some stimulus and a corresponding response, one learns that they go together (or do not go together), and hence the next time that stimulus occurs, that response should (or should not) be engaged in. There are two basic forms of conditioned learning—classical and operant.

Classical conditioning (Does the name Pavlov ring a bell?) Classical conditioning refers to the process of using a natural physiological relationship between a stimulus and response to bring about the learning of the same response to a different stimulus. The concept was developed by Ivan Pavlov, and can be better understood by referring to Figure 11 – 2A. Pavlov did his work with dogs and caused a dog to learn to salivate simply upon hearing a bell by associating that tone for a period of time with

FIGURE 11–2
Learning through classical conditioning

A. Learning by classical conditioning

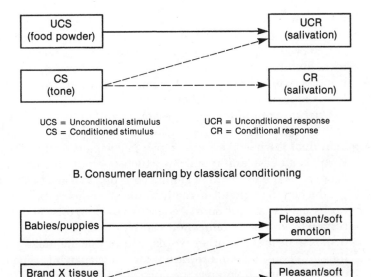

UCS = Unconditional stimulus   UCR = Unconditioned response
CS = Conditioned stimulus   CR = Conditional response

B. Consumer learning by classical conditioning

presentation of food powder to the dog. Dogs (and humans for that matter) automatically form saliva in their mouths when presented with food. The dog has no control over this relationship of food to salivation. If one simply associates some other stimuli (bell) with the food for a period of time, one can teach a dog to salivate by hearing only the tone, with no food present. When this is the case, learning has occurred as the result of classical conditioning.

We suspect that you are wondering what the point of this discussion is with respect to consumer behavior. After all, consumers are not at all like dogs and physiological relationships such as the one described above are not very relevant to most consumer purchase situations. However, classical conditioning does have some very real applications to consumer learning and can explain a great deal of the *associations* made between brand names and other familiar symbols. Turning to Figure 11–2B, we can see an example of consumer classical conditioning. In our society, most people upon seeing a cuddly baby or a cute puppy feel a pleasant, warm, and soft emotion. This is a learned response taught to us by our culture, but it is so well learned that it is, for most of us, an automatic response. When marketers want us to have pleasant feelings for their brands, they may show the brand name and product in association with stimuli known to evoke pleasant emotions. For example, a marketer of tissue paper might do well to show the product in advertisements surrounded with babies or puppies or some combination. Shown often enough, the marketing manager can hope that when you see the product on the supermarket shelf that some of the same pleasant feelings will be aroused. Does this guarantee your purchase? Certainly not, but it does increase the odds of your purchase of that brand. Note that the symbolic associations have to be relevant and meaningful to be effective. One could not, for example, show babies and puppies with cigarettes and expect consumers to react favorably in terms of associative learning.

Operant conditioning Operant conditioning, also known as instrumental learning, differs from classical conditioning primarily in that the individual learner is a more active participant in the learning process. Perhaps an easy example from which operant conditioning can be understood is the problem of getting your dog to learn to sit up. In order to get the dog to respond correctly to the stimulus command "sit up," it is necessary to have the animal engage in the response and then reward the response so that a connection can be made between the stimulus and response desired. In other words, you physically make the dog assume the sitting position (and reward it for doing so) while repeating the stimulus command. If you use the correct reward (probably food) and practice enough, eventually the dog will *learn* to sit up when the command is issued. This procedure is illustrated in Figure 11–3A. Notice that rein-

FIGURE 11–3
Learning through operant conditioning

A. Learning by operant conditioning

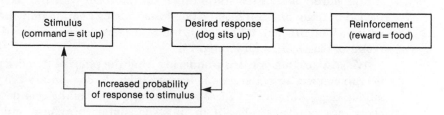

B. Consumer learning by operant conditioning

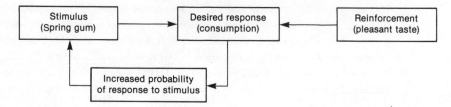

forcement plays a much larger role in operant conditioning than it did in classical. As there is no automatic stimulus-response relationship involved, the subject must first be induced to engage in the desired behavior and then this behavior must be reinforced.

Suppose you are the product manager for American Chicle's new Spring Menthol mint gum. You believe your product has a light, fresh taste that consumers will like. How can you influence them to learn to consume your brand? One approach would be to distribute a large number of free samples through the mail. American cultural values against waste would cause many consumers to chew the gum (desired response). To the extent that the taste of the gum is indeed pleasant (reinforcement), the probability of continued consumption is increased. This is shown graphically in Figure 11-3B.

Operant conditioning generally involves the actual usage of the product. Thus, a great deal of marketing strategy is aimed at securing an initial trial. Free samples (at home or in the store), special price discounts on new products, and giveaways are only a few of the ways marketers try to encourage learning via operant conditioning. As stated before, for successful learning (as measured by repeat purchase behavior) to take place, the product must fulfill the consumer's needs. Otherwise, the reinforcement will be negative and the consumer will learn to avoid (not purchase) the product.

Cognitive learning

The cognitive approach to learning encompasses all the mental activities of humans as they work to solve problems or cope with complex situations. It involves learning ideas, concepts, attitudes, and facts that contribute to our ability to reason, solve problems, and learn relationships without direct experience, repetition, or reinforcement. The following quote should help clarify this type of learning.

> The term cognition emphasizes the symbolic, mental, and inferred (not directly seen) processes of humans. Thus, the sharpening and refining of abstract concepts such as "freedom" and "justice," the search for a solution to a problem, and the use of strategies in games are said to be instances of cognitive processes because they presumably involve mental or symbolic processes on the part of the learner.
>
> Cognition thus typically refers to the class of processes involving such activities as thinking, reasoning, problem solving, and conceptual learning. More generally, reference to cognitive processes implies an active role of the human in learning situations, the use of strategies, and ways in which the learner might organize materials in order to learn and retain them more efficiently. Since it is difficult to think of any human learning situation in which the human is not in some way actively responding, organizing, and reorganizing the materials, human learning will almost always involve some kind of cognitive activity."[6]

---

[6] Ellis, *Fundamentals*, pp. 3–4.

As can be seen from the above, cognitive learning theories are not separate from conditioning theories but rather are an extension of them to enable us to understand more precisely how complex learning occurs. There are simply too many situations that consumers face that cannot be explained by simple conditioning and association. One cannot try out four houses before learning which is the best. One cannot buy one brand of car and discard it the next week like it was a tube of toothpaste, the flavor of which did not appeal to you. Consumers must learn which behavior to engage in prior to engaging in it and frequently have to live with the results for a long time. Trial and error learning simply cannot explain how this type of learning occurs.

In Figure 11−4 we illustrate the components that contribute to learning by cognition as well as provide an example of this type of consumer learning. In Figure 11−4A cognitive learning is shown as goal directed, and the action taken to achieve a desired goal is influenced by an integration of our insights, ideas, and attitudes. Based on the processing of this information, a particular action is taken in order to fulfill a

FIGURE 11–4
Cognitive learning

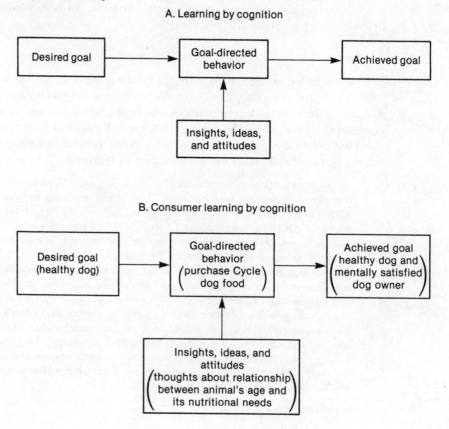

A. Learning by cognition

B. Consumer learning by cognition

certain goal. In terms of consumer learning Figure 11—4B depicts a desired consumer goal as a "healthy dog." By evaluating the available information (i.e., insights, product information, attitudes, etc.), the consumer infers (learns by mental thought) that General Foods' Cycle dog food would help fulfill their desired goal. In this case the achieved goal is a healthy dog as well as a mentally satisfied dog owner. Thus, learning which dog food to purchase was the result of a defined goal and a mental evaluation of alternatives which would achieve that goal.

Another way to understand cognitive learning is to examine how we learn concepts. A *concept* can be defined as a generalized idea that has been developed from specific observations. For example, we have learned that the concept of an automobile is really a label for a class of specific objects, all of which are different but which have certain common, fundamental characteristics. Concept learning, then, is *when two or more differing objects, events, people, and so forth are classified into a single category and given an identifying label.*[7] In order to learn concepts, humans have to be able to process information into defined categories and be able to distinguish differences as well as similarities. This obviously involves a great many complex mental activities that are more than just simple observation and association. Concept learning is an example of the types of learning that must occur at some stage in individual development in order for consumers to effectively cope with the complex and changing environments that they face. Concepts are the basis for learning principles which give us the rules by which we organize and give meaning to the world in which we live.

As we have stated continually, we view the consumer as a problem solver and goal seeker. This means that the consumer is an active, thinking, and learning person involved in responding to situations that may or may not have occurred before. Cognitive learning theories help us to understand how consumers handle complex problems through the acquisition, processing, and even creation of information. Thus, cognitive learning involves learning about situations and behaviors prior to their occurrence, altering and adopting already acquired responses based on new experiences and information, and developing insight and understanding that allow for the creation of new learning experiences.

Other characteristics of learning

Regardless of which approach to learning is applicable in a given marketing situation, there are several general characteristics of learning which are relevant and of interest to marketing managers. We will deal briefly with four of these characteristics: stimulus generalization, stimulus discrimination, extinction or forgetting, and imagery.

Stimulus generalization Once we have learned a particular re-

---

[7] Ibid., p. 137.

sponse that works for us we are able to capitalize on that learning by transferring it to other similar learning situations. In other words, we *generalize* from one stimulus situation to others. This is termed stimulus generalization and rests on the basic principle of *whenever a response is learned in one stimulus situation, other stimuli similar to those in the training situation acquire some tendency to produce that response.*[8] For example, Pavlov was able to have the dog make the salivation response to other stimuli that were similar to the bell tone, say the jingling of keys. Stimulus generalization is really the basis for the transfer of learning and as such is particularly relevant to marketing.

Consider the consumer learning problem that a marketer faces when trying to introduce a new brand into the marketplace to compete with already successful brands. If there is no significant differential advantage for the new brand, consumers must learn that it is at least as good as the existing choices. An important way to bring about this learning is to make the new brand similar to existing brands so consumers can generalize their previous learning. Similar brand names, product shapes, packaging, and advertising can all help to bring this about.

The value of *family branding* strategies is derived from stimulus generalization. As you recall from your marketing management course, a family branding policy is where the same brand name, e.g., General Electric or Campbells, is given to every product in the line. The reasons for doing so are obvious—the consumer can generalize from the successful use of one product in the line to others that have not yet been tried. In the case of Campbells, the products are very similar (soups) and so the transfer is particularly easy. For General Electric, however, the differences between products are significantly larger (toaster versus a refrigerator), yet learning about quality and dependability can be transferred easily. This ability to learn via generalization of the brand name means that the marketer can concentrate on a single stimulus in the promotion campaigns instead of having to develop separate, and expensive, individual brand strategies.

One must remember that if positive and favorable brand attributes can be learned via generalization so can negative and unfavorable ones. Witness the case of Bon Vivant soups.[9] The company had a line of soups, among which was a vichyssoise. Unfortunately, a number of food poisonings were traced to a shipment of Bon Vivant's vichyssoise. Naturally, the product was withdrawn from the market, but consumers also generalized to all of the other soups under the Bon Vivant brand and sales for the entire line were drastically affected.

Stimulus discrimination Stimulus discrimination refers to the pro-

---

[8] Ibid., p. 22.

[9] "Bon Vivant Tells Its Side of the Story," *Marketing Communications* (December 1971), pp. 24–25.

cess of learning to respond *differently* to somewhat similar stimuli. At some point, learning via generalizations becomes dysfunctional because less and less similar stimuli are still being grouped together. At this point consumers need to begin to be able to differentiate between the stimuli. As one noted author has said, "put in marketing terms, discrimination is the process by which buyers strengthen their attachment to a particular brand."[10] For example, the management of Levis feels that consumers should not see their jeans as being just like every other brand. In order to develop a brand loyal market for Levis, consumers had to be taught to differentiate between all the similar brands.

There are a number of ways that marketers do this, not the least obvious of which are the advertising campaigns that specifically point out brand differences, real or contrived. The product itself is frequently altered in shape or design to help increase product differentiation. For example, to serve different consumer needs in the detergent market, Procter and Gamble has created several brands of detergent that include Tide, Cheer, Bold, Gain, Dash, Oxydol, Duz, Bonus, Salvo, and Era. Each brand is distinctive in brand name, packaging, and primary consumer benefit in order to achieve stimulus discrimination and avoid stimulus generalization.

Note that not all marketing managers want to bring stimulus discrimination about for their brands. There is a very definite "me-too" strategy that many companies adhere to in almost every product category. These marketers are willing to accept the market share (a sometimes significant one) gained by simply being as similar to the leading brand as possible. The costs of bringing about stimulus or brand differentiation are high and the me-too firms can be extremely profitable by obtaining a smaller, but less expensive, market share.

Extinction If marketing managers are interested in consumer learning, they should also be concerned with how long that learning lasts. Extinction of learned responses, or forgetting as it is more commonly termed, occurs because the reinforcement for the learned response is withdrawn, or the learned response is no longer used.

How quickly extinction occurs generally appears to be *a function of the importance of the stimulus, the amount and frequency of reinforcement, and the repetition or practice engaged in.* If these three factors seem familiar to you, they should, as we discussed them previously when dealing with the strength of learning. In fact we can make the general statement that the probability of extinction will vary inversely with the strength of learning, that is, the less strong the original learning experience, the higher the probability of extinction or forgetting.

---

[10] J. A. Howard, "Learning and Consumer Behavior," in *Perspectives in Consumer Behavior*, eds. H. H. Kassarjian and T. S. Robertson (Scott, Foresman and Co., 1973), p. 82.

In general, we remember longer information that is important to us, regardless of reinforcement and repetition. However, much of the information given to consumers by marketers is of low importance, and repetition and reward become important factors. We have already discussed the basic effects of repetition and the question now is how does a manager put it to use. Here we are discussing how many repetitions are necessary and how should they be spaced. The primary example of this is the advertising budget. Most firms have fixed dollar budgets and have to allocate them over the year. How many ads do they show and when do they show them for maximum effect? The A. C. Gilbert Company, a toy manufacturer, spread its entire advertising budget equally over a year by appearing on the same cartoon show every Saturday morning.[11] Was this the most effective repetition schedule? There is no necessarily correct answer, of course, but consider that the largest percentage of toy purchasing occurs at Christmas time when increased repetitions might have more impact. The children in the audience might retain the advertised message longer at a time that purchase is more likely to occur. Figure 11−1 suggests that concentrating their advertisements closer to the primary purchasing season would have been a wiser use of scarce advertising dollars.

Imagery   Words, whether a brand name or corporate slogan, create certain images. For example, brand names such as Camel and Rabbit evoke sensory images, or well-defined mental pictures. As a result these words possess a high degree of imagery or mental visibility. This aids learning as words high in imagery are substantially easier to learn and remember than low-imagery words.[12] The theory behind the imagery effect is quite simple. High-imagery words leave a dual code since they can be stored in memory on the basis of both *verbal* and *pictorial* dimensions, while low-imagery words can only be coded *verbally*. Since imagery greatly enhances learning and the speed of learning, the imagery of a brand name represents a critical marketing decision when developing a brand name for a new product.

Conclusions on consumer learning

So far we have examined consumer learning in general terms. We have looked at what learning is and what its role is in the consumer decision process. We explored some basic theoretical approaches to learning, conditioning, and cognition and discussed the kinds of consumer learning situations that can best be explained by each. Finally, we looked at a number of specific learning characteristics—generalization, discrimination, extinction and imagery. Let us now turn to a discussion

---

[11] R. F. Hartley, *Marketing Mistakes* (Grid, Inc., 1976), p. 114.

[12] A. Paivio, *Imagery and Verbal Processes* (Holt, Rinehart and Winston, 1971).

of how consumer socialization occurs and trace individual learning development up through young adults.

CONSUMER SOCIALIZATION

In our earlier discussion of culture (Chapter 4) a distinction was made between acculturation—learning another's culture—and enculturation—learning your own. The process of enculturation is really the process of socialization. Marketing managers have a particular interest in that part of socialization that involves learning to purchase and consume products.

Consumer socialization is learning theory in action and is an important aspect of our study of consumer behavior because so much of our consumption behavior patterns are largely determined by our early learning. Suppose, for example, that you were a brand manager for Gillette in charge of safety razors. We would suspect that you would be very interested in how young men learn a preference for safety razors or electric razors. Do their fathers teach them by serving as role models? Do they learn that the use of one type of shaving device is more masculine than another? Can they be influenced in their product purchases? These kinds of questions are of great interest to marketing managers for many types of products and, on an overall basis, are of interest to all of us in our effort to try and understand consumer behavior. In addition, we shall see that the public policy officials are also very interested in how consumers learn, frequently with the intent to control or regulate marketing activities aimed at influencing young consumers.

Consumer socialization defined

Consumer socialization is defined as the *processes by which young people acquire skills, knowledge, and attitudes relevant to their functioning as consumers in the marketplace.*[13] We are concerned with understanding both what behaviors children learn and how those behaviors are associated with the purchase and use of goods and services. The *what* of consumer learning refers to the content of learning and the *how* refers to the methods by which that content is acquired.

The content of consumer learning can be broken down into two categories—directly relevant and indirectly relevant.[14] By *directly relevant* we mean those aspects of consumer behavior that are necessary for purchase and use to actually take place. In other words, a person has to learn particular skills such as how to shop, how to compare similar

---

[13] S. Ward, "Consumer Socialization," *Journal of Consumer Research* (September 1974), p. 2.

[14] Ibid.

brands, how to budget available income, and so forth. It should be apparent that everyone learns these skills differently as seen by differences in actual behavior. Knowledge and attitudes about stores, products, brands, salespeople, clearance sales, advertising media, coupons, and so forth are also directly relevant consumer learning content necessary to carry out purchase and use activities.

Indirectly relevant consumer learning content refers to everything which has been learned that motivates purchase and use behavior. It is the knowledge, attitudes, and values that cause people to want certain products and that allows them to attach differential evaluations to products and brands. For example, some consumers know (have learned) that when buying a car that Mercedes-Benz is an extremely prestigious brand name and represents the kind of car they would most like to have. They may respond well, therefore, to other brands of cars designed and advertised to be similar to a Mercedes-Benz. Note that this information was not necessary to carry out the actual purchase (directly relevant), but was extremely important in deciding to purchase and what to purchase (indirectly relevant). As pointed out in Chapter 4 on culture, we learn the rules or norms associated with existing in our society, and many of these norms are indirectly related to product purchase and use. One learns, for instance, that because you are a young husband and father, there are many specific activities and behaviors required of you. Therefore, as much as you might want to buy that little red sports car, your only real choice is among various brands and sizes of station wagons.

How children learn to consume

A great deal of work has been undertaken recently to determine how children learn the consumption process.[15] Without oversimplifying the matter too much, we can say that two basic perspectives as to how children learn have been developed: social learning and cognitive development/information processing. We will look briefly at each of these before moving on to an examination of children's learned decision-making abilities from birth until leaving the family of orientation.

Social learning Essentially, there are two social learning processes that influence how children learn—direct instrumental training and imitation. *Direct instrumental training* occurs when a teacher, parent, or other significant individual specifically and directly attempts to bring about certain responses through reinforcement. In other words, a parent may try to directly teach a child which kinds of snack foods that an allowance may be spent on by explicitly stating which foods can be

---

[15] For examples of various studies relating to this question, see S. Ward, D. B. Wackman, and E. Wartella, *How Children Learn to Buy* (Sage Publications, 1977).

purchased (fresh fruits, sugarless gum and candy, and certain kinds of pastries) and which cannot be purchased (potato chips, soft drinks, and so forth). This learning can be accomplished through a series of reinforcements over time, taking either the form of reward (e.g., praise or extra privileges) or punishment (e.g., removal of privileges).

It would appear that this form of social learning is the major way that directly relevant skills, knowledge, and attitudes are learned. As basic education and income levels rise in our society, the extent and diversity of this type of learning experience is bound to increase. Parents and representatives of other institutions, such as the school or church, increasingly seem to be concerned that children learn at an early age how to shop, how to utilize money, how to compare similar products, and so forth. Commercial institutions are also interested in teaching children how to consume. A savings and loan association in Arizona developed a school program complete with "special" money whereby children could learn the value of money in terms of purchasing power. Of course, the children were also taught the value of saving a certain portion of their money, and the association was happy to open special accounts for them and their parents!

Imitation, on the other hand, occurs when the child tries to match behavioral responses to those cues provided by a role model. Imitation frequently, though not always, occurs without direct instruction from the role model and is an extremely important way for children to learn both directly and indirectly relevant skills, knowledge, and attitudes toward consumption. Let us return to our initial example in this section concerning the process by which a young male would decide on the purchase of a manual or electric shaver. For many young boys, the process of learning to shave and what to shave with is developed through imitation of their fathers. Dad is seen shaving and shaving is seen as one of the things a grown-up does. The shaving equipment a child is first exposed to by this very important role model will undoubtedly affect his own learning of what is a proper shaving device. We are not saying that children automatically copy their parents. Many things could cause a young man to use an electric razor instead of a manual one such as his father used. Different skin sensitivity, new technological advances in electric razors, preferences of a stronger role model, or peer group pressures could cause a different purchase choice to be made. However, the initial modeling behavior is still relevant and may, in fact, be the determining influence.

For imitation or modeling to successfully occur, four processes must take place.[16] First, the child must pay attention to the role model. Second, the child must have the necessary skills to understand what the role

---

[16] A. Bandura, "Social Learning through Imitation," *Nebraska Symposium on Motivation,* ed. M. R. Jones (Univeristy of Nebraska Press, 1962), pp. 211–69; and A. Bandura and R. H. Walters, *Social Learning and Personality Development* (Holt, Rinehart and Winston, 1963).

model is doing and be able to actually do it. This is necessary to enable practice to occur. Third, there has to be some form of reinforcement given to the imitation. For example, a young boy's father might encourage attempts to shave (though up to a certain age, without a blade!) but not encourage imitation of other behaviors such as swearing or smoking. Finally, there has to be retention of the learned response, which depends primarily on practice and reinforcement.

Thus, social learning is an actual example of learning theory as discussed earlier in this chapter. Atkin provides us with a good example of observational learning by explaining how children learned from a public service advertisement concerning littering.[17] The advertisements featured various models "pointing out" pollution or littering examples with their fingers and encouraging (harassing?) the offenders to quit. Over 700 children were surveyed, and there was a significant correlation between their exposure to the public service advertisements and their specific behaviors of actually pointing out litter offenders. Similar learning has occurred, to the dismay of many smoking parents, from advertisements directed at children to tell Mommy and Daddy that smoking is bad for them.

Cognitive development/information processing This approach to understanding how children learn differs from the social learning approach in much the same way that we distinguished earlier between the conditioning and cognitive approaches to basic learning theory. That is to say, neither is more correct or relevant than the other. Instead, they explain different aspects and levels of complexity of learning. Cognitive development refers to the stages that children go through in their development of intellectual thought. Information processing refers to the mental activities of perceiving new information and using it in combination with already stored experiences to solve complex, and frequently abstract, problems. The two ideas are inherently tied together because information processing ability seems to be directly tied to stage of cognitive development.

Our knowledge of stages of cognitive development is primarily a result of work done by Piaget.[18] He isolated four primary stages of development as follows:

1. *The period of sensori-motor intelligence* (0–2 years). During this period behavior is primarily motor. The child does not yet "think" conceptually, though "cognitive" development is seen.
2. *The period of preoperational thought* (2–7 years). This period is characterized by the development of language and rapid conceptual development.

---

[17] C. Atkin, "Children's Social Learning from Television Advertising: Research Evidence on Observational Modeling of Product Consumption," in *Advances in Consumer Research III*, ed. B. B. Anderson (Association for Consumer Research, 1976), pp. 513–19.

[18] B. J. Wadsworth, *Piaget's Theory of Cognitive Development* (David McKay Co., 1971).

3. *The period of concrete operations* (7 – 11 years). During these years the child develops the ability to apply logical thought to concrete problems.

4. *The period of formal operations* (11 – 15 years). During this period the child's cognitive structures reach their greatest level of development, and the child becomes able to apply logic to all classes of problems.[19]

Children then, according to Piaget, develop into better and better information processors through natural maturation and through experience. One would expect then that as children grow older they would become more complex problem solvers and deal with increasing amounts and types of information on a more and more effective basis.

A number of marketing studies have used Piaget's stages to explain how children respond to various marketing-related activities. A good example of such a study was one done by Ward on children's reactions to commercials.[20] Children from 5 to 12 years old were interviewed the day after they had seen videotaped programming that represented a typical Saturday morning's viewing for children of that age range. The results are summarized by age groups and closely parallel Piaget's middle two groups.

1. As the child becomes older, the understanding of what a commercial really is increases. Children from 5 to 7 have considerably less understanding or awareness of what a commercial is than do those from 8 to 12.

2. As the child increases in age, the basic purpose of a commercial is better understood. Younger children do not understand that advertisers want to make money off the products and very few children in any of the age groups realized that the programs they view are paid for by advertising.

3. Younger children were generally not able to discriminate between a program and a commercial as well as older children. (Note that this problem is made even more difficult when the presentation, format, and characters are the same between program and commercial such as in animated cartoon shows.)

4. Younger children tend to believe more in the basic truthfulness of commercials they view than do older children.

Other studies have indicated that as children become older they have better recall of brand names.[21] They can also recall more complex, mul-

---

[19] Ibid., pp. 26 – 27.

[20] S. Ward, "Children's Reactions to Commercials," *Journal of Advertising Research* (April 1972), pp. 37 – 45.

[21] R. S. Rubin, "An Exploratory Investigation of Children's Responses to Commercial Content of Television Advertising in Relation to Their Stages of Cognitive Development" (Ph.D. diss., University of Massachusetts).

tidimensional (product feature) advertisements.[22] Further, they become more aware of advertising as a source of new product information and become more selective in which sources they rely on.[23]

Influence of the family

Regardless of how one views children's learning, it must be obvious that the family is an important influence in the learning process. The family, and particularly the parents, are the primary transmitters of directly relevant and indirectly relevant skills, knowledge and attitudes concerning consumer behavior. Ward, Wackman, and Wartella have dealt with this aspect of consumer socialization in some detail and report the results of their own as well as others' research into the family's role in consumer socialization.[24] The following paragraphs represent a summary of these author's findings as well as those of others in the field and should give the reader a feel for the types of influences that parents, especially mothers, have on what and how much children learn about being consumers.

By having mothers fill out a questionnaire concerning their goals for teaching their children to be a consumer, it was found that in the short run, mothers want their children to learn how to handle money and to distinguish quality products. Price/bargain and quality on the other hand were both mentioned as long-term teaching goals.

Methods of teaching children were also considered. The different teaching modes included: (1) prohibiting certain actions, (2) lectures, (3) discussions, (4) being an example, and (5) allowing the child to learn from experiences. It was found that the methods differed little by age group, indicating little attempt on the mother's part to plan direct methods.

Interaction between parents and children in which the parent initiated the interaction included discussing products and discussing commercials. Mothers were questioned as to how often they discuss ideas, such as "how often do you ask the child's preference when buying things?" Results indicated that there was no difference between high, low, and medium frequency of discussion for age groups or socioeconomic status. Discussion of TV commercials was measured as to type of comments made about the advertisement with a distinction made between general and specific comments. More than half of the mothers talk about the ads, although somewhat less frequently with kindergartners; and higher-status mothers report more frequent discussions. The comments are more likely to be general and are frequently negative,

[22] A. D. Leifer et al., "Developmental Aspects of Variables Relevant to Observational Learning," *Child Development* (November 1971), pp. 1509–16.

[23] Ibid.

[24] Ward, Wackman, and Wartella, *How Children*, chap. 7.

which is consistent with another finding that mothers generally have a negative attitude toward commercials directed at children.

Child-initiated interaction was also considered when a child requests a product. Information on frequency of yielding to requests of children showed a positive relationship to age, with the largest increase from the third to the sixth grade. There were no differences by social class.

When reacting to purchase requests, mothers responded in one of four ways: (1) bought what is asked for, (2) discussed and negotiated terms for buying, (3) refused, but explained why, and (4) refused with no explanation. Mothers with older children were more likely to "negotiate," with a concurrent decrease in the "refuse but explain why" response to older children. An increase in the use of the negotiation response and the "refuse but explain why" response was seen with increasing socioeconomic status. Younger children's mothers frequently deny the request, yet explain why.

The family context also offers a child the opportunity for consumption on his or her own. Children's buying role was operationalized by finding out: (1) if the child alone buys the product, (2) the child chooses, but discusses with parents, (3) the parents choose, but discuss with child, and (4) the parents buy. As expected, this buying role was found to increase with age. It was also found that in lower status homes, the child's role was slightly increased.

When the parents were asked how much money a child is provided, it was found that allowances were more frequently provided with increasing age and with social class. Outside earnings increased with age, and it was also found that children of lower social class have more sources of income.

Television, as a source of socialization within the home, was considered a consumption-related experience for children. Viewing time was stable across age groups but decreased as social class increased.

Children's consumer decision making

We have discussed how children become socialized, that is, how they learn to become consumers and what the influence of the family can be. Let us now look at the stages that children go through and describe relevant behaviors that would be of interest to marketing managers. We will use the same basic stages presented in Chapter 9 to explain the family life cycle. We will be interested, however, in the stages prior to an individual moving out of the family of orientation and into the family of procreation. Table 11–1 shows the four stages of interest to us—infant, preschool, preteenager, and teenager.

Infant This category may seem to be relatively unimportant to the marketing manager aside from the direct need for certain products such as baby foods, diaper services, and so forth. It is true that infants up until

TABLE 11–1
Characteristics of the individual in the early stages

Category	General range age	Major lifestyle problems and tasks
Infant	0–2	No expected tasks. Completely cared for by other family members. A major focus of attention and concern by others.
Preschool	3–5	Has developed a definite personality. Can interact and communicate well with others. Still largely cared for but expected to conform to basic family behavior patterns.
Preteenage	6–12	Through interaction with peers and experience with extrafamily institutions (school, church, etc.) a definite lifestyle approach begins to emerge. Task responsibilities, both in and out of the family, begin to be assigned.
Teenager	13–18	Development of an independent lifestyle. Many identification problems. Relationship with family begins to be strained as need for independence increases.

two years or so are extremely dependent on their parents and are not functioning consumers on their own. Yet because of their overwhelming dependency they, in fact, can control a large part of their parents' life. For example, some authors have ingeniously pointed out the "power of the nap" in terms of affecting shopping behavior.[25] Infants have very rigid eating and sleeping schedules which affect all the mother's (and father's frequently) behavior associated with leaving the home. Mothers who have infants need to go shopping between feeding and nap time or when someone trustworthy will watch the child. Recreation alternatives for parents of infants are rather sharply decreased because of their lack of flexibility.

Preschool   From three to five years of age seems to be a particularly important time in consumer socialization. Children have developed language and mobility to the extent that they can interact with others. Dependence on the adult members of the family has been reduced, though obviously the child still needs a great deal of parental support and control. Speech and physical mobility mean that the child can begin to express specific demands and participate in more out-of-home activities such as shopping. Children in this preschool age are most

---

[25] F. D. Reynolds and W. D. Wells, *Consumer Behavior* (McGraw-Hill Book Co., 1977), p. 56.

likely to accompany parents to the grocery store and this is when consumer socialization really begins. Children three to five years old have specific tastes and preferences for certain types of products—specifically foods such as cereals and snacks. They do try to influence the purchase decision and can be relatively successful. It has been found that as the child's age increases, the number of attempts to influence purchase decisions decrease.[26] However, the attempts to influence are more likely to be successful.

Partially because they are not yet in school, children in the three to five age range are exposed to more television advertising. As has been noted before, these children may be more susceptible to advertised product messages because they understand less the purpose and intent of commercials. Television viewing is also subject to social class influence. Generally as the socioeconomic level is increased, less time is spent in viewing.

Preteenage Preteenage covers the age group of 6 to 12 years of age. This means, according to Piaget, that the child can make logical decisions that extend beyond the immediate, perceived situation. Language skills are further improved, and the child becomes aware of more complex, future-oriented problems and goals. Interaction with others outside of the family is also dramatically increased, due primarily to the exposure to others through school. The number of important or significant role models is increased (e.g., teachers, peers, etc.) and the search for independence begins.

Preteenagers are heavy consumers of many kinds of products, such as fast foods, records, clothing, and movies. They seem to demand and are given a fair amount of control over purchase decisions for a limited range of products. As noted before, they make fewer requests to influence purchases but their requests are more likely to be granted. They also are at an age where specifically stated likes or dislikes are acceptable to parents. For example, preteenagers are less likely to be forced to eat certain foods than preschoolers if they express a negative preference. This is also an age where a strong need exists to be like others in the child's peer group. Clothing, sports equipment, entertainment, and other purchase choices are largely determined by what friends or classmates are doing. Children of these ages are consumers in their own right because they normally have their own incomes. Allowances, gifts, and part-time jobs provide preteenagers with disposable income that can represent a sizeable market to local retailers.

Preteens view less television than preschoolers, but not significantly so. We do see a shift in the time they view television, as older children normally are allowed to stay up later at night to watch TV. Therefore, their program preferences tend to shift over time, and they are exposed

---

[26] S. Ward and D. Wackman. "Children's Purchase Influence Attempts and Parental Yielding," *Journal of Marketing Research* (August 1972), pp. 316–19.

to commercials for products substantially different than shown on Saturday morning cartoon shows or on daytime soap opera and game shows. Print media also become more important in the preteenager segment because these children have the ability, and frequently the desire, to read. Specialized magazines such as *Boy's Life* and comic books are directed specifically at this market. Again, the likelihood of exposure to print media and the degree of that exposure are likely to vary directly with the socioeconomic level of the family.

Teenager   The teenager stage encompasses those young people between the ages of 13 and 18. This is an extremely active purchasing group, as well as composing the next mass market that marketers face. In our society children normally live at home until the age of 18 or until they finish high school. At that time, they leave the family of orientation and "become an adult." This leaving is primarily important in terms of attitude and expected behaviors. The young person is expected to contribute to the family income if he or she remains at home or to become self-supporting and find a full-time job. There are exceptions to this generalization, of course, the biggest of which are those people who continue on to college and remain dependent on their parents financially.

Teenagers frequently have a great deal of spending power. Like preteenagers, parents still provide the major financial support. Teenagers, however, often have the time, motivation, and increased skills to find better paying part-time jobs. If they are on allowances, these tend to become larger because the teenager has more needs that require fairly significant amounts of money. Dating, for example, is an encouraged and approved behavior that can be expensive.

Radio is an important media to teenagers. This is not to say that television and print media usage is significantly reduced, just that more time than before is spent listening to the radio. This seems primarily due to the increasing interest in and knowledge of music by teenagers.

Teenagers tend in many family situations to be consulted on major purchases that affect the entire family. Examples of such purchases are the car, vacations, houses, and so forth. The teenager therefore becomes an influencer that the marketer should be aware of, even if he or she is not present during the shopping activity. For example, the purchase of a new or used car in a family that has a teenage driver normally involves input on factors such as style, model, color, and accessories from the teenager. The salesperson would want to be aware of these inputs and respond to them (and hence the teenager) as well as to the adults actually making the final decision.

CHILDREN AND ADVERTISING

Before concluding our chapter on individual development, it is appropriate to comment on the growing concern with the type of influence that marketing activities can have on children's learning. These concerns are voiced by public policy officials, parents, and marketers themselves and revolve mainly around the effects of advertising on children. The basic nature of the debate is to what extent advertising can and does influence children who are unable to properly evaluate and use the information contained in persuasive messages.

For example, in 1975 Hasbro Industries, Inc., came out with the Sno-Man Sno-Cone Machine, a toy for making flavored ice, and promoted it with television commercials that began with the lyric, "Who's the kid with all the friends hanging 'round? The kid with the Sno-Man Sno-Cone."[27] The children's unit of the National Advertising Division (NAD) of the Council of Better Business Bureaus questioned the copy based on the "implication that by owning the toy a child might better his or her peers."[28] In other words, this public policy group was concerned that by using knowledge of consumer behavior (specifically peer group influences) a business firm was able to unfairly influence children. It should be noted that for this particular case, Hasbro was able to supply the NAD with sufficient evidence that children were not responding to peer group pressure and the complaint was dropped. However, "the advertiser was requested to communicate an 'ambience of sharing' as clearly as possible in the future."[29]

The Federal Trade Commission in 1978 recommended that proceedings should be undertaken to determine which of the following actions should be taken:

1. Ban all televised advertising for any product which is directed to, or seen by, audiences composed of a significant proportion of children who are too young to understand the selling purpose of, or otherwise comprehend or evaluate, the advertising;

2. Ban televised advertising directed to, or seen by, audiences composed of a significant proportion of older children for sugared food products, the consumption of which poses the most serious dental risks;

3. Require that televised advertising directed to, or seen by, audiences composed of a significant proportion of older children for sugared food products not included in (2) be balanced by nutritional and/or health disclosures funded by advertisers.[30]

These relatively dramatic (or in the view of advertisers affected by the actions—drastic) actions were a result of an intensive research effort on the part of the FTC to determine what the effect of advertising might be on children, particularly with respect to sugared foods. Part of the report is

---

[27] "A Four Year Review of the Children in Advertising Review Unit, June 1974 through June 1978 (National Advertising Division, Council of Better Business Bureaus, Inc., New York), p. 14.

[28] Ibid.

[29] Ibid., p. 15.

[30] FTC Staff Report on Television Advertising to Children (Federal Trade Commission, February 1978).

summarized below that appears relevant to our discussion of consumer learning.[31]

Summary of the FTC Staff Report on Television Advertising to Children

    I. Children's exposure to TV commercials.
   1. In 1977, the average American child aged 2 through 5 watched 25 hours and 36 minutes of TV per week.
   2. Older children, aged 6 through 11, watched 25 hours and 41 minutes per week.
   3. The National Science Foundation Report estimates that:
      a. Children 2 through 5 view 20,476 commercials per year.
      b. Children 6 through 11 view 19,236.
   4. According to the NSF report, of the range of products promoted directly to children:
      a. 25 percent is for candy/snacks.
      b. 25 percent is for cereal.
      c. 10 percent is for eating establishments, primarily fast-food restaurants.
   A. The preparation of the TV commercials directed to children and the selling techniques they use.
   1. The preparation of commercials.
      a. Commercials developed from direct testing and observation of child audience.
      b. Techniques from child psychology are used to determine the most efficient ways to induce demand.
   2. Selling techniques used.
      a. Magical promises that a product will build muscles or improve athletic performance.
      b. The chase or tug-of-war sequence in which one character tries to take a product away from another.
      c. The use of music, singing, and dancing.
      d. The use of super heroes.
      e. The voice of authority.
      f. The voices of children agreeing with the announcer.
      g. Depictions of children outperforming adults.
      h. Animation.
      i. Peer group acceptance appeals.
      j. Selling by characters who also appear in the programming.
   II. Impact of TV advertising for sugared foods and other products on children.

---

[31] Ibid.

1. TV advertising exerts a strong influence over children.
2. The strongest determinant of that influence is the child's age.
3. Children watch commercials before they are interested in programs because commercials are often the best produced and most imaginatively conceived moments on TV.
4. Children tend to prefer, and ask their parents to buy, the products promoted to them.
5. Children are frequently successful in these purchase requests.
6. TV commercials are frequently misunderstood by the child audience.
   a. Children have difficulty in differentiating commercials from programming.
   b. Children show little understanding of the purpose of commercials to create demand.
   c. Children repose indiscriminate trust in commercial messages especially if they fail to recognize selling purpose, or otherwise understand or evaluate the commercial.

A. Children's confusion regarding TV advertising.
   1. TV advertising and the preschooler.
      a. The preschooler has limited capacity for reasoning.
      b. The child is unable to put himself/herself in the place of another person to see that his/her viewpoint is only one of many possible viewpoints.
      c. Thinking focuses on only one feature at a time.
      d. TV appears real to little children. They may believe there are "real little people" in the set.
      e. Children may believe a person speaking from the set is speaking to them personally.
      f. Even the animated fantasy character is perceived in some sense real and in some sense adult, so that they are to be listened to, learned from, and imitated.
      g. They have difficulty distinguishing an advertisement from the product being advertised.
      h. They can parrot an advertisement but rarely understand what the message means.
   2. Television advertising and the school-age child.
      a. The inability of many children to differentiate between television programs and commercials (especially between the ages of 5 and 8).
      b. The trust reposed in television commercials by children who do not perceive their selling purpose or cannot otherwise comprehend or evaluate them.

    c. A tendency to believe the commercials as truthful messages rather than persuasive messages.

Our intention here is not to build a case either for or against the FTC position on advertising to children. It is apparent that children are influenced and do learn from television advertising. The question that we as marketing managers and members of society should be concerned with is whether or not that learning is positive and meaningful.

SUMMARY

Consumers must learn almost everything related to being a consumer—product existence, performance, availability, values, preference, and so forth. Marketing managers, therefore, are very interested in the nature of consumer learning, both for adult purchasers and for children who are undergoing consumer socialization.

Learning is basically defined as the process that results in behavior, immediate or expected, which comes about from experience or practice, real or conceptualized, in response to stimuli and/or situations. Learning is dynamic and adaptive and results in changes in behavior. The strength of learning depends on three basic factors—importance, reinforcement, and repetition or practice. Importance refers to the value that the consumer places on the information to be learned—the greater the importance, the greater the learning. Reinforcement is anything which increases the likelihood that a desired response will be repeated in the future—the greater the reinforcement (up to a point), the greater the learning. Repetition or practice refers to the number of times that we are exposed to the information or that we practice a behavior. Repetition increases the strength and speed of learning. All three factors are directly related to each other. That is, less repetition is necessary for very important and heavily reinforced messages and so forth.

Two basic types of learning, conditioning and cognition, are used by consumers. There are two forms of conditioned learning—classical and operant. Classical conditioning refers to the process of using a natural physiological relationship between a stimulus and response to bring about the learning of the same response to a different stimulus. Operant conditioning differs in that the individual learner is a more active participant in the learning process. In order for the participant to learn to make a certain response from a variety of responses, it is first necessary to bring about the desired response and then to reinforce that response choice. Reinforcement plays a much larger role in operant conditioning than it does in classical conditioning. As there is no automatic stimulus-response relationship involved, the subject must first be induced to engage in the desired behavior and then this behavior must be reinforced.

The cognitive approach to learning encompasses the mental activities of humans as they work to solve problems or cope with complex situations, such as learning to buy a home. Cognitive learning involves the learning of ideas, concepts, attitudes, and facts that contribute to our ability to reason, solve problems, and learn relationships without direct experience, repetition, or reinforcement.

Stimulus generalization is one way of transferring learning by generalizing from one stimulus situation to other, similar ones. Family branding is an excellent example of the use of stimulus generalization by marketers. Stimulus discrimination refers to the opposite process of learning to respond differently to somewhat similar stimuli. Marketers interested in building brand loyal customer segments must bring about the ability to discriminate between like brands.

Extinction, or forgetting, is also of interest to marketing managers. Extinction is directly related to the strength of original learning, modified by continued repetition. That is, extinction will occur more quickly the less important the information or behavior, the less reinforcement, and the less repetition it has had.

Consumer socialization deals with the processes by which young people (from birth until 18 years of age) learn how to become functioning consumers. How children become socialized (learn their own culture with respect to consumption) is very important to marketers who are interested in selling products to young people now or in the future. Consumer socialization deals with the learning of both directly relevant purchasing skills (budgeting, shopping) and indirectly relevant skills (symbols of quality and prestige for example).

There are two perspectives as to how children learn—social learning and cognitive development/information processing. Social learning deals with direct training and also the imitation of role models with no direct training involved. Cognitive development/ information processing refers to the development stages that children go through in terms of developing their mental activities and abilities to perceive and use information. Piaget's four primary stages of development are useful for categorizing cognitive development learning. They are sensorimotor intelligence (0–2 years), preoperational thoughts (2–7 years), concrete operations (7–11 years), and formal operations (11–15).

The family is a major influence in the learning process for young people. The family, and particularly the parents, is the primary transmitter of directly relevant and indirectly relevant learning concerning consumer behavior. Children's interactions with parents in terms of purchase requests and the granting of those requests change fairly dramatically as children get older. When one looks at the stages (infant, preschool, preteenager, and teenager) children go through, it is easy to see the many lifestyle problems and tasks that are due to age and stage in the life cycle. These variations result in many different marketing problems and opportunities.

Public policy officials, parents, and marketing managers have become concerned about the effects that television advertising can have on children's learning and consumption activities. The Federal Trade Commission has proposed controls over children's TV advertising, and the debate has begun as to what extent advertising can and does influence children who are unable to properly evaluate and use the information contained in persuasive messages.

REVIEW QUESTIONS

1. What is meant by "consumer behavior is learned behavior"?
2. What factors affect the strength of learning? How are these factors related to each other?
3. Distinguish between learning via classical conditioning and that which occurs via operant conditioning.
4. What do we mean by cognitive learning and how does it differ from the conditioning theory approach to learning?
5. What is meant by stimulus generalization? When is it used by marketers?
6. What is meant by stimulus discrimination? Why is it important?
7. What is extinction and why are marketing managers interested in it?
8. What is consumer socialization and how is knowledge of it useful to public policy officials as well as marketing managers?
9. What do we mean when we say that children learn "directly relevant" and "indirectly relevant" consumer skills and attitudes?
10. How do children learn as explained by social learning theories?
11. What are the developmental stages postulated by Piaget, and how are they relevant to an understanding of children's learning?
12. In what ways does the family influence children's consumption learning?
13. What types of influences do children in each of the four stages— infant, preschool, preteenager, and teenagers have on the consumption decisions of the family as a purchasing unit?
14. What direct, personal consumption decisions do children in each of the four stages make that are of interest to marketing managers?
15. Why are public policy officials concerned with the possible effects of advertising on children's learning?
16. For what products does television advertising seem to impact on children the most and what selling techniques are used to create this impact?

DISCUSSION QUESTIONS

1. What product and use factors would be important for Jeff to present to consumers in order to get them to learn to purchase a moped and the Motron brand specifically?

2. Based on your answer to question 1 above, what role do you think importance, reinforcement, and repetition will play, individually and in combination, in bringing about strong learning about Motron?

3. In what ways could Jeff and other moped marketers influence children's learning about the potential purchase of a moped? Develop a specific marketing strategy for preteenagers and one for teenagers.

4. Almex and Company has recently introduced a new coffee-flavored liqueur in direct competition with Hiram Walker's tremendously successful Kahlua brand.[32] Almex and Company has named its new entry Kamora and is packaging it in a similar bottle to that of Kahlua, using a pre-Columbian label design. The ad copy for Kamora reads—"If you like coffee—you'll love Kamora." Explain Almex's marketing strategy in terms of learning theory.

5. The FTC has required manufacturers to produce corrective advertisements in cases in which the manufacturer deceived the public with a particular claim or implied claim that was not true. The purpose of the corrective ad is to properly inform the public so they are not deceived in their perceptions of a particular brand. When this is accomplished, the firm may remove the corrective ad. This is based on the assumption that new learning has occurred. Some feel that after the corrective ad is removed it is only a matter of time before consumer perceptions of the falsely advertised product will return to their prior level as shown below.[33] Discuss learning in this case and why or why not consumer beliefs will return to levels prior to exposure of a corrective ad.

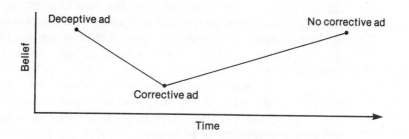

[32] This problem is based on "Kahlua's High Sales Greet New Rival," *Advertising Age* (April 12, 1979), p. 48.

[33] A. Sawyer, "The Need to Measure Attitudes and Beliefs over Time: The Case of Deceptive Advertising," in *Marketing 1776–1976 and Beyond*, ed. K. Bernhardt (American Marketing Association, 1976), pp. 380–85.

6. Discuss stimulus generalization and discrimination with respect to a firm's branding strategy. Identify five brand names that encourage learning by utilizing stimulus generalization and five brand names that avoid this type of learning. Why would the marketers of these respective products either encourage or discourage stimulus generalization?

7. What effect do television commercials aimed at children seven and under have on their socialization process? How does this contribute to their behavior as teenagers and young adults? What role should the government play in regulating television advertisements aimed at children seven and younger?

PROJECT QUESTIONS

1. Pick a consumer convenience product, perhaps a personal care product such as a deodorant or mouthwash, and create advertising copy stressing (a) a positive reinforcement and (b) a negative reinforcement.

2. Pick a small sample of friends and interview them to find out which type of reinforcement appeal (from #1 above) would be most effective. To do this you might present each friend with one of the appeals and then ask them to respond to the following question: What is your overall reaction to this advertisement?

   Unfavorable __ : __ : __ : __ : __ : __ : __ Favorable

   How likely would you be to try this product based on this advertising appeal?

   Very likely __ : __ : __ : __ : __ : __ : __ Very unlikely

3. Visit a children's toy store and examine various types of toys that seem to be marketed to specific age groups. Do you find any correspondence between these age groups and those postulated by Piaget? How do marketers of toys such as these appeal to their consumers?

4. Identify three advertisements, one based on cognitive learning, another based on operant learning, and the third based on classical conditioning. Discuss the nature of each advertisement and how it utilizes a certain type of learning.

5. Develop a short questionnaire to measure children's depth of awareness and understanding of television commercials shown on Saturday mornings. Interview four children, two in a 5 to 7 age

group, and two in an 8 to 12 category. Discuss the results in terms of differences between the two groups in number of commercials recalled, specific information recalled, and ability to differentiate between commercials and programs.

12

Individual characteristics: Motivation and personality

Thomas J. Lipton, Inc., recently decided to introduce Lipton *Lemon Tree,* a powdered lemonade flavored drink mix, into the growing, but highly competitive powdered drink market.[1] Consider some of the questions the product manager must have asked in deciding if and how to introduce this product: Why do consumers purchase powdered drink mixes? Why do they purchase lemonade flavored powdered drink mixes? Are existing brands completely satisfying all consumers? These questions all deal with motivation. That is, they focus on the goals sought by consumers in a specific purchase situation.

Consumer *motivations* are the energizing force that activates behavior and provides purpose and direction to that behavior. *Personality* reflects the common responses (behaviors) individuals make to a variety of recurring situations. The two concepts are closely interrelated and are frequently difficult to separate. For example, consumers who are *self-confident* (a personality characteristic) are more likely to have a *need for assertion* (a characteristic of motivation) because the two individual characteristics are closely related.[2]

---

[1] L. Edwards, "Powdered Drinks Market Still Sizzling," *Advertising Age* (March 5, 1979), p. 1.

[2] L. Robinson, "Consumer Complaint Behavior: A Review with Implications for Further Research," paper presented at the Third Annual Conference on Consumer Satisfaction/ Dissatisfaction and Complaining Behavior (1978).

The purpose of this chapter is to examine the nature of consumer motivations and personality and to describe how these individual characteristics energize and direct consumer behavior.

MOTIVATION

The term *motivation* should be familiar to you since you have used it and heard it used many times. Parents and teachers want to motivate students to learn; coaches motivate their players to give 100 percent; we often wonder what a person's real motives are when they tell us something; and we question the motives of marketers who try to persuade us to purchase their products.

The nature of motivation

As the above examples imply, motivation is the reason for behavior. A motive is a *construct representing an unobservable inner force that stimulates and compels a behavioral response and provides specific direction to that response.*[3] Thus, like most constructs in consumer behavior, we cannot see a motive. We can only infer the existence of motives from the behaviors of individuals.

Motivation is viewed as an inner *force*. It is commonly referred to as an urge, wish, feeling, need, and most appropriately, a motive.[4] The word *force* implies a dynamic, active nature as well as the power and ability to *stimulate* and *compel* behavior. When consumers are motivated by definition their physical and/or mental makeup is activated. In this way, we can almost feel motivation in a very real physical and mental sense. This stimulation is not without direction as consumers use goal-directed behavior to resolve problems and fulfill personal needs. For motivation to be useful in marketing practice then, a marketing manager must understand what motives (inner forces) stimulate what types of behavior (direction) and how these motives and behavior are influenced by the specific situations in which consumers engage in goal-directed, problem-solving behavior. The marketer who can discern this information is naturally in the best position to respond to consumer needs.

To illustrate the nature of consumer motivation and goal-directed behavior consider consumer motives in the purchase of clothing. Consumers with a strong need for self-expression may be motivated to purchase clothing that expresses or symbolizes status because they have a strong need to express their identity (or desired identity) to others. On

---

[3] R. F. Thompson, *Introduction to Physiological Psychology* (Harper & Row, 1975), p. 295.

[4] C. N. Coffer and M. H. Appley, *Motivation: Theory Research* (John Wiley and Sons, Inc., 1964), p. 5.

the other hand, consumers with a strong need for affiliation may purchase a certain wardrobe in order to feel more comfortable in their relationships with people they want to be like or be liked by. While these motivations may be strong, they are still dependent on the situation. For example, a consumer with a high need for affiliation may not be guided by this motivation in a purchase of underwear if the purchase or use of this product is unlikely to be observed by others.[5] Likewise, individuals who have a strong need for achievement demonstrate achievement-related behavior in situations they perceive as ego involving or evaluative, but not in situations they perceive as nonevaluative.[6] Therefore, we need to keep in mind that while motivations are energizing forces which contribute significantly to goal-directed behavior, motives compelling behavior in one situation may not exist or be quite different than motives stimulating behavior in another situation.

Innate versus learned motivations It was once believed that behavior was primarily innate and the result of instinctive motivations. That is, biologically based instincts such as sex, hunger, and thirst were thought to be the only needs that motivated behavior. While we all can recognize the existence of such biological needs, it should also be evident that a great many more of our needs are psychological in nature and have been learned.

Learned needs or motives can be considered to be psychologically based rather than physiologically based. These are motives that we learn throughout life but primarily through socialization in early childhood. Since every individual's personal development and socialization is slightly different, so are the motives that relate to our particular lifestyles and patterns of behavior.

To understand the distinction between biological or innate motives and psychological or learned motives, we can examine our lunchtime behavior. An innate hunger motive may account for our actually eating lunch, but the type of food we purchase, the manner in which we eat the food, how long we take to eat, and what we do while we are eating are all learned behaviors derived from our culture, childhood socialization, and reference groups. Thus, it is important for marketing managers to recognize that while some behavior is motivated by innate needs, learned motivations generally guide the expression of that behavior. For example, a thirsty consumer's purchase of a particular brand of soft drink on a hot summer day may reflect both the consumer's innate need to satisfy thirst as well as a learned need for self-expression. In this situation, the marketer cannot control the consumer's thirst, but the marketer can influence the consumer's choice of soft drink if the con-

---

[5] G. Fennell, "Motivation Research Revisited," *Journal of Advertising Research* (June 1975), p. 25.

[6] J. W. Atkinson, "The Achievement Motive and Recall of Interrupted and Completed Tasks," *Journal of Experimental Psychology* (1953), pp. 381–90.

sumer feels the brand of soft drink consumed reflects a desired identity.

General motives

Before going further in our discussion of motivation, it will be useful to present and discuss a summary of the general motivations that seem most relevant to consumer behavior. This is not to say that a study of the many individual theories of motivation would not be helpful; we simply feel it is the results provided by these theories that are most useful in understanding consumer behavior rather than the theories themselves. Therefore, rather than discuss theories of motivation in terms of Freud's channelization of the libido,[7] Alder's striving for superiority,[8] Fromm's escape from loneliness,[9] Sullivan's need for human relationships,[10] Horney's need to cope with anxiety,[11] and so on, we prefer to summarize the results of these theories in terms of the needs they represent and the impact these needs appear to have on consumer behavior.

We see two categories of basic motives or needs as being especially relevant to marketing managers—internal, nonsocial motives and external, social motives.

Figure 12–1 lists these motives along with a short description of each. The basic distinction between each category rests on the nature of the need. Internal, nonsocial motives reflect needs that individuals have with respect to themselves strictly as individuals, apart from others. Many of these needs are information based. That is to say, they indicate what kind of information we need, in what form we need it, and how we should process it in order to make the world around us meaningful and psychologically comfortable.

External, social motives, on the other hand, deal with human needs directly related to interactions with others in our world. Many of the reasons we engage in purchase behavior are based on our relationships with other people, and the external, social motives are related to our interactions with these other individuals.

Remember that these are categories of general motives that underlie specific consumer problems and decision-making situations. In other words, it is not always possible to trace the purchase of a product directly back to one of these general motives. For example, when a consumer runs out of salt and then purchases Mortons salt, it might not be particularly relevant for the marketing manager of Mortons to try to

---

[7] C. S. Hall and G. Lindzey, *Theories of Personality* (John Wiley and Sons, Inc., 1970).

[8] H. L. Ansbacher and R. Ansbacher, *Individual Psychology of Alfred Alder (Basic Books, 1956).*

[9] E. Fromm, *Escape from Freedom* (Holt, Rinehart and Winston, 1941).

[10] H. S. Sullivan, *The Interpersonal Theory of Psychiatry* (Norton, 1953).

[11] K. Horney, *Neurotic Personality in Our Times* (Norton, 1937).

FIGURE 12–1
General motives relevant to the practice of marketing

Internal, nonsocial motives or needs	
Consistency:	The need for internal equilibrium or balance.
Causation:	The need to determine who or what causes the things that happen to us.
Categorize:	The need to establish categories or mental partitions which provide frames of reference.
Cues:	The need for observable cues or symbols which enable us to infer what we feel and know.
Independence:	The need for feeling of self-governance or self-control.
Curiosity	The need for variety and difference.
External, social motives or needs	
Self-expression:	The need to express self-identity to others.
Ego-defense:	The need to defend or protect our identities or egos.
Assertion:	The need to increase self-esteem.
Reinforcement:	The need to act in such a way that others will reward you.
Affiliation:	The need to develop mutually satisfying relationships with others.
Modeling:	The need to base behaviors on those of others.

Source: adapted from W. J. McGuire, "Psychological Motives and Communication Gratification," in *The Uses of Mass Communications: Current Perspectives on Gratifications Research*, eds. J. G. Blumler and C. Katz, (Sage Publications, 1974), pp. 167–96.

determine which of these general motives led to that purchase. The purchase in this case was motivated by routine depletion. The brand choice, however, may reflect a need for security or acceptance that is provided by a nationally branded product. Or, the brand choice simply could reflect habit ("I've always bought Mortons").

However, general motives can be useful to the marketing manager in understanding many purchases. For example, marketers of premium beers, wines, and liquors know that the basic reasons (motives) that people spend more money for brands that many times they cannot physically differentiate are a direct result of external, social motives. Knowledge of these motives provides specific information that can be used in promotional campaigns, outlet selection, and pricing strategies.

Let us now look in more detail at each of the basic motives that seem applicable to the practice of marketing.

Internal, nonsocial motives

Need for consistency Many motives revolve around the need for internal equilibrium or balance. The basic desire here is to have all facets or parts of an individual consistent with each other. These facets include attitudes, behaviors, opinions, self-images, views of others, and so forth. Following a major purchase, a consumer may have feelings of dissonance (feelings inconsistent with his or her purchase) and be motivated to seek additional information to reduce these feelings of inconsistency.[12] Thus, this concern for "did I make the right purchase?" must be reduced to establish a comfortable balance between feelings, attitudes, and behavior. The need for consistency, particularly with respect to purchase behavior, is discussed in depth in Chapter 19 in the section on postpurchase dissonance.

This need can also affect the consumer decision process. Consistency theorists have pointed out that new and different information is frequently viewed as being dangerous to a presently held position and may therefore be ignored by consumers. This greatly enhances the need for familiar and credible sources in message presentation in order to improve the chances of communication of information (See Chapters 10 and 13).

Need to attribute causation   This set of motives deals with our need to determine who or what *causes* the things that happen to us. Do we attribute the cause of a favorable or unfavorable outcome to ourselves or to some outside person or force? If a consumer finds that one brand of shampoo controls his or her dandruff while other brands do not, the consumer may attribute the causality of dandruff control to a particular brand. If the consumer consistently finds this same distinction between one shampoo and all others, the consumer will become more confident in this attribution since it is consistently reinforced.

The need to attribute cause has led to an area of research known as *attribution theory.*[13] This approach to understanding the reasons consumers assign particular meanings to the behaviors of others has been used primarily for analyzing consumer reactions to promotional messages (in terms of credibility).[14] Knowing that consumers will attribute cause to a message and, therefore, judge the credibility of the message

---

[12] See W. H. Cumming and M. Venkatesan, "Cognitive Dissonance and Consumer Behavior: A Review of the Evidence," *Journal of Marketing Research* (August 1976), pp. 303 – 8.

[13] See F. Heider, *The Psychology of Interpersonal Relations* (John Wiley and Sons, Inc., 1958); H. H. Kelley, *Attribution in Social Interaction* (General Learning Press, 1971); and H. H. Kelley, "The Process of Causal Attribution," *American Psychologist* (February 1973), pp. 107 – 28; R. W. Mizerski, L. L. Golden, and J. B. Kernan, "The Attribution Process in Consumer Decision Making," *Journal of Consumer Research* (September 1979), pp. 123 – 40.

[14] See R. B. Settle and L. L. Golden, "Attribution Theory and Advertiser Credibility," *Journal of Marketing Research* (May 1974), pp. 181 – 85; R. E. Burnkrant, "Attribution Theory in Marketing Research: Problems and Prospects," in *Advances in Consumer Research II,* ed. M. J. Schlinger (Association for Consumer Research, 1975), pp. 465 – 70; R. A. Hansen and C. A. Scott, "Comments on Attribution Theory and Advertiser Credibility," *Journal of Marketing Research* (May 1976), pp. 193 – 97; L. L. Golden, "Attribution Theory Implications for Advertisement Claim Credibility," *Journal of Marketing Research* (January 1977), pp. 115 – 17; and R. E. Smith and S. D. Hunt, "Attribution Processes and Effects in Promotional Situations," *Journal of Consumer Research* (December 1978), pp. 149 – 58.

source requires marketers to present source information such that correct causation is easy for the consumer to assess. The need for causation has also proven useful in understanding biased evaluations of sales personnel.[15]

Need to categorize Consumers have a need to be able to categorize and organize information and experiences in some meaningful yet manageable way. As a result, we establish categories or mental partitions which provide frames of reference which allow us to process large quantities of information. Prices are often categorized such that different prices connote different categories of goods. Automobiles over $10,000 and automobiles under $5,000 elicit two different meanings because of information categorized on the basis of price level. Likewise, beer prices at $1.25, $3.00, and $4.95 a six-pack elicit three different meanings due to categorization of the price and associated quality of the beer. The categorization process and marketing practices based on this process are described in some detail in Chapter 10.

Need for cues These motives reflect needs for observable cues or symbols which enable us to infer what we feel and know. Impressions, feelings, attitudes, and so forth are subtly established by viewing our own behavior and that of others and drawing inferences as to what we feel and think. In many instances, clothing plays an important role in presenting the subtle meaning of a desired image and consumer lifestyle. For example, in the late 1960s, many people who identified with the values and lifestyles of the counterculture had strong preferences for a certain style of dress since it fulfilled a need for external cues which helped establish and reinforce a particular identity.

Need for independence Here, we are concerned with an individual's need for independence or feeling of self-governance. This is derived from a human need to establish a sense of self-worth and meaning by achieving self-actualization. This need has grown in importance in the American culture as many feel that in a highly technological society we are in danger of losing our identity and individuality. Marketers have responded by providing products that suggest that you "do your own thing" and "be your own person." This, in essence, is the underlying theme of Camel's cigarette advertisements. The value of information overall is enhanced by the need for independence, because more information can help consumers achieve independent judgments more readily.

Need for novelty While it would seem to be logical and proper to assume that people tend to engage in machinelike behavior in order to simplify and standardize a complex world, there seems to be strong evidence that, at least occasionally, we seek variety and difference simply

---

[15] S. Banks, "An Attributional Experiment on Sexual Biases towards Sales People," *Proceedings* (American Marketing Association, 1979).

out of a curiosity need. This may, in fact, be the prime reason for a great deal of brand switching and so-called impulse purchasing. This need is clearly illustrated in an outdoor advertising study.[16] Prior to an advertising campaign, a telephone sample of 350 people revealed that only one half of 1 percent could name the 23rd president of the United States. Following this survey, 14 billboards (with copy areas 12 feet by 25 feet) were used to pose the question: "Who was the 23rd president?" After three weeks of this billboard exposure, a second telephone sample revealed that now 7.71 percent knew the 23rd president. Since the advertisement did not provide the answer, it is clear that curiosity caused some individuals to seek out the answer. We are not going to tell you who the 23rd president was; perhaps your curiosity will lead you to find out.

External, social motives

Need for self-expression These motives are externally oriented and deal with the need to express one's identity to others. Self-expression seems to be a vitally important motivating force for some consumers nearly all of the time, and for almost all of us, some of the time. We feel the need to let others know by our actions (which include the purchase and display of goods) who we are and what we are. The purchase of many products, particularly clothing and automobiles, allows consumers to express an identity to others since these products have symbolic or expressive meanings. Thus, the purchase of the latest in ski wear probably reflects much more than a desire to remain warm while skiing.

Need for ego-defense The need to defend our identities or egos is another important external, social motive. We all have a self-concept that in some manner enables us to express our identity and lifestyle (see Chapter 14). This may not be our ideal identity but it is one that we have found that we can realistically maintain and one that works for us. Therefore, when our identity is threatened, we are motivated to protect our self-concept and utilize defensive behaviors, attitudes, and so forth. Again, many products can provide some ego-defense. A consumer who feels insecure may rely on well-known brands for all socially visible products to avoid any chance of making a socially incorrect purchase. This strategy serves to protect the consumer's ego.

Need for assertion This reflects a consumer's need for engaging in those types of activity that will bring about an increase in self-esteem as well as one's esteem in the eyes of others. Motivation theorists holding this view of man describe life as competitive and hold that individuals are motivated to achieve control or dominance. In terms of complaint behavior, we find that individuals who feel they have a greater span of

---

[16] W. C. Hewett, "The Significance of Human Curiosity in an Outdoor Advertising Experiment," *Journal of Business* (January 1975), pp. 108–10.

control and are generally more self-confident are more likely to complain, and thus have a greater need to assert themselves when they are dissatisfied.[17]

Need for reinforcement   Colin Fletcher, in *The Winds of Mara*, described the reinforcement motive quite well as: "when certain actions turn out well and others badly, then it is a good idea, next time, to point yourself toward past success."[18] We quite often are motivated to act in certain ways because we were rewarded for doing so earlier by others. The purchase of products specifically designed to be used in public situations (clothing, furniture, artwork, and so forth) are frequently sold on the basis of the amount and type of reinforcement that will be received. For example, a clothing ad might indicate that "your friends will all marvel at how sophisticated you look."

Need for affiliation   Another well-developed external, social motive is a need for affiliation. By affiliation, we mean the need to develop mutually helpful and satisfying relationships with others. The need here is to share and to be accepted by others. As we saw in Chapter 8, group membership is a critical part of most consumer lives, and many consumer decisions are based on the need to maintain satisfying relationships with others. Marketers frequently use such affiliation based themes as, "your kids will love you for it," in advertisements.

Need for modeling   The need for modeling reflects a tendency to base behavior on that of others. Modeling theorists point out that we seem naturally motivated to take on the behaviors of those around us or at least react to those behaviors around us in some noticeable fashion. Since we are all conformists to some degree, the need to model or copy certain roles helps us fulfill other needs such as role adoption, self-expression, or adapting. The need for modeling is particularly important in setting up marketing operations in a foreign country, where the sales force must model their behaviors in accordance with the roles existing in the culture of the foreign country. Without effective modeling the entire operation faces a greater chance of failure (see Chapter 4).

The modeling motive emphasizes the need of persons to adopt roles or add new roles to their self-concept. The basic feeling is that one's self identity or ego is enhanced. These roles reflect the individual's goal orientations or their perceptions of ideal self-image. The women's movement is in part motivated by the need in many women to adopt new roles which extend their self-concept. Marketers have been responsive to this need by portraying women in a wider variety of roles and by developing specific products which enhance expression of these roles (see Chapter 5).

---

[17] Robinson, "Consumer Complaint."

[18] C. Fletcher, *The Winds of Mara* (Alfred A. Knopf, 1973), p. 9.

Motivational conflict

As you might guess, with the many motives we have and the many situations in which these motives are activated, there are frequent conflicts between motives. Multiple motivations and conflict among these motivations are common since we have limited resources in terms of time, money, and effort, yet we are constantly being reminded of attractive and desirable activities, products, and services.

The resolution of a motivational conflict often affects consumption patterns. Therefore, in many instances the marketer can analyze situations which are likely to result in a motivational conflict, provide a solution to that motivational conflict, and attract the patronage of those consumers facing the motivational conflict. There are three types of motivational conflict of relevance to marketing managers.[19] Each is described below.

Approach-approach motivational conflict In an approach-approach motivational conflict, a consumer faces a choice between two attractive alternatives. The more equal this attraction, the greater the conflict. For example, a consumer who recently received a large income tax refund (situational variable) may be torn between a vacation in Hawaii (perhaps powered by the curiosity motive) and an expensive grandfather clock for the living room (perhaps powered by the need for self-expression). Such a conflict could be resolved by a timely advertisement designed to encourage one or the other action. Or, a product modification, such as "fly now, pay later," could result in a resolution whereby both alternatives are selected. Since individuals in this type of conflict like both alternatives, they are very susceptible to external influences, both personal (friends) and commercial (salespersons), toward one or the other option.

Approach-avoidance motivational conflict In an approach-avoidance motive conflict, the consumer faces both positive and negative consequences in the purchase of a particular product. A consumer who is concerned about gaining weight yet likes beer faces this conflict. The development of lower calorie beers, in part, reduces this conflict and allows the weight sensitive beer consumer to do both—consume beer and also control calorie intake. This is a common type of conflict in purchasing many consumer products, since acquiring the benefits represented by the product (approach) requires that we surrender purchasing power (avoidance). This often results in postdecision dissonance (see Chapter 19).

Avoidance-avoidance motivational conflict An avoidance-avoidance motive conflict is one in which the consumer faces two undesirable alternatives. This occurs for most students the night before an exam: you

---

[19] Based on K. Lewin, *A Dynamic Theory of Personality* (McGraw-Hill Book Co., 1935), pp. 88—91.

neither want to study nor fail the exam. When a consumer's old washing machine finally fails, the same conflict occurs. The person may not want to spend money on a new washing machine nor go without one. The availability of credit is one way of resolving this motivational conflict. Likewise, many heads of households would view life insurance as an avoidance-avoidance conflict; they want financial security for their families in the event of death but they do not want to spend their hard-earned money for the cost of this protection. Many life insurance programs attempt to reduce this conflict by creating both an investment and life insurance policy. The conflict is greatly reduced in this case by shifting the focus of the purchase from death and cost, two negative features, to return on investment and retirement income, two positive features.

Marketing strategy and motives

The preceding pages have discussed a number of types of motives or needs. Each was discussed independently of the others. It is critical to recognize that most behaviors, including consumption behaviors, are in response to multiple motives. A consumer may order a Coors beer when visiting a tavern with a group of friends because the person (1) is thirsty (physiological motive); (2) has enjoyed the taste of Coors in the past (reinforcement motive); (3) is insecure and thinks Coors is accepted by the group (ego-defense and affiliation); and (4) also feels that people with good judgment drink Coors (expressive). It requires substantial research and insight to balance a product's benefits (physical and psychological) with the motives of a defined target market.

PERSONALITY

While motivations are the energizing force that makes consumer behavior purposeful and goal directed, the personality of the consumer guides and directs the behavior chosen to accomplish goals in different situations. As we mentioned earlier, it is often very difficult to distinguish between motivation and personality since both concepts are similar in nature and interrelated in terms of the effects each has on consumer behavior.

Personality deals with those *relatively long-lasting personal qualities that allow us to cope with and respond to the world around us.* Behavior is an outcome of personality, and many personality theories are presented as general theories of behavior. We can easily (though perhaps not always accurately) describe our own personality or the personality of a friend. For example, you might say that one of your friends is "fairly aggressive, very opinionated, competitive, outgoing, and witty." What you have described are the behaviors your friend has exhibited over time across a variety of situations. These characteristic ways of responding to a wide variety of situations should, of course, also include responses to marketing strategies. It is for this reason that personality has been of interest to marketing managers for many years.

For some time there has been controversy in the field of psychology as to the exact nature of personality, the value of studying such a broad area, and the problems with measurement.[20] Much the same disenchantment has also been evident in the marketing literature as to the predictive use of personality.[21] However, the concept is a very real and meaningful one to all of us on a daily basis. People do have personalities! Personality characteristics exist in those we know and help us to describe and differentiate between people. Furthermore, as we will see shortly, personality characteristics can be used to help structure successful marketing strategies.

Personality theories

As was the case with motivation, there are numerous theories of personality.[22] However, these numerous theories can be categorized as being either individual theories or social learning theories.[23] Understanding these two general approaches to personality will provide an appreciation of the potential uses of personality in marketing decisions.

Individual personality theories All the individual personality theories have two common assumptions: (1) that all individuals have internal characteristics or traits and (2) that there are consistent differences between individuals on those characteristics or traits that can be measured. The external environment or events around us (situations) are not considered in these theories and are assumed not to influence personality based behaviors. Most of these theories state that the traits or characteristics are formed at a very early age and are relatively unchanging over the years. Differences in individual theories center around the definition of which traits or characteristics are the most important and most enduring. Examples of some of the better-known individual theories of this school are provided by Freud, Allport, Cattell, Murray, and Rogers.

Let us look briefly at Cattell's theory as a representative example of the individual approach.[24] He classifies traits as being one of three possible types—ability or performance capability (intelligence, coordination); dynamic or interest and motivation; and temperament (emotional reac-

---

[20] For overviews of these arguments, see W. Mischel, *Personality and Assessment* (John Wiley and Sons, Inc., 1968); and J. B. Bavelas, *Personality: Current Theory and Research* (Brooks/Cole Publishing Co., 1978).

[21] H. H. Kassarjian, "Personality and Consumer Behavior: A Review," *Journal of Marketing Research* (November 1971), pp. 409–18.

[22] See C. S. Hall and G. Lindzey, *Theories of Personality*, 2d ed. (John Wiley and Sons, Inc., 1970).

[23] See Bavelas, *Personality*.

[24] Hall and Lindzey, *Theories*, chap. 10.

tion, energy). These traits are acquired at an early age through learning or are inherited. A unique aspect of Cattell's approach is the delineation of *surface traits or observable behaviors* that are similar and cluster together and *source traits* that represent the causes of those behaviors. Cattell felt that if one could observe the surface traits that correlate highly with one another, they would identify an underlying source trait. For example, the surface traits of vocabulary, arithmetic ability, and reasoning might be the result of a source trait of general mental ability. Similarly, a source trait of emotional stability may account for the surface traits of poise, calm composure, and lack of hypochondria (imaginary illnesses).[25] Figure 12−2 gives examples of some of Cattell's major source traits.

While Cattel's theory is representative of multitrait personality theories (more than one trait influences behavior), there are a number of single trait theories. Single trait theories stress one trait as being of overwhelming importance. Some examples of single trait theories are those that deal with dogmatism, authoritarianism, anxiety, and locus of control.[26] Let us look more closely at one of these, locus of control.

This single trait theory deals with the extent to which people believe that they or some outside force controls the important activities in their lives.[27] At one extreme, individuals themselves are in complete control of their lives and the events that affect them. At the other end of the continuum, individuals feel as if they have no control over their life but are subject to luck, fate, or what have you. One could imagine the kinds of behaviors that feelings such as these could influence. For example, the need for, use of, and belief in information and information sources could vary widely depending on an individual's feelings of control. Likewise, consumers with a greater locus of control are more likely to take complaint action when they are dissatisfied with a product. Why? By the nature of this personality trait they feel they can exercise control over their discontent and achieve satisfaction.

Social learning theories Social learning theories, as opposed to individual ones, emphasize the environment as the important determinant of behavior. Hence, there is a focus on external versus internal factors. Also, there is little concern with variation between individuals in terms of individual traits. Systematic differences in situations, in stimuli, or in social settings are the major interest of social theorists—not differences in traits, needs, constructs, or other properties of individuals. Rather than classifying individuals, the social theorists classify situations.[28]

---

[25] Bavelas, *Personality,* p. 47.

[26] Ibid., chap. 13.

[27] J. B. Rotter, "Generalized Expectancies for Internal versus External Control of Reinforcement," *Psychological Monographs, 1966* (1, whole no. 609).

[28] Bavelas, *Personality,* p. 156.

FIGURE 12–2
Cattell's source traits

Reserved; detached, critical, aloof, stiff	vs.	*Outgoing;* warmhearted, easygoing, participating
Dull; low intelligence	vs.	*Bright;* high intelligence
Affected by feeling; emotionally less stable	vs.	*Emotionally stable;* mature, faces reality, calm
Humble; stable, mild, easily led, docile, accommodating	vs.	*Assertive;* aggressive, competitive, stubborn
Sober; Taciturn, serious	vs.	*Happy-go-lucky;* enthusiastic
Expedient; disregards rules	vs.	*Conscientious;* persistent, moralistic, staid
Shy; timid, threat-sensitive	vs.	*Venturesome;* uninhibited, socially bold
Tough-minded; self-reliant, realistic	vs.	*Tender-minded;* sensitive, clinging, overprotected
Trusting; accepting conditions	vs.	*Suspicious;* hard to fool
Practical; down-to-earth concerns	vs.	*Imaginative;* bohemian, absentminded
Forthright; unpretentious, genuine, but socially clumsy	vs.	*Astute;* polished, socially aware
Self-assured; placid, secure, complacent, serene	vs.	*Apprehensive;* self-reproaching, insecure, worrying, troubled
Conservative; respecting traditional ideas, conservatism of temperament	vs.	*Experimenting;* liberal, freethinking, radicalism
Group dependent; a joiner and sound follower	vs.	*Self-sufficient;* resourceful, prefers own decisions
Undisciplined; lax, follows own urges, careless of social rules	vs.	*Controlled;* exacting willpower, socially precise, compulsive, following self-image
Relaxed; tranquil, torpid, unfrustrated, composed	vs.	*Tense;* frustrated, driven, overwrought

Source: Adapted from R. B. Cattell, H. W. Eber, and M. M. Tatsuoka, *Handbook for the Sixteen Personality Factor Questionnaire* (Champaign, Ill.: Institute for Personality and Ability Testing, 1970), pp. 16–17. Reprinted by permission of the copyright owner. All rights reserved.

Personality, then, in this view seems to downplay the impact of the person and concentrate on the environment and the situations the environment produces, the topic of Chapter 3. However, the person is still there and personality is viewed as a set of principles by which an individual interacts with an environment. Social learning theories then deal with how people learn to respond to the environment and the patterns of responses that they learn. As situations change, individuals change their reactions. In the extreme case every intrapersonal interaction may be viewed as a different situation with the result being a different response pattern. Some people may see us as an extrovert and others as an introvert. Each can be accurate in their assessment of our personality because we express different personalities to each person.

A combined approach   In essence, the differences between individual and social theories of personality can be defined as *state* versus *trait*. Individual or trait theorists see behavior as largely determined by internal characteristics common to all persons but existing in differing amounts within individuals. Social or state theories claim just the opposite—situations that people face are the determinants of behavior and different behaviors among people are the result of differing situations. This debate should sound familiar to you, as it provided the basis of Chapter 3 on situations. As we did in that chapter, we will again take the position that *behavior is a result of some combination of individual traits or characteristics and situations that people face*.

While research seems to indicate that individual traits are not good predictors of behavior, our basic intuitions disagree and we look for and expect to see some basic stability in individual behavior across situations. For example, a person who is highly trusting will probably tend to exhibit that trait when faced with a large variety of situations. Certainly some situations would result in less trusting behavior than others, but it seems reasonable to assume that the trusting person will generally act in a more trusting way than the nontrusting person regardless of the situation. Thus, the situation modifies the general trait and together they affect behavior. The outcomes of behaviors can also alter the individual trait. For example, a basically trusting person can, through a series of unfortunate experiences, learn not to be as trusting. A series of specific situations have therefore altered the basic trait.

Bem and Allen provide us with a potentially more accurate and productive approach to using individual traits by proposing that some people are consistent across situations and some people are not.[29] It is a fact of life, they claim, that we will never be able to predict more than some of the people some of the time. The way one goes about doing this is to have individuals identify or classify themselves as to whether or not they are consistent on a particular trait across situations. Those who classify themselves as consistent would be much more predictable on behaviors that relate to that trait. This same reasoning could be applied to the predictive ability of situations. "In short, if some of the people can be predicted some of the time from personality traits, then some of the people can be predicted some of the time from situational variables."[30]

[29] D. J. Bem and A. Allen, "On Predicting Some of the People Some of the Time: The Search for Cross-Situational Consistence in Behavior," *Psychological Review* (November 1974), pp. 506–20.

[30] Ibid., p. 517.

The use of personality in marketing practice

While we each have a variety of personality traits and become involved in many situations which activate different aspects of our personality, some of these traits or characteristics are more desirable than others and some may even be undesirable. That is, in some situations we may be shy when we wish we were bold, or timid when we would like to be assertive. Thus, we all can find some areas of our personality that need bolstering or improvement.

Like individuals, many consumer products also have a "personality." Where one brand of perfume may connote youth, sensuality, and adventure; another perfume may be viewed as modest, conservative, and aristocratic. In this example, each perfume has a distinct personality and each perfume is likely to be purchased by a different type of consumer or for a different situation. Consumers will tend to purchase the product with the personality that is most pleasing to them in both a personal and symbolic way.

Thus, consumers frequently purchase products to reflect their personality or to bolster some important void in their personality. Because these needs may vary from one situation to another, we should keep in mind both the dimensions of personality which are being served and the situation in which it is being served. To illustrate this relationship we will present the following two examples of how personality of the individual and the perceived personality of the product influenced consumer behavior in a particular situation.

Influencing brand preference with personality A study by Anheuser-Busch demonstrates how personality can be presented in a beer commercial to influence consumer brand preferences.[31] In this study, four commercial advertisements were created for four new brands of beer. Each commercial represented one of the new brands of beer and was created to portray the beer as being appropriate for a specific "drinker personality." For example, one brand was featured in a commercial that portrayed the "reparative drinker," a self-sacrificing, middle-aged person who could have achieved more if the individual had not sacrificed personal objectives in the interest of others. For this consumer, drinking a beer serves as a reward for sacrifices. Other personality types, such as the "social drinker" who resembles the campus guzzler and the "indulgent drinker" who sees himself/herself as a total failure, were used to develop product personalities for the other new brands of beer in the study.

Then 250 beer consumers watched these commercials and tasted all four brands of beer. After given sufficient time to see each commercial and sample each beer, consumers were asked to state a brand preference and complete a questionnaire which measured their own "drinker

---

[31] R. L. Ackoff and J. R. Emsoff, "Advertising Research at Anheuser-Busch, Inc.," *Sloan Management Review* (Spring 1975), pp. 1 – 15.

personality." The results showed that most consumers preferred the brand of beer that matched their own drinker personality. (That is, the drinker personality of the brand they preferred was the same as their own drinker personality.) Furthermore, the effect personality had on brand preferences was so strong that most consumers also felt that at least one brand of beer *was not fit to drink.* Unknown to these 250 consumers was the fact that all four brands were the *same* beer. Thus, the product personalities created in these commercials attracted consumers with like personalities. However, the product personalities portrayed for some brands were so distasteful to some consumers that these consumers transferred their dislike for the personality to their perception of the taste of the beer.

Influencing advertising preference with personality In another study, Kassarjian utilized measures of Reisman's inner- and other-directed social character as a basis for creating advertisements.[32] Kassarjian hypothesized that inner-directed individuals would prefer advertisements that portrayed an inner-directed personality. Likewise, he felt that other-directed individuals would prefer ads that portrayed an other-directed personality. In terms of personality, inner-directed people turn to and rely on their own inner values and standards for guiding their behavior, while other-directed persons depend upon the people around them to give direction to their actions. For example, in terms of sports an inner-directed person may be more interested in *individual* sports while an other-directed person may be more interested in *group* sports.

To test the impact of this trait on advertising preferences, Kassarjian created two versions of the same basic advertisement for 27 different products. For each product there was an inner-directed advertisement which featured solitary, personal activities and an other-directed advertisement which featured group or interaction appeals. Figure 12 – 3 provides brief descriptions of 10 of the 27 advertisements used in the study. Two hundred consumers selected one of the two advertisements for each product based on the appeal the ad held for them. Inner-directed individuals, as measured on a test developed by Reisman, tended to prefer the inner-directed advertisements, while other-directed individuals preferred the other-directed advertisements.

Problems in utilizing personality theories While these two examples help us demonstrate how personality can be used to influence brand and advertising preference, both examples were the result of carefully planned marketing studies which utilized appropriate measures of personality for the use intended as well as careful control of the situation and measurement of behavior. Many other studies have been much less

---

[32] H. H. Kassarjian, "Social Character and Differential Preference for Mass Communication," *Journal of Marketing Research* (May 1965), pp. 146 – 53.

FIGURE 12–3 Inner- and other-directed personality appeals for 10 products and services

Product	Inner-directed appeal		Other-directed appeal	
	Slogan	Illustration	Slogan	Illustration
Telephone company	Just dial. Its so easy, fast, and dependable.	Attractive girl holding telephone and staring into space.	The personal touch for every occasion.	Five pictures of young ladies in a variety of situations talking on the telephone.
High-fidelity turntable	Accurate, dependable, quality high-fidelity equipment.	Record player, AM-FM radio in quality cabinet.	In selecting components use the latest high-fidelity equipment.	Turntable in foreground with homemade but attractive cabinet in back.
Ralph's Market	Ralph's—known for the finest quality at the right price.	Food presented on extremely expensive silver serving piece.	Ralph's—the supermarket with the greatest choice.	Paper plates, supper napkins, many types of food in a buffet setting.
Sea & Ski	For proper sun protection—Sea & Ski.	Beach scene with three unrelated couples.	For a desirable vacation glow—Sea & Ski.	Two men and three women water skiing from same boat.
IBM typewriter	You save time and money when you buy IBM typewriters.	Typist in foreground with boss giving orders in background.	Your IBM typewriter is part of the team in progressive management.	Typewriter in foreground. Smiling man and woman in background looking at papers.
Bayer aspirin	Don't spoil your leisure time—Bayer aspirin.	Man working in "do it yourself" workshop.	Don't spoil your leisure time—Bayer aspirin.	Two men holding drinks, talking at cocktail party.
Kodak	For a lasting record.	Man photographing London Bridge.	Share your experiences with friends at home.	Man photographing women in front of building. European travel posters in foreground.
Fairchild's restaurant	The height of sophistication.	Waiter in tuxedo.	Good food, reasonable price, gay atmosphere.	People being served in fancy restaurant.
Community organization	Take an active part in community life, do your part for your country.	Older man in foreground. Seven men sitting around a table in background.	Know what is going on, join a community project.	Seven men in a room drinking in background. Man holding papers in foreground.
Books	Improve yourself. Read and learn.	Dozen books including: My Life in Court, The Outline of History, The Valiant Years, Conversations with Stalin.	Improve yourself; be confident in any crowd.	Illustrations of 11 books including: Lose Weight and Live, Women and Fatigue, Ship of Fools.

Source: H. H. Kassarjian, "Social Character and Differential Preference for Mass Communication," *Journal of Marketing Research* (May 1965), pp. 146–53.

successful. In fact, there is a frequent tendency to consider personality as "unusable" as far as marketing strategy is concerned (the preceding examples should indicate that this is a premature judgment).

There are a number of reasons for the frequent failure of personality to predict consumer behavior. In the first place, the social theorists are at least partially correct in that there are no individual characteristics that are completely enduring and that overpower all situational influences. Many of the studies showing limited or no personality influences did not account for or control situational variation and hence could be expected to provide less than completely predictive results. As one noted researcher in the field has stated, "personality researchers in consumer behavior much too often ignore the many interrelated influences on the consumer decision process, ranging from price and packaging to availability, advertising, group influences, learned responses, and preferences of family members, in addition to personality."[33]

Another reason why personality researchers seem to be unable to predict purchase preference could well be related to the methods of assessing or measuring personality characteristics. All too often researchers would adopt without change a personality measurement instrument that had been developed for a very different reason than to predict consumer behavior. Again, Kassarjian points out that "instruments originally intended to measure gross personality characteristics such as sociability, emotional stability, introversion, or neuroticism have been used to make predictions of the chosen brand of toothpaste or cigarettes."[34] The studies that seem to do a better job with personality usually involve, among other advances, tailor-made assessment instruments that fit the purchase situation being researched.[35] Instead of automatically adopting whatever trait a particular instrument uses, the researcher should select ones that are appropriate to the purchase situation. For example, what would heterosexuality necessarily have to do with brand preference of furniture polish or toilet paper? Probably very little and yet this trait is frequently included on standard instruments.

The potential to use certain personality variables to predict behavior still exists if managers adopt the Bem and Allen approach to predicting some of the people some of the time. There may be certain characteristics, such as seeking adventure, for certain people that would allow us to predict certain brand or image preferences across a variety of purchase situations. Our problem is finding those people who see themselves as consistent on the characteristic. This can be achieved through market research or by using surrogate variables. For example, it may well be

---

[33] Kassarjian, "Personality," p. 416.

[34] Ibid., p. 415.

[35] For an example of such a study, see I. S. White, "The Perception of Value in Products," in *On Knowing the Consumer,* ed. J. W. Newman (John Wiley and Sons, Inc., 1966), pp. 173–86.

that there are at least a fair number of young, single, highly educated individuals who would respond to an adventure-oriented image for products ranging from cologne, to beer, to automobiles, to clothing. Remember that a marketing manager does not need to be able to predict the behavior of everyone in a potential market segment to be successful.

The effect of personality on consumer decision making

Thus far we have discussed personality as it influences preferences for product or advertising attributes. However, personality may also influence the manner in which consumers process product-related information. In this sense, personality acts as a *moderating* or *mediating* variable that can and does change the nature of the decision process. For example, a highly dogmatic (close-minded) individual in certain situations will process information differently than would a less dogmatic individual in a similar situation. People high in dogmatism tend to "prefer to rely heavily on the pronouncements of authorities and tend to accept information primarily on the basis of its source, while low dogmatics tend to act upon their independent evaluation of message content."[36] This would suggest that in constructing an information campaign to be directed toward a more dogmatic audience, careful attention must be paid to the source of the message in order to effectively influence the audience. The task then is to identify audiences that are highly dogmatic. This is not always an easy thing to do. Finding that even a portion of a desired target market has this trait may suggest designing *some* of the promotional message with highly authoritarian sources.

Information processing theorists have found that we learn relatively fixed patterns for experiencing our world (usually termed *cognitive structures*) and these affect behavior much as do other personality characteristics.[37] An example of such an information processing based characteristic is leveling—sharpening. This characteristic is concerned with the degree to which individuals assimilate new stimuli with existing memory. Persons exhibiting high leveling tendencies will tend to lump new information with old, while those on the sharpening end of the continuum tend to hold all individual stimuli separate and intact in memory. This has been found to affect the correct recall of product comparison information on products with a number of different attributes advertised.[38]

---

[36] J. Jacoby, "Personality and Innovation Proneness," *Journal of Marketing Research* (May 1971), p. 246.

[37] J. Bieri, "Cognitive Structures," in *Personality Theory and Information Processing,* ed. H. M. Schroeder and P. Suedfield (Ronald Press, 1971), p. 191.

[38] K. A. Coney, "Leveling—Sharpening: A Cognitive Control Approach to Consumer Information Recall," in *Marketing in Turbulent Times,* ed. E. M. Mazze (American Marketing Association, 1975), pp. 162—66.

Other studies indicate that *cognitive complexity* affects the tendency to change attitudes given new information, with people high in complexity being less likely to change than those with lower complexity.[39] Again, the practical use of this information will largely depend on our ability to determine the degree of complexity of those we are trying to influence. If market segments are composed of persons who vary randomly in their degree of complexity, it will be difficult for us to design appropriate information campaigns. However, if we can determine other variables that are correlated with complexity and that are easier to determine or measure, we could develop more specific persuasive campaigns. For example, there is some evidence that lower cognitive complexity is associated with a higher tendency to react in a socially desirable manner. Heavy users of products whose appeal and use is centered around making oneself socially desirable (i.e., deodorant) may in fact be less cognitively complex and more accepting of new information. Note that this is not a proven fact, merely an indication of the type of effects that personality characteristics might have on information processing and hence consumer behavior.

EXPERIENCES AND EXPECTATIONS

We would be remiss in our explanation of individual characteristics and their effect on consumer decision making if we did not at least briefly discuss personal *experiences* and *expectations.* Here we are dealing with the things or events that have happened or that one expects to happen in the future. We are not talking about outcomes of specific decision-making activities. These are planned for, and while we are not sure exactly how they will work out, we have some control over them. There are any number of things that happen to all of us that we do not control but that have major influences on us. Sudden and major events such as the Vietnam War or a major economic recession occur and affect everyone, though in many different ways. Not only are our values and attitudes affected (changed or strengthened) but our chosen career plans or family plans can be drastically altered. In other words, *all individuals are in part unique because of the things that have happened to them.* Being in a serious accident or winning the state lottery would probably make you a somewhat different person from that point on in your life.

Your expectations of what will happen to you are also individual characteristics that make you unique. *Expectations concerning future income, health, career, and family circumstances definitely can have an effect on the decisions you make today, as well as your evaluation of your present self-image and your relationship to others.* Specific expecta-

---

[39] Bieri, "Cognitive Structures," p. 197.

tions may depend largely on the basic personality characteristics you possess, such as the degree of pessimism or optimism concerning your world.

The point of this discussion concerning experiences and expectations is merely to round out our discussion of individual characteristics and to indicate to you that we will never be able to completely predict individual behavior if for no other reason than we do not know what has happened to everyone in the past or what they expect to happen in the future. In general, we assume that these types of differences cancel each other out for any given market segment or that they have the same general influence on any given group.

SUMMARY

Motivation and personality deal with why and how the consumer behaves in certain ways. Understanding these two aspects of consumer behavior can help managers focus on the goals consumers have in specific purchase situations and identify common behavioral responses that consumers are likely to make.

Consumer motivations are energizing forces that activate behavior and provide purpose and direction to that behavior. In terms of specific product purchases, consumer motivations seem highly dependent on the situation at hand. It is necessary, therefore, to understand what motives stimulate what types of behavior and how these motives and behaviors are influenced by specific situations in which consumers engage in goal-directed, problem-solving behavior.

It is important to note the difference between physiological and psychological motives. Physiological motives are basically innate, biological needs such as hunger and thirst. Psychological or learned motives are needs that we develop over our lifetime but primarily through socialization in early childhood.

General motives can be classified as being either internal, nonsocial in nature or external, social. Internal, nonsocial motives reflect needs that people have with respect to themselves and are largely information based. Examples of these types of motives are the need for consistency, causation, categorization, cues, independence, and curiosity. External, social motives, on the other hand, deal with human needs directly related to interactions with significant others in their world. These motives encompass the need for self-expression, ego-defense, assertion, reinforcement, affiliation, and modeling. These general motives can be extremely useful to marketing managers trying to determine the basic, underlying reasons for the purchase of their product type.

Due to the large number of motives and the many different situations that consumers face, motivational conflict can occur. There are three kinds of motivational conflicts that marketing managers should be aware of and try to reduce or solve for the consumer if possible. In an approach-approach motivational conflict, the consumer faces a choice between two attractive alternatives. In an approach-avoidance conflict, the consumer faces both positive and negative consequences in the purchase of a particular product. And finally in the avoidance-avoidance conflict the consumer faces two undesirable alternatives.

The personality of a consumer guides and directs the behavior chosen to accomplish goals in different situations. Personality is the relatively long-lasting personal qualities that allow us to cope with and respond to the world around us. Though there are many controversies in the area of personality research, we can be assured that personalities do exist and are meaningful to consumers and therefore to marketing managers.

There are two basic approaches to understanding personality: individual theories and social learning theories. Individual theories have two common assumptions: (1) all individuals have internal characteristics or traits and (2) there are consistent differences between individuals on these characteristics or traits that can be measured. Most of the individual theories state that traits are formed at an early age and are relatively unchanging over the years.

Social learning theories, as opposed to individual ones, emphasize the environment as the important determinant of behavior. Therefore, the focus is on external (situational) versus internal factors. Also, there is little concern in social learning theories with variation between individuals in terms of individual traits.

The differences between the individual and social learning theories of personality can be defined as those between state and trait. Individual theorists claim behavior is determined by internal characteristics (traits) common to all persons but existing in differing amounts within individuals. Social theorists claim just the opposite—the situations people face determine behavior. Your text takes the position that behavior really is a result of a combination of traits and situations.

Personality is of use to marketing managers, particularly in influencing brand preference and advertising preference. Products, like individuals, have personalities, and consumers tend to prefer products with personalities that are most pleasing to them in both a personal and symbolic way. It is also apparent that consumers prefer advertising messages that portray their own or a desired personality.

Personality is a controversial area and problems with its use in marketing have become apparent. Much of the research done on personality in marketing was done from purely an individual or trait point of view, failing to include situational influence at all. Also the methods of assessing or measuring personality often have been inaccurate or inappropriate.

Personality also has some direct effects on the consumer decision-making process. It may act as a moderating or mediating variable that can change the nature of the process. This can be shown by the fact that highly dogmatic consumers process information differently than low-dogmatic consumers. In addition, information processing theorists have found that we learn relatively fixed patterns for experiencing our world (cognitive structures) and these act much as do other personality characteristics.

Individual experiences and expectations also play a role in determining behavior. Here we are dealing with the things or events that have happened or that one expects to happen in the future. Every individual is unique in part because of the things that have happened to them or that they expect to happen to them.

REVIEW QUESTIONS

1. Why must motivation provide for both stimulation of behavior and direction of that behavior to be useful for marketing managers?
2. What role does motivation play in the consumer's decision-making process?
3. What is the difference between learned and innate motives? Which are more relevant to consumer activities?
4. What do we mean by general motives? How do they differ from problem-specific motives?
5. What are internal, nonsocial motives and how would knowledge of them be useful to a marketing manager?
6. What are external, social motives and how would knowledge of them be useful to a marketing manager?
7. What is meant by motivational conflict and what relevance does it have for marketing managers?
8. What is personality in a consumer behavior sense?
9. Describe the individual and the social learning theoretical approaches to personality.
10. What are major complaints against the individual approach? How is this approach potentially useful to marketing managers?
11. What do we mean by single trait and multiple trait individual theories?
12. How can knowledge of personality be used to influence brand preferences?
13. How can a knowledge of personality be used to affect consumers' preferences for advertisements?
14. What are some of the major problems marketing managers face when attempting to utilize personality theory?
15. In what way can personality influence the manner in which consumers process product related information?

16. How do cognitive structures such as leveling—sharpening act like personality characteristics and what effects do such structures have on information processing?

17. What role do individual experiences and expectations play in consumer decision making? What effect do they have on a marketing manager's ability to predict that decision-making behavior?

DISCUSSION QUESTIONS

1. Which of the internal motives would seem to be applicable to any promotional campaign that Jeff would set up for Motron? Which of the external motives?

2. Describe a consumer purchase situation for a Motron moped that illustrates the motivational conflict situation of approach-approach? of approach-avoidance? of avoidance-avoidance?

3. What kind of individual personality characteristics would seem to be relevant for a college-age market segment for Motron mopeds? a senior citizen market segment?

4. How might Jeff use his knowledge of personality to develop an advertising campaign for Motron?

5. Using Figure 12—2, discuss how you would use one of the personality source traits in developing a package design for a women's cigarette aimed at the working woman.

6. Discuss the various problems that can be encountered in relating personality to brand purchase behavior. How can each of these problem areas be overcome? How would you suggest that personality be used in product positioning?

7. Discuss how the personality of a consumer affects their decision-making process.

PROJECT QUESTIONS

1. Read the article "Personality and Consumer Behavior: A Review," by H. H. Kassarjian.[40] Which of the approaches reported seems to have the most promise for future research given our discussion of individual versus social learning theories?

2. Develop an advertisement for Motron based on relevant internal and external motives. Be prepared to explain which motives the ad reflects and why they are relevant to the purchase of a Motron moped.

3. Find and cut out two newspaper or magazine advertisements, one that is based on an inner-directed personality and the other based on an other-directed personality. Discuss how the ad copy and illustration each contributed to the personality of the advertisement. Also,

---

[40] *Journal of Marketing Research* (November 1971), pp. 409—18.

discuss what you feel might have been the marketers' rationale in using each personality in positioning each product.

4. For each of the external, social motives identify a brand of product that may be purchased because of this motive. For each brand of product and external motive, discuss how you would go about using this motive in promotion of each brand.

5. Individuals who are open-minded and/or inner-directed are more likely to be innovators in new product adoption. Likewise, those who are highly dogmatic and/or other-directed tend to be late adopters and laggards in the diffusion of innovations. How would you utilize this information in promoting an innovative product? What changes, if any, would you make in your promotion strategy as the product became widely accepted?

Attitudes and influencing attitudes

Du Pont Company budgeted more than $5 million for a major television campaign to be run from February through June 1979. The primary goal of the campaign was "to overcome less than favorable attitudes by many people toward business and chemical manufacturers."[1] What are *attitudes* and why are corporations such as Du Pont so concerned that consumers maintain "favorable" attitudes toward the corporation and its products?

An attitude is *an enduring organization of motivational, emotional, perceptual, and cognitive processes with respect to some aspect of the individual's world.*[2] That is, an attitude is the way we think, feel, and act toward some aspect of our environment such as a retail store, a television program, or Du Pont antifreeze. Attitudes are formed as the result of all the influences we have been describing in the past ten chapters and they represent the basis for the lifestyles individuals pursue. Thus, they are the focal point for a substantial amount of marketing strategy such as Du Pont's television advertising campaign described above. While Du Pont is attempting to change existing unfavorable attitudes, it is more

---

[1] "Du Pont Notes Importance of Chemicals to Consumers," *Advertising Age* (March 5, 1979), p. 63.

[2] D. Krech and R. S. Crutchfield, *Theory and Problems in Social Psychology* (McGraw-Hill Book Co., 1948), p. 152. For discussion of various definitions, see C. A. Kiesler, B. E. Collins, and N. Miller, *Attitude Change* (John Wiley and Sons, Inc., 1969), chap. 1.

common for marketers to attempt to reinforce existing favorable attitudes or to create new attitudes about new or altered products.

In this chapter we will discuss the role that attitudes play in coordinating consumer values with the consumer lifestyles. We will also examine the characteristics of attitudes, the multiattribute attitude model used by marketers, the functions fulfilled by attitudes, and how marketing strategies can be developed to influence attitudes.

VALUES AND ATTITUDES

It is important to recognize that attitudes are different from personal values and beliefs. *Beliefs* encompass what we think or believe about the things that make up the world that we live in. For example, we may believe that Du Pont is a large firm that makes numerous products. *Attitudes* are a more enduring organization of interrelated beliefs that describe, evaluate, and direct action with respect to a particular object or situation. Thus, our attitude toward Du Pont would consist of additional *beliefs,* our *feelings* about the firm, and our behavioral *response tendencies* with respect to the firm. *Values* are not tied to any specific situation or object. Instead, they respresent standards for guiding behavior and influencing beliefs and attitudes. A value that might influence our attitudes toward Du Pont would be a strong preference for natural as opposed to man-made products. We have a large number of beliefs, a smaller number of attitudes, and even fewer values.

Values serve as a basic, integrating framework for our attitudes.[3] Therefore, it is often useful to analyze values rather than, or in addition to, attitudes. Values exist at two levels—global and domain or situation specific. *Global* values are fewer in number and are strongly held, enduring ideals that guide actions across many situations (See chapters 4 and 5). Thus, global values are abstract and generalized. *Domain* or situation specific values, on the other hand, are acquired through experiences in specific situations or domains of activity. For example, individuals acquire values specific to economic transactions through economic

---

[3] See M. Rokeach, "A Theory of Organization and Change within Value-Attitude Systems," *Journal of Social Issues* (January 1968), pp. 13–38; M. Rokeach, *The Nature of Human Values* (Free Press, 1973); M. Rokeach, *Beliefs, Attitudes, and Values* (Jossey Bass, Inc., 1968), pp. 123–32; J. Scott and L. Lamont, "Relating Consumer Values to Consumer Behavior: A Model and Method for Investigation in *Combined Proceedings,* ed. R. C. Curhan (American Marketing Association, 1974), pp. 283–88; V. Lessig, "A Measurement of Dependencies between Values and Other Levels of the Consumer's Belief Space," *Journal of Business Research* (July 1975); D. Vinson, J. M. Munson, and M. Nakanishi, "An Investigation of the Rokeach Value Survey for Consumer Research Applications," in *Advances in Consumer Research IV,* ed. W. D. Perreault (Association for Consumer Research, 1977), pp. 242–52; J. M. Carman, "Values and Consumption Patterns: A Closed Loop," in *Advances in Consumer Research V,* ed. H. K. Hunt (Association for Consumer Research, 1978); and W. R. Darden, O. Erdem, D. K. Darden, and R. Howell, "Consumer Values and Shopping Orientations," paper presented at the Southwestern Marketing Association Conference, Spring 1979.

exchange and consumption; social values through family and group interaction; religious values through religious instruction; and so forth.

An illustration of the potential applicability of an understanding of a market segment's underlying value structure is contained in Figure 13 – 1. To construct this table, students from a western university known

FIGURE 13–1

Global values, domain-specific values, automobile attributes, and the preferred type of automobile for two groups of students with dissimilar lifestyles

Global values	Domain-specific values	Automobile attributes	Preference for type of automobile
More liberal group:			
Exciting life	Lasting products	Unleaded gas	Compact car
Equality	Nonpolluting pro-	High-speed cap-	
Self-respect	ducts	ability	
Forgiving	Health-promoting	Handling	
Intellectual	products	Quality work-	
Logical	Products easy to	manship	
	repair	Advanced en-	
	Quiet products	gineering	
	Help eliminate	Low-pollution	
	environmental	emission	
	pollution		
More conservative group:			
National security	Prompt service on	Smooth riding	Standard-size car
Salvation	complaints	Luxurious in-	
Polite		terior	
Social recognition		Prestige	
		Large size	
		Spacious in-	
		terior	

Source: D. Vinson, J. Scott, and L. Lamont, "The Role of Personal Values in Marketing and Consumer Behavior," *Journal of Marketing* (April 1977), p. 48. Used with permission from the American Marketing Association.

for its liberal lifestyle and attitudes and students from a conservative southern university known for a more traditional lifestyle each completed a questionnaire designed to measure their global values and the domain-specific values they held toward certain products. Figure 13 – 1 shows the global and domain-specific values that were *different* for each group of students and the automobile attributes that were also significantly different for each group in terms of importance. Each student was also asked to state a preference for either a compact-size car or standard-size automobile. The more liberal group had a greater preference for compact cars, which was consistent with their global and domain-specific values. They also indicated a higher preference for automobile attributes consistent with an exciting life while still preferring nonpolluting and long-lasting products. On the other hand, the more conservative group preferred larger, standard-size cars, which was more consistent with their values.[4]

Understanding the values which underlie the preference for compact cars or standard-sized cars has obvious applicability in terms of developing advertising campaigns, product design, and segmentation strategy. As we saw in Chapter 5, a number of widely shared American values appear to be undergoing substantial changes. As these values change, so will related attitudes and behaviors. This in turn will create additional problems and opportunities for marketing managers.

CHARACTERISTICS OF ATTITUDES

Attitudes have a number of characteristics that must be understood before we can effectively influence (create, change, or reinforce) them. In this section, we are going to briefly describe the components of attitudes, consistency among these components, the centrality of attitudes, and the intensity with which attitudes are held.

Components of attitudes

Cognitive component   It is useful to consider attitudes as having three components: cognitive, affective, and behavioral. The *cognitive component* consists of the individual's beliefs and knowledge about the object. For most attitude objects, we have a number of beliefs. For example, we may believe that Du Pont (1) is a large manufacturer, (2) makes a wide variety of chemical products, (3) is publicly held, and (4) is generally quite profitable. Each of these beliefs reflects (not necessarily accurately) knowledge about an *attribute* of the organization. The total configuration of beliefs about the organization (or other object) represents the cognitive component of the attitude toward that particular organization or object.

Affective component   Our feelings or emotional reactions to an object represent the *affective component* of the attitude. A consumer that states "I like Du Pont" or "Du Pont is a terrible corporation" is expressing the results of an emotional or affective evaluation of the firm. The statements above imply an overall evaluation. However, this total reaction is generally based on an evaluation of the firm's performance or characteristic on each attribute. Thus, the statement "Du Pont makes *excess* profits" or "Du Pont makes *dangerous* products" implies a negative affective reaction to specific aspects of Du Pont which in combination with reactions to all other relevant attributes of Du Pont will determine the overall reaction to the firm. On the other hand, attitude statements such as "Du Pont is a progressive, innovative firm" or "Du Pont makes quality prod-

---

[4] D. Vinson, J. Scott, and L. Lamont, "The Role of Personal Values in Marketing and Consumer Behavior," *Journal of Marketing* (April 1977), pp. 44–50.

ucts'' reflect positive feelings that would probably lead to favorable consumer reactions.

Behavioral component A series of decisions to not purchase Du Pont brand items, to recommend other brands to friends, or to support legislation unfavorable to Du Pont would reflect the *behavioral component* of an attitude. Since behavior is generally directed toward an entire object, it is less likely to be attribute specific than either beliefs or cognitions. However, this is not always the case, particularly with respect to retail outlets. For example, many consumers buy grocery items at discount or warehouse type outlets but purchase meats and fresh vegetables at regular supermarkets. Thus, for retail outlets it is possible and common to react behaviorally to specific attributes of the outlet. This is generally difficult to do with products because we have to either buy or not buy the complete product.

Component consistency Figure 13—2 illustrates the three components of attitudes described above. In general, all three components of an attitude tend to be *consistent* with each other. This is of critical importance because it forms the basis for a substantial amount of marketing strategy. Consistency means that if we can influence one component of a consumer's attitude, the remaining components may shift also. As managers, we are ultimately concerned with influencing

FIGURE 13–2

Attitude components and manifestations

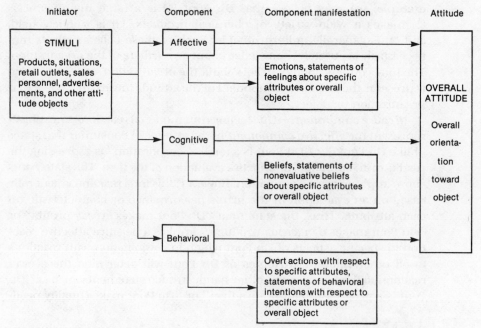

Source: Adapted from M. J. Rosenberg and C. I. Hovland. *Attitude Organization and Change* (Yale University Press, 1960), p. 3.

behavior. We can seldom influence behavior directly. That is, we are not able to physically force consumers to buy our products, but consumers will often listen to our sales personnel, attend to our advertisements, or examine our packages. We can influence their behavior by influencing a belief or feeling about the product if the three components are indeed consistent with each other.

The available evidence indicates that the three components are generally consistent. However, we do not react to products in isolation. As we saw in Chapter 3, the situation (or our attitudes toward the situation) also plays an important role. Consider a beer consumer who believes that Budweiser has a bitter taste (cognitive component) and, not liking a bitter taste, does not like Budweiser (affective component). We would assume that this consumer would not drink Budweiser. In general, our assumption would be correct. Still, there might be many occurrences in which attitudes toward the overall situation would lead to a different behavior pattern.

For example, at a social event where this was the only beer served, the consumer may prefer to consume Budweiser over not having any beer at all. In this situation the consumer may reevaluate the beer's taste (i.e., belief) and conclude it is better tasting than originally thought. This in turn (due to internal consistency) may lead to a more favorable liking (i.e., affect) of the beer and hence a change in attitude. This kind of trial behavior helps illustrate the importance of product samples and promotional incentives designed to encourage the consumer to try a particular brand of product. After trial, the consumer has more tangible, first-hand information about the product on which to base beliefs (i.e., cognitions) and feelings of like or dislike (i.e., affect).

In the example described above, the individual's attitude toward the overall situation led to consumption patterns that would not have been expected based solely on a knowledge of the individual's attitude toward the brand. In this case, the individual consumed a brand toward which a negative attitude was held. In other situations, individuals may fail to purchase objects toward which they have a favorable attitude. You might have a favorable attitude toward a Texas Instrument's *TI 55* hand calculator. However, if you have completed your quantitative coursework, you might not purchase one even if the funds were readily available. You might recommend it to others, compliment a friend who purchased one, or otherwise act favorably toward the brand in *relevant situations.*

Centrality

As described earlier, attitudes are guided in part by our personal values. For example, a consumer with strong personal values toward ecology, thriftiness, and social responsibility would be expected to have favorable attitudes toward recyclable containers. Another consumer who assigned limited importance to these values could also have favorable attitudes, though much less strong, toward recyclable containers.

The connection between a consumer's personal values and attitudes is referred to as *centrality*. The centrality of an attitude reflects how closely that attitude relates to personal values. For the environmentally conscious consumer, attitudes about recyclable containers are more central because these attitudes are closer to personal values. The other consumer does not share the same personal values concerning ecology, thrift, and social responsibility, and as a result the attitudes toward recyclable containers are less central.

The more central an attitude, the more difficult it is to change. To change a very central attitude requires the attitude to become inconsistent with a number of values. Since this is unlikely, the values themselves must be changed or a new attitude made consistent with existing values.

Intensity

The intensity of an attitude is determined by the affective component of an attitude. Intensity refers to how *strongly* the consumer feels. The environmentally conscious consumer could be expected to feel very strongly toward recyclable containers while the other consumer probably would not. In this case the attitude toward recyclable containers held by each consumer differs in intensity. Strongly held attitudes (i.e., intense attitudes) are difficult to change. This is supported by a substantial body of research as well as the intuitive knowledge that it is easier to influence someone who is relatively neutral about an issue than it is to influence someone who feels strongly about the issue.[5]

Most marketing strategies are aimed at creating minor rather than major attitude changes. The tendency is to attempt to shift consumers from indifference to acceptance or from acceptance to preference. To capture a target market with intense negative attitudes toward a brand generally requires a new brand or a major modification of the existing brand. The last section of this chapter provides a brief description of how this was accomplished for Marlboro cigarettes.

MULTIATTRIBUTE ATTITUDE MODEL

As the preceding discussion implied, our attitudes toward most objects are based on our evaluations of and reactions to the various charac-

---

[5] J. L. Freedman, "Involvement, Discrepancy and Change," *Journal of Abnormal and Social Psychology* (1964), pp. 290−95; M. Sherif and C. I. Hovland, *Social Judgment: Assimilation and Contrast Effects in Communication and Attitude Change* (Yale University Press, 1961); C. I. Hovland, O. J. Harvey, and M. Sherif, "Assimilation and Contrast Effects in Reaction to Communication and Attitude Change," *Journal of Abnormal and Social Psychology* (1957), pp. 244−52; L. N. Diab, "Some Limitations of Existing Scales in the Measurement of Social Attitudes," *Psychological Reports* (1965), pp. 427−30; J. Whittaker, "Attitude Change and Communication-Attitude Discrepancy," *Journal of Social Psychology* (1965), pp. 141−47.

teristics or attributes that are associated with the object. A number of approaches have been developed to predict individuals' overall attitudes toward an object from a knowledge of their reactions to the specific attributes associated with the object.[6] Most marketing applications use a version of this approach referred to as *multiattribute models.*[7] A useful formulation of the multiattribute model is:

$$A_b = \sum_{i=1}^{n} W_i \left| I_i - X_{ib} \right|$$

where:

A_b = The consumer's attitude toward a particular brand b.

W_i = The importance the consumer attaches to attribute i.

I_i = The consumer's ideal performance on attribute i.

X_{ib} = The consumer's belief about brand b's performance on attribute i.

n = The number of attributes considered.

The individual's attitude toward a particular brand is based on the sum of how much that brand's performance on each attribute differs from the consumer's ideal performance on that attribute weighted by the importance of that attribute to the consumer. An example will help clarify this model.

Assume that a consumer perceives Budweiser to have the following levels of performance on four attributes:

Budweiser

	(1)	(2)	(3)	(4)	(5)	(6)	(7)	
Low price	I						X	High price
Mild taste	I					X		Bitter taste
High status		X		I				Low status
Low calories	I			X				High calories

In this case this consumer *believes* (i.e., the Xs) that Budweiser is extremely high priced, very bitter in taste, above average in status, and fair in calories. The consumer's ideal beer (i.e., the Is) would be low priced, mild in taste, average in status, and low in calories. Since these attributes are not equally important to the consumer, they are assigned weights

---

[6] M. Rosenberg "Cognitive and Attitudinal Effect," *Journal of Abnormal and Social Psychology* (1956), pp. 367–72; M. Fishbein, "An Investigation of the Relationships between Beliefs about an Object and the Attitude toward That Object," *Human Relations* (1963), pp. 233–40; and M. Fishbein and I. Ajzen, *Belief, Attitude, Intention and Behavior: An Introduction to Theory and Research* (Addison-Wesley Publishing Co., 1975), p. 301.

[7] See W. L. Wilkie and E. A. Pessemier, "Issues in Marketing's Use of Multiattribute Attitude Models," *Journal of Marketing* (November 1973), pp. 428–41.

based on the relative importance *this* consumer attaches to each as shown below:

Attribute	Importance
Price	30
Taste	30
Status	0
Calories	40
	100 points

In this case this consumer considers calories the most important beer attribute with price and taste just slightly less important. The perceived status of a beer is irrelevant to this consumer and is given no weight.

The measurement of beliefs, shown above on a *semantic differential scale,* and importance weights, shown above on a *constant sum scale,* are described in more detail in Chapter 17.[8]

From this information we can index this consumer's attitude toward Budweiser as follows:

$$A_{Bud} = (30)(|1 - 7|) + (30)(|1 - 6|) + (0)(|4 - 2|) + (40)(|1 - 4|)$$
$$= (30)(6) + (30)(5) + (0)(2) + (40)(3)$$
$$= 180 + 150 + 0 + 120$$
$$= 450$$

This involves taking the absolute difference between the consumer's ideal beer attributes and beliefs about Budweiser's attributes and multiplying these differences times the importance attached to each attribute. In this case, the attitude index is computed as 450. Is this good or bad? An attitude index is a relative measure, so in order to determine whether this index reflects a favorable or unfavorable attitude we must evaluate it relative to attitudes toward competing products or brands.

If Budweiser were perceived as the consumer's ideal beer, then all the consumer's beliefs and ideals would be equal and an attitude index of zero would be computed, since there would be *no difference* between what is desired and what is believed by the consumer to be provided. A score of zero indicates an extremely favorable brand attitude since beliefs correspond identically with preferred characteristics. On the other hand, if consumer beliefs and ideals are at extreme opposite ends of the scale for each attribute, there is a maximum difference possible between desired and perceived beliefs. In this example the maximum attitude index would be computed as 600. Thus, an index of 600 in this case reflects the worst possible evaluation and hence implies the least favorable attitude. Therefore, as shown below an attitude index of 450 could

---

[8] For additional techniques and details, see D. S. Tull and D. I. Hawkins, *Marketing Research* (Macmillan Publishing Co., 1980), chap. 9.

be inferred as an unfavorable attitude since it is closer to the unfavorable end of this attitude index scale. It is possible that this score of 450 could be *relatively* favorable, however, if all other competing brands had larger scores.

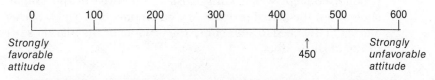

Marketing managers are generally less concerned with the summated score than they are with the individual components of that score. In the above example (assuming the individual was characteristic of a target market), Budweiser would be very concerned about its perceived price and taste since these are important attributes with inadequate performance levels. This is often referred to as a *profile analysis*.

The following applications of profile analysis are typical: (1) General Motors, to develop advertising strategies;[9] (2) Container Corporation of America, to evaluate direct mail approaches;[10] and (3) Du Pont, to evaluate corporate image advertising.[11] It is also commonly used in research on store images.[12] Coca-Cola uses this model (assuming equal attribute importance) in new product development. Consumers rate the product concept (a description of the general characteristics of the product, e.g.,

TABLE 13–1
Profile analysis of the product concept, actual product, and ideal new soft drink

	Target market responses		
Attribute*	Product concept	Actual product	Ideal product
Sweetness (sweet—not sweet)	4.42	3.25	4.17
Flavor (strong–weak)	4.90	3.17	4.63
Color (dark–light)	2.60	4.64	3.16
Aroma (strong–weak)	3.62	3.68	3.64

* Measured on a six-point semantic differential scale.
 Source: Adopted from H. E. Bloom, "Match the Concept and the Product," *Journal of Advertising Research* (October 1977), pp. 25–27.

---

[9] D. A. Aaker and J. G. Myers, *Advertising Management* (Prentice-Hall, Inc., 1975), pp. 125–27.

[10] F. P. Tobalski, "Direct Mail: Image, Return and Effectiveness," *Journal of Advertising Research* (August 1970), pp. 18–25.

[11] R. C. Grass, D. W. Bartges, and J. L. Piech, "Measuring Corporate Image Ad Effects," *Journal of Advertising Research* (December 1972), pp. 15–22.

[12] D. L. James, R. M. Durand, and R. A. Dreves, "The Use of a Multi-Attribute Attitude Model in a Store Image Study," *Journal of Retailing* (Summer 1976), pp. 23–32.

a carbonated, pineapple/lime flavored drink with low calories) prior to trying it, the product after trying it, and their perception of an ideal version of the product.[13] Table 13–1 illustrates part of the results of an initial test of a potential new carbonated drink. As can be seen, the product concept was a fairly close fit on three of the four attributes shown, but the actual product fit well on only one. Thus, Coca-Cola was alerted to the need to alter either the product or the market's perception of the ideal product.

FUNCTIONS OF ATTITUDES

Attitudes persist as important factors in consumer behavior because they are useful in maintaining consistency and add meaning and expression to a consumer's lifestyle. Attitudes also fulfill important functions in terms of helping consumers adjust to difficult situations, express their values, organize their knowledge, and defend their egos in threatening situations.[14] Unless we know the function served by a particular attitude, we are in a poor position to understand or influence it.

The knowledge function

Attitudes serve a knowledge function when they help us organize and simplify the complex and changing world in which we live. One researcher has described this function in this way:

> Individuals not only require beliefs in the interest of satisfying various needs, they also seek *knowledge* to give meaning to what would otherwise be an unorganized chaotic universe. People need standards and frames of reference for understanding their world, and attitudes help to supply such standards.[15]

The knowledge function of attitudes often takes the form of generalizations or stereotypes that may or may not be true. The opinion that "all cola soft drinks taste the same" expresses an attitude about cola soft drinks. This attitude may or may not be correct for the individual that holds it (since taste discrimination varies among individuals). Nonetheless, it will guide the consumer's behavior. Attempts by soft drink manufacturers to convince consumers that their brand does indeed taste different (and better) can focus on the knowledge side of the attitude. Thus, Pepsi-Cola advertises the results of taste tests which show consumers preferring the taste of Pepsi over Coca-Cola. The ads then pre-

---

[13] H. E. Bloom, "Match the Concept and the Product," *Journal of Advertising Research* (October 1977), pp. 25–27.

[14] D. Katz, "The Functional Approach to the Study of Attitudes," *Public Opinion Quarterly* (Summer 1960), pp. 163–204.

[15] Ibid., p. 175.

sent the consumer with the "Pepsi Challenge" to taste the difference themselves.[16]

The knowledge function of attitudes also affects consumer perceptions of where products should be purchased. For example, the marketers of Smile toothpaste wanted to create a high-priced, high-quality attitude toward their toothpaste and first marketed this product much like a cosmetic by distributing Smile through channels used primarily for cosmetics. However, consumers expect to purchase toothpaste in a grocery or drugstore and not at department or specialty stores where they purchase cosmetics. Thus, Smile, like many other such attempts by manufacturers to use uncommon channels of distribution, met with failure because of well-established consumer attitudes built around consumer knowledge of where products should be acquired.

The value expression function

Many attitudes express basic values that the consumer holds and considers to be important. As we saw in Figure 13−1, the global values of liberal students correspond well with certain domain-specific values and desired product attributes. Beliefs about alternative products are then guided by these values such that similar attitudes are also likely to result. Therefore, a consumer with global values that contribute to a domain-specific value that products should be nonpolluting is likely to form a negative attitude toward products which pollute the environment. When this is the case, the attitude is an expression of a basic value.

Because a great many products are symbolic and provide a particular image, consumers having values similar to those expressed by that product image are more likely to hold a favorable attitude toward that product. Thus, in the automobile study cited earlier, consumers who attached importance to the values of social recognition and prestige preferred products that portrayed social status and elitism.

The ego-defense function

While attitudes may serve as a way to express our values, they also are useful in protecting our egos in threatening or uncomfortable situations. Defense mechanisms such as projection, compensation, and rationalization can be useful in developing ego-protective attitudes. Consumers who are insecure may prefer an automobile that delivers power since this aspect of a car and their attitude toward it are protective of their feelings of insecurity. In this situation the consumer's attitude toward automotive power is one that compensates for feelings of insecu-

---

[16] "Pepsi: We're Preferred," *Advertising Age* (July 19, 1976), p. 17.

rity. Other products with symbolic meanings such as clothes, jewelry, and cigarettes may serve as ego-protective products for consumers who feel inadequate, insecure, or low in self-esteem.

The adjustment function

Attitudes also fulfill an adjustment function which allows an individual to adjust to new and different situations in a psychologically consistent manner. While in college, students often identify with a particular lifestyle independent of their major area of study. However, following graduation, business students going to work for a major corporation may adjust their attitude and lifestyle to the new situation created by the environment of the corporation of which they are now a part. Because this change can take place very quickly, it illustrates the relevance of the adjustment function in providing attitudes that help us adjust to new and sometimes unfamiliar situations.

In terms of consumption behavior we often adjust our attitudes in accordance with the social reward or punishment we receive from others. A consumer who purchases a rather exotic pair of pants may develop an indifferent or negative attitude toward the pants after receiving a great deal of teasing from friends. The consumer bought the pants because of personal preference and the belief they would enhance self-image, but after receiving criticisms the buyer adjusted this attitude to one of dislike. Of course, the opposite could also be true when a consumer receives social praise for a particular action or appearance.

INFLUENCING ATTITUDES

Marketing managers are interested in reinforcing existing favorable attitudes, creating favorable attitudes about new or unknown products or brands, and/or changing existing attitudes to more favorable ones. A substantial amount of all marketing strategy is designed to reinforce existing favorable attitudes. In general, the same procedures are used to reinforce, create, or change attitudes. These procedures are primarily aimed at influencing the cognitive or belief component of the attitude. It is implicitly assumed that affect (liking) and behavior (purchase) will follow the creation of desired cognitions. This assumption makes intuitive sense. If you were convinced that a brand contained a desirable attribute, you would be more likely to both like and purchase that brand than otherwise. This was the basic premise used by D'Arcy-MacManus & Masius in designing the successful advertising campaign for Anheuser-Busch's light beers.[17]

---

[17] "A-B Aims to Win by Segmenting Light Beer," *Marketing News* (December 29, 1978), p. 6.

General approaches to influencing attitudes

There are four basic marketing strategies for altering the cognitive structure of a consumer's attitude:

1. Change the belief(s) about the attributes of the brand.
2. Change the relative importance of these beliefs.
3. Add new beliefs.
4. Change the belief(s) about the attributes of the ideal brand.

Each of these strategies is illustrated in Table 13−2 and is described below.

The first strategy involves shifting beliefs about the performance of the brand on one or more attributes. The attitude of the beer consumer with beliefs that Budweiser is overpriced and tastes bitter could be im-

TABLE 13–2

A. Initial belief structure and attitude (attitude = 300)

Attribute	Importance	Ideal	Belief
Price	50	3	5
Taste	50	5	1
Social status	0	3	4
	100		

B. Strategy I: Change beliefs about brand (attitude = 200)

Attribute	Importance	Ideal	Belief
Price	50	3	5
Taste	50	5	3
Social status	0	3	4
	100		

C. Strategy II: Shift attribute importance (attitude = 220)

Attribute	Importance	Ideal	Belief
Price	30	3	5
Taste	30	5	1
Social status	40	3	4
	100		

D. Strategy III: Add beliefs (attitude = 220)

Attribute	Importance	Ideal	Belief
Price	30	3	5
Taste	30	5	1
Social status	0	3	4
Less calories	40	5	4
	100		

E. Strategy IV: Change beliefs about ideal (attitude = 150)

Attribute	Importance	Ideal	Belief
Price	50	3	5
Taste	50	2	1
Social status	0	3	4
	100		

proved. For example, assume the consumer's original belief structure was as shown in Table 13—2A. Based on this structure of beliefs, ideal beliefs, and belief importance, an attitude index of 300 was computed. By shifting this consumer's perception of the taste of Budweiser (perhaps through advertising), this attitude index can be improved. This is shown in Table 13—2B with the index improved to 200 by a favorable change in the perceived taste. Note that it would also be possible to actually change (improve) the flavor of the beer. As noted in an earlier chapter, beer is one of the products towards which many consumers seem to be unable to respond well to physical stimuli changes or differences. Hence, the possible reliance on advertising.

As shown in Table 13—2A, this consumer considers some beliefs to be more important than others. Therefore, another way to change the attitude is to shift the relative importance away from poorly evaluated attributes to positively evaluated attributes. This strategy is illustrated in Table 13—2C, as importance was shifted from price and taste to the social status of the beer.

The third change strategy involves *adding* new beliefs to the consumer's belief structure (i.e., cognition). Let us assume that Budweiser is able to offer one-third less calories in a beer without altering the taste. Let us also assume that our consumer views this as a very favorable new product feature. The addition of this positive feature contributes favorably to a better overall attitude toward this brand of beer. This is illustrated in Figure 13—2D, as the addition of this positive feature resulted in reallocation of relative importance and an improved attitude index. In this case the addition of less calories as a product attribute improved the attitude by shifting importance away from poorly evaluated price and taste attributes to the positively evaluated calorie attribute.

The final change strategy involves altering the perceptions of the ideal brand. For example, Budweiser might attempt to convince our consumer that good beer has a strong taste. The result of succeeding in this strategy can be seen in Table 13—2E. The late 1970s saw many consumers altering their perceptions of the ideal characteristics of products as far as energy consumption was concerned.

Message characteristics and attitude change

Marketers attempt to influence consumer attitudes by providing direct product experience and by using persuasive messages. Direct product experience is encouraged through free samples, money-back guarantees, reduced prices, and so forth. Direct product experience can have a tremendous impact on creating, reinforcing, or changing attitudes. However, it is also expensive, frequently difficult or impossible to implement (e.g., in many states it is illegal to distribute samples of alcoholic beverages), and limited to the short run. Therefore, most firms rely on persuasive messages in addition to, or instead of, direct product experience to influence attitudes. In this section of the chapter, we are going to examine a number of aspects of persuasive messages that can bring about attitude creation, reinforcement, and change.

Source credibility   Influencing attitudes becomes much easier when the source of the message is viewed as highly credible by the target market.[18] This is commonly referred to as *source credibility*. Source credibility appears to be composed of two basic dimensions: trustworthiness and expertise.[19] A source that has no apparent reason to provide other than complete, objective, and accurate information would generally be considered as trustworthy. Most of us would consider our good friends trustworthy on most matters. However, many consumers doubt the trustworthiness of sales personnel and advertisements because it might be to their advantage to mislead the consumer. Remember that the source of a communication can be an identifiable person, an unidentifiable person (a "typical" housewife), a company or organization, an inanimate figure such as a cartoon character, or even the infamous "they."

Although most of us trust our friends, we may not consider them to be credible sources for advice on the purchase of many products. This is because they lack the expertise, knowledge, or experience to provide the required guidance. Sales personnel and advertising managers, on the other hand, generally have the required expertise (but may not be viewed as trustworthy).

Thus, such organizations as the American Dental Association (ADA) which are widely viewed as both trustworthy and expert can have a tremendous influence on attitudes. The remarkable success of Crest toothpaste is largely attributable to the ADA endorsement. Underwriters Laboratories, Good Housekeeping, and other trustworthy and expert sources are widely sought for their endorsements.

Movie stars and athletes are commonly used for endorsements. Fig-

---

[18] C. Goldberg, "Attitude Change as a Function of Source Credibility, Authoritarianism, and Message Ambiguity," *Proceedings of the Annual Convention of the American Psychological Association* (1970), pp. 407–8; E. McGinnies, "Initial Attitude, Source Credibility, and Involvement as Factors in Persuasion," *Journal of Experimental Social Psychology* (July 1973), pp. 285–96; J. McKillip and D. Edwards, "Source Characteristics and Attitude Change," *Personality and Social Psychology Bulletin*, (March 1974), pp. 135–37; W. F. McDaniel and C. Vestal, "Issue Relevance and Source Credibility as a Determinant of Retension," *Bulletin of the Psychonomic Society* (June 1975), pp. 481–82; M. H. Birnbaum, J. Wong, and P. Wong, "Combining Information from Sources That Vary in Credibility," *Memory and Cognition* (May 1976), pp. 330–36; and V. Andreoli and S. Worchel, "Effects of Media, Communicator, and Message Position on Attitude Change," *Public Opinion Quarterly* (Spring 1978), pp. 59–70.

[19] See C. I. Hovland, I. L. Janis, and H. H. Kelley, *Communication and Persuasion* (Yale University Press, 1953); D. Berlo, J. Lemert, and R. Mertz, "Dimensions for Evaluating the Acceptability of Message Sources," *Public Opinion Quarterly* (Winter 1969–70), pp. 563–76; and R. L. Applebaum and K. W. Anatol, "The Factor Structure of Source Credibility as a Function of the Speaking Situation," *Speech Monographs* (August 1972), pp. 216–22.

FIGURE 13–3

Celebrities used as credible sources in product promotions

Celebrity	Product
O. J. Simpson	Treesweet orange juice
Mohammed Ali	Sears Die-Hard battery
Ed McMann	Budweiser beer
Danny Thomas	Norelco coffee maker
Joe DiMaggio	Mr. Coffee (coffee maker)
Robert Redford	Environmental protection
James Stewart	Firestone tires
Joe Namath	Brute mens cologne
Bruce Jenner	Wheaties
Karl Malden	American Express Travelers Checks
Bob Hope	Texaco Oil Company
Robert Conrad	Ever-Ready batteries
Orson Wells	Paul Masson wines
Robert Young	Sanka

ure 13–3 lists several commonly seen company spokesmen. In some cases, the individual is viewed as being an expert, such as Joe Namath for men's cologne. In other cases, the firm is relying on the general believability of spokespersons as well as their image and attention-attracting ability.[20]

Using a company spokesperson creates special risks for the sponsoring organization. Few well-known personalities are admired by everyone. Thus, it is important to be certain that most of the members of the relevant target markets will respond favorably to the spokesperson. An additional risk is that some behavior involving the spokesperson will affect the individual's credibility after he/she is associated with the firm. The American Cancer Society had to stop a series of commercials in which Tony Curtis spoke against cigarette smoking when he was arrested on a marijuana charge. Ideal Toy Corporation apparently lost several million dollars on an Evel Knievel toy line after the stuntman was convicted of beating a reporter with a baseball bat.[21]

Fear appeals Utilization of a credible source relies on perceived trustworthiness and expertise to influence attitudes. Fear appeals make use of *the threat of negative (unpleasant) consequences if attitudes or behaviors are not altered.*[22] While fear appeals have been studied primarily in terms of physical fear (physical harm from smoking, unsafe driving, and so forth), social fears (disapproval of one's peers for incorrect

---

[20] For a discussion of these issues, see H. H. Friedman, S. Termini, and R. Washington, "The Effects of Advertisements Utilizing Four Types of Endorsements," *Journal of Advertising* (Spring 1976), pp. 22–24; and R. B. Fireworker and H. H. Friedman, "The Effects of Endorsements on Product Evaluation," *Decision Sciences* (July 1977), pp. 576–83.

[21] "Motorcycle Migraine," *Fortune* (January 16, 1978), p. 49.

[22] For a review of research findings, see B. Sternthal and C. S. Craig, "Fear Appeals: Revisited and Revised," *Journal of Consumer Research* (December 1974), pp. 22–34.

clothing, bad breathe, or inadequate coffee) are also frequently used in advertising.[23] For fear appeals to be successful, the level of fear induced must not be so high as to cause the consumer to distort or reject the message.[24] In addition, it is critical that the source of the fear-arousing message be viewed as highly credible.[25] An example of an effective use of fear appeals is the antismoking campaign described below.

> The English cancer foundation sponsored a series of advertisements in which cowboys from the United States were interviewed by their physician. Each had been a heavy smoker and a cowboy all his life and, also, each had six months or so to live. In the advertisement, the cowboy was pictured on his horse with tubes running from machines into his body. In the dialogue the physician and cowboy discuss the cowboy's smoking behavior and current condition and conclude that the two are related. The intent of this advertisement was to create fear in a credible manner by having a physician interview an actual heavy smoker who has been given a short time to live.[26]

Humorous appeals At almost the opposite end of the spectrum from fear appeals are message appeals built around humor. While in the past humor was not used a great deal in advertising communications, a recent study found that approximately 15 percent of the television advertisements examined were built around a humorous theme.[27] These types of messages are particularly effective at gaining attention.[28] Yet for humorous appeals to be effective in terms of influencing beliefs and behavioral intentions, the following performance criteria must be met:

1. The brand must be identified within the opening ten seconds, or there is a danger of inhibiting recall of important selling points.
2. The type of humor makes a difference. Subtlety is more effective than the bizarre.
3. The humor must be relevant to the brand or key idea. Recall and persuasion are both decreased when the linkage is not made.
4. Humorous commercials that entertain by belittling potential users do *not* perform well.[29]

---

[23] See M. Ray and W. Wilkie, "Fear: The Potential of an Appeal Neglected by Marketing," *Journal of Marketing* (January 1970), pp. 59–62.

[24] J. R. Stuteville, "Psychic Defenses against High Fear Appeals: A Key Marketing Variable," *Journal of Marketing* (April 1970), pp. 39–45.

[25] Sternthal and Craig, "Fear Appeals."

[26] "Marlboro 'Sandbagged' by U. K. Showing Mixing Ads, 'Cowboys' with Cancer," *Advertising Age* (November 15, 1976), p. 1; " 'Death in the West' Headed for Boot Hill, PM Suit Hopes," *Advertising Age* (January 31, 1977), p. 1.

[27] J. Kelly and P. Solomon, "Humor in Television Advertising," *Journal of Advertising* (Summer 1975), pp. 31–35.

[28] B. Sternthal and C. Craig, "Humor in Advertising," *Journal of Marketing* (October 1973), pp. 12–18.

[29] H. Ross, Jr., "How to Create Effective Humorous Commercials, Yielding Above Average Brand Preference Change," *Marketing News* (March 26, 1976), p. 4.

Humor, when well done, can gain attention, influence attitudes, and increase sales. As the first three points above imply, the humorous message must remain focused on the brand or key selling point. Otherwise, it may distract from the message you are trying to communicate. In addition, the humor must not be directed at the users of the product.

Drawing a conclusion Should an advertisement explicitly recommend a course of action or draw a firm conclusion (sometimes referred to as a "hot" message) or should it present information and leave it up to the consumer to draw a conclusion (a "cool" message)? Research findings indicate that the hot message is generally more effective at influencing attitudes, particularly in the short run. However, cool messages gain in effectiveness with repetition and may be preferred by respondents. Also, cool messages are more effective with some target groups, such as the highly educated.[30]

Nonovert appeals Word-of-mouth communications from relatives, friends, or peers are important sources of information that can have a very substantial influence on consumer beliefs. The source in this case is personal and trustworthy. Marketers have tried to create this same effect in message presentation through "slice of life" or nonovert appeals.[31]

These generally involve a real-life situation with ordinary people who would not be perceived as spokespersons for a company. The viewer of this message presentation is in effect overhearing a conversation between two or more people who are talking about a particular brand of product. For example, two consumers discussing the benefits of a new brand of detergent are not speaking directly to the viewers; instead the viewers are overhearing a conversation between two individuals much like themselves. There is evidence that beliefs can be positively influenced under these conditions.[32]

Distraction Consumers frequently counterargue with advertisements and other messages that conflict with their existing attitudes. That is, a consumer committed to driving a private automobile may counterargue with a message promoting bus transportation something like:

Advertisement: Let us do the driving, it's less stressful!

Consumer: Yea, and I can listen to some bore next to me chatter.

Advertisement: And there are no parking problems.

Consumer: Of course not; you drop me off five blocks from my office.

---

[30] See H. Hadley, "The Non-Directive Approach in Advertising Appeals," *Journal of Applied Psychology* (April 1963), pp. 496−98; "Ads without Answers Make the Brain Itch," *Psychology Today* (November 1975), p. 78.

[31] K. Roman and J. Maas, *How to Advertise* (St. Martin's Press, 1976), pp. 23−24.

[32] E. Walster and L. Festinger, "The Effectiveness of 'Overheard' Persuasive Communications," *Journal of Abnormal and Social Psychology* (1962), pp. 395−402.

The impact of counterargument is often to *strengthen* the consumer's initial attitude. Therefore, marketers are interested in reducing counterarguments.

One way of achieving this goal is with *distraction*.[33] This can be done with the use of humor.[34] Or it may be done with the presentation of competing stimuli such as background music or noise.[35] While distraction can reduce counterargumentation, it also can reduce attention and comprehension of the message.[36] Therefore, it is very important to thoroughly pretest messages using this approach.

Repetition Repetition of a message clearly enhances learning (see Chapter 11). There are many reasons why repetition of the message has a positive influence on attention and, in many cases, on attitudes. Since there are a variety of factors involved, we have listed below those that are most useful in understanding the role of repetition as an influence on attitudes:

1. Because of situational distractions and message complexity, it is often necessary to repeat a message several times before information is comprehended.
2. Through repetition, information is moved from short-term memory into long-term memory.
3. Continued association of an attitude (feeling or belief) with a brand through repetition increases the strength of that attitude (i.e., affect).
4. Repetition reduces forgetting by continually reinforcing the message.[37]

The effects of repeat exposure of a message on consumers have been demonstrated in both print and electronic media in terms of increased message attention and comprehension.[38] As a message is repeated, atten-

---

[33] L. Festinger and M. MacCoby, "On Resistance to Persuasive Communication," *Journal of Abnormal and Social Psychology* (1964), pp. 359–66; and J. Freeman and D. Sears, "Warning, Distraction, and Resistance to Influence," *Journal of Personality and Social Psychology* (1965), pp. 262–66.

[34] Sternthal and Craig, "Humor in Advertising."

[35] J. Engel, R. Blackwell, and D. Kollat, *Consumer Behavior,* 3d ed. (Dryden Press, 1978), p. 425.

[36] M. Venkatesan and C. Haaland, "The Effect of Distraction on the Influence of Persuasive Marketing Communications," in *Insights into Consumer Behavior,* ed. J. Arndt (Allyn and Bacon, 1968), pp. 55–66; D. Gardner, "The Distraction Hypothesis in Marketing," *Journal of Advertising Research* (1970), pp. 25–30; and S. Bither, "Effects of Distraction and Commitment on the Persuasiveness of Television Advertising," *Journal of Marketing Research* (1972), pp. 1–5.

[37] A. Mitchell and J. Olson, "Cognitive Effects of Advertising Repetition," working paper no. 49, (College of Business Administration, Pennsylvania State University, October 1976).

[38] "Frequency in Broadcast Advertising: 1," *Media/Scope* (February 1962).

tion and comprehension of the message increase; when the exposure is removed, awareness and comprehension decrease.[39]

The effect repeat exposure has on awareness is shown in Figure 13–4. In this example, a department store advertised a special promo-

FIGURE 13–4

Message awareness and comprehension on each of five days of message presentation

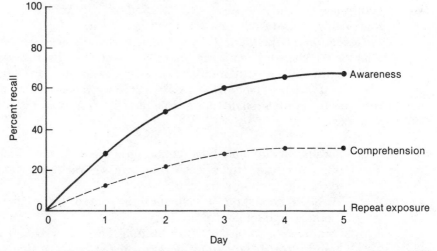

Source: R. Best, "Optimizing Policies for Marketing Promotions," working paper, University of Arizona (1978).

tion in a university newspaper for five consecutive days. Thus, the target audience was a well-defined segment of the store's market, and the newspaper was read by three out of every four students of the over 30,000 attending the university. As shown in the figure, after the first exposure to the department store's message, 37 percent of the readership recalled the ad. Following the second exposure 52 percent recalled seeing the ad, and the proportion increased for each of the remaining three days but at a slower rate of change. Following the last exposure, 67 percent of the readership recalled the advertisement.[40]

Comprehension of the important message content (store name and merchandise on sale) followed a similar pattern. However, as shown in Figure 13–4, less than 30 percent of the readership comprehended the message content after five exposures. This low level of comprehension was probably due to the fact that the advertisement contained too much information, had a format similar to a competing store's advertising

---

[39] H. Zielske, "The Remembering and Forgetting of Advertising," *Journal of Marketing,* (January 1959), p. 240; and E. Pomerance and H. Zielske, "How Frequently Should You Advertise?" *Media/Scope* (September 1958), pp. 25–27.

[40] R. Best, "Optimizing Policies for Marketing Promotions," working paper, University of Arizona (1978).

format, and positioned the store name in the ad such that it could not be readily seen in a quick exposure of the advertisement.

The study described above illustrates the impact that repetition can have on the cognitive (belief) component of attitudes. Other studies have shown that repeat exposure can directly influence the affective (liking) component of an attitude without altering the belief.[41] That is, repeated exposures to a product or style may increase our liking of the product or style. Of course, use of repeat exposure must be done carefully as over-exposure has been shown to create a boomerang effect in which the initial positive effects on attitudes are weakened by reactance against overexposure to the same message.[42]

Amount of information   The amount of information presented in a marketing communication should be controlled for two reasons. First, when too much information is presented the consumer can become overwhelmed and unable to sort out the information. When this is the case confusion results and information is not correctly comprehended. This is exactly what happened in the department store advertisement discussed above; a combination of too much information and confusing information format greatly reduced consumer comprehension of important aspects of the message.

A second reason to limit the amount of information presented in a message is related to information overload (see Chapter 10).[43] This is illustrated in Figure 13−5.[44] In this case students processed different amounts of information, some important and some unimportant, in evaluating alternative brands of 10-speed bicycles. As shown in Figure 13−5, choice accuracy increased as the amount of information used in decision making increased to a point and then decreased as more information was added to the information processing task.

Order of presentation   Because the learning of most marketing messages, particularly advertisements, involves a low-involvement learning process, the order of presentation of information presented in the ad is critical to the message's success.[45] Important information, like the brand's name and/or key ideas, should be presented at the very beginning and/or end of the ad message, as information presented in the

[41] R. Zajonc, "The Attitudinal Effects of Mere Exposure," *Journal of Personality and Social Psychology* (1968), pp. 1−27.

[42] R. Miller, "Mere Exposure, Psychological Reactance and Attitude Change," *Public Opinion Quarterly* (1976), pp. 229−33.

[43] J. Jacoby, D. E. Speller, and C. A. Kohn, "Brand Choice Behavior as a Function of Information Load," *Journal of Marketing Research* (February 1974), pp. 63−69.

[44] R. Best, "Choice Accuracy as a Function of Information Load, Choice Variance, and Discrimination Power," working paper, University of Arizona (1978).

[45] H. E. Krugman, "The Impact of Television Advertising: Learning without Involvement," *Public Opinion Quarterly* (1965), 349−56; and H. E. Krugman, "Memory without Recall, Exposure without Perception," *Journal of Advertising Research* (August 1977), pp. 7−12.

352

FIGURE 13–5
An example of information overload

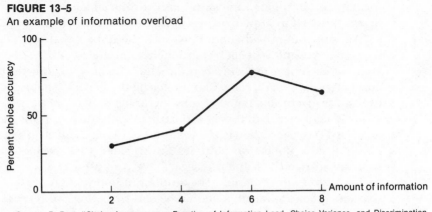

Source: R. Best, "Choice Accuracy as a Function of Information Load, Choice Variance, and Discrimination Power," working paper, University of Arizona (1978).

middle of a message is not recalled as well in a low-involvement learning process. This is illustrated in Figure 13 – 6. This demonstrates the effects of "primacy" (material presented first) and "recency" (material presented last) in low-involvement learning. That is, for much information presented in advertisements that consumers are not interested in, the highest level of recall is for information presented at the beginning and end of the message. Thus, brand name and/or key sales points are generally presented early in a message and are often repeated at the end of the message.

One-sided versus two-sided messages Marketers, in advertisements and sales presentations, generally present only the benefits of their product without mentioning any negative characteristics it might possess or any advantages a competitor might have. These are *one-sided*

FIGURE 13–6
Recall of message presentation as a function of the order in which message information is presented

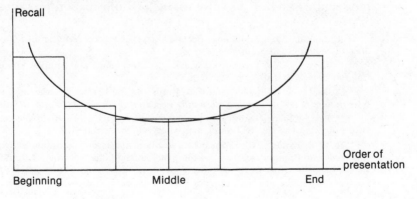

messages since only one point of view is expressed. The idea of a *two-sided message,* presenting both the good and bad points, is counterintuitive and most marketers are reluctant to try such an approach. However, two-sided messages are generally more effective than one-sided messages in terms of changing a strongly held attitude. In addition, they are particularly effective with highly educated consumers. One-sided messages are most effective at reinforcing existing attitudes.[46]

Tha Marlboro story[47]

It is appropriate to close this chapter with a brief description of a classic marketing program which had a major impact on consumer attitudes. Close your eyes and think of Marlboro cigarettes. What comes to mind? Is it an effeminate, sissy cigarette with an ivory tip or a red beauty tip? Not hardly when one thinks of the Marlboro Man!

Philip Morris began marketing Marlboro in 1924 as an extremely mild, filter cigarette with either an ivory tip or a red beauty tip! It was advertised in a very plush atmosphere and was widely used by women. By the 1950s the image described above was firmly established. In addition, all filter cigarettes were viewed as somewhat effeminate.

By the mid-1950s it was becoming increasingly apparent that filter cigarettes would eventually take over the market. Philip Morris decided to make Marlboro acceptable to the heavy user market segment—males. To accomplish this, everything but the name was changed. A more flavorful blend of tobaccos was selected along with a new filter. The package design was changed to red and white with an angular design (more masculine than a curved or circular design). One version of the package was the crush-proof box. Again, a very rugged, masculine option.

The advertising used "regular guys," not professional models, who typified "masculine confidence." The Marlboro cowboy (a real cowboy) was introduced as "the most generally accepted symbol of masculinity in America." To lend credence to the new brand it was tied to the well-known Philip Morris name with "new from Philip Morris" in the introductory advertising.

How successful was it? What did you think of a few minutes ago when asked to think about Marlboro? Think how drastically attitudes had to be changed to bring about such a dramatic product image shift. *Attitudes can be created, changed, and reinforced given an understanding of what attitudes do for consumers and how attitudes are structured.*

---

[46] See C. Hovland, A. Lunnsdaine, and F. Sheffield, *Experiments on Mass Communication* (Princeton University Press, 1948), chap. 8.

[47] Based on E. L. Brink and W. T. Kelley, *The Management of Promotion* (Prentice-Hall, Inc., 1963), pp. 161–65.

SUMMARY

Attitudes can be defined as the way we think, feel, and act toward some aspect of our environment. They are a result of all the influences discussed so far in the text and represent the basis for the lifestyle individuals pursue. Attitudes, therefore, are the focal point of a great deal of marketing strategy.

Attitudes are different from values and beliefs but have an important interrelationship. Beliefs are what we think or believe about our world and values represent standards for guiding behavior and influencing beliefs and attitudes. Thus, values serve as an integrating framework for attitudes that are drawn from a large number of beliefs.

The understanding and use of attitudes is clearer when they are looked at as having three component parts—cognitive, affective, and behavioral. The cognitive component consists of the individual's beliefs or knowledge about the object. Feelings or emotional reactions to an object represent the affective component of the attitude. The behavioral component reflects overt actions and statements of behavioral intentions with respect to specific attributes of the object or the overall object. In general, all three components of an attitude tend to be consistent with each other. Thus, if marketing managers can influence one component, the other components may also be influenced.

Centrality refers to the connection between a consumer's personal values and attitudes. Generally, the more central an attitude, the more difficult it is to change. Intensity of an attitude refers to how strongly the consumer feels about the attitude object. As with centrality, intense attitudes are generally more difficult to change.

Attitudes toward most objects are based on evaluations of and reactions to the various characteristics or attributes that are associated with the object. Multiattribute attitude models have been developed to predict overall attitudes based on reactions to specific attributes. These models are typically constructed such that the overall attitude consists of the sum of how much that brand's performance on each attribute differs from the consumer's ideal performance on that attribute weighted by the importance of that attribute to the consumer.

One important way to view attitudes is to consider the function served by a particular attitude. Attitudes serve a knowledge function when they help us organize and simplify the complex and changing world in which we live. Many attitudes express basic values that the consumer holds and thus fulfill a value expressive function. As opposed to value expressive, attitudes may serve in such a manner as to protect our egos in threatening or uncomfortable situations. Attitudes also fulfill an adjustment function which allows an individual to adjust to new and different situations in a psychologically comfortable manner.

Marketing managers are interested in reinforcing existing favorable attitudes, creating favorable attitudes about new or unknown products or brands, and/or changing existing attitudes to more favorable ones. There are four basic strategies for influencing attitudes by altering the cognitive structure of a consumer's attitude. First, it is possible to change the belief(s) about the attributes of the brand. Second, one might change the relative importance of these beliefs. Third, new beliefs could be added to the present attitude. And finally, the belief(s) about the attributes of the ideal brand could be changed.

Marketers attempt to influence consumer's attitudes by providing direct product experience and by using persuasive messages. Because direct product experience is so expensive, frequently difficult to implement, and limited to the short run, most firms rely on persuasive messages.

Source credibility is one way to manipulate messages and thus influence attitudes. Source credibility appears to be composed of two basic dimensions: trustworthiness and expertise. Influencing attitudes becomes much easier when the source of the message is viewed as highly credible by the target market.

Fear appeals make use of the threat of negative consequences if attitudes or behaviors are not altered and therefore are useful in persuasive messages for certain types of products. While fear appeals have been studied primarily in terms of physical fear, social fears are also used in advertising. Humorous appeals can also be effective in influencing attitudes. However, the humorous message must remain focused on the brand or main selling point to be effective.

The effects of drawing a conclusion for the audience (a hot message) or leaving the consumer to draw the conclusion (a cool message) seem to be highly dependent on the target group. Overall, hot messages seem somewhat more effective, at least in the short run. Word-of-mouth communications from friends and peers have always been influential, and messages portraying this type of situation (nonovert appeals) seem to be effective.

Repetition of a message clearly enhances learning and has a large influence on attitudes. Repetition has been shown to directly influence the affective component without altering the belief. One must be careful of boomerang effects from overexposure. The order of presentation also can affect attitudes, particularly recall. Generally, we remember the first and last parts of the message better than the middle. Two-sided messages are generally more effective than one-sided messages in terms of changing strongly held attitudes.

REVIEW QUESTIONS

1. What are values and how are they related to attitudes?
2. What is the difference between global values and domain-specific values?
3. What are beliefs? What role do they play in the formation of attitudes?
4. What are the key characteristics of cognitive, affective, and behavioral components of attitude? How are they related in terms of consistency?
5. Under what circumstances (i.e., situations) would consumers be inconsistent in terms of their attitude toward a particular brand of a product?
6. What roles do centrality and intensity play in your attitudes toward different television programs?
7. What are the key elements of the multiattribute attitude model?
8. What functions do attitudes perform for consumers?
9. What are the different strategies a marketer could utilize in an attempt to change attitudes?
10. What message strategies can marketers use in an attempt to gain attention and alter attitudes toward a given stimulus?
11. When using fear appeals how should source credibility be used in creating a message intended to change attitudes?
12. How should humor be used in message presentation?
13. What effects are created by drawing a conclusion, nonovert appeal, and distraction in terms of gaining attention and influencing attitudes?
14. What is meant by primacy and recency? How does it apply to attitude change?
15. What is meant by information overload?
16. Explain the difference between one-sided and two-sided communication. When would you use each and why?
17. How can repetition be used to influence attitudes?

DISCUSSION QUESTIONS

1. How would global and domain specific values of different segments of the American culture contribute to attitudes toward mopeds?
2. How would you recommend that Jeff obtain a multiattribute attitude measure of student attitudes toward mopeds?
3. What aspect of your attitude would have to change in order for your attitude toward mopeds to improve? That is, would you recommend changing existing beliefs, shifting the importance of beliefs, shifting the ideal desired from beliefs, or adding new beliefs?

4. How might a severe gasoline shortage (i.e., situation) change your attitude toward mopeds? How would the components of multiattribute model change?

5. Of the various message strategies presented in this chapter which would be most effective, and why, in changing attitudes toward mopeds among three different market segments—students, housewives, and retired consumers?

6. In terms of structure, what would you recommend in designing a communication strategy to change attitudes?

7. Review the American values described in Figure 5−1. Pick five values that you believe are undergoing change in America. What product-related attitudes do you think will be affected by these shifts?

8. Discuss the functions attitudes serve and how consumers may utilize each function in purchasing an automobile.

9. Discuss how you would use source credibility and fear appeal in developing an attitude change strategy for parents who abuse their children. Would you build your message around an affective component, cognitive component, or both? How would you measure the success of an advertisement built around your attitude change strategy?

PROJECT QUESTIONS

1. Develop a multiattribute attitude model to measure student attitudes toward transportation alternatives. Then measure the attitudes of five students in terms of their attitude toward using the bus, a car, bicycle, and moped. Following the attitude measurement ask the students to rank their preference for each mode of transportation. Then compute attitude measures for each student and compare these measures with their preferences. Each student's most-favorable attitude should correspond with their preferred mode of transportation. Also, examine differences in the cognitive structure (i.e., beliefs, ideals, and weights) of students with different attitudes and preferences. Can you explain why they have different attitudes and preferences? In each case, what would you have to alter to improve the student's attitude toward their least-preferred mode of transportation?

2. Measure another student's ideal beliefs and belief importance for breakfast cereals. Examine these ideal beliefs and importance weights and then develop a verbal description (i.e., concept) of a new brand of breakfast cereal that would satisfy this student's needs in a breakfast cereal. Next, measure that student's attitude toward the concept of breakfast cereal you have developed in your verbal description. How did you do in this marketing exercise? If you went

wrong, how would you change things to improve your new product concept?

3. Find and cut out of a magazine or newspaper two advertisements, one which is based on an affective component and the other based on the cognitive component. Discuss the motive of each ad in terms of its copy and illustration and what effect it creates in terms of attitude. Also, discuss why the marketer might have taken that approach in each advertisement.

4. Identify a television commercial that uses a humorous appeal and then interview five other individuals not enrolled in your class and measure their (1) awareness of this commercial, (2) recall of brand advertised, (3) recall of relevant information, (4) liking of the commercial, and (5) the preference for the product advertised. Then evaluate your results and assess the level of communication that has taken place in terms of these five consumers' exposure, attention, comprehension, and preferences for this product and commercial.

14

Lifestyle

"More than a beautiful place to live —it's a way of life." This is a key promotional phrase used to describe Westlake Hills, Prudential Insurance Company of America's planned residential-industrial-commercial community of 25,000 near Los Angeles. The community is strictly regulated even to the point of requiring a specified level of lawn maintenance. One analyst describes it as follows: "The Westlake lifestyle can be defined as a social ethic emphasizing recreation, sociability, and materialism." As one consultant to Westlake expresses it: "No question about it. They are buying an identity here."[1]

In the example described above, the organization is deliberately marketing and the consumers are purchasing more than houses. What is being purchased is a lifestyle or at least a major portion of one. Although the lifestyle implications of purchasing a home in Westlake Hills are substantially more blatant than for most consumer purchases, it is a major contention of this text that *consumers make consumption-related decisions in order to maintain and/or enhance their lifestyles*. That is, our purchase and utilization (or nonpurchase or nonutilization) of many products is based on our perception of the impact this behavior will have on our lifestyle.

---

[1] Based on J. Dreyfus, "Paradise at a Price: Required Conformity in Suburbia," *The Arizona Republic* (February 25, 1979), p. SL2.

359

THE NATURE OF LIFESTYLE

Lifestyle is defined simply as *how one lives*. One's lifestyle is a function of inherent individual characteristics that have been shaped and formed through social interaction as one moves through the life cycle. Thus, lifestyle is influenced by the many factors we have discussed in the past 11 chapters—situations, culture, social class, reference groups, family, and individual characteristics and abilities. Therefore, this chapter will serve as somewhat of an overview of the combined impact that these influences have on the way we live. The remainder of the text is devoted to an analysis of how consumers actually make purchase decisions designed to maintain or enhance their lifestyles. Figure 14–1 illus-

FIGURE 14–1
Lifestyle and the consumption process

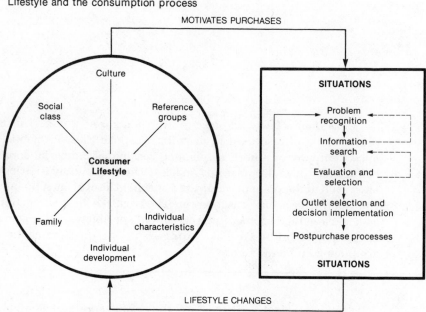

trates the variables that influence and make up consumer lifestyles and the relationship that lifestyle has to the decision-making process.

As the figure indicates, lifestyle has a dual role for consumers. First, it is a basic motivator (desire to enhance or maintain present lifestyle) for many purchase and use activities. That is, the need to make purchase decisions arises from who we are and what we are and the problems and opportunities that we face in life. For example, one of the authors of this text established himself as a "swinging bachelor" shortly after taking a teaching job after graduation. For him, this image involved a modified version of the standard "bachelor's pad," the pursuit of tennis and other recreational activities, clothing purchases, and so forth. His lifestyle and thus his purchases differed dramatically from those exhibited by the other two authors when they took their first teaching jobs (one was married with a working wife and the other was married with three young children).

The second aspect of lifestyle that interests marketing managers is its changing nature as a result of the consumer decision process. Again, Figure 14−1 points out that the results of decisions that consumers make about products provide motivational and attitudinal information that can alter or reinforce lifestyles. Over time, through learning, our lifestyles undergo changes. This is easiest to see when we examine young consumers, particularly through the first few stages of the family life cycle. The experiences we have, the situations we face, and the increasing exposure to a wider variety of others' lifestyles bring about the possibility of lifestyle changes.

When lifestyle changes do occur, they usually bring to light new consumption-related problems and/or opportunities that in turn necessitate new consumer decisions. The process then is dynamic and constantly changing because of the decisions that consumers make as well as changes in the determinants of lifestyle themselves. For instance, changes in cultural values can bring about lifestyle changes, as can moving through the stages of the family life cycle.

It is relevant to note at this point that lifestyle for any given individual is not constantly and dramatically changing. Human beings would probably not be able to stand constant changes without having to endure high levels of anxiety and frustration. Hence, lifestyle changes occur for most of us most of the time in a fairly gradual, almost nonconscious manner. The most dramatic and sudden lifestyle changes are probably brought about by outside events such as wars and depressions or individual experiences of a dramatic nature such as serious injury, marriage, graduation, birth of children, divorce, employment changes, or death of a spouse. Aside from such experiences, we can expect that dramatic lifestyle changes for most individuals are few and far between. Furthermore, the probability of change decreases with age (except, of course, for the major change that often occurs at retirement).

We are going to examine two major aspects of lifestyle in this chapter. First, the self-concept will be examined as the internal or psychological manifestation of lifestyle. Then, we will examine how lifestyle is currently measured through the use of psychographics. Earlier chapters, particularly Chapters 4 through 9, have provided descriptions of parts of the lifestyles of selected groups such as social strata, subcultures, families with young children, and so forth.

SELF-CONCEPT

The self-concept as defined by Carl Rogers, "may be thought of as an organized configuration of perceptions of the self which are admissible to awareness. It's composed of such elements as the perceptions of one's characteristics and abilities; the percepts and concepts of the self in relation to others and to the environment; the value qualities which are perceived as associated with experiences and objects; and goals and ideals which are perceived as having positive or negative valence."[2] In other words, your *self-concept is composed of the attitudes you hold toward yourself.* The behavioral component of these attitudes is reflected in your lifestyle. Thus, the self-concept serves as the basis for one's lifestyle.

The self-concept is really divided into four basic parts, as shown in Figure 14–2: *actual* versus *ideal* and *private* versus *social.* The actual/

FIGURE 14–2
The self-concept

	Actual concept	*Ideal concept*
Private self	Real self ⟶	Ideal self
Social self	Real others ⟶	Ideal others

ideal distinction refers to your conception of *who I am now* and *who I would like to be.* The private self refers to *how I am or would like to be to myself,* while the social self is *how I am seen by others or how I would like to be seen by others.* We then are able to see four separate self-concepts as follows:

Real self—how I actually see myself now.

Ideal self—how I would like to see myself.

and

Real others—how I perceive others actually see me.

Ideal others—how I would like to have others see me.

As Figure 14–2 further shows, there is a very definite relationship between the real and ideal self and between the real and ideal others. In both cases, we strive to move our real (actual) self-concept toward our ideal self-concept. A basic motivation then, according to self-concept theorists, is to achieve the ideal self-concept. This need to move toward

---

[2] C. Rogers, *Client Centered Therapy* (Houghton Mifflin Co., 1951). See also R. C. Wylie, *The Self Concept* (The University of Nebraska Press, 1961).

the ideal is true for the individual's own self-concept as well as for the concept that others have of the individual.

The distinction between private and social self-concepts is an important one. The private self-concept alone cannot explain all of the lifestyle behavior that we see individuals engage in. This is exemplified in the following quote:

> Two systems have now developed, both of which determine behavior. The one, based on self-actualization, approaches or avoids depending on whether or not the resulting experience is seen as one which will enhance the person. The other, based on the need for positive regard, approaches or avoids depending on whether or not the resulting experience is seen as one which will meet with approval from significant others (or from the self, when the viewpoint of others has been internalized). Needless to say, the person often encounters situations in which one basic need says "approach" while the other says "avoid." Learning a new skill, for example, often means embarrassment in the early, awkward stages, but, when accomplished, adds to the competence of the individual.[3]

In other words, we engage in behaviors (such as product purchases) if we think those purchases will enhance the attainment of our ideal image—private and/or social. The advertisement copy presented in Figure 14−3 appears to be based on this approach. In other words, the Excalibur is appropriate for those desiring a private or social self-concept of a confident, self-assured, unique individual with refined taste.

The self-concept is, in fact, the personal manifestation of the lifestyle for any individual, since the self-concept denotes the totality of one's attitudes, feelings, perceptions, and evaluations of oneself. The self becomes a value around which life revolves, so the individual's evaluation of the self greatly influences behavior.[4] Furthermore, since the self-concept grows from interactions with parents, peers, teachers, and significant others, self-enhancement will depend upon the reactions of these people. Thus, the individual will strive for and direct behavior toward obtaining a positive reaction from these significant others (see Chapter 8).

The use of the self-concept by marketing managers is explained by the following logical model of the relationship between the self and product purchase:

1.   An individual has a self-concept of himself.
2.   The self-concept is of value to the individual.
3.   Since the self-concept is valued, the individual will strive to enhance the self-concept.

---

[3] P. J. Geiwtz, *Non-Freudian Personality Theories* (Brooks/Cole Publishing Co., 1969), p. 87.

[4] E. L. Grubb and H. L. Grathwol, "Consumer Self-Concept, Symbolism and Market Behavior: A Theoretical Approach," *Journal of Marketing* (October 1967), pp. 22−27.

FIGURE 14–3
Ideal image oriented advertisement

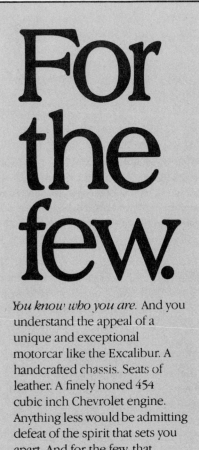

For the few.

You know who you are. And you understand the appeal of a unique and exceptional motorcar like the Excalibur. A handcrafted chassis. Seats of leather. A finely honed 454 cubic inch Chevrolet engine. Anything less would be admitting defeat of the spirit that sets you apart. And for the few, that would be unthinkable. *Excalibur.*

Used with permission from Excalibur Automobile Corporation.

4. The self-concept is formed through interaction process with parents, peers, teachers, and significant others.
5. Products serve as social symbols and, therefore, are communication devices for the individual.
6. The use of products as symbols communicate meaning to self and to others, causing an impact on the intra-action and/or interaction processes and, therefore, an effect on the individual's self-concept.
7. Therefore, consumer behavior of an individual will be directed toward

furthering and enhancing of the self-concept through the consumption of goods as symbols.[5]

A substantial amount of research has been conducted on the self-
concept as it relates to product or brand choice. It has been found that
there is congruence between owners' perceptions of their automobiles
and their perceptions of themselves.[6] The same study also found that,
for the most part, people who own one brand of car have different
perceptions of owners of other brands. This was specifically shown to be
true with the owners of Volkswagens and Pontiac GTOs.[7]

Another study included self-concept along with ideal self-image in
evaluating socially consumed versus privately consumed products, and
most and least preferred products.[8] It was found that most consumers
preferred brands that were similar to their self-concepts, thus further
supporting previous studies.

In summary then, the self-concepts that individuals have of
themselves—real and ideal, private and social—serve as a guide for many
of the product and brand choices made. As marketing managers strive to
develop new products and new appeals for consumers, they would do
well to keep in mind this important lifestyle variable. Products that
are seen as being possibly expressive of self-image will be judged by
consumers on "how well they help to make me what I want to be and
how I want others to see me." Seagrams Distillers Company understands this concept as shown by the simple copy of some of its most
successful blended whiskey advertising—"What a man serves is often a
reflection of the man."

PSYCHOGRAPHICS

Operationalizing or measuring lifestyle has been and continues to be
a major problem. Until recently, the few attempts to measure lifestyle
involved detailed depth interviews and questionnaires administered to a
generally limited sample. Social Research, Inc., of Chicago has conducted several classic studies using this approach.[9] However, the expense and time involved with this methodology have limited its usefulness.

---

[5] Ibid.

[6] A. C. Birdwell, "Influence of Image Congruence on Consumer Choice," in *Reflections on Progress in Marketing,* ed., L. G. Smith (American Marketing Association, 1964), pp. 290–303.

[7] E. L. Grubb and G. Hupp, "Perception of Self, Generalized Stereotypes, and Brand Selection," *Journal of Marketing Research* (February 1968), pp. 58–63.

[8] I. J. Dolich, "Congruence Relationships between Self Images and Product Brands," *Journal of Marketing Research* (February 1969), pp. 80–84.

[9] See L. Rainwater, R. P. Coleman, and G. Handel, *Workingman's Wife* (Oceana, 1959); and R. F. Coup, S. Greene, and B. B. Gardner, *A Study of Working-Class Women in a Changing World* (Social Research, Inc., 1973).

Psychographics is the primary way that lifestyle has been made operationally useful to marketing managers today. Psychographics is a way of describing (graphics) the psychological (psycho) makeup or lifestyle of a consumer or consumer segments. Psychographic research is quantitative research intended to place consumers on psychological—as distinguished from solely demographic—dimensions.[10] Psychographics is a method of describing the total lifestyle of a consumer in a quantitative manner such that statistical comparisons and predictions can be made. One should not assume that there is no qualitative aspect of psychographics. On the contrary, psychographics tries to define the qualitative aspects of consumer lifestyle. One of the advantages of the psychographic approach is that those qualitative aspects of lifestyle are translated into quantitative (number) terms and hence are much more useful in marketing decision making. As with all measurement tools in marketing, there are some problems with the psychographic technique. Managers are cautioned to be fully aware of both the advantages and disadvantages of psychographics before using the results.

Marketers engaged in psychographic research have a large number of dimensions of lifestyle to draw from in their attempts to develop a picture of the consumer. As you will see, demographics are included in psychographic consumer profiles but only as one aspect of lifestyle. Let us look at some of the more frequently used psychographic dimensions.

1. *Demographics* (see Chapter 6). Data on the demographic characteristics of the consumers such as sex, age, ethnic, social, economic, family, and occupation categories.
2. *Attitudes* (see Chapter 13). Evaluative statements held about other people, ideas, products, and so forth. Expression of feelings toward the tangible and intangible items that make up a person's lifestyles.
3. *Values* (see Chapters 4 and 13). Widely held beliefs that affirm what is desirable and have some impact on activities.
4. *Personality traits* (see Chapter 12). Characteristic and relatively enduring ways of responding to the environment.
5. *Activities and interests.* The nonoccupational behaviors that consumers devote time and effort to, such as hobbies, public service groups and causes, church, sports, and so forth.
6. *Usage rates.* The amount of any product category under consideration that the consumer uses in a specified purchase. Typically described as heavy, medium or light usage.

These variables are measured via standard demographic and product usage questionnaires in conjunction with AIO (activity, interest, and

---

[10] W. D. Wells, "Psychographics: A Critical Review," *Journal of Marketing Research* (May 1975), pp. 196–213.

opinion) inventories. AIO inventories consist of a large number (often as many as 300) statements with which respondents express a degree of agreement or disagreement.[11] In general, the items on the AIO inventory measure aspects of lifestyle relevant to the product category under consideration. For example, a manufacturer of floor tiles might include items on home entertainment, the behavior and role of children in the home, pet ownership and attitudes, usage of credit, interest in fashion, and so forth. The value of such lifestyle information on a particular target market is easy to visualize.

Tables 14 – 1 and 14 – 2 show both demographic and psychographic profiles of heavy users of shotgun shells. Note how much information the product manager has about the most significant part of the market segment. This information would be of interest to anyone dealing with the sale of shotguns (manufacturers and retailers) or other hunting equipment, as well as to others such as those who organize hunting trips, own hunting lodges, and so forth.[12]

The demographics paint a good but incomplete picture of the heavy user of shotgun shells. When we go beyond them, we can begin to make some determinations as to what kind of person our good customer is and what appeals might work best. For instance, could you make some predictions as to the type of television shows and magazines our heavy user probably watches and subscribes to? Other activities that are associated with hunting are shown that may help the advertiser develop stronger appeals and more relevant settings for shotgun ammunition advertising. Our heavy user also appears to be somewhat self-indulgent, willing to accept risk, and relatively conscienceless, all of which may be of great interest to the public policy official concerned with hunting safety, game laws, and so forth.

Figure 14 – 4 provides us with an example of a general lifestyle segmentation study performed by the Newspaper Advertising Bureau.[13] This study was not done with respect to the purchase of any particular product. Rather its intent was to try for an overall picture of male consumers. Pick a product such as wine and using the information in Figure 14 – 4 determine the potentially most profitable (in terms of usage) market segments(s) for wine in general. Next, consider if there would be a difference in your choice based on whether you were selling an inexpensive pop wine (Ripple), a low-priced table wine (Gallo's Hearty Burgundy), or an expensive vintage wine (Stag Leap's Cabernet Sauvignon). Could

---

[11] For details see S. Mehrotra and W. D. Wells, "Psychographics and Buyer Behavior: Theory and Recent Empirical Findings," in *Consumer and Industrial Buying Behavior*, eds. A. G. Woodside, J. N. Sheth, and P. D. Bennett (Elsevier North/Holland, Inc., 1977) pp. 49 – 65.

[12] For a complete discussion of this example, see Wells, "Psychographics," pp. 197 – 99. Our discussion is abstracted from Wells' article.

[13] Ibid., p. 201.

TABLE 14-1

Demographic profile of the heavy user of shotgun ammunition

	Percent who spend $11 or more per year on shotgun ammunition (141)*	Percent who don't buy shotgun ammunition (395)*
Age		
Under 25	9	5
25–34	33	15
35–44	27	22
45–54	18	22
55–or over	13	36
Occupation		
Professional	6	15
Managerial	23	23
Clerical–sales	9	17
Craftsman	50	35
Income		
Under $6,000	26	19
$6,000–10,000	39	36
$10,000–15,000	24	27
$15,000 or over	11	18
Population density		
Rural	34	12
2,500–50,000	11	11
50,000–500,000	16	15
500,000–2 million	21	27
2 million–or over	13	19
Geographic division		
New England—Mid-Atlantic	21	33
Central (North, West)	22	30
South Atlantic	23	12
East South Central	10	3
West South Central	10	5
Mountain	6	3
Pacific	9	15

* Number in parentheses indicates sample size.
Source: W. D. Wells, "Psychographics: A Critical Review," *Journal of Marketing Research* (American Marketing Association, May 1975), p. 197.

you develop advertising messages for each wine type and groups based on the information given you?

Another example is shown in Table 14–3. This was the result of a study conducted for a regional brewer of beer in the youth (18–25 years) market. Note the differences between the heavy and light drinker segments. "The heavy beer drinker is less of a risk taker, is less supportive of a permissive society, is less optimistic, and thinks of himself as more physically active in his life."[14] If the brewer in question was trying

[14] T. C. Kinnear and J. R. Taylor, "Psychographics: Some Additional Findings," *Journal of Marketing Research* (November 1976), pp. 422–25.

TABLE 14–2

Psychographic profile of the heavy user of shotgun ammunition

Base	Percent who spend $11 or more per year on shotgun ammunition (141)*	Percent who don't buy shotgun ammunition (395)*
I like hunting	88	7
I like fishing	68	26
I like to go camping	57	21
I love the out-of-doors	90	65
A cabin by a quiet lake is a great place to spend the summer	49	34
I like to work outdoors	67	40
I am good at fixing mechanical things	47	27
I often do a lot of repair work on my own car	36	12
I like war stories	50	32
I would do better than average in a fist fight	38	16
I would like to be a professional football player	28	18
I would like to be a policeman	22	8
There is too much violence on television	35	45
There should be a gun in every home	56	10
I like danger	19	8
I would like to own my own airplane	35	13
I like to play poker	50	26
I smoke too much	39	24
I love to eat	49	34
I spend money on myself that I should spend on the family	44	26
If given a chance, most men would cheat on their wives	33	14
I read the newspaper every day	51	72

* Number in parentheses indicates sample size.
  Source: W. D. Wells, "Psychographics: A Critical Review," *Journal of Marketing Research* (American Marketing Association, May 1975), p. 198.

to stimulate light drinkers into heavier consumption, information such as this would be useful in the development of advertising appeals. The study also illustrates the difficulty one would have in bringing about such consumption conversion. Heavy and light beer drinkers are very different people in terms of lifestyle!

Psychographics is a commonly used tool by consumer goods companies as well as by advertising agencies. General Foods used psychographics to help determine dog food preferences (one of the results being Cycle dog food).[15] Ford Motor Company's success with Pinto was also the

---

[15] P. W. Bernstein, "Psychographics Is Still an Issue on Madison Avenue," *Fortune* (January 16, 1978), p. 80.

FIGURE 14–4
Eight male psychographic segments

Group I.   The quiet family man (8 percent of total males)

Here is a self-sufficient man who wants to be left alone and is basically shy. Tries to be as little involved with community life as possible. His life revolves around the family, simple work, and television viewing. Has a marked fantasy life. As a shopper he is practical, less drawn to consumer goods and pleasures than other men.

Low education and low economic status, he tends to be older than average.

Group II.   The traditionalist (16 percent of total males)

A man who feels secure, has self-esteem, follows conventional rules. He is proper and respectable, regards himself as altruistic and interested in the welfare of others. As a shopper he is conservative, likes popular brands and well-known manufacturers.

Low education and lowest socio-economic group, mostly older than average.

Group III.   The discontented man (13 percent of total males)

He is a man who is likely to be dissatisfied with his work. He feels bypassed by life, dreams of better jobs, more money, and more security. He tends to be distrustful and socially aloof. As a buyer, he is quite price conscious.

Lowest education and lowest socioeconomic group, mostly older than average.

Group IV.   The ethical highbrow (14 percent of total males)

This is a very concerned man, sensitive to people's needs. Basically a puritan, content with family life, friends, and work. Interested in culture, religion, and social reform. As a consumer he is interested in quality, which may at times justify greater expenditure.

Well educated, middle or upper socioeconomic status, mainly middle-aged or older.

Group V.   The pleasure oriented man (9 percent of total males)

He tends to emphasize his masculinity and rejects whatever appears to be soft or feminine. He views himself a leader among men. Self-centered, dislikes his work or job. Seeks immediate gratification for his needs. He is an impulsive buyer, likely to buy products with a masculine image.

Low education, lower socioeconomic class, middle-aged or younger.

Group VI.   The achiever (11 percent of total males)

This is likely to be a hardworking man, dedicated to success and all that it implies, social prestige, power, and money. Is in favor of diversity, is adventurous about leisure-time pursuits. Is stylish, likes good food, music, etc. As a consumer he is status conscious, a thoughtful and discriminating buyer.

Good education, high socioeconomic status, young.

FIGURE 14–4 (continued)

Group VII. The he-man (19 percent of total males)

He is gregarious, likes action, seeks an exciting and dramatic life. Thinks of himself as capable and dominant. Tends to be more of a bachelor than a family man, even after marriage. Products he buys and brands preferred are likely to have "self-expressive value," especially a man-of-action dimension.

Well educated, mainly middle socioeconomic status, the youngest of the male groups.

Group VIII. The sophisticated man (10 percent of total males)

He is likely to be an intellectual, concerned about social issues, admires men with artistic and intellectual achievements. Socially cosmopolitan, broad interests. Wants to be dominant, and a leader. As a consumer he is attracted to the unique and fashionable.

Best educated and highest economic status of all groups, younger than average.

Source: W. D. Wells, "Psychographics: A Critical Review," *Journal of Marketing Research* (May 1975), p. 201.

TABLE 14–3
Illustrative beer-related psychographic findings

		Scale values*	
	Psychographic scales	Light drinker†	Heavy drinker
I.	Risk-taking		
	I like to fly	6.1‡	3.4
	Buying stocks is too risky	4.8	8.7
	I often try new brands	5.7	3.9
	Taking chances can be fun	5.1	2.2
II.	Permissive society		
	Hair length and clothing styles describe the nature of a person	2.1	4.2
	Hippies should be dealt with severely	3.4	7.2
	Discipline is lacking in people	4.1	6.7
	Marijuana smokers should not go to jail	6.8	2.4
III.	Optimism		
	I approach a new day with excitement	7.4	3.9
	My best life accomplishments have yet to occur	6.2	4.7
	I do not do well at most things I've tried	2.4	5.6
IV.	Active life		
	I look for an active stimulating life	4.7	6.2
	I go hunting	3.5	4.4

* Ten-point rating scale; higher numbers indicate a higher score on the scale.

† Light drinker consumes one to nine bottles per week, and the heavy drinker consumes ten or more bottles per week.

‡ Mean scale values are reported; all reported scores are significantly different at the .01 level by a z-test for differences between means.

Source: T. C. Kinnear and J. R. Taylor, "Psychographics: Some Additional Findings," *Journal of Marketing Research* (American Marketing Association, November 1976), p. 422.

partial result of psychographic research. Initially, the car was positioned as a "frisky, carefree little car" like a pinto pony, but research showed that consumers wanted a "practical and dependable little car."[16]

THE USE OF LIFESTYLE IN MARKETING

Psychographics has proven useful to marketing managers because it allows them to define and differentiate market segments based on lifestyle characteristics. The need for more than demographic information is summarized in the following quotation:

> Based on demographic data, it (market research) may tell us a lot about the age, income, education, and family size of prospective customers—but it doesn't tell us anything about their attitudes and living styles. It can't clearly differentiate between swingers and standpatters, between militant feminists and women with traditional values, between those who admire Ralph Nader and those who identify with Archie Bunker.[17]

In other words, by using psychographics as a marketing tool to measure lifestyles, it has been possible to develop market segmentation strategies that use lifestyle as the basis for segmentation. Studies have been done on a wide range of products such as cable TV,[18] eye makeup,[19] shortening,[20] nonprescription drugs,[21] vacations,[22] credit cards,[23] financial services,[24] and fashion clothing.[25] In addition, psychographics have been used in the analysis of media usage.[26]

We have already noted how lifestyle segmentation and segment de-

---

[16] Ibid.

[17] Ibid., p. 78.

[18] C. C. Binkert, J. A. Brunner, and J. L. Simonetti, "The Use of Life Style Segmentation to Determine if CATV Subscribers Are Really Different," *Journal of the Academy of Marketing Science* (Spring 1975), pp. 129–36.

[19] W. D. Wells and D. Tigert, "Activities, Interests and Opinions," *Journal of Advertising Research* (August 1971), pp. 27–35.

[20] Ibid.; and "How Marketing Research Can Avoid Missing Opportunities in the Cosmetic Jungle," *Marketing News* (January 16, 1976), p. 5.

[21] R. Ziff, "Psychographics for Market Segmentation," *Journal of Advertising Research* (April 1971), pp. 3–10.

[22] W. R. Darden, W. D. Perrault, Jr., and M. T. Troncalli, "Psychograhic Analysis of Vacation Innovators," *Review of Business and Economic Research* (Winter 1975–76), pp. 1–18.

[23] J. T. Plummer, "Life-Style Patterns and Commercial Bank Credit Card Usage," *Journal of Marketing* (April 1971), pp. 35–42.

[24] "Describe Six Psychographic Segments of Canadian Financial Services Market," *Marketing News* (October 22, 1976), p. 5.

[25] E. A. Richards and S. S. Sturman, "Life-Style Segmentation in Apparel Marketing," *Journal of Marketing* (October 1977), pp. 89–91; and "Vassarette Finds Psychographics First Research Understood, Used," *Marketing News* (February 24, 1978), p. 7.

[26] See K. E. A. Villani, "Personality/Life Style and Television Viewing Behavior," *Journal of Marketing Research* (November 1975), pp. 432–39; and W. O. Bearden, J. E. Teel, Jr., and R. M. Durand, "Media Usage, Psychographic and Demographic Dimensions of Retail Shoppers," *Journal of Retailing* (Spring 1978), pp. 65–74.

scription have benefited specific brands, such as Cycle dog food and the Ford Pinto. Lifestyle analysis can be of use to marketing managers on a much broader scale that bridges many specific product and use situations. For example, we looked at eight male psychological segments earlier in this chapter and noted that marketers for a large number of products might find those lifestyle characterizations useful. Let us now look at an even more specific example of lifestyle analysis and its relationship to marketing management decisions.

As pointed out in Chapters 5 and 9, women's roles in the American culture have changed dramatically over the past few decades. These changes have presented marketing managers with a variety of opportunities and problems which can be better understood through lifestyle analysis. Tables 14−4, 14−5, 14−6 and 14−7 present lifestyle informa-

TABLE 14–4
Demographic profile of traditional and modern women*

Item	Traditional	Modern
Age—		
Under 25	34%	66%
25–34	36	64
35–44	44	56
45–54	48	52
55 and over	58	42
Education—		
Some college and higher	40	50
High school and lower	60	50
Employment—		
Employed	26	56
Not employed	74	44
Family income—		
Under $4,000	4	4
$4,000–8,000	16	13
$8,000–10,000	10	10
$10,000–15,000	32	27
$15,000–20,000	18	24
$20,000–or over	20	22
Dwelling unit—		
Apartment	5	11
One family home	83	76
Other	12	13

* $p < 0.05$.
Source: F. D. Reynolds, M. R. Crask, and W. D. Wells, "The Modern Feminine Life Style," *Journal of Marketing* (American Marketing Association, July 1977), p. 39.

tion on modern and traditional women and working and nonworking women.[27] Note from the tables that traditional and modern women's lifestyles vary fairly systematically and that these differences tend to

[27] F. D. Reynolds, M. R. Crask, and W. D. Wells, "The Modern Feminine Life Style," *Journal of Marketing* (July 1977), pp. 38−45.

TABLE 14–5 Lifestyle profile of the modern woman

| | Percent agreeing* | | | | | |
| | Total | | Working | | Nonworking | |
Statement	Trad.	Mod.	Trad.	Mod.	Trad.	Mod.
Traditional roles: Home and work:						
A woman's place is in the home	68%	30%	62%	27%	69%	34%
A working world is no place for a woman	28	9	21	8	30	10
I am a homebody	77	62	61	55	78	70
Traditional roles: Family relations:						
Men are smarter than women	29	18	29	19	28	17
The father should be the boss in the house	81	59	83	60	81	58
A wife's first obligation is to her husband, not her children	74	67	71	66	75	68
Children are the most important thing in a marriage	60	45	57	47	60	43
Young people have too many privileges	80	72	80	72	81	71
If children are ill in bed, parents should drop everything to see to their comfort	82	69	83	67	82	72
When making important family decisions, consider the children first	58	52	60	50	58	53†
Orientation toward housekeeping activities:						
Our home is furnished for comfort, not style	92	88	91	88†	93	89
The kind of dirt you can't see is worse than the kind you can see	79	74	77	75†	80	73
I like to save and redeem saving stamps	78	72	75	73	79	74
My days follow a definite routine—eating meals at the same time each day, etc.	70	62	66	57	71	68†
Meal preparation should take as little time as possible	37	44	44	47†	35	42
I never eat breakfast	30	35	28	38	30	32†
I always bake from scratch	44	37	39	38†	46	35
I went out to breakfast instead of having it at home at least once last year	46	57	49	63	46	51†
I cooked outdoors at least once during the past year	81	85	83	91	82	79†
Satisfaction with life:						
I wish I could leave my present life and do something entirely different	22	30	23	29†	22	32
My greatest achievements are still ahead of me	56	70	62	73	54	66
Physical attractiveness:						
I like to feel attractive to members of the opposite sex	79	89	80	88	79	90
I want to look a little different from others	66	72	69	71†	65	73
All men should be clean shaven every day	76	67	76	67	75	67
There are day people and night people; I am a day person	72	67	76	66	70	67†
I like to think I am a bit of a swinger	18	39	20	32	18	29
A drink or two at the end of a day is a perfect way to unwind	18	23	16	24	19	22†
Had a cocktail or drink before dinner at least once last year	56	69	55	74	64	67†
Had wine with dinner at least once during the past year	53	64	52	66	54	61

Travel proneness:					
I would feel lost if I were alone in a foreign country	75	64	75	61	74	67
I would like to take a trip around the world	59	74	64	77	54	71
I would like to spend a year in London or Paris	25	39	30	37	25	38
Mobility:						
We will probably move at least once in the next five years	32	41	32	40	33	43
Attitudes toward transportation:						
I have often thought of buying a subcompact car	42	50	42	51	42	48‡
I like sports cars	30	47	31	49	29	45
Financial outlook:						
Five years from now our family income will probably be a lot higher than it is now	60	70	62	73	59	65
Women don't need more than a minimum amount of life insurance	42	32	35	31†	44	33
I am considering buying life insurance	13	22	15	23	13	19
Attitudes toward American business:						
Americans should always try to buy American products	78	68	77	69	78	66
I admire a successful businessman more than a successful artist or writer	33	25	32	25	32	23
Views toward events and situations:						
Everything is changing too fast today	69	62	70	59	68	65†
There is too much emphasis on sex today	90	81	94	79	89	84
I am in favor of very strict enforcement of all laws	94	89	91	90†	95	89
Police should use whatever force is necessary to maintain law and order	76	62	77	61	75	62
Communism is the greatest peril in the world today	71	55	71	55	71	54
The United States would be better off if there were no hippies	64	46	65	43	64	50
I think the women's liberation movement is a good thing	41	61	39	60	42	62
Activity patterns:						
I have somewhat old-fashioned tastes and habits	91	81	90	79	92	84
I went to the movies at least once in the past year	68	79	74	81	67	76
I like science fiction	37	53	36	53	38	54
I visited an art gallery or museum at least once last year	45	52	42	54	47	48†
I gave a speech at least once during the past year	23	30	23	34	24	24†
I attended school at least once during the past year	22	32	30	39	21	24†
I attended church at least once during the past year	89	82	90	84	89	81
Went to a pop concert at least once last year	7	18	11	20	5	15
I did a crossword puzzle at least once last year	73	78	70	79	74	77
I played cards at least once during the past year	80	86	77	88	82	84†
I went swimming at least once last year	57	67	60	71	57	62†
I went bowling at least once last year	30	39	34	41†	30	37
I went skiing at least once during the past year	4	7	4	8	5	5†

* p ≤ 0.05 unless otherwise indicated.   † p ≥ 0.10.   ‡ p ≤ 0.08.
Source: F. D. Reynolds, M. R. Crask, and W. D. Wells, "The Modern Feminine Life Style," *Journal of Marketing* (American Marketing Association, July 1977), pp. 42–43.

TABLE 14–6
Media differences

| | Percent exposed* | | | | | |
| | Total | | Working | | Nonworking | |
Category	Trad.	Mod.	Trad.	Mod.	Trad.	Mod.
Radio program format						
Heavy rock	8%	20%	8%	19%	8%	21%
Popular music—top 40	44	56	48	58	44	55
Television program favorites						
"Waltons"	42	32	41	30	42	34
"Little House on the						
Prairie"	33	24	31	22	34	28
"Happy Days"	16	20	14	21	17	19[b]
Daytime game shows						
(in general)	12	8	14	8	11	10
Magazines (read one or more issues in last four issues)						
Cosmopolitan	10	16	12	19	9	12†
Glamour	7	13	6	25	7	10†
Playboy	9	19	11	19	9	18
Psychology Today	3	6	2	6	3	6
Redbook	27	34	22	34	29	34†

* p < 0.05 unless otherwise indicated.
† (NS) = p > 0.10.
Source: F. D. Reynolds, M. R. Crask, and W. D. Wells, "The Modern Feminine Life Style," *Journal of Marketing* (American Marketing Association, July 1977), pp. 44–53.

show up rather dramatically in such important decision areas as media preferences and product usage. Of course, there are many product categories for which there are no significant differences between modern and traditional lifestyles. The real importance of recognizing different lifestyles is not the fact that two different women purchase different products or brands, but *how one must appeal to two different lifestyles in order that they will purchase the same brand:*

> For a large number of consumption categories, modern women do not differ from traditional women in purchasing behavior, or the differences that do exist can be explained by employment status. In this study, women responded to 58 product use questions. Only 12 differences were significant after employment status was controlled. Thus, for most products and brands, the marketer must reach women of both orientations at the same time. *The task becomes more subtle than changing the brand;* it requires focusing more exclusively upon the promotional program and its components—themes, advertisement setting, characters and communicators, music and/or artwork, tone of voice, and appeals—to ensure

TABLE 14–7
Selected product usage

| Product | Percent using weekly or more often* | | | | | |
| | Total | | Working | | Nonworking | |
	Trad.	*Mod.*	*Trad.*	*Mod.*	*Trad.*	*Mod.*
Lipstick	87%	80%	91%	82%	85%	79%
Hairspray	62	56	64	61ᵇ	61	51
Eye makeup	48	62	54	67	46	56
Suntan lotion (summer)	28	40	49	51†	31	41
Artificial sweetener	33	8	32	29†	33	27
Beer	9	12	7	12	9	11†
Flavor-filter cigarettes	8	12	8	11†	8	13
Menthol-filter cigarettes	7	11	7	10†	7	11
Cold or allergy tablets	39	48	46	48†	37	48
Gasoline (personally purchased)	78	83	83	89	76	76†
Regular (stick) margarine	87	81	87	80	88	83†
Ready-to-eat cold cereal	94	90	95	89	94	91†
Prepared breakfast	96	93	96	91	96	95†

* $p < 0.05$.
† (NS) = $p > 0.10$
Source: F. D. Reynolds, M. R. Crask, and W. D. Wells, "The Modern Feminine Life Style," *Journal of Marketing* (American Marketing Association, July 1977), pp. 44–53.

the portrayal of roles and motives that are congruent with either of these two quite different life styles.[28]

SUMMARY

Lifestyle serves as the major focal point of the consumer decision-making process and can be defined simply as how one lives. Lifestyle is a function of one's inherent individual characteristics that have been shaped and formed through social interaction as one moves through one's life cycle.

Lifestyle has two important characteristics for marketers. First, it is a basic motivation for many purchase and use activities. Secondly, because of changing environments and the results of decisions that consumers make about products, lifestyles are altered or reinforced. Therefore, over time and due to learning, lifestyles undergo change.

The self-concept can be defined as the attitudes one holds toward himself or herself and, as such, serves as the basis for one's lifestyle. The self-concept is really composed of four basic parts: The real self,

[28] Ibid., pp. 44–45.

how I actually see myself now; the ideal self, how I would like to see myself; the real other, how I perceive others actually see me; and the ideal other, how I would like to have others see me. Consumers strive to move the real (actual) self-concept toward the ideal. The need to achieve the ideal becomes a motivating force. To the extent that marketers can tie products to the ideal concept, purchase of those products would be seen by consumers as a good way to help attain their ideal self concept.

Psychographics is the primary way that lifestyle is made operationally useful to marketing managers today. This is a way of describing the psychological makeup or lifestyle of consumers by assessing such lifestyle dimensions as activities, interests, and opinions. While there are certain operational problems with psychographic measurement, it is a widely used tool by consumer goods companies and advertising agencies.

REVIEW QUESTIONS

1. What do we mean by consumer lifestyle? What factors determine and influence that lifestyle?
2. What relationship exists between consumer lifestyle and consumer decision making?
3. What is the self-concept? How does it act as a motivating force for consumer behavior?
4. Define psychographics and explain how it is potentially useful to marketing managers.
5. What types of variables do marketing managers use to construct a psychographic instrument?
6. How is lifestyle used by marketers in developing segmentation strategies?

DISCUSSION QUESTIONS

1. How could Jeff use the self-concept to explain purchase motivation for mopeds for the precollege market (16 – 19 years old)?
2. Would it be possible for Jeff to develop market segments on the basis of lifestyle for his Motron moped? Why or why not?
3. The example in this chapter on the modern feminine lifestyle concluded that for many products and brands, the marketer must reach women of both orientations (modern and traditional) at the same time. Why is this true and what difficulties are involved?
4. Cosmetic manufacturers attempt to fit their products to the mental picture their customers hold of themselves.[29] In 1973, Revlon intro-

[29] "Cosmetics: Kiss and Sell," *Time* (December 11, 1978), pp. 86 – 96.

duced Charlie in response to the changing lifestyle of females. In 1977, Revlon responded to another shift in lifestyle by introducing Jontue, "Sensual . . . yet with a touch of innocence." Discuss how Revlon could have used psychographics in detecting these respective changes in lifestyle.

5. With respect to question 4, discuss how Revlon could have used measurements of target consumers' ideal self-concept in developing the brand names Charlie and Jontue.

6. How does consumer lifestyle change at different stages of an individual's family life cycle? Discuss which of eight male psychographic profiles shown in Figure 14−4 best describes different stages of the family life cycle for *male* consumers.

7. The following quote is from Paul Casi, president of Glenmore distilleries:

> Selling cordials is a lot different from selling liquor. Cordials are like the perfume of our industry. You're really talking high fashion, and you're talking generally to a different audience—I don't mean male versus female—I'm talking about lifestyle.[30]

   a. In what ways do you think the lifestyle of cordial drinkers would differ from those who drink liquor, but not cordials?

   b. How would you determine the nature of any such differences?

   c. Of what use would a knowledge of such lifestyle differences be to a marketing manager introducing a new cordial?

PROJECT QUESTIONS

1. Develop an advertisement based on each of the four parts of the self-concept for a moped. Define the market segment the ad is aimed at and explain how it reflects the self-concept.

2. Develop a relevant psychographic instrument to be used to measure the lifestyle of the market segment noted above. (Hint: Use the basic variables described in the chapter.)

3. Read "Psychographics: A Critical Review" by Wells.[31] What problems seem to exist in the use of psychographics? Compare this article to the one by Bernstein.[32] Does real life use of psychographics exist?

4. Using the psychographic scales listed in Table 14−3, construct a questionnaire to measure the endorsement of these statements by light and heavy beer drinkers on your campus. Utilize the same

---

[30] N. F. Millman, "Glenmore Moves to Follow Up Amaretto Success," *Advertising Age* (June 25, 1979), p. 4.

[31] *Journal of Marketing Research* (May 1975), pp. 196−213.

[32] "Psychographics Is Still an Issue on Madison Avenue," *Fortune* (January 16, 1978), p. 80.

ten-point rating scale and definition for a heavy beer drinker shown below Table 14−3. Then have light and heavy beer drinkers evaluate these statements in terms of how much they agree or disagree with them and compare the results obtained by the class with those shown in Table 14−3.

5. Develop 15 statements related to the attitudes, interests, and opinions of students on your campus. Then, using a five category *agree−disagree* scale, interview five other students not enrolled in this class. Then, using all the information collected by the entire class, divide up the individuals surveyed into groups based on similarity. For two groups of reasonable size that are dissimilar in agreement with AIO statements, discuss what campus activities would appeal most to each group. Are there new activities these groups would enjoy using if available?

SECTION FOUR
consumer decision process

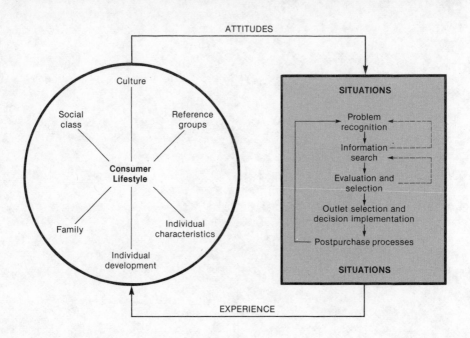

U p to now we have been concerned with the various sociological and psychological factors that can contribute to different patterns of consumer behavior. Though these various kinds of influences can each play a significant role in behavior, it has been our premise that all behavior takes place within the context of a situation. Therefore, behavior may vary among consumers as well as for the same consumer from one situation to another.

Of particular importance to marketers is how situations and internal and external sources of influence affect the consumer purchase decision process. That is, how do these influences contribute to the recognition of consumer problems, the search for information, evaluation of alternatives, and selection of an alternative method of purchase and place of purchase. Following purchase, how do these influences contribute to product use, satisfaction, and disposition as well as the motivation to repurchase the same brand or product. These are all very relevant areas of behavior that the marketing manager must understand and utilize in developing a marketing program that is designed to serve the unique needs of a particular segment of consumers.

The consumer decision process, as outlined in this section and the figure at left, is composed of a sequential process of problem recognition; information search; brand evaluation, selection, and decision implementation; and use, satisfaction, disposition, and repurchase motivation. Chapter 15 deals with the first stage of this process, problem recognition. Our discussion of problem recognition will focus on how it occurs and contributes to information search. Information search constitutes the second stage in the consumer decision process and it is discussed in Chapter 16. The nature of consumer information search and those factors that influence different levels of prepurchase information search will be considered. Chapter 17 examines the brand evaluation and selection process. Chapter 18 deals with outlet selection and the in-store influences that often contribute to brand switching. The final stage of the consumer decision process, presented in Chapter 19, involves behavior after purchase including postpurchase feelings, use behavior, satisfaction, disposition, and repurchase motivation. Throughout these five chapters we will attempt to present what consumers do at different stages of the consumer decision process, what factors contribute to their behavior, and what actions can be taken by marketers to affect their behavior.

15

Problem recognition

From 1975 on, a substantial amount of publicity appeared concerning the potentially harmful effects of fluorocarbons in aerosal products on the upper atmosphere. Gillette Company, with a large number of aerosal personal care products, hair sprays, and deodorants, began studies to determine the impact of this publicity on their consumers. Between 1976 and 1977, increasing numbers of consumers recognized a problem—a difference between their desired state (a healthy environment) and their existing state (a deteriorating environment). As a result of this problem recognition, these consumers were rejecting all forms of aerosal products. By carefully monitoring problem recognition with respect to their product category, Gillette Company was able to shift successfully from fluorocarbons to hydrocarbon aerosals.[1]

With problem recognition we begin our explanation of the consumer decision-making or problem-solving process. So far, we have been primarily concerned with explaining the factors that go into the makeup of consumer lifestyle, for it is this lifestyle that is the primary cause of decision making. In other words, our focus to date has been on what consumers are and what makes them that way. For the rest of the text we will be looking at *how* consumers actually make the decisions necessary to solve their consumption problems in order to maintain and enhance their lifestyle.

---

[1] "Research Helps Sell New Aerosal Products, Says Gillette's Lopater," *Marketing News* (July 8, 1978), p. 9.

Remember that a marketing manager cannot directly shape or manipulate the culture, the family institution, an individual's personality, or any of the other factors discussed so far. But managers can understand these factors in order to affect the decision process in a positive manner. As we shall see in the next chapters, it is possible to structure informational campaigns based on consumer lifestyle knowledge, such that consumers can be persuaded to behave more favorably toward a particular product, service, or social activity. Once a marketing manager understands, to the extent possible, the external and internal forces that shape consumer lifestyle, that manager can more effectively influence the consumer's decision-making activity.

A day rarely passes in which a consumer fails to recognize a consumption problem. Routine problems of depletion, such as the need to get gasoline as the gauge approaches empty or the need to replace a frequently used food item, are readily recognized, defined, and resolved. The unexpected breakdown of a major appliance like a refrigerator or stove creates an unplanned problem which is also easily recognized but is often more difficult to resolve. Recognition of other problems may take longer as they may be subtle and evolve slowly over time, such as the decision to buy a recreation vehicle or microwave oven.

Problem recognition is the first stage in the consumer decision process, and it must occur before decision making can begin. In each of the situations described above, *the recognition of a problem was the result of a discrepancy between a desired state and an existing state that was sufficient to arouse and activate the decision process*. Once a problem is recognized, it must be defined such that it is then possible to begin an information search for feasible ways to solve the problem. The kind of action taken by consumers in response to recognized and defined problems relates directly to the situation, its importance to the consumer, and the dissatisfaction or inconvenience created by the problem. This chapter focuses on four main issues: (1) the process of problem recognition, (2) the types of problem recognition, (3) uncontrollable determinants of problem recognition, and (4) marketing strategies based on the problem recognition process.

THE PROCESS OF PROBLEM RECOGNITION

Consumers must make decisions in order to maintain or enhance their lifestyle. Central to every consumer decision is problem recognition. Without the recognition of a problem, there is no need for a consumer decision. This condition is illustrated in Figure 15 – 1 when there is no discrepancy between the consumer's desired state (what the consumer would like) and the existing state (what the consumer perceives as already having or existing). On the other hand, when there is a perceived discrepancy between a consumer desire and the perceived existing state, recognition of

FIGURE 15–1

The process of problem recognition

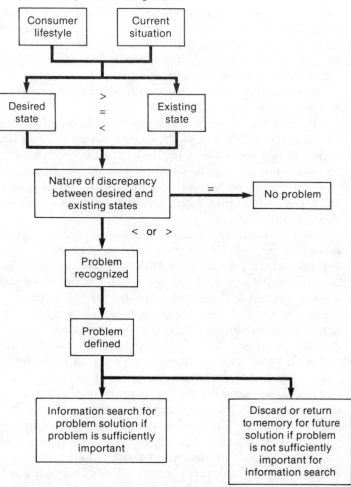

a problem occurs.[2] As indicated in Figure 15–1, anytime the desired state is perceived as being greater than (>) or less than (<) the existing state, a problem has been recognized. Any time the desired state is equal to (=) existing state, no problem exists and hence no decision needs to be made.

At the heart of the problem recognition process is the degree to which

---

[2] R. Anderson and J. Hair, Jr., "Consumerism, Consumer Expectations, and Perceived Product Performance," in *Proceedings 3d Annual Conference,* ed. M. Venkatasah (Association for Consumer Research, 1972), pp. 67–69; and R. Olshavsky and J. Miller, "Consumer Expectations, Product Performance and Perceived Product Quality," *Journal of Marketing Research* (February 1973), pp. 19–21.

a desired state is out of alignment with an existing state. In Figure 15—1, consumer desires are represented as the result of a variety of internal (personality, learned experiences, attitudes, etc.) influences that are manifested in the lifestyle of the consumer.[3] In addition, the current situation (time pressures, physical surroundings, and so forth) influences the desired state of affairs. Perceptions of an existing state are also highly individualized and vary in relation to a consumer's lifestyle and current situation. When these two states are out of alignment, problem recognition occurs.

The problem recognition process is based on information processing (see Chapter 10). That is, problem recognition involves the decision, "Is there a difference between my desires and my current situation?" Stimuli relevant to the existing situation (hunger pangs, friend's new clothes compared to my older ones) and the desired situation (no hunger pangs, clothes at least as nice as my friend's) must be processed for problem recognition to occur.

The motivation to resolve a particular problem depends upon two factors; *the magnitude of the discrepancy between the desired and existing states and the importance of the problem*. An individual could desire to have a car that would average at least 20 miles per gallon while still meeting certain size and power constraints. If the current car obtains an average of 19.5 miles per gallon, a discrepancy exists, but it may not be large enough to motivate the consumer to proceed to the next step in the decision process.

On the other hand, a large discrepancy may exist and the consumer may not proceed to information search because the *relative importance* of the problem is small. A consumer may desire a new Lincoln Continental and own a six-year-old Pinto. The discrepancy is large. However, the relative importance of this particular discrepancy may be small compared to other consumption problems such as those related to housing, utilities, and food. Relative importance is a critical concept because all consumers have budget constraints, time constraints, or both. Only the relatively more important problems are likely to be solved. In general, importance is determined by how critical the problem is to the maintenance of the desired lifestyle.

The role of relative importance can be seen in a package decision made by General Foods. Consumers indicated that cereal packages did not fit well on their pantry and cabinet shelves. In response, General Foods introduced compact cereal boxes, which eventually failed. The problem, although recognizable, was of relatively little importance to customers.[4]

---

[3] W. Wells and G. Gubar, "The Life Cycle Concept of Marketing Research," *Journal of Marketing Research* (November 1966), pp. 353—63.

[4] E. Tauber, "Discovering New Product Opportunities with Problem Inventory Analysis," *Journal of Marketing* (January 1975), p. 69.

Once the problem is recognized it must be defined in such a way that the consumer can actually initiate action that will bring about a relevant problem solution. Note that in many cases problem recognition and problem definition occur simultaneously, such as a consumer running out of coffee. But consider the more complicated problem involved with status and image or how we want others to see us. For example, you could feel something was wrong with your expression of a desired image but be unable to define exactly what was wrong. In other words, you would not be able to define the problem even though you recognized that you did have a problem. An analogous situation is the sales manager who mistakenly says that the company's problem is one of declining sales. In reality the sales decline was only a symptom that allowed the manager to recognize a problem existed. The problem cannot be solved until it is defined, that is, until we know what caused the sales decline.

Like our sales manager, consumers will not know where to begin problem solution until the problem is adequately defined. This may involve information search with the sole purpose of identifying exactly what is wrong. Note again that this difference between problem recognition and problem definition probably only occurs in more complex situations, particularly in relation to matters of self-image.

To illustrate the entire process of problem recognition consider the following example. You live ten miles from campus and feel that the cost of operating your car to drive back and forth to classes and campus activities is prohibitive. It is also extremely difficult to find a parking space. It is too far to walk and you really do not like to spend much time and physical effort in getting back and forth to school.

Clearly, a problem exists for you. In a very real sense, your existing state is greater than your desired state, that is, you have and are using more resources than you need to use or want to use. You have recognized the problem due to an analysis of your present position and with the help of external information. The problem is defined as being a need for a less expensive yet convenient means of transportation for your commuting. Now if the relative importance is sufficient, you would begin some type of information search in order to determine feasible alternative ways to solve the problem.

TYPES OF PROBLEM RECOGNITION

It will be of help to us in understanding the process of problem recognition if we can develop a taxonomy or classification scheme of types of problem recognition. Figure 15–2 provides such a classification scheme based on two factors: (1) immediacy of required solution and (2) whether or not the problem was expected. There are two levels of each of these factors, thereby giving us a matrix of four problem types — routine, emergency, planning, and evolving.

FIGURE 15–2

Types of problem recognition

Expectancy of problem \ Immediacy of solution	Immediate solution required	Immediate solution not required
Occurrence of problem expected	Routine	Planning
Occurrence of problem unexpected	Emergency	Evolving

Immediacy of required problem solution is a relevant variable in determining types of problem recognition because it helps define the decision time horizon. The length of the decision process as well as the intensity of effort put into that process is directly related to how soon a problem solution is required. *Whether or not the problem is expected* to occur or comes as a complete surprise will also have a direct impact on the decision process. This variable will at least partially determine the sources of information used, number and type of alternatives considered, and so forth.

It must be remembered that the types of problem recognition discussed here are heavily affected by the importance of the problem for each consumer. In other words, not all routine problems (immediate solution required/occurrence expected) are the same. One can run out of toothpaste and automobile tires at the same time and can have expected to do so (both defined as routine problems), but still have different decision processes because tires are typically a more important purchase.

Routine problems

As shown in Figure 15–2, a routine problem is one in which *the discrepancy between the desired and existing states is expected to occur and where an immediate problem solution is required*. The majority of problems consumers recognize and solve each day come under this classification. Most food purchases and purchases of inexpensive household items, for example, are expected and the need for replacement is immediate. Additionally, many more expensive products such as automobile tires (indeed even the automobile itself), insurance, and so forth can also fall under this classification. The important characteristics are that the problem occurrence, in this case depletion (the previous solution is used up), is expected and that when depletion occurs a replacement must be purchased within a limited time. Hence, one can recognize that an insurance policy ends on a certain day and that repurchase must occur immediately so that coverage will be continuous. With problems of this routine type, we often find consumers recognizing the problem and solving it prior to the time of complete depletion. In other words, I may make an insurance purchase decision before the policy actually expires or buy a pound of coffee before I actually run out.

Given the differences between individuals and between purchase and use situations, it is impractical to classify the problem types in terms of product types. The purchase of car insurance could be either a routine problem or an emergency depending on what caused the depletion (normal expiration or sudden cancellation). By the same reasoning, car insurance purchase might also be described as a planning problem if an immediate solution is not required.

In general, however, those low commitment products characterized as convenience goods are associated with routine problem recognition. Problem recognition is primarily stimulated by normal depletion, but brand dissatisfaction may be just as potent a problem cause as depletion. It is evident by the tremendous amount of brand switching exhibited by consumers of low commitment products that some level of discrepancy frequently exists between the desired and the existing states provided by products of this type. For example, consumers not totally satisfied with their present brand of shampoo may try several other brands in search of a brand which will reduce the discrepancy between the desired performance of a shampoo and the observed performance of the brands they have used.

If enough consumers share the same problem and are identifiable, the marketer may respond with a separate marketing program. For example, Johnson Wax used mail panel data to discover that oiliness was a hair care problem of many women. Further research indicated that this was a particularly important problem among younger women and that existing products were not successfully dealing with the product. As a result, Johnson Wax developed Agree Shampoo and Agree Creme Rinse, both of which are very successful.[5]

Likewise Cycle dog food was developed by General Foods in response

---

[5] "Key Role of Research in Agree's Success Is Told," *Marketing News* (January 17, 1979), p. 14.

to a segment of dog owners concerned about the health of their dogs and the nutrition they receive from dog food.[6] There are four versions of Cycle: Cycle 1—for puppies up to one year; Cycle 2—for young adult dogs; Cycle 3—for overweight dogs; and Cycle 4—for older dogs. These were all developed because a significant number of consumers felt existing solutions (brands) were inadequate (i.e., their desired state exceeded existing states).

Emergency problems

Emergency problems are characterized primarily by the fact that their *occurrence is unexpected and an immediate solution is required*. For example, when your four-year-old refrigerator breaks down you are faced with the necessity of purchasing a new (or used) one to replace it or purchasing major repair services. In either case, the problem demands an immediate solution and will necessitate a different kind of decision-making process than other problem types. Generally, there will be a substantially shorter information search, less use of commercial information sources, a smaller number of brands considered, a differing importance placed on product attributes (availability and delivery may now be more important than price), fewer retail outlets visited, and so forth.

It is likely in some situations that emergency problems may bring about temporary problem solutions. In other words, the problem will not be solved satisfactorily and in effect becomes a planning or evolving problem. In fact, lease/rent products are often used as temporary solutions to emergency problems. Some firms such as the Seven-Eleven Corporation provide solutions to emergency problems by remaining open after normal store hours.

Planning problems

An extension of the routine problem is the planning problem which occurs *when the problem occurrence is expected, but an immediate solution is not required*. The effect on the decision-making process is to lengthen it, encouraging more information search (increasing the probability of engaging in information search), increasing the number of alternatives to be considered, and so forth.

Recognition of this type of problem, even though expected, does not necessarily mean that consumers actually spend a great deal more time in active decision making. It may be that the active decision process is broken up into more specific segments that take place at distinctly different times. For instance, even if you know that a transportation prob-

---

[6] P. Bernstein, "Psychographics Is Still an Issue on Madison Avenue," *Fortune* (January 16, 1978), p. 80.

lem involving the purchase of an automobile may arise a year from now, you may not spend a year actively searching for a solution. But you may, at least indirectly, be affected because you will probably be more susceptible to advertisements concerning automobiles and word-of-mouth information from friends about their experiences.

Evolving problems

We define evolving problems as those where *the problem occurrence is unexpected but no immediate solution is required*. In fact, the time frame for solution may stretch into years. Recognition of these types of problems may be very subtle and take considerable time for the discrepancy between desired and existing states to develop.

An example of recognition of an evolving problem occurs in the process of fashion adoption. For many consumers, the adoption of a new fashion evolves over a considerable period of time. Early awareness of a particular fashion innovation would not necessarily result in a discrepancy between what is desired and the existing state of consumer's fashion clothing. As the fashion spreads, the beginning of a discrepancy can occur and continue to grow until an external search and evaluation of the fashion takes place. This type of problem recognition and consumer purchase was particularly evident in the adoption of wire rim glasses as a fashion in the late 1960s and early 1970s. The fashion originated in a counterculture youth movement in the mid-1960s. However, manufacturers of eyeglasses, recognizing the American culture's strong identification with youthfulness and independence, turned this into a marketing opportunity as they promoted this product as a fashion that connotated this orientation and consumer lifestyle.[7] Eventually, even some of the most conservative individuals recognized the discrepancy and purchased wire rim glasses.

UNCONTROLLABLE DETERMINANTS OF PROBLEM RECOGNITION

A discrepancy between what is desired by a consumer and what the consumer has is the necessary condition for problem recognition. A discrepancy can be the result of a variety of factors that influence consumer desires, perceptions of the existing state, or both. These factors are often beyond the direct influence of the marketing manager, for example a change in family composition. Marketing efforts such as advertising can also influence problem recognition. In this section of the chapter we are going to review some of the uncontrollable factors that affect problem recognition. Most of these factors have been covered in detail in

---

[7] J. Sood, *Situations in Marketing* (Business Publications, Inc., 1976), pp. 7, 8.

earlier chapters of the book. In this section we are going to relate them more directly to the problem recognition process. We will discuss the marketing manager's utilization of the problem recognition process in the final section of this chapter.

Factors influencing the desired state

There are many factors that can affect a consumer's lifestyle and desires. The most important of these factors are: (1) changing family characteristics, (2) changing financial conditions, (3) changing financial expectations, (4) changing reference groups, (5) novelty or sensation seeking behavior, (6) changing situations, and (7) individual development.

Changes in family characteristics create changes in lifestyle and dramatic changes in consumer desires. As shown in Chapter 9, after marriage substantial changes occur in the desired state for housing, home furnishings, leisure activities, and numerous other products.[8] The birth of a child also alters needs, attitudes, and consumer lifestyles such that consumer desires change.[9] For example, the addition of a first child often results in a recognition of a need for greater financial security and the subsequent purchase of life insurance to reduce a discrepancy between desired financial security and perhaps an existing lack of such security. An increase in the felt need for saving may also occur, thus limiting disposable income.

Changes in financial status[10] and/or *changes in financial expectations*[11] can also affect a consumer's desired state and subsequently contribute to a discrepancy between desired and existing states. A salary increase, large tax return, inheritance, or anticipation of any of these can cause the consumer to change desires such that an existing state is less satisfying. Some automobile retailers take advantage of income tax refunds by advancing a down payment to individuals who have filed a return but have yet to receive the refund. While this type of discrepancy is often the result of personal financial gain, a financial loss[12] or changing economy[13] can also change consumer expectations and result in problem recognition on the part of many

---

[8] R. Ferber, "Family Decision Making and Economic Behavior," in *Family Economic Behavior: Problems and Perspectives,* ed. E. B. Sheldon (J. B. Lippincott Co., 1972), pp. 29−61.

[9] Wells and Gubar, "Life Cycle Concept."

[10] F. Juster and P. Wachtel, "Uncertainty Expectations and Durable Goods Demand Models," in *Human Behavior in Economic Affairs,* eds. B. Strumpel, J. Morgan, and E. Zahn (Jossey-Bass, Inc., 1972), pp. 321−45.

[11] E. Mueller, "The Desire for Innovations in Household Goods," in *Consumer Behavior: Theoretical Sources,* eds. S. Ward and T. Robertson (Prentice-Hall, Inc., 1973), pp. 354−84.

[12] Ibid.

[13] E. Kelley and L. Scheeve, "Buying Behavior in a Stagflation/Shortage Economy," *Journal of Marketing* (April 1975), pp. 44−50.

fixed-income consumers. In periods of rapid inflation many families are forced to cut back on extras, such as entertainment, and to purchase different quality levels of other products, such as food, in order to resolve problems created by a decrease in purchasing power.

A *change in reference groups* is also likely to alter a consumer's lifestyle which in turn can affect desires (see Chapter 8). This happens to many college students following graduation. Quite often in just a matter of a few days, a student's environment and major point of reference changes from the college campus to the corporate environment of a business. The conspicuous difference in clothing and behavior quickly influences new employees as they discover many discrepancies between their previous lifestyle and reference groups and the lifestyle exhibited by their new reference group. These discrepancies create recognizable problems which new employees will resolve in order to adjust to the explicit and implicit standards of their new reference group.[14]

A less obvious factor that influences problem recognition is the *desire for novelty or desire for change.*[15] In one study, approximately a third of those who switched to a new brand did so simply because they wanted a change, even though they were satisfied with their present product.[16] In another study, 15 percent who bought a new product did so because it was new.[17] Thus, novelty-seeking behavior is an important cause of problem recognition. It appears that at least some consumers are what has been termed *sensation seekers.*[18] These consumers respond more readily to new concepts[19] and symbols represented in the form of clever package designs and new products.[20]

An individual's *current situation* strongly influences the desired state of affairs (see Chapter 3). An individual with limited time may desire that a retail store provide ample parking and fast service, while a similar individual with more time may desire friendly service and wide selection. During cold weather many people prefer hot drinks, while hot weather makes cold drinks more desirable. During normal weather

[14] A. B. Cocanougher and G. D. Bruce, "Socially Distant Reference Groups and Consumer Aspirations," *Journal of Marketing Research* (August 1971), pp. 379–81.

[15] M. Venkatesan, "Cognitive Consistency and Novelty Seeking," in *Consumer Behavior: Theoretical Sources,* eds. S. Ward and T. Robertson (Prentice-Hall, Inc., 1973), pp. 354–84.

[16] E. Katz and P. F. Lazarsfeld, *Personal Influences* (New York: Free Press, 1955).

[17] G. Haines, "A Study of Why People Purchase New Products," in *Science, Technology and Change,* ed. R. Haas (American Marketing Association, 1966), pp. 685–97.

[18] G. Klonglan and E. Coward, "The Concept of Symbolic Adoption: A Suggested Interpretation," *Rural Sociology* (March 1970), pp. 77–83.

[19] R. Herrmann, R. Warland, and E. Carpenter, "Consumer Adoption and Rejection of Imitation Food Products," Pennsylvania State University Agricultural Experiment Station, Bulletin 79 (1972).

[20] R. Mittlestaedt, S. Grossbart, W. Curtis, and S. Devere, "Optional Stimulation Level and the Adoption Decision Process," *Journal of Consumer Research* (September 1976), pp. 84–94; and G. Miaoules and N. D'Amato, "Consumer Confusion and Trademark Infringement," *Journal of Marketing* (April 1978), pp. 48–55.

an individual may desire the flexibility of private transportation. A shift to snow and ice may change the desired state to one of reliability and safety. Situational variables are an important factor in problem recognition.

Finally, *individual development* (see Chapter 11) can influence the desired state. It is difficult to separate individual development from associated changes in reference groups, family life cycle, and so forth. It appears to influence the desired state independently of these other factors. For example, with increasing maturity, excitement and adventure appear to become less desirable. Thus, an advertisement by the Old West Regional Commission aimed at older vacationers stresses that "the pace is strictly relaxed."

Factors influencing the existing state

Consumer perceptions of the existing state can also be affected by many influences which contribute to a discrepancy and recognition of a problem. Factors beyond the control of marketers which can influence perceptions of the existing state include: (1) normal depletion, (2) dissatisfaction with existing solutions, (3) individual development, and (4) the efforts of consumer groups and governmental agencies.

Normal depletion is the cause of most routine problems as frequently used foods and household items are used up and need to be replaced. Depletion can also be more subtle, such as the need for an oil change or the replacement of a tire that is beginning to show wear. With most problems of this type, the condition of depletion is easily recognized and resolved with a consumer purchase.

A discrepancy between desired and existing states can also be the result of *consumer dissatisfaction* with the existing state. This dissatisfaction with an existing state can be the result of either instrumental performance, expressive performance, or both.[21] *Instrumental performance* relates to the physical performance of the product, while *expressive performance* is evaluated in terms of the nonmaterial, psychological dimensions of the product. If both dimensions of performance are not satisfactory, consumer dissatisfaction with the product results. For example, Ryan found that for a clothing purchase to be satisfactory, it must perform well on the dimension most important to the consumer, and it must reach a minimum level on all the other dimensions.[22] He found that clothing dissatisfaction was most readily related to a failure in instrumental performance, such as a poor fit. Once the instrumental performance is satisfied, usually to some minimum level of performance, dissatisfaction can still occur when the clothing fails to provide the

---

[21] J. Swan and L. Combs, "Product Performance and Consumer Satisfaction: A New Concept," *Journal of Marketing* (April 1976), pp. 25–33.

[22] M. Ryan, *Clothing: A Study in Human Behavior* (Holt, Rinehart and Winston, 1966), pp. 183–85.

FIGURE 15–3
The creation of problem recognition based on a price discrepancy

Toys

Manufacturer and toy	Average Price Consumer's Reports	LaBelles Oracle Rd. Fort Lowell	Fed Mart Campbell Fort Lowell	Jewelcor Broadway	Levy's El Con	Globe Grant Rd. First Ave.	K-Mart Valencia	Woolco 22nd St. Alvernon	Zody's Craycroft Broadway
Fisher Price Lift & Load Depot, ages 2-6	15.00	14.77	12.99	12.47	14.80		11.88	12.96	
Mattel's Sew Perfect sewing machine; ages 6 & up (needs batteries)	16.00	13.97	11.99	11.97					
Tonka Mighty Dump	12.00	8.97	7.99	9.77		7.97	10.97	7.97	14.99
Kenner's Jaime Sommers Bionic Woman with mission purse	13.00	11.47	7.49	6.97		9.97	8.77		
Kenner's $6 million man with Bionic grip	9.00	9.47	7.49	6.97	7.50	7.46	7.44	8.97	
Sunday Tuesday Taylor Ideal Toy Corp.	9.00	7.97			8.00		6.88		
Mego Corp.'s Biotron (needs batteries)	16.00	15.47			13.50				
Schaper Super Jock basketball		6.97	5.99	4.92	8.00			6.96	
football		6.97	5.99	4.92		6.96		6.96	9.99
baseball	9.00				9.80			8.96	
Schaper Max Machine (needs batteries)	15.00	11.97		9.99			15.96		
Nerf football		2.87	2.49	2.64		2.47	2.97	2.96	
flying hero		2.27		1.96	2.00	2.79			2.99
Monopoly		4.97	3.99	4.97	4.00	4.47	4.44	4.86	5.99
Baby dolls Kenner Baby Heartbeat		11.97			12.00	12.97	10.44	10.22	
Ideal Baby Rub-a-dub		11.97			12.00	9.96	9.97		13.99
Mattel Baby Come Back		12.97	10.99	10.97			11.56		
Kenner Baby Alive		11.97					10.88		

Source: *Arizona Daily Star* (November 1977). Used with permission.

desired expressive performance.[23] In other words, if your friends do not respond to you as a result of your clothes in the way you wanted them to.

The normal processes of *individual development* may alter our per-

---

[23] M. Horn, *The Second Skin: An Interdisciplinary Study of Clothing* (Houghton Mifflin Co., 1968), p. 12.

ceptions of our existing states. This is particularly true with respect to our physical attributes. As we age many of us experience complexion problems, weight problems, heart and/or stomach problems, and hearing problems. Likewise, our mental development may lead to dissatisfaction with our existing reading material or music collection. Development of skills such as racquetball or guitar may lead to dissatisfaction with our current equipment.

Finally, with increasing concern for consumer welfare, *consumer groups and many governmental agencies* attempt to cause a particular type of problem recognition among consumers. The goal is to produce a dissatisfaction with current solutions that are unhealthy, dangerous, or ecologically unsound. For example, the American Cancer Association spends a substantial amount of effort in attempting to create dissatisfaction with the current state of affairs among cigarette smokers. Publicity generated by consumer groups and others was the cause of the problem recognition involving aerosol sprays described at the beginning of this chapter.

Examine Figure 15−3 which ran in the Tucson *Arizona Daily Star* prior to Christmas. Zody's, which is perceived by many to be a discount store, had the highest price on every item in the comparison that it carried. This could easily generate problem recognition among Zody's customers (i.e., by affecting their perception of the existing state—high prices instead of low prices).

MARKETING STRATEGY AND PROBLEM RECOGNITION

Marketing managers have two general approaches available to them with respect to problem recognition. First, they need to know what problems consumers are facing in order to develop a marketing mix to help solve those problems. This requires that they measure problem recognition. Second, marketers will, on occasion, want to activate problem recognition.

Measuring problem recognition

Consumer problems may be either manifest or latent. A *manifest problem* is one of which the consumer is aware. A *latent problem* is one of which the consumer is not aware. This concept is very similar to the concept of a felt need discussed in the innovation section of Chapter 8. An example will make this distinction clear.

Timberlane Lumber Co. acquired a source of supply of Hoduran Pitch Pine. This natural product lights at the touch of a match even when damp and burns for 15 to 20 minutes. It will not flare up and is therefore relatively safe. It can be procured in sticks 15 to 18 inches long and 1 inch in diameter. These sticks can be used as is to ignite fireplace fires, or they can be shredded and used to ignite charcoal in charcoal grills.

Prior to marketing the product, Timberlane commissioned a marketing study to estimate demand and guide in developing marketing strategy. Two large samples of potential consumers were interviewed. The first sample was asked how they lit their fireplace fires and what problems they had with this procedure. Almost all of the respondents used newspaper, kindling, or both, and almost none experienced any problems. The new product was then described, and the respondents were asked to express the likelihood that they would purchase such a product. Only a small percentage expressed any interest. However, a sample of consumers that actually used the new product for several weeks felt it was a substantial improvement over existing methods and expressed a desire to continue using the product. Thus, the problem was there (because the new product was strongly preferred over the old by those who tried it), but most consumers were not aware of it. This is a *latent problem*. Before the product can be successfully sold, the firm must activate problem recognition.

In contrast, a substantial percentage of those interviewed about lighting charcoal fires expressed a strong concern about the safety of liquid charcoal lighter. These individuals expressed great interest in purchasing a safer product. This is a *manifest problem*. Timberlane need not worry about problem recognition in this case. Instead, it can concentrate on illustrating how its product solves the problem that the consumers already know exists.

As indicated above, marketing strategy will vary depending on whether the problem is manifest or latent. A wide variety of approaches are used to determine the problems consumers are facing.[24] The most common approach is undoubtedly intuition. That is, the manager can analyze a given product category and logically determine where improvements could be made. Thus, soundless vacuum cleaners or dishwashers are logical solutions to potential consumer problems. The difficulty with this approach is that the problem thus identified may be latent or of low importance to most consumers.

The most common research approach is *surveys* which ask relatively large numbers of individuals about the problems they are facing. This was the technique used by Timberlane in the example above. A second common approach is to utilize *focus groups*.[25] Focus groups are composed of 8 to 12 similar individuals, that is, male college students, female lawyers, or teenage girls, brought together to discuss a particular topic. A moderator is present to keep the discussion moving and focused on the topic, but otherwise the sessions are free flowing.

---

[24] For details, see D. S. Tull and D. I. Hawkins, *Marketing Research* (Macmillan Publishing Co., 1980).

[25] Ibid.

Both surveys and focus groups tend to take one of three approaches to problem identification: activity analysis, product analysis, or problem analysis. *Activity analysis* focuses on a particular activity such as preparing dinner, maintaining the lawn, or (as in the previous example) lighting the fireplace fire. The survey or focus group attempts to determine what problems the consumers feel occur during the performance of the activity.

Product analysis is similar but examines the purchase and/or use of a particular product or brand rather than an activity. Thus, consumers may be asked about problems associated with using their lawn mower or their popcorn popper. Curlee Clothing used focus groups to analyze the purchase and use of men's fashion clothing. The results indicated a high level of insecurity in purchasing men's clothing. This insecurity was combined with a distrust of both the motivations and competence of retail sales personnel. As a result, Curlee initiated a major effort to train retail sales personnel through specially prepared films and training sessions.[26]

Problem analysis takes the opposite approach from the previous techniques. It starts with a list of problems and asks the respondent to indicate which activities, products, or brands are associated with those problems. Figure 15−4 illustrates the results of one study using this approach.

Reacting to problem recognition

Once a consumer problem is identified, the manager may structure the marketing mix to solve the problem. This may involve product development or alteration, modifying channels of distribution, changing pricing policy, or revising advertising strategy. For example, a large number of people must minimize their salt intake. Many of these individuals are aware of the problem (minimizing salt intake) but are not aware of the products that can assist with this process. Tums utilizes the following advertising copy to indicate that this product can help with this problem:

GET A LOT OF RELIEF FROM HEARTBURN.
WITHOUT A LOT OF SODIUM.

When you get a touch of heartburn and you've got to watch your salt (sodium) intake, get relief with Tums.
Tums has only a trace of sodium—less than 3 milligrams per tablet. A lot less than many other antacids. (You should always read the labels.)

---

[26] D. I. Hawkins, "Curlee Clothing Company" (Harvard Intercollegiate Case Clearing, 1972), no. 9−572−618.

FIGURE 15–4

Results of a problem inventory analysis about food products

1. The package of _____ doesn't fit well on the shelf.
   Cereal 49%
   Flour 6
2. My husband/children refuse to eat _____.
   Liver 18%
   Vegetables 5
   Spinach 4
3. _____ doesn't quench my thirst.
   Soft drinks 58%
   Milk 9
   Coffee 6
4. Packaged _____ doesn't dissolve fast enough.
   Jello/gelatin 32%
   Bouillon cubes 8
   Pudding 5
5. Everyone always wants different _____.
   Vegetables 23%
   Cereal 11
   Meat 10
   Desserts 9
6. _____ makes a mess in the oven.
   Broiling steaks 19%
   Pie 17
   Roast/pork/rib 8
7. Packaged _____ tastes artificial.
   Instant potatoes 12%
   Macaroni and cheese 4
8. It's difficult to get _____ to pour easily.
   Catsup 16%
   Syrup 13
   Gallon of milk 11
9. Packaged _____ looks unappetizing.
   Hamburger helper 6%
   Lunch meat 3
   Liver 3
10. I wish my husband/children could take _____ in a carried lunch.
    Hot meal 11%
    Soup 9
    Ice cream 4

Source: E. Tauber, "Discovering New Product Opportunities with Problem Inventory Analysis," *Journal of Marketing* (American Marketing Association, January 1975), p. 70.

Agree Shampoo and Agree Creme Rinse were developed only after research indicated consumers were experiencing a problem with oily hair. Self-service gas stations, warehouse food stores, and generic food items have all evolved as responses to consumer reactions to increasing prices.

As you approach graduation, you will be presented with opportunities to purchase insurance, acquire credit cards, and solve other problems associated with the onset of financial independence and a major change in lifestyle. These opportunities, which will be presented through both personal sales contacts and advertising media, reflect various firm's knowledge that many individuals in your situation face problems that their products will help solve.

Weekend and night store hours are a response of retailers to the consumer problem of limited weekday shopping opportunities. This problem has become particularly important to families with working wives.

As we have seen, competition, consumer organizations, or governmental agencies occasionally introduce information in the marketplace that triggers problem recognition that particular marketers would prefer to avoid. The American tobacco industry has made strenuous attempts to minimize consumer recognition of the health problem associated with cigarette smoking. For example, a recent Newport cigarette advertisement shows a happy, laughing couple under the headline: "Alive with pleasure." This could easily be interpreted as an attempt to minimize any problem recognition caused by the mandatory warning at the bottom of the advertisement: "Warning: The Surgeon General has determined that cigarette smoking is dangerous to your health."

The examples described above represent only a small sample of the ways in which marketers react to consumer problem recognition. Basically, each firm must be aware of the consumer problems it can solve, which consumers have these problems, and the situations in which the problems arise.

Activating problem recognition

There are occasions when the manager will want to influence problem recognition rather than react to it. In the earlier example involving the fire starters, Timberlane would have to activate problem recognition in order to sell the product as a fireplace starter. There are two basic approaches to causing problem recognition. These are *generic problem recognition* and *selective problem recognition*. These are analogous to the economic concepts of generic and selective demand. Generic problem recognition involves a *discrepancy which a variety of brands within a product category can reduce*. Selective problem recognition involves a *discrepancy which only one brand within a product category can reduce*.

Generally, a firm will attempt to influence generic problem recognition when the problem is latent or of low importance *and* it is early in the product life cycle, the firm has a very high percentage of the market, external search after problem recognition is apt to be limited, or if it is an industry wide cooperative effort.

Consider the advertising copy in Figure 15–5 which appeared on the back of the program at a major women's basketball game. In this case,

FIGURE 15–5
An attempt to influence generic problem recognition

Used with permission from Blue Ribbon Sports.

the focus is primarily on generating a recognition of the discrepancy between the existing state for many female junior high, high school, and club basketball players (wearing men's shoes) and the desired state (wearing shoes made especially for women). The product is relatively new in the life cycle, Nike is widely distributed, and the advertisement attempts to limit and direct external search.

Door-to-door sales for such products as encyclopedias and vacuum cleaners attempt to arouse problem recognition in part because the salesperson can then limit external search to one brand. Cooperative advertising ("Everybody needs milk") frequently focuses on generic problem recognition. Likewise, virtual monopolies such as U.S. Tobacco in the moist snuff industry (Skoal, Copenhagen, Happy Days) can focus on generic problem recognition because any sales increase will probably come to their brands. However, a smaller firm that generates generic problem recognition for its product category may be generating more sales for its competitors than for itself.

Figure 15−6 illustrates an attempt to influence selective problem recognition. Notice that the advertisement focuses heavily on Allstate and how Allstate may cost less for the same coverage (desired state) than your existing insurance (existing state). This is in sharp contrast to the Nike advertisement shown in Figure 15−5. In the Nike ad which at-

FIGURE 15–6
An attempt to influence selective problem recognition

Used with permission from Allstate Insurance Company.

tempts to influence generic problem recognition, the brand name is not in the headlines and only appears twice in the copy. Firms attempt to cause selective problem recognition to gain or maintain market share, while generic problem recognition generally results in an expansion of the total market.

How can a firm influence problem recognition? Recall that problem recognition is a function of (1) the *importance* and (2) *magnitude* of a discrepancy between a desired state and an existing state. Thus the firm can attempt to influence the size of the discrepancy by altering the desired state or the perceptions of the existing state. Or, the firm can attempt to influence the perception of the importance of an existing discrepancy.

Most marketing efforts attempt to influence the desired state. For example, the Nike advertisement in Figure 15−5 is devoted primarily to stressing the advantages (desired state) of a basketball shoe designed specifically for women. Many new products, such as Agree Shampoo were developed in response to consumer descriptions of desired states. Marketing efforts are then devoted to convincing consumers that the product can provide the desired state.

It is also possible to influence perceptions of the existing state through advertisements. Many personal care and social products take this approach. "Even your best friend won't tell you . . ." or "Mary is a great worker but her coffee . . ." are examples of messages designed to generate concern about an existing state. The desired state is assumed to be fresh breath and good coffee. These messages are designed to cause individuals to question if their existing state coincides with this desired state.

The final approach to influencing problem recognition is to change the importance associated with an existing discrepancy. The American Cancer Society devotes considerable effort toward persuading smokers (most of whom express a desire to quit—problem recognition) that it is important to quit immediately. Likewise, many Americans express a desire to conserve energy yet, in many cases, this desire is not strong enough to influence important consumption decisions such as the use of public transportation versus a private automobile.

SUMMARY

Problem recognition is the first, essential step in the consumer decision process. It involves the existence of a discrepancy between the consumer's desired state, what the consumer would like, and the existing state, what the consumer perceives as already existing. Both the desired state and the existing state are influenced by the consumer's lifestyle and current situation. If the discrepancy between these two states is sufficiently large and important enough, the consumer will begin to search for a solution to the problem.

There are four broad types of problems that confront consumers based on the immediacy of the required solution and whether or not the problem was expected to occur. These are: (1) routine problems which are expected to occur and which require an immediate solution, (2) emergency problems which are not expected and which require an immediate solution, (3) planning problems which are expected to occur and which do not require an immediate solution, and (4) evolving problems which are not expected and which do not require an immediate solution. It is important for marketing managers to be aware of the type(s) of problem recognition which lead to the purchase of their products, since type of problem recognition influences the type and amount of information search.

A number of factors beyond the control of the marketing manager can affect problem recognition. The desired state of affairs is commonly influenced by (1) changing family characteristics, (2) changing financial conditions, (3) changing financial expectations, (4) changing reference groups, (5) need for novelty, (6) changing situations, and (7) individual development. The existing state is influenced by (1) normal depletion, (2) dissatisfaction with existing solutions, (3) individual development, and (4) the efforts of consumer groups and government agencies.

Before marketing managers can respond to problem recognition generated by outside factors, they must be able to measure problem recognition. Surveys and focus groups using activity, product, or problem analysis are commonly used to measure problem recognition.

Once managers are aware of problem recognition patterns among their target market, they can react by designing the marketing mix to solve the recognized problem. This may involve product development or alteration, a change in store hours, a different price, or a host of other marketing strategies.

Marketing managers often want to influence problem recognition rather than react to it. They may desire to generate generic problem recognition, a discrepancy which a variety of brands within a product category can reduce; or selective problem recognition, a discrepancy which only one brand in the product category can reduce. Most attempts by marketers to generate problem recognition focus on altering the desired state of affairs. This is attempted through messages showing the advantages that the state of affairs provided by a particular product can bring.

REVIEW QUESTIONS

1. When does problem recognition occur?
2. What is the difference between a latent problem and a manifest problem? Why is this distinction important?

3. What can happen after a problem is recognized?
4. What is the role of information processing in problem recognition?
5. How does lifestyle relate to problem recognition?
6. What influences the motivation to resolve a particular problem?
7. What factors can be used to classify consumer problems?
8. What is a routine problem? a planning problem? an emergency problem? an evolving problem?
9. What are the main uncontrollable factors that influence the desired state? Give an example of each.
10. What are the main uncontrollable factors that influence the existing state? Give an example of each.
11. How can you measure problem recognition?
12. In what ways can marketers react to problem recognition? Give several examples.
13. How does generic problem recognition differ from selective problem recognition? Under what conditions would a firm attempt to influence generic problem recognition? Why?
14. How can a firm influence problem recognition? Give examples.

DISCUSSION QUESTIONS

1. How could Jeff stimulate problem recognition in terms of creating a discrepancy between the desired and existing states of alternative modes of transportation? Would you recommend focusing on the desired state through a desired lifestyle or focusing on the existing state in terms of expectations and perceived levels of performance provided by alternative modes of transportation? Be specific. Also, how would you stimulate search and evaluation of Jeff's brand of moped?
2. What type of problem is created by increasing gasoline prices? Discuss this problem in terms of how it is recognized by different segments of society. What will have to happen to make this problem more readily apparent and how will this effect the image of moped?
3. What factors will contribute to problem recognition for the new employee following graduation? How would each of these factors affect your lifestyle and contribute changes in your desired state for many products and services? Which products and services might you now view as less satisfactory, causing you to seek better solutions in the form of more personally satisfying products and services?
4. Discuss what types of marketing promotions a firm might use in attempting to stimulate an evolving type of problem recognition.
5. Discuss the types of products that resolve specific problems that occur for most consumers at different stages of their family life cycle.

6. Discuss how you would measure problem recognition among joggers.

PROJECT QUESTIONS

1. Interview five other students and identify three consumer problems that they have recognized and defined. For each problem recognition determine: (a) The relative importance of the problem; (b) How the problem occurred; (c) What caused the problem (i.e., change in desired or actual states), (d) What type of problem recognition each problem is (i.e., routine, emergency, planning, or evolving), (e) What action they have taken, and (f) What action is planned in order to resolve each problem.

2. One of the major consumer problems that many consumers face is in the area of automotive repair. Develop a questionnaire to measure problem recognition, importance, and action planned to resolve this problem. Then interview five other students. In evaluating your results along with the results obtained by other members in your class determine the degree to which this is a problem and the degree to which students plan to take some action to resolve the problem. Also, try to estimate the percentage of students who will never resolve this problem and the dollar value of this loss.

3. Using the classification scheme shown in Figure 15–2, list five products that would be purchased in response to each type of problem recognition. Then compare the products you have identified with those identified by other students in the class.

4. Utilizing the problem inventory list in Figure 15–4, remove statements 2 and 10 and have several fellow students fill in the blanks in order to assess student perception of recognizable food-related problems. Then determine as a class if there is any consensus in terms of a particular problem recognition among the students interviewed.

5. Find and cut out of a newspaper or magazine an advertisement that is attempting to deal with problem recognition. Analyze the advertisement in terms of the type of problem and what action the ad is suggesting. Also, discuss any changes you would recommend to improve the effectiveness of the ad in terms of dealing with problem recognition.

16

Information search

University Hospital, an independent corporate entity, is the 380-bed principal teaching hospital of Boston University's School of Medicine. Several years ago, it became clear that the public was confused about the identity of University Hospital. The hospital had had a variety of names in the past and was not called University Hospital until 1965. The current name suggests a student health center to some individuals, and its location adjacent to Boston City Hospital caused confusion for others. Finally, much of the general public was uncertain about the nature and role of teaching hospitals in general.

As a result of the public's lack of understanding, University Hospital's occupancy rate and fund-raising efforts were not as successful as they could have been. The primary problem was that the public would not seek out information about hospitals even when confronted with illness. Thus, the hospital's management realized that it was their responsibility to place relevant information within easy reach of the consumer. The initial marketing effort involved newspaper preprints inserted into newspapers throughout the hospital's region. This annual effort is supplemented by a three-time yearly publication called, "Healthful Hints from University Hospital." Consumers can subscribe to this publication at no charge. The "Healthful Hints" publication is promoted via announcements on radio and television as well as by newspaper and direct mail advertisements.

As a result of the efforts described above (as well as additional communications programs), the public's understanding of University

Hospital has increased, as has its occupancy rate. And there has been a more favorable reception given to its fund-raising activities. The underlying reason for this success was the recognition that most consumers would not seek out information about University Hospital. Once this was understood, the hospital's management was able to develop a promotional campaign based on the target market's pattern of information search.[1]

Consumers are involved in an ongoing and seemingly never-ending recognition of problems and opportunities; so internal and external search for information and solutions to these problems is a continuing process. However, the search for and acquisition of information is not free.[2] Information search involves the mental as well as physical activities which consumers must perform in order to make decisions and accomplish desired goals in the marketplace.[3] It takes time, energy, money, and can often require giving up more desirable activities. The benefits of information search, however, often outweigh the cost of search. For example, search may produce a lower price, a preferred style of merchandise, a higher quality product, a reduction in perceived risk, or greater confidence in the choice. In addition, the physical and mental processes involved in information search are, on occasion, rewarding in themselves.[4]

There are many factors which affect consumer information seeking behavior, including activities by the marketer. Marketing managers attempt to both encourage and discourage information search by consumers. For example, in the automotive industry, customer loyalty to a particular brand of automobile is frequently encouraged by the firm. Such brand loyalty results in less information search and alternative brand evaluation.[5] On the other hand, a retail drugstore that advertises discount prices on prescription drugs is attempting to create a discrepancy between desired and existing prices paid and thus stimulate external search and evaluation and hopefully the purchase of prescription drugs at their retail store.

Chapter 10 described information processing and how an individual

---

[1] D. R. Giller, "Hospital Joins Marketing World," *Advertising Age* (April 2, 1979), pp. S—1, S—12.

[2] A. Downs, "A Theory of Consumer Efficiency," *Journal of Retailing* (Spring 1961), pp. 6—12; and W. Bender, "Consumer Purchase Costs—Do Retailers Recognize Them?" *Journal of Retailing* (Spring 1966), pp. 1—8.

[3] R. Kelly, "The Search Component of the Consumer Decision Process—A Theoretic Examination," in *Marketing and the New Science of Planning*, ed. C. King, (American Marketing Association, 1968), p. 273.

[4] E. M. Tauber, "Why Do People Shop?" *Journal of Marketing* (October 1972), pp. 45—48.

[5] P. Bennett and R. Mandell, "Prepurchase Information Seeking Behavior of New Car Purchases—the Learning Hypothesis," *Journal of Marketing Research* (November 1969), pp. 430—33.

derives and stores meaning from stimuli in the environment. In that chapter, we focused on the process of reacting to a particular stimulus. In this chapter, our concern is with the conditions that lead an individual to seek out certain types of stimuli for processing. We are going to examine seven questions related to information search:

1.   What is the nature of information search?
2.   What types of information are sought?
3.   What sources of information are used?
4.   How extensive is external information search?
5.   Why do consumers engage in external search?
6.   What conditions affect the level of external information search?
7.   What marketing strategies can be developed based on patterns of search behavior?

NATURE OF INFORMATION SEARCH

In Figure 16—1, we have reproduced the information processing model developed in Chapter 10. Problem recognition occurs via a comparison of an existing state with a desired state. The determination of the existing state involves the perception process which provides information to current memory. Information on the desired state is also fed into current memory from either the perception process or retention

FIGURE 16–1
Information processing for consumer decision making

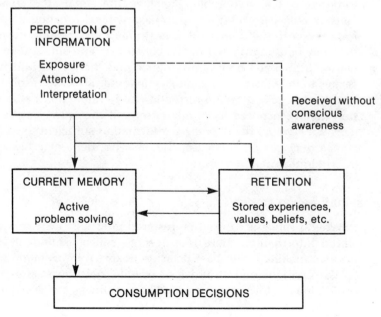

(long-term memory). Once the problem is recognized, relevant information from retention is brought into current memory to determine if a satisfactory solution is known (the decision rules involved in this decision are described in the next chapter). This is *internal search*. If no satisfactory solution is known, then the perception process is focused on stimuli relevant to the resolution of the problem. This is *external search*.

Internal information search

A great many recognized problems are resolved by the consumer through internal processing of information. That is, the consumer may simply recall from retention stored information related to a particular problem and use this information to resolve the problem. For example, a consumer that suddenly acquires a cold may recall that Dristan nasal spray provided relief in the past. This consumer may also recall that a drugstore on the way home from work carries Dristan. The purchase could then be made using only internal search. Of course, the internal search could have been more complex—such as recalling several brands which performed with varying degrees of effectiveness in a variety of situations.

Internal information search is an activity that is not observable and is very difficult for marketers to measure. Nevertheless, marketers can still influence internal search through advertising and other marketing efforts. For example, after a new car purchase a customer may feel vulnerable. The firm that treats the customer with considerable care after the purchase will be creating a very positive impression in the mind of that customer. This positive experience will probably be remembered by the consumer, and subsequent purchases will be influenced by this experience and the stored information that relates to it. On the other hand, a consumer about to resolve a problem based solely on internal information and evaluation of stored information may be exposed to an advertisement that suggests the purchaser does not have all the necessary information sufficient to make a brand choice decision. In this case, the advertisement may have stimulated external information search.

External information search

When problems can not be resolved internally with an evaluation of stored information, there is a need to collect additional information prior to making a purchase decision. External information can include (1) the opinions and attitudes of friends, neighbors, and relatives, (2) professional information provided in pamphlets, articles, and books, or

(3) marketer-generated information presented in advertisements and displays and by sales personnel. Thus, external information search involves the collection of additional information by utilizing the perception process as shown in Figure 16–1.

TYPES OF INFORMATION SOUGHT

Recall from Chapter 2 that a consumer decision requires information on (1) the appropriate evaluative criteria for the solution of a problem, (2) the existence of various alternative solutions, and (3) the performance level or characteristic of each alternative solution on each evaluative criterion. Information search, then, seeks each of these three types of information.

Suppose you are provided with a sum of money with which to purchase a 35mm camera, perhaps as a graduation present. Assuming that you have not been in the market for a camera recently, your first thoughts would probably be: "What characteristics do I want in a camera?" You would then engage in internal search to determine the appropriate characteristics. These characteristics are your *evaluative criteria*. If you have had limited experience with cameras, you might also engage in external search to learn which characteristics a good camera should have. You could check with friends, read *Consumer Reports* and/or talk with sales personnel. Thus, one potential objective of both internal and external search is *the determination of appropriate evaluative criteria*. We provide a detailed discussion of evaluative criteria in the next chapter.

After (and while) searching for appropriate evaluative criteria, you would probably search for appropriate alternatives—in this case brands or, possibly, stores. Again, you would start with an internal search. Based on this search, you might in effect say to yourself: "I know that Canon, Vivitar, Pentax, Minolta, Olympus, and Nikon all make cameras. After my brother's experience, I'd never buy a Pentax. I've heard good things about Canon, Nikon, and Minolta. I think I'll check them out."

The six brands that you thought of are known as the *awareness set*. The awareness set is composed of three subcategories of considerable importance to marketers. The three brands that you have decided to investigate are known as the *evoked set*.[6] An evoked set is those brands one will consider for the solution of a particular consumer problem. If you do not have an evoked set for cameras, or lack confidence that your evoked set is adequate, you would probably engage in external search to learn about the available alternatives. If you are initially satisfied with the

---

[6] B. Campbell, "The Existence of Evoked Set and Determinants of Its Magnitude in Brand Choice Behavior," in *Buyer Behavior: Theoretical and Empirical Foundations*, eds. J. Howard and L. Ostlund, (Alfred A. Knopf, Inc., 1973), pp. 243–44.

evoked set, additional information search will be focused on the performance of the brands in the evoked set on the evaluative criteria. Thus, the evoked set is of particular importance in structuring subsequent information search.

The brand that you found completely unworthy of further consideration is a member of what is called the *inept set*.[7] Brands in the inept set are actively disliked by the consumer. Positive information about these brands is not likely to be processed even if it is readily available.

Vivitar and Olympus were brands of which you were aware but were basically indifferent toward. They compose what is known as an *inert set*. Consumers will generally accept favorable information about brands in the inert set, although they do not seek out such information. Brands in this set are generally acceptable when preferred brands are not available.

Consumers with substantial product knowledge are likely to use more evaluative criteria and require more brands in their evoked set to satisfy these evaluative criteria.[8] On the other hand, consumers with smaller evoked sets may have a single criterion guiding their brand selection. Also, as the information processing task becomes more difficult, more evaluative criteria may be added but fewer brands are considered in order to manage the information processing task and arrive at a brand choice decision.[9]

Table 16—1 illustrates the size of the awareness, evoked, inert, and inept sets of one group of consumers for four product categories. Notice that, in all cases, the evoked set is substantially smaller than the awareness set. Since it is generally the evoked set from which consumers make final evaluations and decisions, marketing strategy which focuses only on creating awareness may be inadequate.

In order to choose among the brands in the evoked set, the consumer compares them on the relevant evaluative criteria. This process requires the consumer to gather information about each brand on each pertinent evaluative criterion. In our camera example, you might collect information on the price, ease of loading, and quality of lens for each brand you are considering.

In summary, consumers engage in internal and external search for (1) appropriate evaluative criteria, (2) the existence of potential solutions, and (3) the characteristics of potential solutions.

---

[7] C. Narayana and R. Markin, "Consumer Behavior and Product Performance: An Alternative Conceptualization," *Journal of Marketing* (October 1975), pp. 1—6.

[8] F. May and R. Homans, "Evoked Set Size and the Level of Information and Processing in Product Comprehension and Choice Criteria," in *Advances in Consumer Research IV*, ed. W. D. Perrault, Jr. (Association for Consumer Research, 1977) pp. 172—75.

[9] J. Belonax and R. Mittlestaedt, "Evoked Set as a Function of Number of Choice Criteria and Information Variability," in *Advances in Consumer Research, V*, ed. H. K. Hunt (Association for Consumer Research, 1978), pp. 48—51.

TABLE 16-1

Awareness, evoked, inert, and inept brand sets for four different product classes

Product class	Minimum	Maximum	Average
Toothpaste			
Awareness	3	11	6.5
Evoked	1	4	2.0
Inert	0	8	2.0
Inept	0	6	2.5
Mouthwash			
Awareness	1	6	3.5
Evoked	0	3	1.3
Inert	0	5	1.2
Inept	0	3	1.0
Deodorant			
Awareness	1	11	6.0
Evoked	0	4	1.6
Inert	0	8	2.4
Inept	0	8	2.0
Beer			
Awareness	3	24	10.6
Evoked	0	13	3.5
Inert	0	15	4.7
Inept	0	18	2.4

Source: C. Narayana and R. Markin, "Consumer Behavior and Product Performance: An Alternative Conceptualization," *Journal of Marketing* (October 1975), P. 4.

SOURCES OF INFORMATION

Refer again to our rather pleasant example of receiving cash with which to purchase a 35mm camera. We suggested that you might check with friends, consult *Consumer Reports,* or talk with sales personnel to collect relevant information. These represent the three primary sources of information available to consumers: (1) *personal sources,* such as friends and family; (2) *professional sources,* such as consumer groups and government agencies; and (3) *marketing sources,* such as sales personnel and advertising.

As the decision becomes more important to the consumer and the evaluative criteria become more subjective (style as opposed to price), the reliance on personal and professional sources tends to increase. The use of sources of information also varies as personal characteristics change. For example, Table 16 — 2 shows a significant increase in the use of *Consumer Reports* as an information source for microwave ovens as education increases. However, overall generalizations concerning the relative importance of each potential source of information are not justified. As we saw in Chapter 8, opinion leaders (personal information sources) are critical for some product categories and less important for

TABLE 16-2
Information sources consulted prior to purchasing a microwave oven

	Education level		
Percent of respondents who:	High school or less	Some college	Completed college
Visited retail outlets	54%	44%	48%
Read magazine ads	9	8	10
Read newspaper ads	6	8	5
Watched television ads	8	11	6
Read *Consumer Reports*	3	9	17
Talked with friends....................	20	26	23

Source: *Cooking Appliance Purchase and Usage Patterns* (Newsweek, Inc., 1978), p. 27.

others. It is important for the marketing manager to determine the sources of information used for the product under consideration by the appropriate target market and to react accordingly.

DEGREE OF EXTERNAL INFORMATION SEARCH

Marketing managers are particularly interested in external information search as this provides them with direct access to the consumer. How much external information search do consumers actually engage in? Because convenience goods like soft drinks, gum, and candy are generally purchased without much search effort, our discussion will focus on the information search associated with shopping goods which are more likely to involve external search.

Four different measures of external information search have been used: (1) number of stores visited, (2) number of information sources used, (3) number of alternatives considered, and (4) overall or combination measures. Each of these measures of search effort assesses a different aspect of behavior, yet each measure supports one observation: *external information search is skewed toward limited search with the greatest proportion of consumers performing little external search prior to purchase.*[10]

Number of stores visited

The number of stores visited is the most frequently used measure of external search. Surveys of shopping behavior have shown that over 60 percent of all durable purchases are made generally after visiting only one

---

[10] J. W. Newman, "Consumer External Search: Amount and Determinants," in *Consumer and Industrial Buying Behavior*, eds. A. Woodside, J. Sheth, and P. Bennett (Elsevier North-Holland, Inc., 1977), pp. 79–94.

store.[11] For example, one-stop shoppers account for approximately 60 percent of the purchases of new automobiles and major household appliances; 60 to 80 percent, for various items of apparel and small appliances; and 85 to 90 percent, for cookware, towels and sheets, and toys.

Figure 16−2 shows the number of stores visited before the purchase of small appliances.[12] In this case 77 percent of the small appliance

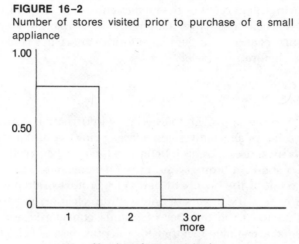

FIGURE 16–2
Number of stores visited prior to purchase of a small appliance

Number of stores visited

Source: Derived from J. Udell, "Prepurchase Behavior of Buyers of Small Appliances," *Journal of Marketing* (American Marketing Association, October 1966), pp. 50–52.

buyers visited one store, 19 percent visited two stores, and 4 percent made three or more store visits before purchase. Obviously, most of these consumers perceived very little benefit from extending the search beyond one store visit. This could be due to a high cost of additional search, strong loyalty to a particular brand or store, little difference perceived between brands, or some combination of these and other influences.

Number of information sources used

Because the number of stores visited offers only a very limited perspective on external search, it is important to look at the number of information sources used prior to purchase. Sources of information include personal sources, like relatives, friends, and neighbors; pub-

[11] Ibid.

[12] J. Udell, "Prepurchase Behavior of Buyers of Small Appliances," *Journal of Marketing* (October 1966), pp. 50−52.

lished information found in pamphlets, articles, and books; and marketer information made available through advertising, sales promotion, and personal selling. Though this measure of information search is considerably different from the number of stores visited, the same level of information-seeking behavior has been observed. For example, over a third of the buyers of major appliances and new automobiles use one source of information prior to purchase.[13] In the automobile study, 15 percent of these buyers used no external source of information before buying; 30 percent of the buyers consulted one source before purchase; 26 percent used two sources of information; 18 percent used three sources; and 12 percent used four or more external sources of information before purchase.[14]

Number of alternatives considered

Another approach to evaluating information search is to examine the number of alternatives considered prior to purchase. Like the two previous measures of search behavior, the number of alternatives considered also shows a limited amount of prepurchase search. For example, 42 percent of the buyers of new refrigerators evaluated one brand, and 71 percent of the buyers of new vacuum cleaners evaluated one brand.[15] In Table 16–3 the number of brands considered and number of stores visited are shown together for the purchase of refrigerators and electric irons. One-store shopping was almost twice as frequent for electric irons (82 percent) compared to refrigerators (42 percent), and on the average, fewer brands of electric irons were examined (an average of 2.52 for refrigerators and 1.65 for electric irons). This limited amount of brand evaluation and store search is undoubtedly related to both a lack of effort on the part of consumers and the effectiveness of marketing and sales efforts on the part of manufacturers and retailers.

Combination measures

Because each of these measures of external search deals with a different aspect of search behavior, it is also useful to examine the total search effort to evaluate more completely the search behavior of consumers. Based on three separate studies that span over 20 years, we can classify consumers in terms of their total external information search as (1)

[13] G. Katona and E. Mueller, "A Study of Purchase Decisions," in *Consumer Behavior: The Dynamics of Consumer Reaction,* ed. L. Clark (University Press, 1955), pp. 30–87; and J. Newman and R. Staelin, "Prepurchase Information Seeking for New Cars and Major Household Appliances," *Journal of Marketing Research* (August 1972), pp. 249–57.

[14] Ibid.

[15] W. Dommermuth, "The Shopping Matrix and Marketing Strategy," *Journal of Marketing Research* (May 1965), pp. 128–32.

TABLE 16–3

Number of stores visited and number of brands evaluated before purchase of refrigerators and electric irons

Number of brands examined	Number of stores visited					
	1	2	3	4	5 or more	
Refrigerators						
1.................	36%	5%	—	—	—	41%
2.................	3	6	2%	1%	1%	13
3.................	3	3	5	5	1	17
4.................	—	2	3	3	3	11
5 or more........	—	—	5	5	8	18
	42%	16%	15%	14%	13%	100%
Electric irons						
1.................	62%	2%	1%	—	—	65%
2.................	11	3	1	1%	—	16
3.................	5	1	3	1	—	10
4.................	4	—	1	1	1%	7
5 or more........	—	1	1	—	—	2
	82%	7%	7%	3%	1%	100%

Source: W. Dommermuth, "The Shopping Matrix and Marketing Strategy," *Journal of Marketing Research* (American Marketing Association, May 1965), p. 130.

nonsearchers, (2) information searchers, and (3) extended information searchers.

Nonsearchers (60 percent) Nonsearchers are buyers who engage in little or no external information search before the purchase of durable goods. An early study of information search classified 65 percent of the shoppers of major durables as nonsearchers based on the buyer's attempt to look at products owned by others and seek advice, read advertisements or articles, and visit several stores before purchase.[16] Another study found that 49 percent of the buyers of major durables did little or no information search;[17] and a third study classified 65 percent of the buyers of major durables as nonsearchers.[18] Thus, as shown in Table 16 − 4, there is considerable agreement in terms of the relative magnitude of nonsearchers in spite of differences in the buyers surveyed, measurement scales, and time at which the study was conducted.

Information searchers (30 percent) In Table 16 − 4 we can see that 25 percent to 38 percent of the major appliance buyers observed in these three studies could be classified as information searchers because their

---

[16] Katona and Mueller, "Purchase Decisions," pp. 30 − 87.

[17] Newman and Staelin, "Prepurchase Information," pp. 19 − 29.

[18] J. Claxton, J. Fry, and B. Portis, "A Taxonomy of Prepurchase Information Gathering Patterns," *Journal of Consumer Research* (December 1974), pp. 35 − 42.

TABLE 16–4
Information search behavior of three classifications of major appliance buyers

Search behavior	Katona and Mueller (1955)	Newman and Staelin (1972)	Claxton, Fry and Portis (1974)	Approximate Average
Nonsearchers	65%	49%	65%	60%
Information seekers	25	38	27	30
Intense information seekers	10	13	8	10

behavior demonstrated a moderate level of search. For example, Claxton and his associates classified 27 percent of their major appliance buyers as "thorough and balanced" information searchers because as a group they averaged three types of information sources used and visited an average of four stores prior to purchase. Thus, this segment of buyers performed what might be thought by many as a reasonable information search by consulting multiple sources and multiple stores prior to making a fairly important and expensive consumer purchase decision.

Extended information searchers (10 percent) By far the smallest group of major appliance buyers are those classified as extended information searchers. These buyers sought a great deal of information before purchasing. In the Katona and Mueller study these buyers sought information from others, noted advertisements, read articles, and visited multiple stores before purchasing. While their search effort was considerable, it was also balanced in terms of sources of information. Claxton and his associates classified 8 percent of their shoppers as extended information searchers, but their search was less balanced as they used an average of two sources of information and visited an average of eight stores before purchase.

Conclusions on degree of external information search

It is clear from the above discussion that most consumers engage in minimal external information search immediately prior to the purchase of consumer durables. The level of search for less important items is even lower.[19] As we will see in the next section, limited information search does not *necessarily* mean that the consumer is not following a sound purchasing strategy.

COSTS VERSUS BENEFITS OF EXTERNAL SEARCH

Why do 60 percent of the buyers of major appliances described above do little or no external search, while 10 percent of the buyers engage in

[19] Katona and Mueller, "Purchase Decisions," pp. 30–87.

extensive external search? The answer lies in the differences between the buyers in terms of their awareness and perceptions of the benefits and costs of search associated with a particular situation.

The benefits of external information search can be tangible such as a lower price,[20] a preferred style, or higher quality product;[21] or the benefits can be intangible in terms of reduced risk,[22] greater confidence in the purchase,[23] or even providing enjoyment.[24] Perceptions of these benefits are likely to vary with the consumer's experience in the market, media habits, and the extent to which the consumer interacts with others or belongs to differing reference groups. Therefore, one explanation as to why 60 percent of the major appliance buyers do little or no search is that they do not perceive discernible benefits resulting from such an effort. To the extent that such benefits are not perceived, consumer motivation for information search is greatly reduced.

On the other hand, external acquisition of information is not free, and many consumers may engage in little or no search because the costs of search exceed the perceived benefits. For example, assume you are buying a fairly expensive toy as a Christmas present for a younger brother or sister. Since you do not have a lot of time to do your shopping, you go to a department store close to where you live. You find the toy you would like to purchase but the price is $2 or $3 more than you expected to pay, and you think you can buy the same toy at another store five miles away at a lower price. Whether you buy the toy at that store and pay a higher price or go to the other store depends on the costs you attach to the extra search effort in that particular situation. For some, the benefit (a possible $2 or $3 savings) would exceed the cost (monetary, time, and psychological) of traveling five miles to visit another store and they would make the required effort. Others may attach greater costs to this additional search effort, and because these costs appear to exceed the potential or expected benefits, they would not engage in additional search. Thus, another explanation for the limited amount of search effort displayed by many consumers could be based on a high perceived cost of search relative to the potential or expected reward.

The costs of search can be both monetary and nonmonetary. Monetary costs include out-of-pocket expenses related to the search effort such as the cost of transportation, parking, and time-related costs which

---

[20] G. Stigler, "The Economics of Information Search," *Journal of Political Economy* (June 1961), pp. 213–25; and D. I. Hawkins and G. McCain, "An Investigation of Returns to Different Shopping Strategies," *Journal of Consumer Affairs* (Summer 1979), pp. 64–74.

[21] D. Cox and S. Rich, "Perceived Risk and Consumer Decision Making—a Case of Telephone Shopping," *Journal of Marketing Research* (November 1964), pp. 32–39; and Dommermuth, "Shopping Matrix," pp. 128–32.

[22] Cox and Rich, "Perceived Risk," pp. 32–39.

[23] P. Green, "Consumer Use of Information," in *On Knowing the Consumer*, ed. J. W. Newman (John Wiley and Sons, Inc., 1966), pp. 67–80.

[24] Tauber, "Why Do People Shop?" pp. 45–48.

include lost wages,[25] lost opportunities,[26] charges for child care, and so forth. Nonmonetary costs of search are less obvious but may have an even greater impact than monetary costs. Almost every external search effort has implicit in it the cost of physical and psychological strain. Frustration and inner conflict between the search task and other more desirable activities, as well as fatigue, are real psychological and physical costs that may shorten the search effort.[27]

FACTORS INFLUENCING THE LEVEL OF EXTERNAL SEARCH

The preceding discussion emphasized that external information search occurs when the expected benefits of the search are greater than the perceived costs of the search. In this section, we are going to examine three basic types of factors that influence the expected benefits and/or perceived costs of search: market characteristics, consumer characteristics, and situational characteristics.

Market characteristics

Market characteristics play a major role in determining the expected benefits and costs of information search. Market characteristics include price differences, product differentiation, branding, level of advertising, store location, sales personnel, point-of-purchase displays, and packaging and labeling.

Price The price of a product and the price differences among equivalent brands in a product class are perhaps the most influential factors in stimulating consumer search.[28] If the price of a product were trivial to the individuals involved or if the price difference among competing alternatives were negligible, there would not be an economic incentive to carry out an external search. A number of studies have shown that the higher the price level of the product category, the greater the amount of external information search.[29] For external search to be justified on eco-

[25] G. Becker, "A Theory of the Allocation of Time," *The Economic Journal* (September 1975), pp. 493–517.

[26] B. Marby, "An Analysis of Work and Other Constraints on Choice of Activities," *Western Economic Journal* (September 1970), pp. 213–25; and J. Mincer, "Market Prices, Opportunity Costs, and Income Effects," in *Measurement Economies,* ed. D. Patinkin (Stanford University Press, 1964).

[27] Bender, "Consumer Purchase"; Downs, "Consumer Efficiency," pp. 6–12; and T. Lanzetta and V. Kanareff, "Information Cost, Amount of Payoff, and Level of Aspiration as Determinants of Information Seeking in Decision Making," *Behavioral Science* (1962), pp. 459–73.

[28] Stigler, "Information Search," pp. 213–25.

[29] L. Bucklin, "Testing Propensities to Shop," *Journal of Marketing* (January 1966), pp. 22–27; Udell, "Prepurchase Behavior," pp. 50–52; Dommermuth, "Shopping Matrix," pp. 128–32; and A. Kleimenhagen, "Shopping, Specialty or Convenience Goods?" *Journal of Retailing* (Winter 1966–67), pp. 32–39.

nomic grounds, prices for the product category must be high enough so that a reasonable price savings can be obtained.[30] However, external search via telephone shopping has been found to be economically viable for relatively low-priced products.[31]

To illustrate the effect price can have on stimulating information search, consider the prices of five popular toys available in some 36 retail stores in Tucson, Arizona, approximately six weeks before Christmas in 1976. For the five toys shown in Table 16−5 prices varied from $51.27 to

TABLE 16-5
Price range of five toys

	Market prices	
Product	Low	High
Play Family Sesame Street	$12.97	$ 27.50
Magic Jewel	10.44	26.50
Weeble Treasure Island	12.99	24.00
Monopoly	3.88	9.00
The Six Million Dollar Man	10.99	18.95
Total	$51.27	$106.05

Source: Derived from "Fourth Annual Toy Survey," Tucson Consumers Council (1976).

$106.05. The price magnitude of the toys is considerable, but even more astonishing are the price differences. For many consumers concerned with the high cost of Christmas, this information published each year by the Tucson Consumers Council is extremely useful in stimulating external information search and lowering the cost of purchase.

As mentioned before, the costs of search to a particular consumer must also be considered before we can judge the amount of search effort justifiable in a particular purchase. In a simulation study of the toy market described above, an extended search effort was warranted only when the costs of search were fairly low.[32] This was partly due to the shape of the price distribution in this market. Other studies have reached similar conclusions.[33]

Product differentiation Instead of, or in addition to, price differentials, many product categories are characterized by variations in product features, style, and/or appearance. When consumers perceive a consid-

---

[30] L. Telser, "Searching for the Lowest Price," *American Economic Review* (1973), pp. 41−49; and M. Rothschild, "Searching for the Lowest Price When the Distribution of Prices Is Unknown," *Journal of Political Economy* (July−August 1974), pp. 689−711.

[31] Hawkins and McCain, "Investigation of Returns."

[32] R. Best, J. Cady, and G. Hozier, Jr., "Searching for the Lowest Price," *Arizona Review* (January 1978), pp. 1−7.

[33] Hawkins and McCain, "Investigation of Returns."

erable and important difference among brands based on a difference in features, style, and/or appearance, external information search is increased.[34] Highly differentiated products for which consumers engage in relatively extensive external search include clothing,[35] new furniture,[36] and automobiles.[37] For example, in a study of shopping for new living room furniture only 22 percent visited just one store before purchase.[38] Likewise, a study of the purchase of fashion-oriented clothing (women's hats) found substantial use of a variety of information sources.[39]

Branding The strategy behind branding a product is essentially one of encouraging repeat purchase and discouraging external information search. That is, a positive brand name can be easily stored in retention and retrieved for use in purchase decisions. For example, in a study of automobile purchases, external information seeking decreased as the number of repeat purchases of a particular car (i.e., brand) increased.[40] An analysis of information search among buyers of new cars and major appliances also showed that those with one brand in mind at the outset of the decision process averaged substantially less information seeking than those who initially considered two or more brands.[41] Thus, branding coupled with brand satisfaction can reduce information search.

Level of advertising Advertising is a potential source of information about product availability, features, prices, and places of purchase.[42] Since advertising is a relatively low cost source of information for the consumer, we would expect that it would be widely used. In addition, we might suspect a different pattern of external information search for products characterized by readily available advertising messages. However, the actual use of advertising messages by consumers is not clear.

A number of studies indicate that advertising is not a widely used information source. For example, only about 10 percent of the buyers of shoes and personal accessories report checking advertisements;[43] only

[34] Cox and Rich, "Perceived Risk," pp. 32–39; and Dommermuth, "Shopping Matrix," pp. 128–32.

[35] W. Dommermuth and E. Cundiff, "Shopping Goods, Shopping Centers, and Selling Strategies," *Journal of Marketing* (October 1967), pp. 32–36.

[36] B. LeGrand and J. Udell, "Consumer Behavior in the Marketplace—an Empirical Study in the Television and Furniture Fields with Theoretical Implications," *Journal of Retailing* (Fall 1964), p. 32; and Claxton et al., "Taxonomy of Prepurchase," pp. 35–42.

[37] Newman and Staelin, "Prepurchase Information," pp. 19–29.

[38] LeGrand and Udell, "Consumer Behavior," p. 32.

[39] C. King, "Communicating with the Innovator in the Fashion Adoption Process," in *Marketing and Economic Development,* ed. P. Bennett (American Marketing Association, 1965), pp. 425–40.

[40] Bennett and Mandell, "Prepurchase Information," pp. 430–33.

[41] Newman and Staelin, "Prepurchase Information," pp. 19–29.

[42] P. Nelson, "Information and Consumer Behavior," *Journal of Business* (March–April 1970), pp. 311–39; and P. Nelson, "Advertising Is Information," *Journal of Political Economy* (July–August 1974), pp. 729–54.

[43] G. Fisk, "Media Influence Reconsidered," *Public Opionion Quarterly* (1959), pp. 83–91.

19 percent recall obtaining information from advertisements in making food purchases;[44] and in the purchase of home appliances such as radios, hair dryers, toasters, and coffee makers, only 25 percent consulted newspaper ads, 15 percent read magazine advertising, 14 percent saw television advertising, and 7 percent listened to radio advertising before buying.[45] These figures are consistent with those shown for microwave ovens in Table 16–2.

Before we conclude that advertising has no effect, we should consider some contradictory evidence. Until very recently many states prohibited the advertisement of prescription drugs and eyeglasses. In both cases, states that prohibited price advertising of these products had significantly higher overall prices and a greater price difference among identical products than states that allowed such advertising.[46] Advertising in these cases was used by consumers to the extent that the overall price structure of the market was affected. Thus, the availability of advertising does appear to affect the search process and the price paid for some goods.

Store distribution　The number, location, and distances between retail stores in the market affect the number of store visits a consumer will make before purchase.[47] Because store visits take time, energy, and in many cases money, a close proximity of stores will increase this aspect of external search. On the other hand, if stores are few in number and relatively distant from one another, constraints on time and/or the costs of search may be such that fewer stores will be visited prior to purchase. The advent and growth of shopping malls has reduced this cost of external search among the stores in each mall.

Availability of sales personnel　Product categories vary considerably in the amount of personal selling involved. In those categories where sales personnel are available, they serve as an important information source. For example, in one investigation of customer-salesperson interaction, the average transaction lasted 23 minutes during which 75 percent of the time was spent giving information and providing clarification. Based on the amount and nature of information exchanged between customer and salesperson, 80 percent of the purchase outcomes could be determined from the interaction. Sales information on the limit of price concessions, delivery, styling, and warranty all contributed posi-

[44] L. Bucklin, "The Information Role in Advertising," *Journal of Advertising Research* (September 1965), pp. 11–15.

[45] Udell, "Prepurchase Behavior," pp. 50–52.

[46] J. F. Cady, "Restricted Advertising and Competition: The Case of Retail Drugs," *American Enterprise Institute for Public Policy Research* (March 1976), pp. 1–20; B. Rosenthal, "Retail Drug Price Competition," *Congressional Record House* (March 19, 1973); and L. Benham, "The Effect of Advertising on the Price of Eyeglasses," *Journal of Law and Economics* (October 1972), pp. 337–52.

[47] Nelson, "Advertising," pp. 729–54. See also G. S. Cort and L. V. Dominguez, "Cross-Shopping and Retail Growth," *Journal of Marketing Research* (May 1977), pp. 187–92.

tively to the chances of a customer purchase; when the salesperson "knocked" competitive brands, attempted to change price limits, made frequent reference to quality, or continually mentioned price, a purchase was less likely.[48]

Extent of point-of-purchase displays Point-of-purchase displays offer another potential source of information. In one study, 82 percent of 5,000 consumers indicated seeing at least two displays during a store visit, 44 percent said they used the display to make a purchase decision, and 33 percent purchased one or more of the items displayed.[49] Point-of-purchase displays have been shown to increase brand switching by 30 percent in drugstores[50] and 39 percent in liquor stores.[51] In another study the purchase of nonfood grocery store products was increased by 37 percent over normal shelf purchases by the use of displays without motion; by using displays with motion, purchases were increased by 83 percent over the normal shelf purchases.[52] Point-of-purchase displays appear to attract attention and provide information that is used by many consumers in their purchase decisions.

Packaging and labeling requirements A final source of information available to the consumer that varies across product categories is the label of a packaged good. Labeling of ingredients in descending order based on volume has been required for most food products for over 50 years. In the event a product has been fortified with nutrients and/or makes a nutritional claim, the manufacturer is now required to provide nutritional labeling. The addition of nutritional information to many food products was heralded as a major accomplishment and important move toward the full and complete disclosure of useful product information.[53] A number of studies, including some done by the Food and Drug Administration (FDA), have indicated that consumers want nutri-

[48] R. Willett and A. Pennington, "Customer and Salesman: The Anatomy of Choice and Influence in a Retail Setting," in *Science Technology and Marketing,* ed. R. Haas (American Marketing Association, 1966), pp. 598—616.

[49] "Awareness, Decision, Purchase," Point of Purchase Advertising Institute, New York, 1961, p. 14.

[50] "Drugstore Brand Switching and Impulse Buying," Point of Purchase Advertising Institute, New York, 1961, p. 14.

[51] "Package Store Brand Switching and Impulse Buying," Point of Purchase Advertising Institute, New York, n.d.

[52] "Motion Moves More Merchandise," Point of Purchase Advertising Institute, New York, n.d., p. 3. Also see "How In-Store Merchandise Can Boost Sales," *Progressive Grocer* (October 1971), pp. 94—97; "How the Basics of Special Display Affect Sales and Profits," *Progressive Grocer* (January 1971), pp. 34—45; and "How to Make Displays More Sales Productive" *Progressive Grocer* (February 1971), pp. 34—45.

[53] G. Bymers, "Seller-Buyer Communication: Point of View of a Family Home Economist," *Journal of Home Economics* (February 1972), p. 59; and A. Berloian, "Nutrition Labels: A Great Leap Forward," *FDA Consumer* (September 1973), p. 1.

tion labeling, claim they would use it, but seldom actually use it or understand it correctly in brand choice decisions.[54]

For example, one study found that only 25 percent of consumers studied were aware of the nutrition label, 15 percent understood it, and 10 percent used it in a purchase decision.[55] An FDA study found that 33 percent of the consumers they interviewed looked for ingredient labeling and only 5 percent looked for nutrition labeling.[56] Another study reported that the greatest impact of detailed nutrition labeling was a more favorable perception of product quality.[57] In a more recent study, Day has noted that the only apparent effect of nutrition labeling has been to increase consumer confidence in nutritionally labeled food products.[58]

Thus, while packages and labels are a potential source of information and the amount of data available on them varies widely across product categories, they do not appear to have a major impact on the external search process.

Consumer characteristics

While market characteristics have a major impact on external information search, a variety of consumer characteristics also affect perceptions of expected benefits, search costs, and thus the need to carry out a particular level of external search. In the following discussion we will look at the consumer characteristics of learning and experience, personality, perceived risk, social status, and age and stage in the family life cycle as these variables relate to external search.

Learning and experience   A satisfying experience with a particular brand is a positively reinforcing process (see Chapter 11) which increases the probability of a repeat purchase of that brand and decreases the likelihood of external search. As a result, external search is greater for consumers having a limited purchase experience with brands in a

---

[54] R. Lenahan, J. Thomas, O. Taylor, D. Call, and D. Padberg, "Consumer Reaction to Nutrition Labels on Food Products," *Journal of Consumer Affairs* (Summer 1973), pp. 1—4; U.S. Food and Drug Administration, "Consumers Talk about Labeling," *FDA Consumer* (February 1974); U.S. Food and Drug Administration, "The Food Labeling Revolution," *FDA Consumer* (April 1974); P. Daly, "The Response of Consumers to Nutrition Labeling," *Journal of Consumer Affairs* (Winter 1976), pp. 170—78; G. Day, "Assessing the Effects of Information Disclosure Requirements," *Journal of Marketing* (April 1976), pp. 42—52; and R. Best and J. McCullough, "Evaluation of Food Labeling Policies through Measurement of Consumer Utility," in *Advances in Consumer Research V*, ed. H. K. Hunt (Association for Consumer Research, 1978), pp. 213—19.

[55] Lenahan et al., "Consumer Reaction."

[56] U.S. Food and Drug Administration, "Consumers Talk."

[57] E. Asam and L. Bucklin, "Nutrition Labeling for Canned Goods: A Study of Consumer Response," *Journal of Marketing* (April 1973), pp. 32—37.

[58] Day, "Assessing the Effects."

particular product category.[59] For example, many new car buyers, based on a satisfying experience with a particular brand of automobile, repurchase that brand with very little information search.[60] The learning effect is particularly evident in studies of choice behavior where information search decreases very rapidly as consumers gain experience with a new brand set. This effect on information search and brand preference has been observed for products such as bread,[61] beer,[62] shirts,[63] and hairsprays.[64]

Personality and self-concept Motivation to carry out an external search is also influenced by the personality and self-concept of the consumer. For example, shoppers who see themselves as deliberate information seekers are more likely to engage in extensive external search prior to purchase than shoppers with a different self-concept.[65] Self-perceptions of household roles influence external search among women. Those who see themselves as traditionalists do little search and tend to do what their parents had done; women who see themselves as liberalists engage in less search as more time is devoted to other, nonhousehold activities; and those women who see themselves as the "mother" are strongly concerned with family welfare and have the strongest tendency to engage in an information search.[66]

Information search has also been related to consumer personality and predisposition in terms of enjoyment derived from shopping,[67] depending on others for information and advice[68] and open-mindedness and self-confidence.[69]

Perceived Risk We mentioned earlier that information search can

---

[59] P. Green, M. Halbert, and J. Minas, "An Experiment in Information Buying," *Journal of Advertising Research* (September 1964), pp. 17–23; and G. Hughes, S. Tinic, and P. Naert, "Analyzing Consumer Information Processing," in *Marketing Involvement in Society and the Economy,* ed. P. McDonald (American Marketing Association, 1969), pp. 235–40.

[60] Bennett and Mandell, "Prepurchase Information," pp. 430–33.

[61] W. Tucker, "The Development of Brand Loyalty," *Journal of Marketing Research* (August 1964), pp. 32–35.

[62] J. McConnell, "The Development of Brand Loyalty: An Experimental Study," *Journal of Marketing Research* (February 1968), pp. 13–19.

[63] J. Swan, "Experimental Analysis of Predecision Information Seeking," *Journal of Marketing Research* (May 1969), pp. 192–97.

[64] J. Sheth and M. Venkatesan, "Risk-Reduction Processes in Repetitive Consumer Behavior," *Journal of Marketing Research* (August 1968), pp. 307–10.

[65] R. Kelly, "The Search Component of the Consumer Decision Making Process—a Theoretic Examination," in *Marketing and the New Sciences of Planning,* ed. C. King (American Marketing Association, 1968), p. 273.

[66] L. Bucklin, "Consumer Search, Role Enactment, and Market Efficiency," *Journal of Business* (October 1969), pp. 416–38.

[67] Katona and Mueller, "Purchase Decision."

[68] Newman and Staelin, "Prepurchase Information."

[69] Green, "Consumer Use," pp. 67–80.

be motivated when the search effort is rewarded financially with a lower price paid. In many instances perceptions of risk due to performance of the product can also motivate greater information search prior to purchase.[70] For example, high fashion clothing items have greater perceived risk associated with them, and, as a result, more information is sought prior to purchase.

It is important to keep in mind that risk is subjective and may vary from one consumer to another as well as vary for the same consumer from one situation to another. For example, the purchase of a bottle of wine may not involve much risk when buying for one's own consumption. However, the choice of wine may involve considerable risk when buying wine for a dinner party for one's boss. To deal with risk in this particular situation, the consumer may buy the most advertised brand, the brand used before and found to be satisfactory, a well-known brand, a brand recommended by a friend whose opinion is respected, or the most expensive brand. Thus, we can see in this situation that the risk of buying an inappropriate wine for an important occasion could greatly influence the information search and brand choice decision. When perceived risk is high, consumers also try to reduce risk through personal and/or neutral sources of information such as the Good Housekeeping Seal, Underwriter's Laboratory, U.S.D.A. Choice, and other credible endorsements.

Social status variables As we saw in Chapter 7, social status exists along a number of dimensions in our society. Education, occupation, and income are the major dimensions. External search has been found to increase with increases in each of these categories. A direct relationship between level of education completed and amount information seeking has been found for buyers of major appliances,[71] new furniture,[72] homes,[73] new cars,[74] and food products.[75] When occupation was used as a measure of social class, the same relationship was found for

---

[70] See J. Jacoby and L. Kaplan, "The Components of Perceived Risk," in *Proceedings 3d Annual Conference,* ed. M. Venkatesan (Association for Consumer Research, 1972), pp. 382–93; T. Redelius, "Consumer Rankings of Risk Reduction Methods," *Journal of Marketing* (January 1971), pp. 56–61; S. Cunningham, "Perceived Risk and Brand Loyalty," in *Risk Taking and Information Handling in Consumer Behavior,* ed. D. Cox (Harvard University Press, 1967), pp. 507–23.

[71] Katona and Mueller, "Purchase Decisions"; and *Cooking Appliance Purchase and Usage Patterns* (Newsweek Inc., 1978), p. 27.

[72] Claxton et al., "Taxonomy of Prepurchase."

[73] D. Hempel, "Search Behavior and Information Utilization in the Home Buying Process" in *Marketing Involvement in Society and the Economy,* ed. P. McDonald, (American Marketing Association, 1969), pp. 241–49.

[74] Newman and Staelin, "Prepurchase Information."

[75] J. Pearce, "Are Americans Careful Food Shoppers?," *FDA Consumer* (September 1976).

major durables.[76] External search is greatest among middle-income individuals.[77]

The FDA conducted a study to determine the amount of information used by food shoppers by giving a shopper one point for each shopping aid used — making a shopping list, reading for specials, checking lists of ingredients, using unit pricing, looking for open dates, and using nutritional labeling. In a nationwide survey, 1,664 shoppers were interviewed and categorized as low, medium, or high in terms of amount of informa-

TABLE 16–6
Demographic characteristics of three classifications of shoppers in terms of their use of information prior to purchase of food products

Demographic characteristics	Amount of information used		
	Very little	Moderate	A great deal
All food shoppers	22%	50%	28%
Sex			
Female	20	50	30
Male	32	48	20
Education			
Less than High School	45	44	11
High School	20	51	30
College	14	52	34
Age			
18–34	20	50	31
35–49	19	52	29
50 and over	26	48	26
Race			
Nonblack	20	51	29
Black	35	42	23
Socioeconomic status			
Low	34	46	19
Medium	16	53	31
High	14	50	36
Nutrition knowledge			
Low	32	48	20
Medium	21	49	30
High	12	53	35

Note: Total percentages may not add to 100 due to rounding.
Source: J. Pearce, "Are Americans Careful Food Shoppers?" *FDA Consumer* (September 1976).

tion used; and in Table 16−6 these results are shown in relation to consumer characteristics. The results of this survey show that among col-

---

[76] Katona and Mueller, "Purchase Decisions"; and Newman and Staelin, "Prepurchase Information."

[77] Newman and Staelin, "Prepurchase Information"; and G. R. Foxall, "Social Factors in Consumer Choice: Replication and Extension," *Journal of Marketing Research* (June 1975), p. 62.

lege-educated shoppers only 14 percent were classified as low, while 45 percent of those not finishing high school were classified as low. The reverse is also true as only 11 percent of the shoppers who did not finish high school were classified as high in amount of information used, while 34 percent of the college-educated shoppers were classified as high. The socioeconomic status category provides similar results.

Age and stage in the family life cycle   Age of the shopper has also been found to be related to information search, but inversely. That is, external search appears to decrease as the age of the shopper increases.[78] This is reflected in Table 16−6 as the greatest percentage of shoppers who were classified as high in amount of information used were in the 18 to 34 age group and the smallest percentage of these shoppers were people 50 or over. This may be explained in part by increased learning and product familiarity with age.

Situational characteristics

As was indicated in Chapter 3, situational variables can have a major impact on search behavior. For example, recall that one of the primary reactions of consumers to crowded store conditions is to minimize the extent of external information search.[79] Temporal perspective is probably the most important situational variable with respect to search behavior. As the time available to solve a particular consumer problem decreases, so does the amount of external information search.[80] Gift-giving situations (task definition) tend to increase perceived risk which, as we have seen, increases external search.[81] Each of these variables is described in detail in Chapter 3.

MARKETING STRATEGIES BASED ON INFORMATION SEARCH PATTERNS

Internal search

Consumers generally respond to the recognition of a problem by checking long-term memory (retention) to see if a satisfactory solution is

---

[78] Hempel, "Search Behavior"; Katona and Mueller, "Purchase Decisions"; and Newman and Staelin, "Prepurchase Information."

[79] G. D. Harrell and M. D. Hutt, "Crowding in Retail Stores," *MSU Business Topics* (Winter 1976), pp. 31−39.

[80] See P. Wright, "The Harassed Decision Maker: Time Pressures, Distractions, and the Use of Evidence," *Journal of Applied Psychology* (October 1974), pp. 555−61.

[81] M. Vincent and W. G. Zikmund, "An Experimental Investigation of Situational Effects on Risk Perception," in *Advances in Consumer Behavior III*, ed. B. B. Anderson (Association for Consumer Research, 1976), pp. 125−29.

known. If a satisfactory solution is not known, then retention is scanned for appropriate evaluative criteria, potential solutions (evoked set), and information on the characteristics of the evoked set. Given the relatively limited amount of external information search described earlier, it appears that many consumers make decisions based solely or primarily on stored information. Therefore, marketers must attempt to influence the internal search process.

The simplest decision situation is problem recognition ("I am almost out of toothpaste") followed by internal information search which produces a single satisfactory solution ("I need to buy another tube of Close-Up soon"). This is known as *brand loyalty*. Since brand loyalty is primarily an outcome of a previous purchase, we treat it in detail in Chapter 19. At this point, we should note that marketers generally attempt to create loyalty to their brand so that sales will not be lost during the purchasing process. This requires consistent quality control so that each experience with the brand is reinforcing (see Chapter 11). In addition, the distribution system must be sound to avoid out-of-stock situations. Consumers have been found to purchase other brands of their evoked set in order of preference when their preferred brand was not available.[82] When no member of the evoked set is available, consumers may choose randomly from the inert set.[83] In either case, the purchased brand may replace the previously preferred brand in future purchases.

Just as marketers desire consumer loyalty to their brand, they hope to minimize loyalty to competing brands. Attracting brand loyal consumers away from competing brands may require a product alteration, a major price reduction, or the utilization of free samples. Since the percentage of consumers loyal to a given brand is generally low, marketers tend to concentrate more on influencing the evoked set.

Marketers want their brand to be considered acceptable by members of their target market. However, you may recall from Table 16 – 1 that most consumers consider only a few brands acceptable. For example, in Table 16 – 1 we can see that the average number of brands of toothpaste that consumers could recall was 6.5. However, the average number they would consider purchasing was only two. Since the evoked set guides further information search, how can a marketer place a brand in a consumer's evoked set?

The first step is to determine precisely where the brand stands among

---

[82] D. I. Hawkins and R. Best, "Utilization of Preference Choice Probabilities in Market Share Forecasts," paper presented at the 1975 Southwestern Marketing Association Conference.

[83] R. Best, "Validity and Reliability of Criterion-Based Preferences," *Journal of Marketing Research* (February 1978), pp. 154 – 60.

the target market.[84] Consider the three toothpaste brands A, B, and C as shown below:

How brand is perceived by target market	Brands		
	A	B	C
Unaware	60%	20%	10%
Awareness	40	80	90
Inert	20	60	20
Inept	5	5	55
Evoked	15	15	15

Each brand is in the evoked set of 15 percent of the market. However, the strategies to increase market share for each brand would differ significantly. Brand A needs to increase awareness, and Brand B needs to convert indifference into acceptance. Brand C may have to bring out a complimentary brand or make a major alteration in the existing brand to reduce the percentage of the market that considers their product to be inept.

Although the specific strategies involved in each of the three examples described above would differ, they would have to influence the consumer *at a time during which the consumer was not actively seeking the information*. Recall that the evoked set guides subsequent information search. Therefore, entry to the evoked set must often be gained prior to active problem recognition. This involves low-involvement learning (see Chapter 11) and the use of stimulus and tie-in factors to attract attention to the firm's messages (see Chapter 10). A vast amount of consumer advertising by manufacturers is designed to place or retain the firm's brand in the evoked set during a time when the consumer is not involved in a selective information search.

In addition to influencing the evoked set, messages aimed at the consumer during nonsearch may attempt to influence the perception of the appropriate evaluative criteria ("Be sure to check the warranty before you buy") or to associate performance characteristics with the brand ("Charmin is so squeezably soft"). The latter is also a very common goal of consumer goods advertising.

External search

Marketers can attempt to encourage external search so they can take advantage of existing search patterns. Encouraging external search may involve direct attempts to persuade individuals to search such as "Com-

---

[84] See Narayana and Markin, "Consumer Behavior."

pare before you buy" or "Ask someone who owns one." Or it may involve making the information readily available. Such approaches as comparison advertising[85] and unit pricing[86] assist the consumer in external search.

Marketers can utilize the patterns of search behavior existing in their target market for their product category. For example, assume you want to reach young mothers with information about a new skin care product for babies. Your research indicates that (1) "gentleness" and "soft aroma" are two important evaluative criteria, (2) the awareness set is small and the evoked set is limited to one, (3) external search is very common, and (4) women with two or more children and with the youngest child under four are the primary source of external information. This provides excellent guidance for a communications strategy. Of course, like most of the other applications we have discussed in this text, this one is specific to a particular product category and target market.

SUMMARY

Following problem recognition, consumers engage in a search for information on (1) the appropriate evaluative criteria for the solution of the problem, (2) the existence of various alternative solutions, and (3) the performance of each alternative solution on each evaluative criterion. The information search may be internal and involve retrieving information from memory. In addition to the internal search, consumers frequently engage in external search which involves consulting friends, professional sources, and/or advertisements.

For most product categories, most consumers have an evoked set which guides the search process. That is, when faced with a problem, most consumers can recall a limited number of brands that they feel are probably acceptable solutions. These acceptable brands, the evoked set, are the only ones that the consumer seeks additional information on during the remaining internal and external search process. Therefore, marketers are very concerned that their brands fall in the evoked set of most members of their target market. A substantial amount of advertising has this as its primary objective.

---

[85] See W. Wilkie and P. Farris, "Comparison Advertising: Problems and Potential, *Journal of Marketing* (October 1975), pp. 7 – 15; T. Shimp, "Comparison Advertising in National Television Commercials: A Content Analysis," in *Marketing in Tubulent Times*, ed. E. M. Mazze (American Marketing Association, 1975, pp. 504 – 8; R. D. Wilson, "An Empirical Evaluation of Comparative Advertising Messages: Subject's Responses on Perceptual Dimensions," in *Advances in Consumer Research III*, ed. B. B. Anderson (Association for Consumer Research, 1976) pp. 53 – 71; L. L. Golden, "Consumer Reactions to Comparative Advertising," *Advances in Consumer Research III*, ed. B. B. Anderson (Association for Consumer Reserch, 1976) pp. 63 – 67.

[86] See J. E. Russo, "The Value of Unit Price Information," *Journal of Marketing Research* (May 1977), pp. 195 – 201; J. M. Carman, "A Summary of Empirical Research or Unit Pricing in Supermarkets," *Journal of Retailing* (Winter 1972 – 73), pp. 63 – 76.

In addition to their own experiences and memory, consumers can seek information from three major types of external sources: (1) personal sources such as friends and family, (2) professional sources such as consumer groups, paid professionals, and government agencies, and (3) marketing sources such as sales personnel and advertising. The fact that only one of these three information sources is under the direct control of the firm suggests the need to pay close attention to product performance and customer satisfaction after the purchase.

Available evidence suggests that explicit external information search after problem recognition is somewhat limited. This emphasizes the need to communicate effectively with consumers prior to problem recognition. External search tends to increase as the importance of the purchase increases (often reflected in the price of the item) and as the risk involved in the purchase increases (reflected in part in the price of the item and the consumer's prior knowledge about the item). Individual characteristics such as education, self-concept, and past experiences, as well as market characteristics such as price range, brand variation, and level of advertising also affect the amount of external search.

It is often suggested that consumers should generally engage in relatively extensive external search prior to purchasing an item. However, this view ignores the fact that information search is not free. It takes time, energy, money, and can often require giving up more desirable activities. Therefore, consumers should engage in external search only to the extent that the expected benefits such as a lower price or a more satisfactory purchase outweigh the expected costs.

Firms generally want to minimize the external search engaged in by their current consumers. They attempt to do this in part by generating brand loyalty. In addition, marketers want their brand to be considered when consumers do engage in external search. This is generally approached by attempting to move one's brand into the target market's evoked set. This requires extensive marketing efforts at a time during which the consumer is not actively seeking information on the product.

REVIEW QUESTIONS

1. When does information search occur? What is the difference between internal and external information search?
2. What kind of information is sought in an external search for information?
3. What are evaluative criteria and how do they relate to information search?
4. How does a consumer's awareness set influence information search?

5. What role do the concepts of evoked set, inert set, and inept set play in a consumer's information search? Why are some brands in a consumer's evoked set and others in the inert or inept sets?

6. Of the products shown in Table 16−1 which product class is most likely to exhibit the most brand switching? Explain your answer in terms of the information provided in Table 16−1.

7. What are the primary sources of information available to consumers and what effect does each have on information search?

8. Discuss the different ways in which external information search can be evaluated.

9. Using the information presented in Table 16−3 discuss the differences in information search for refrigerators and electric irons. What factors might contribute to these differences?

10. How do nonsearchers, information searchers, and extended information searchers differ in their search for information? Which category of consumers appears most rational to you and why?

11. What factors might contribute to the search effort of consumers who are essentially one-stop shoppers? How do these factors differ in terms of how they influence information searchers and extended information searchers?

12. What factors have to be considered in the total cost of purchase? How might these factors be different for different consumers?

13. Explain how different market characteristics affect information search?

14. How do different consumer characteristics influence a consumer's information search effort?

15. How do grocery shoppers who use a great deal of information differ from shoppers who use very little information? (See Table 16−6.)

16. How do situational characteristics influence a consumer's prepurchase information search?

DISCUSSION QUESTIONS

1. How can Jeff evaluate the information search of potential buyers? How could he utilize the concepts developed in this chapter in terms of sources of information, awareness and classification of brands, and information sought in the purchase of mopeds and other competing products?

2. What marketing strategies would you recommend to Jeff that moped dealers use to stimulate shopper search such that potential buyers would include mopeds in their evoked set of alternative choices?

3. How would you assess the moped industry in terms of the marketing characteristics that influence shopper search? Of these characteristics, which should be changed in order to be more effective, and how

should they be changed in order to effectively influence the information search and purchase of Jeff's brand of moped?

4. What factors contribute to the size of an awareness set, evoked set, inert set, and inept set? How can these factors be used to explain differences in the size of these respective sets for toothpaste and beer?

5. Discuss those factors that may contribute to external information search and those factors which act to reduce external search for information before purchase of a new stereo and pair of shoes.

6. Is it ever in the best interest of a marketer to encourage potential customers to carry out an extended prepurchase search? Why or why not?

7. Discuss those consumer characteristics that affect prepurchase search and the nature of their effect.

8. Discuss the patterns of behavior that are revealed in Table 16−6 in terms of the relationship between demographic characteristics and amount of information used in the purchase of food products.

PROJECT QUESTIONS

1. Interview five other students (not in your class) and measure their evaluation of mopeds in terms of awareness, and as an evoked, inert, or inept transportation alternative. Also, ask them if:
   a. They have ridden on a moped.
   b. They know someone who has a moped.
   c. They have ever looked at one in a store.
   d. They would consider buying one if the price of gasoline reaches $4 a gallon.

   Assess your results in terms of how each student evaluated mopeds in relation to each student's degree of exposure to mopeds and buying intentions under the situation of $4 per gallon gasoline prices. To get a more complete picture of this marketing situation, the class should pool their results and make an overall assessment.

2. For the same four products listed in Table 16−1, ask three other students to list all the brands they are aware of in each product category. Then have them indicate which ones they would regularly consume (evoked set), which ones they were indifferent toward (inert set), and which brands of those they listed they strongly disliked and would not purchase (inept set). Arrange your results like they are shown in Table 16−1 and evaluate the similarities and differences between your results and those shown in Table 16−1.

3. Develop a short questionnaire designed to measure the information search consumers engage in prior to purchasing an automobile. Your questionnaire should include measures of variety of information sought as well as sources which provided this information. Also

include measures of the relevant consumer characteristics which might influence information search, as well as some measure of past experience in terms of automobile purchase. Then interview five consumers using the questionnaire you have developed. Analyze each consumer's response and then classify each consumer in terms of information search as either a nonsearcher, information searcher, or extended information searcher. Finally, the class should pool their classifications to get a more accurate picture of the search effort exhibited by consumers interviewed by the class.

4. Develop a questionnaire that measures the relative frequency with which consumers purchase their favorite soft drink and the size of their evoked, inert, and inept sets. Then interview five other students not enrolled in your class and obtain this information. Next, graph the relationship between the relative frequency of favorite soft drink purchases and the size of each respondent's evoked set, inert set, and inept set. Interpret your findings and compare them with the results found by others in your class.

17

Alternative evaluation and selection

The market for bubble gum in the United States is almost $400 million a year. The Wrigley Company recently announced plans to introduce a new brand of soft bubble gum—Hubba Bubba. According to a company executive, Hubba Bubba will offer "a real breakthrough, a difference nobody has." This difference is "amazing no-stick bubbles," which means that popped bubbles will not stick to the blower's face. The company will spend in the area of $10 million for media advertising during the product's first year.[1]

It is clear from the above example that Wrigley executives believe that the "stickiness" of bubble gum's bubbles is or can become an important factor in a particular target market's selection of a brand of bubble gum. Their product design and promotion decisions are based on this belief about how consumers evaluate brands of bubble gum.

In this chapter, we are going to analyze the evaluation and selection of a solution from among the available alternatives. We will concentrate on four main areas. First, the nature and characteristics of evaluative criteria (the features the product *should* have) will be described. Evaluative criteria are particularly important since consumers select alternatives based on their relative performance on the appropriate evaluative criteria. After examining evaluative criteria, we will focus on the ability of

---

[1] L. Edwards, "Wrigley Throws New Items into Battle for Market Lead," *Advertising Age* (April 2, 1979), p. 3.

consumers to judge the performance of products on key evaluative criteria. Next, we will examine the decision rules that consumers use in selecting one alternative from those considered. Finally, we will look at some of the marketing strategies that affect patterns of alternative evaluation and selection.

EVALUATIVE CRITERIA

Evaluative criteria are *the various features that a consumer looks for in response to a particular type of problem.* Wrigley executives clearly believe that stickiness is or can become an evaluative criterion for bubble gum. In the purchase of a 35mm camera, you might be concerned with the cost, weight, ease and speed of loading, and quality of lens. These would be your evaluative criteria. Someone else could approach the purchase of a 35mm camera with an entirely different set of evaluative criteria. In this section of the chapter, we are going to examine (1) the nature of evaluative criteria, (2) the measurement of evaluative criteria, and (3) the role of evaluative criteria in marketing strategy.

Nature of evaluative criteria

Evaluative criteria can differ in type, number, and importance. The type of evaluative criteria a consumer uses in a decision varies from *objectively specified* cost and performance type criteria to *subjective* criteria based on factors related to suitability such as style, color, prestige, and brand and retailer image. The number of evaluative criteria used in a consumer decision is generally less than six.[2] In some instances the number of criteria used may go substantially higher, largely depending on the product in question.[3] Naturally, for fairly simplistic products like toothpaste, soap, or facial tissue the number of evaluative criteria used in decision making are few. On the other hand, the purchase of an automobile, stereo system, or house may involve several criteria that the consumer would want to evaluate prior to purchase.

Whether there are few or many evaluative criteria, the criteria are likely to differ in their importance to the consumer, with one or two criteria standing out above all the others.[4] Though we often assume that

---

[2] J. Engel, R. Blackwell, and D. Kollat, *Consumer Behavior* (Dryden Press, 1978), p. 369; R. Allison and K. Uhl, "Influence of Beer Brand Identification on Taste Perception," *Journal of Marketing Research* (August 1964), pp. 36–39; and L. Anderson, J. Taylor, and R. Holloway, "The Consumer and His Alternatives: An Experimental Approach," *Journal of Marketing Research* (February 1966), pp. 62–67.

[3] M. Fishbein, "Attitude, Attitude Change, and Behavior: A Theoretical Overview," in *Attitude Research Bridges the Atlantic,* ed. P. Levine (American Marketing Association, 1975), p. 376.

[4] D. Cox, "The Measurement of Information Value: A Study of Consumer Decision Making," in *Emerging Concepts in Marketing,* ed. W. S. Decker (American Marketing Association, 1962), pp. 414–15; and F. Hansen, "Psychological Theories of Consumer Choice," *Journal of Consumer Research* (December 1976), p. 133.

the cost of a product would be one of the primary evaluative criteria used in brand selection, greater emphasis is frequently placed on less tangible criteria.[5] For example, in selecting a hair shampoo one consumer may look for dandruff control and therefore place great importance on that performance attribute relative to price, while another may not even consider dandruff control in evaluating shampoos, yet use price as a measure of a shampoo's quality.

To illustrate more realistically the possible range and type of evaluative criteria in consumer decision making, each of 13 hair shampoos and five of their respective cost and performance attributes are listed in Table 17–1. The staff of *Consumer's Research Magazine* evaluated these

TABLE 17–1
Evaluative criteria used by *Consumer's Research Magazine* in rating hair shampoos

Alternative brands	CR rating	Price (cents per ounce)	Reduction of surface tension in 1 percent water*	Soil removing ability†	Lathering ability in moderately hard water	pH‡
Bright Side	A	8.1	VG	A+	M	6.9
Head & Shoulders	A	17.2	VG	A+	M	7.4
Protein 21	A	18.4	G	A+	M	6.4
Alberto VO₅	A−	12.6	VG	A	M	7.3
Breck Basic with protein	A−	15.4	G	A+	L	7.2
Clairol Herbal Essence with protein	A−	11.1	G	A	M	6.1
Enden Dandruff Remover	A−	17.8	G	A	VL	7.3
Rinse Away Dandruff	A−	17.4	G	A	H	7.2
Breck One Dandruff Shampoo	B	23.2	F	A−	L	7.2
Clairol Great Baby with protein	B	18.2	G	A	M	5.8
Johnson's Baby Shampoo	B	15.6	G	A−	L	6.6
Lustre Creme	B	13.5	VG	A+	VL	7.4
Prell	B	12.4	VG	A	M	7.0

Note: A+ = Above average   VG = Very good   H = High
        A = Average   G = Good   M = Moderate
        A− = Below average   F = Fair   L = Low
                                 P = Poor   VL = Very low
* Reduction of surface tension refers to the ability to get hair wetter and hence allow hair to get cleaner.
† Soil removing ability refers to the ability to remove surface dirt from hair.
‡ pH refers to acidity and is a direct measure of comfort with respect to irritation when in the eye (generally the lower the value, the better).
Source: Developed from "Shampoos with herbs, balsams, protein, and eggs," *Consumer's Research Magazine* (April 1974), pp. 7–10.

13 shampoos on the basis of these criteria and classified them into three preference categories A, A-, or B. In this case we can observe the number of choice alternatives and the different types and number of evaluative

[5] A. Gabor and C. Granger, "Price Sensitivity of the Consumer," *Journal of Advertising Research* (December 1964), pp. 40–44; I. White, "The Perception of Value in Products," in *On Knowing the Consumer,* ed. J. Newman (John Wiley and Sons, Inc., 1966), pp. 101–2; G. Harris, "A Study of Why People Purchase New Products," in *Science, Technology and Marketing,* ed. R. M. Haas (American Marketing Association, 1966), pp. 665–85.

criteria used in brand evaluation. However, we do not know what importance the staff of *Consumer's Research* placed on these different evaluative criteria in order to arrive at their classification of each brand. No matter what importance they attached to each of the evaluative criteria, the importance would only be accurate for a small proportion of consumers, as individuals differ greatly in their selection of evaluative criteria and the relative importance they attach to them.

Examine the evaluative criteria shown in Table 17−1 closely. It is evident that some of the criteria used by *Consumer's Research* would not be used by the average consumer, at least not in the form used by *Consumer's Research*. Think back to your last purchase of shampoo. Were you deeply concerned about the ability of the shampoo to reduce surface tension in water? (Since the ability to reduce surface tension is directly related to cleaning ability, you probably considered it indirectly). Other evaluative criteria are not included in the list. For example, *Consumer's Research* did not consider the convenience or attractiveness of the package, form or color of the shampoo, or aroma. Yet these criteria might be as important to some consumers as the pH.

One criterion that would appear on many consumer lists of evaluative criteria is price. And, in order to enhance the consumer's ability to evaluate relative prices, the unit price (price per ounce) of each brand is provided by *Consumer's Research*. Had just the price and fluid ounces in the container been listed, the price differential between many shampoos would have been more difficult to discern. Therefore, many outlets now provide unit prices on the items they carry. Evidence indicates that this policy results in consumers spending less on the product category and an increase in the market shares of private brands. However, maximum benefits are obtained only when the unit prices are displayed in an easily readable summary list.[6]

Various agencies of the federal government have required that information on specific evaluative criteria be available on the package of certain products. For example, open dating, nutrition labeling,[7] and

---

[6] J. E. Russo, "The Value of Unit Price Information," *Journal of Marketing Research* (May 1977), pp. 193−201. See also C. Block, R. Schooler, and D. Erickson, "Consumer Reaction to Unit Pricing: An Empirical Study," *Mississippi Valley Journal of Business and Economics* (Winter 1971−72), pp. 36−46; J. Carman, "A Summary of Empirical Research on Unit Pricing in Supermarkets," *Journal of Retailing* (Winter 1972−73), pp. 63−71; W. J. Granger and A. Billson, "Consumers' Attitudes toward Package Size and Price," *Journal of Marketing Research* (August 1972), pp. 239−48; H. R. Isakson and A. R. Maurizi, "The Consumer Economics of Unit Pricing," *Journal of Marketing Research* (August 1973), pp. 277−85; W. E. Kilbourne, "A Factorial Experiment on the Impact of Unit Pricing on Low-Income Consumers," *Journal of Marketing Research* (November 1974), pp. 453−55; K. B. Monroe and P. J. LaPlaca, "What Are the Benefits of Unit Pricing?" *Journal of Marketing* (July 1972), pp. 16−22; I. Ross, "Applications of Consumer Information to Public Policy Decisions," in *Marketing Analysis for Societal Problems*, eds. J. N. Sheth and P. L. Wright (University of Illinois, 1974); and J. Russo, G. Krieser, and S. Miyashita, "An Effective Display of Unit Price Information," *Journal of Marketing* (April 1975), pp. 11−19.

[7] K. Monroe and P. Friedman, "Consumer Responses to Unit Pricing, Open Dating and Nutrient Labeling," in *Proceedings 3d Annual Conference,* ed. M. Venkatesan (Association for Consumer Research, 1972), pp. 361−69.

interest rates are required for a variety of products.[8] A major motivation for such requirements is to encourage consumers to increase the importance they attach to these types of evaluative criteria.

Measurement of evaluative criteria

Before a marketing manager or a public policy decision maker can develop a sound strategy to affect consumer decisions, it is necessary to determine (1) which evaluative criteria are used by the consumer, (2) how the consumer perceives the various alternatives on each criterion, and (3) the relative importance of each criterion. Because consumers may not or cannot verbalize their evaluative criteria for a product, it is often difficult to determine which evaluative criteria consumers are actually using in a particular brand choice decision. This is even more of a problem in determining the relative importance consumers attach to their evaluative criteria.

Determination of which evaluative criteria are used   To determine which evaluative criteria are used by consumers in a specific product decision, the marketing researcher can utilize either *direct* or *indirect* methods of measurement. *Direct* methods would include asking consumers what information they use in a particular purchase or, in a focus group setting, observing what consumers verbalize about products and their attributes. Of course, direct measurement techniques assume that consumers can and will provide data on the desired attributes. Recall from the Agree Shampoo example in Chapter 1 that consumers were able to express their concerns about oily hair. However, direct questioning is not always so successful. As we saw in the last chapter, consumers consistently state that they want nutritional labeling but rarely utilize it.[9]

Indirect measurement techniques differ from direct in that they assume consumers will not or cannot tell you directly what their evaluative criteria are. Hence, you must use other (indirect) methods such as projective techniques, which allow the person to indicate what criteria "someone else" might use. The someone else is very probably that person of course, and we have indirectly determined the evaluative criteria used.

Multidimensional scaling (MDS) is a useful indirect technique for determining evaluative criteria. It is an inference technique in which consumers judge the similarity of alternative brands, and then these judgments are processed via a computer to derive a spatial configuration or

---

[8] G. Day and W. Brandt, "Consumer Research and the Evaluation of Information Disclosure Requirements: The Case of Truth in Lending," *Journal of Consumer Research* (June 1974), pp. 21–32.

[9] R. Lenahan, J. Thomas, O. Taylor, D. Call, and D. Padberg, "Consumer Reaction to Nutrition Labels on Food Products," *Journal of Consumer Affairs* (Summer 1973), pp. 1–4; U.S. Food and Drug Administration, "Consumers Talk about Labeling," *FDA Consumer* (February 1974).

perceptual map of these brands.[10] No evaluative criteria are specified; the consumer simply ranks the similarity between all pairs of alternatives and a multidimensional configuration is derived in which the consumer's evaluative criteria are the dimensions of the configuration.

For example, consider the MDS configuration of soft drinks shown in Figure 17–1. This configuration was derived from one consumer's rank-

FIGURE 17–1
Multidimensional scale of consumer perceptions of eight brands of soft drink and evaluative criteria used to differentiate between these brands

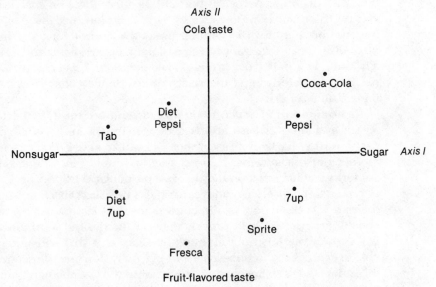

ing of the relative similarity of all pairs of the eight brands. Examining this configuration we can identify axis I as a "sugar versus nonsugar" dimension and axis II as a "cola versus fruit-flavored" dimension. This procedure allows us to identify evaluative criteria by inferring what the consumer used to differentiate between brands.

This procedure reflects only those criteria that differentiate the brands being considered. All eight brands in Figure 17–1 have similar carbonation levels. Carbonation does not, therefore, appear as a dimension. However, reducing or increasing the carbonation level of one of the brands could affect sales dramatically which would indicate that it was indeed an evaluative criteria. Since MDS isolates only criteria that currently differentiate brands, it is not effective for isolating desired but currently nonexistant criteria.

Determination of consumers' judgments of brand performance on

---

specific evaluative criteria There are a variety of methods available for measuring consumers' judgments of brand performance on specific attributes. These include *rank ordering scales, semantic differential scales, Stapel scales,* and *Likert scales.*[11] The semantic differential is probably the most widely used technique.

The semantic differential lists each evaluative criteria in terms of opposite levels of performance, that is, fast-slow, expensive-inexpensive, and so forth. These opposites are separated by five to seven intervals and placed below the brand being considered as shown below.

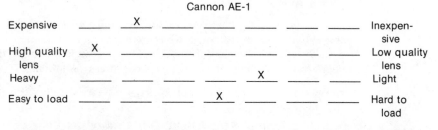

Cannon AE-1

Expensive		X					Inexpensive
High quality lens	X						Low quality lens
Heavy					X		Light
Easy to load				X			Hard to load

The consumers are asked to indicate their judgments on the performance of the brand by marking the blank that best indicates how accurately one or the other term describes or fits the brand. The end positions indicate "extremely," the next pair "very," the middle-most pair "somewhat," and the middle position "neither-nor." Thus, the respondent in the example above evaluates the Cannon AE-1 camera as very expensive with an extremely high quality lens, somewhat light, and neither easy nor hard to load.

Determination of the relative importance of evaluative criteria The measurement of the importance assigned to evaluative criteria can also be measured by either direct or indirect methods. The *constant sum scale* is the most common method of direct measurement.[12] To use this method the consumer is typically given 100 points to allocate to his or her evaluative criteria in accordance with the importance of each criteria. For example, in evaluating the importance of shampoo criteria, a 100-point constant sum scale could be used in the following way:

Evaluative criteria	*Importance (in points)*
Unit price	20
Surface tension reduction	0
Soil removing ability	40
Lathering ability in moderately hard water	30
pH	10
	100

[11] For details, see D. S. Tull and D. I. Hawkins, *Marketing Research* (MacMillan Publishing Co., 1980), chap. 9.

[12] J. Pavasars and W. Wells, "Measures of Brand Attitudes Can Be Used to Predict Buying Behavior," *Marketing News* (April 11, 1975), p. 6; and Tull and Hawkins, *Marketing Research.*

This consumer weighted soil removing ability highest, the lathering ability of the shampoo in moderately hard water second in importance, and unit price and pH third and fourth in importance. The other evaluative criterion was of no relevance to this consumer, as it was assigned zero importance.

One problem with the direct approach is that individuals tend to overweight less important criteria while giving less weight than appropriate to important criteria.[13] One psychologist offered the following explanation for this problem in overweighting minor criteria and underweighting major criteria:

> Possibly our feeling that we can take into account a host of different factors comes about because, although we remember that at some time or other we have attended to each of the different factors, we fail to notice that it is seldom more than one or two we consider at any one time.[14]

An increasingly popular indirect approach to measuring the relative importance of evaluative criteria is *conjoint analysis.* In conjoint analysis, the consumer is presented with a set of products or product descriptions in which the potential evaluative criteria vary.[15] The consumers rank-order these products in terms of their overall preference for them. A computer program then analyzes the preferences in light of the variations in the attributes and the result is a number which reflects the importance of each attribute. For example, speed and range were found to be a particularly important evaluative criteria in fleet operators' comparisons of conventional versus electric vehicles. In fact, these criteria were almost three times as important as the pollution control criterion.[16]

This method of examining consumer evaluative criteria has been used in the study of soft drinks,[17] housing alternatives,[18] travel behavior,[19] health care,[20] and new product design.[21]

---

[13] P. Slovic and S. Lichtenstein, "Comparison of Bayesian and Regression Approaches to the Study of Information Processing in Judgment," *Organizational Behavior and Human Performance* (November 1971), p. 684.

[14] R. Shepard, "On Subjectively Optimum Selection among Multiattribute Alternatives," in *Human Judgments and Optimality,* eds. M. Shelly, II, and G. Bryan (John Wiley and Sons, Inc., 1964), p. 266.

[15] For a simplified overview of the procedure, see Tull and Hawkins, *Marketing Research;* and P. E. Green and Y. Wind, "New Way to Measure Consumers' Judgments," *Harvard Business Review* (July—August 1975), pp. 107—17.

[16] G. Hargreaves, J. D. Claxton, and F. H. Siller, "New Product Evaluations: Electric Vehicles for Commercial Application," *Journal of Marketing* (January 1976), pp. 74—77.

[17] J. McCullough and R. Best, "Conjoint Measurement: Temporal Stability and Structural Reliability," *Journal of Marketing Research* (February 1979), pp. 26—31.

[18] J. Fiedler, "Condominium Design and Pricing," in *Proceedings 3d Annual Conference,* ed. M. Venkatesan (Association for Consumer Research, 1972), pp. 279—93.

[19] J. Davidson, "Forecasting Traffic on STOL," *Operations Research Quarterly* (December 1973), pp. 561—69; and R. Ross, "Measuring the Influence of Soft Variables on Travel Behavior," *Traffic Quarterly* (July 1975), pp. 333—46.

INDIVIDUAL JUDGMENT AND EVALUATIVE CRITERIA

Returning to our continuing effort to select a 35mm camera, suppose quality of the camera was one of your evaluative criteria. The simplest approach would be to apply a direct judgment based on a knowledge of optics, engineering, and craftsmanship. Such direct judgments are commonly applied to many evaluative criteria such as price, color, taste, and so forth. The issue of concern with respect to direct judgments is the ability of individuals to correctly assess the relative performance level of various brands on the evaluative criteria in question.

Few of us possess the necessary skills to make a direct assessment of the quality of a camera. Therefore, many of us would make an indirect judgment by utilizing the reputation of the brand or the price level to *infer* quality. An attribute such as price used to estimate the level of a different attribute such as quality is known as a *surrogate indicator.* Marketing managers need to be aware of the conditions in which consumers use surrogate indicators and the accuracy of these indicators.

Accuracy of individual judgments

The average consumer is not adequately trained to judge the performance of competing brands on complex evaluative criteria such as quality or durability. For more straightforward criteria, most consumers can and do make such judgments. Prices can generally be judged and compared directly. However, even this can be complex. Is a liter of Coca-Cola selling for 59 cents a better buy than a quart selling for 53 cents? Consumer groups have pushed for unit pricing to make such comparisons simpler. The federal Truth-in-Lending law was passed to facilitate direct price comparisons among alternative lenders.

The ability of an individual to distinguish between similar stimuli is called *sensory discrimination.*[22] This involves such variables as the sound of stereo systems, the taste of food products, or the clarity of photos. The minimum amount that one brand can differ from another with the difference still being noticed is referred to as the *just noticeable difference* (j.n.d.). Marketers seeking to find a promotable functional difference between their brand and a competitor's must surpass the j.n.d. in

[20] B. Parker and V. Srinivasan, "A Consumer Preference Approach to the Planning of Rural Health Care Facilities," *Operations Research* (September—October 1976), pp. 991–1025; and Y. Wind and L. Splitz, "Analytical Approach to Marketing Decisions in Health Care Organizations," *Operations Research* (September—October 1976), pp. 973–990.

[21] P. Green and V. Rao, "Conjoint Measurement for Quantifying Judgmental Data," *Journal of Marketing Research* (August 1971), pp. 355–63; P. E. Green and V. Srinivasan, "Conjoint Analysis in Consumer Research: Issues and Outlook," *Journal of Consumer Research* (September 1978), pp. 103–23; and I. Fenwick, "A User's Guide to Conjoint Measurement in Marketing," *European Journal of Marketing,* vol. 2 (1978), pp. 203–11.

[22] J. H. Myers and W. H. Reynolds, *Consumer Behavior and Marketing Management* (Houghton Mifflin Co., 1967), p. 15.

order for the improvement or change to have any noticeable impact on the consumer. On the other hand, a marketer may want to change a product feature but not have the consumer perceive any change and hence not surpass the j.n.d.

The higher the level of the original attribute, the greater the amount that attribute must be changed before the change will be noticed. Thus, a small addition of salt to a pretzel would not distinguish the product from a competitor's unless the competitor's pretzel contained only a very limited amount of salt. This relationship is expressed formally as:

$$j.n.d. = \frac{\Delta I}{I} = K$$

where

$j.n.d.$ = Just noticeable difference
I = Initial level of the attribute
ΔI = Change in the attribute
K = Constant that varies with each sense mode

This formula is known as Weber's law. Values for K have been established for several senses and can be utilized in the development of functional aspects of products.[23] More useful than the formula itself is the general principle behind it—*individuals typically do not notice relatively small differences between brands or changes in brand attributes.* Makers of candy bars have utilized this principle for years. Since the price of cocoa fluctuates widely, they simply make small adjustments in the size of the candy bar rather than altering price. Marketers want some product changes, such as reductions in the size of the candy bars, to go unnoticed. These changes must be below the j.n.d. Positive changes, such as going from a quart to a liter must be above the j.n.d. or it may not be worthwhile to make them (unless advertising can be used to convince people that they exist).

Packaging changes also can be determined by the j.n.d. Many times marketers want to redesign the package and improve it, but they must be careful that the consumer does not translate a change in the package to a change (unless it is positive) in the product quality and performance. Kendall Oil with its Pennsylvania motor oil, Helene Curtis with Everynight shampoo, and White Rock Corporation with White Rock club soda have all recently modified packages while maintaining the favorable image associated with the original package.

Marketers have been particularly interested in the taste aspect of sensory discrimination. Most consumers maintain that taste is their

---

[23] R. L. Miller, "Dr. Weber and the Consumer," *Journal of Marketing* (January, 1962), pp. 57–61.

[24] W. P. Margulies, "Don't Shock Buyers—Subtle Package Updates Are Best," *Advertising Age* (February 19, 1979), pp. 53–54.

primary evaluative criteria for most food and beverage products as well as for cigarettes and related products. In general, we can conclude that accurate taste judgments play only a minor role in determining brand success (unless, of course, the brand is unusually distinct).[25] For example, in one study 60 of 79 consumers were not able to identify Coca-Cola correctly more than twice out of four tries when it was paired with Pepsi-Cola or Royal Crown.[26] Similar tests and results have been reported with cigarettes, beer, and aspirin. Studies such as these suggest that actual taste characteristics may be of less importance than product image. Think for a moment about the advertisements for products such as beers, soft drinks, and so forth. Most such advertisements concentrate primarily on image or nonfunctional aspects of the product (the "Marlboro man" or the "Pepsi generation"). However, they also provide some statement about *why* the brand should *taste* better than a competitor's ("it's beechwood aged").

Use of surrogate indicators

Consumers frequently use an observable attribute of a product to indicate the performance of the product on a less observable attribute. For example, most of us use price as a guide to the quality of at least some products. An attribute used to stand for or indicate another attribute is known as a *surrogate indicator.*

Price has been found to influence the perceived quality of shirts, radios, and aftershave lotion;[27] beer;[28] carpeting;[29] and numerous other product categories.[30] These influences have been large but, as might be

---

[25] An overview of research in this area is in Myers and Reynolds, *Consumer Behavior,* pp. 15−20. See also S. H. Lane, J. Zychowski, and K. Lelii, "Cola and Diet Cola Identification and Level of Cola Consumption," *Journal of Applied Psychology* (April 1975), pp. 278−79.

[26] F. J. Thuzin, "Identification of Cola Beverages," *Journal of Applied Psychology* (July 1962), pp. 358−60.

[27] B. Render and T. S. O'Connor, "The Influence of Price, Store Name, and Brand Name on Perception of Product Quality," *Journal of the Academy of Marketing Science* (Fall 1976), pp. 722−30.

[28] J. D. McConnell, "Effects of Pricing Perception of Product Quality," *Journal of Applied Psychology* (April 1968), pp. 331−34.

[29] B. P. Shapiro, "Price Reliance: Existence and Sources," *Journal of Marketing Research* (August 1973), pp. 287−91; and J. E. Stafford and B. M. Enis, "The Price Quality Relationship: An Extension," *Journal of Marketing Research* (November 1969), pp. 456−58.

[30] See H. Leavitt, "A Note on Some Experimental Findings about the Meaning of Price," *Journal of Business* (July 1954), pp. 205−10; D. Tull, R. A. Boring, and M. H. Gonsior, "A Note on the Relationship of Price and Imputed Quality," *Journal of Business* (April 1964), pp. 186−91; F. Olander, "The Influence of Price on the Consumer's Evaluation of Products and Purchases," in *Pricing Strategy,* eds. B. Taylor and G. Wills (Brandon/Systems Press, 1970), pp. 50−69; Z. Lambert, "Price and Choice Behavior," *Journal of Marketing Research* (February 1972), pp. 35−40; D. Z. Newman and J. C. Becknell, "The Price-Quality Relationship as a Tool in Consumer Research," *Proceedings 78th Annual Conference* (American Psychological Association, 1970), pp. 729−30; J. R. Andrews and E. R. Valenzi, "The Relationship between Product Purchase Price and Blind Rated Quality," *Journal of Marketing*

expected, decline as visible product differences, prior product use, and additional product information increases. Brand name or brand reputation is often used as a surrogate indicator of quality. It has been found to be very important when it is the only information the consumer has available and to interact with or, on occasion, replace the impact of relative price.[31] Store image,[32] packaging,[33] and color[34] have also been found to affect perceptions of quality.

Surrogate indicators are also used for attributes other than quality. For example, the color of ice cream affects perceptions of flavor (a cream-colored ice cream tastes "richer") and the color of liquid detergents is used as an indicator of mildness.[35]

Marketing responses

Marketers recognize and react to the ability of individuals to judge evaluative criteria and to their tendency to use surrogate indicators. For example, most new consumer products are initially tested against competitors in *blind* tests. A blind test is one in which the consumer is not aware of the brand name of the product. Agree Shampoo was not introduced until blind tests indicated it was preferred over a target competitor.[36] These tests enable the marketer to evaluate the functional

Research (August 1970), pp. 393–95; K. Monroe, "The Influence of Price Differences and Brand Familiarity in Brand Preferences," *Journal of Consumer Research* (June 1976), pp. 42–49; and P. Raju, "Product Familiarity, Brand Name, and Price Influence on Product Evaluation," in *Advances in Consumer Research IV,* ed. W. D. Perreault, Jr. (Association for Consumer Research, 1977), pp. 64–71.

[31] J. C. Makens, "Effects of Brand Preference upon Consumers' Perceived Taste of Turkey Meat," *Journal of Applied Psychology* (August 1965), pp. 261–63; I. S. White, "The Perception of Value in Products," in *On Knowing the Consumer,* ed. J. W. Newman (John Wiley and Sons, Inc., 1966), pp. 90–106; Render and O'Connor, "Influence of Price"; J. Jacoby, J. Olson, and R. Haddock, "Price, Brand Name, and Product Composition Characteristics as Determinants of Perceived Quality," *Journal of Applied Psychology* (December 1971), pp. 470–79; D. Gardner, "Is There a Generalized Price-Quality Relationship?" *Journal of Marketing Research* (May 1971), pp. 241–43; and K. B. Monroe, "Buyers' Subjective Perceptions of Price," *Journal of Marketing Research* (February 1973), pp. 70–80.

[32] J. J. Wheatley and J. S. Y. Chiu, "The Effects of Price, Store Image, and Product and Respondant Characteristics on Perceptions of Quality," *Journal of Marketing Research* (May 1977), pp. 181–86; Render and O'Connor, "Influence of Price"; Stafford and Enis, "Price Quality"; and J. R. Andrews and E. R. Valenzi, "Combining Price, Brand, and Store Cues to Form an Impression of Product Quality," *Proceedings 79th Annual Conference* (American Psychological Association, 1971), p. 649.

[33] R. L. Brown, "Wrapper Influence on the Perception of Freshness in Bread," *Journal of Applied Psychology* (August 1958), pp. 257–60; Wheatley and Chiu, "Effects of Price"; and C. McDaniel and R. C. Baker, "Convenience Food Packaging and the Perception of Product Quality," *Journal of Marketing* (October 1977), pp. 57–58.

[34] D. M. Gardner, "An Experimental Investigation on the Price Quality Relationship," *Journal of Retailing* (Fall 1970), pp. 39–40; and Wheatley and Chiu, "Effects of Price."

[35] D. F. Cox, "The Measurement of Information Value: A Study in Consumer Decision Making," in *Emerging Concepts in Marketing,* ed. W. S. Decker (American Marketing Association, 1962), pp. 414–17.

[36] "Key Role of Research in Agree's Success Is Told," *Marketing News* (January 12, 1979), p. 14.

characteristics of the product and to determine if a j.n.d. over a particular competitor has been obtained.

Marketers also make direct use of surrogate indicators. For example, Andecker is advertised as "the most expensive taste in beer." This is an obvious attempt to utilize the price — quality relationship that many consumers believe exists for beer. A marketer stressing the rich taste of a milk product would want to make it cream colored rather than white and a hot, spicy sauce would be colored red.

Marketers utilize brand names as indicators of quality in a number of ways. Elmer's glue stresses the well-established reputation of its brand in promoting a new super glue (ads for Elmer's Wonder Bond say "Stick with a name you can trust").[37] And Texaco ("We're working to keep your trust") focuses almost entirely on the firm's image rather than on product attributes.

Brands that are facing well-established competitors have difficulty convincing consumers of the equality or superiority of their product. In one test, an unknown brand of adding machine and a well-known brand were distributed to a number of users under three conditions: (1) with brand labels removed, (2) with correct brand labels, and (3) with the brand labels reversed. In the blind test (number 1 above), the unknown brand was rated somewhat superior. In the correct label test, the unknown brand was rated somewhat inferior. Finally, in the reversed label test, the unknown brand was rated far superior.[38]

How can a lesser known brand convince a target market that it is equal or superior to a more prestigious competitor? Carnation has sought to convince consumers that its Coffee-mate nondairy creamer tastes as good in coffee as cream does by advertising the results of a well-controlled blind taste test which confirmed this.[39] Sylvania has followed a similar strategy by advertising the results of blind tests between one of its models of television sets and similar models by General Electric, RCA, Sears, Sony, and Zenith.[40] Blitz (versus Budweiser) and Pepsi (versus Coca-Cola) have used similar strategies. In fact the Pepsi — Coca-Cola comparisons touched off a national advertising war with Pepsi claiming a two to one preference over Coca-Cola in blind taste tests, and Coke countering with commercials claiming "one sip isn't enough" and generally trying to discredit the taste test process.[41] Similarly, Perrier is

[37] "Borden after Instant Glue Lead, but Finding No. 1 a Sticky Matter," *Advertising Age* (February 26, 1979), p. 3.

[38] White, "Perception of Value."

[39] "Carnation's Taste Test of Coffee-mate and Cream," in *Marketing Research*, eds. D. S. Tull and D. I. Hawkins (MacMillan Publishing Co., 1980).

[40] "Sylvania's Evaluation of Consumer Preferences for Color Television Pictures," in *Marketing Research*, eds. Tull and Hawkins.

[41] "Coke Touts 2 to 1 N.Y. Margin as Pepsi Changes Dallas Letters," *Advertising Age* (June 28, 1976), p. 2; N. Giges, "Pepsi Co. Ad Insists: No Question—Coke Drinkers Prefer Pepsi," *Advertising Age* (July 19, 1976), p. 2; and "One Sip Not a Taste Test, Coke Tells New Yorkers," *Advertising Age* (August 16, 1976), p. 6.

under attack from Canada Dry which claims that in a blind test, connoisseurs preferred club soda over Perrier.[42]

Advertising the results of blind tests is not the only way to attack a well-known competitor. Appropriate pricing, packaging, promotion, and distribution can establish a quality image with no reference to competitors. However, the approaches described above represent a very direct recognition of the role of surrogate indicators and one approach to utilizing this knowledge.

DECISION RULES

Let us return to our camera purchase for a moment. Suppose you have evaluated a particular model of each of the three brands in your evoked set on price, weight, lens quality, and ease of loading. Further suppose that each brand excells on one attribute but falls short of one or more of the other remaining attributes as shown below:

Brand ranking

Attribute	Canon	Nikon	Minolta
Price	2	1	3
Weight	1.5	3.0	1.5
Lens	3	1	2
Loading	2	2	2

* A rank of 1 is most favorable.

Which brand would you select? The answer would depend upon the decision rule you utilize. We are going to describe five decision rules that consumers frequently use either singularly or in combination: disjunctive, conjunctive, lexicographic, elimination by aspects, and compensatory.

Disjunctive decision rule

The disjunctive decision rule or choice model is used when *only a single evaluative criterion is utilized in selecting a brand.* That is, the consumer would select that brand which performed best based on the consumer's evaluation of one attribute across all brands. For example, from the information presented in Table 17–1, a consumer interested *only* in the lathering ability of a shampoo in moderately hard water would choose Rinse Away Dandruff, because of the 13 shampoos shown, Rinse Away Dandruff shampoo provides the highest evaluative rating on

[42] "Canada Dry Soda Joints Ranks of Perrier Needlers," *Advertising Age* (February 19, 1979), p. 3.

this product attribute. If you were using a disjunctive decision rule with price as the criterion, which brand of camera would you select?

The disjunctive rule is often used by price shoppers to select from among the brands in their evoked set. In addition, it may be used by hobbyists and others seeking excellent performance on one attribute. However, it is probably used most often in combination with the conjunctive decision rule.

Conjunctive decision rule

A conjunctive decision rule is frequently used in combination with other rules, yet it can provide a single brand selection under certain circumstances.[43] The conjunctive choice rule *establishes minimum required performance standards for each evaluative criterion.* For example, assume the information in Table 17−1 represented a consumer's evaluations of the shampoo brands. Further assume a conjunctive choice rule establishing the following cutoff points for the evaluative criteria:

Evaluative criteria	Cutoff point
Price (oz.)	0.12
Reduction in surface tension 1 percent water	F
Soil-removing ability	A
Lathering ability in moderately hard water	M
pH	7.0

Any brand falling below any of these minimum standards would be eliminated from further consideration. In this example, all but two brands are eliminated from further consideration—Bright Side and Clairol Herbal Essence with protein. These are the only two shampoos that meet or exceed the minimum standards established by the consumer who utilizes this conjunctive decision rule. Under these circumstances either brand may be equally satisfying for the consumer in which case 50 percent of the time the consumer might select Bright Side and 50 percent of the time Clairol Herbal Essence with protein. Or, the consumer may choose to use another decision rule to select a single brand from these two shampoos.

Because we have limited ability to process information, the conjunctive rule is very useful in reducing the size of the information processing task to some manageable level by first eliminating those alternatives which do not meet minimum standards. This is often done in the pur-

---

[43] J. Payne, "Heuristic Search Processes in Decision Making, in *Advances in Consumer Research III*, ed. B. B. Anderson (Association for Consumer Research, 1976), pp. 321−27.

chase of such products as homes or rental of apartments, as a conjunctive rule is used to eliminate alternatives that are out of a consumer's price range, outside the location preferred, or that do not offer the features desired in the home or apartment they are seeking. Once alternatives not providing these features are eliminated, another choice rule may be used to make a brand choice among those alternatives that satisfy these minimum standards.

In addition, the conjunctive decision rule is commonly used in a satisfying strategy with an *acquisition by processing brands* procedure (see Chapter 10). That is, the consumer evaluates the brands in the evoked set one at a time. The first brand that meets all the minimum requirements is selected. This is a common approach to the purchase of items of limited importance to the consumer. Finally, the conjunctive rule probably underlies all of the other decision rules. That is, any brand in a consumer's evoked set is assumed to perform at some minimal level on all relevant evaluative criteria.

Lexicographic decision rule

The lexicographic decision rule is an extension of the disjunctive choice rule in that it allows for additional evaluative criteria but only when needed. That is, *if a brand cannot be selected using the consumer's most important evaluative criterion, then the consumer's second most important evaluative criterion would be used to evaluate the remaining alternatives.* If this does not provide a single brand choice, then the procedure would continue in accordance with the order of important evaluative criteria.

For example, assume that a particular consumer ranked "reduction in surface tension" as the most important evaluative criterion; "lathering ability" as the second most important evaluative criterion; and unit price as the third most important evaluative criterion for selecting a shampoo. Using a lexicographic decision rule the first evaluative criterion would provide the consumer with Head & Shoulders and Prell as the two shampoos that scored the highest (i.e., both VG) on this consumer's most important evaluative criterion. Because they are both rated very good, a choice cannot be made between the two brands and therefore the second most important evaluative criterion is brought into the picture to assist in breaking the tie. All other brands are permanently removed from further consideration regardless of other redeeming qualities. In this case both brands were evaluated as moderate in terms of lathering ability. Thus, a choice still cannot be made, and the third most important evaluative criterion is brought into consideration. In this case Prell is less expensive (12.4¢/oz. versus 17.2¢/oz.), and the consumer's choice would be Prell based on a lexicographic choice process.

If you rated ease of loading as your most important criterion, weight second, price third, and quality of lens fourth, which brand of camera would you select using a lexicographic decision rule (based on the hypothetical performance levels presented earlier)?

Elimination-by-aspects decision rule

The elimination-by-aspects decision rule is similar to a combination conjunctive-lexicographic decision rule. The idea behind this decision rule is to eliminate those alternatives that do not possess selected aspects in terms of a brand's attributes. Aspects (i.e., performance characteristics) of attributes that are common to all alternatives are not included since they will not differentiate alternatives in the choice process. For example, in the purchase of a new car a consumer using this decision rule may first select an automatic transmission as a desired aspect of the alternative they seek; this will eliminate all cars that do not have this feature. Given the remaining alternatives another aspect, say an $8,000 price limit, is selected and all cars whose price exceeds this limit are excluded. The process continues until all cars but one are eliminated. The final alternative possesses a feature (i.e., aspect) that no other alternative provides. This unique feature is often referred to as a *determinant attribute*.[44] Thus, a determinant attribute can be critical in the selection of a particular brand. Identification of such attributes is obviously important to a firm's marketing success, since it is this information that often determines brand or store selection. For example, store location and price have been shown to be determinant attributes in selecting a food store, and value for the money, assortment, and quality are determinant attributes in selection of fashion clothing stores.[45]

While this decision rule is closely related to the lexicographic decision rule, elimination by aspects requires no specific ordering of attributes. There is an equal chance of any attribute being considered at each stage of the choice process. An important characteristic of this rule is that the importance of evaluative criteria do not play a major role in the selection of a brand alternative; rather the determining attribute may be a less significant attribute that is unique to only one brand. The following narrative of a television advertisement illustrates the logic of brand selection using elimination by aspects.

> "There are more than two dozen companies in the San Francisco area which offer training in computer programming." The announcer puts some two dozen eggs and one walnut on the table to represent the alternatives and continues: "Let us examine the facts. How many of these schools

---

[44] M. Alpert, "Identification of Determinant Attributes: A Comparison of Methods," *Journal of Marketing Research* (May 1971), pp. 184–91.

[45] S. Arnold, M. Sylvia, and D. Tigert, "A Comparative Analysis of Determinant Attributes in Retail Store Selection," in *Advances in Consumer Research V*, ed. H. K. Hunt (Association for Consumer Research, 1978), p. 663.

have on-line computer facilities for training?" The announcer removes several eggs. "How many of these schools have placement services that would help find you a job?"

The announcer removes some more eggs. "How many of these schools are approved for veterans' benefits?" This continues until the walnut alone remains. The announcer cracks the nutshell and concludes: "This is all you need to know in a nutshell."[46]

The advertisement demonstrates the logic of elimination by aspects in selecting a computer programming school. The advantage of this decision rule is that in choosing among many complex alternatives such as new cars or computer training schools, one typically faces an overwhelming amount of relevant information and this decision rule is easy to use.

Compensatory decision rule

Each of the four previous decision rules are noncompensatory choice rules, since very good performance on one evaluative criterion cannot compensate for poor performance on another evaluative criterion. On occasion, consumers may wish to average out some very good features with some less attractive features of a product in determining overall brand preference in a choice decision. Therefore, the compensatory decision rule states *that the brand that rates highest on the sum of the consumer's judgments of the relevant evaluative criteria will be chosen.* This can be illustrated as:

$$R_b = \sum_{i=1}^{n} W_i B_{ib}$$

where:

R_b = Overall rating of alternative b.
W_i = Importance or weight attached to evaluative criterion i.
B_{ib} = Evaluation of brand b on evaluative criterion i.
n = Number of evaluative criteria considered relevant.

This particular decision rule has been the subject of extensive empirical testing as well as theoretical analysis.[47] Referring again to Table 17–1, assume that a particular consumer views Enden's unit price of 17.8 cents per ounce as very poor because it is a relatively high price and evaluates Enden's pH as good, its soil-removing ability as fair, and lathering ability in moderately hard water as very poor since it is given a rating of very low. To represent these evaluations numerically, we can score an evaluation of very good equal to 5, good equal to 4, fair equal to 3, poor

---

[46] A. Tversky, "Elimination by Aspects," *Psychological Review* (July 1972), pp. 281–99.

[47] See M. Fishbein and I. Ajzen, *Belief, Attitude, Intention and Behavior: An Introduction to Theory and Research* (Addison-Wesley Publishing Co., 1975).

equal to 2, and very poor equal to 1. Then if the consumer weights these evaluative criteria as we illustrated earlier with the 100-point constant sum scale (see page 445), then we can compute a numerical rating for Enden as shown below:

$$
\begin{aligned}
R_{\text{Enden}} &= W_1B_1 + W_2B_2 + W_3B_3 + W_4B_4 \\
&= (20)(1) + (10)(4) + (40)(3) + (30)(1) \\
&= 20 + 40 + 120 + 30 \\
&= 210
\end{aligned}
$$

Of course, a rating of 210 for Enden does not mean much until it is contrasted with the ratings of other brands in the evoked set. For the same consumer, Lustre Creme might rate as:

$$
\begin{aligned}
R_{\text{Lustre Creme}} &= (20)(4) + (10)(4) + (40)(5) + (30)(1) \\
&= 80 + 40 + 200 + 30 \\
&= 330
\end{aligned}
$$

A consumer using a compensatory decision rule and considering only these two brands would select Lustre Creme.

Which decision rules are used by consumers?

While consumers do not necessarily assign explicit numerical weights to the importance of attributes or assign numerical scores to the performance levels of various brands, these choice models are reasonable representations of the decision rules commonly used by consumers in brand selection.

To date, we cannot answer the question as to which rules are used by consumers in which situations. Some research has been done in specific situations that indicates that people *do use* the rules. A marketing manager then will have to determine, for the market segment under consideration, which is the most likely rule and translate that into the appropriate information strategy.

In Table 17 − 2 we have listed eight different decision rules, a verbal description of each, and the number of individuals who used these choice rules in making an automobile brand selection when given seven automobile attributes. In this case 174 undergraduate marketing students evaluated this information in making brand choice decisions. For this task well over 58 percent of the students used a lexicographic rule, whereas a little less than a third used a compensatory rule. Only one student used a conjunctive model, and nine used a conjunctive choice model along with a compensatory model. None of the students used any form of a disjunctive choice model.[48]

---

[48] M. Reilly and R. Holman, "Does Task Complexity or Cue Intercorrelation Affect Choice of an Information Processing Strategy: An Empirical Investigation," in *Advances in Consumer Research IV*, ed. W. D. Perreault, Jr. (Association for Consumer Research, 1977) pp. 185−90.

TABLE 17–2
Brand choice models and their relative use in selecting a brand of automobile based on seven car attributes

Brand choice rule	Verbal description	Percent using this choice rule
Disjunctive	I chose the car that had a really good rating on at least one characteristic.	0 %
Conjunctive	I chose the car that didn't have any bad ratings.	0.5
Lexicographic	I looked at the characteristic that was most important to me and chose the car that was best in that characteristic. If two or more of the cars were equal on that characteristic, I then looked at my second most important characteristic to break the tie.	58.5
Compensatory	I chose the car that had a really good rating when you balanced the good ratings with the bad ratings.	31.0
Disjunctive-conjunctive	I first eliminated any car that didn't have at least one really good score and then chose from the rest the product that didn't have a really bad score on any characteristic.	0
Conjunctive-disjunctive	I first eliminated the cars with a bad rating on any characteristic and then chose from the rest the one with a high score on any characteristic.	0
Disjunctive-compensatory	I first eliminated any car that didn't have at least one really good rating and then chose from the rest of the cars that seemed the best when you balanced the good ratings with the ones that were bad.	1.0
Conjunctive-compensatory	I first eliminated the cars with a really bad rating on any characteristic and then chose from the rest the one that seemed the best overall when you balanced the good ratings with the bad ratings.	5.0

Source: Derived from M. Reilly and R. Holman, "Does Task Complexity or Cue Intercorrelation Affect Choice of an Information Processing Strategy: An Empirical Investigation," in *Advances in Consumer Research IV*, ed. W. D. Perrault, Jr. (Association for Consumer Research, 1977), pp. 185–90.

Selection and usage of a particular information processing strategy did not change when the information processing task was made more difficult by either increasing the number of brands to be evaluated or by randomizing the information provided. Other research has shown that consumers are fairly consistent in their use of decision rules, as identical or very similar rules were used in the selection of different products and stores.[49] However, the time horizon involved[50] and product complexity and product familiarity have been found to influence the decision rules used.[51]

Marketing applications of decision rules

It is important for marketing managers to be aware, if possible, of the decision rules being used by their target market. Suppose that lens quality is the most important attribute to a group of potential camera consumers, with price second most important. If a lexicographic or disjunctive decision rule is being used by a significant portion of this group, the firm *must* meet or exceed the competition on lens quality. If most of the consumers are utilizing a compensatory model, lens quality might be reduced to a point slightly below the competition *if* a more than offsetting price decrease can be obtained.

The type of decision rule used by the target market for the product in question will influence the product design as described above. In addition, the nature and amount of information carried in advertising messages should be influenced by this variable. Advertising based on a conjunctive decision rule would carry information on all the relevant attributes, while advertisements based on a lexicographic rule would stress the most important attributes.

MARKETING STRATEGY AND ALTERNATIVE EVALUATION

It is obvious that marketing strategy must be based on information and assumptions about how consumers evaluate alternatives and make brand selections. We have tried to indicate the relationship between consumer approaches to alternative evaluation and marketing strategies throughout the chapter. In this section we are going to describe a very common, direct utilization of this material in the development of marketing strategy—*benefit segmentation.*

Benefit segmentation involves *segmenting the market for a given product* based on the primary evaluative criterion used or that one

[49] R. Blattberg, P. Peacock, and S. Sen, "Purchasing Strategies across Product Categories," *Journal of Consumer Research* (December 1976), pp. 143–54.

[50] P. Wright and B. Weitz, "Time Horizon Effects on Product Evaluation Strategies," *Journal of Marketing Research* (November 1977), pp. 429–43.

[51] C. W. Park, "The Effect of Individual and Situation-Related Factors on Consumer Selection of Judgment Models," *Journal of Marketing Research* (May 1976), pp. 144–51.

TABLE 17-3
1974 bank benefit segments*

	Segment 1 Front runners (n = 8)	Segment 2 Loan seekers (n = 51)	Segment 3 Representative subgroup (n = 118)	Segment 4 Value seekers (n = 89)	Segment 5 One-stop bankers (n = 78)
Principle benefits sought	· Large · Bank for all · Good advertising	· Good reputation · Loans easily available · Low loan interest	· No differences (about average on all benefits sought)	· High savings interest · Quick service · Low loan interest · Plenty of parking	· Wide variety of services · Convenient hours · Quick service Encourages financial responsibility Convenient branch
Banks favored	· Commercial bank A	· Commercial B · Savings X	· Commercial A · Commercial B	· Savings Y · Savings Z	· Commercial A · Commercial B
Demographic characteristics	· Young · Rent home	· More transient More blue-collar		· Tend to save more	Older
Lifestyle characteristics†	High ability to manage money	· Liberal about use of credit · Positive about bank loans		· Conservative overall lifestyle · Conservative about use of credit Low propensity toward risk taking	· Conservative about use of credit Positive toward checking account

* Because consistency was high between both split halves, the results shown here represent the overall sample.
· Items similarly characterized the same segment in the 1972 survey.
‡ Dimensions represent factor scores of all 196 general and banking-specific lifestyle items.
Source: R. J. Calantone and A. G. Sawyer, "The Stability of Benefit Segments," *Journal of Marketing Research* (American Marketing Association, August 1978), p. 400.

evaluative criterion in a compensatory decision rule that is rated very heavily. For many product categories, consumers could base their decisions on a number of evaluative criteria. These evaluative criteria represent the benefits the consumers hope to derive from the product. Benefit segmentation involves developing a unique marketing strategy for each group of consumers that is seeking a unique benefit.[52]

Consider Table 17–3. It illustrates five potential market segments for bank services based on the primary evaluative criterion utilized (benefit sought).[53] It also indicates that a substantial group, referred to as the "representative subgroup" in the table, are using a conjunctive or compensatory decision rule with nearly equal weights. In addition, it suggests characteristics associated with individuals seeking each benefit. The value of this approach for developing marketing strategy should be apparent in the development of advertising themes, specific attributes desired, evoked set determination, and so forth.

SUMMARY

As and after consumers have gathered information about various alternative solutions to a recognized problem, they evaluate the alternatives and select the course of action that seems most likely to solve the problem.

Evaluative criteria are the various features that a consumer looks for in response to a particular problem. They are the performance levels or characteristics that consumers use to compare different brands in light of their particular consumption problem. The number, type, and importance of evaluative criteria used differ from consumer to consumer and across product categories. Since evaluative criteria are the factors the consumer considers in a purchase decision, it is important for the marketing manager to know which criteria are used by the relevant target market.

The measurement of (1) which evaluative criteria are used by the consumer, (2) how the consumer perceives the various alternatives on each criterion, and (3) the relative importance of each criterion is a critical first step in utilizing evaluative criteria to develop marketing strategy. While the measurement task is not easy, a number of techniques ranging from direct questioning to projective techniques to multidimensional scaling are available.

A number of evaluative criteria such as price, size, and color can be judged easily and accurately by consumers. Others, such as quality, durability, and health benefits are much more difficult to judge. For

[52] R. I. Haley, "Benefit Segmentation: A Decision-Oriented Research Tool," *Journal of Marketing* (July 1968), pp. 30–35.

[53] R. J. Calantone and A. G. Sawyer, "The Stability of Benefit Segments," *Journal of Marketing Research* (August 1978), pp. 395–404.

example, numerous studies have shown that many consumers cannot distinguish between brands of soft drinks, beers, cigarettes, and other products. In such cases, consumers often use price, brand name, or some other variable as a surrogate indicator for quality. To overcome such surrogate indicators, many lesser-known or lower-priced brands advertise the results of (or encourage participation in) blind brand comparisons.

When consumers judge alternative brands on several evaluative criteria, they must have some method to select one brand from among those evaluated. Decision rules serve this function. A decision rule specifies how a consumer compares two or more brands. The five commonly used decision rules are disjunctive, conjunctive, lexicographic, elimination by aspects, and compensatory. The marketing manager must be aware of the decision rule(s) used by the target market since different decision rules require different marketing strategies. For example, a target market using a disjunctive or lexicographic decision rule would require the marketing manager to develop a product that excelled on the most important attribute. If the market used a conjunctive decision rule, a much more balanced product in terms of attribute performance levels would be required.

Marketers recognize and utilize differing consumer preferences for evaluative criteria within the same product category. This is the underlying basis of all segmentation strategies. This utilization of evaluative criteria is most evident in benefit segmentation. Benefit segmentation involves segmenting the market for a given product based on the primary or most important evaluative criterion used by groups of consumers.

REVIEW QUESTIONS

1. What are evaluative criteria and on what characteristics can they vary?
2. What are the ways in which marketing can determine which evaluative criteria consumers use?
3. What are the methods available for measuring consumers' judgments of brand performance on specific attributes?
4. How can the importance assigned to evaluative criteria be assessed?
5. What is sensory discrimination and what role does it play in the evaluation of products? What is meant by a "just noticeable difference"? How have marketers used this concept in marketing products?
6. What are "surrogate indicators" and how are they used in

the consumer evaluation process? How have marketers used "surrogate indicators" in positioning various products?

7. What is a disjunctive decision rule?
8. What is a conjunctive decision rule?
9. What is a lexicographic decision rule?
10. What is an elimination-by-aspects decision rule?
11. What is a compensatory decision rule?
12. How can knowledge of consumers' evaluative criteria and criteria importance be used in developing marketing strategy?
13. How can knowledge of the decision rule consumers might use in a certain purchase assist a firm in marketing products selected by use of this decision rule?

DISCUSSION QUESTIONS

1. Identify the evaluative criteria and the importance a consumer might utilize in evaluating alternative modes of transportation. How could SMC shift consumer judgments (i.e., evaluations) on specific evaluative criteria to improve consumer attitudes toward mopeds? How could SMC shift the importance of specific evaluative criteria to favorably improve attitudes toward mopeds? Also, how could SMC favorably improve attitudes toward mopeds by adding new evaluative criteria? (See Chapter 13.)
2. Identify five products in which surrogate indicators may be used as evaluative criteria in a brand choice decision. Why are the indicators used and in each case how might a firm enhance their use (i.e., strengthen their importance) in the consumer evaluation process?
3. The table below represents a particular consumer's evaluative criteria, criteria importance, acceptable level of performance, and judgments of these evaluative criteria with respect to several brands of mopeds. Discuss the brand choice that this consumer would make when using the lexicographic and compensatory decision rules.

Evaluative criteria	Criteria impor- tance	Level of perfor- mance	Alternative brands						
			Puch	Moto- becane	Motron	Vespa	Cimatti	Garelli	Batavus
Price	35	3	3	2	3	2	3	2	3
Horsepower	10	3	5	4	4	4	2	5	3
Weight	5	2	3	3	3	3	3	3	3
Gas-economy . . .	30	3	2	3	4	3	4	3	3
Color selection . .	15	3	2	5	4	4	2	3	2
Frame	5	2	3	3	3	4	2	3	3

Note: 1 = Very poor; 2 = Poor; 3 = Fair; 4 = Good; and 5 = Very good.

4. Discuss the first four decision rules listed in Table 17−2 in terms of how they would be utilized in selecting a job following graduation.

5. Discuss surrogate indicators that could be used to evaluate the perceived quality of a stereo, aftershave lotion, and lawnmower.

6. Referring back to Table 13−2, discuss the various ways a marketer can attempt to change attitudes and, in effect, change brand evaluation. Discuss each attitude change strategy in terms of how it would affect a consumer's brand evaluation process.

7. In this chapter, we presented a psychologist's explanation as to why individuals often overweight minor criteria. Do you agree or disagree with this explanation? Explain your position and what you would recommend in overcoming the problem when collecting this type of consumer information.

PROJECT QUESTIONS

1. Develop a list of evaluative criteria that students might use in evaluating alternative apartments they might rent. After listing these criteria, go to the local newspaper or student newspaper and select several apartments and list them in a table like the one in Discussion Question #3. Then have five other students you know each evaluate this information and have each indicate the apartment they would rent if given only those alternatives. Next, ask them to express the importance they attach to each evaluative criteria, using a 100-point constant sum scale. Finally, provide them with a series of statements which outline different decision rules (like that shown in Table 17−2) and ask them to indicate the one that best describes the way they made their choice. Compare each participant in terms of their criteria importance and the decision rule they used in making a brand choice.

2. Develop a short questionnaire to elicit the evaluative criteria consumers might use in purchasing a moped. Also, have each respondent indicate the relative importance they attach to each of the evaluative criteria they consider. Then, working with several other students, combine your information and develop a segmentation strategy based on consumer evaluative criteria and criteria importance such that fairly homogeneous market segments are identified. Then develop a marketing communication for each market segment such that their needs would be served by your brand of moped.

3. Set up a taste test experiment to determine if volunteer taste testers can perceive a just noticeable difference between three different brands of cola. To set up the experiment, store each cola in a separate but identical container and label the containers L, M, and N. Then provide volunteer taste testers with an adequate opportunity to evaluate each brand before asking them to state their identification

of the actual brands represented as L, M, and N. Evaluate the results after several volunteers have made taste evaluations. Then evaluate the results and discuss the marketing implications of these results.

4. For a product that is considered high in social status, develop a questionnaire that measures the evaluative criteria of that product, using both a *direct* and an *indirect* method of measurement. Compare the results and discuss their similarities and differences and which evaluative criteria are most likely to be utilized in brand choice.

18

Outlet selection and decision implementation

Fleet-Air manufactures and markets a line of high-quality children's shoes which are distributed through independent shoe stores. Although Fleet-Air had never engaged in consumer advertising, a declining market share made such action desirable in 1978. Prior to beginning the advertising campaign, Fleet-Air conducted research to determine the attributes that mothers of young children found important in purchasing children's shoes. The three most important attributes were found to be service, proper fit, and quality. Note that two of the three important attributes are more closely associated with the retail outlet than with the product itself. As a result of these findings, Fleet-Air developed an ad campaign which stressed both the quality of Fleet-Air shoes *and* the expertise of independent shoe retailers. The advertising campaign produced major sales increases in the test market area and is being expanded nationally.[1]

As the Fleet-Air case described above indicates, consumers must select both specific items (brands) and specific outlets to resolve problems. There are three ways these two decisions can be made: (1) simultaneously; (2) item first, outlet second; or (3) outlet first, item second. The discussion in the preceding chapters has generally assumed that brands were selected and purchased without evaluating alternative

---

[1] N. Giges, "Fleet-Air Shoes Ready to Take on Giants," *Advertising Age* (August 21, 1978), p. 50.

retail outlets. This situation may arise frequently. For example, in our camera purchase described in the preceding chapters, we may select a brand and purchase it from the nearest store that carries that brand. Of course, even in this situation we chose one store from among those carrying the brand (using either a lexicographic or disjunctive decision rule with nearness of location usually being the primary criterion). In this case, the decision sequence was brand choice, store choice. Of course, the store choice portion of the decision could have been much more complex.

It is also common for stores to form our evoked set rather than brands. For example, you might be familiar with one store—Campus Cameras—that sells cameras. You could decide to visit this store and select a camera from among the brands available there. In effect, your initial evoked set would consist of a store rather than brands. The decision sequence in this situation was store choice, brand choice.

A third shopping strategy would be to compare the brands in your evoked set at the stores in your evoked set. The decision would involve a simultaneous evaluation of both store and product attributes. Thus, you might have to choose between a camera that is your second preference at a store with friendly personnel and excellent service facilities versus your favorite camera at an impersonal outlet with no service facilities. The data presented in Chapter 16 on information search suggests that this is the least commonly used strategy.

Both the manufacturer and retailer need to be aware of the decision sequence used by their target market. If the store is selected first, the manufacturer must be concerned with obtaining distribution in the appropriate stores and with strengthening the stores that carry its brand through cooperative advertising programs and similar activities. If the brand is chosen first, the manufacturer can be more exclusive in its distribution, rely less on cooperative advertising and more on brand advertising, placing prominent advertisements in the Yellow Pages showing where the brand is available, and so forth.

The procedure involved in selecting an outlet is exactly the same as the procedure described in the previous chapters for selecting a brand. That is, the consumer recognizes a problem which requires an outlet to be selected, engages in internal and possibly external search, evaluates the relevant alternatives, and applies a decision rule to make a selection. We are not going to repeat our discussion of these steps. However, we do want to examine in some detail the evaluative criteria used by consumers in store selection decisions. In addition, we are going to examine the relationship between certain consumer characteristics and the use of specific evaluative criteria.

It is not uncommon for a consumer to make a brand decision, select a retail outlet, and then purchase a different brand due to in-store influences. Four in-store influences that appear to influence purchase decisions are described in this section of the text—point-of-purchase displays, price reductions, store layout, and stockouts.

After selecting a brand and an outlet, the consumer must complete the transaction in order to acquire the item. In our economy, this frequently involves the use of credit. The final section of this chapter examines the role of credit in the consumer decision process.

STORE ATTRIBUTES AFFECTING STORE CHOICE

As stated earlier, the selection of a specific retail outlet, whether before or after a brand decision, involves a comparison of the alternative stores on the consumer's evaluative criteria. In this section, we are going to examine a number of evaluative criteria commonly used by consumers in store selection decisions.

Outlet location and size as evaluative criteria

The location of a retail outlet such as a supermarket, bank, or restaurant plays an important role in consumer store choice. For example, the major consideration used by the U.S. Postal Service has historically been the cost of the land. Now the Postal Service realizes that most consumers stop at a post office as a secondary stop while on the way to a primary location. Surveys are now being conducted to determine the traffic patterns of postal customers, and these will serve as guides for locating new postal stations.

If all other things are approximately equal in a store selection decision, the consumer will generally select the closest store, since it would provide more convenience to the consumer in terms of time and effort.[2] This provides the store closest to a particular market a substantial advantage in attracting customers.

Likewise, the size of an outlet is an important factor in store choice. Unless a customer is particularly interested in fast service or convenience, larger outlets are preferred over smaller outlets, all other things being equal. The increase in selection in terms of product lines, brands, and models associated with larger outlets appears to be highly desired by many consumers.

These two factors have long been recognized by retailers, and several methods for calculating the level of store attraction based on store size and distance have been developed which predict retail trade fairly accurately. One such model is called the *retail gravitation model* and is useful in determining the share of retail trade that would be attracted to each of

---

[2] G. Olsson, *Distance and Human Interaction: A Review and Bibliography* (Philadelphia: Regional Science Research Institute, 1965).

two shopping areas.[3] This model is based on the distance to each trade area and the size of each trade area. Using these two characteristics, the following method has been devised and proven useful in estimating the market shares of different centers of retail trade:

$$\left(\frac{MS_1}{MS_2}\right) = \left(\frac{S_1}{S_2}\right)\left(\frac{D_2}{D_1}\right)^2$$

where:

MS_1 and MS_2 = Market share of retail centers 1 and 2.

S_1 and S_2 = Size in square footage of retail centers 1 and 2.

D_1 and D_2 = Distance from consumer market to retail centers 1 and 2.

Assume that two comparable centers of retail trade are competing for the purchases of a segment of consumers that live in a particular housing development. If trade area 1 was two miles from the location of this market and had 30,000 square feet of merchandise, and the competing trade area was four miles away but had square footage of 60,000, the ratio of market shares for these two retail centers would be estimated as shown below:

$$\left(\frac{MS_1}{MS_2}\right) = \left(\frac{30,000 \text{ sq. ft.}}{60,000 \text{ sq. ft.}}\right)\left(\frac{4 \text{ miles}}{2 \text{ miles}}\right)^2$$

$$= \left(\frac{1}{2}\right)(2)^2$$

$$= 2$$

This means that the market share of retail center 1 (MS_1) is predicted to be two times greater than the market share of retail center 2 (MS_2). Because the sum of these market shares must add up to one (assuming no other competition), trade area 1 has a market share of 0.67 and trade area 2 has a market share of 0.33. This illustrates the importance of location since retail center 2 is twice as big as retail center 1 but twice as far away, and as a result obtains half as much market share.

In the retail gravitation model, square footage is assumed to be a measure of assortment or breadth of selection of merchandise. This assumption implies that the larger the retail trade area the greater the breadth and depth of the merchandise assortment. Likewise, distance is assumed to be a measure of the effort, both physical and psychological, to reach a given retail area. We all recognize that both these assumptions are only partially correct.[4] Therefore, the gravitational model of retail trade has been extended to include travel time instead of distance, differ-

---

[3] P. Converse, "New Laws of Retail Gravitation," *Journal of Marketing* (October 1949), pp. 379–88.

[4] For example, see C. M. Lillis and D. I. Hawkins, "Retail Trade Flows in Contiguous Areas," *Journal of Retailing* (Summer 1974), pp. 30–42.

ent rates of attraction for different types of products, and the effects of several areas of trade or competing retail shopping within an area of trade.[5] This method of evaluating consumer attraction to retail stores is shown below as:

$$MS_j = \frac{\dfrac{S_j}{T_j{}^{\lambda_j}}}{\sum\limits_{j=1}^{n} \dfrac{S_j}{T_j{}^{\lambda_j}}}$$

where:

MS_j = Market share of store j.
S_j = Size of store j.
T_j = Travel time to store j.
λ = Attraction factor for a particular product category.

To illustrate the usefulness of this method of estimating retail attraction, assume the attraction factor (λ) for a particular type of merchandise was 1.0 and that retail store 1 was 3,000 square feet and 5 minutes away; store 2 was 6,000 square feet and 10 minutes away; and that another competitor, store 3, had a store size of 24,000 square feet but was 20 minutes away. The market shares in this case using this method of estimating consumer attraction would be 0.25, 0.25, and 0.50, respectively, for retail stores 1, 2, and 3. Thus, in this case the overwhelming advantage in the size provided by retail store 3 allows them to attract 50 percent of the purchases despite a relatively long distance from the market of interest.

As other influences can also play a major role in store choice, this basic model has been extended even further to include variables such as consumer sensitivity to driving time and the image of various retail stores in relationship to a consumer's ideal store. In one study the extended retail gravitation model was able to provide accurate predictions of supermarket trade and explained approximately 80 percent of the behavior observed in the choice of supermarkets among some 372 shoppers.[6]

Store image

While location of a retail store is a major influence in consumer store choice, many other retail store attributes are also influential in a consumer's decision to shop at a given store when making a particular purchase. A given consumer's or target market's perception of all of

---

[5] D. Huff, "A Probabilistic Analysis of Consumer Spatial Behavior," in *Emerging Concepts in Marketing*, ed. W. S. Decker (American Marketing Association, 1962), pp. 443–61.

[6] T. Stanley and M. Sewell, "Predicting Supermarket Trade: Implications for Marketing Management," *Journal of Retailing* (Summer 1978), pp. 13–23.

FIGURE 18–1

The dimensions and components of store image attributes

Dimension	Component
Merchandise	Quality
	Selection
	Style
	Price
Service	Lay-away plan
	Sales personnel
	Easy return
	Credit
	Delivery
Clientele	Customers
Physical facilities	Cleanliness
	Store layout
	Shopping ease
	Attractiveness
Convenience	Location
	Parking
Promotion	Advertising
Store atmosphere	Congeniality
Institutional	Store reputation
Post-transaction	Satisfaction

Source: R. Hansen and T. Deutscher, "An Empirical Investigation of Attribute Importance in Retail Store Selection," *Journal of Retailing* (Winter 1977–78), pp. 59–73. Used with permission.

these attributes is generally referred to as the store *image.* In Figure 18–1 we have listed 9 dimensions and some 20 components of these 9 dimensions of store images. The merchandise dimension, for example, takes into account such components as quality, selection, style and price; while the service dimension includes components related to credit, financing, delivery, and sales personnel. These are the dimensions and components thought to represent the major attributes of a store and thus its image.

In one study these 20 store image components were expanded into a list of 41 specific store attributes frequently used in store image and store patronage studies.[7] To evaluate the importance of these attributes, two groups of consumers were asked to rate the importance of each of these 41 store attributes; one group rated the importance of these attributes with respect to department stores and the other rated these attributes for grocery stores. The average rating and rank order in importance for each attribute was then computed for each type of retail store.

Table 18–1 lists the top ten and bottom five rated store attributes for department stores, and Table 18–2 shows the same information for

[7] R. Hansen and T. Deutscher, "An Empirical Investigation of Attribute Importance in Retail Store Selection," *Journal of Retailing* (Winter 1977–78), p. 59–73.

TABLE 18–1

Top ten and bottom five store attributes for department stores

Store attribute	Rank	Mean importance rating*
Dependable products	1	9.58
Fair on adjustments	2	9.38
High value on money	3	9.25
High-quality products	4	9.15
Easy to find items you want	5	9.14
Fast checkout	6	9.14
Helpful personnel	7	9.12
Easy to return purchases	8	9.12
Easy to exchange purchases	9	9.11
Store is clean	10	9.03
.	.	.
.	.	.
.	.	.
Layaway available	37	5.30
Company operates many stores	38	5.01
Store known by friends	39	4.89
Many friends shop there	40	4.58
Store is liked by friends	41	4.57

* The importance of each attribute was rated from 0 (no importance) to 10 (very important) by 267 consumers.
Source: R. Hansen and T. Deutscher, "An Empirical Investigation of Attribute Importance in Retail Store Selection," *Journal of Retailing* (Winter 1977–78), pp. 59–73. Used with permission.

TABLE 18–2

Top ten and bottom five store attributes for grocery stores

Store attribute	Rank	Mean importance rating*
Dependable products	1	9.50
Store is clean	2	9.33
Easy to find items you want	3	9.27
Fast checkout	4	9.23
High-quality products	5	9.10
High value for the money	6	9.05
Fully stocked	7	8.94
Helpful store personnel	8	8.88
Easy to move through store	9	8.88
Adequate number of store personnel	10	8.87
.	.	.
.	.	.
.	.	.
Many friends shop there	37	4.18
Store is liked by friends	38	4.07
Easy to get credit	39	2.58
Layaway available	40	2.09
Easy to get home delivery	41	1.93

* The importance of each attribute was rated from 0 (no importance) to 10 (very important) by 215 consumers.
Source: R. Hansen and T. Deutscher, "An Empirical Investigation of Attribute Importance in Retail Store Selection," *Journal of Retailing* (Winter 1977–78), pp. 59–73. Used with permission.

grocery stores. In both cases, "dependable products" ranked number one in importance to consumers. Beyond that, for department stores we see that value and quality from the merchandise dimension were ranked three and four and the remaining attributes were related to the service dimension except for store cleanliness, which is a physical dimension of a store. Store attributes rated least important were mainly from the clientele dimension.

For grocery stores four of the ten most important attributes related to the merchandise dimension, three attributes were related to a service dimension, and four attributes were related to the physical dimensions of a store. Of the five least important store attributes for grocery stores, three related to the service dimension and two were related to a clientele dimension.

Of course, a marketing manager cannot assume that these ratings would be the same for all potential target markets or store types. However, the manager can investigate the importance of various attributes among the target market(s) of interest. These findings can then be translated directly into marketing strategy. For example, the data in Table 18−2 indicates the importance of having a clean store with fast checkout and an adequate number of helpful store personnel. This suggests that advertising stressing these factors in addition to the traditional price-oriented retail advertising would be effective with this group of consumers.

Image elasticity   The method described above involves simply asking members of the target market to rate the importance they attach to specified store features. This is a useful and popular approach, though consumers' statements of what is important are not always accurate.[8] If actual purchase data are available, perhaps from a panel,[9] consumers' perceptions of a store's attributes can be related directly to their purchasing behavior using multiple regression analysis.[10]

The results of a study using this approach are shown in Table 18−3. This table includes *only* those attributes that were statistically related to differential purchasing (they are similar to the concept of a "determinant attribute" discussed in the preceding chapter). In the case of store 1, consumer evaluations of only two of the ten store attributes considered were significant contributors to store sales. Store 2 had one significant store attribute; store 3 had two, and store 4 and store 5 had three store attributes that were directly linked to consumer purchases. In each case there was a different set of store attributes contributing to the

---

[8] See D. S. Tull and D. I. Hawkins, *Marketing Research* (Macmillan Publishing Co., 1980), chap. 8.

[9] Ibid.

[10] R. Best, G. Albaum, and D. Hawkins, "The Importance of Image Elasticity in Determining the Economic Benefits of Repositioning a Store Image," *Proceedings,* Western American Institute for Decision Sciences (March 1979), pp. 136−39.

TABLE 18–3

Image elasticities of store image attributes that were related to store purchases

Store attribute	Store number*				
	1	2	3	4	5
Honesty	1.76				
Quality					
Price					
Service				0.91	0.75
Easy to find merchandise			1.06		
Helpful employees					
Cleanliness		0.91		1.82	0.82
Pleasant atmosphere	1.22				
Selection				1.47	
Friendliness			1.14		0.44

* Store 1 was a local department store; store 2 a nationwide medium-priced department store; store 3 a nationwide discount store; store 4 a regional department store; and store 5 a nationwide medium-priced department store.

Source: R. Best, G. Albaum, and D. Hawkins, "The Importance of Image Elasticity in Determining the Economic Benefits of Repositioning a Store Image," *Proceedings,* Western American Institute for Decision Sciences (March 1979), p. 136.

sales of a particular store, although store cleanliness had an effect on purchase for three of the five stores.

The store elasticities shown in Table 18–3 are estimated such that a 1 percent change in the target market's perception of the store on that attribute is associated with a percentage change in sales equal to the elasticity figure. For example, assume that the average perception of honesty of this target market for store 1 were to change from 4.10 (on a seven-point scale) to 4.14 (approximately 1 percent improvement). This model would then predict a sales increase to this target market of 1.76 percent. The value of this approach for developing marketing strategies and priorities is obvious. In addition, it provides an indication of the maximum one should spend to achieve a given change in store image.

Retail advertising

Retailers attempt to influence store choice decisions by advertising particular items at reduced prices immediately prior to the time consumers typically purchase those items. One study found that almost 55 percent of over 500 adults surveyed checked newspaper advertisements before purchasing drugstore-type items.[11] Thus, a substantial percentage of consumers do seek store and product information from newspaper advertisements prior to purchase.

---

[11] D. I. Hawkins and J. H. Barnes, Jr., "Comparison of Shopping Behaviors and Attitudes between Employed Females, Unemployed Females, and Employed Males," *1979 Proceedings of the Southwestern Marketing Association Conference* (Citadel Press, 1979).

FIGURE 18-2

The relationship between advertising and time of purchase for grocery products

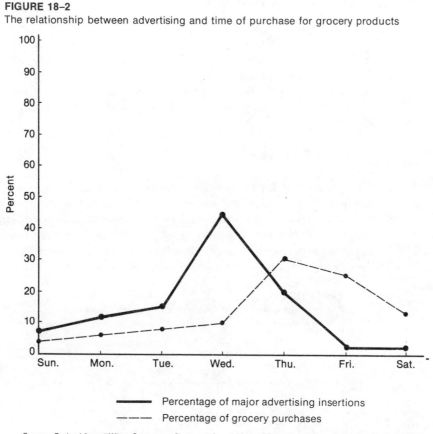

Source: Derived from "When Customers Shop and Super Markets Advertise," *Progressive Grocer* (April 1977), p. 190.

Figure 18−2 illustrates the relationship between retail advertising and the day of the week on which consumers shop for grocery items. Of course, the percentages shown in the figure are aggregate in nature; specific target markets such as employed women may exhibit very different patterns.[12] As Figure 18−2 indicates, peak grocery advertising occurs on Wednesdays with 44 percent of major advertising insertions ocurring on this day. The sales peak is greatest the next day and then declines steadily each day after that.[13] It is clear that grocery retailers attempt to influence store patronage decisions by placing relevant information, generally price discount data, before the consumer just prior to the common or standard times at which store decisions are made.

---

[12] Ibid.

[13] "When Customers Shop and Super Markets Advertise," *Progressive Grocer* (April 1977), p. 190.

CONSUMER CHARACTERISTICS AND STORE CHOICE

The preceding discussion has by and large focused on store attributes independently of the specific characteristics of the consumers in the target market. Some groups of consumers may be particularly concerned with specific attributes of a retail store. In this section, we are going to examine three consumer characteristics that are particularly relevant to store choice: social class, consumer confidence, and family characteristics.

Social class

The purchase of products involves a certain amount of risk that may include both economic and social consequences.[14] Certain products due to their expense or technical complexity represent high levels of economic risk, while other products which are more closely related to a consumer's public image present high levels of social risk. In Table 18−4 cookware and undergarments are shown to be low in both eco-

TABLE 18–4
The economic and social risk of various types of products

Social risk	Economic risk	
	Low	High
Low	Sleepwear Ironing table Undergarments Toys Cookware Hosiery	Vacuum cleaner Electric blender Automobile tires Power tools Men's electric shavers Typewriter
High	Men's dress shirts Costume jewelry Women's blouses and sweaters Handbags Wall decorations Men's dress slacks	Draperies Ladies' coats Stereo hi-fi Men's sports coats Ladies' dresses

Source: V. Prasad, "Socioeconomic Product Risk and Patronage Preferences of Retail Shoppers," *Journal of Marketing* (American Marketing Association, July 1975), p. 44.

nomic and social risk, while men's dress shirts and costume jewelry are low in economic risk but high in social risk.[15] Other products such as

---

[14] R. Bauer, "Consumer Behavior as Risk Taking," in *Dynamic Marketing for a Changing World,* ed. R. S. Hancock (American Marketing Association, 1960), pp. 389−98.

[15] V. Prasad, "Socioeconomic Product Risk and Patronage Preferences of Retail Shoppers," *Journal of Marketing* (July 1975), pp. 42−47.

power tools and typewriters are low in social risk but high in economic risk. Finally, men's sport coats and women's dresses are high in both economic and social risk.

The perception of these risks differs among consumers based in part on the past experience and the lifestyle of the consumer. This is particularly true in how social risks associated with a purchase are viewed by consumers in different social classes.[16] One way of reducing social risk is to shop at retail stores that connote the social prestige desired by the consumer. Thus, consumer choices of retail stores are susceptible to influence from their social class for products that are high in social risk.[17] For example, attitudes toward shopping at discount-type retail stores for products which are low in social risk are very similar for consumers of different social classes. However, for products high in social risk, consumers of different social classes vary significantly in their attitudes toward shopping at discount stores. Specifically, consumers in higher socioeconomic strata are more likely to shop at specialty stores for the purchase of products higher in social risk.[18]

Consumer confidence

The role of consumer confidence and perceived risk can also be important in a consumer's store choice and purchase decision. Consumers who are more self-confident and perceive less risk in an important purchase are more likely to purchase from a new store or specialty store than consumers who are lower in self-confidence and perceive more risk in making a satisfactory purchase. Under these conditions less confident consumers would make their purchases at a well-established department store which in their mind reduces the risk of an unsatisfactory purchase.[19] The combination of higher perceived risk and lower levels of self-confidence experienced by their durable goods consumers suggests that department stores should attempt to further reduce consumer uncertainty through careful merchandising and in-store promotional campaigns that emphasize the assistance that the store provides its customers. In addition, the department store should carry well-known major brands which also serve to reduce perceived risk.[20]

Consumer self-confidence, both general and product specific, affects not only the type of store selected, but also the use of stores versus

---

[16] R. Hisrich, R. Dornoff, and J. Keenan, "Perceived Risk in Store Selection," *Journal of Marketing Research* (November 1972), pp. 453–59.

[17] M. Perry and C. Harmon, "Canonical Analysis of the Relation between Socioeconomic Risk and Personal Influence in Purchase Decisions," *Journal of Marketing Research* (August 1969), pp. 351–54.

[18] Prasad, "Socioeconomic Product," pp. 42–47.

[19] J. Dash, L. Schiffman, and C. Berenson, "Risk and Personality-Related Dimensions of Store Choice," *Journal of Marketing* (January 1976), pp. 32–39.

[20] T. Redelius, "Consumer Ranking of Risk Reduction Methods," *Journal of Marketing* (January 1971), pp. 56–61.

in-house (catalog and telephone) shopping.[21] As we would expect, the more confident a consumer is, the more likely he or she is to shop "at home." This suggests that mail-order and telephone based retailers should attempt to minimize any perceived risks associated with this type of shopping in order to attract consumers with relatively low levels of self-confidence. In response to this need, many catalog retailers have set up toll-free complaint lines and automatic and rapid refunds for unsatisfactory orders.

Family characteristics

Recall from Chapter 9 that various family members may play differing roles in the overall decision process. For example, the wife makes 71 percent of the actual coffee purchases and 84 percent of the pet food purchases. However, in approximately half of these cases, the husband has recognized the need for the purchase and/or selected the brand.[22] Thus, a situation where one family member selects the products and/or brand and a *different* family member selects the retail outlet is not uncommon. Of course, joint decision making with respect to the outlet also occurs as does joint shopping (numerous examples are provided in Chapter 9).

The above discussion indicates that the retailer as well as the manufacturer needs to determine *who* in the families in the relevant target markets are involved with *which* aspects of the decision process. The retailer will generally then want to focus promotional activities on the family member(s) that influences store choice.

IN-STORE INFLUENCES THAT ALTER BRAND CHOICE

It is not uncommon to enter a retail outlet with the intention of purchasing a particular brand and to leave with a different brand. Influences operating within the store induce additional information processing and subsequently affect the final purchase decision. We are going to examine four variables that singularly and in combination influence brand decisions inside a retail store: point-of-purchase displays, price reductions, store layout, and stockout situations.

---

[21] J. M. DeKorte, "Mail and Telephone Shopping as a Function of Consumer Self-Confidence," *Journal of the Academy of Marketing Science* (Fall 1977), pp. 295–306. See also H. E. Spence, J. F. Engel, and R. D. Blackwell, "Perceived Risk in Mail-Order and Retail Store Buying," *Journal of Marketing Research* (August 1970), pp. 364–69; J. C. Cunningham and W. H. Cunningham, "The Urban In-Home Shopper: Socioeconomic and Attitudinal Characteristics," *Journal of Retailing* (Fall 1973), pp. 39–43; F. D. Reynolds, "An Analysis of Catalog Buying Behavior," *Journal of Marketing* (July 1974), pp. 47–51; and P. L. Gillett, "In-Home Shoppers—An Overview," *Journal of Marketing* (October 1976), pp. 81–88.

[22] Jaffe Associates, Inc., *A Pilot Study of the Roles of Husbands and Wives in Purchasing Decisions*, n.d.

The fact that consumers often purchase brands different from or in addition to those planned has led to an interest in *impulse purchases.* Impulse purchases are generally defined as *purchases made in a store that are different from those the consumer planned to make prior to entering the store.* Unfortunately, impulse purchase and even its more accurate substitute, *unplanned purchase,* connotes a lack of rationality or alternative evaluation. However, this is not necessarily true. The decision to purchase Del Monte's rather than Green Giant peas because Del Monte is on sale is certainly not illogical. Nor is an unplanned decision to take advantage of the unexpected availability of fresh strawberries.

Considering impulse purchases as being the result of additional information processing within the store leads to much more useful marketing strategies than considering these purchases to be random or illogical. This approach allows the marketer to utilize knowledge of the target market, its motives, and the perception process to increase sales of specific items.

Point-of-purchase displays

Point-of-purchase displays are common in the retailing of many products, and the impact these displays have on brand sales is often tremendous. In Table 18−5 the impact of a point-of-purchase display in conjunction with a price reduction for a variety of products and brands is shown.

TABLE 18–5
Impact of display on sales for different types of products

Product class	Brand	Percentage increase
Bleach	Clorox	268%
	Private label	393
Facial tissues	Scotties	352
	Private label	291
Fabric softener	Downey	709
	NuSoft	451
Cooking and salad oil	Crisco	626
	Wesson	1,179
Mayonnaise	Hellman's	575
	Cains'	792
Food storage bags	Baggies	240
	Glad	251
Light-duty liquid detergent	Ivory	1,022
	Joy	1,372
Semimoist dog foods	Top Choice	343
	Special Cuts	282

Source: M. Chevalier, "Substitution Patterns as a Result of Display in the Product Category," *Journal of Retailing* (Winter 1975–76), p. 68. Used with permission.

Although the range of percentage increase varies considerably by product class and to a lesser degree by brand within a product class, each of these changes represents a substantial increase in sales. Light duty liquid detergents, Ivory and Joy, achieved greater than a 1,000 percent increase in sales over normal shelf sales. On the other hand, the promotion of food storage bags produced about a 250 percent sales increase for Baggies and Glad, less than one fourth the sales impact created by the two brands of liquid detergent.[23]

Though point-of-purchase displays vary greatly in size, shape, quality of construction, and personal appeal, one study found that even the addition of a simple mobile-type display was sufficient to increase purchases of dairy products.[24] Under normal conditions approximately 30 percent of the store shoppers made cheese purchases at the store's dairy case. When a mobile-type display was used to attract attention to the dairy case, cheese sales increased an average of 30 percent. However, the height and placement of the mobile display was critical. If the mobile was too high (10 feet off the ground) sales were unaffected; when the mobile was too low (7 feet off the ground) sales increased 13⅓ percent; and when the mobile was at an intermediate height (8½ feet), sales increased 30 percent; and when the mobile was overhead the aisle in front of the dairy case, the purchase behavior of shoppers was unaffected.

Time also had an impact on the sales effect of the mobile-type display. Most of the sales increase occurred in the first two weeks the display was utilized. When *new* materials were used each week, the percentage of shoppers buying cheese increased from 20 percent above normal the first week to 30 percent in the fifth week. In addition, the percentage buying milk increased from 40 percent to 60 percent. In both cases the average amount purchased by each shopper was also greater.

Price reductions and promotional deals

Price reductions and promotional deals (coupons, multiple-item discounts, and gifts) are almost always accompanied by the use of some point-of-purchase materials. Therefore, the relative impact of each is sometimes not clear. Nonetheless, there is ample evidence that in-store price reductions affect brand decisions. Table 18–6 illustrates the impact of promotion deals and in-store price reductions for a variety of dairy products. As can be seen, the impact is strong but short run in nature. That is, sales return to near normal after the special is removed.[25]

---

[23] M. Chevalier, "Substitution Patterns as a Result of Display in the Product Category," *Journal of Retailing* (Winter 1975–76), pp. 65–72.

[24] "How to Turn P-O-P into Sales Dollars," *Progressive Grocer* (June 1977), pp. 83–100.

[25] B. C. Cotton and E. M. Babb, "Consumer Response to Promotional Deals," *Journal of Marketing* (July 1978), pp. 109–13. See also J. A. Dodson, A. M. Tybout, and B. Sternthal, "Impact of Deals and Deal Retraction on Brand Switching," *Journal of Marketing Research* (February 1978), pp. 72–81.

TABLE 18–6 Average quantities of selected dairy products purchased by households before, during and after purchase on promotional deal*

Product and situation†	Average quantity purchased			Number of households
	Before	During	After	
Fluid milk (half gals.):‡				
All	5.9	7.5	5.9	623
		28%	0%	
Regular	7.0	8.4	7.0	550
		20%	1%	
Cottage cheese (lbs.):‡				
All	1.3	3.5	1.6	453
		169%	23%	
Regular	3.4	4.7	3.8	117
		38%	12%	
Yogurt (half pts.):‡				
All	1.5	5.4	2.0	195
		258%	33%	
Regular	5.1	9.2	6.1	36
		80%	20%	
Ice cream (half gals.):§				
All	1.3	2.8	1.5	907
		114%	12%	
Regular	2.7	4.0	3.1	324
		46%	13%	
Ice milk (half gals.):§				
All	0.7	2.2	0.7	292
		207%	0%	
Regular	2.8	3.7	2.9	45
		32%	2%	
Novelties (half gals.):§				
All	0.3	1.0	0.4	334
		221%	21%	
Regular	0.8	1.2	1.1	67
		42%	38%	
Processed cheese (lbs.):‡				
All	0.7	2.8	0.7	457
		400%	0%	
Regular	1.6	2.7	2.1	94
		69%	31%	
Natural cheese (lbs.):‡				
All	0.7	2.4	1.0	315
		243%	43%	
Regular	1.2	1.7	1.2	78
		42%	0%	
Butter (lbs.):§				
All	1.3	2.6	1.2	350
		100%	−8%	
Regular	2.6	3.7	2.8	123
		42%	8%	
Frozen toppings (half-pts.):‡				
All	0.4	1.2	0.1	101
		200%	−75%	
Cream products (pts.):‡				
All	1.1	1.9	1.2	125
		71%	6%	

* Percentage figures indicate change from the period before purchase on deal (percent calculated before data rounded). Purchases during the promotional period were significantly greater than those before promotions for all products, at the 1 percent level of probability using a paired t-test. None of the purchases after the promotional period were different than before promotion at the 5 percent level.

† The two situations were: All—indicates those households that were included regardless of whether they purchased the product prior to a purchase on deal; Regular—indicates those households that were included only if they purchased in all three periods.

‡ The period for average purchase was two weeks.

§ The period for average purchase was 30 days.

Source: Reprinted from B. C. Cotton and E. M. Babb, "Consumer Response to Promotional Deals," *Journal of Marketing* (American Marketing Association, July 1978), p. 111.

Not all households respond to price reductions and deals similarly. Available evidence suggests that households with ample resources (a strong financial base rather than a high income) are more likely to take advantage of deals than are other households.[26] Thus, stores oriented toward financially established consumers can anticipate a strong response to price reductions and other promotional deals.

Store layout

The location of items within a store is an important influence in the purchase of both product categories and brands. Typically, the more visibility a product receives the greater the chance it will be purchased.[27] ShopRite grocery stores were forced to alter their standard store layout format when they acquired an odd-shaped lot in Springfield, New Jersey. The modification is shown in Figure 18–3. The major changes involved moving the appetizer-deli section normally located adjacent to the meat section in the rear of the store to a heavy traffic area near the front of the store. As a result, the appetizer-deli section accounts for 7 percent of this store's sales rather than the normal 2 percent. This is important since these items average 35 percent gross margin compared to less than 10 percent gross margin for most store items. ShopRite is using the new layout in all future stores because of its dramatic effect on consumer purchase patterns and store profits.[28]

Stockouts

Stockouts, the store being temporarily out of a particular brand, can obviously affect a consumer purchase decision in that the consumer must then decide whether to buy the same brand but at another store, switch brands, or delay the purchase and buy the desired brand later at the same store. This decision can vary considerably from one consumer to another as well as be affected by the type of product and situation in which the product is needed.

In Table 18–7 we have listed 30 different product classes and five demographically different groups of consumers and the purchase behavior they selected to use in a stockout situation.[29] It seems that each of these consumer groups are somewhat loyal to the shampoo they use, as

---

[26] R. Blattberg, T. Buesing, P. Peacock, and S. Sen, "Identifying the Deal Prone Segment," *Journal of Marketing Research* (August 1978), pp. 369–77. See also David B. Montgomery, "Consumer Characteristics Associated with Dealing: An Empirical Example," *Journal of Marketing Research* (February 1971), pp. 118–20; and F. E. Webster, Jr., "The Deal-Prone Consumer," *Journal of Marketing Research* (May 1965), pp. 186–89.

[27] "How to Turn P-O-P into Sales Dollars."

[28] "Store of the Month," *Progressive Grocer* (October 1976), pp. 104–10.

[29] "Customer's Behavior When Confronted with a Product Stockout at a Supermarket," *Progressive Grocer* (October 1968).

FIGURE 18-3
Grocery store layout

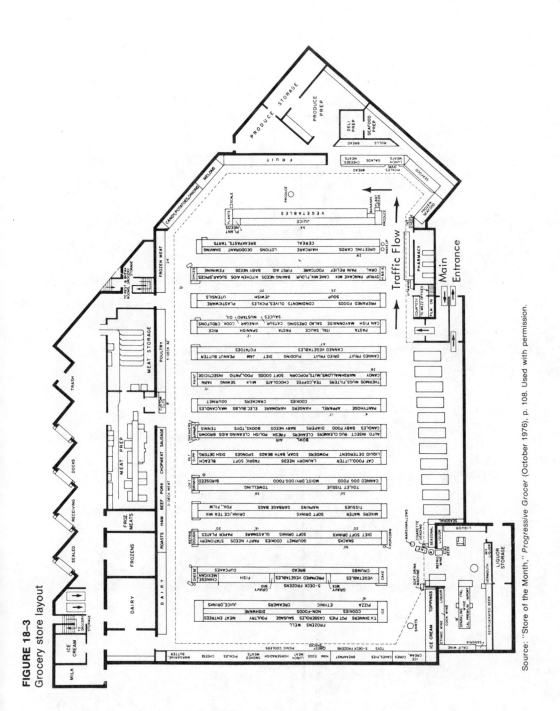

Source: "Store of the Month," *Progressive Grocer* (October 1976), p. 108. Used with permission.

TABLE 18–7

Customer's behavior when confronted with a brand stockout at a supermarket

	Buy elsewhere*					Switch brands*					Buy later at same store*				
Product	1	2	3	4	5	1	2	3	4	5	1	2	3	4	5
Margarine	17%	18%	26%	36%	17%	58%	46%	66%	27%	52%	25%	36%	10%	45%	33%
Cigarettes	75	82	81	83	80	10	4	17	17	5	15	14	2	8	15
Gelatin	13	11	27	10	21	61	50	60	40	49	26	42	13	60	32
Liquid starch	6	9	27	11	28	50	39	54	44	53	44	52	19	56	19
Hand soap	30	21	33	45	30	43	43	53	36	49	26	36	15	27	23
Toothpaste	39	36	63	60	43	52	40	28	30	36	9	24	10	20	21
Cereal	30	28	28	20	24	61	59	58	30	57	9	17	15	60	20
Dog food	61	62	39	25	41	39	38	50	50	44	0	0	11	50	19
Baby food	40	60	48	20	59	40	33	46	40	33	20	7	9	60	7
Deodorant	59	54	67	56	58	36	19	25	33	26	5	27	10	22	16
Shampoo	61	54	66	67	57	26	21	27	33	23	13	25	8	17	20
Regular coffee	46	48	36	27	36	32	28	57	18	33	23	28	6	64	33
Catsup	30	7	26	40	19	57	59	67	40	63	13	35	8	30	19
Mayonnaise	52	7	39	22	27	26	55	51	22	59	22	41	13	67	14

Percent of customers who would

Product															
Instant coffee	33	14	44	11	29	52	36	53	33	50	14	55	4	67	23
Canned tuna	30	19	22	9	18	52	56	67	46	53	17	26	12	55	29
Canned peaches	9	10	11	9	18	73	52	81	36	55	18	38	8	64	27
Peanut butter	17	18	26	20	27	67	46	61	50	58	17	36	14	40	18
Jam	9	21	15	36	21	77	48	77	27	64	14	31	8	46	16
Tomato juice	27	15	17	11	17	68	56	76	44	66	5	30	7	56	17
Toilet tissue	26	28	24	25	22	65	52	63	33	61	9	21	13	50	18
Facial tissue	22	19	19	0	19	70	52	67	33	64	9	30	14	78	19
Aluminum foil	17	18	13	33	15	78	46	80	33	68	4	36	8	44	19
Salad oil	26	11	24	38	20	57	50	67	38	62	17	39	10	38	20
Solid shortening	13	12	27	18	20	65	35	65	50	56	22	54	8	46	27
Canned soup	32	14	33	25	25	46	45	51	33	50	23	41	17	50	25
Canned milk	20	14	15	30	13	70	43	77	30	68	10	43	8	50	20
Canned corn	27	7	18	9	19	55	65	73	55	57	18	31	10	46	24
Canned green beans	18	11	17	29	19	64	61	78	57	57	18	32	6	29	24
Laundry detergents	46	36	51	50	52	38	29	43	30	23	17	43	9	30	27
Waxed paper	13	12	13	20	14	78	65	74	40	73	9	23	13	50	14

Note: The percentages sometimes add up to more than 100 percent due to the fact that some respondents checked "buy elsewhere" and "buy later at the same store," indicating that they would do one or the other but will not switch brands.

* Key to store neighborhood numbers: 1 = Young married; 2 = Blue-collar; 3 = High income; 4 = Black; and 5 = Small town.

Source: "Customer's Behavior When Confronted with a Product Stockout at a Supermarket," Progressive Grocer (October 1968).

a majority of them would shop elsewhere while less than a third would switch brands and less than 20 percent would delay their purchase of shampoo. On the other hand, for canned corn a stockout produced very limited brand loyalty, as most consumers preferred to switch brands at the time of purchase rather than buy elsewhere or delay the purchase. This was particularly true for the high-income consumers in their purchase of canned corn as well as canned peaches, tomato juice, canned milk, canned green peas, waxed paper, and aluminum foil. When brand switching does occur in response to a stockout, the second most preferred brand is generally selected.[30]

The general tendency of consumers to either switch brands or switch stores in response to a stockout indicates the tremendous importance of distribution and inventory management for both manufacturers and retailers. Not only are current sales lost when consumers switch stores or brands, but some consumers may develop preferences for the new store or brand. Thus both current and future market share may be lost in a stockout situation.

DECISION IMPLEMENTATION

Once the brand and outlet have been selected, the consumer must complete the transaction. This involves what we normally call "buying" the product. Traditionally, this involved the surrender of cash to acquire the rights to the product. However, credit plays a major role in consumer purchases in today's society. Without credit, a great many purchases could simply not be made. In 1977, consumer short-term and intermediate-term credit totaled $216,572 million, an increase of $31,063 million from 1976. Retailers accounted for approximately 10 percent of the credit extended to consumers in 1977, but the majority of consumer credit was provided by commercial banks who extend credit to consumers for the purchase of automobiles.[31]

The use of bank credit cards, such as Visa, Master Charge, Diner's Club, and American Express, provide an increasingly popular way of financing a purchase decision. In 1977, $2,600 million of retail credit was extended using the Visa credit card, an increase of 22 percent over the previous year. Likewise, in 1977 Master Charge extended $3,078 million credit to consumers, an increase of almost 19 percent over the amount provided in 1976. The number of retail outlets offering consumers these options increased from 1976 to 1977 by 13.5 percent for Visa and 18.5 percent for Master Charge.[32] The marketing manager of Interbank—

---

[30] D. I. Hawkins and R. Best, "Utilization of Preference Choice Probabilities in Market Share Forecasts," paper presented at the 1979 Southwestern Marketing Association Conference.

[31] "Consumer Credit," *Survey of Current Business* (October 1978), p. S—18.

[32] "Volume Up, Delinquencies Down," *Banking,* pp. 112—13.

operator of Master Charge—points to a 1976 marketing research study they did to offer an explanation for the increasing demand for this method of purchase:

> We have a highly mobile society. People are traveling and moving more. In addition, young people are less likely to be loyal to a particular store. They shop value and price. In one department store we studied, the average age of an account-holder was upper-forties. Our average is mid-thirties Moreover, better than two-thirds of department store cards are issued to women. Master Charge is 50/50.[33]

The average retail purchase was $26.81 for Visa card users and $26.87 for Master Charge in 1977.[34] Thus, it appears that this method of purchasing is used for small dollar purchases of retail goods. Evidence indicates that lower socioeconomic groups frequently use bank credit cards as a form of installment credit. That is, they tend to pay less than the full amount of their monthly bill. Upper socioeconomic groups are more likely to use credit cards as a form of convenience. They charge items rather than pay cash or write checks but they pay the entire bill each month.[35]

Consumer preference for this method of purchase is also being felt in the supermarket area where Jewel, a midwestern grocery chain, tried the Visa card in a 90-day market test but did not continue due to the high cost.[36] However, Ralph's, a West Coast grocery chain, tested it first in their liquor and deli departments for six months in 1975 and decided to continue its use in these departments and extend it to other areas of higher-priced general merchandise. Thus, consumer credit in grocery stores has produced mixed results due to the limited benefits provided consumers and merchants. The vice president of one major chain of grocery stores explained the failure of the bank card as a method of food purchase in the following way:

> Our objective was to increase sales volume and traffic and offer convenience. There was a slight increase in volume, but a customer survey indicated that they were not happy about it. They thought that prices would have to increase. Just 13 percent of our customers who had cards were using them. This amounted to about 5–6 percent of our shoppers, totaling 15 percent of sales.[37]

With the margin on grocery products running about 1 percent, many feel that supermarkets just cannot afford bank cards. There is also a fear that

---

[33] "More Stores Using Bank Cards," *Chain Store Age Executive* (January 1977), p. 26.

[34] "Volume Up, Delinquencies Down."

[35] J. W. Slocum, Jr., and H. L. Mathews, "Social Class and Income as Indicators of Consumer Credit Behavior," *Journal of Marketing* (April 1970), pp. 67–74.

[36] "More Stores Using Bank Cards."

[37] Ibid.

it may be difficult to obtain payment as people may be reluctant to pay for something they consumed some 30 days ago.

Of course, credit not only is a means to purchase a product, it is also a product itself. Thus, the decision to purchase a relatively expensive item may trigger problem recognition for credit. Since a variety of forms of credit are available, the decision process may then be repeated for this problem.[38]

SUMMARY

The consumption process involves the acquisition and use of products to maintain and enhance one's lifestyle. Most consumer products are acquired through some form of a retail outlet. Thus, consumers must select outlets as well as products. There are three general ways these decisions can be made: (1) simultaneously; (2) item first, outlet second; or (3) outlet first, item second. Both the manufacturer and the retailer need to be aware of the decision sequence used by their target market as this will have a major impact on their marketing strategy.

The decision process used by consumers to select a retail outlet is the same as the process described in Chapters 15 through 17 for selecting a brand. The only difference is in the nature of the evaluative criteria used. Outlet location is an important attribute for many consumers with closer outlets being preferred over more distant ones. Larger outlets are also generally preferred over smaller outlets. These two variables, often in conjunction with other variables, have been used to develop "retail gravitation" models. These models can predict the market share of competing shopping areas with reasonable accuracy.

The store's image and the type and amount of retail advertising also exert important influences as evaluative criteria. The major dimensions of store image are merchandise, service, clientele, physical facilities, convenience, promotion, store atmosphere, institutional, and post-transaction factors. Image elasticity is a measure of the impact a change in one of these dimensions would have on sales.

Different types of consumers assign different values to store attributes. Lower social class consumers have differing store preferences from middle-class consumers for some product categories. For example, both groups have similar feelings about shopping at discount stores for low-risk products. However, middle-class consumers are

---

[38] See O. C. Walker, Jr., and R. F. Sauter, "Consumer Preferences for Alternative Retail Credit Plans: A Concept Test of the Effects of Consumer Legislation," *Journal of Marketing Research* (February 1974), pp. 70−78; N. R. Burnstein, "A Comment on Consumer Preferences for Alternative Retail Credit Plans," *Journal of Marketing Research* (November 1978), pp. 639−43; and G. Albaum, "Consumer Reactions to Variable Rate Mortgages," *Journal of Consumer Affairs* (Winter 1979).

much less likely to shop discount houses for items perceived to have a high social risk than are lower-class consumers. Likewise, consumers with a low level of confidence tend to prefer well-known, high-service stores.

Both retailers and manufacturers need to be aware of family purchasing roles. As we saw in Chapter 9, it is common for one member of the family to select the product while a second family member may select the outlet. Thus, the "within family" target market for retailers and manufacturers often differs.

Consumers often purchase a brand or product while in a store that differs from their plans before entering the store. Such purchases are referred to as impulse or unplanned purchases. Unfortunately, both of these terms imply a lack of rationality or decision processes. It is more useful to consider such decisions as being the result of additional information processing induced by in-store stimuli. Such variables as point-of-purchase displays, price reductions, store layout, and brand or product stockouts can have a major impact on sales patterns.

Once both the outlet and brand have been selected, the consumer must acquire the rights to the item. Increasingly this involves the use of credit—particularly the use of credit cards. However, major purchases often require the consumer to make a second purchase decision—"What type of credit shall I buy to finance this purchase?" Financial institutions are increasingly recognizing the opportunities in the consumer credit field and are beginning to utilize standard consumer goods marketing techniques.

REVIEW QUESTIONS

1. In the consumer's decision process, the consumer faces both the problem of what to buy and where to buy it. What alternative ways does the consumer have in accomplishing both of these goals?
2. How does the size and distance to a retail outlet effect store selection and purchase behavior?
3. What are the two models of retail gravitation presented in the chapter? How do they differ?
4. What is a store image and how does it influence store choice?
5. How can a marketing manager use store image measures?
6. What is meant by image elasticity? Of what value is it to a retail store manager?
7. How is store choice affected by a consumer's social class?
8. What is meant by social risk? How does it differ from economic risk?
9. What role does consumer confidence play in store choice?

10. Once in a particular store, what in-store characteristics can influence brand choice? Give an example of each.

11. What role does the method of payment play in the final implementation of a purchase decision?

DISCUSSION QUESTIONS

1. How should Jeff go about measuring the store image of the various retail stores that distribute the Motron? Distributors of his brand of moped include bicycle shops, lawnmower retailers, motorcycle shops, and moped shops. How are the images of these stores going to affect the image of his product in terms of price, quality, and service after purchase?

2. How are social and economic risks likely to affect different prospective buyers of mopeds? Are either types of risk going to affect store choice? If so, in what way? What can Jeff suggest to his retailers to overcome this problem and enhance customer attraction to retail stores offering the Motron?

3. What in-store characteristics could Jeff provide his retailers in order to enhance the probability of purchase among individuals who visit a store? Describe each factor in terms of how it should be used in marketing the Motron and describe its intended effect on the consumer.

4. How would you go about determining the need for credit in the purchase of mopeds? Since credit plays an important part in today's consumer purchase behavior, it is absolutely essential to know if this aspect of the consumer's purchase decision needs greater attention.

5. What are the major marketing strategy implications of Table 18−7?

6. Based on the results presented in Tables 18−1 and 18−2, what store attributes should management pay particular attention to and which store attributes should be given their least attention? What important attributes differentiate department stores from grocery stores?

7. Using the information on image elasticity presented in Table 18−3, how would you advise the manager of store number 4 to improve its store image and sales? Which attribute(s) of store 4 would you focus on and what effect would they have on sales? How would your advice change for store 1?

8. What retail marketing strategies would you recommend for each of the four major categories of products shown in Table 18−4?

9. To what would you attribute the increased sales of deli products when moved to a new location in the store layout shown in Figure 18−3?

10. Using the information provided in Table 18 – 7, in what ways are young married couples different in their purchases than most of the other consumers studied? What reasons can you provide to explain why they display different behavior when facing a stockout of a particular product?

PROJECT QUESTIONS

1. Identify three stores that offer mopeds that students might go to if they were evaluating mopeds for purchase. Estimate the driving time to each store from campus and estimate the approximate square footage allocated to displaying mopeds at each store. Then using this information and an attraction factor of $\lambda = 2$ estimate the market share of each retail store using the customer attraction model. If your estimated market shares were equal to the store's actual share of the student market, what does this imply about the customer attraction model and the marketing mix of each store and its mopeds?

2. Develop a questionnaire to measure a moped's image. Be sure to include those store attributes that would affect consumer decisions to shop at a particular store. Then have three or four other students evaluate the image of a moped marketed by a lawnmower shop, a bicycle shop, and a motorcycle shop. After obtaining your results, form a group with several other students in your class and combine your results to get a more complete picture of how the product image was affected by the type of retail store.

3. For the products listed in Table 18 – 7, interview several students not enrolled in your class and ask them what they would do when faced with a stockout for each product listed: buy elsewhere, switch brands, or buy later at the same shop. Then combine all the results to obtain an estimate of student behavior. Compare student behavior with the behavior of other groups shown in Table 18 – 7 and discuss any similarities and differences.

4. Develop a questionnaire designed to measure the image of two restaurants near campus. Then have several students not enrolled in your class complete your questionnaire. With this information, evaluate the image of each restaurant in terms of similarities and differences.

5. Arrange with a local retailer (convenience store, drug store, etc.) to temporaily install a point-of-purchase display. Then set up a procedure to unobtrusively observe the frequency of evaluation and selection at the display.

19

Postpurchase processes

3M Company introduced Embark, a plant growth regulator, to the commercial market in 1978. Embark, which slows the growth rate of grass, is used on golf courses, cemeteries, college campuses, along highways, and in other areas where it is desirable to minimize the frequency of mowing. In 1979, the firm began to conduct market research on the feasibility of introducing Embark into the consumer market. A company representative described the goal of the research as one of being "sure we position it (Embark) correctly for the consumer. We don't want the consumer to have false expectations about the product or the results."[1]

3M Company's concern that consumers might form unrealistic expectations about Embark's performance and then be dissatisfied after using the product reflects the increasing importance marketers assign to ensuring that consumers are satisfied *after* they purchase a product. In addition, it reflects the realization that marketing activities that occur before the purchase can influence the final evaluation of the product's performance after the purchase. This chapter examines the activities that typically occur after the purchase and describes the steps that marketing managers can take both before and after the purchase to increase consumer satisfaction and future sales.

---

[1] "3M Will Embark on Consumer Area Bid," *Advertising Age* (March 26, 1979), p. 68.

THE NATURE OF POSTPURCHASE PROCESSES

Figure 19−1 illustrates the major processes that may occur after a product is purchased. Each of these processes is covered in detail in this chapter. A brief overview at this point will help clarify the interrelationships. After a purchase, an individual sometimes experiences doubt or

FIGURE 19–1
Postpurchase processes

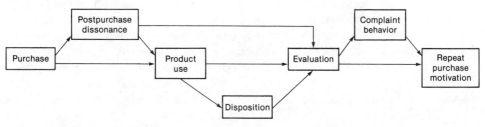

worry about the wisdom of the purchase. This doubt may occur before the product is used and is referred to as *postpurchase dissonance*. The conditions that lead to postpurchase dissonance and the steps that consumers take to reduce dissonance have important implications for marketing strategy which are described in the next section of this chapter.

Not all purchases lead to postpurchase dissonance. Instead, the purchase may be followed directly by usage by either the purchaser or some other member of the purchasing unit, generally the family. In addition, even in those purchase situations that do involve postpurchase dissonance, the dissonance reduction process generally leads to product usage (although it sometimes results in a product return prior to usage). Thus, most purchases are followed by usage. An analysis of product usage patterns can provide marketers with clues to improvements in the marketing mix variables as well as new product ideas. An understanding of how a product is used is particularly important because product usage is the primary influence on evaluation.

Product usage is often accompanied or followed by the disposition of the product or some parts of the product's container or package. Understanding disposition behavior is important because of the increasing concern for solid waste management and energy conservation. In addition, the disposition of the product or its package can influence the evaluation of the product.

As Figure 19−1 shows, evaluation is influenced by postpurchase dissonance, product use, and disposition. Evaluation is also the primary determinant of repurchase motivation. Therefore, a substantial portion of this chapter is devoted to the factors related to favorable and unfavorable evaluations. An unfavorable evaluation can lead to complaint behavior. Such complaints can be addressed to the retail outlet involved, the manufacturer, and/or governmental agencies. The resolution of such complaints can have a major impact on repurchase motivation.

Repurchase motivation is a concern of most marketers. Marketing managers want consumers to repurchase the same product, different products by the same manufacturer (or in the same store) or to recommend the purchase of these products to members of their reference groups. In the final section of the chapter, we examine the various functions that repeat purchases fulfill for consumers as well as the factors that lead to repeat purchasing behavior.

Thus, a number of important processes occur after a purchase is made. These processes culminate in some form of repeat purchase motivation which is of critical importance to most marketing managers.

POSTPURCHASE DISSONANCE

Try to recall the last time you made an important (to you) purchase in which you had to consider a variety of alternatives that differed in terms of the attributes they offered. Perhaps a decision like selecting a college close to home where you would have many friends or one further away but better academically. It is likely that immediately after you committed yourself to one alternative or the other you wondered "did I make the right decision? Should I have done something else?" This is a very common reaction after making a difficult, relatively permanent decision. This type of doubt or anxiety is referred to as *postpurchase dissonance.*[2]

As Figure 19–1 indicates, some, but not all, consumer purchase decisions are followed by postpurchase dissonance. The probability of a consumer experiencing postpurchase dissonance as well as the magnitude of such dissonance is a function of:

1. *The degree of commitment or irrevocability of the decision.* The easier it is to alter the decision, the less likely the consumer is to experience dissonance.
2. *The importance of the decision to the consumer.* The more important the decision is to the consumer, the more likely dissonance will result.
3. *The difficulty of choosing among the alternatives.* The harder it is to select from among the alternatives, the more likely the experience and magnitude of dissonance.[3] Decision difficulty is a function of

---

[2] The basic theory of cognitive dissonance of which postpurchase dissonance is a subset is presented in L. Festinger, *A Theory of Cognitive Dissonance* (Stanford University Press, 1957). An overview is available in W. H. Cummings and M. Venkatesan, "Cognitive Dissonance and Consumer Behavior: A Review of the Evidence," *Journal of Marketing Research* (August 1976), pp. 303–8.

[3] M. Menasco and D. Hawkins, "A Field Test of the Relationship between Cognitive Dissonance and State Anxiety," *Journal of Marketing Research* (November 1978), pp. 650–55.

the number of alternatives considered, the number of relevant attributes associated with each alternative, and the extent to which each alternative offers attributes not available with the other alternatives.

4. *The individual's tendency to experience anxiety.* Some individuals have a higher tendency to experience anxiety (a high-anxiety trait) than do others. The higher the tendency to experience anxiety, the more likely the individual will experience postpurchase dissonance.[4]

Dissonance occurs because making a relatively permanent commitment to a chosen alternative requires one to give up the attractive features of the unchosen alternatives. This is inconsistent with the desire for those features. As we saw in Chapter 12, consumers are frequently motivated to achieve and maintain consistency. Therefore, dissonance is unpleasant and consumers may attempt to reduce it.

Dissonance reduction processes

While we may all experience some level of dissonance after a major purchase, these feelings vary from one consumer to another. This is because no two consumers are likely to find themselves in the same situation in terms of evaluation of alternatives, ability to purchase, need for other alternative purchases, and level of trait anxiety. Also, we should keep in mind that postpurchase dissonance is not an enduring feeling of psychological discomfort but one that is at its greatest magnitude shortly after the purchase. Since dissonance is uncomfortable, the consumer may utilize one or more of the following approaches to reduce feelings of dissonance:

1. Increase the desirability of the brand purchased.
2. Decrease the desirability of rejected alternatives.
3. Decrease the importance of the purchase decision.[5]

The use of the first two methods of dissonance reduction is illustrated in Figure 19–2. This shows the results of a study in which consumers who experienced high and low levels of dissonance ranked their preference for chosen and unchoosen products, in this case record albums. Consumers ranked their album preference prior to choice, immediately after choice, and one week after choice. Consumers experiencing high levels of dissonance increased the desirability of the album chosen (as indicated by increased preference ratings for it) on each subsequent evaluation and decreased the attractiveness of unchosen albums (indicated by lowered preference ratings). On the other hand, consumers

---

[4] S. Oshikawa, "The Measurement of Cognitive Dissonance: Some Experimental Findings," *Journal of Marketing* (January 1972), pp. 64–67; and D. I. Hawkins, "Reported Cognitive Dissonance and Anxiety: Some Additional Findings," *Journal of Marketing* (July 1972), pp. 63–66.

[5] Festinger, *Cognitive Dissonance*.

496

FIGURE 19–2

Preference for chosen and unchosen alternatives for high- and low-dissonance consumers

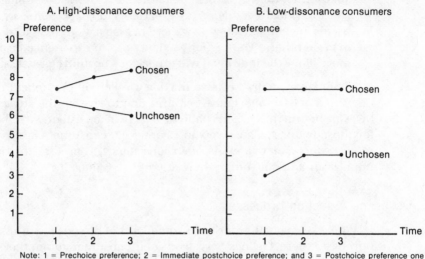

Note: 1 = Prechoice preference; 2 = Immediate postchoice preference; and 3 = Postchoice preference one week later.

Source: Derived from L. LoSciuto and R. Perloff, "Influence of Product Preference on Dissonance Reduction," *Journal of Marketing Research* (American Marketing Association, August 1967), pp. 186–90.

experiencing lower levels of dissonance did not change their evaluation of either chosen or unchosen record albums.[6]

Figure 19−2 also illustrates the closeness between chosen and un-chosen alternatives for high-dissonance consumers, which is one of the primary causes of their dissonance. For low-dissonance consumers the choice was much simpler since their chosen record album was much more preferred than their unchosen record album. Similar results have been found for instant coffee, but in this case the likelihood of experiencing postpurchase dissonance was reduced when brand familiarity was greater.[7] Thus, one way consumers avoid the potential of experiencing postpurchase dissonance is to repurchase familiar brands.

While the period in which a consumer may actively experience post-purchase dissonance may be limited to a couple of days or a week, the effect it has on the consumer may be longer. For example, in one study students ranked their preferences for five swimming suits that differed in style and color.[8] After this preference ranking, half the stu-

---

[6] L. LoSciuto and R. Perloff, "Influence of Product Preference on Dissonance Reduction," *Journal of Marketing Research* (August 1967), pp. 186−90.

[7] J. Cohen and M. Goldberg, "The Dissonance Model in Post-Decision Product Evaluation," *Journal of Marketing Research* (August 1970), pp. 315−21.

[8] R. Mittlestaedt, "A Dissonance Approach to Repeat Purchasing Behavior," *Journal of Marketing Research* (November 1969), pp. 444−46.

dents were asked to choose a swimsuit from the alternatives they ranked third and fourth in terms of preference. The remaining students were asked to select a swimsuit from their third and fifth ranked swimsuits. Presumably, the latter group should experience less dissonance than the former group since their alternatives were not as closely matched. Some time later the subjects were asked to make the decision again, only this time their second preferred swimsuit and the swimsuit the student had selected on the previous occasion were the two included in their choice. In this case 64 percent of the high-dissonance consumers picked the swimsuit they had picked before, the swimsuit that prior to their first choice was less preferred by that consumer. For the low-dissonance consumers, 86 percent switched to their more preferred swimsuit when given that option in the second choice situation. It appears that tough choices, in which dissonance is likely to occur, may produce a level of loyalty to the chosen brand.

Marketing strategies based on dissonance reduction processes Doubts that follow a purchase are often reduced by searching for additional information that serves to confirm the wisdom of a particular choice.[9] There is evidence that both positive and negative information might be sought in a search for additional information.[10] Naturally, information that supports the consumer's choice acts to bolster confidence in the correctness of the purchase decision. On the other hand, consumers may seek out discrepant facts in order to refute them and thereby also reduce dissonance.[11] In either case, the search for information after purchase as a way to reduce uncertainty greatly enhances the role that advertising and follow-up sales efforts can have on consumers. To enhance customer confidence in their brand choice, the Ford Motor Company designs certain advertisements for recent purchasers in the hope that these advertisements will help reduce postpurchase dissonance.[12] The usefulness of this marketing effort has been proven effective in at least one study which showed that owners of new automobiles showed a higher recall of dealer advertisements.[13]

---

[9] J. Adams, "Reduction of Cognitive Dissonance by Seeking Consonant Information," *Journal of Abnormal and Social Psychology* (1961), pp. 74–78; J. Mills, E. Aronson, and H. Robinson, "Selectivity in Exposure to Information," *Journal of Abnormal and Social Psychology* (1959), pp. 250–53.

[10] R. Lowe and I. Steiner, "Some Effects of the Reversibility and Consequences of Decisions on Post-decision Information Preferences," *Journal of Personality and Social Psychology* (1968), pp. 172–79.

[11] J. Freedman, "Preference for Dissonant Information," *Journal of Personality and Social Psychology* (1965), pp. 287–89.

[12] G. Brown, "The Automobile Buyer, Decision within the Family," *Household Decision Making,* ed. N. Foole (New York University Press, 1961), pp. 193–99.

[13] This finding, like many others associated with dissonance studies, is subject to a variety of interpretations, see Cummings and Venkatesan, "Cognitive Dissonance." While dissonance theory may not prove to be the ultimate explanation for those behaviors, it does provide a useful guide for managerial action.

Other marketing efforts have also proven useful in reducing post-purchase dissonance. For example, following the purchase of a refrigerator a letter was sent to some customers, a telephone call was made to others, and the remainder were not contacted.[14] Those that were contacted after purchase were thanked for doing business with the merchant and reassured that they had made a wise purchase. Shortly thereafter, these customers were interviewed and their levels of post-purchase doubt measured. As shown in Table 19−1 the letter pro-

TABLE 19-1

Dissonance and repurchase motivation following a postpurchase sales communication

Postpurchase action	Postpurchase dissonance*	Repurchase motivation†
No contact	2.11	2.08
Letter sent	1.90	2.30
Telephone call	2.31	1.70

* The higher the score, the higher the dissonance.
† The higher the score, the higher the repurchase motivation.
Source: Derived from S. Hunt, "Post-Transaction Communication and Dissonance Reduction," *Journal of Marketing* (American Marketing Association, January 1970), pp. 46–51.

duced the lowest level of postpurchase doubt, and the telephone call produced the highest level of postpurchase doubt. This might imply that the telephone call was disruptive and perhaps created feelings of uncertainty and suspicion by implying that something was wrong.

Marketers need to maximize consumer satisfaction immediately after the purchase. To fail to do so can result in permanent dissatisfaction or at least short-term negative word-of-mouth communications. For example, Table 19−1 clearly indicates an inverse relationship between the level of postpurchase dissonance and the level of repurchase motivation. However, the fact that the phone call increased dissonance indicates that caution (and testing) should be used in selecting a method to help consumers reduce potential dissonance.

PRODUCT USE

Most purchases do not involve postpurchase doubt. Instead, either the purchaser or some other member of the purchasing unit uses the product without first worrying about the wisdom of the purchase. And, as Figure 19−1 shows, even when postpurchase dissonance occurs, it is still generally followed by product use.

---

[14] S. Hunt, "Post-Transaction Communication and Dissonance Reduction," *Journal of Marketing* (January 1970), pp. 46−51.

Observing consumers as they utilize products is an important aspect of product development. For example, observations of consumer modifications of existing bicycles led to the commercial development of the immensely popular "stingray style children's bicycle. However, almost all research of this nature is in an artificial setting and/or is being conducted with the consumer's permission. As a result, few "nonstandard" product uses are observed.

Many firms attempt to obtain relevant information on product usage via surveys using standard questionnaires or focus groups. Such surveys can lead to new product development or indicate new uses or markets for existing products. For example, consumers were using baking soda as a personal deodorant long before Arm & Hammer developed a baking soda based deodorant. Likewise, consumers were using baking soda as an freshner in their refrigerators before such usage was encouraged by Arm & Hammer.

Understanding how products are used can also lead to more effective advertising and supplementary sales. Recall from Chapter 6 that there are major regional variations in how coffee is consumed; that is, with or without cream, in a mug or a cup, and so forth. Thus, a coffee marketer may find it worthwhile to prepare regional versions of the major advertising theme to reflect regional usage patterns. Retailers can frequently take advantage of the fact that the use of one product may require or suggest the use of other products to encourage related purchases. Consider the following product "sets": houseplants and fertilizer, canoes and life vests, cameras and carrying cases, sport coats and ties, and dresses and shoes. In each case, the use of the first product is made easier, more enjoyable, or safer by the use of the related products. Retailers can promote such items jointly and/or train sales personnel to make relevant complementary sales. However, to do so requires a sound knowledge of how the products are actually utilized.

Increasingly stringent product liability laws are also forcing marketing managers to examine *how* consumers use their products.[15] These laws have made firms responsible for harm caused by product failure *not only when the product is used as specified by the manufacturer but in any reasonably foreseeable use of the product*. For example, Parker Brothers voluntarily recalled their very successful plastic riveting tool, Riviton, at a cost approaching $10 million. The reason was two deaths caused by children choking after swallowing one of the rubber rivets. Both Wham-O Manufacturing and Mattel have been involved in similar recalls in recent years.[16] Thus, the manufacturer must design products with both their primary purpose *and* other potential uses in mind. This

---

[15] "The Devils in the Product Liability Laws," *Business Week* (February 12, 1979), pp. 72–78.

[16] C. W. Stevens, "One Producer Finds Recall Is Best Policy for a Hazardous Toy," *The Wall Street Journal* (March 2, 1979), p. 1.

requires substantial research into how consumers actually use the products.

Unfortunately, there are few published accounts of how products are actually used. Marketing managers must generally develop product usage data for their own specific product categories.

DISPOSITION

Disposition of the product or the product's container may occur before (for the container), during, or after product use. Or, for those products which are completely consumed, such as an ice cream cone, no disposition may be involved. Until recent years, only limited attention had been devoted to the disposition process. Ecological and economic concerns have led to an interest in what happens to product packages and to products after the consumer no longer desires to retain them.

Both product and package design affect the disposition decision. For example, some packages are not efficient in terms of consumption behavior since it is difficult to maintain the product's quality once the package has been opened. When this is the case much more of the product will be wasted. White bread is a good example, as little waste is associated with white bread that comes in a standard resealable bread wrapper. However, specialty breads, often in packages that cannot be efficiently resealed, are a major source of waste. As a result, specialty breads account for only 16 percent of the total bread sales but more than 32 percent of all bread waste.[17] Clearly, marketing mix decisions can have a major impact on consumption efficiency.

Package disposition

Millions of pounds of product packages are disposed of everyday. These containers are thrown away as garbage, or as litter, used in some capacity by the consumer, or recycled. Creating packages which utilize a minimal amount of resources is important for economic reasons as well as being a matter of social responsibility. Producing containers that are easily recyclable or that can be reused also has important consequences beyond social responsibility. Certain market segments consider the recyclable nature of the product container to be an important product attribute. These consumers anticipate disposition of the package as an attribute of the brand during the alternative evaluation stage. Thus, the ease of disposition can be used as a marketing mix variable in an attempt to capture certain market segments.

---

[17] W. Rathje, W. Hughes, and S. Jernigan, "The Science of Garbage: Following the Consumer through His Garbage Can," *Business Proceedings* (American Marketing Association, 1976), pp. 56—64.

Studies of individuals using recycling centers reveal two basic sets of motives.[18] One group of consumers recycle certain containers for the financial renumeration. These individuals tend to have lower socio-economic standing.

The second major motive for using recycling centers is a strong concern for ecology. Individuals recycling packages for this reason are generally relatively young, from upper socioeconomic categories, somewhat liberal, and feel they can control their environment. These consumers share many characteristics with what is called the "socially conscious consumer."[19] *Socially conscious consumers* consider the impact of their purchase decisions on the social or physical environment as an important attribute in the decision process.

The socially conscious consumer, including those concerned with recycling, are important for a variety of reasons. First, they represent a sizable, affluent market segment. Second, they tend to be influential and have the potential to influence other segments. Finally, they tend to be politically active and may influence the legal environment in which a firm operates. This is obvious in the increasing number of states banning throw-away bottles and pull-tab cans.

Product disposition

For many product categories, a physical product continues to exist even though it may no longer meet a consumer's needs. A product may no longer function physically (instrumental function) in a manner desired by a consumer or it may no longer provide the symbolic meaning desired by the consumer. An automobile that no longer runs is an example of a product ceasing to function instrumentally. An automobile whose owner decides it is "out of style" no longer functions symbolically (for that particular consumer). In either case, once a replacement pur-

---

[18] See W. G. Zikmund and W. J. Stanton, "Recycling Solid Wastes: A Channels of Distribution Problem," *Journal of Marketing* (July 1971), pp. 34 – 39; R. A. Marquardt, A. F. McGann, and J. C. Makens, "Consumer Responses to the Problem of Disposable Containers," in *Advances in Consumer Research I*, eds. S. Ward and P. Wright (Association for Consumer Research, 1974), pp. 38 – 50; F. E. Webster, Jr., "Determining the Characteristics of the Socially Conscious Consumer," *Journal of Consumer Research* (December 1975), pp. 188 – 96; J. Arbuthnot, "The Roles of Attitudinal and Personality Variables in the Prediction of Environmental Behavior and Change," *Environment and Behavior* (June 1977), pp. 217 – 33; and W. H. Peters, "Who Cooperates in Voluntary Recycling Efforts?" in *Increasing Marketing Productivity*, ed. T. V. Greer (American Marketing Association, 1973), pp. 505 – 8.

[19] See G. Brooker, "The Self-Actualizing Socially Conscious Consumer," *Journal of Consumer Research* (September 1978), pp. 107 – 12; L. R. Tucker, Jr., "The Environmentally Concerned Citizen," *Environment and Behavior* (September 1978), pp. 389 – 418; P. E. Murphy, "Environmentally Concerned Consumers: Demographic Dimensions," in *Research Frontiers in Marketing: Dialogues and Directions,* ed. S. C. Jain (American Marketing Association, 1978), pp. 316 – 20; and P. E. Murphy, N. Kangun, and W. Locander, "Environmentally Concerned Consumers: Racial Variations," *Journal of Marketing* (October 1978), pp. 61 – 66.

chase is made (or even before the purchase) a disposition decision must be made.

Figure 19–3 illustrates the various alternatives for disposing of a product. The three basic decisions are to keep the product, get rid of it temporarily, or get rid of it permanently. As Table 19–2 indicates, the method of disposition varies dramatically across product categories. For example, in almost 80 percent of the cases a used toothbrush was thrown away, but less than 12 percent of the stero amplifiers were disposed of in this manner.

FIGURE 19–3
Product disposition alternatives

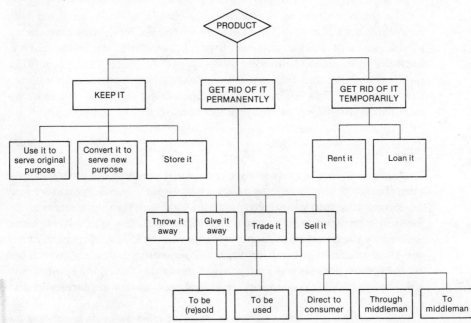

Source: J. Jacoby, C. K. Berning, and T. F. Dietvorst, "What about Disposition? *Journal of Marketing* (American Marketing Association, April 1977), p. 23.

Unfortunately, we know very little about the demographic or psychological characteristics of individuals who tend to select particular disposal methods. One study in this area found few meaningful differences in the characteristics of individuals choosing differing means of disposing of small electrical appliances.[20] It appears that situational variables such as the availability of storage space, the current needs of friends, the

---

[20] M. Burke, W. D. Conn, and R. J. Lutz, "Using Psychographic Variables to Investigate Product Disposition Behavior," *Research Frontiers in Marketing: Dialogues and Directions*, ed. S. C. Jain (American Marketing Association, 1978), pp. 321–26.

TABLE 19–2
Disposition decisions for six products

	Stereo amplifier	Wrist- watch	Tooth- brush	Phono- graph record	Bicycle	Refrig- erator
Converted	1.6%	1.8%	17.2%	9.6%	1.5%	7.5%
Stored	—	28.7	—	32.8	3.1	—
Thrown away	11.5	30.6	79.7	43.2	17.3	22.6
Given away	31.1	23.1		9.6	40.2	19.3
Traded	4.9	5.6		0.8	3.2	20.4
Sold	42.6	5.6		—	17.3	25.8
Rented	—	0.9		—	—	3.2
Loaned	—	—		—	1.5	1.0
Other	8.3	3.7	3.1	4.0	15.9	—
	100.0%	100.0%	100.0%	100.0%	100.0%	100.0%

Source: J. Jacoby, C. K. Berning, and T. F. Dietvorst, "What about Disposition?" *Journal of Marketing* (American Marketing Association, April 1977), p. 26.

availability of recycling or charitable organizations, and so forth *may* be the primary determinant of disposition behavior.

Product disposition and marketing strategy Why should a marketing manager be concerned about the disposition of a used product? The primary reason is that disposition decisions affect the purchase decisions of both the individual making the disposition decision and other individuals in the market for that product category. There are three major ways in which disposition decisions can affect a firm's marketing strategy.

First, disposition must sometimes occur before acquisition of a replacement because of physical space or financial limitations. For example, a family living in an apartment may find it necessary to dispose of an existing bedroom set before acquiring a new one because of a lack of storage space. Or, individuals may need to sell their current bicycle in order to raise supplemental funds to pay for a new bicycle. If consumers experience difficulty in disposing of the existing product, they may become discouraged and withdraw from the purchasing process. Thus it is to the manufacturer's and retailer's advantage to assist the consumer in the disposition process.

Second, frequent decisions by consumers to sell, trade, or give away used products may result in a large used product market which can reduce the market for new products. The manufacturer may want to enter such a market by buying used products or taking trade-ins and repairing them for the rebuilt market. This is common for automotive parts such as generators and, to a lesser extent, for vacuum cleaners.

A *third* reason for concern with product disposition is the fact that the United States is not completely a throw-away society. As we discussed earlier in this chapter, many Americans are very concerned with waste and how their purchase decisions affect waste. Such individuals might be willing to purchase, for example, a new vacuum cleaner if they were confident that the old one would be rebuilt and resold. However, they might be reluctant to throw it away or to go to the effort of reselling it themselves. Thus, manufacturers and retailers could take steps to ensure that products are reused. Such steps could increase the demand for new products while meeting the needs of consumers needing less-expensive versions of the product.

PURCHASE EVALUATION

As we saw in Figure 19−1, a consumer's evaluation of a purchase is influenced by postpurchase dissonance, product use, and product disposition. This does not mean that all purchase evaluations are influenced by each of these three processes. Rather, these three processes are potential influencing factors that may affect the evaluation of a particular purchase. It should also be noted that either the outlet or the product or both may be involved in the evaluation.

Postpurchase dissonance can have a direct influence on the evaluation process prior to the use of the product. As we saw in Table 19−1, repurchase motivation, which reflects a positive evaluation, decreases as postpurchase dissonance increases. In the preceding section, we examined disposition and indicated that, for certain market segments, the availability of ecologically sound disposition alternatives has a major impact on the overall evaluation of the product or product category. In this section, we are going to analyze the relationship between product usage and the evaluation of the purchase decision.

The evaluation process

A particular alternative such as a product, brand, or retail outlet is selected because it is thought to be a better overall choice than other alternatives that were considered in the choice process. Whether that particular item was selected because of its presumed superior functional performance or because of some other feature such as a lower price or more appealing style, consumers have some level of expected performance that the brand should provide. If performance falls short of expectations, dissatisfaction will occur and problem recognition will result.[21] If the discrepancy between performance and expectation is

---

[21] R. Anderson, "Consumer Dissatisfaction: The Effect of Disconfirmed Expectancy on Perceived Product Performance," *Journal of Marketing* (February 1973), pp. 33−44; see also E. Anderson and J. F. Hair, Jr., "Consumerism, Consumer Expectations, and Perceived Product Performance," in *Proceedings 3d Annual Conference,* ed. M. Venkatesan (Association for Consumer Research 1972), pp. 67−79; R. Cardozo, "An Experimental Study of

large and/or the problem it creates is important enough, the consumer will restart the entire decision process. The item causing the problem recognition will most likely be placed in the inept set (see Chapter 16) and no longer be considered.

This has important marketing implications in terms of positioning the level of promotional claims. Since it has been shown that consumer dissatisfaction is a function of the disparity between expectations and perceived product performance, unrealistic consumer expectations created by excessive promotional exaggeration can contribute to consumer dissatisfaction. This relationship between promotional claims, expectations, and purchase evaluations is the reason for the 3M Company's concern about correctly positioning Embark in the consumer market (refer to the beginning of this chapter).

The need to develop realistic consumer expectations poses a difficult problem for the marketing manager. For a brand or store to be selected by a consumer, it must be viewed as superior on the relevant combination of attributes. Therefore, the marketing manager naturally wants to emphasize the positive aspects of the brand or outlet. If such an emphasis creates expectations in the consumer that the product cannot fulfill, a negative evaluation may occur. As we will see in detail shortly, negative evaluations can produce brand switching, unfavorable word-of-mouth advertising, and complaint behavior. Thus, the marketing manager must balance enthusiasm for the product with a realistic view of the product's attributes.

Dimensions of performance   Since performance expectations and actual performance are major factors in the evaluation process, we need to examine the dimensions of product performance. For many products there are two dimensions to performance, instrumental and expressive or symbolic.[22] *Instrumental performance* relates to the physical functioning of the product. This naturally would be important in the evaluation of a dishwasher, sewing machine, or other major appliance. *Symbolic performance* relates to aesthetic or image enhancement performance. For example, the durability of a sport coat is an aspect of instrumental performance, but styling would represent symbolic performance.

Is symbolic or instrumental performance more important to consumers as they evaluate product performance? The answer to this question undoubtably varies by product category and across consumer groups. However, a number of studies focusing on clothing provide

Consumer Effort, Expectations, and Satisfaction," *Journal of Marketing Research* (August 1965), pp. 244 – 49; and R. W. Olshavsky and J. A. Miller, "Consumer Expectations, Product Performance, and Perceived Product Quality," *Journal of Marketing Research* (February 1973), pp. 19 – 21.

[22] J. Swan and L. Combs, "Product Performance and Consumer Satisfaction: A New Concept," *Journal of Marketing* (April 1976), pp. 25 – 33.

some insights into the relationship of these two types of performance to the evaluation process.

Clothing appears to perform five major functions: protection from the environment, enhancement of sexual attraction, aesthetic and sensuous satisfaction, an indicator of status, and an extension of self-image.[23] Except for protection from the environment, these functions are all dimensions of symbolic performance. Yet studies of clothing returns, complaints about clothing purchases, and discarded clothing indicate that physical product failures are the primary cause of dissatisfaction.[24] A recent detailed study of the relationship between performance expectations, actual performance, and satisfaction with clothing purchases reached the following general conclusion: dissatisfaction is caused by a failure of instrumental performance, while complete satisfaction also requires that the symbolic functions perform at or above the expected levels.[25]

These findings certainly cannot be generalized to other product categories without additional research. The conclusion that the performance attributes that lead to dissatisfaction are different from those that lead to satisfaction is interesting.[26] It suggests that the marketing manager should maintain performance at the minimum expected level on those attributes that lead to dissatisfaction while attempting to maximize performance on those attributes that lead to increased satisfaction.

Individual variations in purchase evaluations

A number of individual characteristics appear to affect the outcome of the evaluation process. Consumer feelings of personal competence and efficacy are closely related to satisfaction.[27] Consumers who feel they are competent and effective in life in general are more likely to be satisfied with their purchase of major durables than consumers who are low on these traits. This is consistent with other research which has shown that individuals with high personal competence/efficacy also have a greater satisfaction with life overall.[28] Thus, expressions or feelings of consumer satisfaction and dissatisfaction are attributable in

---

[23] M. J. Horn, *The Second Skin: An Interdisciplinary Study of Clothing* (Houghton Mifflin Co., 1968), p. 12.

[24] M. S. Ryan, *Clothing: A Study in Human Behavior* (Holt, Rinehart and Winston, 1966), pp. 183–85.

[25] J. E. Swan and L. J. Combs, "Product Performance and Consumer Satisfaction: A New Concept," *Journal of Marketing* (April 1976), pp. 25–33.

[26] Such a phenomenon has been studied extensively in relationship to job satisfaction. See F. Herzberg, *Work and the Nature of Man* (World Publishing, 1966).

[27] R. Westbrook, "Consumer Satisfaction as a Function of Personal Competence/Efficacy," unpublished research paper, University of Arizona (1979).

[28] F. Andrews and S. Withey, "Developing Measures of Perceived Life Quality: Results from Several National Surveys," *Social Indicators Research* (1974), pp. 1–26.

part to the nature of individuals themselves. In addition, the more effort consumers exert in the search and evaluation, the more likely they are to be satisfied with the resultant purchase.[29] These individual variations suggest that it may not be feasible nor practical for marketers to deliver complete satisfaction to all consumers all of the time.

When perceptions of product performance match or exceed expectations of product performance, satisfaction occurs and there is less need for information search and evaluation. When this is the case the consumer may repurchase the same brands (shop again at the same outlet) since expectations have been met and there is no need to expend unnecessary effort on finding a better product. When expectations are not met and dissatisfaction occurs, the consumer must decide on a strategy for dealing with the dissatisfaction.

Complaint behavior

Figure 19–4 illustrates the major options available to consumers who are dissatisfied with a purchase. The primary decision is whether to take

FIGURE 19–4
Actions taken by consumers in response to product dissatisfactions

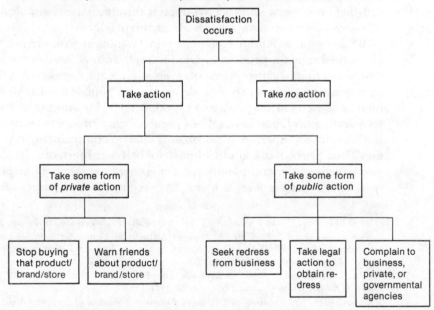

Source: R. Day, "Extending the Concept of Consumer Satisfaction," in *Advances in Consumer Research IV*, ed. W. D. Perreault, Jr. (Association for Consumer Research, 1977), p. 153. Used with permission.

---

[29] Cardozo, "Experimental Study."

some form of action or not. By taking no action, the consumer, in effect, decides to tolerate the dissatisfaction or to rationalize it. A primary reason for taking no action is that pursuing an active course of action requires time and effort that may exceed the perceived value of any likely result.

As Figure 19—4 indicates, action in response to a state of dissatisfaction can be private in nature such as switching brands, products, or stores or warning friends about the product. Or, the action may be public such as demanding redress from the firm involved, complaining to the firm or some other organization, or taking legal action against the firm.

A study of 540 consumers who could recall a case in which one or more of the grocery products they normally purchase were defective, produced 1,307 separate unsatisfactory purchases. In terms of private actions, 25 percent of these unsatisfactory purchases resulted in brand switching, 19 percent caused the shopper to stop buying the product, 13 percent led to an in-store inspection of future purchases and 43 percent produced no private action. These same defects caused the following public actions: 3 percent produced complaints to the manufacturer, 5 percent produced complaints to the retailer, 35 percent resulted in the item being returned, and 58 percent produced no public action.[30] In a similar study of durable goods, 54 percent of the dissatisfied customers said they would not purchase the brand again, and 45 percent warned their friends about the product.[31]

While brand switching and attempting to influence others not to purchase the brand (or product or from the retail outlet) are fairly common responses to a negative purchase evaluation, complaints to the firm or governmental agencies are not very common. Noncomplaint rates are as high as 86 percent for problems experienced by consumers of low-cost, frequently purchased items.[32] For personal care products 89 percent of the consumers experiencing problems take no complaint action.[33] However, this percentage is cut almost in half for most durables as the percentage of noncomplaints for consumers experiencing a problem with household durables is about 50 percent,[34] and 44 percent for new

---

[30] A. C. Nielsen, "Caveat Venditor," *The Nielsen Researcher,* no. 6 (1975), pp. 2—3.

[31] R. L. Day and E. L. Landon, Jr., "Toward a Theory on Consumer Complaining Behavior," paper presented at Symposium on Consumer and Industrial Buying Behavior, University of South Carolina, March 26, 1976.

[32] A. Andreasan and A. Best, "Consumers Complain—Does Business Respond?" *Harvard Business Review* (July—August 1977), pp. 93—101.

[33] B. Diener, "Information and Redress: Consumer Needs and Company Responses—the Case of the Personal Care Industry," working paper no. 75—113 (Marketing Science Institute, 1975).

[34] See D. Caplovitz, *The Poor Pay More,* 2d ed. (Free Press, 1967); B. Mason and S. Himes, Jr., "An Exploratory Behavioral and Socio-Economic Profile of Consumer Action about Dissatisfaction with Selected Household Appliances," *Journal of Consumer Affairs* (Winter 1976), pp. 121—27.

cars.[35] This percentage is reduced even lower for clothing purchases, as only 25 percent of those experiencing a problem do not take some form of complaint action.[36] *There appears to be a difference in complaint behavior that is related to both the cost and social importance of the product.*

In terms of individual consumer complaint effort, analyses of complaint files show that about one fourth of the complainers account for nearly 50 percent of all the complaints.[37] For example, a sample of 2,400 households revealed the frequency of complaints shown in Table 19–3 for some 34 commonly purchased products and services.[38]

TABLE 19–3
Frequency of complaints

Number of complaints	Percent of all respondents	Percent of complainers	Percent of complaints
0	46.8%	—	—
1	25.5	47.9%	23.5%
2	13.0	24.4	23.8
3	8.2	15.4	22.6
4	3.3	6.3	12.3
5	1.5	2.9	7.0
6 or more	1.7	3.2	10.7
	100.0%	100.0%	100.0%

Source: A. Andreasan and A. Best, "Consumers Complain—Does Business Respond?" *Harvard Business Review* (July–August 1977), p. 98. Used with permission.

In this case a little over 50.0 percent of the consumers voiced complaints, and of these, 47.9 percent did it only once, while 3.2 percent complained six or more times. Of course, it is not only how much you complain that brings action but also the manner in which you express your complaint. One study showed that there was a significant difference in response to handwritten and typed complaints about guaranteed products, with typed complaints receiving better responses.[39]

Individual variation in complaint behavior Every study of dis-

---

[35] J. Swan and J. D. Longman, "Consumer Satisfaction with Automobile Repair Performance: Attitudes toward the Industry and Governmental Control," *Proceedings* (American Marketing Association, 1973), pp. 241–48.

[36] M. Wall, "Consumer Satisfaction with Clothing Wear and Care Performance and Consumer Communication of Clothing Performance Complaints," Ph.D. dissertation, Ohio State University, 1974.

[37] L. Robinson, "Consumer Complaint Behavior: A Review with Implications for Further Research," paper presented at Third Annual Conference on Consumer Satisfaction/Dissatisfaction and Complaining Behavior (October 1978).

[38] Andreasan and Best, "Consumers Complain."

[39] M. Bosching, "Manufacturer's Responses to Consumer Complaints on Guaranteed Products," *Journal of Consumer Affairs* (Summer 1976), pp. 86–90.

satisfied consumers has found that a significant percentage do not complain. What individual characteristics differentiate those who complain from those who do not? Noncomplainers are often unaware of available avenues for complaints, feel powerless to act, or do not feel that complaining is worth the trouble. Compared to complainers, they tend to have lower incomes and less education.[40]

A number of personality characteristics also serve to differentiate complainers from noncomplainers: closed-minded (i.e., dogmatic) consumers have a higher propensity to complain;[41] greater generalized self-confidence corresponds with greater amounts of complaint behavior,[42] the more powerless a consumer feels, the less likely he or she is to take a complaint action;[43] and the more an individual believes in our political system to resolve problems (i.e., high political efficacy), the more likely he or she will attempt to resolve a problem by engaging in a complaint behavior.[44]

Marketing strategy and complaint behavior Marketers need to satisfy consumer expectations by (1) creating reasonable expectations through promotional efforts and (2) maintaining consistent quality so that these reasonable expectations are fulfilled. As we have seen, dissatisfied consumers are very likely to switch brands or product categories. In addition, dissatisfied consumers tend to express their dissatisfaction to their friends. Dissatisfaction may cause the firm to lose future sales to the dissatisfied consumer *and* current sales to that consumer's friends.

The evidence presented in this chapter suggests that it is virtually impossible to "please all the people all the time." When a consumer is dissatisfied, the most favorable consequence is for the consumer to communicate this dissatisfaction to the firm but to no one else. This alerts the firm to problems, enables it to make amends where necessary, and minimizes negative word-of-mouth communications. Unfortunately, many individuals do not communicate their dissatisfaction to the firm involved. Furthermore, complaints about products frequently go to retailers and are not passed on to manufacturers.

Many firms attempt to overcome this by establishing and promoting

---

[40] R. Warland, R. Herrmann, and J. Willits, "Dissatisfied Consumers: Who Gets Upset and What They Do about It," *Journal of Consumer Affairs* (Winter 1975), pp. 156−62.

[41] J. Faricy and M. Maxio, "Personality and Consumer Dissatisfaction: A Multidimensional Approach," in *Marketing in Turbulent Times*, ed. E. M. Mazze (American Marketing Association, 1975), pp. 202−8.

[42] Robinson, "Consumer Complaint."

[43] Z. Lambert and F. Kniffin, "Consumer Discontent: A Social Perspective," *California Management Review* (Fall 1975), pp. 36−44.

[44] L. Hill, "Socio-Psychological Dimensions of Complaints to Ombudsman: A New Zealand Analysis," *Proceedings* (American Political Science Association, 1971), pp. 100−9; and K. Friedman, *Complaining: Comparative Aspects of Complaint Behavior and Attitudes toward Complaining in Canada and Britain* (Sage Publications, 1974).

"consumer hot lines"—toll-free numbers that consumers can use to speak with a representative of the firm when they have a complaint.[45] Whirlpool, for example, did this when they installed what was termed a "cool" line for customers having complaints.[46] The idea was that the customer had direct access for the firm and could register complaints and problems immediately therefore "cooling" down "hot" customers. Such activities can neutralize negative feelings and create a positive reaction among a vocal and influential population segment.

REPEAT PURCHASE MOTIVATION

As Figure 19—1 indicates, the evaluation of the purchase decision and the result of any complaint behavior affect the consumer's repurchase motivation. And, as you might expect from the material presented as well as by examining your own behavior, when purchase expectations are fulfilled, there is a tendency to repurchase the brand or product that provided that satisfaction.[47] This is because such an experience is rewarding and therefore reinforcing (see Chapter 11). As we saw in Figure 19—4, dissatisfaction with the purchase may still be followed by repeat purchases. This is because the expected benefits of renewed search and evaluation are less than the expected costs of such activities.

In this section of the chapter, we want to examine the nature of repeat purchasing behavior and the consumer characteristics and marketing activities that influence it.[48]

Nature of repeat purchasing behavior

Repeat purchasing behavior is frequently referred to as *brand loyalty.* Brand loyalty implies a psychological commitment to the brand (much like friendship), whereas repeat purchasing behavior simply involves the frequent repurchase of the same brand (perhaps because it is the only one available, is generally the least expensive, and so forth). Brand loyalty is defined as:

(1) a biased (i.e., nonrandom), (2) behavioral response (i.e., purchase), (3) expressed over time, (4) by some decision-making unit, (5) with respect to

---

[45] State regulatory agencies are also utilizing such lines to learn of consumer problems. See S. L. Diamond, S. Ward, and R. Ferber, "Consumer Problems and Consumerism: Analysis of Calls to a Consumer Hot Line," *Journal of Marketing* (January 1976), pp. 58—62.

[46] Whirlpool Corporation, "Consumer Communications," *Consumer Programs Book,* n.d.

[47] For a good discussion of this topic, see R. A. Westbrook, J. W. Newman, and J. R. Taylor, "Satisfaction/Dissatisfaction in the Purchase Decision Process," *Journal of Marketing* (October 1978), pp. 54—60.

[48] For a more detailed treatment, see J. Jacoby and R. W. Chestnut, *Brand Loyalty: Measurement and Management* (John Wiley & Sons, Inc., 1978).

one or more alternative brands out of a set of such brands, and (6) is a function of psychological (decision-making, evaluative) processes.[49]

It is important to note that there is a great deal of difference between brand loyalty as defined above and repeat purchase behavior. This difference and a marketing strategy based on it is explained by Seagram's president, Frank Berger, as follows:

> The goal of liquor advertising is more than getting a trial and repeat purchase of a product. . . . The consumer must *adopt* the brand. Until that time, he's always vulnerable to competing brands. . . . At Seagram's, we raise prices on all brands continually, reinvesting the profits in advertising to obtain the reach and frequency needed to capture the consumer's brand loyalty.[50]

Figure 19—5 illustrates the potential makeup of the market share for a given brand at one point in time. There are three general categories of purchasers for any given brand: (1) nonloyal repeat purchasers, (2) loyal repeat purchasers, and (3) happenstance purchasers (purchase based on situational factors). As the figure indicates, each of these groups can be further subdivided based on their reactions to competing brands. Since each of these three categories of purchasers may require a unique marketing strategy, a substantial amount of research has been devoted to determining the characteristics of each group (although most studies have treated loyal and nonloyal repeat purchasers as a single group).

Research studies to date have produced two major conclusions. One is that *brand loyalty is a product specific phenomenon* and there is no such thing as a loyalty-prone consumer. That is, a consumer loyal to one brand in a given product category may not display similar loyalties to brands in other product classes. A second conclusion is that *brand loyal consumers express greater levels of satisfaction than less loyal and nonloyal consumers.*[51]

Traditional measures of brand loyalty have been based on measures of repeat purchase of the same brand. Using this measure of brand loyalty, brand loyal consumers *cannot* be distinguished from nonbrand loyal consumers in terms of socioeconomic, demographic, and psychological differences.[52] Also, there is only limited evidence that the loyalty

---

[49] J. Jacoby and D. B. Kyner, "Brand Loyalty vs. Repeat Purchasing Behavior," *Journal of Marketing Research* (February 1973), pp. 1—9.

[50] "Instill 'Brand Loyalty', Seagram Exec Tells Marketers," *Advertising Age* (April 30, 1979), p. 26.

[51] J. Newman and R. Werbel, "Multivariate Analysis of Brand Loyalty for Major Household Appliances," *Journal of Marketing Research* (November 1973), pp. 404—9.

[52] R. E. Frank, W. F. Massy, and T. M. Lodahl, "Purchasing Behavior and Personal Attributes," *Journal of Advertising* (December 1969), pp. 15—24; R. E. Frank, "Correlates of Buying Behavior for Grocery Products," *Journal of Marketing* (October 1967), pp. 48—53; J. S. Coulson, "Buying Decisions within the Family," in *On Knowing the Consumer*, ed. J. Newman (John Wiley and Sons, Inc., 1966), p. 66; R. P. Brody and S. M. Cunningham, "Personality Variables and the Consumer Decision Process," *Journal of Marketing Research* (February 1968), pp. 50—57.

FIGURE 19-5
Market share composition

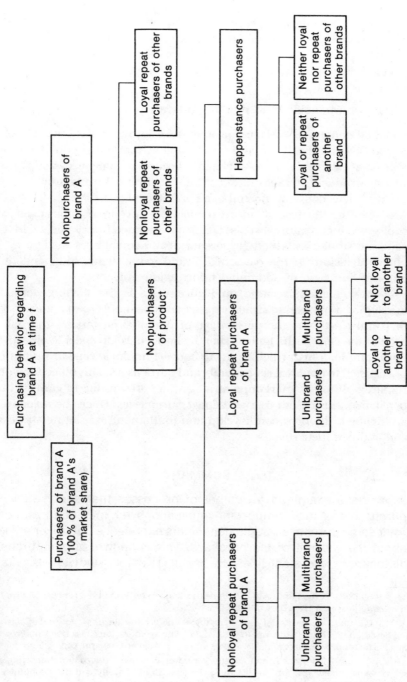

Source: J. Jacoby and R. W. Chestnut, *Brand Loyalty: Measurement and Management* (John Wiley & Sons, Inc., 1978), p. 103. Used with permission.

behavior of an informal group leader affects the brand loyalty of other group members.[53] One factor that is systematically related to brand loyalty is store loyalty. Consumers who are store loyal and thereby shop at relatively few stores are more likely to exhibit greater brand loyalty.[54]

Repeat purchasing behavior and marketing strategy

While consumer satisfaction and store loyalty contribute to repeat purchase behavior, it can also be affected by marketing efforts. In markets where there are many alternative brands, greater price activity, and where products are easily substitutable, brand loyalty tends to decrease.[55] This does not mean that all brand loyal consumers will become less loyal in the face of more choice, greater price differences, and more product features. This fact was evidenced very nicely in two separate studies in which 20 percent of the consumers made a brand choice decision on the basis of a brand name alone, independent of amount and type of additional information available.[56]

A market analysis based on Figure 19−5 is the starting point for developing a marketing strategy based on repeat purchase patterns. The firm must estimate the percentage of potential customers that fall in each of the cells in the figure. Then it should develop specific objectives. For example, a firm might want to convert nonloyal repeat multibrand purchasers to nonloyal repeat unibrand purchasers. This objective would require a different marketing strategy than attempting to convert happenstance purchasers to loyal repeat purchasers. Once the objective(s) are defined, the firm can develop and implement marketing strategies and evaluate their results.

SUMMARY

We have examined a number of processes that occur after the purchase that have important implications for marketing strategy. After some purchases, some consumers experience doubts or anxiety about the wisdom of the purchase. This is known as postpurchase dissonance. It is most likely to occur (1) among individuals with a

---

[53] J. Stafford, "Effect of Group Influences on Consumer Brand Preferences," *Journal of Marketing Research* (February 1966), pp. 68−75.

[54] J. Carman, "Correlates of Brand Loyalty: Some Positive Results," *Journal of Marketing Research* (February 1970), pp. 67−76; T. Rao, "Consumer's Purchase Decision Process: Stochastic Models," *Journal of Marketing Research* (August 1969), pp. 321−29.

[55] J. Farley, "Why Does Brand Loyalty Vary over Products," *Journal of Marketing Research* (November 1964), pp. 9−14; and J. Farley, "Brand-Loyalty and the Economics of Information," *Journal of Business* (October 1964), pp. 370−81.

[56] J. Bettman and J. Jacoby, "Patterns of Processing Consumer Information," in *Advances in Consumer Research III*, ed. B. B. Anderson (Association for Consumer Research, 1975), pp. 315−20.

tendency to experience anxiety (2) after an irrevocable purchase, (3) that was important to the consumer, and (4) involved a difficult choice between two or more alternatives. Postpurchase dissonance is important to the marketing manager because, if not resolved, it can result in a returned product or a negative evaluation of the purchase. Firms often utilize the fact that consumers seek reinforcing information after a major purchase as a basis for advertisements assuring them that they made the proper choice.

Whether or not the consumer experiences dissonance, most purchases are followed by product use. This use may be by the purchaser or by some other member of the purchasing unit. Marketing managers are interested in product use for a variety of reasons. The major reason is that consumers use a product to fulfill certain needs. If the product does not fulfill these needs a negative evaluation may result. Therefore, managers need to be aware of how products perform in use. Monitoring product usage can also indicate new uses for existing products, needed product modifications, appropriate advertising themes, and opportunities for new products. Product liability laws are making it increasingly important for marketing managers to be aware of all potential uses of their products.

Disposition of the product or its package may occur before, during, or after product use. Disposition behavior is becoming increasingly important to marketing managers because of the ecological concerns of many consumers, the costs and scarcity of raw materials, and the activities of federal and state legislatures and regulatory agencies. The ease of recycling or reusing a product's container is an important product attribute for many consumers. These consumers, sometimes referred to as socially conscious consumers, are an important market segment not only because of their purchases but also because of their social and political influence. Product disposition is important to marketing strategy because (1) sometimes disposition must precede the purchase due to financial or space limitations, (2) certain disposition strategies may give rise to a used or rebuilt market, and (3) difficult or unsatisfactory disposition alternatives may cause some consumers to withdraw from the market for a particular item.

Postpurchase dissonance, product usage, and disposition are potential influences on the purchase evaluation process. Basically, consumers develop certain expectations about the ability of the product to fulfill instrumental and symbolic needs. To the extend that the product meets these needs, satisfaction is likely to result. When expectations are not met, dissatisfaction is likely to result.

Taking no action; switching brands, products, or stores; and warning friends are all common reactions to a negative purchase evaluation. The marketing manager would generally prefer that dissatisfied consumers complain directly to the firm (and to no one else). This would alert the firm to problems as well as provide it an attempt to make amends. Unfortunately, only a fairly small, unique set of consumers tend to complain. Developing such strategies as consumer hot lines can increase the percentage of dissatisfied consumers who complain to the firm.

After the evaluation process and, where applicable, the complaint process, consumers have some degree of repurchase motivation. There may be a strong motive to avoid the brand, a willingness to repurchase it some of the time, a willingness to repurchase it all of the time, or some level of brand loyalty—a willingness to repurchase coupled with a psychological commitment to the brand. Marketing strategy does not always have the creation of brand loyalty as its objective. Rather, the manager must examine the makeup of the brands current and potential consumers and select the specific objectives most likely to maximize the overall organizational goals. For example, there may be a greater net payoff associated with converting nonpurchasers to happenstance purchasers than there is with converting repeat purchasers to loyal purchasers. The manager must select the appropriate objective and then develop marketing strategies to accomplish the objective.

REVIEW QUESTIONS

1. What is meant by the disposition of products and product packaging, and why does it interest governmental regulatory agencies?
2. What is postpurchase dissonance? What characteristics of a purchase situation are likely to contribute to postpurchase dissonance?
3. In what ways can a consumer reduce the effect of postpurchase dissonance?
4. In what ways can a marketer help reduce postpurchase dissonance?
5. How does the disposition of products vary in Table 19−2? What factors influence the different patterns of disposition shown in Table 19−2?
6. What is the difference between instrumental and symbolic performance, and how does each contribute to consumer satisfaction?
7. How do consumer feelings of personal competence affect consumer satisfaction?
8. What courses of action can a consumer take in response to dissatisfaction?
9. How does complaint behavior vary across product categories?
10. Using the information shown in Table 19−3, what percentage of the consumers who complain account for approximately 50 percent of the complaints? How do these consumers differ in terms of

demographics from those that do nothing in response to dissatis-faction?

11. How do consumers who complain differ in personality from those that do not complain?

12. What is the relationship between product satisfaction and repur-chase behavior. What is the difference between repeat purchase and brand loyalty?

13. What characteristics have been found to distinguish brand loyal consumers from nonbrand loyal consumers? What effect does store loyalty have on brand loyalty?

DISCUSSION QUESTIONS

1. How could Jeff instruct his retailers to deal with consumers imme-diately after purchase so as to reduce postpurchase dissonance? What specific action would you recommend, and what effect would you intend it to have on the recent purchaser of a Motron?

2. Discuss how Jeff could determine how consumers actually use their moped? How could he use this information to identify potential customers and to develop a marketing program directed at them?

3. How would you go about measuring consumer satisfaction among purchasers of various mopeds? What questions would you ask, and what additional information would you collect and why? How could this information be used by Jeff in evaluating and planning his mar-keting programs?

4. The A. C. Nielsen study cited in this chapter's footnote 30 found that 61 percent of the unsatisfactory purchases of health and beauty aids, such as deodorants, shampoos, or vitamins, were followed by con-tinued purchase of the brand. Only 27 percent of the unsatisfactory purchases of paper products were followed by repeat purchases of the same brand. Why is there such a large difference?

5. Examine Figure 19—5 and pick three distinct conversion objectives (e.g., converting nonloyal repeat multibrand purchases to nonloyal repeat single-brand purchases). Describe the marketing strategies required by each. Use soft drinks as a product category for your discussion.

6. Based on those characteristics that contribute to postpurchase dis-sonance, discuss several product purchases that are most likely to result in dissonance and several that will not create this effect.

7. Examine Table 19—2 and discuss the results in terms of the disposi-tion alternatives used for the products evaluated. What consumer and product characteristics contribute to these differences in dispo-sition behavior?

8. What level of product dissatisfaction should a marketer be content with in attempting to serve a particular target market? What charac-

teristics contribute to dissatisfaction, regardless of the marketer's efforts?

PROJECT QUESTIONS

1. Develop a questionnaire designed to measure consumer satisfaction of a clothing purchase of $25 or more. Include in your questionnaire questions that measure the product's instrumental and expressive dimensions of performance as well as what the consumer wanted in terms of instrumental and expressive performance. Then interview several consumers to obtain information on actual performance, expected performance, and satisfaction. Using this information determine if the consumer received (i.e., evaluation of performance) what they expected (i.e., wanted) and relate this difference to consumer expressions of satisfaction.

2. Develop a survey to measure student dissatisfaction with retail purchases. For purchases they were dissatisfied with, determine what action they took to resolve this dissatisfaction and what was the end result of their efforts.

3. Develop a method of measuring brand loyalty and measure the brand loyalty of several students with respect to shampoo, cereal, and soft drinks.

4. With the cooperation of a major durables retailer, assist the retailer in sending a postpurchase letter of thanks to every other customer immediately after purchase. Then approximately one month after purchase, contact some customers and measure their purchase satisfaction, using a seven-interval satisfaction-dissatisfaction semantic differential scale. Evaluate the results and compare them with those shown in Table 19—1.

5. For the products and disposition alternatives listed in Table 19—2, develop a questionnaire designed to evaluate this same information in either a student or nonstudent population. After collecting this type of information, create a similar table and evaluate the results with respect to those shown in Table 19—2.

6. Develop a questionnaire to be used in a telephone interview designed to measure consumer purchase dissatisfaction and complaint behavior. Sample a consumer population to measure the incidence of purchase dissatisfaction and the type of action taken in response to that dissatisfaction.

20

Managerial overview and future developments in consumer behavior

The marketing program for L'eggs hosiery began with a small mass of wrinkled fabric developed by the Hanes Corporation. Consumer research played the lead in the development of a total marketing program for this product which has been called "the outstanding new product success of the last five years. We [Hanes] talked to women to find out everything we could about hosiery. We did this through focus groups, in-home testing, a national behavior study, and concept testing. And we didn't forget the trade—the buyers, managers, and owners of supermarkets and drug chains. We talked to them about their needs, problems, and opinions."[1] The understanding of consumer behavior that resulted from this research played a major role in the development of the brand name, image, package, point-of-purchase materials, advertising and promotion strategy, media schedule, and distribution for L'eggs pantyhose.

In marketing practice, managers face a wide variety of problems and opportunities that require insightful decisions with regard to product positioning, pricing, advertising, and sales promotion and distribution. As in the L'eggs experience, successful firms generally utilize a knowledge of or research into relevant aspects of consumer behavior in making marketing decisions. That is, for a particular marketing problem or

[1] "L'eggs Success Grew from Rumpled Bit of Cloth," *Marketing News* (December 29, 1978), p. 9.

opportunity, the manager must ask—what aspects of consumer behavior play a role in the acquisition or use of this product? The answer to this question provides direction to the development of specific marketing strategy and tactics.

In many instances, the influence may be external as presented in our discussion of cultural influences, social class, reference group, and family influence. At other times the relevant source or sources of influence may be internal in nature, such as information processing, learning, motivation, personality, or attitudes. Frequently, the marketing manager will see that both external and internal influences are operating on the consumer as the consumption problem is recognized and the purchase decision reached.

The purpose of this last chapter is to summarize for you the major concepts presented throughout this text. We would also like to point out what we feel might be some new developments in consumer behavior over the next five to ten years and how they might be used by managers in making future marketing decisions.

MANAGERIAL OVERVIEW

Figure 20—1 presents a visual representation of the major influences on and steps in the consumption process. Consumer behavior is a process or series of steps taken in response to a problem or opportunity. Basically, individuals and families acquire, utilize, and dispose of prod-

FIGURE 20–1
Overview of the consumption process

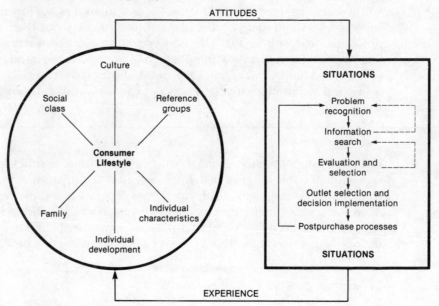

ucts in order to maintain or enhance their lifestyle. Lifestyle is influenced by one's culture, social class, reference groups, family, individual characteristics, and individual development. As Figure 20–1 shows, lifestyle influences consumer decisions and is in turn influenced and altered by the results of those decisions.

While lifestyle is influenced by the factors mentioned above, any given consumption decision must take place within the context of a specific situation. Specific situational influences may result in consumption patterns that one would not necessarily be able to predict from a knowledge of only the consumer. For example, many consumers prefer relatively low prices, but occasionally make purchases at high-priced convenience stores when in a hurry or after regular shopping hours. Situational variables that may influence consumer behavior have been classified as: (1) physical surroundings, (2) social surroundings, (3) temporal perspective, (4) task definition, and (5) antecedent states. The frequent need to purchase a pair of pantyhose in a hurry (temporal perspective) for a party or some other event provides an example of why many women wanted and supported L'eggs distribution in nonconventional outlets such as supermarkets and convenience stores.

Marketing managers must be aware of the situational variables that may influence the purchase and use of their product. However, the internal and external factors influencing lifestyle also can present the creative manager with useful guides to marketing strategy.

EXTERNAL INFLUENCES

Culture

Whenever the market potential for a new product spans more than one country or cultural unit, the manager must realize that one of the most profound influences affecting the products overall success is an accurate understanding of cross-cultural influences. Each market may be unique in terms of social norms and traditions. For example, marketing L'eggs in many foreign cultures would be impossible or would require major changes in the marketing mix since hosiery is not worn, women do not reveal their legs, or such products violate other cultural values. Even if the product itself is acceptable, severe cultural constraints may exist in terms of acceptable distribution outlets, methods of promotion, and pricing. Before expanding L'eggs into foreign markets, the marketing management should acquire the same level of understanding of the behaviors and norms in the proposed market as they acquired for the U.S. market.

Quite often, international product failures are caused by such obvious factors as a failure to understand subtleties of the language or consumer preferences for product form, method of promotion, or place of purchase. Or, the demographic characteristics of the country involved may not be appropriate. Even more frequently, marketing programs fail to reach their potential due to a lack of understanding of cross-cultural variations in values or in nonverbal meanings, such as time, space, friendship, or color.

While it is easy to visualize the appropriateness of a thorough analysis of demographics and cultural values when considering a foreign market, it is equally important to consider these same factors when evaluating the domestic market. The United States is undergoing substantial demographic changes in terms of the age distribution of the population, the distribution of family income, and the geographic distribution of the population. Just as the demographics of the United States (and most other countries) are changing, so are many of the traditional cultural values. Perhaps the value changing most rapidly today is the traditional view of the role of the woman in society. These changes are creating major problems and opportunities for marketing managers. For example, working women, particularly those with full-time jobs, tend to be heavier consumers of pantyhose, such as L'eggs.

An understanding of the culture is also important when examining markets based on subcultures within the larger market. While the United States is a relatively homogeneous society, subcultures based on race, religion, national origin, and geographic location present important opportunities for alert firms. Conversely, failure to understand subcultural variations can be the cause of product and/or promotional campaign failures.

Social stratification

Various aspects of social stratification, such as income, education, or occupation play an important role in many purchase decisions. Therefore, the marketing manager should ask: "What role, if any, does social stratification play in the consumption of my product?" For many products, such as detergents and canned foods, the majority of our social strata will exhibit similar consumption patterns. For other products, such as alcoholic beverages and clothes, various social strata will exhibit sharply differing consumption patterns. For example, pantyhose are purchased most heavily by women with relatively high levels of education from households with high annual incomes.

Reference groups

The power of word-of-mouth communication is well understood in marketing practice. But in many instances, managers have been unable to stimulate and direct it in favor of their brand of product. An understanding of reference group behavior offers considerable potential to marketers who are interested in enhancing word-of-mouth communication. The L'eggs marketing program stimulated trial behavior and word-of-mouth communication by being the first hosiery brand ever to coupon its target market via direct mail.

A challenge that faces every marketing manager is how to reach the appropriate reference group and stimulate specific brand communication within that group. Because opinion leaders within a reference group are influential in communicating product specific information for many product classes, a manager may try to develop a plan for identifying and/or creating opinion leaders in order to accomplish a desired level of word-of-mouth communication. This type of marketing effort is particularly appropriate for many new product introductions, such as L'eggs pantyhose, when the manager feels the product offers a differential advantage over present products on the market. If this benefit is real and accurately perceived by opinion leaders, these opinion leaders in effect become implicit promoters of the firm's product. However, there are frequently a number of problems in identifying and reaching specific opinion leaders for a product class which necessitates the use of other marketing strategies.

Family

In many instances, the actual purchaser of a product may be influenced by other members in the household. This varies by product class, social class, the working status of the wife, and value orientation held by the female head of household. Because these differences affect product, brand, and store selection, marketing managers must understand which members of the household are involved in each stage of the decision process.

A good understanding of husband-wife influence and decision making can be particularly important in developing a marketing program for many durable products since one spouse may initiate problem recognition while the other has a greater influence in actual brand selection. Because each contributes to the purchase, but in different ways, separate marketing programs may be appropriate for each spouse.

Family size and age of children in a family also greatly affect the purchase of particular products. As a result, for many products, the marketing manager needs to be sensitive to differences in the stage of family life cycle of different consumers. Quite often, stage of the family life cycle can be a useful method of market segmentation and the basis for developing marketing programs.

INTERNAL INFLUENCES

Information processing

Consumers must process information provided by the external environment before problem recognition and solution can occur. An understanding of how consumers receive, categorize, store, retrieve, and use information provides insights into how a product might be positioned and advertisements created in order to enhance desired information processing and learning. In addition, an understanding of the limits to individual information processing capabilities will allow the marketing manager to avoid "overloading" consumers with information that they cannot or will not use.

Individual development and learning

The goal of most brand managers is to achieve a desired product position (image) that is differentiated from competing brands and readily learned and preferred by target market consumers. For this reason, marketers often turn to learning theory to gain insights into how consumers learn and what effect learning has on their brand choice behavior. Marketing managers have utilized knowledge of theories of classical conditioning, operant conditioning, and cognitive learning to guide the development of marketing communications. For example, the name, package design, and advertising jingle all fit closely together, which enhanced consumer learning about L'eggs.

Applications of learning theory extend beyond the creation of advertisements. For example, Procter and Gamble minimizes the use of the Procter and Gamble name with their various detergents (Tide, Cheer, Bold, Gain, Dash, Oxydol, Duz, Bonus, and Salvo). The reason for this is, in part, a characteristic of learning called *generalization.* Since Procter and Gamble does not want consumers to generalize or consider all of their detergents as being similar, they do not stress the Procter and Gamble name. General Electric, takes the opposite approach in branding its various appliances. Since toasters, mixers, and so forth clearly serve different purposes, General Electric wants the quality associated with its established appliances to be generalized to any new appliances it might introduce.

Individual characteristics

Because consumers have motivations and personalities that guide their behavior, successful marketers try to understand each so that they can provide marketing programs that offer suitable product benefits and brand personalities consistent with the motives and personalities of target market consumers. There are a wide variety of motivations that *energize* and *direct* consumer behavior. In many situations, the manager may find one or more of these motivations extremely useful in creating a marketing program. Motives are basic consumer needs which products can satisfy, and the more closely marketing efforts relate to these motives in a particular choice decision, the more likely is consumer satisfaction.

While we are all aware that individuals have personalities, we should also recognize that many products have distinct personalities. Of course, this does not happen by accident, as marketers often work very carefully in researching the personality of target market consumers and then attempt to blend that personality into their brand image. While the successful use of personality in marketing is still relatively unpredictable, when properly researched and understood it offers substantial benefits in achieving a desired product position and marketing success.

Attitudes

Marketers have long recognized the importance of consumer attitudes. Because consumers tend to be consistent in their feelings, thoughts, and actions, it is often a marketing goal to build a favorable brand attitude based on the assumption that corresponding behavior would also occur.

While marketers can examine the affective, cognitive, and behavioral components of consumer attitudes, the cognitive component of attitude has proven the most useful in diagnosing problems and developing attitude change strategies. Depending on the circumstances, a manager may wish to alter beliefs about brand attributes, shift the importance assigned to different brand beliefs, add new beliefs, or shift the ideal belief that target market consumers hold.

In other instances, the marketer might find it more useful to examine the function provided by a particular attitude. Because attitudes are used to indicate values, defend egos, provide knowledge, and give expression to one's personality, attempts to change attitudes may be very difficult without understanding the function they fulfill for the consumer.

Once attitudes have been measured or estimated and desirable attitudes specified, a variety of strategies are available to create new attitudes, or reinforce or change existing attitudes. Most of these strategies are based on characteristics of the individuals one desires to influence or the characteristics of the message to be used.

Lifestyle

As we have illustrated in Figure 20−1, consumer lifestyle is the hub of various external and internal influences affecting consumer behavior. Because consumer lifestyle is an expression of these influences, it has frequently been used as a basis for understanding differences in consumer needs and behaviors. Psychographics, the assessment of lifestyle by studying consumers activities, interests, and opinions, is a technique commonly used by marketing managers. Psychographic studies have been used with varying degrees of success to both segment and better understand the markets for a wide variety of products.

The internal manifestation of lifestyle is the self-concept. Consumers have both actual self-concepts and ideal self-concepts. Because many products are symbolic in nature, consumers are frequently attracted to those products with images similar to their ideal or actual self-concept. When this is the case, the marketing manager has a useful tool for developing marketing programs for unique segments of consumers that share a particular ideal self-concept. The information provided by the ideal self-concept of target market consumers is very valuable in product development, branding, product positioning, and developing a communications and retail strategy.

CONSUMER DECISION PROCESS

Problem recognition

Consumers utilize products to maintain or enhance their lifestyle. Problem recognition occurs, therefore, when a consumer perceives a product-related deficiency in maintaining an existing lifestyle or an opportunity to improve that lifestyle. If the perceived problem is important enough, consumers will begin to take action to resolve the problem. Thus, problem recognition is the first step in the consumption process.

Consumers often recognize problems due to factors over which marketers have no control, such as a change in the family makeup (birth of a child) or the failure of an existing product or brand. Marketers may react to such recognized problems by developing appropriate products, changing existing products, prices, or channels of distribution, and so forth. At other times, the marketing manager may wish to stimulate problem recognition. L'eggs advertising has been designed, in part, to create problem recognition by stressing the importance of a stocking that provides "good fit."

Information search

After recognizing a problem, a consumer may purchase a previously satisfactory brand without securing any additional information, or consult numerous personal, professional, and market sources of information. The amount and type of information sought by target consumers is obviously of critical importance to the marketing manager.

Consumers may engage in both internal (memory) and external information search. Consumers seek information on (1) the appropriate evaluative criteria for the solution of a problem, (2) the existence of various alternative solutions, and/or (3) the performance of each alternative solution on each evaluative criterion. For many product categories, consumers limit their search to an evoked set of brands—brands that the consumer is aware of and generally considers to be satisfactory.

Consumers engage in a surprisingly small amount of direct, external search. However, there are large individual differences in this behavior. Marketing activities such as point-of-purchase displays and advertising can increase external search. Marketing managers generally prefer that only consumers of competing brands engage in search prior to purchase. Therefore, many marketing strategies are designed to minimize external search by a firm's existing customers.

Alternative evaluation and selection

Marketing managers must be aware of the evaluative criteria used by consumers in brand choice decisions. A knowledge of these evaluative criteria and the relative importance different segments of consumers assign to them is very useful in understanding consumer wants and developing marketing programs to satisfy those wants.

Equally important is an understanding of the decision rules used by consumers to chose from among various brands. For example, if choice behavior by the target market for a particular product class is predominately disjunctive, the manager needs to maximize the brand's performance on that single evaluative attribute which determines choice. On the other hand, if the brand selection is predominately compensatory, a much different product differentiation strategy is needed.

Outlet selection and decision implementation

Retail managers must base their marketing strategies on the process consumers use to select stores. In addition, marketing strategies developed for products must take into account both the store choice decisions of consumers and the influence of in-store attributes on brand choice.

For the producers of L'eggs, it was absolutely critical to create the proper in-store influence to capture the attention of pantyhose buyers. L'eggs achieved this with an attractive display rack that takes up less than three feet of floor space while conveniently displaying over 200 pairs of pantyhose. A great deal of L'eggs success has to be attributed to the in-store influence of their unique package and display.

The selection of a retail outlet involves exactly the same process as the selection of a brand. The only difference is the nature of the attributes considered. For retail outlets, the attributes of size, location, and image are particularly important. Once a consumer enters a retail outlet, such in-store influences as point-of-purchase displays, price reductions, and even the store layout can influence product category and brand choice.

Once a consumer chooses both the brand and the outlet, the transfer of ownership must occur. Increasingly, this involves the use of various forms of credit. In fact, the need to finance purchases often leads to a second round of consumer decision making after the product is selected.

Postpurchase processes

After an important purchase for which the consumer had difficulty choosing between two or more alternatives, a feeling of anxiety or doubt, called postpurchase dissonance, often occurs. Alert managers can increase customer satisfaction by assisting in the reduction of this dissonance.

While we have only limited data on the actual use and disposition of products, knowledge about such behavior can lead to improved package and product designs, new products, new uses for existing products, and more effective promotional campaigns. The existence of socially conscious consumers suggests the possibility of segmentation strategies based on the ecological aspects of the brand's package, use, and/or disposition.

Throughout postpurchase evaluation, consumers are assessing purchased products to determine if they meet their desires and/or expectations. This leads to either satisfaction or dissatisfaction. Dissatisfaction, of course, can lead to a variety of behaviors, most of which cost the firm current and/or future sales. While dissatisfaction tends to reduce repurchase motivations, satisfaction tends to increase them. In some cases, satisfaction may lead to brand loyalty; that is, the consumer may make a psychological commitment, much like friendship, to the brand.

FUTURE DIRECTIONS IN CONSUMER BEHAVIOR

Throughout this book, we have emphasized how knowledge about consumer behavior is currently being utilized by sophisticated marketing practitioners. While much is known and is being put into practice, even more remains to be learned. In this final section of the book, we want to briefly present a few of the areas of consumer research that we feel will produce useful knowledge in the next five years or so. Our discussion is in no way exhaustive of potential areas of development or meant to be definitive statements of the concepts discussed. Rather, we merely want to expose you to a few of the exciting new areas of consumer research.

Role accumulators

In our presentation of reference groups, we discussed the characteristics of reference groups and how they influence individual behavior. We also discussed how marketers can make use of reference groups by disseminating information to opinion leaders and then depending on the opinion leaders to disseminate information within the reference group. A new concept which offers considerable promise is that of the *role accumulator*.[2]

---

[2] S. Sieber, "Toward a Theory of Role Accumulation," *American Sociological Review* (August 1974), pp. 567−78.

Role accumulators are not necessarily opinion leaders or group leaders; they are simply members of *many* reference groups. Because of the many roles they play as members of different reference groups, the role accumulator acquires more information and is in contact with more people. Thus, there is the potential that the diffusion of innovations as well as information is spread faster when disseminated through role accumulators.[3]

While we do not know much about role accumulators in relation to the dissemination of market information and brand choice behavior, the concept is an exciting one and one that could be easily used in marketing practice. For example, if role accumulators do prove to be good channels of information dissemination, the marketer's task is to identify those individuals that belong to a large number of reference groups and direct information to them based on the belief that they will in turn diffuse this information within the many groups to which they belong. It may also be easier to identify role accumulators than it is to identify opinion leaders, since it may only be necessary to count group memberships rather than measure interaction.

Adult life cycle

The concept of family life cycle should be familiar to you since we discussed it in some detail in Chapter 9. A similar but distinct life cycle concept focuses on what has been termed the *adult life cycle*.[4] As shown in Figure 20–2 and described in Figure 20–3, adults move through different phases of their life independent of family status. Understanding these different stages of adult life cycle allows a marketing manager to fulfill the needs of consumers at different stages of their adult life cycle. Therefore, this concept offers an alternative basis for market segmentation and development of marketing strategy.

To illustrate this concept, consider the stage of "becoming one's own man," which is a key phase of adult life cycle and important in the purchase of many products. Individuals in this stage of their adult life cycle are faced for the first time with the fact that they are growing old. In response to this, adults at this stage of life take up a variety of activities to prolong their identity with youth. A good illustration of this behavior was during the introduction of the Ford Mustang; it was designed for a young audience, but the majority of its purchasers turned out to be middle-aged men looking for youth-oriented symbols to retain a youthful feeling and image.

---

[3] E. Hirschman and M. Wallendorf, "Role Accumulation and Early Adoptions," working paper, Graduate School of Business, University of Pittsburgh, 1978.

[4] See D. Levinson, *The Seasons of a Man's Life* (Ballantine Books, 1978); G. Sheehy, *Passages: Predictable Crises of Adult Life* (E. P. Dutten, 1974); R. Ralston, "The Adult Life Cycle: Its Applicability to Market Segmentation," honors thesis, Arizona State University, 1978.

FIGURE 20–2
Adult life cycle

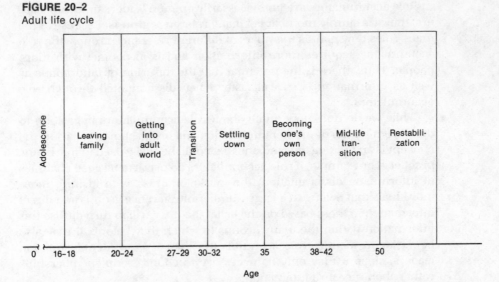

While the concept of an adult life cycle is only partially developed (studies thus far have focused only on males), it supplements the family life cycle and could prove very useful in developing more comprehensive marketing strategy within different stages of a family life cycle.[5]

Family buying center

In many ways, marketers have simplified their marketing programs by developing strategies aimed at the purchasers of products. As discussed in Chapter 9, in our presentation of family influences, a variety of inputs from family members influence that purchase. While marketers have recognized this and often develop separate strategies for each spouse, a model of family purchase behavior as a buying center has not been developed yet. This concept offers a more complete specification of family influences and how they can be used in a particular marketing program.

What has been proposed is the application of organizational buyer behavior to family buyer behavior.[6] That is, taking the concepts and relationships that have been developed in organizational buying and applying this to the family unit. This would involve looking at the family as a small organization with multiple inputs, interests, and role respon-

---

[5] Ralston, *Adult Life Cycle.*

[6] Y. Wind, "On the Interface between Organization and Consumer Buying Behavior," in *Advances in Consumer Research V,* ed. H. K. Hunt (Association for Consumer Research, 1978), pp. 657–62.

FIGURE 20–3 Stages of the adult life cycle

Stages	Life cycle description
1. Leaving the family.	First attempts to break away from traditional family unit. Feelings of freedom, loneliness, unsure of one's self. Seeks peer support and assurance. Not a period of lasting relationships.
2. Getting into the adult world.	An age of reaching toward others. An effort to fashion an initial life structure. The person is more secure with himself/herself. A time for togetherness in marriage. A man is also likely to acquire a mentor—a patron or supporter 8 to 15 years older.
3. Transition.	Confirmation of choices made in 20s— e.g., career. End of novice stage of adulthood.
4. Settling down.	Deeper commitments are made to job and family. More involvement and activity in important aspects of life. Increased drives toward upward mobility and ambition. Still questioning, however. Can be a crisis period.
5. Becoming one's own man.	The mid-life explosion—a second adolescence. Values are questioned, awareness that death will eventually come and that time is running out. The mentor acquired in stage 2 is cast aside. Troubled relationships with wife, family, and friends. Appear to be in a "state of suspended animation."
6. Mid-life transition.	A realization that much of life is now fixed and must be lived with. A period of reflection coming in the form of questions such as "what have I done with my life?" Causes of this soul searching are bodily decline and an increasing sense of awareness of mortality, a sense of aging, and polarity between masculine and feminine.
7. Restabilization.	Stability returns. A softening of feelings and relationships. A tendency to avoid emotion-laden issues. Less concern for either past or future and more with everyday happenings.

Source: Adapted from R. C. Ralston, "The Adult Life Cycle: Its Applicability in Market Segmentation," honors thesis, Arizona State University, 1978.

sibilities. While empirical study of this has not yet occurred, it offers promise in terms of better understanding family purchase behavior and how managers could improve their ability to market to different types of family buying centers.

Imagery and linguistics

Our knowledge of how mental images are formed from information and how linguistics affects consumer learning is almost nonexistent in marketing. Yet, the brand names chosen to represent a product and the information used to position this product are basically linguistic in nature. Research on imagery has already shown great promise in terms of more rapid learning.[7] Words that possess both audio and visual characteristics are learned more rapidly than words with only audio characteristics. Also, logos that correspond well with the brand name and product function are learned more rapidly. In both cases, there are simply more information cues to aid memory and learning of a particular brand name and/or brand information. L'eggs' name, package design, advertising jingle, and function all fit together in a manner that exemplifies this theory. As this research develops it has the potential of contributing greatly to the area of branding, packaging, and marketing communication.

The psycholinguistic structure of messages also offers a great deal of promise in terms of increased learning.[8] The structure of language does affect learning and as this research develops and is applied to marketing, it has the potential of making a significant impact in the construction of marketing communications used in advertising and sales promotion.

Cognitive response memory

Consumer research in the areas of memory, cognitive structure, and cognitive response are in their infancy, yet they offer a great deal of potential in marketing practice over the next five to ten years. Studies relating unaided recall of brands and brand information to memory and cognitive structure may assist future marketers in product positioning

---

[7] A. Pavirio, *Imagery and Verbal Processes* (Holt, Rinehart and Winston, 1971); K. Lutz and R. Lutz, "Imagery-Eliciting Strategies: Review and Implications of Research," in *Advances in Consumer Research V*, ed. H. K. Hunt (Association for Consumer Research, 1978) pp. 611–20; J. Rossiter and L. Percy, "Visual Imagery Ability as a Mediator of Advertising Response," in *Advances in Consumer Research* ed. H. K. Hunt (Association for Consumer Research 1978), p. 621–29; B. Calder, "Cognitive Response, Imagery, and Scripts: What Is the Cognitive Basis of Attitude?" in *Advances in Consumer Research V*, ed. H. K. Hunt (Association for Consumer Research, 1978) pp. 630–34.

[8] J. Bransford and J. Franks, "The Abstraction of Linguistic Ideas," *Cognitive Psychology* (1971), pp. 331–50.

and marketing communications.[9] As more becomes known about the relation between memory and cognitive structure, marketers may utilize cognitive response (i.e., free elicitation of product specific information) as a basis for market segmentation such that specific marketing programs can be developed for segments of the market that differ in cognitive structure and memory.

Disposition

Marketing programs are generally developed around what consumers want and do and how they feel prior to purchase and after purchase, but very little is actually known about how they consume and dispose of products. At first, you might wonder what can a marketer possibly learn from a study of consumer dispositions? This is how archeologists study the consumer behavior of ancient civilizations. The lifestyle of a culture, subcultures, social classes, geographic regions, and individual families is partially evident in their disposition behavior.[10]

In the future, we may see a more formal study of disposition behavior and how marketers can improve marketing programs based on what is disposed and how much. This may, in turn, lead to new products, modified products, formulations, packaging, and methods of disposal.

CONCLUSION

"When leisure suits came out, we stuck to the traditional suit, thinking our customer would buy them no matter what the latest trends were. We were dead wrong. We got caught with our pants down."[11]

---

[9] See B. Posher, "The Retrieval of Sentences from Memory: A Speed-Accuracy Study," *Cognitive Psychology* (July 1976), pp. 291–310; D. Norman, *Memory and Attention: An Introduction to Human Information Processing,* 2d ed. (John Wiley & Sons, Inc., 1976); E. Johnson and J. Russo, "The Organization of Product Information in Memory Identified by Recall Times," in *Advances in Consumer Research V,* ed. H. K. Hunt (Association for Consumer Research, 1978) pp. 79–86; J. Olson, D. Toy, and P. Dover, "Mediating Effects of Cognitive Responses to Advertising on Cognitive Structure," in *Advances in Consumer Research V,* ed. H. K. Hunt (Association for Consumer Research, 1978) pp. 72–78; and R. Lutz and J. Swasy, "Integrating Cognitive Response and Structure and Cognitive Response Approaches to Monitoring Communications Effects," in *Advances in Consumer Research IV,* ed. W. Perreault, Jr. (Association for Consumer Research, 1977), pp. 363–71.

[10] See J. Jacoby, C. Berning, and T. Dietvorst, "What about Disposition?" *Journal of Marketing* (April 1977), pp. 22–28; M. Burke, W. Conn, and R. Lutz, "Using Psychographic Variables to Investigate Product Disposition Behaviors, in *Research Frontiers in Marketing: Dialogues and Directions,* ed. S. Jain (American Marketing Association, 1978), pp. 321–26; M. DeBell and R. Dardis, "Extending Product Life: Technology Isn't the Only Issue," in *Advances in Consumer Research VI,* ed. W. Wilkie (Association for Consumer Research, 1979), pp. 381–85; and J. Hansen, "A Proposed Paradigm for Consumer Disposition Processes," *Journal of Consumer Affairs* (Summer 1980).

[11] A quote from an executive at Montgomery Ward in United Press International, "Men's Clothiers Zero in on Ages 28 through 40," n.d.

Our journey through consumer behavior is now at an end. Or perhaps, for those of you with aspirations of successful careers in marketing, it is just beginning. The purpose of this text has been to give you a fundamental understanding of and curiosity about how people behave with respect to consumption activities. We firmly believe that for anyone to actively, successfully, and happily practice the art and science of marketing, this understanding and curiosity are basic prerequisites. Therefore, we have tried to present you with a usable, managerial understanding of who consumers are and how they go about making decisions. Hopefully, we have done this in such a way that your curiosity about human behavior has been raised to a level that will make you ask new questions and try to develop new answers to the many difficult problems marketing managers face. Without this basic curiosity concerning why people do what they do, the practice of marketing will probably always be a fairly dull process for you. However, if you are excited and interested in people as consumers, your work will be fulfilling and you will be less likely to "get caught with your pants down." Have fun!

REVIEW QUESTIONS

1. How do each of the external influences affect lifestyle and consumer behavor?
2. How do each of the internal influences contribute to consumer behavior and the development of marketing strategy?
3. What role do attitudes play in consumer behavior and marketing strategy?
4. What is the consumer decision process and how can knowledge of it be used in the development of successful marketing strategy?
5. What are *role accumulators* and what potential do they offer in the development of marketing strategy?
6. What is the adult life cycle and how would it be useful to marketers?
7. What is the nature of imagery and linguistics in learning and why would marketers be interested in their effects on consumers?
8. What is cognitive response memory and what is its potential use in marketing?
9. What value would a study of disposition provide marketers?

Author index

535

Subject Index

543

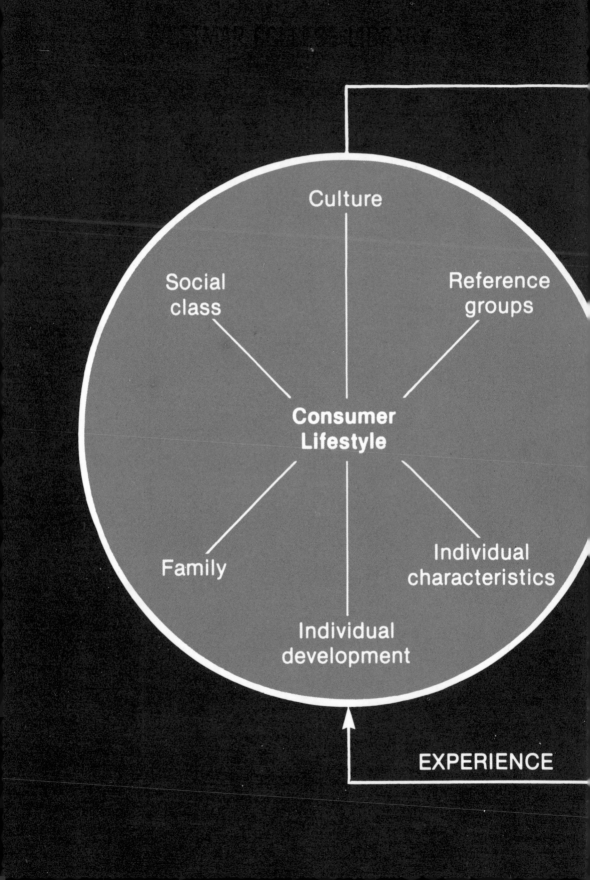